THE HANDBOOK O … S

The Handbook of Service Industries

Edited by

John R. Bryson

Professor of Enterprise and Economic Geography, School of Geography, Earth and Environmental Sciences, University of Birmingham, UK and Distinguished Research Fellow, Foundation for Research in Economics and Business Administration (SNF), Bergen, Norway

Peter W. Daniels

Professor of Geography and Dean of Physical Sciences and Engineering, School of Geography, Earth and Environmental Sciences, University of Birmingham, UK

Edward Elgar

Cheltenham, UK • Northampton, MA, USA

Published by
Edward Elgar Publishing Limited
Glensanda House
Montpellier Parade
Cheltenham
Glos GL50 1UA
UK

Edward Elgar Publishing, Inc.
William Pratt House
9 Dewey Court
Northampton
Massachusetts 01060
USA

A catalogue record for this book
is available from the British Library

Library of Congress Cataloguing in Publication Data
The handbook of service industries / edited by John R. Bryson and Peter W. Daniels
p. cm.—(Elgar original reference)
Includes bibliographical references and index.
1. Service industries. I. Bryson, J. R., 1963– II. Daniels, P. W.

HD9980.5.H358 2007
338.4—dc22

2007000148

ISBN 978 1 84064 948 2

Printed and bound in Great Britain by MPG Books Ltd, Bodmin, Cornwall

Contents

Contributors

Jonathan V. Beaverstock Professor of Economic Geography, Department of Geography, Loughborough University, UK.

William B. Beyers Professor, Department of Geography, University of Washington, Seattle, WA, USA.

John T. Bowen Associate Professor, Department of Geography and Urban Planning, University of Wisconsin, Oshkosh, WI, USA.

John R. Bryson Professor of Enterprise and Economic Geography, School of Geography, Earth and Environmental Sciences, University of Birmingham, UK and Distinguished Research Fellow, Foundation for Research in Economics and Business Administration (SNF), Bergen, Norway.

Peter W. Daniels Professor of Geography and Dean of Physical Sciences and Engineering, School of Geography, Earth and Environmental Sciences, University of Birmingham, UK.

Alan V. Deardorff John W. Sweetland Professor of International Economics, Department of Economics, University of Michigan, Ann Arbor, MI, USA.

Peter Enderwick Professor of International Business, Auckland University of Technology, Auckland, New Zealand.

Jean Gadrey Emeritus Professor of Economics, University of Lille, France.

Jeremy Howells Professor, ESRC Centre for Research on Innovation and Competition (CRIC), University of Manchester, UK.

T.A. Hutton Associate Professor, School of Community and Regional Planning, University of British Columbia, Vancouver, Canada.

Sven Illeris Department of Geography, Roskilde University, Denmark.

Thomas R. Leinbach Professor of Geography, Department of Geography, University of Kentucky, Lexington, KY, USA.

Linda McDowell Professor of Human Geography, School of Geography, University of Oxford, UK.

Ian Miles Professor, ESRC Centre for Research on Innovation and Competition (CRIC), University of Manchester, UK.

Andrew Murphy Senior Lecturer in Marketing, Department of Commerce, Massey University, Palmerston North, New Zealand.

Ikujiro Nonaka Professor, Graduate School of International Corporate Strategy Hitotsubashi University, Japan; Xerox Distinguished Professor in Knowledge, IMIO, UC Berkeley, CA, USA; Visiting Dean and Professor, Center for Knowledge and Innovation Research, Helsinki School of Economics, Finland.

Vesa Peltokorpi Graduate School of International Corporate Strategy, Hitotsubashi University, Chiyoda-ku, Tokyo, Japan.

Pascal Petit Centre d'Études Prospectives d'économie mathématique appliquées à la planification (CEPREMAP) and Research Director at the Centre National de Recherche Scientifique (CNRS), Paris, France.

Grete Rusten Senior Researcher, Foundation for Research in Economics and Business Administration (SNF), Bergen, Norway.

Saskia Sassen Ralph Lewis Professor of Sociology, University of Chicago, IL, USA and Centennial Visiting Professor, London School of Economics, UK.

Dai Senoo Associate Professor, Department of Industrial Engineering and Management, Tokyo Institute of Technology, Japan.

Metka Stare Senior Research Fellow, Centre for International Relations, Faculty of Social Sciences, University of Ljubljana, Slovenia.

Nico Stehr Karl-Mannheim Professor for Cultural Studies, Zeppelin University, Friedrichshafen, Germany; Fellow, Center for Advanced Cultural Studies, Essen, Germany.

Robert M. Stern Professor Emeritus of Economics, Department of Economics, University of Michigan, Ann Arbor, MI, USA.

Barney Warf Professor, Department of Geography, Florida State University, Tallahassee, FL, USA.

1 Worlds of services: from local service economies to offshoring or global sourcing

John R. Bryson and Peter W. Daniels

Introduction

In the economically developed world, the majority of all jobs, often more than 75 per cent, involve some form of service work (Bryson et al., 2004b). Furthermore, some 9 in 10 of all new jobs are also in services, particularly in Europe, North America, Japan, Australia and New Zealand, as well as in newly industrialised countries such as Singapore or Korea. This Handbook provides a state-of-the-art account of this transformation which has been under way for more than 40 years – the shift away from manufacturing to service employment. There are important differences between national economies in the outcomes and consequences of the shift from manufacturing to services so that there are different types of service economy (see Chapters 4 and 5).

It is worth noting at the outset the common mistake of assuming that the transformation of economies towards services is a phenomenon of the twentieth century. The social sciences have paid too little attention to the role they played during the Industrial Revolution or earlier. The considerable rise in the importance of services in the latter half of the nineteenth century has been largely ignored. A case example is the United Kingdom. Using fire office registers to undertake an investigation into the structure of London's economy between the years 1775 and 1825 Barnett, for example, provides an unusually detailed historical investigation from which it is concluded that:

> service industries made no less contribution to the British economy during the Industrial Revolution than manufacturing, and that nowhere was this more true than in London. Its service economy was on a very large scale, serving the nation as a whole as well as the capital . . . London's service industries underpinned both its own and the national manufacturing and commercial infrastructure and at the same time contributed to the new 'commercialisation of leisure'. (Barnett, 1998: 183)

During the late eighteenth century, London was already being transformed into a key world city, a process that has since continued up to the present and its status as a global city (see Chapter 11). Deane and Cole (1962: 166, 175) calculated that in 1851 some 45.3 per cent of the UK's national income was derived from service activities (trade, transport, housing, the professions, civil service and so on). The structure of employment in the UK changed dramatically during the nineteenth century as a result of technological innovation and the increasing maturity and extension of the capitalist system. Employment growth occurred in occupations that facilitated the exchange of goods and services between producers and consumers. Between 1881 and 1901 the number of business clerks increased from 175 000 to 308 000, bank officials from 16 000 to 30 000 and insurance officials and clerks from 15 000 to 55 000 (Marsh, 1977: 124). During the nineteenth century, international trade was continuously impeded by financial problems until it was enabled and supported by the establishment of bill markets and banking facilities of the kind associated with the flow of tea and silk from China to Europe between 1860 and 1890 (Hyde, 1973). As the UK was becoming an industrialised society it was simultaneously being transformed into a service economy; the growth of manufacturing employment went hand in hand with the growth of service employment. This was an ongoing transformation and it is evident in many different indicators of social and economic transformation. An unusual indicator is provided by Cameron (2002) as part of a detailed social history of one street in Solihull, West Midlands (UK). He explores the economic and social history of every house in this street's history between 1904 and 1984. The analysis reveals a shift away from manufacturing towards services that began during the interwar period. Even before 1918, 20 per cent of the heads of household held professional (white-collar) jobs (Table 1.1).

The capitalist economic system is in a constant state of flux as new technologies and ways of organising production, distribution and even consumption are developed. Enhanced competition, adjustments to the organisation of production, and developments in information and communication technologies (ICTs) alter the ways in which the majority of people experience work; who works, for how much, how often, and where (see Chapters 17, 18 and 19). Most social scientists would acknowledge that these economic trends are not easily separated from a range of complex, non-economic changes. Non-economic factors have not become more important but rather, social scientists have become more attuned to conceptualising the economy and the economic as culturally and socially embedded (Granovetter, 1985). Understanding the dynamics of the evolving capitalist economic system is a complex task for two reasons. First, capitalism continues to re-invent itself at scales ranging from the organisation of a single workplace to the emergence of new international divisions of labour. Second, the methodologies, technologies and theoretical frameworks deployed by social scientists have dramatically increased and in some cases have even been transmogrified. These two changes are not necessarily related. The 'cultural turn' experienced by many social sciences does not mean that non-economic factors have become more important; rather they have become increasingly visible to social scientists. Warf (2004: 85) summarises these changes by suggesting that 'capitalism has changed ontologically – it has become more flexible and globalized – and because our way of understanding it has changed as social science has become epistemologically more self-conscious'. The processes that have been identified in recent research may not therefore be new phenomena: they reflect a construction of a particular world view that foregrounds some features of the economy and backgrounds others.

Table 1.1 Employment of heads of household, Ashleigh Road, Solihull, 1904–1984

	Professional	Manufacturers	Craftspeople & commercial managers	Merchants	Total
Up to 1918	5	9	7	4	25
1918–39	13	20	5	17	55
1945–64	20	10	1	9	40
1965–84	17	4	Nil	7	28
Total	55	43	13	37	148

Source: Cameron (2002: 23).

There can be no question that capitalism has changed and will continue to change; however, it is difficult to achieve agreement on the nature and extent of these changes. At one level, 'time–space compression' conveniently reworks the intra- and inter-firm geographies of firms and corporations (Harvey, 1989: 147) while, at another level, new international divisions of labour continue to evolve (Bryson and Rusten, 2005). These ongoing adjustments are not surprising as time–space compression and evolving divisions of labour have been extant for centuries. Servan-Schreiber (1969) noted more than 30 years ago that the compression of time and space was fundamental to the challenges that America had to face over the next 10 years. But the pace of change is escalating and it offers new opportunities for the developing, transition and developed market economies (see Chapters 8, 9 and 10). A good example is Ireland's 'Tiger economy', which has exploited a niche within the global economic system for software development and specifically cultural and language localisation of generic software packages. In its 2005 review of Ireland's economy, Forfás, Ireland's national body responsible for providing policy advice on enterprise, trade, science, technology and innovation, drew attention to the rapidity of change as well as the ongoing shift towards service employment and exports. It noted:

> The pace of change in the global economy continues to increase. Firms in Ireland are facing competitive challenges more comprehensive and unremitting than at any point in our recent economic history and competition is set to be as intense at the high end as it is at the lower end. Many parts of China, India, South East Asia and Central Europe are now targeting the kinds of high-tech manufacturing and services activities – electronics, software, financial and other services and pharmaceuticals – that have driven Ireland's growth over the last 15 years. For example, the number of foreign R&D units in China has increased from a standing start in 1993 to 700 today; China's total spending on R&D climbed from \$21 billion in 1996 to an estimated €102.6 billion in 2004 (1.44 per cent of GDP) and, in absolute terms, is now behind only that of the USA (\$312.5 billion) and Japan (\$112.7 billion). (Forfás, 2005: 1)

Manufacturing employment in Ireland continues to decline, but this is more than offset by net gains in internationally traded services; in 2005 some 2812 jobs were added to total employment in financial and other international services, an increase largely accounted for by firms in consulting, software and other computer-related services. Ireland's total market share in services increased markedly from 0.4 per cent in 1993 to 2.2 per cent in 2004, making it the 14th largest exporter of services in the world.

Forfás considers that Ireland 'now faces an unprecedented challenge to grow the high-paid jobs and knowledge-intensive investment needed to sustain our performance into the future' (ibid.: 2). This is not, however, confined to Ireland; the majority of the advanced economies have been facing this challenge for well over 20 years. Service employment that adds significant value to production and economic systems that are physically grounded elsewhere in the world economy have become part of the mantra of local economic development policies in the developed market economies. The argument is that the decline in low-value manufacturing employment can be more than offset by geographically 'sticky' service functions that are locally embedded in centres of creativity (Florida, 2002). These regional and national development policies are founded upon a set of assumptions concerning the locations of added-value service functions that are currently being tested as services are increasingly integrated into the global economic system (see Chapter 7). It is too early to argue that high-paid service jobs are protected from foreign competition and that services will not follow manufacturing jobs to lower-cost locations.

Defining services

Scholars have found it extremely difficult to construct a rigorous definition of services (see Chapter 2). Originally the category of 'services' was as a 'residual' that embraced everything that was not included in the primary (extractive) or secondary (manufacturing) sectors of the economy. This has encouraged attempts to define and identify services on the basis of their primary characteristics, of which two are supposed to delimit them from other forms of economic activity. First, the output of a service is ephemeral or non-material (for example, a lecture or theatrical performance) and, second, the production and consumption of a service occurs simultaneously. There are obvious difficulties with both these characteristics: some services are not ephemeral and do have materiality (software, or even a haircut) and some can be stored (software, servicing of a machine).

It is important not to become too distracted by the search for a precise definition of services. It is certainly an important activity for those involved in measuring the economy, for example national statistical agencies or economists interested in improving productivity measures for services, but perhaps less so for scholars more generally. It is easy to become distracted by classification issues at the expense of understanding process. In any case, the pace of economic change dictates constant refinement of classifications to accommodate the ongoing 'extended division of labour' (Sayer and Walker, 1992).

All attempts to classify services also recognise the complexity and diversity of the business activities that need to be included (see Chapters 2 and 3). A simple classificatory schema of service activities identifies five different types:

1. consumer services that provide services for final end-users;
2. producer and business services that provide intermediate inputs into the activities of private and public sector organisations;
3. public services provided directly by the state or indirectly by the private sector and not-for-profit organisations;
4. not-for-profit organisations working beyond the confines of the state; and
5. informal services or unpaid service work that is often predominantly undertaken by women, and which is a vital element of people's daily lives.

Each type describes a heterogeneous collection of service functions. The focus of this Handbook is predominantly on producer services. They comprise several distinctive sectors (law, accountancy, market research, technical consultancy and so on) as well as a very broad size-range of firms. Producer services make an important contribution to economic development as they contribute directly to the creation of added value; they contribute to a national economy's balance of payments through exports and have also experienced dramatic growth rates both in employment as well as new firm formation.

It is usually assumed that producer service firms perform an important role in knowledge creation, as well as in shaping regional competitiveness. However, it is easier to assert this relationship than it is to successfully test its existence because it is difficult, and perhaps impossible, to develop objective measures of the impacts that producer service firms have on client companies or on overall regional competitiveness. The problem centres around the difficulty of isolating the impact of the input provided by a producer service firm from a whole range of other intra-client variables such as the ability and competence of its management team (Bryson et al., 1999). It is important to understand the types of expertise and knowledge that producer service firms provide to their clients (see Chapter 16) in that they are commercial enterprises in their own right that must place their own business interests before those of their clients; like all commercial enterprises, producer service firms are concerned with maintaining or enhancing their own profitability.

Conceptualising the shift towards service employment

There are many different ways of conceptualising the shift towards service employment. Part of the shift may be explained by the process of deindustrialisation, which is related to the existence of manufacturing cost differentials and variations in employment and environmental legislation. Manufacturing employment shifts to low-cost locations, leaving behind a pool of unemployed production workers and ultimately the creation of alternative employment opportunities that are either in public or in private services. An alternative explanation attributes the growth in service employment to changes in the behaviour of clients or to the enhanced complexity of the business world (Bryson et al., 2004b). The former explanation is grounded in industrial decline while the latter highlights a set of positive drivers behind the growth of service work. The deindustrialisation explanation is linked to debates about the rise of service-led or -dominated economies in which a set of theories as well as assumptions regarding those sectors that create wealth and those that are considered as parasitic are central (see Chapter 6). Although they are quite complex, these debates are fundamental to the development of the discipline of economics and economic geography and have also become integrated into everyday or lay understandings of economies.

Over time the social sciences have reconfigured the ways in which wealth creation or added value are conceptualised. Classical political economists like Adam Smith and David Ricardo drew a distinction between productive and unproductive labour (see Chapter 6). According to Smith (1776 [1977]: 429–30) 'there is one sort of labour which adds to the value of the subject upon which it is bestowed: there is another which has no such effect. The former, as it produced a value, may be called productive; the latter, unproductive labour'. He used this simple bipolar division of labour to argue that a whole range of service activities are essentially unproductive, even going as far as to argue:

> The labour of some of the most respectable orders in the society is, like that of menial servants, unproductive of any value, and does not fix or realize itself in any permanent subject; or vendible commodity, which endures after that labour is past, and for which an equal quantity of labour could afterwards be procured. The sovereign, for example, with all the officers both of justice and war who serve under him, the whole army and navy, are unproductive labourers. They are the servants of the public, and are maintained by a part of the annual produce of the industry of other people. Their service, how honourable, how useful, or how necessary soever, produces nothing for which an equal quantity of service can afterwards be procured. The protection, security, and defence of the commonwealth, the effect of their labour this year will not purchase its protection, security, and defence for the year to come. In the same class must be ranked, some of the gravest and most important, and some of the most frivolous professions: churchmen, lawyers, physicians, men of letters of all kinds; players, buffoons, musicians, opera-singers, opera-dancers, etc. The labour of the meanest of these has a certain value, regulated by the very same principles which regulate that of every other sort of labour; and that of the noblest and most useful, produces nothing which could afterwards purchase or procure an equal quantity of labour. Like the declamation of the actor, the harangue of the orator, or the tune of the musician, the work of all of them perishes in the very instant of its production. (Ibid.: 430–31)

Many of these 'unproductive' jobs are services. This division between 'productive' and 'unproductive' labour is, however, outdated and very much an eighteenth- and nineteenth-century conceptualisation of the economy.

The neoclassical economists tried to shift the debate forward; all labour was in fact productive. To Marshall '[a]ll labour is directed towards producing some effect', but even he took the view that '[w]henever we use the word *Productive* by itself, it is to be understood to mean productive of the means of production, and of durable sources of enjoyment' (Marshall, 1920: 56). Many service activities have transitory impacts on their clients and, in this context, it is important to distinguish between those that are directly integrated into the production process (producer services) and those that are targeted at final consumers (consumer services). The former are part of the value-creation chain while some of the latter may only be involved in the transfer of money around an economy rather than its creation. Conceptually, it is difficult to differentiate between productive and unproductive labour since all labour activity contributes to value creation or retention. This is an important point in so far as some seemingly 'unproductive' heavily localised services actually ensure that money continues to circulate within a local or national economy and, in these terms, they act as a form of import substitution.

The work of the classical economists still underpins everyday popular conceptions of service activities. Many lay observers and even some academics consider that manufacturing creates wealth and that services are essentially parasitic activities. Indeed, the assumption of a dependent relationship between manufacturing and service activities is still entrenched in much of the academic literature and the popular press. This mode of thinking is enshrined in 'economic base theory' which is founded on the belief that in order to survive and grow, a region or nation must earn external income. Economic base theory divides an economy into two sectors: basic activities which produce goods which are consumed outside the area or region, and 'dependent' or service activities which provide services (retailing, banking and so on) to the local population (Haggert et al., 1977). The total employment in a region or national economy is a product of these two types of activities. Service growth is dependent on an expansion of 'basic' activities, an assumption that underpins numerous attempts to model economic activity such as Ira S. Lowry's model of the urban economy as well as many regional policy initiatives (Wilson, 1974; Webber, 1984). Such has been the influence of economic base theory on conceptualising economic relationships that the 'service sector is one of the least understood portions of our global economy' even though 'no economy can survive without a service sector' (Riddle, 1986: 12). In a similar vein 'it is incorrect to view services as essentially "nonbasic" by contrast with supposedly "basic" manufacturing industry . . . [*and this is*] supported by a growing body of theoretical and conceptual analysis *and* detailed empirical research' (Urry, 1987: 6).

Economic base theory seriously understates the contribution that services make to a local economy. Many producer services are exported and even some consumer services bring income into a local economy or, at worst, ensure that expenditure and related multipliers are retained within an area. The conventional categorisation of an economy into 'non-basic' services and 'basic' manufacturing therefore misrepresents the current structuring of economic behaviour for at least two reasons.

First, services contribute to economic growth in a variety of ways; they are traded locally, regionally, nationally and internationally. They are also heavily wrapped around and integrated into the production processes of manufactured goods as well as services; they add value by smoothing the relationship between production and consumption, for example via market research, product design (Bryson et al., 2004a), development and testing, and advertising. Services are also directly involved in innovation (Howells, 1999) (see Chapters 2 and 15 as well as Part IV).

Second, manufacturing is undergoing a complex process of hybridisation whereby the categories of manufacturing and services are becoming increasingly blurred (Daniels and Bryson, 2002). Manufacturing has become more like a service in which product customisation and the 'service' experience of the product are an essential part of the symbiosis that exists between production and consumption. Some manufacturing companies are directly responsible just for the design and marketing of their product; the actual production is subcontracted to a contract manufacturing company. Many products are useless without embedded services. Apple's iPod or computers more generally have limited or even no use value without their embedded software as well as content (music, film and so on). Another good example is the design and manufacture of elevators; much of the added value in their production does not come from manufacturing but rather from service contracts because, legally, all elevators in the developed market economies must be covered by an annual service contract (Giarini, 2002). To Giarini this implies that the economic theory of value needs to be reconstructed to include a temporal dimension. In this context, elevator manufacturers have two profit streams. First, profit obtained from the production, sale and installation of elevators and, second, an annual stream of profits that come from servicing the elevator throughout its life.

The United Kingdom: a service economy?

The shift towards service employment should not be equated with the demise of manufacturing or the complete displacement of direct production with service work. Many economies are still dominated by the development, design, manufacture and sale of goods; the absence of manufacturing with a national economy would be a serious obstacle since everyday life as well as service work is supported by a complex array of products. Many of these products must be manufactured or customised locally, for example, products that are difficult or impossible to transport or production processes that require close contact between producers and consumers.

After the Second World War, manufacturing employment encountered gales of creative destruction (Schumpeter, 1942) that eventually culminated in, what some commentators have termed, the 'crisis of Fordism' (Gaffikin and Nickson, 1984). This led to the ongoing reduction in manufacturing employment and a shift towards a diverse collection of service jobs. But this does not mean that the UK was becoming a service economy: in this regard it is important to distinguish employment from economic output. These two variables are not necessarily related or they are related in unexpected ways. Currently, the shift towards service-dominated economies is first and foremost a shift or restructuring in employment rather than an outcome of the complete demise of manufacturing. At issue is productivity. As already noted, the category of 'services' includes an extremely diverse group of business activities; from extremely highly paid professional work to elementary occupations. The common denominator is that, unlike manufacturing, much of this work deploys people-based skills or what is commonly termed 'embodied labour' (Bryson et al., 2004b). Such is the heterogeneity of service work that it includes business functions in which productivity is very high and increasing as a result of an interaction between work practices and new technologies (such as the introduction of people-facilitated as well as automated call centres) alongside a range of occupations in which productivity improvements have been either non-existent or extremely low (see Chapter 6). The latter are labour-intensive activities such as face-to-face interactions between service providers and clients for which productivity improvements are extremely difficult to achieve. As a result, overall productivity improvements in the service side of the economy have as a general rule been much lower than for manufacturing. The implication is that this productivity differential partly explains the shift from manufacturing to service work.

In 2004, manufacturing exports from the UK amounted to £158 billion or 55 per cent of total exports (Mahajan, 2005: 23). Yet manufacturing directly accounted for just 3.3 million jobs or around 16 per cent of total employment with a further 3 million jobs dependent on the sector. The gross value added (GVA) created by manufacturing increased by 26 per cent over the period from 1992 to 2003 (Figure 1.1) but value added increased at much faster rates in other sectors of the economy. This means that other sectors were growing at a much faster rate than manufacturing even though in absolute rather than relative terms the contribution of manufacturing to the overall economy increased over this time period. In 1999, manufacturing's contribution to total GVA fell below 20 per cent and by 2004 its share had fallen to 14.9 per cent. Reductions in the share of GVA also took place in agriculture, mining, energy, the public sector and transport and communications.

These figures demonstrate that the decline of manufacturing has been overemphasised within developed market economies such as the UK. That said, it is crucial to recognise that a complex restructuring of economic activity is occurring in which new types of economic activity such as computer services or information management are flourishing alongside the development of innovations in existing services, for example in insurance, banking and retailing (see Chapters 19 and 20). This restructuring reflects, first, the externalisation of previously in-house services to independent providers and, second, the ongoing development of an extended division of labour. The latter arises from the growing complexity of production as well as service innovations that have been and are being developed by service providers in an effort to refine product differentiation in the marketplace.

While most of the key manufacturing sectors have therefore declined in relative terms, and some in absolute terms (for example, footwear, knitted goods, leather goods, manmade fibres, wearing apparel), the service sector has expanded whether measured by employment or as GVA. Between 1992 and 2003, GVA increased by 354.3 per cent in computer services, 221.5 per cent in other business services and 225.6 per cent in market research and management consultancy (Figure 1.1 and Table 1.2). In 2003, computer services accounted for 2.9 per cent of total GVA (£28.7 billion). Over the past decade, growth in the UK economy has been led by service industries; nine of the top 10 fastest-growing industries between 1992 and 2003 were services (see Table 1.2). An inexorable decline in manufacturing employment has been offset by employment gains in services.

Service work: personality as a commodity

Manufacturing workers are usually invisible in the final act of end-user consumption. Consumers are aware that manufactured goods are produced by people, but it is unusual

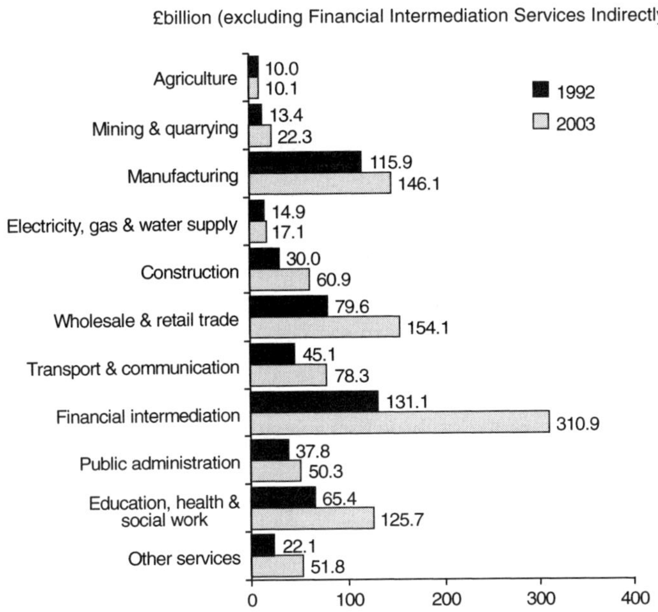

Source: Mahajan (2005: 23).

Figure 1.1 Comparison of GVA at current basic prices by industry, 1992 and 2003

Table 1.2 The top 10 fastest-growing industry groups in terms of GVA between 1992 and 2003 (weighted by per cent growth and £m)

Input–Output no.	Input–output group name	Change 1992–2003 %	Change 1992–2003 £m
107	Computer services	354.3	22,401
114	Other business services	221.5	23,900
101	Insurance and pension funds	220.7	15,915
121	Recreational services	152.3	17,032
103	Owning and dealing in real estate	164.0	11,550
104	Letting of dwellings	105.4	39,814
111	Market research, management consultancy	225.6	7,813
88	Construction	103.1	30,911
92	Hotels, catering, pubs, etc.	117.4	17,623
91	Retail distribution	101.6	28,342

Source: Mahajan (2005: 27).

for manufacturing workers to have direct contact with final consumers. In many manufacturing processes, consumers are distanced from producers; individual workers remain invisible in the production process and their identities are hidden behind a company name or brand. The majority of service workers will have some form of direct or indirect contact with their clients or customers. The 'facing' or 'embodied' nature of service work differentiates it from manufacturing although not necessarily from craft production processes.

Service workers rent their 'smiles', emotions, expertise, appearance and emotional intelligence as well as their muscular capacity for wages, salaries or consultancy fees (Bryson et al., 2004b). The service relationship is founded upon a series of skills that are required to deploy the body and personality (facial muscles, body language, voice and so on) in such a way as to maximise the economic benefits that can be obtained from an exchange based on people skills (Wharton, 1993). Muscular capacity based on strength has been supplemented by embodied expertise part of which is acquired via the educational system, part by socialisation, and part by genetic inheritance. Individuals without the correct embodied expertise are increasingly in danger of being partially or completely excluded from the world of face-to-face service work (McDowell, 2004a) (see Chapter 21).

The diversity of the service economy includes services that are intended for final consumption (consumer and public services) as well as intermediate services that contribute to the creation of wealth in other parts of the economy. Many of these services are supplied and consumed locally in a process of face-to-face co-production. This type of 'facing-based' economic relationship in which both parties to a transaction are co-located, usually defines the traditional service relationship which is based on embodied expertise centred on the ability of the service provider to enter into a relationship with a client. In the academic literature, heavily embodied services have conventionally been considered as having low productivity levels since it is impossible to substitute embodied expertise with machines (Bryson et al., 2004b).

Thus, producer service firms are established by individuals who are attempting to capitalise on their expertise, personality, reputation and network of contacts. Much of this work is performed at the client's premises or even remotely via ICTs. Producer service workers enjoy stimulating creative environments, including the delights of rural environments (Beyers and Lindahl, 1996a). This means that producer service firms can be established in relatively remote locations and still provide services to local, national and even sometimes to international clients.

Success in the world of producer services is attributable to three interrelated factors:

1. Individuals and firms must acquire and continue to develop technical expertise.
2. There needs to be an ability to transform technical expertise into something that has commercial value by providing distinctive inputs into the activities of client firms.
3. People-focused skills involving presentation and communication techniques are key skills; these can be subsumed under the terms 'impression management' or 'client relationship building'.

The first factor is relatively easily acquired while the second might come with experience, but the third factor is difficult to develop in someone who does not have the right personality or even the appropriate accent and/or appearance.

The academic literature on service work is heavily influenced by Arlie Hochschild's (1983) seminal work on the commercialisation of emotions in face-to-face service encounters. Hochschild was inspired by C. Wright Mills's (1953) classic work, *White Collar Work*. Wright Mills was one of the first sociologists to explore the complexity and diversity of service work in his analysis of the new American middle class. Although neglected in the recent literature it does deserve to be incorporated into current analyses of emotional labour as well as studies of the offshoring of service activities. For example, Wright Mills notes:

> When white-collar people get jobs, they sell not only their time and energy but their personalities as well. They sell by the week or month their smiles and their kindly gestures, and they must practice the prompt repression of resentment and aggression. For these intimate traits are of commercial relevance and required for the more efficient and profitable redistribution of goods and services. Here are the new little Machiavellians, practicing their personable crafts for hire and for the profit of others, according to rules laid down by those above them. (Ibid.: xvii)

Wright Mills developed the concept of the 'personality market' which describes the 'shift from skills with things to skills with people' (ibid.: 182) and central to this shift is the enhanced importance of the psychological dimensions of service work.

In this account of the new world of work, men and women 'are to be shaped' (ibid.: 183) and their personalities managed, by themselves and by others. Wright Mills noted that hundreds of white-collar workers employed by the Schenley Distillers Corporation were sent on a personality course in order to learn greater friendliness and enhanced people skills. White-collar workers were increasingly trained to exploit their bodies and personalities to such an extent that:

> In one large department store, a planted observer said of one girl: 'I have been watching her for three days now. She wears a fixed smile on her made-up face, and it never varies, no matter to whom she speaks . . . When a customer approached, she immediately assumes her hard, forced smile. It amazes me because, although I know that the smiles of most salesgirls are unreal, I've never seen such calculation given to the timing of a smile. (Ibid.: 184)

Central to Wright Mills's work on white-collar work is the realisation that a new labour aristocracy is springing up based on personal charm. This argument resonates with that made by McDowell in this book (see Chapter 21).

Part of the account of white-collar work presented by Wright Mills concerns the ways in which service workers acquire prestige or social esteem. This is not easy to unravel in that it is part of the process by which service workers construct their identities. There are many different processes implicated in the acquisition of prestige by white-collar employees but perhaps the most important are associated, as the label implies, with their dress. Many white-collar workers wear street clothes at work and according to Wright Mills, white-collar women spend more on clothes than 'wage-working women [blue-collar workers] of similar income' (ibid.: 241). The point is that for many white-collar workers their employment enables and requires them to wear street clothes at work. They may have similar incomes to factory workers but have higher prestige as their dress is one indicator of lifestyle and identity. Other ways in which prestige is achieved is via association with the name of a firm and with customers. Thus, secretaries do not construct their identity in terms of what they do, but rather with the company that employs them, and salespeople will try to borrow prestige from contact with high-status customers.

Fundamental to Wright Mills's account of white-collar work is the enhanced importance of formal education in determining an individual's life conditions. Formal education in secondary school and at university has for the 'new middle class . . . replaced property as the insurance of social position' (ibid.: 245). Education and the ability to succeed in the 'personality market' by capitalising on one's personalities underlies an individual's ability to compete in the service world (Bryson et al., 2004b).

Global sourcing or offshoring

The most recent literature on service activities (OECD, 2005) highlights the enhanced significance of internationalisation (see Chapter 7 and also the chapters in Part III) and, not least, the increasing ability of service providers to follow manufacturing by *offshoring or global sourcing* elements of their production systems (see Chapter 14). This is defined as the relocation of back- or front-office business processes to lower-cost locations. The term 'offshoring' is used in the USA and the UK and it does not have to entail the relocation of service work overseas; it can refer to relocations within the same continental landmass. An alternative term, 'global sourcing', has been developed to describe this process which can take two forms. First is foreign direct investment whereby a company establishes a foreign affiliate to provide a service, for example the call centres established by British Telecom in Bangalore and Hyderabad. Second, a firm may outsource the service to a third-party supplier which can either be locally owned or managed or be a foreign affiliate of another transnational corporation.

Global sourcing is closely related to developments in ICT. New technology has the potential to create entirely new services or to challenge the relationship that conventionally exists between the co-production of a service in time and space. Initially, replacing some employees with machines increased the efficiency and profitability of service firms located in developed market economies, but local expensive labour was still a central component of the production system. Nevertheless, the development of new technology and associated service production systems offered the possibility of relocating production from high- to low-cost production locations and, in the case of services, to locations with relatively low labour costs, for example India and China. Service production could thus follow manufacturing in the development of a 'second global shift' (Dicken, 2003) or a 'new international division of "service" labour' (NIDSL).

A number of factors lie behind the decision to send a particular service activity offshore. First, the service must be capable of some degree of standardisation that does not require face-to-face interaction with consumers. Second, the inputs and outputs required to deliver a service must be capable of being traded or transmitted with the assistance of ICT (OECD, 2005: 12). Third, some service activities are not fixed in space and can be provided either as a form of foreign trade or by the temporary relocation of a service worker to a client's premises, for example management consultancy or various forms of auditing (see Chapter 22). Fourth, specialist services can be provided from central locations with consumers travelling to avail themselves of the service. In many cases such services would be provided within the confines of a nation state, but some of these services are being consumed by a form of service-based travel, for example, education (secondary and tertiary), plastic surgery and a whole range of other surgical operations.

Unlike the first 'global shift', the geography of the second shift is determined by the educational and language abilities of service workers located in low-cost locations (United Nations, 2004: 165). For the English-speaking world this means that potential suppliers must be able to provide English-speaking employees, making the geography of the second global shift different from the first. It is not only constrained by language but also by cultural nearness, or the ability of foreign service suppliers to relate to customers located in other countries.

The global sourcing of services involves call centres that are providing relatively basic services (account management, travel agency and so on) and data processing, as well as a range of highly skilled white-collar work such as accountancy and legal services (Table 1.3). The trend to send the latter, high-value, jobs to places like India is starting to escalate. In January 2005, JP Morgan Chase, Intel and Microsoft announced plans to create some 7500 jobs in India in high-value tasks such as research and development and the processing of complex derivative trades. In the early years of this century such jobs would have been created in the United States. JP Morgan's strategy involves having 20 per cent of its workforce in India by the end of 2007. Cost is one of the key drivers behind this shift to India where industry analysts estimate that costs are about 40 per cent below US levels (Wighton, 2006: 4). Another key attraction is the availability of highly skilled staff that are being produced by the Indian higher education system. In order to limit its exposure to one country, JP Morgan is exploring other 'offshore locations' in Eastern Europe, China and the Philippines.

The global sourcing of both manufacturing and service work is complex as it involves more than just a simple dualism between onshore/offshore locations. In many instances, firms blend onshore, offshore and nearshore delivery systems to maximise the benefits that accrue from each of these locations. Offshoring represents the development of a complex and sophisticated 'second global shift' that is exploiting the cost and expertise differentials that exist between countries. The example of JP Morgan suggests the development of a geographical business strategy that is based around the creation of a service delivery system that blends outputs from different locations. These new ways of organising the delivery of high-value services urgently require further research.

The structure of the Handbook

It is not our intention in this section to provide a detailed overview of every chapter that is included in this Handbook. However, it is perhaps worth describing the framework that

Table 1.3 Jobs that have been sent offshore from the UK

Call centres	Business systems
Customer services	Graphics services
Out of hours claims (call centre)	Documents production
Back-office administration	Underwriting
Back-office processing	Technical lists
E-commerce	Equity research
Credit control	Business analysts
Internet services	Legal secretaries
Internet claims	Software development
Business services	City analysts
Accounts	Legal secretarial
Finance	Rail timetable enquiries
Human relations	Transcription services (voice and shorthand)
IT	

has been used to construct the collection. During the planning stage it was decided that a key feature would be a focus on the diversity of social science perspectives on services as well as accounts of different types of service economy. This has been a difficult task in so far as it has not always been possible to identify or persuade a colleague from a particular discipline or country to contribute to the collection. The Handbook includes contributions from some of the most influential geographers, economists, sociologists and management scientists that have been working for sustained periods on different aspects of the service sector. The geographical diversity is slightly more limited as the majority of the contributions come from developed market economies. At one level, this reflects the research priorities of colleagues in countries that have yet to experience a dramatic shift towards service employment. At another level, colleagues in developing or transition economies are concerned with understanding other problems that they are facing, for example, accession to the European Union, poorly developed infrastructure, or unequal trading relationships.

The Handbook is organised into five parts, each including chapters written from a variety of different perspectives. An exception is Part V which includes contributions only from geographers.

In Part I, five chapters provide a conceptual overview of the shift towards service work and activities. Together, these chapters provide a sophisticated and complex set of conceptual and theoretical explanations for the ongoing transformation of capitalism towards an information or service economy. Illeris explores the basic characteristics of services and argues that this economic category is still of value in understanding economies. This perspective is developed by Howells in a detailed account of the relationship between services and innovation. Key to his argument is the emphasis that he places on the diversity of the service economy as well as the difficulties involved in studying services; government statistics still do not capture the diversity and complexity of the service sector. A nuanced part of his argument is the contrast he identifies between research that confuses service 'production' with the 'effects' of services. This is an important point in that it highlights the relationship between service producers and consumers and the importance of co-production.

The chapter by Gadrey suggests that there are different types of service economy. America is often considered to be the archetypical service society (see Chapter 8). He argues that other models exist that may be more relevant for Europe's search for a path that will lead to the creation of high-quality jobs and services as well as greater social cohesion. In his analysis he identifies three distinctive models of national economies or service societies: the Anglo-Saxon, Nordic and continental European models. This theme is further developed by Stehr in an account of the different theories that have been developed to explain the shift towards an information age. Stehr concludes by arguing that the emergence of knowledge societies does not mean that modern societies are becoming uniform social and intellectual entities. Knowledge as a capacity for action allows for, and encourages, the co-existence and interdependence of historically distinct forms of social organisation and thought. The emphasis is on both the diversity and inherent complexity of knowledge economies. Finally, Petit revisits the debates regarding the differences that exist between manufacturing and services. A central part of the argument is based around productivity differentials that form the basis of W.J. Baumol's well-known model of unbalanced growth related to productivity differentials. In Baumol's model, services are considered to be stagnant while manufacturing is progressive and able to benefit from progressive productivity improvements. Petit questions whether some trends in work organisation and in consumption patterns in services can help us to foresee the end of the productivity paradox.

In Part II, the development of specific service economies is explored in considerable detail. The intention is to present a set of chapters that examine a similar set of issues but in different geographical settings. Five chapters present detailed accounts of the global service economy (Daniels), services and regional development in the United States (Beyers), services in the Asia-Pacific (Hutton), services in the transition economies of Eastern Europe (Stare) and, finally, Sassen revisits the debate regarding global cities as key sites for advanced producer services.

Part III explores service trade and the shift from the local to global production of services. Three chapters written by geographers (Chapter 12), economists (Chapter 13) and a management scientist (Chapter 14) review this debate but from very different perspectives. The first chapter, by Leinbach and Bowen, explores the role of transport networks in connecting people and firms together in the world economy. The focus is on service delivery associated with freight movements. This is followed by a detailed analysis by Deardorff and Stern of the barriers to international trade in services as well as the policy debates regarding the liberalisation of service trade. Finally, Enderwick explores the growing internationalisation of service activities, and the ways in which these operations are managed by multinational service firms. He argues that developments in ICT have created vast new opportunities for the international exchange of services long considered location bound. This is an important point, and Enderwick develops a nuanced argument by suggesting that these trends are not unique to services and lend support to the view that convergence between the various sectors of the advanced economies is under way. This convergence does not mean that the distinctive characteristics of services, long the subject of academic analysis, no longer matter; rather he suggests that they matter less in terms of international business activity.

In Part IV, the relationship between services, technology and innovation is explored by management scientists (Chapters 15 and 19) and geographers (Chapters 16, 17 and 18). Miles provides a detailed account of his ongoing research into innovation and knowledge-intensive service firms. His analysis begins by considering what sorts of service firm can be described as being most knowledge intensive. He then considers innovation within these firms, and finally their contribution to innovation in their clients. The relationship between clients and suppliers of producer services expertise is developed by Bryson and Daniels in a chapter that explores the types of external expertise that are used by British small and medium-sized enterprises (SMEs). The emphasis is on placing traded producer service expertise in the context of untraded forms of external advice that are used by SMEs to support their business activities. Rusten and Bryson continue the SME theme by exploring developments in ICT and its contribution to the foundation and functioning of industrial clusters. In this context, developments in ICT have removed some of the advantages that are attributed to a location in a cluster but they may also bind clustered firms further together or even create local agglomerations. The last two chapters in this section provide detailed case studies of service innovations. Murphy explores the ways in which services have been bound up in the processes of innovation that comprise the internet – past, present and future. He addresses this complex issue through the organising framework of the notion of 'disruptive innovation': a change in technological capabilities and attributes that undermines the basis upon which products, companies, or industries are organised and add value. The chapter by Nonaka et al. shifts attention away from ICT-enabled relationships to shop-based retailing. They provide a theoretically grounded and context-specific illustration of how one successful convenience store chain has innovated over time in co-evolution with its environment.

The focus of Part V is on service employment or on some of the distinctive people-based characteristics that are fundamental to understanding the service economy. Warf begins by challenging a fundamental conflict that exists in the service literature. The focus of many journal papers and books has been on the localisation of service activities. This emphasis can be traced back to some of the most influential papers (Hill, 1977) that stress that services are produced and consumed at the same time and in the same place. Warf takes as his point of departure the question of how and why some forms of service production are concentrated in a small handful of locales while other services freely roam the globe, creating a constantly changing kaleidoscope of new locales. This issue is fundamental to understanding the ongoing offshoring or global sourcing of service activities. McDowell develops the emphasis placed by Warf on embodied expertise by reviewing the literature on emotional labour in the context of a detailed investigation of sex, gender and sexuality in the service sector. In this she argues that some individuals, predominantly young males, are excluded from the world of service work on the basis of their accent, dress and attitudes to work. Beaverstock takes a very different perspective by exploring the working worlds of highly paid and extremely mobile professionals. He investigates the geography of mobile accountants and argues that the global circulation of professional staff is a business system used for the cross-border transfer of knowledge, expertise and professionalism. McDowell and Beaverstock develop both aspects of Warf's argument, with McDowell focusing on localised service employment and Beaverstock exploring service professionals who are able to roam in specific parts of the globe.

PART I

CONCEPTUAL PERSPECTIVES

2 The nature of services

Sven Illeris

Introduction

The questions to be discussed in this chapter concern the basic characteristics of services. First, is it useful to consider services as one of the main categories of all economic activities and products, a class on the highest level of classification? Here, it should be noted that the word 'services' has several meanings. Two are relevant in this book; however, this double use of the word has rarely caused confusion:

- services are a group of activities: trading, playing, driving and so on; and
- services are also the products or results of these activities: sales, concerts, journeys and so on.

Second, how can services be defined? In scientific work, precise definitions of the concepts used should of course be aimed at. However, it is not easy to arrive at a satisfactory definition of services, and the search for it has consumed much time.

Third, a broader discussion is engaged on the main characteristics of services as well as the implications of these characteristics for the ways in which services function in societies and the ways we can study them. In this connection, the borderline cases between services and other activities and products are scrutinised. One implication is the object of a special discussion, namely the question whether services create wealth. This question has played an important role in the history of economics, and an attempt is made to state how far it has been answered today.

Fourth, since services arguably constitute the most heterogeneous of the high-level categories of economic activities and products, subclassifications need to be considered. The most important subclassifications are presented and briefly discussed.

In the last section of this chapter, its main conclusions are briefly summarised.

Is 'services' a useful category?

The tertiary sector as a whole and the various kinds of services, like all phenomena, should be understood in their context and not be studied as isolated, rigid categories. However, even within a holistic perspective, it is necessary to structure our objects in order to get some understanding of them and act purposefully. We need to classify phenomena, trying to define categories which are as homogeneous and as different from other categories as possible; and label categories: historians delimit periods, biologists define classes, genera, species and so on. We start by defining a small number of very broad categories on a high level, and then subdivide them into narrower categories on lower levels. Biological species can in principle be defined unambiguously as groups of individuals able to produce fertile offspring. But such clearcut classifications are the exceptions rather than the rule. More often than not, class boundaries are rather blurred.

Which categories best capture the economic structure of societies and the fundamental changes that they undergo? The traditional division of economic activities is as follows:

- a primary sector producing goods directly from natural resources;
- a secondary sector modifying material goods; and
- a tertiary sector (also called services) of activities which do not produce or modify material goods.

This classification was already inherent in the writings of the French physiocrats, Adam Smith, Jean-Baptiste Say and Karl Marx (see, for example, Delaunay and Gadrey, 1987; Allen and du Gay, 1994; Hill, 1999), and was finally entrenched by Fisher (1935), Clark (1940) and Fourastié (1949). These authors attached a number of characteristics to each of the sectors, and the division into the three sectors is now the basis of statistical data all over the world.

It was only when the secondary sector in the 1970s showed signs of stagnation and the tertiary sector emerged as the possible future growth sector that the social sciences started to study services in greater depth. A need was then felt to make the nature of the object clear. Given the strong position of Marxism in the 1970s, which considered services to be non-productive or parasitic, it was also necessary for scholars with an interest in them to argue the legitimacy of their work. This is not the place to repeat the arguments against Marx and Adam Smith – their position on this question is hardly defended by anybody today. I shall refer only to Hill's observation (1999) that it is connected with the fact that up to the middle or the end of the nineteenth century, the accumulation of capital was seen as the yardstick of wealth – an idea that can be traced back to mercantilism – while economists now see the satisfaction of human needs as the ultimate goal of the economy.

Thus the 1980s became a decade with lively discussions on the nature of services. In the 1990s, these debates continued in a way which some would call a refinement of our understanding, while others might call it hairsplitting and sterile.

One question that has been discussed is whether the three sectors really constitute the best high-level classification of economic activities. This explicitly confronts the question of whether 'services' is a useful category. It is felt to be a problem that the boundaries between the three categories undoubtedly are blurred, especially the one between the secondary and the tertiary sectors. It is difficult to find characteristics which all services and no other activities have. And tertiary activities are very heterogeneous; cleaning a floor is something very different from Nobel prize-level scientific research.

For these reasons, some authors have argued that the concept of services is not appropriate. In particular, it is rightly argued that secondary (manufacturing) activities tend to become more and more similar to services (Hatchuel, 1994). At the same time, it is argued that services become increasingly industrialised or standardised – which is true in some cases, but it is not shown to be the prevailing trend.

Against these criticisms I would argue that we need classifications even if it is impossible to make them clearcut and totally satisfactory. That high-level categories are heterogeneous is unavoidable – more homogeneous categories must then be found on lower hierarchical levels. The question then is whether a better high-level classification than the three-sector division can be suggested.

If an all-purpose subdivision of services into a few classes existed, these classes might conceivably be promoted to top-level categories. But that is not the case: it will be shown later that a number of subclassifications of services compete, and none of them has been accepted to cover all purposes.

Other attempts to improve the high-level division into three sectors have involved defining a fourth sector. Thus, Gottmann (1961) suggested separating out from the tertiary sector the sophisticated, highly qualified services which he termed the 'quarternary' sector. This suggestion has not had much success, possibly because of data problems: it cuts right across even low-level categories, for instance between routine accountants and lawyers, working for small firms and households, and the 'knowledge-intensive business services' of the same industries.

Another attempt in the same vein was made by Porat (1977) to distinguish an 'information' sector, separating out from both the secondary and the tertiary sectors those activities that produce equipment for and services dealing with information. Inevitably this attempt also met data problems – Porat quotes a study of hospital nurses showing that 60 per cent of their time was spent on gathering and processing information and 40 per cent on patient care such as changing bandages. However, with abundant resources, the Porat report overcame these problems in the USA, and similar studies were made in other countries. It was a weakness that Porat did not distinguish between routine information and knowledge, but this was remedied by Baumol et al. (1989). The interest in this approach has tended to be on the decline, but de Bandt and Dibiaggio (2002) have recently revived it, pointing out that both the service and the information research traditions contribute to the understanding of the emerging new type of economy.

Another approach has been to distinguish a sector that comprises creative activities such as writing and publishing, composing and playing music, creating works of art, devising computer programs, making scientific discoveries, developing new industrial processes and so on. Such activities and their transmission to, and absorption by, consumers have the character of services. But their distribution in most cases operates via embodying them in (mass) media such as books, newspapers, records, disks, tapes, films, computer memories and so on, which have the character of goods – they can be stored, transported, owned and sold. However, their value and price depend on the service contents, not on the physical qualities of the medium. This author has argued (Illeris, 1989) that they constitute the most important borderline case between goods and services. Hill (1999) has suggested that the originals – but not the copies – should be considered a separate category which he called 'intangible goods'. However, Gadrey (2000) has argued that there is no reason to classify the originals and the copies differently.

To conclude, in spite of the weaknesses of the structuring of the economy into primary, secondary and tertiary activities, and the sound arguments behind some alternative suggestions, it seems that none of these has been accepted by societies in general and the scientific community in particular. The publication of the present book is just one piece of evidence. This inertia may partly be due to the fact that statistical classifications are difficult to change, but it is possibly also the case that the weaknesses of the traditional classification are felt to be less significant than those of the alternatives. Even if this is the case, ongoing inconsistencies in the official classification such as placing publishing in the secondary sector and other media in the tertiary sector should be remedied.

One aspect should be added to this discussion of the category of services, in which it has been assumed that service production is an economic activity. So it is, of course. However, Allen and du Gay (1994) have called attention to what they call the 'hybrid' identity of service relations (this concept will be explained later), which are at the same time economic and cultural activities, due to the social interaction required for the production and consumption of many of them. The consequence is that the quality of the service relation depends as much on the social qualifications of the service producers – for example, their ability to create trust and to negotiate – as on their professional qualifications. This corresponds to observations made in the 'service management' literature (Normann, 1984). The hybrid identity of service relations also corresponds with the satisfaction of the middle layers of 'Maslow's pyramid of needs'. The basic physiological needs of food, clothing and shelter are primarily satisfied by goods-producing economic activities. Once they have been satisfied, social, emotional and security needs get priority, and this is where the 'hybrid' services are demanded. In economic terms, this is also expressed in Engel's law: the richer people are, the higher is the share of services in their total consumption. The highest layers, for example, the needs for appreciation and self-realisation, have nothing to do with economic activities, a fact sometimes forgotten by economists.

The definition of services

As already mentioned, the traditional definition is that service (or tertiary) activities are those which do not produce or permanently modify material goods. As *The Economist* (1985) puts it, you can sell them and buy them, but you cannot drop them on your feet ('A GATT for services', 12 October).

Undoubtedly, this is also what non-scientists mean when they use the word services. And if at all possible, scientific definitions should avoid differing from the ordinary language, to limit misunderstandings and to keep the gap between experts and other people narrow.

Examples illustrating that service products are immaterial – or 'intangible' – could be 'teaching', 'cleaning', 'curing' or 'selling': there is no physical product which can be isolated from the process of producing it and the process of consumption or use. In contrast to such goods as vegetables, chairs and machines, which have an independent existence after their production and before their consumption or use, services cannot be stored, transported, owned or sold by somebody. Services are produced and consumed in one process, they are 'perishable' or 'ephemeral'. For this process, Eiglier and Langeard (1987) use the word 'servuction', whereby the consumer often plays an active role, which influences the quality of the service: students must actively absorb the teaching; the client must give the consultant information about the firm. One may speak of co-production.

One critique of the traditional definition, expressed by some economists, is that the immateriality of services is a rather accidental characteristic. The fact that the possibility of ownership is overlooked is to them more fundamental. Broussole (2000) notes that even the concept of theft has a different sense in services. As a stowaway on a ship, you can obtain transport without paying for it, but you cannot take it away and sell it.

For other scholars, it is more unsatisfactory that the traditional definition of services – in developed countries by far the largest of the three high-level sectors – is defined negatively, as a residual. Several attempts have been made to reach a more positive definition. Most of these focus on service production as relations between service producers and service users: between teacher and student, physician and patient, seller and buyer, consultant and client.

Among these attempts, Hill's definition (1977: 318) has widely been recognised as the most satisfactory one, though rather unwieldy. It is basically a definition of service products, but also mentions the activities that create them: 'A service may be defined as a change in the condition of a person, or of a good belonging to some economic unit, which is brought about as the result of the activity of some other economic unit, with the prior agreement of the former person or economic unit'. Gadrey (2002) has illustrated the definition as the triangle in Figure 2.1. Through the service intervention, the service provider A changes the condition of an object (goods, information, individual or organisation) C belonging to the service user B (individual, firm, public body), at the latter's request.

Hill's definition has clearly influenced the UN 1993 System of National Accounts in which the criterion of immateriality has been abandoned. But it still defines services negatively: 'Services are not independent entities over which it is possible to establish ownership rights. Their commercialisation cannot be dissociated from their production' (1977: 318).

However, some authors have recently attacked Hill's definition. As regards the concept of service relation, de Bandt and Dibiaggio (2002) call it 'not such a good idea' to define services in this way, since co-production is found in industrial activities, too, and because service relations contribute to economic development only if they imply a production of more complex knowledge through interaction between complementary competences.

Gadrey (2000) argues that there are many services with little or no relation between the producer and the user. In addition, the fact that Hill's definition relates only to the process

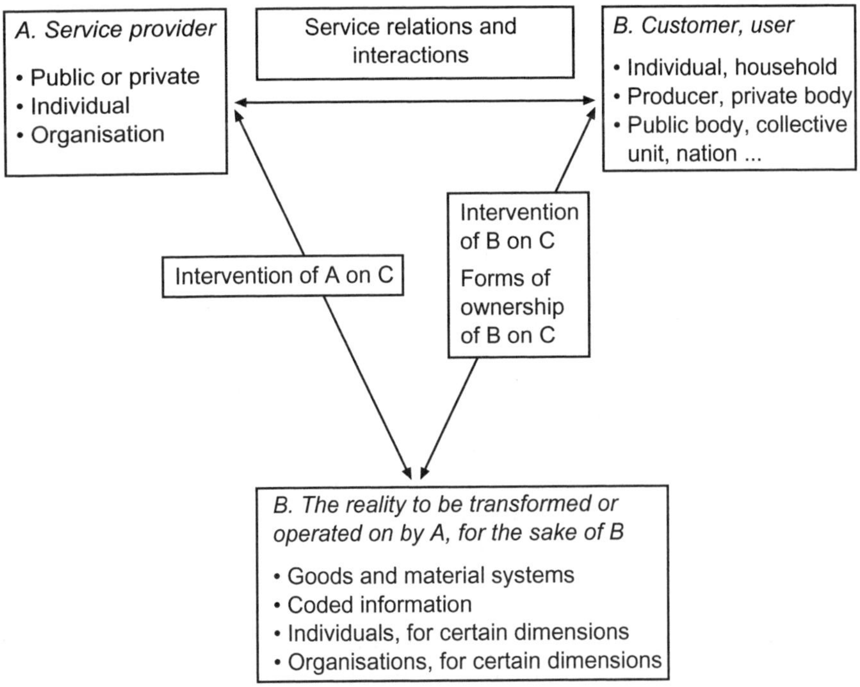

Source: Hill's (1977) definition as illustrated by Gadrey (2002)

Figure 2.1 The service triangle

and not to the output is for him another reason to reject it. Furthermore, Gadrey stresses the narrowness of Hill's central element of the 'change of condition', which he prefers to call the 'useful (long term) effect' – but observes that many service providers do not provide such effects (hotels, retailers, telecommunication companies). In retailing, the goods do not belong to customer B, and many services are produced whether there are customers requesting them or not (public transport). Finally, Gadrey argues that he cannot accept the lack of an entity existing independently of the producer and the user as a criterion, since it depends on social conventions about what is an 'entity'. While Gadrey's other arguments are convincing, I find this one formalistic – generally it is quite clear what an independent entity is.

With these concerns in mind, Gadrey goes on to suggest an alternative definition which includes as one subcategory the 'change-of-condition' or intervention type of services, while other subcategories are services which offer temporary provision of a technical capacity that is regularly maintained (for example, hotel room, car rental, supermarket shelves) or provide human capacities involved in some performance (for example, cultural). His definition of the production of services is thus: 'when an organisation A which owns or controls a technical or human capacity sells (or offers without payment in the case of non-market services) to an economic agent B the right to use that capacity for a certain period in order to produce useful effects on an agent C or on goods that he owns or for which he is responsible' (Gadrey, 2000: 384). One type of service not covered by this definition must be added, namely when a household itself employs a wage earner to look after its goods or its persons (or possible persons towards whom it has the duty of care). Gadrey stresses that some services are covered by more than one of the propositions of the definition, thus some relational services are covered by the intervention and performance rationales, and some postal services by the intervention and technical capacity rationales. Figure 2.2 illustrates this. The services which offer a technical capacity often show considerable gains in productivity, and many of them need not locate in proximity to the service users – a problem which will be discussed later.

Where does this discussion of definitions of services leave us? Beside the traditional one, at least two – Hill's and Gadrey's – have been suggested and supported with thorough theoretical arguments. Several others could be added.

Both Hill's and Gadrey's definitions are very complicated and difficult to use. But they both ignore an important group of services, namely the 'pure public services' such as general government, police and defence which serve society as a whole, not individual persons or firms. As regards police and defence, it may even be argued that they do not carry out activities all the time: their primary purpose is simply through their existence to deter undesirable phenomena, such as crime. It now seems clear that the relation concept and Hill's definition leave out too many services.

To conclude, there is something awkward about our approach to the definition of services. Biologists have taken the characteristics of organisms as their point of departure and then defined classes as those having similar characteristics; new knowledge about the characteristics – for example, DNA studies – has sometimes led to revised conclusions about the definitions of classes. But as regards services, the point of departure is the concrete conclusion: there is virtually no disagreement about which activities are services and which are not. The discussion is about finding the tacit premises that correspond to our conclusion.

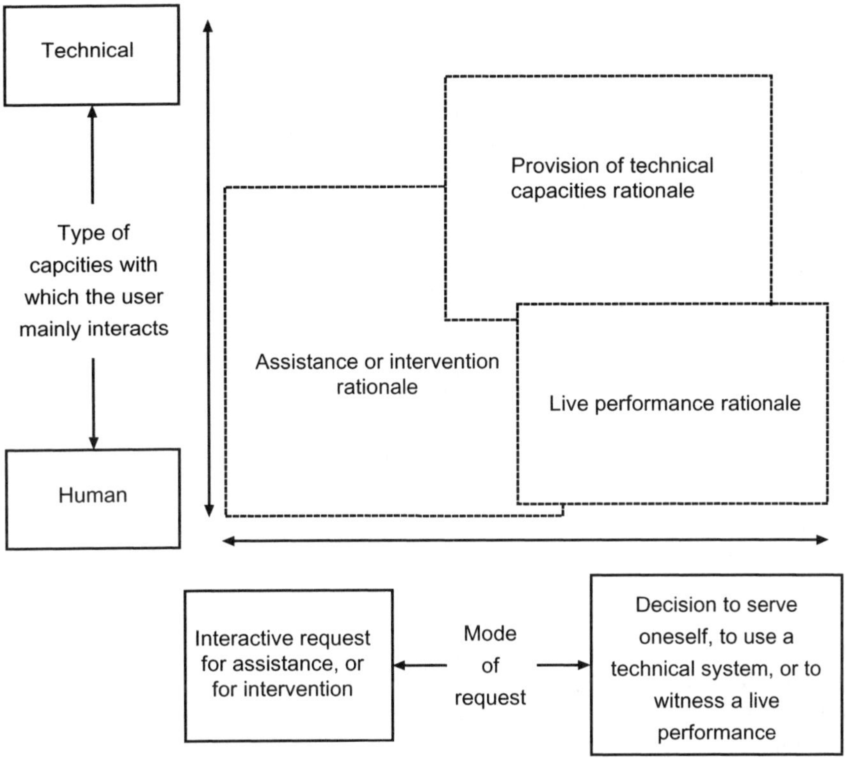

Figure 2.2 *Gadrey's three demand rationales*

These tacit premises were certainly not the complicated constructions suggested in the discussion. They were rather the simple ideas of immateriality and impossibility of ownership (these two characteristics are normally linked) of the traditional definition. So the question is whether there is any good reason why we should not return to the traditional definition and then, as we often have to in social sciences, accept that it is not perfect, and that there are borderline cases and exceptions. These will now be discussed.

Characteristics of services and their implications

Services have a number of characteristics, which again imply important consequences. Some of them have already been mentioned in connection with the discussion of definitions. They will be indicated more systematically now, beginning with the fundamental characteristics of many services.

First, the lack of an entity that can be distinguished – a material good that can be stored, transported, owned and sold – means that it makes little sense to measure the product itself (for example, teaching) and hence that the basic economic concepts of GDP and productivity are difficult to apply. On the other hand, it is possible to distinguish the effects, which constitute the reasons why users demand services, and which may be very durable, as in the case of teaching. There is a whole literature discussing the problems of productivity measurement in services (for example, Gadrey, 1996; Illeris, 1996).

Second, the fact that many services have the character of relations between producers and users means that they must be present at the same time and place, face to face – though contemporary telecommunications in some cases may relax this constraint. Since the travel costs (including time costs) of persons remain high, especially if the partners have to meet frequently, and since they normally have to share a common language and other codes, this fact makes it necessary for service producers to locate in the proximity of users. This also explains why internationalisation of services rather takes the form of setting up affiliates (with native staff) in the customer country than the form of trade. Another consequence is that service producers often have a local monopoly, which tends to slow down productivity growth. Finally, if demand is fluctuating over time – as in transport systems or in assistance systems for accidents – it is expensive to avoid the building of queues at some times and low productivity growth due to low uses of capacity at others.

Third, service relations mean that the activities are often labour intensive, with limited possibilities for economies of scale, for standardisation and for productivity increases. Their quality depends heavily on the professional and social qualifications of the personnel. 'Care' services for children, disabled and elderly people provide examples. Two services are never quite identical, which contributes to the problems of comparing productivity over time and space.

Fourth, the more the service has the character of co-production, the effect of which depends on the service user as well as on the producer, the more each service is unique. As every teacher and student knows, there are never two identical teaching lessons. This means that both parties must engage in the relation in a state of uncertainty, and that some mutual trust is required. Incidentally, the surrounding circumstances also play a role – a visit to Disneyland may be drowned out by rain. The consequence is that the normal market model is not applicable – its basic, though sometimes forgotten, assumption of identical products is not fulfilled (de Bandt, 1994). Of course, the parties will try to reduce the uncertainty, for instance by agreeing on the use of certain methods. Governments also protect customers in opaque markets, for instance by laying down authorisation rules for service providers such as physicians and lawyers.

Fifth, the effect of a service is often irreversible – one may think of a surgical operation (Gadrey, 1994).

Sixth, as already mentioned the final consumption of services does not satisfy the most basic human needs, hence they have a relatively high income elasticity (Engel's law). On the other hand, in developed societies the consumption of many services – not least those produced by governments – fluctuates little over business cycles, so they constitute the most stable part of the economy.

Other characteristics of services are of a less fundamental kind, but still important for their economic, social and geographical consequences.

Most persons engaged in service occupations perform non-manual, white-collar work on salary terms. Exceptions are the manual work and employment on wage terms in transport occupations (including internal transport within firms), repair occupations, cleaning and so forth. The fact that service activities employ a high percentage of women may be a consequence of this, and a derived effect is the large number of part-time jobs.

It has often been assumed that service activities involve relatively more qualified and more low-skilled jobs than goods production, but relatively fewer medium-skilled jobs. This may be correct in the US, where many unskilled workers have 'bad jobs' in service activities. In Western Europe, where minimum wages are higher, service personnel tend generally to be better qualified than manufacturing personnel (Illeris, 2002; see also the analysis by Gadrey in this book, Chapter 4).

The relatively low capital intensity of most service activities means that it is comparatively easy to start new firms (low entry barriers). Consequently, most new firms created are in the service sectors (not least when countries change from planned economies – with low priorities given to services – to market economies). In most private service sectors, there are many very small firms. Large firms, for example, in accounting and management consultancy, tend to organise themselves in ways that leave many decisions to the operative staff. There are, however, sectors with predominantly large corporations and traditions of strict hierarchical organisation, for example, banks, transport companies and retail chains.

Service activities use few natural resources and little energy. They cause little pollution, compared to agriculture and manufacturing. But again, there are exceptions, for example, transport and in some cases tourism.

The participation of users in service relations and the need for trust between service producers and users makes it difficult for service producers to monopolise expertise. Knowledge tends to leak, and legislation on patents and copyrights is difficult to enforce.

The borderline between goods and services

It has already been mentioned that the borderline between goods and services is blurred, and that some authors have even suggested the definition of a fourth top-level sector consisting of elements from both the secondary and the tertiary sectors. Here, some activities containing characteristics of both sectors will be discussed, beginning with some concrete examples and followed by a more general discussion of the border area.

Restaurants are traditionally classified as service activities, though some customers primarily buy prepared meals and only secondarily buy the use of the premises and the serving of the meals (especially in fast-food eating places). Butchers' shops were originally classified as secondary sector firms in the International Standard Industrial Classification (ISIC), but are now treated as retail trade. Repair activities have also been reclassified from the secondary to the tertiary sector. Indeed, the production and repair of goods may very often be similar activities and carried out by the same firms and workers. But otherwise, repair activities have many of the characteristics of services, and they correspond very well to Hill's definition.

Of course, the borderline has always been crossed by intermediate inputs required to produce a good or a service. Some service inputs are necessary to produce goods (management, book-keeping and so on). In recent years, the amount of service inputs to produce goods for final consumption has increased and now typically represents 70–80 per cent of the total costs, from research and development to disposal of the waste when the useful time of the good is over.

Another borderline problem is that the product which is sold to final consumers comprises both goods and service elements. It has always been the case in restaurants, as already mentioned. But now many such packages are marketed (Giarini, 2001): cars sold with after-sales service; computer packages of hardware and software; turn-key factories or institutions are exported including the training of their personnel. Of course, some packages may include only services, such as packaged tourist trips with travel, hotel accommodation, sight-seeing and so on. Usually, it is possible to distinguish between a core product (for instance, air transport from one city to another) and peripheral services (such as booking, baggage registration, serving of meals and drinks, offer of newspapers and so on).

The recognition that many services do not function without the support of material goods, and vice versa, has led several authors to talk of a 'goods–services continuum' (which does not exclude the above-mentioned view that it makes sense to distinguish between goods and services). Thus Barcet (1987: 37) distinguishes five possibilities:

- pure goods, which can be used independently of any services, for example, food;
- mixed goods, which can only be used in combination with some services, for example: instructions for how to use a machine;
- goods–service complexes, where both components are mutually dependent, for example, hardware–software packages;
- services depending on goods support. Thus trade depends on having goods to trade (in consumption statistics, the purchase of goods is classified under consumption of goods, not under consumption of services); and
- pure services, for example, a management consultation.

Barcet and Bonamy (1999b) mention that innovations often combine goods and services in new ways.

These recent approaches stress the complementarity between goods and services. In the 1980s, there was more focus on the question of whether services and goods could substitute for each other, for example, the use of public transport versus the purchase of private cars (Gershuny, 1978).

Do services create wealth?

An important question in connection with the nature of services, already mentioned at the beginning of this chapter, is whether services create wealth. It depends on what is meant by 'wealth'. To Adam Smith and Karl Marx, wealth was human labour accumulated in products that can be owned. Today, wealth is understood as a high degree of satisfaction of human needs. Barcet and Bonamy (1999a) stress that the value of services is in their effects, which are often long term, but which are difficult to measure and even to evaluate, and which in special cases consist of impeding undesirable events (for example, police services) or of reducing some costs. De Bandt (1995), on the other hand, maintains that pure public services do not create economic wealth and are always financed by governments or voluntary contributions rather than sold on a market.

The Smith–Marxian opinion corresponds to the deep-rooted popular notion that such people as wholesalers, bureaucrats and speculators are parasites. One often hears even highly educated people say: 'We cannot live by taking in each other's laundry' – or as the saying goes in Denmark: 'We cannot live by shaving one another' – which is not wrong, but the same is true of *all* economic activities: we cannot live by making, for instance, chairs for one another, either. The division of labour starts by me shaving you, and you making chairs for me. Today, the Smith–Marxian notion is not very useful: we would not have our contemporary wealthy society if we did not have services. The notion that services are not productive must be abandoned (Sayer and Walker, 1992).

On the other hand, the neoclassical point of view that wealth equals the price that can be obtained is not satisfactory either. This may be illustrated by an example from town planning: it is sensibly attempted to plan cities in such a way that – given that people must be able to reach a certain number of places (work, shopping, leisure activities, social contacts and so on) – the volume of traffic is minimised. In other words, we do not accept that even if transport can be sold on a market, and is taken into account as a contribution to GDP, it creates wealth.

There is still a need for theoretically well-based criteria which make it possible to distinguish between economic activities that create wealth and those which do not create wealth. It seems that the question primarily, but not exclusively, concerns services.

Classification of services

As mentioned at the beginning of this chapter, services are extremely heterogeneous. So much so that it has been necessary to consider whether a quarternary sector, an information sector or a media sector should be separated from other services at the highest level of classification of economic activities. What is to be discussed now are subdivisions into more homogeneous classes on a lower level. Service analysts have been busy suggesting such classifications, especially in the 1980s. Here only the most widely cited examples will be mentioned.

Service firms and establishments may be classified into sectors (industries) according to their most important product. This principle is a source of inaccuracy, since many firms produce several products – even mixtures of goods and services. Japanese critics have stressed the eurocentrism of the principle; East Asian firms tend to have broad arrays of products. Alternatively, service activities may be classified according to the occupations (job types) of the individual persons. This will be discussed later.

Among the sectoral classifications, we should first mention the UN's ISIC. The present version is from 1990 and is on a 2-digit level identical with the first revision of the EU Nomenclature des Activités dans les Communautés Européennes (NACE Rev.1). It is also used in the 1993 UN System of National Accounts. Its main service classes – using current scientific rather than the official statistical terminology – are:

- G Trade, repair of household goods;
- H Hotels and restaurants;
- I Transport and communications;
- J Financial activities;
- K Real estate, leasing and business services;
- L Public administration;
- M Education;
- N Health and social services;
- O Waste treatment, associations, recreative, cultural and sport activities, personal services;
- P Domestic services; and
- Q Diplomacy, international organisations.

The statistical offices of individual countries more or less follow this classification. However, many still use the old ISIC from 1968, which was rather poor with regard to the classification of services.

A widely used classification of services is according to user sectors, namely into 'producer services' and 'household services' (or 'intermediate services' and 'consumer services'). The former class consists of all firms which primarily sell to firms and public institutions, while the term 'business services' is used in a narrower sense, now often including only knowledge-intensive business services (KIBS).

The problem with this classification is that many sectors sell to both firms and households, for example, hotels, transport companies, banks and insurance companies. Another problem is that some services serve neither producers nor households directly, namely the 'pure public services' of general government, justice, police and defence. Some manifestations of religion, art and pure science may be included in this category, too.

Another widely used classification is based on ownership: 'private services' and 'public services'. However interesting this distinction is from a political point of view, its weakness is that the borderline is different from country to country and from one period to another.

A related distinction is according to the method of financing: that is, 'marketed' and 'non-marketed' (tax-financed) services. In most West European countries, some public services are marketed – public transport – while some privately owned welfare services are largely government financed. In France, health services are classified as marketed services.

Combining the user and ownership criteria in a rather pragmatic way, Browning and Singelmann (1975) devised a classification which captures some of the most important variations and has been widely used. It has four service groups:

- *Distributive services* transport and communications, wholesale and retail trade.
- *Producer services* finance, insurance, business services.
- *Social services* health, welfare services, education, postal services, government.
- *Personal services* domestic and personal services, hotels and restaurants, repairs, entertainment.

From a geographical point of view, the fundamental distinction is between activities which can sell to customers irrespective of distance and bring incomes to the area where they are located ('basic activities'), and activities which can sell to clients only within a limited area and hence are restricted in their development by their customers' purchasing power ('non-basic activities'). In contemporary societies, there are services in both groups, and it has become necessary to define a third one ('indirectly basic activities'): services which only sell to local customers, but are necessary for the interregional and international competitiveness of the latter.

The service management literature has its own discussions of appropriate classifications of services, based on such criteria as:

- equipment or people focus;
- customer contact time per transaction;
- degree of customisation of the service;
- degree of discretion (judgement) which front-office personnel can exercise in altering the service package or process;
- front office or back office as source of value added; and
- product (what) or process (how) focus.

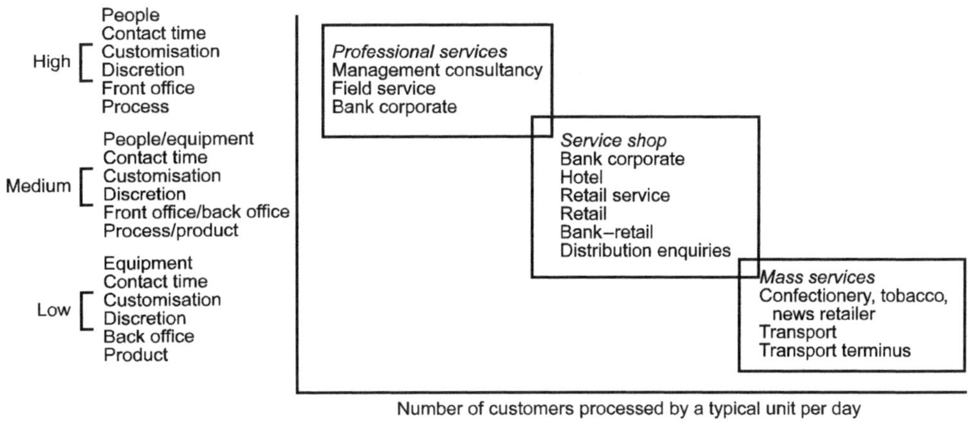

Source: *Silvestro et al. (1992)*

Figure 2.3 The three types of services

Silvestro et al. (1992) found that for management strategy purposes, service organisations could be classified into three types on the basis of the number of customers served per day. Each of these three types – 'professional services', 'service shop' and 'mass services' – would then have similar scores on all the six original dimensions, as shown in Figure 2.3.

Turning to *occupational* classifications, it should be recalled that the possible 'quarternary' and 'information' categories are primarily based on occupations. The UN has produced an International Standard Classification of Occupations (ISCO), but only a few countries publish data according to it. The main service classes are:

- 0/1 Professional, technical and related workers;
- 2 Administrative and managerial workers;
- 3 Clerical and related workers;
- 4 Sales workers; and
- 5 Service workers.

Hill's definition (1977) distinguished between things and persons as the object of the services, while Porat, in the same year, separated out information services. This line of thought has been followed by several authors (Illeris, 1985; Barcet, 1986; Delaunay and Gadrey, 1987), who more or less independently of one another classified services on the basis of their object.

More often than not, the object-based classes have been cross-classified with a distinction between individualised and standardised activities. In this way, one arrives at the following classes, which have been used to study skill and productivity as well as geographical issues:

- A Object: Goods — A1 Individual: Cleaning, hotels, restaurants, repair, renting
  A2 Standardised: Goods transport, retailing, wholesale
- B Object: Information — B1 Individual: Management, consulting, research, culture

	B2 Standardised: Back offices, routine administration, telecomm.
• C Object: Persons	C1 Individual: Education, health, care, sports, bodycare
	C2 Standardised: Transport of persons
• D Pure public services:	General government, police, defence, justice

Education – especially of children and adolescents – is here viewed as a person-related activity, in which social and psychological aspects are important, not as a sheer transfer of information.

Generally, goods- and person-related services as well as individual information services require proximity between the service producer and the service user or serviced thing. Hence, there is little internationalisation in these activities. However, standardised information services are increasingly liable to be transmitted via telecommunications and are exposed to international competition; as an example, one may mention the adult learning programmes now being developed by universities. However, technological progress allows more and more individualised and complicated electronic information transmission. Many activities have changed over time, for instance retailing from a rather individualised to a more standardised activity.

In genuinely individualised service production, it is only to a limited degree possible to increase productivity, and employment tends to increase, while the opposite is the case in standardised service activities.

Classification according to object may of course be cross-classified with the producer/household dimension, as has been done by Miles (1993).

Conclusions

In this chapter, the basic characteristics of services have been discussed. A main question is whether services constitute a useful category at the highest level of classifying economic activities and products. It is concluded that in spite of the problems connected with the concept, nobody has been able to suggest a better one. It should be added that service activities, besides having an economic nature, at the same time are social and cultural activities.

The precise definition of services has attracted much debate. The traditional definition is that service activities are those which do not produce or modify material goods. This definition has been criticised, but so have the alternative definitions that have been proposed. The author suggests that we stick to the brief and practical traditional definition.

In his mind, the following broader discussion of the main characteristics of services and the implications of these characteristics is more fruitful. Among these it may be mentioned that the immateriality of services implies that measurement of the products and of the productivity in service activities pose grave problems. This again makes the application of the general market model difficult.

In this connection, the many borderline cases between services and goods are discussed. It is concluded that instead of focusing on possible substitutions between them, recent approaches tend to stress their complementarity.

The old question of whether services create wealth is briefly taken up. On the one hand, the Smith–Marxian notion that services are not productive must be discarded. On the other, the author cannot accept the neoclassical view that the criterion of wealth is what can be sold on a market. There is a need for further theoretical work.

The final section of the chapter deals with the classification of services. It is concluded that for different purposes, different classifications are useful. No one classification has been accepted as being appropriate for all or even most purposes.

3 Services and innovation: conceptual and theoretical perspectives

*Jeremy Howells**

Introduction

The study of services and innovation remains a neglected area of study. Compared with the study of innovation in the manufacturing realm, the corpus of researchers in services interested in innovation remains small and fragmented, albeit they are experiencing steady growth. Why should this be so? Obviously much depends on history. Innovation in services was largely ignored, in large part because of the artefact, embodied and manufacturing-based paradigms that have remained dominant in innovation studies up until the present day. However, this begs the question of why it has taken so long for new conceptual frameworks to emerge in service innovation.

There are four factors which are presented as being involved in this lag, which also relate more widely to the study of services, but have had a particular impact on service innovation research. First, and most obviously, is that the study of services overall remains a neglected area of research. This is despite the constant refrain by researchers working on services that services make up such a large segment of economic activity within industrialised economies. And this is not a new position (although its relative size is). Even by the early twentieth century, service activity was such a size and significance economically in parts of Europe and North America that it made up something like a quarter to a third of gross domestic product (GDP) in countries in these two continents. It is therefore strange how little active study of the sector was undertaken even after the middle of the twentieth century. This neglect arguably continues. In David Landes's otherwise excellent and thought provoking historical tome, *The Wealth and Poverty of Nations*, published in 1998, no separate mention of services is provided in the index to the book and the significance of services in economic development in the text is at best indirect.

Leading on from this is the ongoing prevailing view of services being passive economic and innovative activities (Hipp, 1999: 163). Services are therefore all too frequently seen as being laggards (Miles, 1993: 661) and as consumers (albeit often significant consumers) of innovations produced by manufacturing firms. This view of services lacking merit or signifying real value (however expressed) goes back as far as Adam Smith (1776) himself who noted: 'The labour of the menial servant . . . does not fix or realise itself in any particular subject or vendible commodity. His services generally perish in the very instant of their performance, and seldom leave any trace or value behind them'.[1] Indeed, Landes echoes this view of services being lesser activities in his review of the decline of leadership by the British in industry. He notes 'As for new technologies and manufactures, well, jobs were opening up *in lesser lines*' (Landes, 1998: 453; my italics). He goes on to quote J.H. Clapham who noted that as branches close down, people leave them and move 'to some expanding occupation, say chocolate-making or chorus singing' and notes these new lines may not have the same social and economic value as their older employments. Thus,

Landes emphasises that many of the new lines (and he includes services in them) do not have the same payoff in skills, knowledge and high-wage jobs as some high-tech items. He circumscribes this observation by noting that neoclassicists may have the right view in that a dollar's worth of hamburger (or in this case, a service) is the same as a dollar's worth of computer chip. Landes, however, sadly does not explore this further or indeed the fact that some services may also be of a 'higher value' to the economy. In relation to multiplier and trade effects, which can be seen as one indicator of economic impact, the view that services are lagging economic activities with low multiplier effects has recently been challenged. Services have been found to have made a very strong contribution to the expansion of the economic base of local economic areas in the United States (Beyers, 2003: 22; see also Beyers, 2002a: passim).[2]

Third, as services have grown within the economy, they have simply become too big a 'sector' to study in any meaningful or coherent form. The sheer size and significance of the sector within the economy creates its own problems. Services not only account for an increasing share of the economy, but they are also far from homogeneous. In addition, they also interact among themselves and with other sectors of the economy (notably manufacturing) in complex ways. Thus, there is a significant challenge in reporting the diversity of activities covered by the service sector, and to provide an informed commentary on the innovation trends across these diverse activities. With such size and diversity, it is perhaps surprising that anyone could hope to cover satisfactorily such a heterogeneous and diverse set of industries with a single monomorphic model or paradigm. Fourth, is the inherent difficulty of studying intangible, disembodied changes over time which covers a key dimension in many service innovations. Whereas indicators and metrics of tangible products and equipment and their innovation may be difficult to survey, it is even harder when intangible changes are sought to be measured. Traditional across-the-board surveys of innovation, most notably the Community Innovation Survey (CIS) undertaken by the European Commission, have only very imperfectly captured innovative activity in services.

To these four factors may be added a fifth, namely that researchers in the field of innovation and services have been perhaps too cautious in generating new concepts and ideas relating to services and innovation. Some commentators have felt that service researchers have been too hidebound in seeking to merely adapt and apply manufacturing-centred innovation paradigms, without seeking to develop and explore totally new models and theories. This last aspect will be covered in more detail below, but raises a more fundamental issue in the generation of new concepts and ideas in the study of services and innovation which will be explored later.

Services and innovation and service innovation

The remit of this chapter covers services and innovation. However, 'services and innovation' as a term is not the same as 'service innovation' and this distinction needs to be emphasised before this review and analysis moves on. All types of innovation affect and make an impact upon service activities and in this respect services are no different from other forms of economic activity. As such, tangible and embodied forms of technological innovation in the form of, for example, new plant and equipment can and do have a significant impact on service industries and activities (Cell C, Table 3.1). This has been especially studied in relation to the effect of information technology (IT) goods and equipment on services (see an excellent review by Pilat, 2001 on this), although this is not necessarily positive in employment terms. Thus, Evangelista and Savona (2003: 471), using 1993–95 CIS II data, found a positive impact of information and communication technologies (ICTs) in Italy in most innovative and knowledge-intensive sectors, but negative impacts in all financial-related sectors (see also Sirilli and Evangelista, 1998).

However, as Tether et al. (2001b: 1120) caution, we should be wary of privileging the impact of ICTs as the major impact of innovation in services. Non-technological innovation in the form of disembodied, non-tangible and organisational change clearly has an important role here. Indeed, disembodied, non-tangible innovations are particularly seen as being in the realm of service industries (Cell D) and these are often 'read' as being 'service innovations' in many studies and texts. For other economic sectors, namely the primary (agricultural) and secondary (manufacturing) sectors, both tangible, embodied innovations (Cell A) and intangible, disembodied innovations (Cell B) also apply, although in much of the innovation literature (although not in management studies) the focus on innovation has been on tangible, embodied innovations or 'technological innovation'.

This basic typology of innovations, outlined in Table 3.1, provides a simple delineation of different types of innovation in relation to services and other economic sectors. However, within these basic types there can be considerable variation. Thus, non-technological innovations can cover a wide range of managerial and organisational changes. In turn, they can vary widely according to scale, ranging from inter-firm, organisational changes right through to changes in work practices at the group and individual levels.

This basic typology also links in with the other key distinctions or dimensions that have been used to describe and analyse innovation within service activities, namely: (a) product, (b) process and (c) delivery innovation. These distinctions have been formalised in the 'Oslo Manual' (OECD, 1997a) and used in the CIS surveys across Europe, but remain open to debate in services. Some would argue that the distinction and co-relation between (a) product innovations and (b) process innovations, is not so clear-cut in the service arena. Thus, there has been much discussion about the co-relationship between product and process innovations within services. Some see that product innovations can be introduced without accompanying process innovations, although others view this is as unlikely (Tether and Hipp, 2002).[3] A study by Djellal and Gallouj (2001) confirms the difficulty of distinguishing between product and process innovations in services. Indeed, Gallouj (2002: 40) goes further by noting: 'If the protagonists believe that the product they are paying for and from which they are benefiting is the immediate act of service delivery, then process and product are virtually one and the same thing'.[4] While more fundamentally still, Petit (1986: 9) argues that it is often very difficult to identify the 'product' when it comes to analysing service dynamics.

Table 3.1 Services and innovation: a basic typology

	'Technological': tangible, embodied innovations	'Non-technological': intangible, disembodied innovations
Primary, secondary (manufacturing)	A	B
Tertiary + (services)	C	D

In turn, delivery innovations, (c), are sometimes seen as a subset of process innovations, (b), (see, for example, Howells and Green, 1988: 164–5), while disembodied forms of organisational innovation are also included under (b) together with more specific production activities of services. In turn, Fraunhofer ISI (2000: 1 and 13) has identified two forms of organisational innovation, namely 'managerial innovations' and 'structural innovations'. Managerial innovations are those innovations that involve the creation of new organisational forms or management methods within the organisation.[5] By contrast, structural innovations are complementary innovations brought in to help the organisation adapt its structure to accommodate new technologies – genuinely novel, disembodied changes which may involve re-assemblage, or recombinations (Gallunc and Rodan, 1998) of other organisational innovations.

Other typologies have been attempted which, for example, seek to introduce the notion of radicalness (incremental versus radical process innovations). In relation to the issue of radicalness, Barras (1990: 219) was trying to inject a longer-term perspective and interpretation of service innovation and its wider impact, which could indeed also be linked to the notions of innovation trajectories and long-wave theory. The problem with such an analysis and typology of service innovation is that it is difficult to articulate and determine which are going to be the really radical innovations, and more particularly when they are going to make an impact on the economy, until a significant amount of time has elapsed after the event.

Finally, it should be noted that Table 3.1 provides only a basic conceptual typology of innovations. In reality, most innovations combine and use both technological and non-technological innovations and indeed have cross-sectoral involvements as well (see below). Thus, the whole issue of outsourcing and externalisation has had a big impact on the growth and development of services in general (Heshmati, 2003) and in particular service sectors (see, for example, MacPherson, 1997; Coe, 2000) and is a process which involves complex arrangements and configurations of both hard (tangible) and soft (intangible) innovations to be effective. As such, real-world innovations rarely wholly reside in one cell, but involve subtle and varied combinations of others.

Existing concepts and models

Existing concepts and theoretical perspectives of services and innovation have been grouped together according to various dimensions. Notably, Gallouj (1997, 2002), Bryson and Monnoyer (2004; following Gallouj) and Tether (2003) have grouped their reviews on the basis of three broad types. For Gallouj, and Bryson and Monnoyer these relate to: the 'technologist', the 'service-oriented' and the 'integrative' approaches. Tether (2003) adopts a broadly similar taxonomy, again identifying three basic approaches: a 'traditional' view of services; the 'Lille' school; and an emergent, less-defined view centred on 'strategic positioning' (and Austrian and evolutionary economics more generally; Tether, 2003: 482–3). Studies seen to adopt a 'technologist' approach of innovation in services are seen to focus on the introduction of artefact, hardware-driven technologies and systems into service firms and organisations. Tether's 'traditionalist' view directly parallels that of Gallouj's 'technologist' approach, and emphasises the supplier-dominated perspective associated with sectoral taxonomies of technological activities and linking this with the work of Evangelista (2000) and Miozzo and Soete (2001) seeking to extend and refine Pavitt's (1984) earlier taxonomy. This view of innovation in services is arguably still held as the dominant paradigm for those working *outside* the services research community (Howells, 2000a).

By contrast, 'service-oriented' approaches have sought to move away from what might be seen as merely adapting manufacturing-centred innovation models to instead focusing on the peculiarities of service innovation and how this might lead to new conceptualisations of innovation processes in relation to service activity. The service-oriented approach and Tether's Lille school, associated with the work of Gallouj and others (Gallouj and Weinstein, 1997; Gadrey and Gallouj, 1998; Sundbo, 1998; Sundbo and Gallouj, 2000; den Hertog, 2000; Djellal and Gallouj, 2001), are similar; the research team based at Lille has done so much work to highlight the distinctiveness of service innovation and to move the debate away from earlier supplier- and technologist-dominated models of service innovation. The service-oriented, Lille perspective also links in with the particular focus on knowledge intensive business services (KIBS; see, for example, O'Farrell and Moffat, 1991; O'Farrell and Wood, 1999; Miles, 1994, 2000b; Bettencourt et al., 2002) in relation to client-oriented service innovation. However, as we have noted, Gallouj (2002: 18) as part of this Lille school now sees himself as moving away from this approach. In developing this view of distinctiveness and differentiation, Tether also believes that the Lille approach goes too far in emphasising the highly differentiated, bespoke nature of service provision with its close relationship with clients. Much of this perspective may have been derived from the particular empirical probe of such work, which was often focused on rather specialised, knowledge-intensive services, which in turn relied on client-intensive relationships, and the co-production of services. Tether's own empirical work has obviously been important in guiding his position here and his critique of the Lille school – in particular, his highlighting the often standardised and low-technology nature of many service outputs (see also Ducatel, 1999) and the more in-house and independent, rather than co-produced, basis of innovative activity (Tether, 2003).

The emergence and rise of the 'service-oriented' approach and its focus on what might be termed the 'high peaks' of service activities in terms of knowledge intensity, innovativeness and client-intensive relationships is, however, understandable in a Kuhnian sense, in that it was seeking to reject the previous traditionalist paradigm which saw services as simply being passive, supplier-dependent and non-innovative sectors. The development of the service-oriented paradigm was as much (if not more) about *rejecting* the traditionalist paradigm, as in creating a necessarily coherent new one (Kuhn, 1962: 77). In seeking to cast out the traditionalist paradigm, proponents of the new paradigm were almost obliged to focus on selecting firms, activities and sectors that readily and most starkly contrasted with previous notions of what services and innovation were about. The privileging in the 'service-oriented' paradigm of co-production and client-intensive arrangements in service innovation may also have been influenced by the substantial amount of research by geographers and others (Tordoir, 1994; Quinn and Dickson, 1995; Cornish, 1996; Bettencourt et al., 2002; Wood, 2002a, 2002b, 2002c). This work highlighted the importance of co-production between service providers and uses in relation to location and spatial trends (as well as the impact of telecommunications in de-coupling the need for co-location of service production and use; Illeris, 1994).

Finally, the 'integrative' approach recognises the convergence of goods and services in both their production and consumption and seeks to develop an integrated theory to cover both segments of the economy. In this third set of approaches identified by Gallouj and Tether (Gallouj's 'integrative' and Tether's 'strategic positioning' approaches) also have similarities with each other, but they are not so closely related. Both stress the often close links between manufacturing and services in provision, consumption and strategy (see, for example, Howells, 2000a, 2001, 2004; Tether et al., 2001b; Daniels and Bryson, 2002; Gallouj, 2002; Tether, 2003; Bryson and Monnoyer, 2004) which Gallouj seeks to privilege as part of his aim 'to reconcile goods and services in a single innovation theory' (Gallouj, 1997: 123). However, it goes beyond this simple conceptual aspiration – it also relates to the deep, practical realities associated with the fact that it is often becoming difficult to distinguish between manufacturing and service companies; the two 'grand' sectors are becoming increasingly blurred (Gallouj, 2002: 1). However, as Howells (2004: 22–3) notes, much of this close inter-linkage of goods and services and in relation to their production and consumption has long been recognised, although it certainly has not been adequately articulated within service innovation research until now.

In the case of the 'strategic positioning' approach, Tether seeks to highlight a number of key dimensions influencing and characterising service innovation. These are that: (i) service firms are highly conditioned by their task environment and competitive position; (ii) nonetheless, though, service firms can exhibit a wide variety of strategies within these different environments; and (iii) they deploy a mixture of 'hard' and 'soft' technologies in achieving their desired strategic managerial innovations. In identifying this third perspective, Tether also seeks to stress the wider evolutionary process of change occurring within service activities and in particular, the close intertwining (or rather inseparability), of product and process innovations and combinatorial aspect of combining both hard and softer technologies (as against the primarily 'soft' technology approach provided by the service-oriented or Lille approaches; compare den Hertog et al., 1997: 33) to yield new service innovations and the somewhat more independent and stand-alone nature of service providers. The combinatorial aspect of manufacturing and services and hard and soft technologies, therefore, appears in both the integrative and strategic positioning approaches, although the former focuses more on the innovation process *per se*, while the strategic approach views innovation within the wider realm of strategy and competitive position of the firm.

The first two contrasting approaches pick up a theme highlighted by Hart and Service (1993) in relation to conceptual developments associated with marketing theory and services. They noted that some marketing academics have felt that services do not warrant a separate conceptual approach to general marketing and this has parallels, as we shall see, with the 'technologist' approach. Others believe that accepted research techniques applied in manufacturing sectors do not provide effective insights into service sectors (ibid.: 50) and this has parallels with the 'service-oriented' approach. Gallouj (2002) goes on to note that these three main approaches can be seen as part of a natural 'life cycle' in the theoretical development of service innovation. Gallouj, not surprisingly on this basis, sees the integrative approach as the most desirable approach and adopts it as a framework for his own studies on service innovation (ibid.: 27 and 1).

The three-stage framework is clearly appealing. Early studies, imbued with manufacturing-dominated paradigms focus on how the adoption of technological innovations, most notably IT equipment, had an impact on service sectors in terms of employment and organisation (see above). The growth and diffusion of service automation was one such theme (Collier, 1983; Holland, 1985). From this we have what might be seen as the reactive, 'service-oriented' phase seeking to assert the distinctiveness of services and the inadequacies of previous models based on manufacturing. Finally, we have what might be termed the reconciliation, 'integrative' phase; manufacturing-based innovation models may have something to say about services (while it may also be hoped that innovation models derived from the study of service activities may have implications for how we perceive innovation processes within manufacturing). This is coupled with the acknowledgement that there is much inter-linkage and overlap between services and manufacturing and the eventual prospect of a holistic model of innovation covering both manufacturing and service activities. Studies can in turn be readily slotted into this framework, although perhaps not quite as easily as might be expected. As noted earlier, studies seeking to investigate the adoption of IT and impact of productivity changes on this process would be seen as part of this technologist approach.[6]

Clearly the third stage has been much harder to determine. The third paradigm is still emergent and, as yet, ill defined. Indeed, this is reflected in the number of studies that have been attributed to this 'third way'. Thus, Bryson and Monnoyer (2004: 214–16) can identify only a few studies (Howells, 2000a; Gallouj, 2002; Daniels and Bryson, 2002) which may be seen as adopting an 'integrative' approach. Equally, Tether (2003: 484–5) only quotes his own multi-authored work (Tether et al., 2001a) and that of Howells (2000a) and Uchupalan (2000). Because such approaches are so relatively new and sparse, they are therefore understandably difficult to articulate fully.

Indeed, given the relative youthfulness of service innovation research, this can equally be applied to the other approaches, which indeed should not be seen so much as clear-cut phases of service innovation research, but rather as one of incremental development. It is still too early to judge how clearly identifiable these different phases in service innovation research are and there is continuing overlap. Although one can discern a shift towards the last two approaches, with the last set of linked, 'emergent' approaches ('integrative' and 'strategic positioning') certainly being the last to emerge, research within all three frameworks is still very active. In terms of distinctiveness, although there are differences between the second and third set of paradigms, how far it is a clear shift, or whether it is a more gradual evolution, is difficult to discern. Given the paucity of work in this area, empirical research in all three areas will continue to be highly valued and can only add to a general richness of understanding in service innovation. In this way it may be more useful to see the groups of research around these paradigms as accretions of work helping to lay the foundations for future research in a vertical way, rather than starting afresh each time in a more linear, block-building and horizontal way.

Services and innovation: wider relations

So far this chapter has reviewed the literature on service innovation in a focused but isolated fashion. It should be noted, though, that researchers in this field have drawn on two wider branches of research: service and innovation research and this is apparent in the development of the service innovation field outlined above. As also noted, in relation to the issue of client relationships and work proximity, research into the relationship between geography, work organisation and service development has been an important and longstanding influence on more specific service innovation research, but also vice versa. Indeed, research into the field of geography and services in relation to innovation and technological change has paralleled the conceptual development of the three service innovation paradigms noted above. Thus the first phase of work centred on the impact of technological change, and specifically IT, on the general organisation and location of services. The main focus of this work lasted until the early 1990s, but still continues today. The role of IT in the emergence of 'back-office' units is one example here (Baran, 1985), but also more generally in how developments in telecommunications may lead to the decentralisation of service activities (see, for example, Hepworth et al., 1987; Howells and Green, 1988) and its more general internationalisation (Langdale, 1985).

By the early 1990s, there was a growing acknowledgement that the impact of IT and other technologies was highly differentiated between sectors, but also between firms and organisations within sectors. There was a growing realisation that how firms used the technologies and adapted their work structure and the 'hard' technologies they acquired, were important in the organisational and geographical development of their activities. Internal disembodied, organisational innovations were therefore acknowledged as important elements in how service firms utilised these externally acquired technologies. Above all, close client proximity, at least in relation to higher-order business and professional services, were seen as important delimitators of how firms shaped their organisational structures (Illeris, 1994; Tordoir, 1994). Thus, more recently, Wood (2002c: 997) in relation to consultancy services noted that consultancy inputs were most likely to exert an innovative effect when there is close and continuous interaction of client and consultant expertise. However, other proponents have sought to emphasise the process of spatial de-coupling away from the requirement for close interaction and proximity (Sampson and Snape, 1985; Cornish, 1996; Quinn and Dickson, 1995; see also Rusten et al., 2004b). The rise of back-office functions within service activities was highlighted more starkly with the rise of call centre operations in the UK and elsewhere. These call centres were using very much an established technology, but in new (disembodied) ways and were in turn having a profound impact on both regional and national economies (Marshall and Richardson, 1996; Richardson and Marshall, 1999; Bristow et al., 2000; Richardson et al., 2000).

The issue of disembodied processes and work organisation therefore came more to the fore in such research, with the realisation that non-technological innovation of how firms operated and organised themselves was important here, as were the barriers to such developments (Tucker and Edmundson, 2003). This phase of research again strongly parallels the service-oriented paradigm of service innovation research more specifically. Latterly, this research has evolved further into a more qualitative interest, particularly at a more individual or group level on how changes in work practices and innovation are affecting organisations and workers alike (Miozzo and Ramirez, 2003; Ramirez, 2004). How an individual feels about working in a call centre has a profound impact on much larger firm issues, such as staff turnover, labour productivity and levels of service which in turn influence firm growth and performance (Wickham and Collins, 2004). It is only really now that these more 'localised' workplace and work practise effects arising from, and being part of, such disembodied innovation processes, are starting to be recognised as key elements in service innovation research.

In relation to integrative and emergent paradigms, it could be argued that in some ways geographical and regional economics has long recognised the close interaction between manufacturing and services. This centres not only on studies examining linkages between business and producer services and manufacturing (see, for example, Keeble et al., 1991; MacPherson, 1997), but also attempts to analyse employment, multiplier and trade effects arising from manufacturing and services and their interaction in local areas and regions (Beyers and Alvine, 1985; Beyers, 2000; Wernerheim, 2004). It also more directly involves the relation between service innovation and urban and regional development (for example, Howells and Green, 1986; Muller and Zenker, 2001; Thiel, 2002; Wood, 2002c; Rubalcaba-Bermejo and Gago, 2003) in terms of how innovation will affect future economic growth and development.

Wider relations in the context of intellectual property (IP) regimes of services and regulatory framework have been explored both in terms of how IP may influence and shape service innovation, but also as an indicator for service innovation (Andersen and Howells, 2000; Miles et al., 2000; Blind et al., 2003). It has often been commented upon that services have much weaker IP regimes and this will impede and restrict their innovative progress. Whereas manufacturing and science-based firms, producing tangible goods, have benefited from a strong patent regime, service firms have lacked an effective IP regime, associated with trademark or copyright legislation, for example, from which to protect more intangible innovations. Recent evidence suggests that service firms do not rate the lack of effective intellectual property rights as a major hurdle in innovation (see, for example, Tether, 2003), but it could also reflect the fact that they use other mechanisms, such as secrecy, short cycle times and new product innovations closely coupled with complex and tacit forms of work organisation (Andersen and Howells, 2000). This may also explain why, although trademark and copyright data for service enterprises may have some usefulness as indicators for innovative activity in services, their applicability and wider utility, as yet, remain limited (Blind et al., 2003).

Services and innovation has also been explored in relation to the systems of innovation approach. This exploration has been undertaken in a number of ways. First, the role of services as part of the innovation and technological infrastructure (Howells, 2000b; Muller and Zenker, 2001); second, the way that services may form and react differently within an innovation system (Howells and Roberts, 2000; Sundbo and Gallouj, 2000); and, third, by more directly representing services as a sectoral system of innovation (Tether and Metcalfe, 2003). All three interrelated perspectives have sought to reassess and rearticulate the systems of innovation approach in the light of what research in service innovation has revealed about services in the innovation approach. Thus, in brief: no longer should services be seen as simply passive, support elements within the innovation system; services involve more loosely coupled but interactive overlapping systems of innovation; and services display different sectoral characteristics and identity from traditional manufacturing sectors. However, in asserting some of the distinctive and peculiar (in comparison to manufacturing) characteristics, these studies can also be seen as reinserting services and service innovation within the wider fabric of the innovation system and the economy more generally. As such, they can be seen as emerging to form part of a more holistic approach of service innovation research that has developed over recent years.

Conclusions: old and new challenges

Before identifying potentially new issues to be considered in service innovation research it is important to recognise old, but continuing, challenges. The most significant and all-embracing of these, echoed in the constant refrain by researchers studying services over the years, is the lack of adequate data, indicators and methods to analyse services and service innovation. As Greenfield noted in 1966, there is a 'dearth of data' (p. 10) in the services field and an 'attempt should be made to develop as much information . . . for services as we have for goods' (p. 130). It is no different today. Thus, the European Commission in December 2003 noted 'serious deficiencies in our understanding of the structure of the services sector and the factors influencing the growth of services enterprises remain. The available statistical material does not reflect appropriately the dominant position of services in the economy' (Commission of the European Communities 2003: 36). Services are difficult to study and conceptualise. A priori model building (followed by empirical testing) may be seen as a more elegant way to proceed by academics, but much can be gained from a posteriori model development generated from the analysis of data and statistics. However, for this to occur comprehensive datasets and robust indicators are required, both of which service research, as a whole, and service innovation research, in particular, still lack.

Closely related to this challenge is one noted by Hill (1977) where much service research confuses service 'production' (and the processes involved with this), with the 'effects' of service. Arguably, most existing service innovation indicators have focused on service processes rather than service effects. It could be argued that this criticism does not apply only to service innovation. Many indicators applied to the manufacturing realm also examine what Hill sees as innovation 'production' rather than innovation 'effects'. However, it is certainly much easier to measure the effects of, say, a new machine tool which can produce 'x' more components ('quantity' effect) or produce them more accurately (within a few microns; 'quality' effect). In a narrower sense, this neglect on effects could be interpreted as indicating more work being required on service productivity effects. It is difficult to dispute that more research needs to be undertaken on such effects, but innovation effects cover much more than what is traditionally perceived as productivity effects (what may be summarised as the efficient use of factor inputs). It also covers the *value* (qualitative as well as quantitative effects) of consuming a service innovation to the consumer, whether it is a personal, household or intermediate service. Consuming a service may therefore yield benefits in terms of saved time or improved resources, but it can also mean much more than this, and this is where the constant refrain of the service sector productivity paradox comes in. Much of this paradox is exactly because services are consumed not just for their productivity cost effects, but also for their contribution to value creation.

Wood's (2002b: 112) comments are illuminating here:

> Value arises primarily from the applications of knowledge through human expertise and ingenuity . . . These tend to be 'low-productivity', labour and especially expertise-intensive functions drawing on financial, planning, design, strategy, marketing, logistical, and many other skills . . . Far from imposing a 'cost disease' on production, as the classic Baumol argument suggests (Baumol 1985), this may represent an efficient aggregate division of labour to serve, and also drive market change.

Innovation (certainly in the early stages of its development and application) may therefore require more labour-intensive support from specialist service providers than old-established methods.

If the effects, rather than simply the process, of service innovation require more emphasis and study, so does the consumption process as an aspect of service innovation require more emphasis. A key aspect of how services are defined relates to their consumption, while how services are consumed represents an important dimension in the innovativeness of a service (Howells, 2004). Indeed this is implicitly, if not explicitly, assumed in much of the client-intensive service studies, which highlight the importance of the client (consumer) in many service-oriented innovations. It also provides part of the reason why so many specialist business services with close client interaction have done so well and grown so fast (Wood, 2002b). Arguably, such service firms have grown so rapidly not only because of their specialist knowledge and bespoke generation and delivery of services to the firm, but also in their ability to *articulate* new wants, and reformulate existing demands, for their clients.

This emphasis on consumption also ties in with the Austrian approach which seeks to stress that the actor's (consumer's) views are important in relation to innovation. Thus, the concept of what an innovation is and whether it can be considered as an innovation depends as much on the (subjective) assessment of the consumer as of the producer (O'Driscoll and Rizzo, 1985) and how it is used (Robertson and Yu, 2001). The benefits (effects) of service innovation (or innovation more generally) may therefore often depend as much on how the innovation is consumed as how it is produced. In a sense this represents going one stage further than simply focusing on the absorption of an innovation (see Cohen and Levinthal, 1990) and suggests that more attention should be paid to the wider consumption and use of service innovations (both internally and externally to the firm in relation to intermediate consumption and services but also in terms of final consumption by individuals and households). In addition, it is argued that the consumption of services, and how this relates to service innovation, holds one of the keys to the onward development of the third, 'emergent' phase of service innovation research outlined above.

Notes

* Thanks go to comments made by various members of the services team at the Institute of Innovation Research. The views expressed are the author's alone.

1. Volume I, Book II, Chapter III, p. 330: 'Of the accumulation of capital, or of productive and unproductive labour' in Adam Smith (1776), *An Inquiry into the Nature and Causes of the Wealth of Nations*, 1976 edn edited by R.H. Campbell and A.S. Skinner with W.B. Todd, Oxford University Press, Oxford.
2. Although it is revealing that William Beyers started to challenge the laggard economic nature of services as far back as the mid-1980s (see, for example, Beyers and Alvine, 1985; see also the even earlier contributions of Daniels, 1983; Coffey and Polèse, 1989; Illeris and Phillipe, 1993), but this has still not gained much recognition outside the relatively small realm of service researchers and government advisers.
3. This discussion is not necessarily unique to services; even in manufacturing literature some assert that product innovations will require process change and innovation to accompany their implementation, however slight that might be (Kraft, 1990: 1030).
4. This is used as the basis of a broader critique of Saviotti and Metcalfe's (1984) analysis of technological indicators in relation to services.
5. This, in turn, has parallels with Henderson and Clark's (1990) concept of 'architectural' innovations.
6. Although the positing by Gallouj (1997: 136–7; see also Bryson and Monnoyer (2004: 210)) of Barras's (1986, 1990) work as being a 'technologist' approach is somewhat at odds here, given that although his work does concentrate on the impact of technological innovation on a service sector (financial services), it also seeks to reject the manufacturing-driven product life-cycle by seeking to affirm the reverse life-cycle concept in a service situation. Surely there is some part of a 'service-oriented' dimension to his analysis by seeking to reject a previously held manufacturing-centred life-cycle paradigm?

4 National economies and the service society: the diversity of models

Jean Gadrey

Introduction

A 'growth regime' dominated by services became established in some countries earlier than in others. This is particularly true of the USA, a country that has for a long time been thought of as a 'model' and which has been the main point of reference for those in Europe seeking to identify the economic policies most likely to encourage the creation of wealth and jobs in services. However fascinating the American model may be, it is not the only one. Other models exist, and they may be more relevant to the search for a European path to the creation of high-quality jobs and services, one that takes greater account of social cohesion.

Our analysis leads to the identification of three models of national economy and service society: the Anglo-Saxon, Nordic and continental European models. Terminology of this kind is found in the work of other authors who have sought to construct international typologies, notably that of Esping-Andersen in *The Three Worlds of Welfare Capitalism* (1990). Esping-Andersen's three worlds or 'regimes' are denoted as follows: liberal (closest country: United States), corporatist (closest country: Germany) and social-democratic (Sweden, Scandinavian countries). Our typology produces groupings that are, in some cases, close to those of Esping-Andersen. However, the criteria we use are somewhat different, since our typology is based not on the characteristics of the welfare state but on the quantitative and qualitative structures of employment in services. Our approach is closer in some respects to that of Castells and Aoyama (1994) and Aoyama and Castells (2002), whose analysis relates to only seven countries and does not, therefore, enable them to construct a typology.

Three criteria will be used initially in order to separate out developed Western countries in terms of the type of economy and service society prevailing in each one. The purpose of these criteria is to identify contrasting situations on the basis of empirical data, without yet offering any interpretation of these contrasts, a task reserved for later sections of this chapter. The first criterion is, quite simply, the 'quantitative' structure of the service sector, as measured by the relative share in employment of the main activities that make it up. The second, more qualitative criterion is job quality and skill levels in services. The third and final criterion is the relative importance of market and non-market services in the service sector as a whole.

The structure of the service economy by major activity: three types

In order to carry out a comparative analysis of national service sector employment structures by industry, the various activities that make up the service sector have to be grouped together to form a limited number of major subsectors. Our starting point here will be a fairly widely accepted division of the service sector (which has its roots in older studies by

Singelmann (1977) and is used particularly by Castells and Aoyama) into four main subsectors: distributive services (transport, communications and trade), personal services, producer services and social services (broadly defined to include essentially education, health and public administration). However, since it is our objective to reveal contrasts in terms of service employment structures between the countries under study, trade and personal services will be added together to form the TPS subsector. In our view, Singelmann's classification is ill-suited to dealing with employment issues in services: in terms of the types of jobs and working conditions they offer, trade services are much closer to personal services than transport and communications. We shall confine ourselves to comparative data on two major subsectors, namely TPS (the two largest elements of which are retailing, and hotels and catering) and social services. It is these two subsectors that provide the most contrasting results. Briefer reference will be made to producer services, another interesting case.

The analysis will also be restricted to countries with highly developed service economies, that is those in which the share of services in total employment was close to or greater than 65 per cent in the year 2000. This excludes the four Southern European countries and Ireland. The purpose of this restriction is to reduce as far as possible the influence of the general level of tertiarisation in national economies (correlated statistically to the level of economic development) on the internal structure of the service sector. Finally, Japan will be excluded from the analysis on the grounds that its service economy is highly specific.

In the light of these points, examination of the data (Table 4.1 and Table 4A.1) immediately reveals the existence of two strongly contrasting groups of developed countries. The first group is made up of English-speaking countries – the USA; Canada (Ca); Australia (Aus); and the UK (sometimes described as 'Anglo-Saxon', a term whose appropriateness is debatable but which may indicate similarities in the type of private and public governance norms and culture). The USA is the most extreme example here; the European representative, obviously, is the UK. The second group consists of the Nordic countries – Sweden (S); Norway (Nor); Finland (Fin); and Denmark (DK). Somewhat curiously, both these groups include countries that hold world records for the share of service employment. In virtually all of them, services accounted for more than 70 per cent of total employment in the year 2000, the only exception being Finland, which was not far behind. Both groups of countries, therefore, consist of service economies par excellence, although it is not the same services that predominate. Their structures differ principally in two ways: in the share of trade and personal services and in that of social services.

Table 4.1 Share of TPS and social services in certain national economies with highly developed service sectors (1997–98) as a % of total employment

	USA	Ca	Aus	UK	S	DK	Nor	Fin	NL	F	DE	B
TPS	28.2	24.8	26.6	24.7	18.1	19.6	17.0	18.1	23.3	21.7	21.4	20.9
Social services	24.7	25.4	25.2	25.3	34.0	31.7	33.7	28.1	28.1	28.7	24.7	30.7

Sources: For Canada, Australia and Norway, own calculations based on OECD (2002b) for 1998, with employment in sector O of CIT13 ('other collective, social and personal services') being divided up on the basis of 75% for social services and 25% for personal services. For the other countries: own calculations, based on Storrie, in Anxo and Storrie (2001).

The first difference between the so-called 'Anglo-Saxon' service economy structure and the Nordic type is in the relative share of the TPS sector. In approximate terms, the Anglo-Saxon type of service economy structure has a TPS sector that, in 1997, accounted for between 25 and 28 per cent of total employment, compared with only 17 to 19 per cent in the Nordic type. This is an enormous difference for countries with similar standards of living (except for the USA, whose per capita GDP is considerably higher). And in the case of the USA, it is not even possible to invoke, by way of explanation, a law stating the existence of a 'natural' link between a higher standard of living and a higher share of total employment for the TPS sector. First, among developed countries there is no significant statistical correlation between these two variables. Second, the Western European countries in which the TPS sector has the highest share of employment tend to be the least-developed ones with the smallest service sectors (not included in the table): Spain (28.3 per cent of employment in the TPS sector in 1998), Greece (27.1 per cent), Portugal (24.5 per cent) and Italy (24.5 per cent).

The second striking contrast between these two types of service economy structure concerns the share of social services in total employment. Broadly speaking, in the Anglo-Saxon type of structure of the late 1990s, social services accounted for around 25 per cent of employment, compared with 30 to 35 per cent in the Nordic type. Or, to put it another way, Sweden has about 10 percentage points less employment than the USA in the TPS sector, but 9 percentage points more employment in social services. Using the data presented by Storrie (Anxo and Storrie, 2001), the share of the main subsectors in social services, namely education, health and social welfare (unfortunately not separated out) and public administration, can be examined in great detail. These data show that the differences between the two types are small in the case of education, with the Anglo-Saxon type having a slightly higher share (about 7.6 per cent of employment, compared with between 6.5 and 7.3 per cent in the Nordic countries). They are slightly greater in public administration (between 4.5 and 6 per cent of employment in the Anglo-Saxon type, compared with between 6 and 8 per cent in the Nordic type). In the 'health and social welfare' subsector, the differences are very great, with a share of 11.5 per cent of employment in the USA (despite the high share of the health sector, which means that employment in social services excluding health is very low) and 11 per cent in the UK, compared with 19.6 per cent in Sweden, 16.7 per cent in Denmark and 14.6 per cent in Finland.

There is in fact a third contrast (ibid.) between these two polar types of service economy structure, but it is less pronounced and less significant for our interpretation for the diversity of models of the service economy. It concerns the share of business services. This figure is greatest in the English-speaking countries, with a share of 15.1 per cent in the USA in 1997 and 14.3 per cent in the UK. This compares with between 11 and 12 per cent in the Nordic countries, but also with 10.5 per cent in Germany and 11.8 per cent in France. A share of 14.1 per cent in the Netherlands rather puts this country in a class of its own; according to this criterion, and the share of employment in trade, the structure of the Dutch service economy is closer to the Anglo-Saxon type than to the Nordic type, whereas the opposite is the case when it comes to the share of personal and social services. Overall, the differences between the two polar types of service economy structure are of the order of 3 percentage points of employment in the business services sector, compared with 8 to 9 points in the TPS sector and 7 to 8 points in social services. This is the justification for focusing on the last two subsectors in order to investigate the most pronounced contrasts. Between these two poles there is a less homogeneous continental group.

The two extreme types of service economy structure are differentiated from each other primarily by the values for a pair of variables, namely the share of the TPS sector and that of social services in total employment. These values are high and low, respectively, in the Anglo-Saxon type of structure and low and high, respectively, in the Nordic type. The other major service subsectors play only a secondary role in this contrast. The other developed countries can be located in terms of their distance from these two poles. Among the EU15 member states with the most highly developed service sectors, Germany (DE) and France (F) are located in intermediate positions (Table 4.1). By these criteria, Belgium (B), which has a highly developed service economy, has a structure close to that of France. The Netherlands (NL) is somewhat atypical, and ultimately closer to France than to the Nordic countries according to this first criterion. The share of the TPS sector in France and Germany, as well as in Belgium, is fairly low, which places these countries closer to the Nordic than to the Anglo-Saxon type. However, as far as the overall share of social services is concerned, Germany is at the (relatively low) level of the English-speaking countries, whereas France is located about midway between the two types.

The second contrast: job quality and skill levels

This criterion is more difficult than the previous one to express in terms of comparative indicators, since the international classifications that rank jobs in terms of skill levels (occupational classifications, level of training required, and so on) and quality (pay, status, job security, social protection, working conditions and so on) are much vaguer than those relating to individual industries. Nevertheless, there are various studies of countries that are representative of the three groups already identified upon which we can draw. They are sufficiently clear and convergent in their conclusions to reveal, once again, a sharp contrast between the dualist Anglo-Saxon type, of which the USA is the exemplar, and the Nordic type, with the same set of European countries, including France and Germany, lying somewhere in between.

The status (or quality) of service jobs

The Anglo-Saxon type differs from the Nordic type in having a far greater share of very low-quality service jobs, measured in terms of pay, social protection, labour turnover rates and working conditions (including working time). Thus the contrast does not relate to the 'average' (in the English-speaking countries there is a significant concentration of high-quality, extremely well-paid jobs) but rather to the existence of a large concentration of very low-quality jobs. A study by the OECD (Organisation for Economic Cooperation and Development, 2001b) showed that in 1999 the employment rate in services (share of the population working in services in the working-age population as a whole) was very significantly greater in the USA than the average for the European Union, but that this 'surplus' was divided up into an excess of 7.5 percentage points in low-wage activities and an excess of 6.9 percentage points in high-wage activities (with similar rates for average-wage jobs). This gives some idea of the extent of wage dualism in the American service sector. In all the countries, the lowest-quality jobs are concentrated in retailing and market services to households. It is in these activities in particular that the Nordic countries differ most in terms of pay, 'generous' social protection and working conditions. In Sweden, the low rates of pay in retailing and personal services were of the order of €10 per hour in 2002, whereas the federal minimum wage in the USA was $5.15, or approximately €5.3 in purchasing power parities.

Even the undeniably 'inferior' status of part-time employment, which is highly concentrated in services and is very largely women's work even in the Nordic countries (which means that significant gender inequalities persist there), is of much higher quality in the Nordic type. Sweden is the EU15 member state that has the highest average weekly working time for female part-timers (25 hours), in contrast not only to the English-speaking countries (UK, Ireland) but also to Germany and the Netherlands. In this second group of countries, the average weekly working time for female part-timers is between 18 and 19 hours (Letablier and Lurol, 2000). If 'student jobs' are excluded, most female part-timers in Sweden (who are often employed in the public sector, particularly in health, education and care services for children and the elderly) work between 25 and 32 hours per week. Moreover, such 'long' part-time arrangements are generally reversible for those women who, having begun their working lives in full-time employment and subsequently opted for parental leave for each child and then decided to go part-time in order to devote more time to their children, wish later to return to a full-time job (usually the same position). Employers are obliged to accept these 'full-time returners', particularly since the vast majority of employees are trade union members and women play a very important role in the trade unions (to say nothing of the 43 per cent of women in the Swedish parliament). This does not prevent a significant proportion of female part-timers in Sweden wishing to work full-time or attempts being made to reduce the part-time rate among women (which, incidentally, has not increased since the 1980s).

Skill and vocational training in services

The contrast between the two types is no less pronounced in this respect. Once again, the Anglo-Saxon type, unlike the Nordic type, is characterised by a marked dualism (here with regard to skills and vocational training). Lester Thurow (1989) long ago denounced the deskilling mode of development that characterises household services in the USA, contrasting it even at that time with the Swedish model.

In their comparative study of 'national systems of production and innovation', Amable et al. (1997) note that the USA, Canada and Australia, three countries that, in their typology, fall within the scope of the 'market system', are characterised by a low level of continuing training. This sets them apart from Germany and the Scandinavian countries, which have efficient retraining/reskilling systems for workers who, for whatever reason, have to be mobile. Although these researchers are not concerned specifically with services, their analysis can, nevertheless, be applied to them. The European research coordinated by Bosch and Lehndorff (2001) revealed very high skill levels, unmatched anywhere else, in the social services sector in Nordic countries, particularly among health workers and home helps for the elderly. In the Scandinavian countries and the Netherlands, public standards of quality and vocational training are high, even when homecare services for the elderly are delegated to the private sector or to community organisations. In Sweden, those engaged in such work require three years' vocational training. Conversely, in other countries, and more particularly in the English-speaking countries, the current trend in health and other social services is to cut costs by creating large numbers of non-professional jobs requiring no specialist training. These workers, who are frequently described as 'assistants' or 'auxiliaries', have no specific skills or qualifications. Thus the fastest-growing occupations[1] identified in the employment projections published by the American Bureau of Labor Statistics include a multitude of jobs of this type whose skill requirements are summarised as 'short-term on-the-job training' or, at best, 'moderate-term on-the-job training'.

The third contrast: market versus non-market services

The most highly developed service economies under study here differ fairly markedly from each other with regard to a criterion which, for simplicity's sake, we shall denote by the adjectives 'market' and 'non-market'. It will be assumed that there are two extreme theoretical situations. In the first, services are provided by private companies in a competitive market with little public regulation. In the second, services are produced by the state or by public institutions and funded out of taxation or by means of other 'compulsory levies'. In this second situation, services are (virtually) free at the point of delivery; there is no market or market competition and recipients are granted 'rights' or 'entitlements' to the services. This is the case, for example, with free state education. Between these two extreme theoretical situations, there are innumerable hybrid situations that differ essentially in the extent to which they are subject to state regulation, which in turn is frequently correlated with the extent to which the activities in question are funded, directly or indirectly, out of the public purse.

Four indicators will be used in order to identify the differences between national service economies on the basis of this third criterion (Table 4.2). These indicators are linked, but only partially, so that they complement one another without overlapping. The first is the share of public sector employment in total national employment. Following the ILO study (1999), public sector employees are defined as those working for central or local government or for state enterprises, whether wholly owned by the state or those in which the state has a majority share. The second indicator is state and social security revenue as a share of GDP. This revenue is made up primarily of 'compulsory levies' (the term compulsory clearly indicating a distancing from the market), plus various other sources of income, including the operating surpluses of state enterprises. The third indicator is public expenditure, excluding social security benefits, as a share of GDP. This sum, which directly funds state services and those who provide them, more accurately reflects the state's share *in the production of services* than the 'redistributive' element used to fund social security cash benefits, which we shall bring into play later for other purposes. The fourth indicator is the level of public expenditure, again as a share of GDP, devoted to education and health, the two enormous service activities that lie at the heart of the UNDP's (United Nations Development Programme) notion of 'human development'.

Examination of the data relating to these four criteria further reinforces the contrast between the Anglo-Saxon and Nordic forms of service economy. In the first type, the competitive market mode of regulation plays an overwhelmingly dominant role in services. The second is characterised by a vast volume of services that are either wholly public in nature or involve a high level of public expenditure and regulation. Once again, most of the other countries are in an intermediate situation when measured in terms of these four indicators of public involvement in the provision of services.

In order further to clarify this contrast between the two polar types, we could have used other variables, including the respective shares of public and private funds in the financing

Table 4.2 *Indicators of the relative shares of market and non-market services in countries with highly developed service sectors*

	USA	Ca	Aus	UK	S	DK	Nor	Fin	NL	F	DE	B
1. Public-sector employment (% of total)	16.0	20.1	21.1	18.9	37.9	26.2	37.6	28.5	–	24.1	19.2	–
2. State revenue (% of GDP) in 2001	30.7	39.8	32.7	39.0	57.0	53.6	56.1	46.2	42.1	47.4	43.0	46.9
3. State expenditure excluding social security benefits (% of GDP) in 1999	17.7	22.9	24.9	23.4	36.1	34.8	29.2	29.2	30.4	31.1	27.2	27.0
4. Public expenditure on health and education (% of GDP)	11.1	13.5	11.5	11.1	14.9	15.0	14.7	12.7	11.1	13.3	12.7	9.4

Sources: 1: ILO (1999), except for France (Tableau de l'économie française 2002, INSEE; Anxo et al. 2001); 2 and 3: OECD *Economic Outlook* (2002, no. 72) and OECD (2002a); 4: estimates based on UNDP (2002), by summing the share of public expenditure on education in GNP and that of public expenditure on health in GDP.

of research, of pay-as-you-go and fully-funded pension schemes, public and private health insurance and so on. This would merely have confirmed the wideness of the gulf that separates them in respect of this third characteristic of the service economy.

From empirical types to interpretative models

By combining the three groups of criteria examined above (relative shares of trade and personal services, job quality and skill levels and relative shares of market and non-market services), three groups of countries can be identified on the basis of their service economy. At this stage, the differences arise only from the conjunction of empirical criteria, without any attempt being made to look for causal relationships or interdependencies between the descriptive variables used.

The main question that rears its head at this stage is the following: can this diversity of types of capitalist economies within highly developed economies be interpreted on the basis of one-way, reciprocal or systemic relationships of causality between a limited number of economic and social 'factors' that go beyond the three descriptive criteria outlined above?

Examination of existing studies and of the available data leads us to favour an explanation in which a major role is played by two types of 'societal norms', each of which exerts a strong influence on the form the service economy takes in a particular country. We define such norms as widely shared cognitive frameworks, often implicit, that in general have a long history. They are values, notions of what is good and fair. It is virtually impossible to identify them *directly* anywhere other than in legal enactments and speeches. However, they can be identified *indirectly* on the basis of some of their outcomes (and the high degree of acceptance of those outcomes) in the countries in question over long periods of time. This is what we shall do here.

The two types of societal norms that play this role here, and which will enable us to develop 'interpretative models' of the service economy *and society*, are, first, those relating to equality and national solidarity and, second, those relating to gender and the family (the notion of the societal gender norm is borrowed from Letablier and Lurol (2000)). Those in the first category relate to equality (or inequality) and solidarity between classes and social groups (as well as between generations and territories) within a country, and we shall confine ourselves here to economic equality and solidarity. Gender norms also concern equality, but this time between men and women, in the economic, domestic and political spheres.

In our view, the heart of the theoretical problem of the diversity of national models of the service economy and society, and in particular the strong and enduring dichotomy between the Anglo-Saxon and Nordic types, lies in these two sets of norms. A society with very high levels of class and gender inequalities cannot have the same service economy as a more egalitarian society. Other factors may be influential and help to shift the models in this direction or that, but – this in any case is the hypothesis we are going to test – these two types of norms are the most reliable 'predictors' of the type of service economy that exists in a given country.

In the final section of this chapter, evidence will be provided in support of this argument. Before that, however, we shall present a limited number of empirical indicators of the current state of the two types of societal norms we have adopted.

Some indicators of equality and gender norms

The issue of concern to us here will not be addressed by drawing up a balance sheet of all the forms of economic and social equality or inequality in the countries under investigation. We shall confine ourselves to the indicators shown in Tables 4.3 and 4.4.

Table 4.3 shows six synthetic indicators of economic inequality and national and, in the case of the last two indicators, international solidarity. The term 'solidarity' encompasses the notions of inequality reduction, universal financial protection against the main economic insecurities (unemployment and poverty, illness, old age, and family benefits) and sustainable development (inter-generational solidarity with regard to the preservation of natural resources). This is why 'generosity' indicators pertaining to social protection, state aid to developing countries and CO_2 emissions per inhabitant are given here.

By far the strongest contrast between the Anglo-Saxon and Nordic models is in the indicators relating to national equality and solidarity norms. The USA holds all the records in the developed world when it comes to poverty, inequality and economic selfishness (rows 5 and 6). The average interdecile earnings ratio ranges from 12 to 17 in three of the four English-speaking countries (Canada is less unequal), compared with a range of only 5.1 to 5.7 in the four Nordic countries. Poverty rates range from 12 to 17 per cent in the Anglo-Saxon type, compared with a range of 5 to 9 per cent in the Nordic type. The share of expenditure on social protection in GDP is about 50 per cent higher in the Nordic countries, while the share of state spending on development is three to 10 times higher in those countries, with the exception of Finland.

Table 4.3 *Six indicators of societal equality and solidarity norms*

	USA	Ca	Aust	UK	S	DK	Nor	Fin	NL	F	DE	B
1. Income inequality (average interdecile ratio*)	16.6	8.5	12.5	12.3	5.4	5.7	5.3	5.1	9.0	9.1	7.1	7.3
2. % poor people (less than 50% of median income)	16.9	12.8	14.3	13.4	6.6	9.2	6.9	5.1	8.1	8.0	7.5	8.2
3. IPH-2 2002 classification (17 countries)**	17	12	14	15	1	5	2	4	3	8	6	13
4. Expenditure on social protection (as % of GDP)	12.6	12.6	8.0	13.5	18.9	17.7	15.5	17.9	12.6	18.4	18.9	15.7
5. State aid to developing countries (as % of GDP, 2000)	0.10	0.25	0.27	0.32	0.80	1.06	0.80	0.31	0.84	0.32	0.27	0.36
6. CO_2 emissions, in tonnes/head of population (1998)	19.9	15.3	17.9	9.2	5.5	10.1	7.6	10.3	10.5	6.3	10.1	10.0

Notes:
* Average interdecile ratio means (see UNDP reports): total income of the 10th decile/total income of the first decile.
** IPH-2 : UNDP (synthetic) index of human poverty, in its 2nd variant adapted for developed countries.

Sources: 1, 2, 3, 5, 6: UNDP (2002); 4: OECD (2001a). The expenditure in question is 'social security transfers' paid by governments in 1999 (and in a few cases 1998).

It will also be noted that 'social security transfers' in the Nordic countries (row 4) are close to those in the countries of continental Europe (excluding the Netherlands), although they are considerably higher than in the English-speaking countries. One of the reasons for this is that 'passive' expenditure linked to unemployment (benefits) is lower when unemployment is itself low, as is the case in the Nordic countries (again with the exception of Finland) and the Netherlands. The same applies to social security benefits linked to poverty, for which there is less need when there are few poor people, all things being equal in terms of notions of solidarity.

Table 4.4 brings together 10 indicators of gender and family norms which, once again, all reveal differences between the English-speaking and Nordic countries that are in some cases weak (indicators 1 and 2) and in others much more pronounced (most of the other indicators). The most marked differences lie in the areas of women's political representation and gender equality at work and with regard to domestic work and childcare (rows 6 to 9).

Overall, the English-speaking countries are sometimes 'better' (in strict equality terms) than those in continental Europe (particularly with regard to criterion 2) and sometimes 'less good'. The classifications in rows 6 and 7 will be explained and commented on in the following section. The relative similarity of the figures for France and Germany in Table 4.4 conceals differences that would be very significant if a distinction was made

Table 4.4 Ten indicators of gender and family norms

	USA	Ca	Aust	UK	S	DK	Nor	Fin	NL	F	DE	B
1. Female participation rate* in 2000	58.8	60.1	55.8	52.8	62.5	61.7	59.1	57.0	45.4	48.5	47.9	39.7
2. Female participation rate* as % of male rate	81.0	82.0	77.0	74.0	89.0	84.0	84.0	86.0	66.0	76.0	69.0	66.0
3. Difference between m. and f. participation rates (25–54 year olds) in 2001	14.9	12.0	18.5	15.0	5.0	7.8	8.1	6.0	19.6	15.4	16.0 (27.0)	20.1
4. % of women in national parliaments** (2000)	13.0	26.0	27.0	17.0	43.0	38.0	36.0	36.0	32.0	11.0	28.0	26.0
5. Iterative Proportional Fitting (IPF)*** classification 2002 (66 countries)	11	7	10	16	3	4	1	5	6	–	8	14
6. Classification by public support for gender equality at work	17	13	15	12	1	2	4	3	9	5	7	6
7. Classification by public support for the nuclear family	18	12	16	13	9	7	4	10	11	3	2	1
8. Participation rate for women with children (1999), in %	61.0	–	45.0	56.0	78.0	84.0	73.0	59.0	61.0	56.0	51.0	69.5
9. Childcare (0–3 years of age), in %	–	–	–	2.0	33.0	48.0	31.0	21.0	8.0	23.0	2 0 (41.0)	30.0
10. Male participation in domestic work (%)	30.0	–	–	–	40.0	35.0	–	–	–	31.0	31.0	–

Notes: * Women aged 15 and over; ** average of two percentages in two-chamber systems; *** Synthetic indicator of female participation in economic and political life. France is not included in the classification because of a lack of data.

Sources: 1, 2, 3, 5: UNDP (2002); 4: OECD (2002b); 6, 7: Korpi (2001), for 18 countries; 8: OECD (2001b). Figures are for mothers with at least one child under 6 years of age (except Denmark: under 10; Rubery et al. (2001)); 9: Plantenga and Hansen (1999): in the case of EU15 and Norway only, the figures relate to the number of places in public facilities (or those receiving significant public funding) as a share of the number of children in the 0–3 age group in the mid-1990s; 10: France and Sweden: Anxo et al. (2001). Domestic work here includes care of others (children, parents etc.). In the case of the USA, figures are taken from studies cited by the same authors, without any guarantee of comparability. For Germany: Beblo (1999). For Denmark: Bonke and Koch-Weser (2001). In all these countries, the data relate only to men and women living as couples.

between Eastern and Western Germany, which is done only in row 9 (where the first figure is for Eastern Germany and the second for Western Germany) and row three, where the second figure refers to the situation in West Germany in 1990. The participation rate for mothers with children under 10 years of age was 50 per cent in Western Germany and 88 per cent in Eastern Germany in 1996 (Rubery et al., 2001).

Equality and gender norms and models of the service economy and society

The aim of this section is to provide indications of the way in which societal equality and gender norms influence, together or separately, the relative importance of trade and personal services and social services sectors. We can start in a basic and purely economic way. In a service economy, like the USA, where the earnings of the richest 10 per cent are about 17 times greater than those of the poorest 10 per cent, the wealthiest people have an enormous personal economic interest (ratio of the estimated utility of the service to the price paid) in 'having themselves served' by people who earn 17 times less than they do. Earnings inequalities not only create inequalities in consumption and wealth. They also make all low-skill services very inexpensive and hence encourage an expansion of such services, since their relative cost is more or less indexed to the lowest wages, which in this model are also (with the statutory minimum wages) the lowest incomes. The wealthiest people in Nordic economies obviously have less of an interest in purchasing a wide range of personal services (whether provided by mutual agreement between individuals or, more importantly, by companies), since the average interdecile earnings ratio is only 5.3. If we go beyond the extremes, that is the top and bottom 10 per cent, and look at the top and bottom 20 per cent, the average interquintile earnings ratio, at 9.0, is still enormous in the USA. It is only about 3.6 in the Nordic countries. In any very egalitarian country, this fact alone constitutes a considerable economic incentive for the development of market personal, domestic and trade services, home deliveries, catering services and so on. Conversely, the predominance of egalitarian norms is an obvious obstacle to the creation of jobs in these kinds of services. The most egalitarian countries obviously need hotels and restaurants, a retail trade, certain home deliveries and so on. However, because of the dominant norms relating to equality (and notably wage equality), the choices that are made tend to result in (i) the limitation of such services to what is 'strictly necessary' (a notion that itself is rooted in a norm), (ii) modes of organisation that make less-intensive use of low-skill labour and more-intensive use of both capital and skill labour in these services and (iii) the virtual non-existence of a whole series of 'menial service jobs' in which people are employed to perform functions that consumers have every interest in performing themselves or to which they attach little value.

There are virtually no cleaning ladies in Sweden, largely because there is neither supply nor demand. On the supply side, Swedish women aspire to something better than privately negotiated jobs without prospects and they have opportunities to realise those aspirations. And students seeking work (mainly during university holidays) also have better opportunities open to them than menial service jobs, particularly since most of them have an adequate income (€1500 per month) thanks to a very favourable funding system based on state-subsidised loans that can be repaid over the course of the working life at very attractive rates of interest. All students can take out the loans, irrespective of their parents' means. On the demand side, if companies were to offer such domestic services, the cost per hour would be exorbitant (around €20, given the levels of wages and social security contributions), all the more since the earnings differentials are low. Furthermore, since there are good-quality public childcare facilities and (professional) home help services for the elderly (see below), 'servants' jobs' are virtually non-existent.

The existence of pronounced income inequalities also results in household services, as well as certain social services, functioning in a dualistic, 'two-speed' way, with a tier of sophisticated services that the wealthiest consumers can afford and a low-price, low-quality tier for those of more modest means. The social segmentation of production and of the market becomes very pronounced in hotels and restaurants, leisure and cultural activities and even in health, education and justice when such services are delivered largely through the market. The USA is the only developed country in which the share of private health expenditure exceeds that of public expenditure (55 per cent compared with 45 per cent). In all the other countries under study here, the share of private health expenditure is between 15 and 30 per cent (UNDP, 2002). To take another example, the cost of a year's study at a major private university in the USA, such as Princeton, is between $28,000 and $30,000, including tuition fees and accommodation. Even in a less prestigious private university, the cost is of the order of $20,000 to $25,000. In other words, even with a fairly well-developed scholarship system for students from less well-off backgrounds, this 'service' remains inaccessible to a large number of potential users, who will have to do without or opt for less prestigious public universities (which themselves are far from being free, incidentally).

Equality norms also influence the scale of social service provision and the relative shares of market and non-market services. First, in an egalitarian country, there will tend to be a view that most social services (particularly education, health, childcare and home help services for the elderly) must be accessible to all citizens at an affordable price (or at no cost) and with few gradations of quality. Access to such services becomes a universal right, which encourages their diffusion to all segments of the population and to all regions. This is why the extent of social service provision is all the greater the lower the inequalities, with a very high statistical correlation (Bosch and Lehndorff, 2001). Moreover, since there can be no question of organising the provision of these services on a 'two-speed', two-tier basis, quality standards and skill levels will be high. Consequently, these 'universal' social services are, first, expensive (and, being both universal and expensive, they will play a considerable role in the economy) and, second, very highly regulated by the public authorities in order to ensure their universality. Now, the more strictly services are regulated and the higher their relative cost, with little segmentation permitted, the less likelihood there is that the private sector will have any interest in investing in them and bringing competition into play. Price competition very quickly comes up against universal quality standards, while no provider seeking to compete on quality can rely on the usual weapon of segmentation. Generally speaking, the stronger the equality and solidarity norms, the more the state (together with other public institutions, particularly those responsible for social protection) will tend to be 'visible', over and above its sovereign functions.

The role of gender and family norms

The role of these norms is more complex, but no less important. One well-known finding of studies on the growth of services is the link that exists between the increase in women's labour market participation and the development of a whole range of public or private 'substitution' services. In many cases, most of the jobs created in these service activities are taken by women and result from the outsourcing of domestic tasks previously performed predominantly by women. This type of finding is neither incorrect nor without its uses, but it makes very little contribution to a real understanding of the diversity of types of service economy that we have identified, notably because it makes no distinction between the egalitarian and inegalitarian modes of female labour market participation. In particular, an investigation of issues around the reconciliation of paid work and family life may very well produce good results for the English-speaking countries (OECD, 2001b), but this is because no distinction is made between the egalitarian and inegalitarian forms of reconciliation. In seeking to go further, we shall draw on the analysis of the Swedish researcher Korpi (2001), who has developed a synthetic classification of 18 developed countries. The criteria adopted are the existence and scale of public measures that support a dual-earner family model, in which the occupational status of the man and woman are as equal as possible, enabling them to contribute as equally as possible to household economic resources. To this end, Korpi uses four main indicators: (i) care services for very young children (under two years of age); (ii) paid maternity leave; (iii) home-care services for the elderly (in the absence of such services, it is often the daughters of the elderly who are supposed to provide the care); and (iv) paid paternity leave. Korpi acknowledges the difficulties surrounding the availability of certain data, which means he has to make do with an imperfect ordinal classification, albeit one that is still capable of revealing trends and contrasting types.

In itself, the classification is very clear (Table 4.4, row 6). At the top are the four Nordic countries. At the bottom are the English-speaking countries (the UK, Canada, Australia and, in 17th place, the USA). Japan, Switzerland and New Zealand are also part of this bottom group. This analysis provides a supplement to the data most commonly used in international comparisons of gender equality at work, which compare male and female activity rates while ignoring arrangements or measures that may enable women's mode of economic activity (occupational status, continuity, career) to be similar to that of men.

Korpi's analysis also makes use of another, more traditional dimension, namely the significance of family policies 'in general'; that is, public arrangements and measures intended to support the nuclear family that do not take gender equality into consideration or may even work explicitly against such equality in the case of certain arrangements that assume mothers will stay at home or encourage them to do so. The classification he obtains is very different from the preceding one (Table 4.4, row 7). This time, Belgium, Germany and France head the table in an interesting reversal of the continental European group, followed by a rather heterogeneous group of countries including the Nordic ones, together with Italy and the Netherlands, and, finally, the English-speaking countries (with the USA bringing up the rear) and Japan.

By combining these two criteria, Korpi ends up with a diagram in the form of an 18-country typology that classifies countries on the basis of their family and gender norms. Three types emerge fairly clearly. The first is the market-oriented model, which equates largely to our Anglo-Saxon model. Countries of this type are characterised by the weakness of both their general family policies and their policies on gender equality at work. The model furthest removed from this one is the dual-earner model, to which the four Nordic countries are allocated. They are characterised by strong public support for gender equality (particularly at work) and fairly significant but not exceptional support for the family. The third, more heterogeneous type is described as the general family support model because of the great significance of norms governing support for the nuclear family. Such support is neutral with regard to gender inequalities, or may sometimes reinforce them.

One cannot but be struck by the congruence between this typology and the one we drew up on the basis of completely different criteria. In order to interpret this high level of agreement between the two, we are going to show, as we did for societal equality norms, that different types of gender and family norms encourage the development of different types (and different volumes) of services.

Let us begin with the market-oriented model, in which there is little support for the family and virtually no public support for gender equality (the English-speaking countries). The economic incentive for women to enter the labour market is high, particularly during periods of economic growth, because of the low level of family benefits or of 'familialist' tax and social security deductions. However, since there is very little in the way of policy measures to promote gender equality at work, the 'natural' tendency, given the history of the family in developed countries, is for women to be employed – whether full- or part-time depends in particular on labour needs – in jobs that remain very inferior to those of men in terms of both status and pay. In this model, women are mainly employed in low-skill jobs in retailing and market services to households, as well as in the least highly valued segment of social services. Because of the inadequate provision of child- and homecare services for the elderly, they tend to leave the labour market or to seek 'short-hours' part-time jobs when they have young children to look after (see the participation rates for women with children in the UK, Table 4.4) or they need to care for elderly parents. For all these reasons, most of them do not have a career worthy of the name and there is a considerable gap between men's and women's earnings (Rubery et al., 2001, Table 5.5, p. 54). The low pay levels in women's jobs and the tendency for women to be concentrated in market personal services, retailing and the low-skill segment of social services reinforce the dualism of jobs, skills and earnings. Moreover, if there are significant general earnings inequalities, as is indeed the case, the two types of norms combine to produce the characteristics of the Anglo-Saxon service economy. These include: the very important role played by the TPS sector (which is very highly feminised), dualistic and relatively underdeveloped social services, low average job quality and low levels of skill and earnings in these sectors and the predominance of the market mode of regulation as a result of the deliberately low profile maintained by the state and, in particular, the voluntary limitation of its power to reduce class and gender inequalities.

For its part, the dual-earner model, which provides strong support for gender equality at work and significant but not exceptional support for the family in general, also very much encourages female participation in the labour market. In the year 2000, participation rates for women aged 15 and over were between 57 and 62.5 per cent in the four Nordic countries and between 53 and 60 per cent in the four English-speaking countries shown in Tables 4.3 and 4.4. However, the emphasis on equality in the labour market means that this high level of economic activity among women takes a different form, with much less divergence between the occupational profiles of men and women. Significant discrimination still exists, even in Sweden (Anxo and Johanson, 1995). Nevertheless, it is true to say that there is less discrimination than elsewhere. In this model, women tend to be employed in service jobs that require significantly higher skill levels and command higher pay than in the market-oriented model, which helps to reduce earnings inequalities in general. Women's employment is less concentrated in market services in the TPS sector but is spread over a number of other sectors, including social services, which are highly developed, have high skill levels and are almost entirely public and strongly regulated by the state. In this sector in particular, women are in a particularly good position to remain in continuous employment (and hence to have a career) while still having time for domestic work and childcare (which is also more equally shared with men), even if, at certain periods in the life course, they opt for 'long' part-time jobs that are 'reversible' and therefore less damaging to careers (although they are still discriminatory). Thus discrimination persists, particularly with regard to part-time work and the high concentration of women's jobs in the (enormous) public sector. However, in the current state of affairs, this second inequality tends rather to reduce the differences between men's and women's careers and earnings. Consequently, the existence of a large non-market sector also meets with approval among women, since it is one means of promoting equality in the labour market, in parallel with its allotted role within the equality and solidarity norm, which is to make good-quality social services universally available.

Finally, there is the group of countries in which the general family support model prevails, with its modest or low level of support for gender equality at work. The main countries in this group are Belgium, France and Germany. In the last-named country, there is a considerable difference between the eastern and western parts, which means that statistics for the country as a whole conceal contrasting situations. The traditional family model with marked inequalities between men and women in the labour market is, in reality, much more firmly entrenched in Western Germany than in France. Be that as it may, female participation rates in this group of countries, which is more heterogeneous than the two previous ones, are relatively low, particularly relative to male rates. On the one hand, certain family and fiscal policies have contradictory effects on female labour market participation or on the incentives for women to work part-time in personal services and retailing. On the other, the relatively high level of support for gender equality in some of these countries (particularly in the social services sector, where provision is not marketised) considerably improves things compared with the wage discrimination that exists in the English-speaking countries and limits dualism in services to some extent. In reality, this group is fairly fragmented. It is more a collection of intermediate national cases, which remain diverse and located somewhere between the polar models and their basic norms. This is as true of Korpi's typology as it is of ours.

Conclusion

Our analysis, now concluded, has led to the development of two principal, fairly contrasting models of the service economy and society characterised by empirical indicators of the structure of service activities and employment and by the role played by two types of societal norms and their associated regulatory mechanisms and institutions. These norms are not, of course, immutable. They can evolve and even suffer periods of instability, and no attempt has been made in this chapter to outline their history. It is obvious, for example, that societal gender norms at the beginning of the twenty-first century are no longer the ones that prevailed in the 1950s, and the same is true of equality norms. The most we can say at the current stage of development is that those that predominate in the two most contrasting models have been in existence for at least two or three decades and seem to be fairly robust.

These two models are potential candidates in the search for a European path to the service economy and society. The Anglo-Saxon model has greater economic and political power, which is reflected in particular in the USA's very effective interventions in the World Trade Organisation in support of the international liberalisation of services that could potentially affect virtually all public services, social services (education and health) and culture, as well as social protection, pensions and so on. The Nordic model, which has a fairly impressive record in terms of economic performance, innovation and social cohesion, is seen as David facing Goliath. Nevertheless, nothing is predestined, however unequal the contest may seem.

Note

1. Among the 30 fastest-growing occupations the following require only on-the-job training: social and human service assistance, personal and homecare aides, medical assistants, physicians and assistants, home health aides, physiotherapist aides, occupational therapist aides, physiotherapist assistants and dental assistants.

APPENDIX 4.1

Table 4.A1 Economic, scientific and technological indicators (2000)

	USA	Ca	Aus	UK	S	DK	Nor	Fin	NL	F	DE	B
Service sector (%), 2001	75.2	74.4	74.2	73.4	73.8	71.1	71.8	66.7	73.4	72.2	64.8	73.1*
GDP/per capita ($000PPP**)	34.1	27.8	25.7	23.5	24.3	27.6	29.9	25.0	25.7	24.2	25.1	27.2
Annual growth in per capita GDP, 1990–2000	2.2	1.9	2.9	2.2	1.6	2.1	3.1	2.4	2.2	1.3	1.2	1.8
Unemployment	4.0	6.8	6.3	5.5	4.7	4.7	3.4	9.8	2.6	9.5	7.5	7.0
Inflation 90-00 (annual growth)	2.7	1.7	2.1	2.9	1.9	2.1	2.2	1.5	2.4	1.6	2.2	1.6
Nos employed in R&D/ 1000 inhabitants	4.1	3.0	3.3	2.7	4.5	3.2	4.1	5.0	2.5	2.7	2.9	2.3
Computers / 1000 inhabitants	585	390	465	338	507	432	491	396	395	305	336	344
Computers connected to internet/1000 inhabitants	295	77	86	28	67	63	101	102	102	19	25	29
Mobile telephones/ 1000 inhabitants	398	285	447	727	717	631	751	720	670	493	586	525

Note: * In 1999; ** purchasing power parities.

Sources: UNDP (2002), except for the first row (OECD).

5 Theories of the information age

Nico Stehr

> In some way or other, any knowledge, and especially all common knowledge of identical objects, determines in many ways the specification (*Sosein*) of society. But all knowledge is ultimately also conversely determined by the society and its structure. (Max Scheler, 1924 [1990]: 17)

Introduction

It is virtually impossible to transcend the contestation and the conflation of the terms 'information' and 'knowledge' in much of the discussion about the information age. However, in the context of an examination of some of the important theories of the information age, it is unavoidable to take up the contentious question of the meaning of, as well as the relation between, knowledge and information. At this juncture, the main puzzle of the theoretical discourse on the role of knowledge and information in social action is whether it is even possible and sensible to distinguish between them. The conceptual distinction between information and knowledge, which is in any case at best relative, appears to be most difficult, if not impossible to sustain in the light of the fact that these notions are often employed as virtual equivalents.

Many dictionaries simply define information as a certain kind of knowledge. A similar symmetry between information and knowledge is evident if one defines information as 'knowledge reduced and converted into messages that can be easily communicated among decision agents' (Dasgupta and David, 1994: 493). In other definitions of information and knowledge, information is simply conceptualized as a subspecies, as an element or the raw material of a number of knowledge forms. For example, information is codified as well as indirect knowledge (see Borgmann, 1999: 49), or knowledge is defined as the cumulative stock of information (Burton-Jones, 1999: 5); similarly, knowledge in general is seen to extend to 'tacit knowledge' (see Polanyi, 1967: 204–6) and other forms of knowledge (Dosi, 1996: 84). In short, the outcome of many efforts to define knowledge and information appears always to lead to the same result: knowledge and information become indistinguishable.

Following such usage in this chapter, I plan to present my argument covering theories of the information age in a number of steps. First, I shall describe some of the intellectual precursors that give rise to the notion that we are living in an information or knowledge age. Second, I shall enumerate some of the perspectives that lead to the idea of modern societies as knowledge or information societies. Third, the usage of the term 'knowledge' as a capacity for action is explicated in greater detail. Fourth, in the core sections of the chapter, I deal with the theory of the knowledge and information society as well as some of its competitors such as the network society. I shall present the argument that advanced societies are best conceptualized as knowledge societies, last but not least because economic growth, social change generally but also the nature of social conflicts are increasingly generated by knowledge (Stehr, 2001, 2002). That is, knowledge does not merely open up the secrets of nature and society but is becoming a key element in the socioeconomic world.

The origins of information/knowledge age

John Stuart Mill (1806–73), in *The Spirit of the Age*, published in 1831 after his return to England from France, where he had encountered and taken in the philosophy of history in the political thinking of the St.-Simonians and of the early Comte, affirms his conviction that progress is possible in society as the result of the intellectual accomplishments of his own age. But progress and the improvement of social conditions are not, Mill argues, the outcome of an 'increase in wisdom' or of the collective accomplishments of science. They are rather linked to the general diffusion of knowledge throughout society:

> Men may not reason, better, concerning the great questions in which human nature is interested, but they reason more. Large subjects are discussed more, and longer, and by more minds. Discussion has penetrated deeper into society; and if greater numbers than before have attained the higher degrees of intelligence, fewer grovel in that state of abject stupidity, which can only co-exist with utter apathy and sluggishness. (Mill 1831 [1997]: 8)

Mill's observations in the mid-nineteenth century, a period he regarded as an age of profound moral and political transition, and in particular his expectation that such beneficial consequences for society as increased individual choice for a greater number of people (and hence emancipation from 'custom') will be the result of a broader diffusion of knowledge and education, but not necessarily scientific knowledge in the narrow sense of the term, resonate with the idea of modern society as a 'knowledge society'.

By the same token, the notion that we have begun to live in an 'information age' often refers to the same historical period, yet the notion of the information age emphasizes the growing presence of certain technical devices and tools in society that allow the much more rapid communication of information and knowledge than was the case in previous periods. Thus, in a recent exhibition devoted to the 'Information Age' in the Smithsonian National Museum of American History, it is argued that the modern information age began with Samuel Morse's invention of the telegraph transmitter and receiver in 1837. It was the first instrument to transform information into electrical form and transmit it reliably over long distances (see also Darnton, 2000).

The promise of more knowledge and information cannot really be separated either from its counter image, for example, from the fears and the darkness associated with a lack of knowledge, or from the allegedly mistaken or false use of knowledge even when it is available in abundance. The general point here is that much is gained from an analytical point of view that confronts a particular perspective with its opposite, its negation or competitor. Such conscious confrontation also serves as a useful reminder that knowledge tends to be contestable and is developed in response to contenders that after a time may only be implicitly accessible, especially as a certain form of knowledge acquires authority and power. The mixture of fears and warnings with blessings and compliments exhibits a trait of virtually all forms of knowledge, namely its controversial nature and the fact that it was, and is, developed in opposition to other forms of knowing. The exclusion of other means and purposes is inevitable. In the case of knowledge, the contestable context is provided for, on the one hand, by arguments that question or promote knowledge *per se* and, on the other, by opinions that at times differ sharply on the uses to which knowledge ought to be put. In contemporary society, doubts about the social consequences of knowledge are bound to give rise to a new field of political activity, namely knowledge politics concerning the regulation and control of new knowledge and technical artifacts (Stehr, 2004).

Knowledge society predecessors

In retrospect, some ancient societies may be described as knowledge societies. Ancient Israel, for example, was founded upon its law-like Torah knowledge. And in ancient Egypt, religious, astronomical and agrarian knowledge served as the organizing principle and the basis of authority. More recently, Marxist theories of society have assigned decisive importance to the (cultural) forces or means of production for societal development since 'man's understanding of nature and his mastery over it by virtue of his presence as a social body . . . appears as the great foundation-stone of production and of wealth, so that general knowledge becomes a direct force of production' (Marx, 1939–41 [1973]: 705). Max Weber's seminal inquiry into the unique features of Western civilization stresses the pervasive use of reason to secure the methodical efficiency of social action. The source of rational action and, therefore of rationalization, is located in particular intellectual devices.

The theory of industrial society, as developed by Raymond Aron (1962 [1967]), which encompasses both socialist and capitalist forms of economic organization as a single social reality of industrial civilization, accentuates first and foremost the extent to which science and technology shape the social organization of productive activities. Even more recent theories of postindustrial society, in particular those of Daniel Bell, have elevated theoretical knowledge to an axial principle of society. That 'rational knowledge', fabricated in one system, apparently travels with great ease and without loss across the boundaries of social systems, for instance, from science into the economy or state institutions, is hardly ever questioned.

The first to employ a related term, 'knowledgeable society', appears to have been Robert E. Lane (1966: 650). Lane's conception of a knowledgeable society, however, is closely tied to a particular theory of science and it reflects the excessive optimism of the 1950s and early 1960s that (social) science will help to bring about a society in which commonsense has been replaced in major social institutions by scientific reasoning. Lane argues that the members of such a knowledgeable society will be guided in their conduct, if not always consciously, by the standards of 'veridical truth'.

In the late 1960s, Peter Drucker, in *The Age of Discontinuity* (1969), refers to 'knowledge society'. Drucker regards knowledge as central to modern society and as the foundation of its economy and of social action. Daniel Bell also employs this term in the context of his discussion of the emergence of postindustrial society, a designation he himself prefers. Bell at times uses knowledge society interchangeably with 'postindustrial society', since he regards knowledge as a 'fundamental resource' of postindustrial society.

The theory of postindustrial society recognizes a particular central principle, viewed as a kind of dominant logic, which allows the observer to impose a specific conceptual order on vast societal developments of modern (Western) society. Bell describes his theory as concerned primarily with changes in the social framework of 'society', that is, its social structure which analytically, along with polity and culture, comprises society. The social structure of a society refers, more specifically, to its 'economy, technology and the occupational system' (Bell, 1973: 12) and the structure of social roles. The kind of changes in the social structure Bell attempts to chart primarily are those induced by the 'axial principle' of his theory of society, namely 'the centrality of theoretical knowledge' (ibid.: 14). Theoretical knowledge has a dual function. It is both the source of innovation and a foundation for policy formation in society. For Bell the axial principle is likened to 'director of social change' in and for postindustrial society.

Postindustrial society is no longer organized around the coordination of individuals and machines for the production of commodities, but around knowledge. It is a game between persons. Postindustrial society witnesses a shift from the production of commodities to the tertiary or service sector and a corresponding decline in the pre-eminence of the occupations of the manufacturing sector of society. One important contrast, therefore, is that a desirable standard of life in postindustrial society is no longer defined by the quantity of goods but by the quality of life as reflected in ready access to services and amenities such as health, education, leisure, and the arts (see ibid.: 166). The kind of work individuals increasingly perform requires theoretical knowledge. The chief 'resource of the post-industrial society is its scientific personnel' (ibid.: 221).

The knowledge referred to in virtually all theories of modern society that elevate knowledge to prominence, and the groups of individuals that are seen as acquiring influence and control by means of this knowledge, tend to be conceptualized narrowly. This does not mean, however, that such a concept lacks cultural centrality and public or political influence. On the contrary, the narrower notion of knowledge and the often accompanying stress on the role of technical innovation that attributes enormous efficacy to scientific and technical knowledge resonates strongly with the dominant public as well as political conception of knowledge, information and its role in society. The narrow definition of knowledge is also a testimony to the success of the scientific community in installing a particular conception of knowledge as the dominant public concept of knowledge. Whatever the limitations of this 'scientistic' conception of knowledge, its centrality clearly reflects the diminishing social role of nonscientific conceptions of knowing and forms of knowledge.

In much the same way, a systematic *sociological* reflection about the nature of 'theoretical knowledge' (and its interrelation with technology) is virtually absent from Bell's *The Coming of Post-Industrial Society*. The concept of knowledge found in Bell's work is formulated in deference to a philosophy of science dominant a few decades ago that describes knowledge as objective, truthful and in conformity with reality. Knowledge is treated as a black box. Paradoxically, there is the tendency to overestimate the efficacy of 'objective' technical-scientific or formal knowledge. We are not offered a sociological perspective of the knowledge process. The central question about knowledge posed by the theory of postindustrial society is a functionalist one: what are the consequences of objective knowledge for both society and the individual, and how can these results of knowledge be apprehended? The lack of sufficient detail and scope in explicating the social role of knowledge results in a deficit of accounts for the reasons of the growing demand for more and more knowledge in modern societies, for the ways in which knowledge travels, for the rapidly expanding groups of individuals in society who in some way or another live off knowledge, for the many forms of knowledge considered pragmatically useful and the various effects knowledge may have on social relations. Since the constitutive mechanism of 'knowledge' is defined in a restrictive objectivist manner, the social, political and economic consequences to which these theories allude tend to be confined to rather straightforward effects that include the hope for (or the fear of) highly rationalized forms of social action. A more adequate understanding of knowledge requires that one opens the black box.

Therefore, I should like to introduce in greater detail a contrasting concept of knowledge that will be employed in explicating the idea of modern society as a knowledge society.

Knowledge about knowledge

I shall define knowledge as a 'capacity for action'. The term 'knowledge' is derived from Francis Bacon's (1581–1626) famous observation that knowledge is power (a somewhat misleading translation of Bacon's Latin phrase: *scientia est potentia*) (1597 [1924]). Bacon suggests that knowledge derives its utility from its capacity to set something in motion. Knowledge as a symbolic 'system' structures reality. Knowledge is a model for reality. Knowledge illuminates and is able to transform reality. The term 'potential', that is, capacity, is employed to describe the power of knowing. Knowledge is becoming. Knowledge acquires its social distinction last but not least because of its ability to transform reality.

Knowledge, as a generalized capacity for action, acquires an active role in the course of social action only under circumstances where such action does not follow purely stereotypical patterns, or is strictly regulated in some other fashion. Knowledge assumes practical significance under conditions where social action is, for whatever reasons, based on a certain degree of freedom in the courses of action that can be chosen. Karl Mannheim (1929 [1936]: 102) defines, in much the same sense, the range of social conduct generally, and therefore contexts in which knowledge plays a role, as restricted to spheres of social life that have not been routinized and regulated completely. For, as he observes, 'conduct, in the sense in which I use it, does not begin until we reach the area where rationalization has not yet penetrated, and where we are forced to make decisions in situations which have as yet not been subjected to regulation'.

Knowledge is not a reliable 'commodity'. It tends to be fragile and demanding, and has built-in insecurities and uncertainties. Despite its reputation, knowledge is virtually never uncontested. Science is in many instances incapable of offering cognitive certainty. This is to say that scientific discourse has been depragmatized: that it cannot offer definitive, or even true, statements (in the sense of proven causal chains) for practical purposes, but only more or less plausible and often contested assumptions, scenarios and probabilities. Instead of being the source of reliable trustworthy knowledge, science becomes a source of uncertainty (Grundmann and Stehr, 2000). The uncertainty linked to scientific findings is not an expression of ignorance, or of a (temporary) deficit of knowledge. Uncertainty is a constitutive feature of knowledge, as it is of the contexts in which knowledge must operate.

Knowledge has of course always had a function in social life; that human action is knowledge based might be regarded as an anthropological constant. Social groups, social situations, social interaction and social roles all depend on, and are mediated by, knowledge. Relations among individuals are based on knowledge of each other. Indeed, if, like the interactionist tradition in sociology, we regard such a general notion of knowledge as the foundation stone of social interaction and social order, we would find that the possibility of social interaction itself is based on situation-transcendent knowledge shared among the individuals engaging in social action. Power, too, has frequently been based on knowledge advantages, not merely on physical strength. Societal reproduction, furthermore, is not just physical reproduction but, in the case of humans, always cultural, that is, reproduction of knowledge.

It is precisely the enhanced social, political and economic significance of scientific knowledge and technological artefacts in modern society that calls for an analysis of its essential features in terms of knowledge. More specifically, I shall indicate how economic capital – or, more precisely, the source of economic growth and value-adding activities – increasingly relies on knowledge. The transformation of the structures of the modern economy on the basis of knowledge as a productive force constitutes the 'material' basis and justification for designating advanced modern society as a knowledge society.

Knowledge societies

In this section I shall explicate and explore the idea that present-day society or, more precisely, the type of society that appears to be emerging as industrial society gives way, is best conceptualized as a 'knowledge society'. But why I regard this term as more fruitful than competing terms and approaches (such as information society or postindustrial society) requires some justification. Present-day society may be described as a knowledge society because of the penetration of all its spheres by scientific and technical knowledge (Stehr, 1994).

Past theorists of society provide designations for the assembly of those attributes of social relations they regarded as constitutive of the specific nature of their particular society. They therefore spoke of capitalist, industrial or postindustrial society. It is for quite similar reasons that one is able to label the now emerging form of society as a knowledge society since it is increasingly clear that knowledge is the constitutive identity-defining mechanism of modern society.

The historical emergence of knowledge societies does not occur suddenly; it represents not a revolutionary development, but rather a gradual process during which the defining characteristics of society change and new traits emerge. Even today, the demise of societies is typically as gradual as was their beginning, even if some social transformations do occur in spectacular leaps. But most major social changes continue to evolve gradually, at an uneven pace, and they become clearly visible only after the transition is already over. The proximity of our time to significant social, economic and cultural changes, however, makes it highly likely that what is now beginning to come into view is of extraordinary present and future significance.

Moreover, knowledge societies do not come about as the result of some straightforward uni-modal unfolding. They are not a one-dimensional social figuration. Knowledge societies become similar by remaining or even becoming dissimilar. New technological modes of communication break down the distance between groups and individuals, while the isolation of particular regions, cities and villages remains. The world opens up and creeds, styles and commodities mingle; yet the walls between incompatible convictions about what is sacred do not come tumbling down. The meaning of time and place erodes even while boundaries are celebrated.

Until recently, modern society was conceived primarily in terms of property and labor. Labor and property (capital) have had a long association in social, economic and political theory. Work is seen as property and as a source of emerging property. In the Marxist tradition, capital is objectified, encapsulated labor. On the basis of these attributes, individuals and groups were able or constrained to define their membership in society. In the wake of their declining importance in the productive process, especially in the sense of their conventional economic attributes and manifestations, for example as 'corporeal' property such as land and manual work, the social constructs of labor and property themselves are changing. While the traditional attributes of labor and property certainly have not disappeared entirely, a new principle, 'knowledge', has been added which, to an extent, challenges as well as transforms property and labor as the constitutive mechanisms of society.

Theories of societies, depending on their constitutive principles, mirror these quintessential social mechanisms in the chosen shorthand for the historical era they claim to describe and represent. Thus, bourgeois or capitalist society was originally viewed as a society of owners. Later it became a 'laboring society', and it is now evolving into a knowledge society.

Daniel Bell (1973: 346) argues that the 'symbolic' onset of postindustrial society may be traced to the period since the end of the Second World War, although he admits that it would be foolish to give precise dates for the origins of these major social transformations. According to Bell, it was in this era that a new consciousness about time and social change began to emerge. Block and Hirschhorn (1979: 368), who also inquire into knowledge, science and technology as the new productive force of postindustrial society, argue that a qualitative shift that even then began to affect the economic system has its origins in the 1920s. At least in the United States, the input of labor, time and capital had already begun to diminish while output had started to rise. In economic terms, knowledge had become a crucial source of (added) value. Finally, Radovan Richta (1969: 276) and his colleagues date the beginning of the profound transformation of modern society (at least of its state-socialist variety) to the profound impact of the scientific and technological revolution in the 1950s.

The society of societies

The emergence of knowledge societies signals first and foremost a radical transformation in the structure of the economy. Productive processes in industrial society are governed by a number of factors that appear to decline in significance as preconditions for a changing and especially a growing economy: the dynamics of the supply and demand for primary products or raw materials; the dependence of employment on production; the importance of the manufacturing sector that processes primary products; the role of manual labor and the social organization of work; the role of international trade in commodities; the function of time and place in production and of the nature of the limits to economic growth. The most common denominator of the changing economic structure is a shift away from an economy largely driven and governed by 'material' inputs into the productive process and its organization, toward an economy in which the transformations of productive and distributive processes are increasingly determined by 'symbolic' or knowledge-based inputs. The development and impact of modern information technology exemplifies these transformations (and not only in the sphere of economic activities). They include the dematerialization of production that represents lessened constraints on supply, lower and declining cost, and a redefinition of the social functions of velocity, time and place (see Perez, 1985; Miles et al., 1988).

The economy of industrial society, in short, is primarily a *material* economy and that gradually changes into a monetary economy. Keynes's economic theory, particularly his *General Theory* (1936), reflects this transformation of the economy of industrial society into an economy substantially affected by monetary matters. But, as more recent evidence indicates, the economy described by Keynes must now be understood as a *symbolic* economy. The structural changes of the economy and its dynamics increasingly reflect the fact that knowledge is becoming the leading dimension in the productive process, the primary condition for its expansion and for a change in the limits to economic growth in the developed world. In the knowledge society, most of the wealth of a company is embodied in its creativity and information. In short, for the production of goods and services, with the exception of the most standardized commodities and services, factors other than 'the amount of labor time or the amount of physical capital become increasingly central' (Block, 1985: 95) to the economy of advanced societies.

The focus of any sociological analysis of modern society must therefore be the peculiar nature and function of knowledge in social relations as well as the carriers of such knowledge together with the resulting changes in power relations and sources of social conflict. In sociology, however, virtually all classical theorists are proponents and even architects of scientism. This even applies to the ways in which knowledge is conceptualized in theories of society designed to capture the unique features of present-day society. For example, Bell (1968: 156–7) acknowledges: 'every modern society now lives by innovation and growth, and by seeking to anticipate the future and plan ahead'. Innovations are driven by theoretical discoveries, while the commitment to growth is linked to the need for planning and forecasting.

But why knowledge or information despite these reflections is supposed to play such an exposed role in modern society remains open or is not even raised as is the case in many contributions to the theory of the information society: 'why should it be information, embracing both goods and services, that has come to dominate the world's largest and most advanced economies?' (Beniger, 1986: v). Bell is optimistic that science (including social science) will affirm these expectations. 'The rise of macroeconomics, and the new codifications of economic theory, now allow governments to intervene in economic matters in order to shape economic growth, redirect the allocation of resources and . . . engineer a controlled recession in order to redeploy resources' (Bell, 1968: 158). Indeed, toward the end of the 1960s, Keynesian economics and interventionist economic policies appeared to have solved for the foreseeable future the problem of planning and controlling national macroeconomic developments. Yet only a few years later, the economists and governments alike bemoaned the absence of any economic policy able to deal with the problem of simultaneous unemployment and inflation. The Keynesian consensus gave rise to what may be regarded as the persisting crisis in economics and economic policy. Bell's claim that the social sciences will be able to deliver and implement ('codify') useful practical knowledge has proved to be much too optimistic.

What justifications are there to designate the presently emerging society a knowledge society rather than a 'science society' (Kreibich, 1986), an 'information society' (for example, Nora and Minc, 1978 [1980]), 'postmodernization' (see Inglehart, 1995), a 'network society' (Castells, 1996) or as 'scientific-technological civilization' (Schelsky, 1961)? There are several important reasons that argue for 'knowledge society' as the term of choice. I shall begin with a brief discussion of the idea that we are living in an age of the technical state or in a technological civilization before I turn to the perspective that modern society is an information society.

The technical state

In the 1960s, both conservative and neo-Marxist thinkers conjured up the image of the impending spiritless technical state and society as technical rationality extends its relentless influence to all sectors of modern life. The domination and closure achieved by the pervasive power and authority of science and technology mark the beginning of a singular type of society and the end of individual freedom and of subjectivity. Individuals are in danger of being totally absorbed into a repressive set of productive relations and absolute domination exercised by the state with the help of new forms of control.

Two prominent accounts are representative of this perspective of the possible rise, the internal make-up and the consequences of the technical state. Herbert Marcuse's influential statement of the theme found, most fully developed, in his *One-Dimensional Man* (1964) and Helmut Schelsky's (1961) thesis that advanced industrial society is a powerful instance of 'scientific civilization' as first expounded by him in a lecture in 1961 entitled 'Man in scientific civilization'. Although Marcuse and Schelsky stood for radically opposed political philosophies and goals, they arrived, in their description of the social consequences of modern science and technology, at essentially the same position. Both descriptions are self-exemplifying in that they display some of the very intellectual practices, namely universality, control and prediction, that the authors otherwise castigate as representative of a scientistic spirit out of control. Although Marcuse's and Schelsky's theories of advanced society today are somewhat forgotten and rarely invoked when attention or critique turns to the key features of modern society, especially its built-in flaws and risks, I shall briefly consider their views and point to convergences with theories of the information and the network society. Among the most notable common denominators is their description of the nature of modern technology as an instrument of social and political action.

Modern technology represents a particular logic and this logic necessarily becomes the dominant logic of human life. One of the significant consequences of such a conception of technology is that the traditional 'logic' of technology reverses itself. That is, technology as a producer of mere means of human action becomes a producer of ends or meaning, or what is but the same, 'means' of action determine its ends and prefigure the direction of social change. Schelsky describes technology as an intellectual process that dissects varied natural objects into their elementary parts in order to re-assemble them according to the principle of the least effort or maximum efficiency. The result of modern technological construction, therefore, is a novel product or process with artificial features and, in analogy, an artificial human being.

The reversal of the means/ends relationship is particularly noticeable in the arena of the authority or power relations in society. More specifically, Schelsky postulates, as a decisive feature of scientific civilization, that power relations are depersonalized; traditional relations of power between individuals and groups, as well as the legitimating belief systems in modern society, exercise power based on political norms and laws, and are replaced by 'iron necessities' of the scientific civilization and these, which is crucial, are 'not arrived at as political decisions and are incomprehensible as based on normative or ethical considerations' (Schelsky, 1961: 22). These developments imply, of course, that democratic decision making becomes impossible because the place of the sovereign citizen is taken by technical necessities that make political contest and discourse superfluous. Power relations take on qualities that make them appear unassailable. Schelsky predicts a concentration and consolidation of state power that therefore evolves into a 'technical state'. The state increasingly monopolizes all means of power based on technology, the necessary financial resources and the (technical) necessity for coordination within its control. It follows that such a state no longer needs politics and politicians in the conventional sense of the term because decisions are taken, or occur, in an almost automatic and self-regulated process. Therefore the notion of the technical state converges, in significant respects, although convergence does not signal identity, with the analysis and the thesis of the increasing societal dominance of technical rationality in advanced society by a number of authors who belong to the group of critical theorists.

Marcuse, for one, observes that the scientific mind and the transformation of its knowledge into scientific-technical rationality in advanced industrial society produce an ensemble of things and objectified social relations that have turned the project of emancipation from the domination of nature and control into its opposite. Marcuse (1964: 146) argues that these outcomes are inherent in pure science and that 'scientific-technical rationality and manipulation are welded together into new forms of social control'. Outside the world of objective things and social relations one encounters only a world of values but since they or their metaphysical basis cannot be verified, the subjective domain is not real, but is objective and weak and ultimately counts for little in the affairs of life.

The power of knowledge and information

The Achilles' heels of the theory of scientific-technical civilization and of instrumental rational control, in which 'technology becomes the subject of history', to use a formulation by Günther Anders (1956 [1980]), is the rather conventional notion of the nature of advanced technology and technological expertise, which animates all of its utopian promises and rationalistic designs. The domination by technology and by technical expertise requires a degree of cognitive coherence and commonality of interest, which in fact cannot be observed among technical experts, or in discourse that rests on the authority of the claims of scientific knowledge. Experts do not act in a unified manner, nor is expertise undivided, nor for that matter, will it ever be if such consensus is to emerge on a voluntaristic basis. It is important to recognize that most 'technical controversies have (taken) the form of a competition between two plausible *interpretations* of a situation . . . and technical expert controversy has many of the features of theoretical controversy in science' (Barnes, 1985: 106). Scientists, engineers, experts and counselors are far too fragmented intellectually, displaying allegiances to varied groups in society, to seriously represent a stratum on the verge of collectively dominating society. Barnes (ibid.: 11) concludes that modern society, though dominated by science, is not ruled by scientific experts: 'Expert assertions today must be expressed in a scientific/technical idiom; that is essential, just as centuries ago a religious idiom was essential. But it no more guarantees that a scientist will be believed today than it guaranteed that a priest would be believed long ago'.

A related and equally dubious assumption of the utopian designs of the impending technical state concerns the conviction that the growth in knowledge and information occurs in patterns that assure its orderliness and therefore prompts greater transparency and rationality of conduct in situations drenched in intelligence. However, the proliferation of knowledge does not invariably mean the reduction of ignorance and increase in certainty. On the contrary, a gain in mere intelligence may well constitute an explosion in confusion, uncertainty and unpredictability. As a result, in the sphere of organizations, for example, an 'increasing share of organizational resources goes to intelligence function; structural sources of intelligence failures become more prominent; doctrines of intelligence – ideas about how knowledge should be tapped and staff services organized – become more fateful' (Wilensky, 1971: 174).

The information society

Wiio (1985) indicates that the term 'information society' was first used in a report to the Japanese government in 1972. The suggestion that contemporary society is an information society frequently is an exemplar of a modern version of technological determinism convinced that a society ought to be named after the technical device that allegedly closely controls its development. The devices are often seen as highly efficient, without flaws and as imposing their logic on the user. The discussion about the information society is typically animated by a related concern, namely that the 'production, processing, and transmission of a very large amount of data about all sorts of matter – individual and national, social and commercial, economic and military' (Schiller, 1981: 25) gives rise to fresh forms of domination and subordination. We are warned that a new order 'is being forced upon an unsuspecting world by advances in telecommunications' (Angell, 1996: 81), that individuals are increasingly paralysed by an overload of information in the new media or that we are in the midst of a deepening social crisis that results from inequality of access to information and from the impoverished content of information itself. Yet every society transmits information and in every society such dissemination is stratified. Little is said by the information society theorists about the genesis of the substance of information, the media of communication, the changes brought about by the actual content of the information that is communicated or, for that matter, about the extent to which the information technology devices are user defined and user led. Nor are discussions about the information society usually concerned with questions of solidarity and authority or whether any economic effects of the spread of communication technologies and information, especially when defined as a material commodity or simply as 'thing-like' (Schement and Curtis, 1995: 2), cannot just as well be accommodated within more conventional neoclassical economic discourse, namely as processes best understood in terms of long-established and familiar market- and commerce-based criteria.

The network society

In a series of imaginative and empirically grounded studies, Manuel Castells (1996) has suggested that modern society constitutes a network society on the basis of the massive use of information and communication technologies in all spheres of social life. The innovations in the field of communication and information technology represent, not unlike the eighteenth century industrial revolution, a fundamental change in the material structure or the forces of production, the social structure and culture of society. The information revolution of the present-age or the transformation of the 'material culture' of modern society since the decade of the 1980s amounts to a historically new formation of capitalism. The new society or network society in which the state continues to occupy a decisive function, originates as the result of a new technological paradigm and therefore a dynamic process that is propelled by information processing or informationism. In short, 'in the new, informational mode of development the source of productivity lies in technology of knowledge generation, information processing, and symbol communication' (Castells, 1996: 17). In contrast to the notion of mass society and the nature of social control and regulation usually seen to operate in such a society, for example the presence of essentially *vertically* functioning mass media, one should also be cognizant of the development and presence of horizontally operating media and that means of media controlled by the end user.

Given Castells's description of the network society with its essential dependence on the operation of communication technologies, the questions that arises is in what way if any does his term of 'network society' differ from that of the more frequently used term, the 'information society'? And, in what ways does Castells's analysis differ from the straightforward assertion that computers create a new society (for example, Dizard, 1997: 20)? The difference to which Castells points and which in his own assessment constitutes a progressive conceptual step forward in our analytical understanding of modern society and the notion of the information society in particular, operates in analogy to the distinction between 'industry' and 'industrial'. At first glance, such a differentiation would not appear to yield much in the way of differences. 'Information' and 'informational' results, Castells suggest, in distinct ways of viewing and knowing. The concept of information or, as he calls it, the 'communication of knowledge' implies nothing more or less than the assertion that information is of importance in all possible social formations or represents an anthropological attribute found in all societies. In contrast to information, 'the term informational indicates the attribute of a specific form of social organization in which information generation, processing, and transmission become the fundamental sources of productivity and power, because [of the] new technological conditions emerging in this historical period' (Castells, 1996: 21). The term 'information' which Castells locates on the same conceptual plane as knowledge remains but skin deep or on the surface while the concept 'informational' refers to the probability that social action is somehow effected in its inner constitution by information or that social organization of social conduct is transformed based on the utilization of information.

In what kind of society do we live?

The close alliance of Castells's theory of society with the development of information and communication technologies as well as his conscious conflation of knowledge and information, make it rather difficult to detect any firm and decisive differences between the notion of an information and a network society. After all, for most observers, especially in the media, the information revolution is understood as a technical one, in the first instance. The gadgets change but not the socio-cognitive frames, the ideologies, the language of entitlements and scientific regimes. Although Castells is not a strict proponent of technological determinism it is almost unavoidable that one discovers a number of theses in his study that tend to resonate with the paradigm of technological determinism that stresses the consequences of the technical product rather than the social processes of innovation. But on the whole there are numerous thoughtful and imaginative observations to be found in his study, for example, Castells's insistence that the idea of information itself reconstitutes and refashions human activity.

None the less, as Alain Touraine (1984 [1988]: 104) has argued convincingly, the specificity of a particular society should not hinge on a given technology: 'It is just as superficial to speak of a computer society or of a plutonium society as it is of a steam-engine society or an electric motor society. Nothing justifies the granting of such a privilege to a particular technology, whatever its economic importance'. But Touraine's alternative designation of modern society as a 'programmed society' resonates with Castells's notion of a network society in as much as that concept also stresses the symbolic transformation. Touraine (ibid.: 104) insists that the idea of a programmed society aptly captures changes under way in modern society, because his imagery highlights the capacity of society to 'create models of management, production, organization, distribution, and consumption, so that such a society appears, at all its functional levels, as the product of an action exercised by the society itself'.

The notion of postindustrial society is perhaps equally ill suited to capture the realities of present-day social and economic transformations. To some extent the term is even misleading because 'industry' or the manufacturing sector of the economic system of modern societies, though they are being transformed to be sure, are certainly not disappearing altogether. The decline of industrial society is not identical with deindustrialization, as is occasionally claimed. If attention is paid exclusively to the diminishing employment in the industrial sector (Therborn, 1995: 71–2) and/or the closure and shrinkage of entire branches of the manufacturing sector, such a claim may of course be made. However, employing the conventional differentiation among economic *sectors*, the contribution of the industrial or manufacturing sector to the total output, the value added, has remained remarkably constant in the economies of most industrial countries.

As a result, interpretations of Bell's theory of postindustrial society that refer to the 'economic predominance of the service sector in contrast to the industrial and agricultural sectors' (Huntington, 1973: 163) as one of the central features distinguishing postindustrial society from its predecessors, identify a characteristic of the modern economy that is not really new or fail to recognize that the changes in the employment among sectors does not necessarily signal a change in the economic importance of sectors in terms of their contribution to gross national product. It is accurate that the production in industry has changed significantly but it is not the case that this sector has almost disappeared and has been dramatically surpassed in its importance for the overall economy. Life without 'industry' is as unimaginable as is life devoted to leisure only. As a result, Touraine's (1984 [1988]: 104) conception of postindustrial society concentrates less on the demise of industry but on the transformation of the products generated and the consequences they assume for society:

> The passage to postindustrial society takes place when investment results in the production of symbolic goods that modify values, needs, representations, far more than in the production of material goods or even of 'services'. Industrial society had transformed the means of production; postindustrial society changes the ends of production, that is, culture.

In a recent analysis of cross-sectional data, which is part of a series of studies dating back to the early 1970s, on values and beliefs of the public in 43 societies representing 70 percent of the world's population, Ronald Inglehart (1995) proposes that the dramatic shift in the direction of social change in the past quarter of a century is impressive evidence that we have entered an era of *postmodernization*. Its origins are to be found in the unprecedented achievement of economic security coupled with the safety net of the welfare state, first in Western Europe and North America and then incipiently in Southeast Asia. The cultural and political feedback that may be observed in these societies manifests itself in a decline of the authority of religion and the state, a persistence of individualism, an emphasis on non-economic values and as a shift from scarcity values to security values as well as a rejection of all forms of power.

According to Inglehart, in the political realm, postmodernization is linked to democratization. Finally, a diminished confidence in the social role of science and technology is noted as a characteristic attribute of the emerging postmodern worldview. Inglehart's argument about the dawn of postmodernization gives primary weight to certain economic accomplishments, especially the achievement of economic security for large segments of the public. The level of economic security attained corresponds to equally unprecedented levels of subjective well-being. Precisely because the public in advanced societies take their material existence for granted, 'they are not aware of how profoundly this supposition shapes their worldview' (ibid.: 385). Although Inglehart refers to a wide spectrum of cultural changes as indicative of postmodernization, he stresses, in contrast to most other postmodernity theorists, that it is economic transformations that make postmodernization possible.

Pierre Bourdieu (1979 [1984]: 55–6) offers similar observations about the cultural consequences of growing economic well-being but refers more to shifts in lifestyle:

> As the objective distance from necessity grows, life-style increasingly becomes the product of what Weber calls the 'stylization of life', a systematic commitment which orients and organizes the most diverse practices – the choice of a wine or a cheese or the decoration of a holiday home in the country.

But the changes that are more significant for modern society and that are captured in the knowledge society perspective are developments that occur with respect to the forms and dominance of knowledge itself. The focus is not merely on science, but on the relationships between scientific knowledge and everyday knowledge, declarative and procedural knowledge, knowledge and non-knowledge, and on knowledge as a capacity for social action.

In the context of influential recent discussions on the impact of science on society, for example as part of an attempt to devise an accounting scheme for its social impact (see Holzner et al., 1987), the nature of the impact of science and technology on social relations and society tends to be conceptualized in a restrictive fashion as well. In most conventional accounts, science and technology are said to generate, first and foremost, if not exclusively, new but fixed types of possibilities, resources or constraints for practical action. There is believed to be an asymmetric relationship between the distinctive spheres of the social systems of science, technology and social institutions. Scientific reasoning and technology artefacts impose their logic on social conduct and beliefs in more or less definitive ways. In some variants of technological determinism, the general effects for society are described as beneficial, perhaps enhancing the logic of human action; in other cases, the primary concern is much more with the destructive forces of technical and scientific rationality and therefore the extent to which the sphere of human action – outside of science and technology – mimics its rationalized world (see Grint and Woolgar, 1997).

Concluding remarks

The concept of knowledge employed in this chapter designed to describe various theories of the information age is much broader than is the case in most theories of the contemporary age as a postindustrial society, a technical state, a network or an information society; and to list only a few of the multiple outcomes of knowledge as a capacity for action, *additional* knowledge mostly generated in modern societies by science and technology permits new forms of social action, but also eliminates old forms of action; science and technology affect the experience of action while also assuring the 'survival' (in the sense of continued relevance) of existing forms of action, and even generate occasions that affirm traditional action and diminish or add to control regimes.

The concept of scientific knowledge advanced here and therefore the idea that our era is best described as a modern knowledge society is therefore quite distant from any notion of technological or scientific *determinism*. Technological determinism often is part and parcel of the theory of the information, postindustrial or network society. None the less, the constraining features of science and technology are by no means underestimated or neglected in perspectives that describe advanced society as a knowledge society. But in contradistinction to most arguments in favor of technological and scientific determinism, and the theories of society associated with such views, the crucial point about knowledge societies is that science and technology possess strong attributes that allow for effective resistance to one-dimensional and homogeneous transformation and therefore efforts to concentrate or even monopolize modern science and technology as a capacity for action. Science and technology have important enabling features that can be harnessed not only by the already powerful: these increase the number of available strategies, heighten flexibility or limit the ability of the powerful to exercise control; by the same token, for others, such features constitute constraining forces that limit choices, reduce options and impose penalties and risks. In short, the impact of scientific knowledge and technical artefacts occurs within and hence is contingent upon situational constraints.

It is therefore by no means contradictory to maintain that knowledge societies can simultaneously become more standardized and more fragile. Generally, it is important to avoid overstating the extent to which modern science and technology are forces that merely operate as means of control and regulation and therefore constrain human agency and delimit social action. They do all of these things, but there are other consequences as well. A perhaps even more significant outcome, as we shall show, is exactly the opposite, namely an increase in the essential fragility of society. Science and technology not only enter relational fields of social action of groups that display an interest in maintaining the status quo but they enter the domain of opposing social forces and are employed for entirely different purposes.

The emergence of knowledge societies does not mean that modern societies are becoming uniform social and intellectual entities. Knowledge as a capacity for action allows for and encourages the co-existence and interdependence of historically distinct forms of social organization and thought. Knowledge societies do not spell the end of ideology or of irrationality. Nor is scientific knowledge, as a cultural ensemble, merely a way of deciphering the world; it is also a model for the world.

6 The political economy of services in tertiary economies

Pascal Petit

Introduction

For a long time the distinction has been clear in everyday language between goods and services. Is this distinction blurring in tertiary economies which have nearly 75 per cent of employment in service activities? To begin with, the debate around services, which dates back to the early developments of economics, was on the value they created. They were blamed for being non-productive activities. The main reason for such a judgement was that they could not be stored, therefore they could not be exchanged in further transactions and so did not contribute to the wealth of nations, as agricultural and industrial products did. For Adam Smith (1776 [1977]: 430), the perishable characteristic of tertiary production was thus the real problem: '[they] perish in the very instant of their performance'. As services could not contribute to an increase in the volume of exchange, they were considered by classical economists as unproductive. Simultaneity of act of production and consumption nullifies the value of work dispensed: '[services] seldom leave any trace or value behind them' (ibid.: 430).

Karl Marx continued this distinction between productive and unproductive labour. But he placed it in the context of an analysis of the circuit of value in which the worker's labour power, and not his service, determined value. Some did express different views. For example, John Stuart Mill (1848) pointed out that educational and medical provision had a favourable effect upon producers and thus indirectly upon production. The duration of this effect seemed more important to him than the non-material aspect of services.

Considerations over the unproductive nature of services somehow disappeared with the development of the neoclassical perspective[1], only to come back in the 1930s and in the postwar period when it was stressed that services enjoy much lower productivity gains and therefore dampen growth processes.[2] This idea, very present in the stages of growth literature, was clearly expressed in Baumol's (1967) seminal paper on unbalanced growth. It assesses that, all things equal, lower productivity gains in services lead to slower economic growth and to a growing concentration of employment in services in a world where goods and services are only components of final demand and remain in constant proportions. The classical debate over the unproductive nature of services was finally replaced by debates over the dynamics of productivity in services. A central issue in that respect has always been the measurement (in volumes or in real terms) of services necessary to appreciate productivity gains. In a world where services account for nearly 75 per cent of employment, where service activities have been deeply transformed and differentiated, this measurement issue has become somehow crucial.

In this new division of labour the distinction between goods and services in many cases faded away for ordinary citizens. This is not so much the case of classic services rendered to people (standard examples of which are J. Fourastié's hairdresser, W.J. Baumol's singer and A.C. Pigou's valet) but of new services in the field of business services or of personal services, linked either with the use of some goods or of some equipment. Services are in effect continuously evolving, transforming into new ones while maintaining old adapted forms.[3]

One can track this flow of evolving service activities under three main items. They appear to be linked either (i) with businesses, externalising all kinds of activities from research and development or management functions to more peripheral tasks, or (ii) with domestic activities from personal care, leisure or education and health; notwithstanding (iii) a large set of intermediary activities like distribution, insurance and banking, transport and communication which address both firms and citizens and constitute the logistics of market economies.[4]

To this 'functional' mapping of service activities one should add another important distinction between public and private services, which draws a line, varying with history, across the three sets above. The mapping of these interrelated expansions of diverse categories of services helps us to follow the current trends in the division of labour. The assessment of the quality changes in all these activities has become a major issue. It conditions the measurement of productivity and thereby of growth accounting and income distribution. Such assessments on the quality of services much depend on the knowledge of the potential users. These appreciations thus require some conventional agreements to become standard measures.

Such issues are at the core of the contemporary questioning on growth and distribution in fully fledged service economies. It is around the formation of such measurement conventions that one should see the present phase in the political economy of services.

This chapter tries to present various aspects and stages in this contemporary building of service economies. First, we concentrate on the current debates attached to services and their apparent stagnancy or low productivity gains. Beyond Baumol's model of unbalanced growth, which took for granted the low productivity in services and mechanically derived its consequences on employment and growth, one is now faced with a productivity paradox that is more pronounced in services. It raises among other things a measurement issue which is obviously linked with the different values attached to quality changes in services. It calls in turn for a comprehensive come back on the rationales grounding the very notion of services. In order to do so the following section first reviews the renewal of the debate over the very definition of services which took place in the last three decades and then links the development of various forms of services at the interplay of three spheres of activities, namely economic, political and domestic. This broad perspective, where services play a function of intermediation between different spheres, helps us to understand both what are the common needs of modern economies and why these economies may differ in organising these various service functions. We then proceed to question whether some trends in work organisation and in consumption patterns in services can help us to foresee the end of the productivity paradox and the lasting or transitory nature of some dualism. Finally, a short conclusion suggests that positive outcomes for the two issues just mentioned may require some radical turn in policies to support some learning processes on the demand side, ensuring a development of service activities which could really take advantage of the specific knowledge and tastes of their customers to improve continuously their quality in a commonly acknowledged way.

The problems with services

In this section we shall not question the definition of services and will simply take them as given items in national accounts. On this basis, we shall consider four questions, successively debated, which are linked with the development of services. The first one takes the long-term perspective of the growth stages analysis and questions the tertiary stage. The second question comes back to a more contemporary perspective on the stagnancy of productivity in services and the unbalanced growth patterns which follow. The third considers the organisational issue raised by the fact that the productivity paradox is maximum in services and the fourth turns back to the issue of the unmeasurable nature of most services.

A tertiary stage of growth

The theory of the three stages of economic growth – primary, secondary and tertiary – was initially formulated by A.G.B. Fisher (1939), then developed by Clark (1940) and Fourastié (1949), and finally reformulated in a different form by Rostow (1953). The theory is based on two straightforward assumptions on production and consumption in order to link economic growth to the development of a service economy. As far as production is concerned, productivity gains (production or added value per head) are assumed to be higher in industry than in the service sector. As for consumption, the income elasticity of demand for services has to be greater than that of demand for goods. This assumption was soon criticised. The fact that income elasticity of demand for services is greater than one does not imply anything about changes in volume. Most empirical studies, from Fuchs (1968) to Gershuny and Miles (1983), deny a more rapid growth in the volume of final demand for services. To be more precise, in an analysis of consumption by purpose, there is a rapid increase of expenditure (in constant prices) on leisure, education, housing and health. But within each purpose, purchase of goods grows faster than purchase of services. This indicates a trend towards goods being substituted for services – a trend that lies at the root of the material development of our societies.

Furthermore, the stage of growth approach assumes a fixed ranking between the productivity gains to explain the relative growth of the three sectors over a long period of time. In fact the relative positions of these aggregate productivity levels changes, and relative shifts in employment trends do occur over the long term. The extra productivity gains in agriculture were especially marked in the postwar period, ending with a sharp and continuous reduction in the share of agricultural activities for over 50 years. Meanwhile the share of both industry and services grew until the mid-1970s to early 1980s, when trends in industry and service employment parted with a growing share in service jobs while the share of jobs in industry started to decline. This was seen as a sign of deindustrialisation.[5]

The question is then how to explain this parting between the employment trajectories in industry and services. It coincided with a slowdown in economic growth with reduced productivity gains in both sectors, still leaving a net result in employment in services while provoking a net decline in manufacturing employment.

So far, drawing on the experience of the developed economies in the 1980s and 1990s, the tertiary stage of growth seems to be associated with slower growth. Furthermore, it also seems to be associated either with high levels of unemployment or with large numbers of working poor. This situation may be transitory. But one should then assess which factors are preventing more rapid growth and full employment. The debate over the limits of the Baumol model of unbalanced growth gives some insights on these conditions.

Unbalanced growth

Within a two-sector model, Baumol (1967) tried to account for the growth of service employment and the slowdown in economic growth. This looks like a follow-up of the above approach in growth stages concentrating on some stylised facts about the tertiary phase at a time when a large share of the population had come to live in towns and agglomerations; an urban world facilitating the diffusion of services.

The model itself is based on three assumptions: (i) the productivity gains are exogenous and intrinsically larger in industry than in services; (ii) the final demands in goods and services are in a fixed proportion and there is no intermediary use; and (iii) wages are constant and similar in both sectors, and prices are determined by a similar mark-up over the wage costs of production (there is no intermediary consumption, no trade and no tax). It follows that employment will concentrate in services and the economic growth will progressively slow down to the lowest productivity level. Interestingly this simple model has been tested many times, revealing some limitations. A first comprehensive test of the hypotheses, in 1981, found that new services led to high productivity gains in a first phase, followed by a progressive decline to a lower level of productivity gains more in accordance with the initial assumptions of the model. The authors thus spoke of 'asymptotically stagnant activities'. Meanwhile if new services continue to emerge, with high productivity gains in their first phase, then it changes the overall picture of the productivity dynamics. Conversely the hypothesis on the constancy of the ratio of final demands in goods and services seemed more robust.

Later reviews of the model stressed the potential impact of the absence of intermediary use (see Petit, 1986; Oulton, 1999; Baumol, 2002). When business services are developing strongly, as in the last two decades, not to account for such intermediary consumption in assessing the dynamics of economic growth may be misleading. Moreover, the assumptions on similar wages across sectors are certainly at odds with the observation of increasing wage inequalities, especially favoured by low wages being concentrated in some service activities.

More generally, Wolff (2002), trying to explain the productivity gains in services, found that they were not correlated either with human or with physical capital. This led to speculation as to whether the measures of productivity gains were accurate. By and large this debate over the model of unbalanced growth stressed the importance of various organisational issues (impact of innovations, of externalisation, of subcontracting and of intermediary use, not to mention sector-specific wage formation). Beyond that it hinted at the dubious nature of measurement in real or volume terms of a great number of the activities under review.

It may also be the case that productivity gains in the service and industry sectors are interdependent. This is most apparent in the very long term, in the benefits that the labour force derives from an efficient health service and education. But it is also clear in a mid-term perspective that services contributing to economic integration (transport, telecommunications, business, banks, insurance) constitute the logistic base for the internal organisation of companies (Williamson, 1975) and therefore contribute to their productivity. Furthermore, it has often been noticed that once the internal division of labour within the enterprise (between research, personnel and production, for instance) had favoured the development of oligopolies, a reorganisation of these oligopolistic structures by product division facilitates the use of external services.

Obviously, and following Baumol's later work (2002), his 1967 model is somewhat crude to account for the multidimensional role of services in contemporary economies. Looking at the intensity of the productivity paradox in services confirms the importance of this organisational issue. (See Box 6.1.)

BOX 6.1 UNBALANCED GROWTH: BAUMOL'S MODEL WITH INTERMEDIARY INPUT

Given a closed economy with sector 1 producing goods, with an intermediary input of services, which are produced in a sector 2 which does not require any intermediary input, we have the following balance sheet of resources and uses:

$$X_1 = D_1$$

$$X_2 - cX_1 = D_2,$$

where D_i are final demands in product i and cX_1 the intermediary input of services in production of sector 1. If one assumes that both products are priced by application of a common mark-up over current wage costs of production:

$$p_2X_2 = N_2w(1 + r)$$

$$(p_1 - cp_2)X_1 = N_1w(1 + r).$$

Then labour productivities (here defined as X_i/N_i) can be expressed as follows:

$$\pi_2 = \frac{w}{p_2}(1 + r)$$

$$\pi_1 = \frac{w(1 + r)}{(p_1 - cp_2)}.$$

We make the following assumptions on the growth rates of these productivities:

$$\dot{\pi} = 0 \quad \text{productivity is stagnant in sector 2,} \tag{6.1}$$

$$\dot{\pi}_1 = a\dot{X}_1 + b \quad \text{productivity in manufacturing enjoys economies of scale.} \tag{6.2}$$

Meanwhile, Engel's law applies regarding final spending in both products:

$$p_2\dot{D}_2 = v(p_1\dot{D}_1 + p_2\dot{D}_2). \tag{6.3}$$

If we now express in growth rates the relations accounting for the equality in volume and value of supply and demand, assuming also that w and r are constant:

$$\dot{X}_1 = \dot{D}_1 \quad (6.4)$$

$$\dot{X}_2 = \dot{D}_2 \frac{D_2}{X_2} + \dot{X}_1 \frac{cX_1}{X_2} \quad (6.5)$$

$$\dot{p}_2 = 0 \quad (6.6)$$

$$\dot{\pi}_1 = -\dot{p}_1 \frac{p_1}{p_1 - cp_2} + \dot{p}_2 \frac{cp_2}{p_1 - cp_2}. \quad (6.7)$$

We then have a linear model of 7 relations with 8 unknown growth rate variables, which can be solved taking the growth rate of demand for goods *D*1 as an exogenous parameter:

$$\dot{X}_1 = \dot{D}_1, \dot{\pi}_2 = 0, \dot{p}_2 = 0, \dot{\pi}_1 = a\dot{D}_1 + b, \dot{p}_1 = -(a\dot{D}_1 + b)(1 - ck).$$

If $c = 0$ we get the standard results of the Baumol model with a declining relative price of goods and a growing demand for services.

If $c > 0$, we have an intermediary input of services; then configurations exist (regarding coefficients and initial conditions) where Baumol's law does not apply and where an increase in the demand for goods is followed by a lesser extension in the final demand for services:

$$\dot{D}_2 = \frac{v(1-\alpha)}{1-v\alpha}[\dot{D}_1(1 - a + ack) + (ck - 1)]$$

$$\dot{X}_2 = \frac{D_2}{X_2}\dot{D}_2 + c\frac{X_1}{X_2}\dot{D}_1,$$

where:

$$k = \frac{p_2}{p_1} \quad \text{and } \alpha = \frac{p_2 D_2}{p_1 D_1 p_2 D_2},$$

leading to the elasticity of the demand for services:

$$e(D_2 D_1) = \frac{v(1-\alpha)}{1-v\alpha}(1 - a + ack).$$

Hence:

$$e(D_2, D_1) < 1 \text{ if } k > \frac{\frac{1}{v} - a\alpha + a - 1}{ac(1-\alpha)} \quad \text{and } \alpha < 1/v.$$

Source: Adapted from Petit (1986).

A productivity paradox at its maximum

The productivity paradox has been debated since the early 1980s. It gained its celebrity from Robert Solow's concise remark in 1987, when receiving his Nobel prize, that we see computers everywhere except in statistics, meaning that in most countries the diffusion of information and communication technology (ICT) equipment did not lead to the expected productivity gains. From the early 1990s, case studies showed how a mix of new equipment and organisational changes could lead to marked improvement in productivity or profit. Whether it was becoming a widespread phenomenon and whether the productivity paradox was no more has been strongly debated ever since. If examples of successful technological changes at firm level, providing that they have been coupled with relevant organisational changes, have been numerous (see Brynjolfson and Hitt, 2000; Greenan et al., 2001) the balance sheet at sectoral level is much less straightforward. That is, the slow productivity growth implies that the productivity paradox still affects to a considerable extent service industries which have been long-time large users of ICTs. The magnitude of the gains in the 1990s for both manufacturing and service industries, according to whether they use or produce ICTs, is very telling in that respect (see Table 6.1).

The figures in Table 6.1 stress that productivity gains have been especially strong in ICT-producing sectors and especially weak in services classified as non-ICT sectors. Van Ark makes a distinction between ICT-producing industries, intensive ICT-using industries and the rest of the economy (the 'non-ICT' sector (2001:1)). Table 6.1 clearly shows the strong dynamics of productivity gains over the 1990s in ICT-producing manufacturing industries. Gains are also apparent in ICT-producing services.[6] Results are rather mediocre for ICT-using industries of all kinds throughout the 1990s, much in line with the non-using industries, with the clear exception of the using services in the US over the 1995–2000 period. The productivity paradox is thus manifest in all these activities, using ICTs without any

Table 6.1 Labour productivity growth (value added per person employed, by industry group, 1990–1995 and 1995–2000 in percentage)

	ICT-producing		ICT-using[a]		Non-ICT		
	Manufacturing	Services	Manufacturing	Services	Manufacturing	Services	Others
1990–1995							
FR[b]	10.0	2.6	3.3	0.5	3.4	−0.3	1.6
UK	15.8	5.6	2.1	2.5	4.0	1.5	6.1
EU	11.1	4.4	3.1	1.1	3.8	0.6	2.7
USA	15.1	3.1	−0.3	1.9	3.0	−0.4	0.7
1995–2000							
FR[b]	15.0	6.2	1.9	0.7	2.7	0.1	1.1
UK	16.1	5.2	1.7	2.6	0.5	0.9	1.5
EU	13.8	6.5	2.1	1.4	1.5	0.2	1.9
USA	23.7	1.8	1.2	5.4	1.4	0.4	0.6

Note: a. excluding ICT producing; b. 1999. See appendix (Table 6A1.1) for the partition of industries between ICT producing, using and non-using.

Source: Van Ark (2001).

Table 6.2 GDP shares of ICT-producing, ICT-using and ICT-non-using industries

Year	ICT producing		ICT using[a]		ICT non-using		
2000	Manufacturing	Services	Manufacturing	Services	Manufacturing	Services	Others
FR	1.4	4.1	5.0	20.3	11.8	47.8	9.7
UK	1.8	5.3	5.8	21.5	9.8	44.7	11.1
EU	1.6	4.3	5.9	21.1	11.9	44.7	10.5
USA	2.6	4.7	4.3	26.3	9.3	43.0	9.8

Notes: a. excluding ICT producing; b. 1999. See appendix (Table 6A1.1) for the partition of industries between ICT producing, using and non-using.

Source: Van Ark (2001).

clear effect. The exception of the US services is a point in question, which results from both changes in measurement practices[7] and efficient structural transformations, as in the distribution industries (the Wal-Mart effect).

Also important in this overall discussion on growth dynamics is the fact that ICTs have no indirect effects on the productivity of ICT-non-using activities. Externalities of, let us say, large network services, for instance, could have helped to increase productivity in activities benefiting from their services (obviously the data shown in Table 6.1 are not pointing in that direction).

If one takes into consideration the relative weight of the industry divisions under review (see Table 6.2), industries with low productivity gains are highly preponderant. The unbalanced nature of the growth paths of contemporary economies is therefore worrying. Industries where productivity is directly boosted by ICTs represent less than 8 per cent of GDP. Regarding service industries, only telecommunications figure in this dynamic core of the economy; the others are split between ICT-using (such as trade, banks, insurance) and non-using (such as transportation, health and education). However, this conclusion very much depends on the validity of the measurement of the productivity gains in question.

Measurement difficulties

It may well be the case that we should not take at face value national accounting in real terms on which the above measures of productivity gains are based. In effect, as stressed by Griliches (1994) and Gadrey (1996), a lot of our measures in real terms are ill defined. Either we confuse output with input measures, or we are not able to take into account quality changes that have deeply transformed the products since the accounting framework was established. The weight of non-measurable sectors has by now far bypassed that of measurable sectors in most countries (see Table 6.3). Data on productivity show that gains have been much higher over the last 20 years in the measurable sector. The idea that real growth has been underestimated in non-measurable sectors cannot be discarded. Wölfl (2003) reviews empirical studies on this measurement bias and shows that assuming only a zero productivity growth when in activities where it was counted negative could lead to sizeable rebalancing of productivity gains between sectors. Such assumptions could lead to the revaluation of aggregate productivity growth in the 1990s by some 0.5 point for the US and up to 1 point for the European Union. The correction

Table 6.3 Nominal output share and labour productivity growth of measurable and non-measurable sectors of the economy, 1980–1998

	France		Germany		UK		US	
	MS	UMS	US	UMS	US	UMS	US	UMS
Share of sector in current GDP								
1980	39	61	44	56	45	55	37	63
1988	30	70	33	67	32	68	28	72
GDP per hour worked (1980 = 100)								
1990	155	124	134	121	153	116	138	107
1998	209	129	178	137	203	139	172	115

Notes:
MS = measurable sector (agriculture, mining, manufacturing, utilities, transport and communication);
UMS = non measurable sector (construction, wholesale and retail trade, finance, insurance and business services, other services and government).

Sources: Groningen Growth and Development Centre sectoral database; NIESR (National Institute of Economic and Social Research) sectoral database; and STAN new database.

seems particularly marked for business services. Indeed, most services belong to the non-measurable category; only transport and communication are considered as measurable. The uncertainty that follows bears strongly on policy making.[8] But to escape such doldrums requires the stimulus of political debates on values, ends and means, all of which takes us back to the roots of the political economy of services.

The three orders of activities and the world of services

At this stage one is tempted to link this uncertainty on the measurement in real terms of services with some specificity of their own. In effect, discussions in the academic world on the true nature of services have been going on for decades, at least since the Second World War, when these activities appeared to play an increasing part in the growth process of modern economies. These debates tended to emphasise various 'technical criteria'. Gadrey (2000), in his clear critiques of these controversies, distinguishes three main characteristics that typify services as opposed to goods: their non-materiality, the fact that they are co-produced and the fact that they cannot be stocked. These criteria point at similar aspects of service activities but they fail to express some specificity that would help to substantiate a difference in nature from goods. However, the definition proposed by Hill (1977) was a clear step forward. A service was defined as a change in the condition of a person, or a good belonging to some economic unit, which is brought about as a result of the activity of some other economic unit, with the prior agreement of the former person or economic unit. It implies a productive operation following a transaction (on the price and content of the operation) between a provider and a user. Delaunay and Gadrey (1987) rightly added to this definition that no transfer of property occurs in the transaction, in order to distinguish the service products in question from the services rendered by employees within firms. If the definition thus completed is effective, it remains rather abstract and gives no intimation concerning the specific role that services fulfil. One can extend this definition to get a more substantial one, in accounting for the specific role that services play at the interfaces between the three spheres of activity that comprise human activities, namely economic, political and domestic.

The economic order is the order of market relations and monetary exchanges. The domestic order refers to familial and personal activities. The political order concerns all the activities linked with the government of the city or of the nation state, the enforcement of law and order as well as defence and international relations.

Human history presents itself in large phases where these orders are combined in various ways. Through the industrialisation process, the modern era of nation states has witnessed an extensive development of the economic sphere which manifests itself through new relations with the political and domestic spheres. Service activities are the main components of these interfaces, for example public services that function as intermediaries between the economic and domestic spheres.

Household catering activities appear in relation with domestic activities. The extension of the wage–labour relationship has placed them in a complementary relation with economic activities as they are a substitute for domestic tasks.

Finally, with regard to economic activities, one finds services of a different nature which either have allowed for the expansion of economic activities, offering true logistics for development (in transport, communication, finance and distribution) or conversely have allowed firms to extend their division of labour both internally (within firms) and externally (among firms), at national and international levels. Such an analytical framework helps to account for the bulk of public services as well as for the public concern that accompanies some services and manifests itself under various forms of tutelage – characteristics which have little to do with Hill's (1977) definition of services. Placing service activities at the interfaces of the three spheres of activity helps to show their evolution in a long-term perspective. In effect it corresponds more or less precisely with the four different types of services: producer, distributive, personal and social services (used in Tables 6.4 , 6.5 and 6.6) that can be mapped in relation to the above interfaces (as shown in Figure 6.1), assuming that distributive services as general logistics belong to the three interfaces.

Each period is characterised by the relative importance and dynamics of these various service activities at the interfaces of the three spheres. In such a perspective the evolution of service activities combines movements of expansion and of substitution between the various categories of services. We shall not go back to the nineteenth century, when service jobs were mainly in domestic and public services, but will present a rapid overview of the contrasting phases in the development of the various interfaces presented by the steady growth of service jobs in the twentieth century. This presentation of the evolution of service jobs will help to show how congruent are the various phases in the architecture of service interfaces with the main traits of the growth regimes.

At the turn of the twentieth century, in most industrialised countries, the share of domestic services was still dominant in the total service employment. By the interwar period the rise of intermediation (finance activities plus distributive services, for example, trade, transportation and communication) had gained in importance and changed the prevailing trend of services. Detailed statistics on services are still few and it is difficult to make comparisons at an international level. The structure of service employment in the second half of the twentieth century is documented much more fully.

Table 6.4 Service employment by subsector in the Fordist period (as a percentage of total employment in 1960/1973 /1987)

	Producer services	Distributive services	Personal services	Social services	Total services
France					
1960	3.5	16.5	7.9	16.0	44.1
1973	6.0	18.6	7.5	19.2	51.3
1987	9.0	20.1	7.9	26.4	63.4
Germany					
1960	3.4	17.5	7.4	10.3	38.6
1973	5.2	18.1	6.5	16.3	46.1
1987	7.7	18.1	8.1	21.6	55.4
Japan					
1960	3.3	18.5	7.5	8.2	37.4
1973	6.5	23.3	8.9	10.5	49.1
1987	10.2	25.1	10.2	13.0	58.6
Netherlands					
1960	4.2	20.4	8.5	14.7	47.8
1973	7.3	20.5	6.5	22.8	57.7
1987	10.8	21.3	6.5	28.4	69.1[a]
Sweden					
1960	3.5	19.5	8.4	16.3	47.7
1973	5.1	19.8	6.6	26.2	57.7
1987	7.2	19.2	5.9	35.1	67.3
UK					
1960	4.4	20.6	8.0	15.8	48.8
1973	6.5	20.1	7.9	20.8	55.4
1987	10.4	21.3	10.1	25.3	67.0
USA					
1960	6.4	22.2	11.3	21.2	61.1
1973	8.7	21.5	10.9	25.3	66.4
1987	13.6	21.5	12.5	26.0	73.5
Average					
1960	4.1	19.3	8.4	14.6	46.5
1973	6.5	20.3	7.8	20.2	54.8
1987	9.8	20.9	8.7	25.1	64.5

Note: a. Includes 2.1 per cent temporary workers employed at employment agencies who cannot be allocated to one of the four subsectors.

Sources: Elfring (1992); see also OECD *Employment Outlook*, June 2000, Annex 3A for details on Elfring's classification.

Table 6.4 thus shows that most of the growth in services in the 1960s comes from the expansion of social and producer services, while distributive and personal services stay at a similar level, even if within these sectors the activities themselves are greatly transformed (with some old trades or practices disappearing and new ones emerging). First, it indicates

Table 6.5 Service employment by subsector in the post-Fordist period (as a percentage of total employment in 1989/1994 /1998)

	Producer services	Distributive services	Personal services	Social services	Total services
France					
1989	2.4	0.0	1.0	2.6	5.9
1994	0.1	−0.2	0.5	0.8	1.3
1998	11.9	19.9	8.3	29.2	69.2
Germany					
1989	0.7	–	–	–	–
1994	1.7	–	–	–	–
1998	10.9	19.9	7.1	24.8	62.6
Japan					
1989	1.7	−0.2	–	–	2.1
1994	1.5	0.3	–	–	2.2
1998	22.6	26.8	–	–	59.4
Netherlands					
1989	1.8	0.6	0.5	0.0	2.9
1994	1.3	−0.7	−0.4	−1.0	−0.8
1998	14.3	22.0	6.2	27.6	70.2
Sweden					
1989	–	–	–	2.1	–
1994	0.8	0.4	0.1	2.8	−0.1
1998	12.2	19.4	5.9	24.3	70.9
UK					
1989	2.4	−0.5	−0.1	3.2	5.1
1994	1.2	−0.2	0.5	0.2	1.6
1998	14.7	21.8	9.2	25.7	71.4
USA					
1989	0.2	−0.1	0.5	1.8	2.5
1994	0.9	0.0	−0.1	−0.1	0.7
1998	15.8	21.2	12.1	24.8	73.8
Average					
1989	1.7	1.3	−0.5	0.9	4.4
1994	−0.2	1.2	0.2	0.2	1.5
1998	24	11.4	21.3	9.2	63.5

Source: OECD *Employment Outlook*, June 2000, Annex 3.C.

a large expansion in social services which are at the interface of the public and domestic spheres (emphasising here the public tutelage aspect without denying that health and education activities also concern economic activities). Second, it shows the rise of a bulk of business services accompanying an expansion of the market sphere in a more urbanised and concentrated environment which allows mainly for the externalisation of peripheral tasks by firms (see Bonamy and Daniels, 1993). The 1980s seem to display similar trends

Table 6.6 *Service employment by subsector and type of capitalism (% of total employment in 1998)*

Type of capitalism	Producer services	Personal services	Social services	Total services
Market based				
USA	15.8	12.1	24.8	73.8
UK	14.7	9.2	25.7	71.4
Canada	16.5	11.7	22.3	69.9
Australia	14.7	11.8	22.2	73.3
Social democratic				
Denmark	11.4	5.8	31.2	69.5
Finland	11.3	6.2	28.0	64.2
Sweden	12.2	5.9	33.4	70.9
Meso-corporatist				
Japan	22.6	–	–	59.4
Korea	9.3	–	–	59.7
Core European Union				
France	11.9	8.3	29.2	69.2
Germany	10.9	7.1	24.8	62.6
Netherlands	14.3	6.2	27.6	70.2
Belgium	11.7	6.8	29.8	70.2
Alpine				
Austria	10.5	9.2	21.7	73.3
Switzerland	15.3	10.0	24.3	69.2
Mediterranean				
Italy	9.3	8.0	22.0	60.8
Greece	7.4	10.4	17.7	58.8
Spain	9.0	11.8	18.5	61.7
Portugal	5.5	10.7	16.2	50.2

Note: Distributive services where employment shares are rather similar have not been reported.

Sources: OECD *Employment Outlook*, June 2000, Annex 3.C; typology of capitalism drawn from Amable and Petit (2001), see Appendix 6A2.

(see Table 6.4) but the 1990s (see Table 6.5) clearly show that the growth in social services has noticeably slowed down, while the rise in producer services accelerated. It accompanies on one side a new phase of extension of the market sphere, with the development of new complex business services, helping firms to externalise complex tasks and access new means of operation. It gives more firms a global reach and constitutes the logistics of the current phase of internationalisation (see Bryson and Daniels, 1998b).[9] On the other side the slowdown in the growth of social services manifests the effect of an ongoing pressure, since the 1980s, to reduce public expenditure and public involvement in the provision of services. If such a policy can explain the reduction in social services in the second half of the 1990s in some countries, it is far from being universal and does not specifically affect countries with a high level of employment in those sectors. This observation reflects the

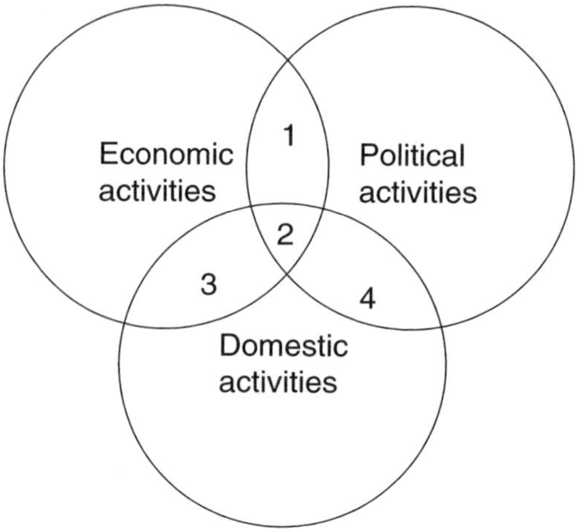

Figure 6.1 The three spheres of services activities and their interfaces: (1) producer, (2) distributive, (3) personal, (4) social

fact that countries differ greatly in the distribution of employment in the various services. In other words the interfaces that the various types of services constitute, reflect different varieties of capitalist economies. If one retains the typology, established in Amable and Petit (2001), on the basis of a broad set of characteristics, and if we compare the shares of service employment within and between these groups of countries (see Table 6.6) we see to what extent this distribution of service employment is in accordance with the typology of capitalist forms.

Market-based economies are thus clearly at the forefront in developing producer services, with the Mediterranean group lagging behind. In social services, countries of the social-democratic group are clearly ahead, followed by the core European group.

Conversely, personal services are more developed at both ends of the more tertiarised countries (the market-based group) and the less tertiarised (the Mediterranean group). The distribution of employment between the various services is thus telling of some differences in general patterns of development.[10] Clearly this last comment does not apply to two outlier groups, the meso-corporatist group where Japan and Korea, although quite different from all the others, are still different from each other, and the Alpine group where the same remark applies.

This diversity shows us the limits set to any generalisation of the trends regarding the structure of employment in services. At first sight it looks as if we had reached in most developed economies such high levels of employment in services that the growth of the overall share of services might well slow down. However, there are good reasons to foresee some continuation of past trends and further increases in the share of services. The reason is partly linked with the Baumol argument (productivity growth is superior in goods-producing sectors) but the growth in business services limits the validity of the argument. In fact the expansion in producer services is likely to continue as it partly follows from the trend in the international division of labour whereby manufacturing activities tend to be largely delocalised, at least for the less sophisticated parts of production. Externalisation and internationalisation will all boost further growth of business services. Furthermore, it corresponds to a wide variety of jobs and functions, from the more highly qualified to the less qualified.

Distributive services are bound to continue to transform themselves, due to the diffusion of new modes of organisation and use of ICTs, but by and large in these large network services these transformations may not affect the overall high levels that they now display.[11] The quality of the jobs may be at stake and may vary from one model of capitalism to another. The main distinctions between the various types of capitalism will most likely come from the distribution between personal and social services (see Table 6.6).

Social services may resume their relative growth, despite a widespread neo-liberal will to lower taxes and reduce the range of activities under direct public tutelage: first, because health and education demands are bound to grow in rich ageing societies; and second, because of the need to develop other social services, at the interface of the political and domestic spheres of activity, corresponding to developing needs in terms of leisure, training, the care of both young and old people, as well as the preservation of natural resources. Youth employment schemes have illustrated the variety of such tasks. The creation of such activities is also a good means of promoting social integration. At a time when proponents of a minimum income aim at reinforcing citizenship and social links, the creation of various kinds of jobs in charge of civic tasks may appeal to all types of capitalism.

The existence of some latitude in the organisation of service production, be it social or producer, or even personal services, leaves some uncertainty about the forms of development of advanced industrial economies, whatever the type of capitalism. The wide range of organisational and technological choices (from time-sharing options to ICT designs, not withstanding the status of jobs) lends support to fears of partial downgrading in wages and conditions of work. The normalisation of these conditions had stabilised demand and facilitated a steady expansion of demand and production during the postwar period. The fall in growth on a global scale, which led to unemployment and a re-evaluation of the wage–labour nexus and its systems of social security, in turn sets off a real risk of deterioration in wages and working conditions for some jobs in countries where service sector activities now represent nearly two-thirds of total employment. During a period of slow growth, a service economy obviously runs the risk of developing a dual society.

Service economies in uncharted waters

Slow growth and dualistic trends have been at work for over two decades while services expanded, experiencing broad technological and organisational changes. The question is then to what extent have these transformations been channelling such divides? Has it been specific to some activities or countries? A related issue is to know whether the dualistic trends are temporary and linked to the diffusion of new forms of organisation and new techniques or correspond to a more permanent transformation.

Lessons from organisational changes

General assessments on technical and organisational changes in services in the last two decades enable us to see to what extent the diffusion of a new technological system centred around ICTs, as well as the growing internationalisation of economic transactions (which is not reduced to trade ratios) and the rise in education levels of the workforce, help to develop dualist tertiary economies. Wolff (2002) has constructed interesting indices of technological activity with skill change, stressing an important stylised fact applying across the board for all developed economies and showing to what extent modern tertiary economies can also be termed 'knowledge-based' economies. Starting with a Dictionary of Occupational Titles, Wolff has defined an index of substantive complexity to quantify activities according to their occupational structures.[12] This index over the 1950–90 period in the US was found to be clearly higher in stagnant services (zero productivity growth) than in non-stagnant sectors (goods producing plus transportation, communication and utilities). An index of worker skill (as the mean years of schooling) led to similar results (that is, higher in stagnant activities), as did an index based on the number of 'knowledge workers' in an industry. A rather different indicator, based on the degree to which the occupational structure shifted over time, also pointed to the importance of changes in stagnant activities. This characterisation can be pursued looking at the levels of investment. The growth in equipment per person engaged in production (PEP) was higher among stagnant activities. More precisely, in the 1987–96 period, if goods producers and progressive services had the highest capital ratio per PEP, these ratios had been growing faster in stagnant services. If one retains only ICT equipment, stagnant services seem to have invested three times more than non-stagnant activities. This confirms that the productivity paradox is the highest in stagnant services. The conclusion for the US at this period is that the more knowledge- and ICT-intensive activities there are, the more such activities are stagnant. These findings seem to apply to most developed economies.

Meanwhile it is also clear that all these service activities have been deeply and apparently innovatively transformed in the process. Could it be the case that organisational mismatches blur the impact of these transformations?

Such a conclusion does not stem straightforwardly from studies on organisational changes. Lorenz and Valeyre (2004), looking at organisational changes in Europe on the basis of a European survey on working conditions undertaken in March 2000 by the European Foundation for the Improvement of Living and Working Conditions in 15 member states,[13] have constructed by means of data analysis a typology of four organisational forms:

- 'learning', covering 39.1 per cent of the employees surveyed and defined by an over-representation of the variables indicating autonomy, problem solving and learning on the job;
- 'lean' (28.2 per cent), defined by team work, quality management, learning but with less autonomy, more control and workplace constraints;
- 'Taylorist' (13.6 per cent), quite the opposite of the learning group with tight control and no autonomy at work; and
- 'traditional' (19.1 per cent), more or less a residual, heterogeneous group incorporating all kinds of traditional working conditions, including crafts.

This typology of work organisation[14] shows that in services (see Table 6.7), learning forms of work organisation and traditional organisation (a miscellaneous residual category) are over-represented, while lean production and Taylorist forms of organisation tend to be under-represented.

However, forms of organisation are far from being entirely determined by the sector of the firms. Both the size of the establishment and the structure of occupational categories

Table 6.7 Forms of work organisation in stagnant services

	Learning organisation	Lean production	Taylorism	Traditional organisation
Wholesale/retail trade	41.5	20.4	11.7	26.4
Hotels and restaurants	29.7	25.8	16.6	27.9
Financial services	58.1	21.5	3.4	16.9
Business services	57.6	18.7	6.9	16.7
Personal services	39.7	18.9	7.6	33.8
Average, whole economy	39.1	28.2	13.6	19.1

Source: European Foundation for the Improvement of Living and Working Conditions, Third Working Conditions Survey, March 2000; see Lorenz and Valeyre (2004).

Table 6.8 Forms of work organisation: national differences

Type of capitalism	Learning organisation	Lean production	Taylorism	Traditional organisation
Market economies				
UK	34.8	40.6	10.9	13.7
Social democratic				
Denmark	60.0	21.9	6.8	11.3
Finland	47.8	27.6	12.5	12.1
Sweden	52.6	18.5	7.1	21.7
Core European				
Belgium	38.9	25.1	13.9	22.1
Germany	44.3	19.6	14.3	21.9
France	38.0	33.3	11.1	17.7
Netherlands	64.0	17.2	5.3	13.5
Mediterranean				
Greece	18.7	25.6	28.0	27.7
Italy	30.0	23.6	20.9	25.4
Portugal	26.1	28.1	23.0	22.8
Spain	20.1	38.8	18.5	22.5
Average EU	39.1	28.2	13.6	19.1

Source: Adapted from Lorenz and Valeyre (2004, Table 6).

are important determinants of the forms of organisation. There is also, on top of these effects, a strong country effect, which is difficult to disentangle from the other effects.[15] Table 6.8 presents these country effects on the basis of Lorenz and Valeyre's (2004) work, within the frame of the overall typology of capitalism used in Table 6.7. To scale the relative influence of these various factors in opting for a learning form of organisation, Lorenz and Valeyre use a multinomial regression which stresses the importance of national factors, with social-democratic countries and core European countries being much more open to this form of organisation.

The two assessments used so far remain puzzling. We tend to value the learning mode of organisation as more prone to productivity enhancements, but even for countries that are so inclined, stagnant services remain stagnant. One is led to conclude that either it is too soon for the learning processes to deliver sizeable results or all forms of work organisation retained so far are inappropriate. It may also be the case that within a sector and even for a given form of organisation some firms are successful, others are not and the overall balance on productivity in a sector does not show up positively. A precise answer would require more investigation across sectors and countries. In effect we know that work organisation in services is both country and sector specific. Accounts for changes over the 1990s (which is a crucial period of adaptation for the 'knowledge-based' economies) bring some support, albeit moderate, to the idea of dualist trends, either within or between firms. In a shift share analysis distinguishing within and between sector effects an OECD assessment on the changes in the characteristics and quality of service sector jobs (in OECD *Employment Outlook*, 2001, ch. 3: 98) stresses that most changes in part-time work, temporary work or tenure jobs (a) occur within sectors and (b) concern countries very differently, even if on average the changes bear mainly on countries of the core European group and secondarily on the countries of the Mediterranean group. Nevertheless, the adjustments are moderate and partly resort to some catching up with practices more common on average.[16] By and large these changes in the characteristics of the jobs do not account for the scale of the failures that the persisting stagnancy of 'stagnant' services represent.

A two-sided view on market failure

Two perspectives can be taken to discuss problems of 'market failure' in services. One focuses on the provision of these services and on the asymmetry of information that makes it less secure. The other looks at the demand side and checks whether needs are satisfied. Both perspectives are complementary. The past two decades have seen a large development of the first approach with the new industrial economics, which applies in the first place to the kind of services dealt with in this chapter. In many situations in effect the problem is to lead agents, by means of rules, to meet some objectives in an uncertain environment, when it is not possible to check their performance. A whole literature on principal–agent problems has thus accompanied the deregulation of public services in the 1980s and 1990s. The other approach has been much less developed. Needs of the users, their capacity to access services and to use them efficiently, have been taken for granted. Only in the cases of education and health did it seem relevant to question the capabilities of users and the associated learning processes. In most other cases, it has largely been assumed that once networks had been set up, providers could take care of the content, appreciate the needs and satisfy them. However, debates on needs are not unprecedented. At the beginning of the twentieth century the discussions on universal services, regarding access to electricity or telephone networks, were key issues in organising the industries and the public intervention in these fields. Such debates vanished with the maturation of the industries in question. Their development became more and more driven by the producers, who came to dominate the logic of most technological choices, fixing norms and orienting innovations with very little interaction with users. France gives good examples of such dominance in its public services, enhanced by its interventionist centralised mode of governance. By comparison, this user perspective has been largely missing in the processes that forge the contemporary technological and organisational changes in services.

The question is not so much how to access some services but, more crucially, how to make use of them strategically as some 'qualified' users can. The tentative question we want to raise is whether this underdevelopment is at the origin of a lack of shared values or principles to orient and appreciate quality changes and therefore real growth in tertiary economies. One may think that this lack of consensus is tied to a general trend towards product differentiation, implying that the quality improvement for one user is not so for another one. Indeed this may well be the case, but depending not only on the person but also on the conditions in which this person may be living at the time of use. Such sophistication is obvious in the case of services using yield management pricing. They discriminate according to the willingness of customers to pay for a defined product (specified in time and space). It does not depend exclusively on the straightforward characteristics of the user but very much also on his/her strategic capacity to take the best options in specified conditions. There is a 'consumer' skill involved in the process which has to be acquired. Not all potential users are in the same position in that respect. The perspective on the demand side is therefore highly dynamic, implying personal and collective learning processes. The mismatch between the two market failure approaches may well depend on the lack of a bridge between a static perspective of asymmetric information in the provision of services and a dynamic perspective of unbalanced learning processes in the development of strategic demands in a world of differentiated products (combining goods and services). Such a tentative hypothesis, were it validated, would be central for policy making.

Towards new political terrains

Our conclusion leads us to stress the need to adjust our political debates on economic growth and welfare to the context of the present phase of tertiary development.

Economies with over two-thirds of their activities in services, while experiencing the diffusion of a new technological system, are bound to face new challenges. The puzzle in that respect lies in the fact that these transformations still do not adopt a well-identified growth pattern. The last two decades seem at first sight to support the view given by Baumol of an unbalanced growth pattern, due to the size of a stagnant sector despite the ongoing technological change and the general rise in education.

This is somewhat misleading as at the same time changes in institutional contexts have also taken place, in particular following a trend of deregulation which deeply concerned all network services. This last phase of expansion of services was also accompanied by a relative growth in business services and, to a lesser extent, in social services.

This evolution in the division of labour among firms limits the validity of the model of unbalanced growth. So does a pervasive technological change around the ICTs which transforms the nature of all products. Meanwhile new modes of organisation have been set to organise the provision of services.

None of these transformations frees cumulative forces of economic growth that could have been tracked down. There was no sign in any country of learning processes leading to some taking off, even if there were clear differences among countries regarding modes of adjustment.

The assumption that the real failure concerned the development of demand therefore gains ground – all the more so if the problem lies more with some failure to forge new learning processes. A broad comparison with what happened in the postwar phase of

Fordism may be telling. The growth in services which greased the running of the manufacturing engine of growth, fuelled, in a cumulative way by market expansion and economies of scale, a balanced extension of personal and social services. Redistributive fiscal policies were a basic tool favouring this broad-based development. It could be read in terms of co-evolving interfaces between the domestic and economic spheres of activity on one side and domestic and political spheres on the other. The last 20 years of the post-Fordist period saw a sustained extension of business services at the interface of the economic and political spheres, redefining the rules of the game and the forms of competition. But this extension has not been met with a parallel extension of the interface between the political and domestic spheres that would balance out the redefinition of the rules of competition and of property rights. This metaphorical account aims to point at the kind of deficit that has developed in parallel with the change in the forms of competition. The recognition of new rights regarding ecology, education, health and more broadly the quality of life in the urban or rural environment, could have helped to forge a new citizenship. This extension of the political terrain would in turn have helped the debate on new policy objectives, giving common bases to appreciate changes in welfare.

These perspectives would have guided the setting up of learning processes, broadening the scope of demand and the strategic capabilities of users/citizens. In this process, politics would have found the means of redistributive action at a time when it is not only a fiscal issue but also one that involves information and knowledge. Such a process can take many forms in terms of employment and different types of 'work' organisation. In a world deeply marked by liberalisation policies and ideology, it may largely call for non-governmental organisations, subsidised or not. Beyond the diversity of solutions, this chapter points at the stakes that such a redefinition of the political terrain represents, to turn the contemporary service economies that are plagued with built-in dualism and growing stagnancy into buoyant knowledge-based economies.

Notes

1. This does not imply that the neoclassical approach, which attaches little theoretical importance to the distinction between goods and services, is satisfactory. The Walrasian model of exchange presupposes a clear distinction between prices and quantities of merchandise. Transactions are all supposed to be located and potentially reversed since they are subject to property rights. Excess supply is supposed to lead to an accumulation of stocks. Characteristics of products and agents are clearly identifiable and are not affected by transactions. All of which is rather unrealistic when applied to services.
2. In the national accounts of socialist countries, a distinction was made between material and non-material production, services that contribute directly to production (transport, trade and so on) were classified under activities related to the production of goods.
3. While the new chases much more the old in the world of goods.
4. The building industry is not considered here as services; an exception can be found in Clark (1940).
5. And all the more so in that there was an absolute decline in manufacturing employment even if its share of GDP remained constant. On the deindustrialisation debate in the 1970s and 1980s, see Rowthorn and Wells (1987).
6. With the exception of the US service industries in the second half of the 1990s.
7. Fears of mismeasurement underassessing quality changes and thus overestimating price inflation and therefore social transfers led in the mid-1990s to the setting up of a commission by the American Senate Finance Committee, headed by Professor Boskin. Its report (Boskin et al., 1996) acknowledged a sizeable mismeasurement, recommended some changes in statistical procedures but chiefly underlined areas of uncertainty.
8. The Boskin et al. report (1996), mentioned above, hinted at the fact that mismeasurement was of the order of magnitude of the by then worrying federal budget deficit.
9. The importance of services in foreign direct investment is one sign of this process.

10. The typology has been established in the base of a wide-ranging set of variables quite distinct from these categories of service.
11. In support of such an assumption, note that the standard deviation of the distribution of the share of employment in distributive services is the lowest of the four types of service.
12. The index was found to be correlated with general education, specific vocational training, data handling, and personal aptitude (intelligence, verbal and numerical abilities).
13. Some 1500 active persons have been surveyed in each state at their place of residence. The exploitation of this survey by Lorenz and Valeyre has been limited to employees in firms with more than 10 employees in manufacturing and service activities, excluding agriculture, fishing, public administration, social security, health, education and social work.
14. It differs from the Wolff criteria in that it focuses on work organisation schemes more than on qualification of factors.
15. The borders between activities especially in services are thus highly country specific.
16. Notwithstanding noticeable exceptions such as the rise in temporary work in Spain and France or the rise in part-time work in Ireland, Belgium and Germany.

APPENDIX 6.1

Table 6.A1 Industries by ICT categories

Industry	Manufacturing	Services
ICT-producing industries	Computers Semiconductors Communication eq. Fibre optics Instruments Radio and TV eq.	Telecommunications Computer services
ICT-using industries	Electrical machinery Watches & instruments Apparel Misc. manufacturing Aircraft Machinery Railroad and other Printing & publishing Ships	Securities trade Retail trade Wholesale trade Banks R&D Professional services Renting of machinery Insurance
Non-ICT sectors	Chemicals Rubber & plastics Textiles Basic metals Stone, clay & glass Petroleum & coal Motor vehicles Leather Fabricated metals Wood Paper Food & beverages	Real estate Transportation Hotels & restaurants Private households Government Other business services Health Education Repairs Personal & social serv.
Other non-ICT sectors Agriculture Utilities Construction Mining	–	–

APPENDIX 6.2 Six types of capitalism defined by their social system of innovation and production (SSIP)

1. A group comprising those countries that best embody the market-based SSIP – including former members of this SSIP (United States, Great Britain, Canada Australia), now joined by Norway.
2. A group comprising those countries that embody the social-democratic SSIP. The list includes the former countries from this SSIP (Finland, Sweden, Denmark), minus Norway.
3. The meso-corporatist SSIP, with Korea now joining Japan.
4. The 'European integration' (or 'public') SSIP, made up of the countries that already belonged to this SSIP (France, Germany, the Netherlands), minus Italy, but now including Belgium and Ireland.
5. An 'Alpine' variant of the preceding SSIP, comprising Austria and Switzerland.
6. A 'Mediterranean' variant of the European SSIP, comprising Spain, Italy, Greece and Portugal.

Source: Drawn from Amable and Petit (2001).

PART II

THE DEVELOPMENT OF SERVICE ECONOMIES

7 A global service economy?

*Peter W. Daniels**

Introduction

Traditionally, most services have been 'non-tradable' in that they require buyers and sellers to be in the same place at the same time. Dental treatment, for instance, is impossible to deliver across a distance. Services that centre on the exchange, storage, processing and retrieval of information broadly defined do not, however, necessarily require physical proximity. They have been non-tradable because some types of information (such as music before the discovery of recording media) could not be stored, other forms of information incorporated in bound documents (books, reports, atlases, censuses) could be stored but could not be transmitted easily or economically, and by custom and habit some information such as that associated with accounting, design, or marketing activities was processed by firms in-house. Information and communication technologies (ICTs) have removed many of these traditional practices and constraints to make many services much more tradable. All kinds of information can be digitally stored, much lower cost and faster telecommunications allow the instantaneous exchange of digitised information with voice communication almost anywhere around the globe where the infrastructure is in place. Companies and individuals are beginning to use electronic media to produce, access and to consume services that have previously involved face-to-face or some form of direct contact. In addition, because knowledge can be codified, standardised and digitised, it allows greater disaggregation (or fragmentation) of the service production process. Opportunities are then created for the location of these fragmented production processes in geographically disparate places to take advantage of cost, quality, economies of scale or other factors. The scope for producing a service in one location and consuming it in another, whether simultaneously (for example, information provided via call centres) or at a different time (for example, data entry, software development), is greatly increased. New ICTs certainly make services more transportable but they also allow the tasks involved in service production to be simplified with the consequence that they can be relocated more easily.

Alongside the revolution in the tradability of services, ICT has also been a catalyst for acceleration in service sector productivity (especially in finance, insurance, retail trade, and transport and communications). If recent evidence from the US is a precursor for international trends (Triplett and Bosworth, 2004), service industries are no longer the 'stagnant sector' dominated by slow growth in the rate of output per capita. The application of technology to production by progressive services (Baumol et al., 1989) has enabled a broad-based rise in US service productivity that incorporates 24 of 29 individual service sectors analysed by Triplett and Bosworth. Services now account for more than 75 per cent of US gross domestic product (GDP) and are the most innovative and dynamic part of the economy; they created more than 19 million jobs in the US during the last decade of the twentieth century. By comparison, employment in the goods-producing sector remained at the same level (stagnant) although output per employee continued to rise. At another level, since 1980 business services have been among the fastest-growing sectors in the advanced economies in terms of employment and value added; they contributed to about the same share of GDP as manufacturing in the European Union (EU) in 2000 and had a higher share in GDP than manufacturing in the US in 2001 (WTO, 2004). More recent data for the EU15 confirm that this trend is not just confined to the US (European Commission, 2004).

These two developments are among a number that have underpinned the remarkable shifts to services in employment or in the structure of national economies, as well as their growing involvement in internationalisation. 'Going global' has adopted an inexorable inevitability during the decade spanning the end of the twentieth and the beginning of the twenty-first century.[1] If globalisation is characterised as increases in the volume, speed and geographical scale of transnational interactions (Held et al., 1999) there is no question that services have been increasingly implicated in this process in recent years (Aharoni and Nachum, 2000; OECD, 2000; Michalova, 2001; Chanda, 2002; Cuadrado-Roura et al., 2002; Mann, 2003; UNCTAD, 2004a). This is partly a function of their sheer visibility, as based on their contribution to national economic growth and employment or their importance in national economic output, even though there remain significant differentials in the scale and diversity of service activities in the economies of low-, medium- or high-income countries. It is also linked to the pervasive engagement with services across the full spectrum of the production process (Bryson and Daniels, 1999; Bryson et al., 2004b). Almost without exception, the global picture is one of growth that is dependent on the expansion of services while manufacturing and/or primary industries are growing more slowly or even contracting.[2] Globalisation is implicated in the emergence of a global service economy but, at the same time, services are themselves facilitators of the globalisation process (see Rubalcaba-Bermejo and Cuadrado-Roura, 2002). This chapter will focus on the economic (Perraton, 1997; Arestis et al., 2003; Chang, 2003) and technological (Henderson, 1989; Howells and Wood, 1993; Archibugi and Michie, 1997; Castells, 2000; Unni, 2000) dimensions of services 'going global, acknowledging that there are also some fascinating cultural (Bowden, 2003; Dolfsma and Dannreuther, 2003; Sandvoss, 2003), political (Amin and Thrift, 1994; Beresford, 2000; Chang, 2003) and environmental (OECD, 1997; Chung, 1998) issues.

The key dimensions of service globalisation can be usefully summarised into four groups (Rubalcaba-Bermejo and Cuadrado-Roura 2002) (Table 7.1). Very prominent is a group (A) that is centred on the international flows of factors of production such as human resources, finance capital, foreign direct investment (FDI), or international trade which in the case of services may occur as cross-border transactions (supplier and client remain in home and host locations), consumption abroad (supplier moves to host location, or client moves to location of supplier), and service transactions that take place within firms with establishments in more than one country (intra-firm trade). A second important dimension of service globalisation is a group incorporating various types of network (B) from the informal (social) to the formal (joint ventures) or organised around physical infrastructure such as intra-corporate telecommunications systems. The globalisation of services also requires frameworks (C) that promote the process; these may be provided by international organisations such as the World Trade Organisation (WTO) or the United Nations Committee on Trade and Development (UNCTAD) that are committed to liberalising the rules on international trade in services or devising ways in which the less-advantaged countries can

Table 7.1 Services 'going global': the four dimensions

A: Flows	A1: Foreign direct investment A1.1 Mergers and acquisitions A1.2 Investment in land/construction on 'greenfield' sites A2: International trade A2.1: Cross-border transactions (supplies, purchases) A2.2: Consumption outside home country (e.g. international tourism) A2.2: Intra-firm transactions A3: Movement of factors of production A3.1: Movement of human resources A3.2: Provision of foreign capital
B: Networks	B1: Agreements B1.1: Joint ventures, franchising, formal and informal networks B2: Agreements among foreign affiliates B3: Technology transfers B3.1: Knowledge transfer B3.2: International R&D
C: Frameworks	C1: Standardisation of services C2: Diversification of global services C3: Bilateral and multilateral trade frameworks (e.g. GATS) C4: Service directives (e.g. EU financial services)
D: Brands and trademarks	D1: Integrating branding strategy across international markets D2: Developing service brands and design for international markets D3: International trademark registration (e.g. Madrid Protocol)

Source: Derived from Rubalcaba-Bermejo and Cuadrado-Roura (2002, Fig. 2.1: 43).

engage more effectively with the global service economy. The notion of frameworks for the internationalisation of services also incorporates tendencies for some kinds of services to become more easily tradable (as information technology has become more important for example). Finally, Rubalcaba-Bermejo and Cuadrado-Roura (2002) identify reputational capital or brands and trademarks (D) as a contributor to service globalisation; in many ways this is more critical for services since the absence of a tangible 'product' implies that potential clients must rely on awareness of the company name (and recommendations on this basis from others) as a measure of the potential benefits of using a service provided by management consultant X rather than Y.

The simple model of the dimensions of service globalisation suggested by Rubalcaba-Bermejo and Cuadrado-Roura provides a useful context for exploring a process that is inevitably complex and in which there is considerable interdependence between each of the groups (A–D). There is a risk that a matrix of this kind conveys a sense of uniformity to the process of service globalisation; in addition to the sources of variation noted by Rubalcaba-Bermejo and Cudrado-Roura, there are spatial, temporal and other influences that dictate the development of 'global service economies' rather than a 'global service economy'. The notion of a global service economy conveys a level of interaction, integration, or reach between world regions or by individual service firms that belies the real level of fragmentation or even the exclusion of certain places and regions. It is much more realistic to think of 'global service economies' which may be converging to create a truly global

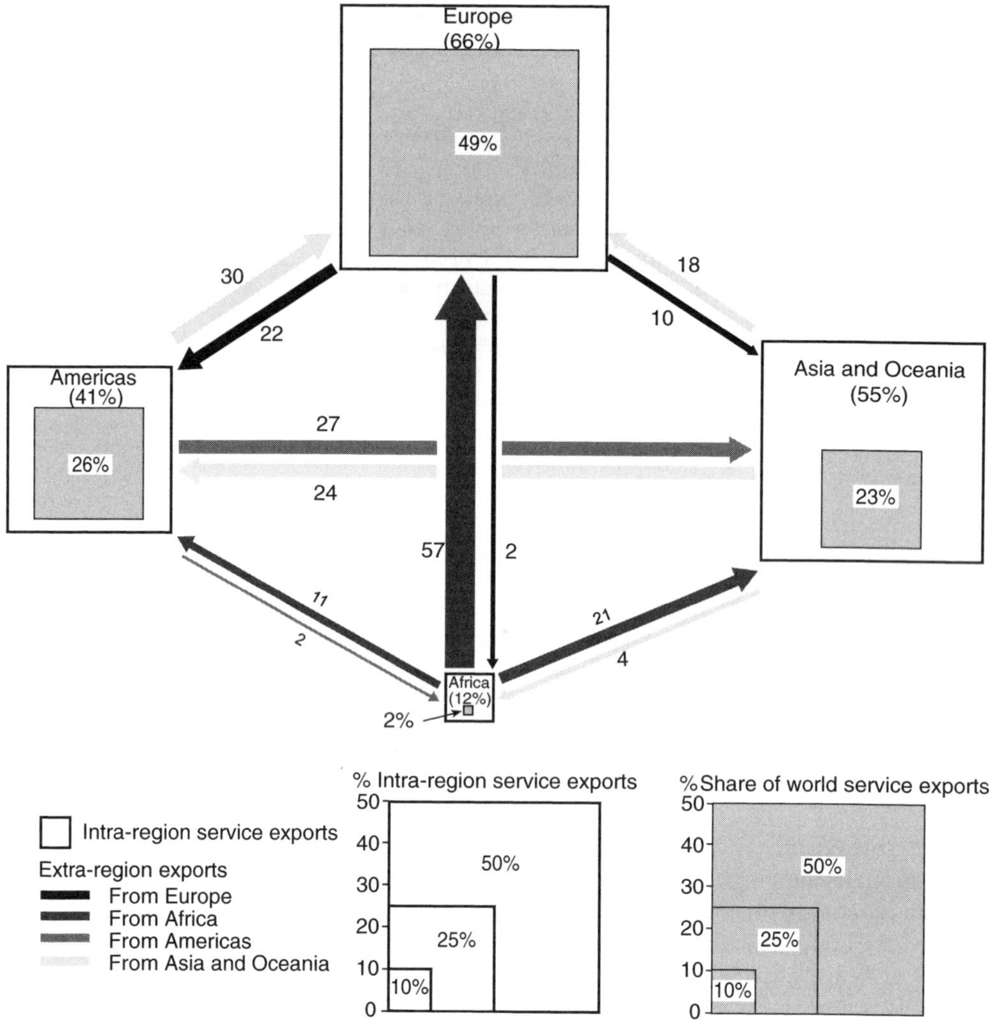

Source: OECD (2002).

Figure 7.1 World and intra-regional shares of service exports, 2000

service economy but that process still has some way to go. These will be examined below under the rubric of 'infrastructure'.

The evidence pointing to a number of global service economies is only broadly indicative because comprehensive service trade flow data, for example, are still not available, but earlier analyses demonstrating the regional foci of global merchandise trade (Poon, 1997; Poon et al., 2000) suggest that similar features might be displayed by services. Apart from Africa, almost half or more of the export of services from the Americas, Europe, and the Asia-Pacific and Oceania are to other countries within those regions (Figure 7.1). It is estimated than in 2000 more than two-thirds of service exports took place between European partners and almost 55 per cent between countries in Asia and Oceania. At individual country level, more

Table 7.2 Regional comparisons of sales and assets, Global 1000 companies, 1994 and 2004

Regional group	No. of companies[1]			Sales (US$m)[2,3]			Assets (US$m)[2,3]		
	1994	2004	Change (%)	1994	2004	Change (%)	1994	2004	Change (%)
EU	252	262	3.9	2,117	5,089	140.4	8,405	26,468	214.9
NAFTA	401	466	16.2	2,297	6,031	102.5	8,031	22,515	180.3
Asia-Pacific	331	222	−32.9	3,259	3,006	−7.8	10,947	10,827	−0.1
Other[4,5]	22	57	259.1	169	566	234.9	913	3,619	296.3
Total	1006[6]	1007[7]	–	8,522	14,691	72.4	28,296	63,429	124.2

Notes:
1. Based on market value on 31 May 1994, 2004.
2. Returns for 1994 fiscal year, translated at 31 May 1994 exchange rates.
3. Returns for 2003, translated at 31 May 2004 exchange rates.
4. 1994: Norway (1 company), South Africa (4), Switzerland (17).
5. 2004: Brazil (5 companies), Chile (1), India (8), Israel (2), Norway (5), Russia (9), South Africa (11), Switzerland (16).
6. The global ranking of six companies reflects the combining of group results in the UK (4 companies), Belgium (1), France (1), Netherlands (4), Sweden (1), Switzerland (1).
7. The global ranking of seven companies reflects the combining of group results in the UK (7 companies), Australia (3), Netherlands (3), US (1).

Sources: *Business Week* (International Edition), 11 July 1994; (European Edition), 26 July–2 August 2004.

than 53 per cent of Australian service exports and 43 per cent of service imports in 1999–2000 involved markets in Asia and Oceania (OECD, 2002). Equivalent proportions for Japan were 37 and 34 per cent, respectively. Some 48 per cent of UK service exports are destined for European partners, with almost 60 per cent of imports originating from sources within Europe (1999–2000).[3] The rationale for significant regionalisation of service and manufacturing trade flows can be illustrated using a comparison of the regional distribution in 1994 and 2004 of the sales and assets of the global 1000 companies compiled by *Business Week* (Table 7.2). The EU and NAFTA (North American Free Trade Agreement) have increased their share of the top 1000 companies from 65 to 73 per cent along with large-scale changes in assets and sales (especially by companies headquartered in the EU). Meanwhile, leading service and manufacturing companies based in the Asia-Pacific have lost ground, especially in sales. Although companies in the top 1000 based outside these three regions have increased in number between 1994 and 2004, they comprise less than 6 per cent of the total in 2004.

The remainder of this chapter starts from the premise that the ability of service firms to achieve a truly global reach is influenced to a significant degree by the opportunities and constraints associated with an environment made up of hard and soft infrastructure. The role of infrastructure such as the national investment climate or the availability and quality of business or financial services is considered. This is followed by a brief but important discussion of the alternative modes of international delivery of services, especially the growing role for mode 4 (the movement of natural persons[4]). These two sections provide the context for the use of some empirical evidence that demonstrates their limiting effects on the global flows of services trade and FDI.

Infrastructure and the global reach of services

It has been suggested that the potential for moving towards a global service economy as opposed to more discrete regional service economies (with some interdependencies) is a function of the coherence that can be achieved in the service trade rules brokered and monitored by organisations such as the WTO. In one of its most recent annual overview of trends and issues in world trade, it emphasises that trade policies and rules are in themselves of little use unless the 'macroeconomic conditions, infrastructure and infrastructural services, the functioning of domestic markets and the robustness of institutions are [acknowledged as] key determinants of the ability of countries to benefit from engagement in the international economy' (WTO, 2004: iii).

Infrastructure and related services influence the global reach of services in a variety of ways and are listed by the WTO (ibid.: 148) as follows:

1. The cost and quality of infrastructural services are important determinants of the volume and value of international trade through the impact they have on cross-border transaction costs.
2. Because sectors differ in terms of how intensively they use infrastructural services, the quality and cost of such services also affect patterns of comparative advantage and international specialisation. Reliable and cost-effective infrastructure services are, for example, more important for trade within international production networks in advanced industries than for trade in non-perishable commodities.
3. Trade in infrastructural services may improve the quality and cost effectiveness of such services, and when that is the case it will stimulate trade in other sectors through the transaction cost channel. Infrastructural services, with the exception of business services, are subject to market imperfections such as network externalities, significant scale economies and coordination failure.
4. The interaction between infrastructure services and trade involves regulation which is a very information-intensive activity; good telecommunications improve the ability of regulators to cooperate at the international level.

Depending on the context and the service activity involved, infrastructure may either act as an enabler of global or regional service interactions, or it may operate as an impediment. The range of infrastructural variables is considerable: from hard infrastructure such as telecommunications or transport to soft infrastructure such as human resources or the investment climate. Only a small number of the possible infrastructural considerations will be examined here, namely telecommunications, the financial sector, business services, and the investment conditions in potential host economies.[5]

Telecommunications

Good telecommunications services are vital for the comparative advantage of the growing number of activities in the service sector whose tradability has been transformed by ICT (Warf, 1995b; Graham, 1999; Wheeler et al., 2000). Developments in telecommunications infrastructure (fixed-line telephony, mobile telephony, the internet and a number of related services) promote cross-border trade in services. Effective telecommunications provide a low-cost channel for searching, gathering and exchanging information which, in turn, is a key input to all economic activities. Hardly any business today can operate without telecommunications. A few years ago, before the internet bubble burst, it was widely believed that the internet would initiate the death of distance and access to markets would, effectively, only be limited by the trade barriers created by countries with differing trade priorities (Capling and Nossal, 2000; Cairncross, 2001; Tharakan and Van Beveren, 2003). This version of the impact of telecommunications on international transactions may materialise in the long run, but during the interim there are a number of obstacles (such as social and educational obstacles/inertia) to overcome.

Since ICTs are now one of the key foundations of our societies and economies it is crucial that access to them is as uniform as possible; in practice, there is a 'digital divide' which means that the 'have-nots', whether they be countries or individuals, are denied the option to participate in new ICT jobs, in e-government, in ICT-improved healthcare, in ICT-enhanced education, or in ICT-enabled transactions by a growing variety of services that were not tradable until the advent of ICT (James, 1999). The digital divide has attracted widespread attention with reference to its meaning, its parameters, and the policies required to achieve change (see, for example, Bridges.org, 2001; Sidorenko, 2001; Haqqani, 2003). It is a complex problem that encompasses physical aspects such as the availability of fixed-line telecommunications, access to computers, training, and local circumstances such as social conditions (poverty, basic literacy). The spread of internet users among the world's population is much more unequal than that of the use of other ICT such as TV or telephones. The inequality of internet usage is even bigger than the spread of GDP between the world's rich and poor countries, and larger than disparities in other technologies such as televisions (G8, 2001). The scale of the digital divide in 2003 is shown in Table 7.3 which shows that Africa, in particular, but also Asia are well behind the Americas (especially North America) and Europe in terms of users per 10,000 inhabitants or the number of personal computers per 100 inhabitants.

The amount of bandwidth (which includes submarine and other international cables and satellite links) available to a country provides an indication of how much information can quickly travel from one country to another. International bandwidth is vital since non-US users of the internet are effectively limited by their country's total international bandwidth. In late 2000 the bulk of internet connectivity linked the US with Europe (56 Gbps) and, to a lesser extent, the US with the Asia-Pacific region (18 Gbps). Africa had very little bandwidth reaching Europe (0.2 Gbps) and the USA (0.5 Gbps). But the picture is changing rapidly as countries like India, once dependent on limited and expensive international communications infrastructure, have rapidly become well-connected to the rest of the world; its international submarine cable capacity will have grown from 31 Gbps in 2001 to 541 Gbps by the end of 2004 – a 17-fold increase in three years (TeleGeography, 2004). But access to this bandwidth comes at a premium price; capacity prices from the US to India, for example, are still five to 10 times higher than on the US to Hong Kong route.

Price is one of a number of factors affecting ICT use; its affordability is related to the basic cost of the technology relative to per capita income. For example, in 2001 access costs (internet service provider: ISP, and telephone call costs) were almost four times as expensive in the Czech Republic and Hungary as in the United States (during off-peak hours; peak prices are even higher) (OECD, 2001a). Even if the price of using the internet is reduced, connection speeds are often relatively slow, so that it takes longer to download e-mail and web pages, is expensive, and fewer people and businesses can participate. Web pages (and e-mail) are also increasingly graphics heavy, and require very large file

Table 7.3 Information technology penetration, world regions, 2003

	Internet				PCs	
Region	Hosts total	Hosts per 10,000 inhab.	Users (k)	Users per 10,000 inhab.	Total (k)	Per 100 inhab.
Africa	243,171	3.01	9988.2	123.67	9453	1.28
Americas	122,555,360	1450.21	217,549.4	2,574.80	239,717	28.95
Asia	13,390,474	37.08	211,201.6	584.25	154,935	4.36
Europe	18,358,407	230.41	176,232.4	2,211.84	167,430	21.44
Oceania	3,034,390	968.49	11,607.4	3,704.74	13,188	42.40
World	157,858,802	258.66	626,578.9	1,027.92	584,723	9.86

Notes:

1. *Internet hosts* refer to the number of computers directly connected to the worldwide internet network. Note that internet host computers are identified by a two-digit country code or a three-digit code generally reflecting the nature of the organisation using the internet computer. The number of hosts is assigned to economies based on the country code although this does not necessarily indicate that the host is actually physically located in the economy. In addition, all other hosts for which there are no country code identification are assigned to the United States. Therefore the number of internet hosts shown for each country can only be considered an approximation. Data on internet host computers are from Internet Software Consortium and RIPE (Réseaux IP Européens).
2. Internet *users* is based on nationally reported data. In some cases, surveys have been carried out that give a more precise figure for the number of internet users. However, surveys differ across countries in the age and frequency of use they cover.
3. The reported figure for internet users is divided by the total population to obtain *users per 100 inhabitants*. Countries that do not have surveys generally base their estimates on derivations from reported internet service provider (ISP) subscriber counts, calculated by multiplying the number of subscribers by a multiplier.
4. *PCs* shows the estimated number of personal computers (PCs), both in absolute numbers and in terms of PCs per 100 inhabitants. The figures for PCs come from the annual questionnaire supplemented by other sources.

Source: ITU, 2003 (www.itu.int/ITU-D/ict/statistics/at_glance/Internet03.pdf). Accessed 14 October 2004.

sizes; these are not a problem for countries with steadily increasing bandwidth (such as in North America and much of Europe), but for other countries it means that, all other things remaining equal, it is actually becoming more expensive to use the internet over time. Even if positive cost and capacity changes can eventually smooth out disparities in internet access, human capital and technical training capacity, based on longstanding international divisions on investment in education, including such factors as staff development programmes, technical training in schools, and secondary and tertiary enrolment, will prolong the digital divide.

Although the digital divide continues to be wide, both within and between national economies, a structural shift in infrastructure is starting to close the gulf (World Bank, 2003b). Fixed-line services have long commanded the largest market share and require costly expenditure on infrastructure. The advent of mobile telephony has introduced lower network infrastructure costs that are quite modest in comparison to fixed lines. It has therefore been much easier for suppliers of mobile services to expand in existing markets or to enter new markets, with increased competition also driving down prices. Mobile lines have therefore increased much faster than fixed lines since 1995 although fixed-line services still have the largest market share. But mobile communication has expanded especially quickly in the less-developed countries that have low densities of fixed-line networks; in some cases they now account for more than half of total telecommunications revenues (OECD, 2001a; ITU, 2004). The digital gap may be narrowing but there is still a chasm between the most- and least-connected economies (WTO, 2004). The number of fixed and mobile telephone lines per 1000 inhabitants in the top 10 countries ranges between 640 and almost 900; in the bottom 10 countries it ranges between 3 and 0.3.

Business services

In its comprehensive analysis of the global infrastructure that facilitates trade (both of services and merchandise), the WTO draws particular attention to business services (ibid.). This broad category includes computing and data processing, professional services, marketing services, technical services, leasing and renting, labour recruitment and operational services. As the WTO (ibid.: 142) notes 'for almost every function performed in a modern business, there exist specialized companies providing the function in the form of a business service [so that] an increasing number of manufacturing and service firms choose to purchase or outsource business services from external suppliers rather than producing the services themselves'.[6] Not only does outsourcing support established business services, it also stimulates innovation, entrepreneurship and further specialisation in the types of business service available. There are a number of ways in which business services contribute to global trade (see ibid.: 142–7 for a detailed discussion).

Business services help to lower barriers to entry and assist with the transfer of technology. In their capacity as highly specialised external suppliers they can reduce the procurement costs for non-core functions (that may also be strategically important) not just for large transnational corporations (TNCs) but also for small and medium-sized enterprises (SMEs). Take the example of boat design: a small boatyard could not normally expect to sustain its own viable, internal team; by purchasing design services from a specialised engineering firm a boatyard SME has access to specialised marine architects, engineers and other experts who can provide state-of-the-art knowledge and technology.[7] In consumer goods industries, packaging, brand development and marketing are often key strategic functions that determine market price, and thus the profitability of the producer. Such functions are increasingly outsourced to specialised service providers, with availability particularly important for SMEs (OECD, 2000). As a result, jobs in business services are directly created while others are simultaneously generated or indirectly created by those sectors that use their expertise (Daniels, 2000). The external purchase of specialised business services by SMEs as well as larger companies and TNCs often helps them access new production, process and organisational technology and to comply with customers' quality requirements and standards required by legislation.

The direct and indirect impact of business services on job creation is replicated for international trade in these services (Noyelle and Dutka, 1988; Goodwin and Neal, 1990; OECD, 1996) while indirect effects arise from the way in which they act as intermediaries between potential exporters and foreign customers. They help to lower transaction costs and to improve productivity and competitiveness in client companies. Marketing services help to match producers in one country with customers in another, while technical and management services help producers in countries with a shortage of skills to improve productivity and become more competitive. There is also complementarity between cross-border supply, following client firms overseas, FDI and the movement of natural persons in the business services sector (see below).

The role of business services as 'infrastructure' is emphasised when their involvement in the production process (measured as their share in total intermediate demand) is examined. In the case of the manufacturing sector, input–output analyses show that the share of business services has increased from 5 per cent in 1972 to 20 per cent in 1998 in the Netherlands and from 3 per cent in 1968 to 14 per cent in 1997 in the UK. Business services accounted for more than 10 per cent of the intermediate consumption of services by manufacturing in France, Germany and Japan in 2003 (OECD, 2003b). Data for the US car industry show that it has shifted its core functions from vehicle manufacturing of cars to research and development (R&D), design and marketing of cars with as much as 88 per cent of total gross output consisting of intermediate inputs. This has shifted the car industry's core activities from manufacturing to services; General Motors, for example, posted an overall net loss of $US1.1 billion for the first quarter of 2005 but Acceptance Corporation, the GM unit responsible for financial services, made a profit of $US728 million, only slightly down from the $US764 million recorded in the first quarter of 2004 (Daniels and Bryson, 2002).

The WTO (2004) concludes that even countries that do not possess comparative advantage in business services can still benefit from trade in those services. Since imports of business services invariably rely on firms being directly represented or entering into joint ventures in the host economies, there is a potential for additional jobs to be created. Trade in business services will also facilitate better links between domestic firms and any foreign customers in other industries to such an extent that it stimulates exports in other sectors. Finally, because financial or telecommunications services require much closer local (national) regulation, the barriers to entry for these services are much higher than for business services. This means that any progress with trade liberalisation can elicit a more rapid response from domestic and incoming business services along with scope for increased levels of trade.

Financial services

The globalisation of services is also dependent on the financial services sector (banks, insurance, securities, asset management and financial information). This component of the infrastructure shapes the efficient allocation of resources across time and space and is an important intermediary in the process of transferring the ownership of a product across borders or hedging the risk that is integral to international trade flows (Sidaway and Bryson, 2002). Financial services, in common with business services, 'oil' international trade transactions while themselves being engaged in international trade. The latter promotes competition between suppliers; an influx of foreign banks, for example, may create competitive pressures that encourage local banks to seek a reduction in their overhead costs with knock-on benefits for their clients, as well stimulating improvements in domestic supervision and regulation (Konopielko, 1999; Levine, 2001; WTO, 2004). Access to, performance and costs of financial services vary enormously among countries. For example, the countries with the highest ratio of private sector credit to GDP are primarily high-income countries; there are several low-income countries where credit to the private sector is almost non-existent. There are also large differences in the interest margins reported by financial services at each end of the spectrum, providing another indicator of the divergence in finance-related transaction costs that firms face in different parts of the world (see WTO, 2004, Table IIB.10: 136). The degree to which national financial services markets are regulated tends to be linked to their openness to international trade in services (and merchandise) (IMF, 2002a).

It is also worth noting one of the key pieces of supporting architecture for world trade in services (and in goods) is the 'letter of credit'. Although there are several types of letter of credit, their basic function is to provide an undertaking by a bank to make a payment to a named beneficiary within a specified time, against the presentation of documents which comply strictly with the terms of the letter of credit (SITPRO, 2004). The main advantage of a letter of credit is that it provides security to both the exporter and the importer, although this must be weighed against the additional costs resulting from bank charges. The use of the letters of credit as a tool to reduce risk has grown substantially during the last 10–15 years. Commercial letters of credit are used primarily to facilitate foreign trade and invariably act as the primary payment mechanism for a transaction.

Investment climate

The national investment climate is another crucial infrastructural factor. A recent study demonstrates how this varies widely between countries, shaping their attraction for inward investment, the potential for service firms to prosper, and for new ones to be set up (World Bank and International Finance Corporation, 2004).[8] The creation of electronic one-stop shops for new businesses, shrinking regulatory delays by weeks, improving credit registries, and increasing the flexibility of labour laws promote economic growth, including new firm formation and raising trade potential. Many of the less-developed countries make it twice as difficult as developed countries for entrepreneurs to start, operate, or close a business. They also provide far fewer intellectual property rights protections compared with those available to businesses in the advanced economies (Anderson and Gallini, 1998).[9] During 2003, the latter implemented three times as many investment climate reforms as poor countries, with European nations especially active. Of the 58 countries (out of 145 surveyed) that reformed and relaxed business regulation in 2003, less than a third were poor or lower-middle-income economies (World Bank and International Finance Corporation, 2004).

The influence of modes of supply of services

The effectiveness of infrastructure such as business or financial services, the investment climate, or telecommunications depends in significant part on the modes of supply of services. The General Agreement on Trade in Services (GATS) identifies four modes of service transactions, depending on the territorial presence of the supplier and the consumer at the time of the transaction.[10] The GATS modes are equivalent of the flows (A) cited by Rubalcaba-Bermejo and Cuadrado-Roura (see Table 7.1). Mode 1 (cross-border) and mode 3 (commercial presence) are often recognised as the key mechanisms for supplying services to international markets and, although service trade data disaggregated by modes of supply are not available, it is possible to calculate a rough approximation using balance of payments and information on foreign affiliates trade (FATS). Estimates indicate that, at least for certain types of services, the supply via mode 4 (temporary movement of natural persons providing a service) is by no means as small as usually assumed (McLaughan and Salt, 2002; Mattoo and Cazaniga, 2003). For example, UK imports of commercial services from India via mode 1 in 2000 (estimated value $US340 million) were significantly lower than those supplied via mode 4. Likewise, cross-border imports of computer services to the US from China and the Philippines were insignificant ($US9 million and $US10 million, respectively) by comparison with those delivered in the form of movement by natural persons ($US260 million and $US60 million, respectively). Although the available data are far from comprehensive it does suggest that the movement of natural persons as a mode of supplying services internationally is important, especially for developing countries. The implication here is that it may compensate for some of the competitive disadvantages that they encounter because of the kinds of infrastructural deficiencies discussed earlier, and which have a greater impact on trade in services via modes 1 and 3. However, the impact of mode 4 mobility on trade may differ from the estimates derived from studies of international migration (Goto, 2000; Martin, 2001; Drinkwater et al., 2002; ILO, 2003). The WTO (2004: 52) outlines the possibilities as follows:

> [A] worker moving abroad temporarily might have a higher propensity than a permanent migrant to import from his country of origin, as he or she has probably not yet adapted to local products (stronger preference effect). As regards exports, on the one hand a worker who temporarily works abroad might not stay long enough to acquire the appropriate knowledge of the local market (destination market) to set up new trade links (weaker information effect). On the other hand, (if he stays long enough) on his return to his home country, he might begin to import a product that he has discovered during his stay abroad. Or, a short stay abroad might be needed to establish links with foreign distributors and importers (stronger information effect). Overall, the final effect of Mode 4 mobility on exports may theoretically be higher or lower than that of migration. The question requires empirical analysis.

There has been some very narrowly focused research on the international migration of managers and professionals (Beaverstock, 1989, 1990; Beaverstock and Smith, 1996) but there is clearly a requirement for more comprehensive research on the mode 4 international movement of both skilled and less-skilled service workers.

The temporary movement of natural persons as a mechanism for delivering services is assuming even greater importance because of the rapid expansion of offshoring and outsourcing by large manufacturing and service firms. Country restrictions on the temporary movement of workers are longstanding but as the demand is increasing so is the diversity of the restrictions and regulations. There are usually requirements for certain levels of education or skills, the temporary migrants may be required to work for the same pay rates as host-country workers and to experience the same working conditions, the visa conditions may not allow family members to accompany the temporary migrant, the duration of the stays permitted will vary according to the type of entrant (for example, temporary visitors for business, intra-corporate transferees, specialty occupation workers) as well as country of origin. Each country has its own priorities, preferences and policies with respect to mode 4; the issues surrounding it and efforts by the WTO to broker agreement among member countries (bilateral or multilateral) that will lead to a more transparent and less restrictive regime have been painfully slow. Through mode 4 trade, skills and knowledge embodied in foreign personnel may be accessed at lower than domestic 'production' costs. This may help to overcome skills and general labour shortages, overall as well as in specific sectors, and thereby help to promote economic growth. By requiring foreign suppliers to comply with domestic market and other regulations, potential entrants are deprived of an economic advantage. The net effect is a reduction in mode 4 trade and its potential to create benefits both for local service suppliers and local users as well as preventing some countries from competing by use of the mode 4 delivery model.

Regional service economies?

The brief exploration of some of the infrastructural factors that shape global flows of trade and FDI in services suggests that a truly integrated global service economy is an aspiration rather than a reality. At the very least, there are too many country variations in factor endowments or differences in levels of openness to international service transactions and investments. On top of this, while international statistical coverage of services continues to be incomplete,[11] it is estimated that commercial services account for only approximately 20 per cent of world trade; a statistic that has hardly changed since the mid-1990s. In 2003, world commercial trade increased by 12 per cent to $US1.8 trillion but this was less than the equivalent rate for merchandise trade (16 per cent and $US7.3 trillion, WTO, 2004).[12] This is part of an ongoing pattern of a mixed performance by services since 1985 in which two of the three major categories of commercial services, travel and transport, have a reduced share of world exports; only 'other services' have increased their share of world exports from some 6 per cent in 1985 to almost 10 per cent in 2002. The 'other services' category is a diverse mix of mainly knowledge and information services, some of which have made dynamic contributions to export growth (especially since 1995). These include, in descending order of export growth rate between 1995 and 2002, computer and information services; financial services; insurance; personal, cultural, and recreational services; and royalties and licence fees.

It is possible to examine the level of participation of different world regions in commercial service exports and imports (Feketekuty, 1988; OECD, 2001b; Freund and Weinhold, 2002; IMF, 2002a). For reasons linked to the infrastructure factors discussed earlier, Western Europe and North America are the leading net exporters of commercial services and have consistently occupied this position (although the levels have varied from year to year). The other world regions are net importers of commercial services but this does not mean that they are dependent on Western Europe or North America. It is necessary to have data on bilateral commercial service trade flows to examine the relative importance of intra- versus inter-regional flows; the OECD made such data available for the first time in 2002 (OECD, 2002). There are caveats attached to the data but the estimates illustrated earlier (Figure 7.1) demonstrate that intra-regional services trade is very significant for three of the four regions used for the analysis. Thus, although Europe is a leading exporter of commercial services (over 50 per cent of total world exports in 2003), almost two-thirds of the exports are between country partners within the region. In the Asia and Oceania region almost 55 per cent of the exports are within the region, followed by the Americas with 42 per cent. Only Africa, where infrastructural factors are still a major impediment (even though changes are occurring), has a very small intra-regional share (just 12 per cent) of commercial service exports.

But the picture is inevitably more complicated than this because a significant share, estimated at 40 per cent or more, of cross-border service trade is undertaken by the foreign affiliates of TNCs (OECD, 1999a; Karsenty, 2000b; Fernandez, 2001; Arkell, 2002). This also serves as a reminder that if service trade is mediated by foreign subsidiaries it means that some form of FDI is involved. Indeed, a better assessment of global and regional trends in service transactions is obtained if FDI is included (UNCTAD, 1998, 2004a;

Mallampally and Zimny, 2000; Grünfeld and Moxnes, 2003). According to Mallampally and Zimny (2000: 25) the 'importance of FDI as an instrument of globalization is much greater in services industries . . . because . . . many are not tradable and establishing foreign affiliates is often the only way of accessing foreign markets'. This refers to the mode 3 (commercial presence) delivery of services which, even though service TNCs for example are still less transnationalised than their manufacturing counterparts, has been expanding rapidly in recent years.

There has been a consistent shift of FDI towards services (Figure 7.2). For the OECD area the main recipients of FDI into their service sector are generally the countries that figure prominently in FDI flows overall: the United States (US$800 billion 1990 and 2002), Germany (US$400 billion), the United Kingdom (US$250 billion) and France (US$240 billion). The vast majority of the service sector net outflows are down to three countries: the United Kingdom, Japan and France. Each generated net outflows in excess of US$2000 billion each between 1990 and 2002. Other significant service sector net exporters of FDI are Canada, the Netherlands and Switzerland. The prominence of the service sector in net overall outflows to the rest of the world (more than US$1 trillion) is very striking with as much as 75 per cent of all the net outflows between 1990 and 2002 due to service sector investment. In 1990 just less than half of world FDI stock was classified as services, but by 2002 the share had risen to 60 per cent with an estimated value of more than $US4 trillion and as the 'transnationalization of the service sector in home and host countries lags behind that of manufacturing, there is scope for a further shift towards services' (UNCTAD, 2004a: xx). In the first half of the 1990s, two sectors (trade, which includes retail and wholesale distribution, and financial intermediation) generally accounted for two-thirds of service sector FDI in the OECD area (Figure 7.3). The share

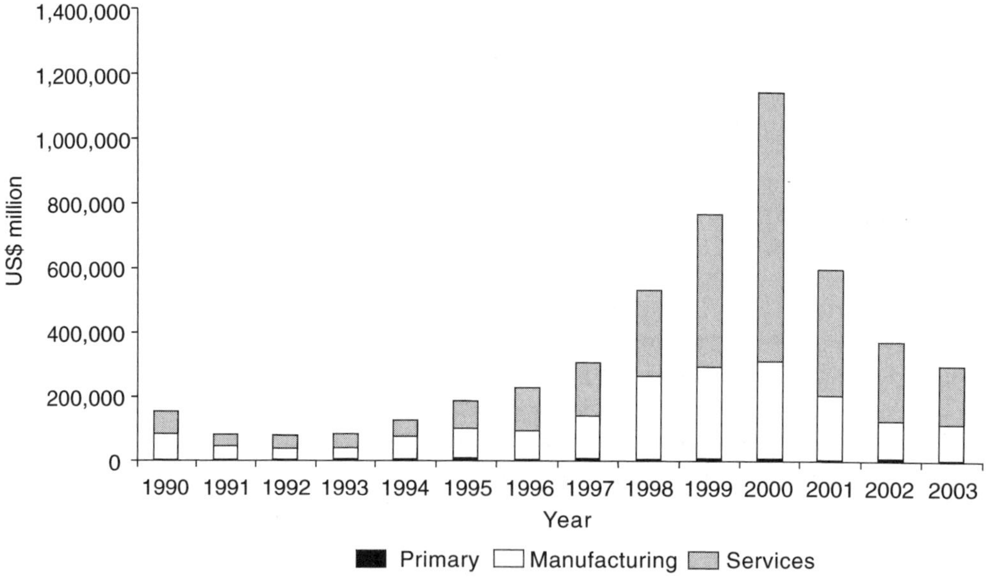

Source: UNCTAD (2004a).

Figure 7.2 Share of services in inward FDI, 1990–2003, OECD countries

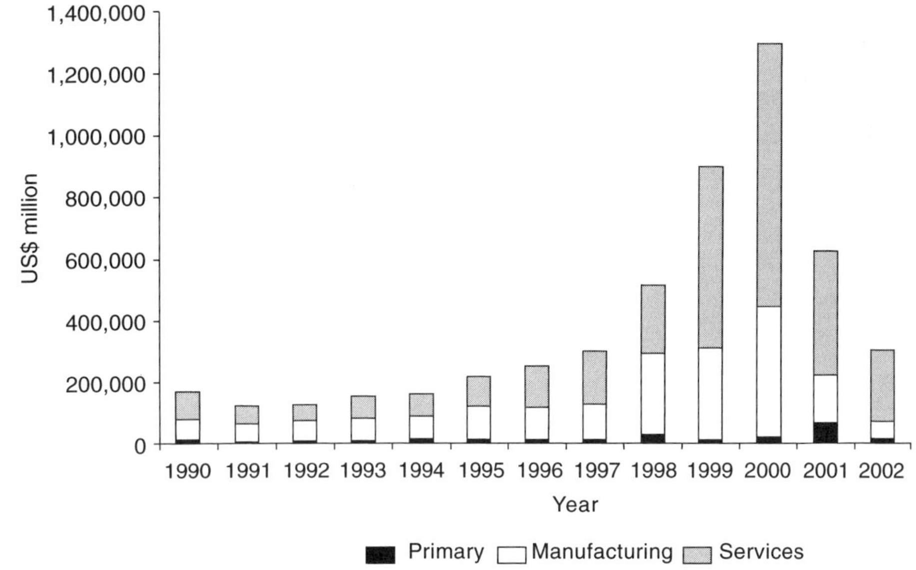

Source: UNCTAD (2004a).

Figure 7.3 Shift of cross-border mergers and acquisitions towards services, 1990–2002, OECD countries

of these sectors had declined to one-third of the total in 2002 as the largest recipient of FDI had become the business services sector. Privatisation, mobile telecommunications, and more sophisticated multimedia technology also boosted the share of the transport and communication sectors which rose from virtually nil in 1990 to just less than 16 per cent of service sector FDI flows in 2002.

Since most service FDI is market seeking, developed countries still attract a major share of inward flows and these are therefore dominated by North America and Western Europe. Historically, these regions have also tended to be the principal source of outward flows of service FDI, but since the early 1990s the global balance has been changing very slowly as FDI sourced in developing countries has visibly begun to grow. The latter accounted for just 1 per cent of outward FDI stock in 1990 but this had increased to 10 per cent in 2002. Unfortunately, bilateral data on FDI that parallels the OECD service trade data is not available; suffice to note that developed countries account for an estimated 72 per cent of the inward stock of services, developing economies 25 per cent, and the countries of Central and Eastern Europe just 3 per cent. There has been a shift in regional origin of outward flows towards the developing countries but, in broad terms, the unbalanced regionalisation typical of inward flows remains.[13]

The structural shift of FDI away from manufacturing towards services has seen a parallel shift in cross-border mergers and acquisitions (M&As) towards services (Figure 7.4) (UNCTAD, 2000; Kang and Sakai, 2001; Lindblom and von Koch, 2002). One is essentially a function of the increasing share of services in economies generally, while the other is a response to the introduction of national privatisation programmes for services such as telecommunications, water and electricity supply, or the deregulation of banking and

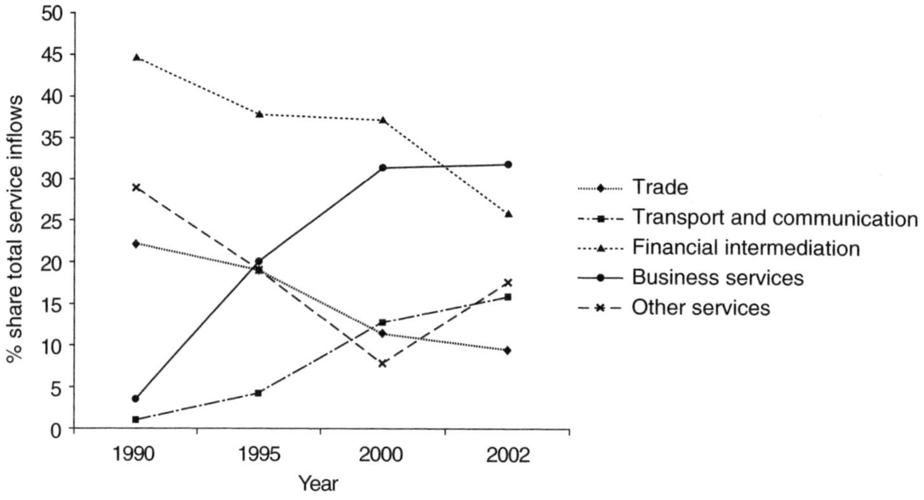

Source: UNCTAD (2004a).

Figure 7.4 Trends in the sectoral structure of service FDI, 1990–2002, OECD countries

financial services from the mid-1980s onwards and especially during the 1990s. Financial services and telecommunications TNCs based in the US and in Europe have dominated worldwide M&A activity until very recently; business and professional services are also involved but their share of total activity has been consistently between 10 and 15 per cent (UNCTAD, 2000). The attraction of M&As for service firms is that they are buying into established business with embedded knowledge of local/regional markets and established links with clients without risking the capital and human resources necessary when investing in a greenfield development.

International production by services can also avoid the risks associated with greenfield investment or M&A by entering into partnerships, franchise arrangements or management contracts. These are non-FDI arrangements that are utilising the intangible, knowledge-based, proprietary assets of service TNCs that can be delivered and exchanged on the basis of tightly specified management contracts that ensure quality and protection of proprietary information in the delivery of the service without putting capital at risk (Hoy and Stanworth, 2002; UNCTAD, 2004a). The scale of these arrangements, which are prominent in retailing (Sanghavi, 1990; Phillips, 1996; Alexander and Doherty, 2002), car-rental, hotel and some business and professional services, relative to other forms of international service transactions (cross-border trade flows, mode 4 flows or FDI) is not, however, fully known (for example, they are not included in data on the activities of the foreign affiliates of service firms) (Fernandez, 2001; Arkell, 2002).

According to Dunning and McKaig-Berliner (2002: 8) all these changes are testament to the growing need for service firms to 'access or tap into complementary resources, capabilities and markets which . . . enable them to better utilize their existing competitive advantages [and] to a greater or lesser extent, firms from all countries are diversifying the geography of their strategic asset-seeking activities'. They suggest that studies of the geography of accessing or creating competitive advantage, at least with respect to professional business service firms, has generally been neglected (Nachum, 1999) even though this is a group of activities that has been increasing its FDI faster than any other. Using a seven-point Likert scale from 0 to 6[14] used by a sample of respondents to a worldwide survey of 96 professional service firms,[15] it emerges that the ranking of geographical sourcing of competition-enhancing assets ranged between 2.39 and 2.52. Their responses suggest that rather less than 50 per cent of these advantages are derived from their foreign activities and there is little difference when the respondent firms are grouped into activities that are typically high-, average- and low-knowledge capital intensive. Within these groups, however, customer needs, links with local customers and clients, and access to unskilled labour were competition-enhancing assets from foreign sources, especially for firms with average- or below-average-knowledge capital intensity (Dunning and McKaig-Berliner, 2002). Overall, the propensity of professional business service firms to access competitive advantages from foreign locations is positively related to their degree of transnationality,[16] and also varies by the country of origin and forms of FDI that they have undertaken. While there were variations by activity type and home region in the assessments by firms of the likely change in the relative importance of the competitive advantages acquired as a direct result of their foreign operations, the study concludes with the observation that 'most significantly of all, only two of the 94 respondents giving information on this point thought that the foreign sourcing of their competitive assets would become relatively less important over the first four years of the present [twenty-first] century' (ibid.: 34).

Even though there has been a shift in the activities driving the development of a global economy, most notably expressed by the marked increase in the service share of FDI, they remain relatively less transnationalised than manufacturing. There were only 20 service TNCs among the world's 100 largest non-financial TNCs in 2002 and just four of these (three French companies in retail, businesses services and telecommunications and a Japanese company in the wholesale trade) had a Network Spread Index (NSI)[17] above the overall average of 17.93 (Table 7.4). The majority of the remaining TNCs are in the media (5), retail (5) and telecommunications sectors (5). An Internationalisation Index (II)[18] also shown in Table 7.4 demonstrates, however, that a low NSI does not necessarily equate with a low proportion of foreign affiliates ($r = 0.47$) so that Wal-Mart, for example, is present in only a small number of potential host economies (NSI = 4.62) but almost 80 per cent of its affiliates are located overseas. At the top of the services list, the French retailer Pinault-Printemps Redoute SA has an above-average NSI but a below-average II score.[19] Another French conglomerate, the Publicis Group, is the only business service firm with above-average NSI (it has offices in 50 countries worldwide) and II scores; it is the world's second-largest media group and the fourth-largest communications group.

From a regional perspective, service FDI in 1990 primarily involved a circuit of inward and outward investment among the developed countries where many of the emerging service TNCs had their headquarters. Almost all worldwide outward FDI originated in the developed countries and for most of the activities at least 60 per cent of inward investment originated from other developed countries. The developing economies were at best marginal, especially as sources of FDI, although by 2002 there were indications that their share of inward investment, especially in business activities, construction, health and social services, and other services was larger than in 1990 and their position as sources of outward investment was also stronger, notably in some of the services that have increased

Table 7.4 NSI and II: leading non-financial TNCs, 2002

Company	Country of ownership	Sector	No of host countries	NSI[1]	II[2]
Pinault-Printemps Redoute SA	France	Retail	52	26.67	60.04
Publicis Group SA	France	Business services	50	25.64	83.26
France Telecom	France	Telecommunications	42	21.54	53.26
Mitsui & Co Ltd	Japan	Wholesale trade	42	21.54	53.26
		Average (Top 100)	*35*	*17.93*	*65.46*
Bertelsmann	Germany	Media	34	17.44	54.18
AOL Time Warner Inc	United States	Media	24	12.31	54.31
News Corporation	Australia	Media	20	10.26	94.47
Thomson Corporation	Canada	Media	19	9.74	95.03
Vivendi Universal	France	Media	17	8.72	44.14
Metro AG	Germany	Retail	26	13.33	32.16
Carrefour SA	France	Retail	18	9.23	42.68
McDonald's Corporation	United States	Retail	14	7.18	45.45
Royal Ahold SV	Netherlands	Retail	10	5.13	47.64
Wal-Mart Stores	United States	Retail	9	4.62	79.27
Telefonica SA	Spain	Telecommunications	20	10.26	62.96
Vodafone Group Plc	United Kingdom	Telecommunications	20	10.26	40.74
Telecom Italia	Italy	Telecommunications	16	8.21	38.89
Verizon Communications	United States	Telecommunications	13	6.67	6.58
NTL Inc	United States	Telecommunications	4	2.05	97.18
Mitsubishi Corporation	Japan	Wholesale trade	30	15.38	49.50

Notes:
1. NSI = no. of host economies/no. of potential host economies (no. of economies in receipt of stock of inward FDI in 2002).
2. II = number of foreign affiliates/number of all affiliates*100.

Source: UNCTAD (2004a), extracted from Annex Table A1.4: 279–80.

their FDI in the developing economies (such as hotels and restaurants, business activities and trade) (UNCTAD, 2004a; see also UNCTAD, 2004b).

Cross-border trade, FDI and a new international division of labour

While intra-regional service trade and FDI flows are still the dominant pattern, there are now signs that something approaching global integration of service production (and therefore trade) is emerging (Feenstra, 1998). As noted earlier, the globalisation of software and services, enhanced IT use, the formation of new activities in new sectors, and job creation are interdependent (Mann, 2003). With the standardisation of service production methods or the setting up of sophisticated knowledge and information databases there are opportunities to disaggregate the production or the delivery of services into discrete, but interdependent, stages. Most important, these stages do not need to be undertaken at contiguous locations but can be configured globally to produce a new international redistribution of certain types of service work.

Emblematic of this trend is the shift offshore of information-technology-enabled services such as telephone banking and IT technical support centres from the US and Western Europe to India, the Philippines, South Africa, Mauritius, Ghana, China and the Caribbean. The range of service activities engaging in offshoring is also broadening to include health services (for example, the Caribbean and South Africa), education services (South Africa), legal and other business services (India), and shipping services (the Philippines) (te Velde, 2004). In other words, the offshoring of service production to developing countries is beginning to have a redistributive impact on the economies of developed and developing countries alike. It is the continuation of a trend that began some 15 years ago when US-based airline and insurance companies began transferring routine ticket- or claims-processing functions offshore to locations in the Caribbean or to the Irish Republic. These modest early developments have since diversified to include other sectors such as business and professional services, health and recreational tourism, education, or software services; all have become potentially significant new sources of service export revenue for countries that until recently have not been very well integrated into the global service economy.

But this trend is also seen as a threat both to the hegemony of the leading service-producing countries and to the future of service jobs in those economies (DTI, 2004; Kirkegaard, 2004; Landefeld and Mataloni, 2004; van Zoest, 2004). It has provoked major political and labour market debates in those countries, mainly English speaking such as the US, the UK and Australia, that have witnessed a marked increase in service offshoring in recent years (see, for example, DTI, 2003; Federal Reserve Bank of Boston, 2004). In the case of the US it has been estimated that 250,000 to 500,000 business service jobs were moved overseas between 2001 and 2004 (Federal Reserve Bank of Boston, 2004). These shifts took place at a time when the US economy was experiencing the weakest period of job growth since 1945 and, not surprisingly perhaps, observers were quick to make a link with job relocation overseas. In practice, such job relocation contributed rather modestly to US employment performance and this is expected to continue in the longer term (ibid.). This is in part because the trade and investment flows that facilitate foreign outsourcing trigger offsetting equilibrating forces, or insourcing (Slaughter, 2004). A similar conclusion has been mooted for the UK where:

> Anxiety about job losses in the new service sectors – like call centres – that seem to be threatened by 'offshoring' is understandable. However, by running an open and flexible economy we have ensured that, for the last seven years, every job loss has been matched, and more, by a job gain: in every region of the UK, unemployment is down and employment is up, by 1.9 million jobs across our country as a whole. As technology and trade develop, the challenge is to step up the active support we offer to people to continue updating their skills, and to business to continue improving their competitiveness. People need to be able to gain job-focused skills training and improve their chances of a sustainable, productive place in the workforce. (DTI, 2004: 11)

The growth in offshoring has changed the competitive environment for domestic service firms. In response they have a number of options that include: competing directly with offshore providers, focusing on areas of their activities where offshoring has disadvantages, using offshoring as a component of their own service offer, acting as a channel of value-added distributor for other offshore services, or viewing offshoring companies as a market for their services.[20]

Table 7.5 Average annual employment growth rate (%) of US parent and foreign affiliates, US service MNCs, 1989–1999

Industry	Change in US parent employment	Change in foreign affiliate employment	Change in all US employment
Legal services	15.4	5.8	1.3
R&D and testing services	8.3	9.8	1.3
Accounting and auditing services	0.6	10.9	2.2
Engineering and architecture services	−0.6	7.3	2.3
Computer and data-processing services	6.8	22.4	9.8
All industries	1.6	4.0	1.8

Source: US Bureau of Economic Analysis, after Landefeld and Mataloni (2004).

Multinational corporations (MNCs) are often viewed as leading the way in offshore outsourcing. While data on the gains and losses from international trade and investment by US MNCs are not available (DTI, 2003; Landefeld and Mataloni, 2004), the Bureau of Economic Affairs (BEA) is able to track where US MNCs are locating their activities, their imports and exports (including origins and destinations), the ratio of domestic to foreign content, and the remuneration rates paid to employees in the US and abroad. Thus, although there has indeed been a small increase in the foreign share of US MNC output, investment and employment, around 75 per cent remains concentrated in the US (Landefeld and Mataloni, 2004). None the less, US service MNCs have generally increased employment at their foreign affiliates at a higher rate than at the US parent establishments or the aggregate rate for all industries (Table 7.5). Because the baseline numbers are different, absolute employment in the home activities of US multinationals (all sectors) increased by 4.7 million (1988–2002) compared with 3.5 million in their foreign affiliates. During the same period, affiliates of foreign-owned MNCs located in the US increased their employment by some 3.1 million. Such insourcing has been largely overlooked and underanalysed and makes contributions to the host economy in two ways (Slaughter, 2004). First, there is a direct effect that takes the form of the jobs created by these subsidiaries and, second, the investment in R&D, physical capital and international trade make US workers and the overall economy more productive. Indeed, between 1997 and 2002, wholesale and retail trade, transportation and warehousing, information, and non-bank finance and insurance services experienced rising subsidiary employment at a rate faster than other firms in these industries, such that in all four industries the subsidiary share of total US employment rose. Existing subsidiaries can expand by building new facilities or by adding capacity to existing facilities and there is also the creation of new subsidiaries when a foreign-owned service multinational develops a greenfield enterprise in the host country. A subsidiary can also be created when a foreign service multinational merges with, or acquires part or all, of an existing domestic service enterprise in which there is no FDI (ibid.).

The picture is of course much more complicated than suggested by basic evidence of this kind. There are several causes for changes in the balance between home and overseas employment within MNCs. The availability of low-cost labour is only one of several factors including: different rates of economic growth in domestic versus overseas locations; overseas market opportunities for services that cannot be delivered by cross-border exports; differences in productivity between parent establishments and foreign affiliates; variations in the outsourcing by the home-country parent to affiliated or non-affiliated overseas companies; outsourcing by the parent company to a home-country supplier that is not also a home-country parent company; and changes in host-country policies towards direct investment. The importance of security considerations is also a variable; by spreading their activities among several locations, service firms (or for that matter manufacturing ones) are reducing risks in an age of geopolitical uncertainty. FDI experts still see the bulk of relocations occurring for lower value-added corporate functions: processing activities followed by logistics and supply functions are the most frequently mentioned corporate functions likely to relocate abroad (UNCTAD, 2004b). Their predictions also vary significantly by region: the relocation of high value-added functions such as R&D was much more frequently mentioned in the case of developed than developing countries. Processing, logistics and supply activities are considered the most important function likely to be relocated to developing countries.

Conclusion

The internationalisation of tradable service activities is well under way but a truly global service economy has yet to emerge. In the sense that globalisation involves the closer economic integration of nation states or the creation of networks of production and distribution by TNCs that allows them to enable uniform access to their expertise everywhere, there remain many obstacles. The purpose of this chapter has been to explore some of developments such as those in ICT that have enabled the global reach of service firms to be extended way beyond that imaginable as little as 20 years ago. ICT manufacturers and services have themselves been instruments of globalisation while simultaneously underpinning the opportunities for client firms and others more generally to use ICT to devise completely new services, to produce and deliver those services in innovative and cost-effective ways, to improve productivity, or to undertake transactions that benefit from improved coordination and control as well as space–time compression.

Yet, for all the advantages and new opportunities proffered on service industries by ICT, it has been demonstrated that capitalising upon them to create a truly global service economy is rather difficult. There are a variety of constraints that have been outlined, including those that might be classified as host-country attributes such as the investment climate, the quality and availability of business or financial services, the telecommunications infrastructure, and the degree to which national economies are open or closed towards fostering cross-border trade or investment by service firms. It has been suggested that one of the most important considerations with respect to the latter is the role performed by different modes for supplying services internationally. In particular, the increasing importance of enabling the movement of natural persons (mode 4) to support the growing demand for global outsourcing and offshoring of a wide variety of non-core business tasks (such as customer support, technical support, bookkeeping, insurance claims processing, database management, software maintenance and so on) illustrates the scope for maintaining a significant gulf between the global aspirations of some service TNCs and the practical reality. At the global level there are a number of regional service economies that are more or less better integrated internally than externally; for example, Western Europe, North America (including Mexico), or East Asia (Japan, Korea, Hong Kong, China and so on). These regionally integrated service trade blocs are not free-standing; in some instances there are also major cross-regional service flows based on tourism, financial transactions, currency dealing, or the activities of business and professional service firms (such as between Western Europe and North America). In view of the size and geographical reach of service TNCs in, for example, transport, banking, computer services or professional services it may be more fruitful to think in terms not of regional service economies or a global service economy, but of service TNC economies. But even here the attainment of a truly integrated global reach will only be possible if international protocols and agreements that affect trade in services or FDI can be agreed and then consistently interpreted and applied by individual countries.

Notes

* I am indebted to Dr David Shaw (Honorary Research Fellow, Services and Enterprise Research Unit, University of Birmingham) for assistance with the compilation of the data summarised in Table 7.2.

1. For services, 'going global' takes two basic forms that are a function of the tradability of their output; those not requiring the physical presence of the supplier and/or the client can be measured as flows by value (payments and receipts) or volume (tourist flows, for example), but for services where the supplier requires a physical presence it is more usual to measure this as foreign direct investment (by value).
2. A possible exception is China, but recently published data from the first economic census indicates that not only is the Chinese economy bigger than expected but that much of the discrepancy is explained by improved service data. China's service sector in 2004 was more accurately measured as representing 41 per cent of the economy, rather than 32 per cent. Manufacturing represented 46 per cent of the economy, rather than 53 per cent as previously calculated. Since 1998, almost 8.5 million new jobs (three times the number lost in manufacturing) have been created in China, mostly in retailing, distribution, health and local/state government services (Saxonhouse, 2006).
3. World trade in commercial services increased by 16 per cent, to $2.1 trillion in 2004, mainly stimulated by a strong recovery in transportation and travel services following the collapse brought about by the events of 11 September 2001 in the US. This was an acceleration of growth for the third year in a row and the largest increase since 2000. The indications are that commercial services trade grew faster in Asian economies than in North American or European economies, although the US remained the world's largest exporter and importer of commercial services (WTO, 2005).
4. The term 'natural persons' is the legal designation for people moving temporarily to a country for the purpose of providing a service (mode 4).
5. While the emphasis here is on ICT infrastructure, it is also the case of course that ICT is a sector in its own right that includes ICT services and ICT manufacturers. The use of ICT throughout the value chain enables firms to increase their overall efficiency, extends their potential market reach, and makes them more competitive. ICT is an important contributor to global wealth and prosperity in its own right; in 2000, the ICT sector's value added in the EU amounted to €443 billion of which 75 per cent was for ICT services and 25 per cent for ICT manufacturing.
6. This also resonates with the past as well as the present. As the UK became a major manufacturing economy during the second half of the nineteenth century it also initiated a transition to a service economy because without the enabling role of services such as transport, insurance, banking and other professional activities the international trade in commodities and products that was so vital to the process of industrialisation would have been inhibited.
7. This is not to say it is impossible; there are for example one-person boat design firms that outsource construction to boat-building firms.
8. The top 20 economies in terms of ease of doing business are New Zealand, United States, Singapore, Hong Kong/China, Australia, Norway, United Kingdom, Canada, Sweden, Japan, Switzerland, Denmark, Netherlands, Finland, Ireland, Belgium, Lithuania, Slovakia, Botswana and Thailand.
9. Protection of intellectual property rights is a major challenge; it affects location and investment decisions for R&D services, some business and professional services, software and computing services, among others (see, for example, Commission on Intellectual Property Rights, 2002).

10. From the perspective of an 'importing' country A, the modes are: 1. *Cross-border* – a user in country A receives services from abroad through its telecommunications or postal infrastructure. Such supplies may include consultancy or market research reports, tele-medical advice, distance training, or architectural drawings; 2. *Consumption abroad* – nationals of A have moved abroad as tourists, students or patients to consume the respective services; 3. *Commercial presence* – the service is provided within A by a locally established affiliate, subsidiary, or representative office of a foreign-owned and -controlled company (bank, hotel group, construction company and so on); 4. *Movement of natural persons* – a foreign national provides a service within A as an independent supplier (for example, consultant, health worker) or employee of a service supplier (for example, consultancy firm, hospital, construction company) (source: www.wto.org/english/tratop_e/serv_e/cbt_course_e/c1s3p/1_e.htm#boxa, accessed 20 October 2004).
11. Nevertheless, the measurement of services is now better than it was 20 years ago. In order to keep things moving forward the UN Statistics Commission invited the OECD in March 2003 to collaborate on the coordination of development work on service statistics by a variety of international organisations and international expert groups. It is hoped that one outcome will be proposals for a strategy for service statistics which address key issues such as: how current coordination mechanisms can be made more efficient to avoid duplication of effort and to ensure coverage of essential issues, and how to communicate conceptual/methodological outputs to all the countries that need them.
12. Given that service inputs are increasingly embodied in merchandise design, production and distribution, the significance of these trends should not be overstated.
13. Data on bilateral flows or stocks of FDI by sector (transport, travel, other services) are not available in sufficient detail for pairs of countries to be able to make a comparison with the data on bilateral flows of commercial services trade (see www.unctad.org/fdistatistics, accessed 22 October 2004).
14. Zero on the Likert scale indicates that the advantages are sourced mainly from the home location; six indicates that the advantages are sourced mainly from abroad.
15. The survey population comprised 448 firms ranked in the top 25 to top 83 in the appropriate industry rankings for accounting/auditing, advertising, architecture, engineering, information technology, investment and financial services, law/legal firms, management consulting, market research, and reinsurance services. They were located in large and small EU countries, the US, Japan, other countries and developing countries (see Dunning and McKaig-Berliner, 2002: Tables 1-3, 3-5).
16. The transnationality of each firm is measured using the Transnationality Index. The index measures the degree to which a TNC divides its activities between its home country and various host countries in which it has affiliates. It is calculated as a simple arithmetic average of the ratio of foreign-to-total assets, sales and employment.
17. NSI = number of host economies/number of potential host economies. The latter is taken to be the number of economies which were in receipt of stock of inward FDI in 2002. On the development of this index, see Ietto-Gillies (1998).
18. II for a TNC = the ratio of foreign to the total number of affiliates.
19. These indices must be used carefully. McDonald's Corporation is a major global retailer but because it operates primarily through franchising arrangements its NSI score of 14 and II score of 45.45 understates its position as an international service TNC.
20. It is important to recognise that only a proportion of service work is suitable for offshoring. There are at least three circumstances where offshoring of certain service functions/activities is unsuitable. First, where there is a major advantage in having a particular activity performed close to the company, notably where an ongoing and regular dialogue between supplier and client is essential. Second, if the value of an activity far exceeds the cost of providing it, control, communications (common language and culture), and speed of response become more important and there are advantages in retaining the activity in the home country. Third, a home country may continue to have areas of unique expertise such as that which arises from relationships with very specialised business sectors (for example, the City of London), with universities, or simply because a cluster of expertise has grown to such an extent that it acts as a significant barrier to entry for new providers/competitors (City of London Corporation, 2005).

8 Services and regional development in the United States

William B. Beyers

Introductory comments

This chapter presents an overview of the development of the service economy in the United States. At the moment, the United States is the world's largest economy – as measured by gross national product – and it is also the world's largest service economy. Three-quarters of the workforce in the United States are currently employed in the services, a share that is among the highest in all countries.

What types of services have been the source of employment growth in the United States, and how important are these services in the overall context of employment change? How have geographic patterns of employment change been associated with the growth of service industries? How has the overall distribution of service employment been changing in the US economy? These questions will be explored in this chapter through the use of employment data that provide useful insights into patterns of regional development driven by service industries in the United States. Documentation of the dynamics of the US service industry will help us better understand the changing role of services as leading agents of change at the regional level, and also to identify regions exhibiting similar patterns of structural change.

The growth and development of the service economy will be addressed via a number of themes in this chapter. In the next section some broad national-level statistics are presented on the long-run change in the structure of the US economy. Several themes are explored with regard to the growth and development of the service economy, including the role of innovation and technological change, shifting geographic patterns of service employment, and the importance of trade in services. This section is followed by a detailed description of regional trends over the 1985–2000 period. This period is long enough for us to identify the regions that have done well recently in the national economic context, as well as those that have not fared so well. This section identifies key sectoral factors associated with strong and weak regional performance. The final section provides a brief summary and comments about the future development of the service economy in the United States.

Background

Broad trends in national employment

The US economy has been dominated by service employment for more than 70 years. The march from an economy dominated by goods production to one dominated by service production has been a theme explored by many scholars over the last half-century or more. Fisher (1939) and Clark (1940 [1957]) observed the historical transition of national economies away from 'primary' and 'secondary' industries by 1940, and wrestled with the emergence of a growing share of employment in 'tertiary' – or in current parlance 'service' activities. Fisher contemplated the evolution of the Australian and New Zealand economies away from their traditional economic strengths in goods production, and struggled to place the role of services in their evolution. Clark, addressing the structural change towards the services for more than 30 years in a series of revisions of his classic *The Conditions of Economic Progress*, realized that the term 'services' was too simple, and that the service component of the economy was undergoing specialization that mirrored the way that primary and secondary activities had specialized in an earlier era (Clark, 1940 [1957]).

Figure 8.1 documents the composition of employment in the United States over the course of the twentieth century. In 1899 only about 34 percent of national employment was in services, while by 2001, service employment had risen to almost 75 percent of total employment. In this period, the absolute level of national employment grew enormously, from 27 million in 1899 to over 135 million wage and salary employees in 2001.[1] It is clearly evident in this figure that farm and mining employment has dropped continuously since 1899. Manufacturing shows an expansion in its proportion until the post-Second World War timeframe, and then has fallen as a share of total employment. Construction employment, considered by Clark to be a part of the services, has expanded slightly in its share of employment over the past half-century (ibid.: 491).

The composition of the service component of employment has been documented in a more detailed manner over time. The early census data did not disaggregate service employment into categories that we commonly utilize today. As the United States began

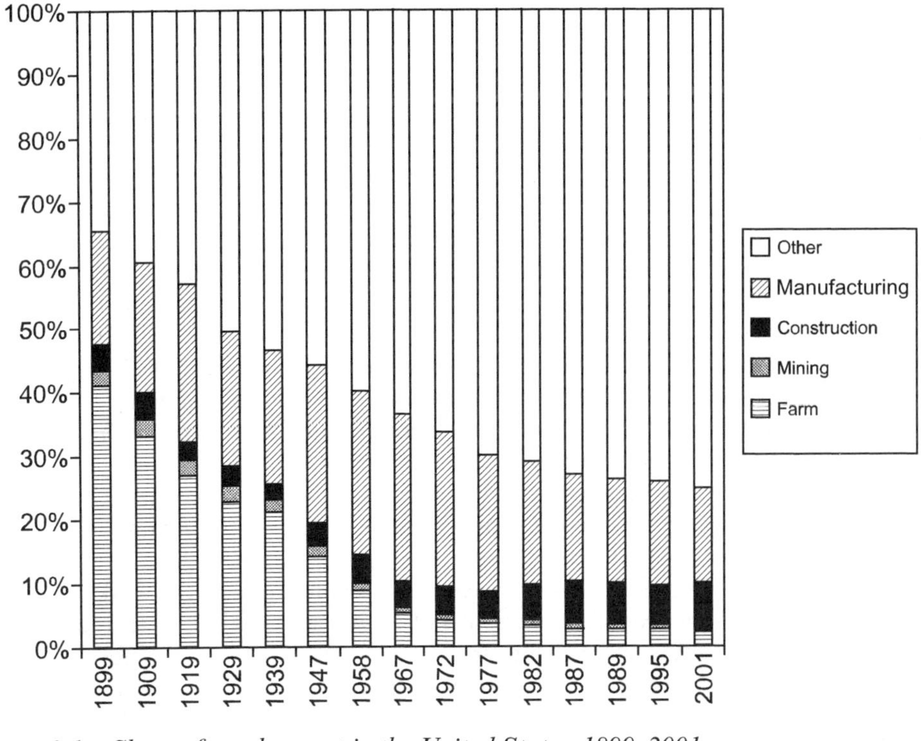

Figure 8.1 Share of employment in the United States, 1899–2001

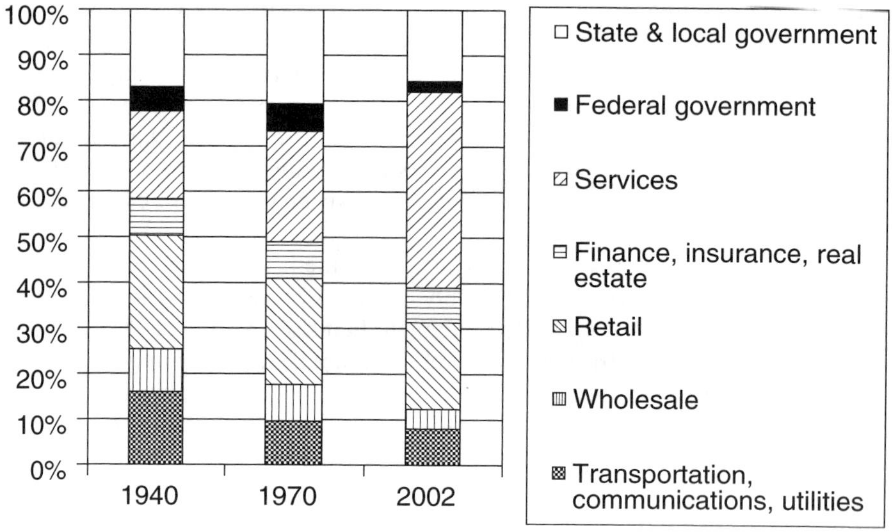

Source: US Census Bureau, *Historical Statistics of the United States* (the 1976 special document); US Bureau of Economic Analysis; US Bureau of Labor Statistics.

Figure 8.2 Composition of service employment in the United States, 1940–2002

to separate in the census measures of the population from measures of business activity, there has been a gradual expansion of the level of detail for the types of work included in the services. Prior to 1940 there was little detail in the census regarding categories of employment within the services. Figure 8.2 presents an estimate of the share of employment within broad lines of service industries from 1940 through 2002. This figure clearly indicates the changing proportions of employment within broad lines of services, including public services. Over the 1940–70 period, a key trend was the relative expansion of the public sector, at the federal, state and local government levels. The distributive services (transportation, communications and utilities; wholesale trade) declined in their relative share, while retailing and finance, insurance and real estate maintained their relative shares. The 'services' division used by the federal statistical agencies clearly shows an expansion in the 1940–70 period. After 1970, government evidences a declining share of employment, as is also the case within the distributive services and retailing. In this most recent period, the 'services' category has undergone explosive growth, with a dramatic increase in its share of employment.

The category 'services' in Figure 8.2 has been disaggregated in various ways by scholars. An influential approach to this disaggregation was offered by Singelmann, who tied the classification to market categories (Singelmann, 1978). In Figure 8.3, three categories have been created, based on Singelmann's scheme, and also influenced by the work of Noyelle and Stanback (1983). Producer services are lines of service activity that sell their output primarily to business and government clients. In some classifications a more embracing definition is used for producer services; these broader definitions include financial, insurance and real estate services, as well as services to transportation (Beyers, 1989). Health services include hospitals, offices of physicians of various kinds, and associated care facilities.

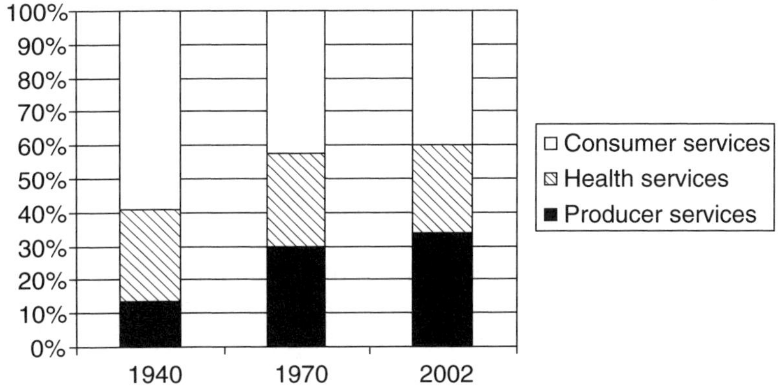

Source: US Census Bureau, *Historical Statistics of the United States* (the 1976 special document); US Bureau of Economic Analysis; US Bureau of Labor Statistics.

Figure 8.3 Disaggregation of service division employment

Consumer services in this figure include accommodation, consumer repair services, educational services, social services, amusements, motion pictures, and museums and zoos. This figure clearly shows the relative growth of producer services over the last 60 years. Absolute employment growth within all three of the sectors included in Figure 8.3 has been strong, given the strong relative growth of service division employment over this time period.

Figures 8.1–3 clearly indicate the strong expansion of service employment. The trend here has been one of a gradually diversifying portfolio of service employment. The service sector has not just expanded proportionally, it has undergone a continual shift in the mix of services. Having documented this shifting mix, let us now turn to research that has attempted to explain why there has been this evolution in the structure of the service economy, and what the geography of growth in the service economy has been in recent decades. Given the very strong role of service employment growth in regional economies, it is also relevant to consider how services are positioned in the economic base of regional economies. These topics are addressed in the next subsection.

Understanding service employment development

The preceding subsection has documented the growth and development of the service economy in recent decades, as measured by employment. Clearly, people working in the service economy – whether as non-farm proprietors or as wage and salary employees – are supplying services to clients demanding their services. This market environment must be viewed in dynamic terms, with simultaneous processes of service innovation, technological development in capital required to produce services, a changing social division of labor, and changing patterns of demand by household consumers, businesses and governments. Research in the United States (and elsewhere) has elucidated aspects of these themes in recent years, as a part of efforts to explain the development of the service economy.

Innovation In 1988 the National Academy of Sciences highlighted the importance of innovation in services with a two-volume set of papers focusing on the changing structure of service industries in the US, and the interaction between technology and innovation in the process of service industry development (Guile and Quinn, 1988a, 1988b). James Quinn, a pioneer in US service research, made the case for the importance of innovation:

> Because the value of all products or services is created solely in the mind (i.e., a jewel, an opera, a Ferrari, a sightseeing tour, or a stylish coat may have little functional value relative to its high price), the growth of a services economy is limited only by the capacity of the human mind to conceive of activities as having high utility. (Quinn, 1988: 25)

This process of innovation can occur in various environments. These are nicely summarized by Sundbo and Gallouj (2000) in a recent study of service innovation in Europe. There is no reason why the processes they catalog are not operative in the United States. They identify six broad service innovation trajectories: (i) the classic research and development (R&D) pattern with a formal R&D department; (ii) the service professional pattern (where the innovation emerges from the project of rendering the service); (iii) the organized strategic innovation pattern (where there is an inhouse commitment to innovation but no formal R&D department); (iv) the entrepreneurial pattern (based on a radical innovation, where the main activity is to sell the radical innovation); (v) the artisan-type pattern (small firms in operational services such as hotels, cleaning) that typically make modest adjustments; and (vi) the network pattern (where multiple firms in an industry work together to effect change). They note that the processes of innovation in the services follow these various pathways such that:

> We can conclude that there is a system of innovation in services, but it is a loosely coupled system and there is a variation of patterns within the system. The system is not a national system, and the varied and loosely coupled character of the system makes it difficult to use it as a basis for political regulation and stimulation. (Ibid.: 64)

They also emphasize the interdependence between the client and the service supplier in this innovation process:

> However, the service innovation system keeps some of its own elements:
>
> - The customer encounter as core driver
> - Many small, non-reproduced changes
> - Person to person contact (non technological) will remain a core characteristic for much service innovation
> - A relatively loosely-coupled organization system, characterized by less R&D, more corporate entrepreneurship, strategic guidance, and service professional trajectories. (Ibid.: 65)

Other scholars also emphasize the importance of clients in this service innovation process. Behara (2002) argues that firms need to develop competency to manage creativity and innovation with their clients. In a similar vein, Boone (2000: 107) concludes: 'Our findings also indicate that managing knowledge about the customer and the process is key to technology-driven service product innovation. Process innovation appears to be an important vehicle for bringing together knowledge about the customer and the process'.

Thus, as in manufacturing, there is evidence of both service product and service process innovation, and over time service product innovation has led to the development of lines of service industries that simply did not exist in earlier eras. However, it is important to recognize the simultaneous dynamism in the capital stock used to produce services, and in particular the central role of information technologies (ITs) that have allowed changes in communications between the service provider and clients, as well as in the service production process. Beyers and Lindahl (1996b) found that changes in IT possibilities caused clients to have changing expectations of what their producer service suppliers should be producing, and that producer service establishments were changing the nature of their services as a result of changing IT capabilities. An example of a case study documenting the impact of one IT technology – cellular telephones – is the work of Brunn and Leinbach (2000). While they concentrate on the industrial success of Nokia, they also anchor their paper around the demand for this IT product in a rapidly changing production environment, including service industries. The restructuring potential of IT has been discussed widely, with many dramatic visions of how industrial activity and regional production systems are likely to be modified (Castells, 1996; Tapscott, 1996; Wheeler et al., 2000). In recent years in the United States the cumulative impacts of IT have been associated with increased productivity in a wide range of industries increasingly reliant on these technologies, leading to the label 'new economy' to characterize the current production system trajectory (Beyers, 2002b).

Demand Simultaneous with processes of innovation in the production of services has been a changing pattern of demand. The changing mix of service industry employment documented above is an indicator of this shifting pattern of demand, favoring the relative growth of some lines of service production, and the simultaneous relative decline in output of other services. The bases for this shifting composition in the demand for services has also been the subject of considerable research in the United States, particularly by staff at the Bureau of Labor Statistics (BLS). This agency tracks development of the labor force in the United States, and is the primary source of forecasts about the expected pattern of growth of industries and occupations in the US economy. These forecasts have a significant influence in the development of training institutions that aim to supply types of workers anticipated to be needed in a growing economy.

Hatch and Clinton (2000) and Goodman and Steadman (2002) (BLS staff members), have examined changing demands within the services division (see Figures 8.2 and 8.3). Their work helps us to understand recent structural change in service employment in the United States, and will be reviewed in some detail. They note that the markets of industries in this division are split between personal consumption expenditure by households, and demands of businesses and government. They observe a modest decline in sales on personal consumption account from 53 to 51 percent between 1988 and 2000, and a modest rise in the share of sales to businesses from 45 to 48 percent. (The balance represents exports.) The growth in business services was found to be related to three key forces: contractual labor arrangements (for example, temporary help), increased construction activity, and changing IT. Regarding personnel supply they note that mere growth of output in industries relying on temporary help would expand demand for such services, but they also note the tendency of managers in client industries to have shifted the composition of their labor force to use more temporary workers (Goodman and Steadman, 2002: 8). Beyers and Lindahl (1999) found the same trend in a survey of producer service establishments.

Hatch and Clinton (2000: 13) also note the rise in the use of temporary help:

> Employment opportunities exploded in the help supply industry as more firms relied on temporary help as a way to manage labor more effectively. Businesses adopted the concept of 'just-in-time-labor,' similar to just-in-time production which is common in the automobile industry. Labor supplied by the help supply industry enabled firms to quickly adjust their labor forces to stay competitive.
>
> Firms expanded demand for temporary workers, especially for more highly skilled ones. During the 1980s, firms typically used temporary workers for more repetitive clerical and menial-labor tasks. This practice transformed during the next decade as companies routinely purchased the services of highly skilled workers from temporary agencies to meet their diverse needs in areas such as financial services, healthy services, telecommunications, and information technology.

Regarding the impact of the growing use of temporary help (one of the largest growth segments within producer services), Goodman and Steadman (2002: 8) write:

> Contractual arrangements instead of direct hiring also contribute to the growth of management services. Unlike the formerly typical scenario of a consulting company leaving management with a report and then ceasing to be involved, modern consultants often contribute actively to the transformation of a business process, and may leave some of their own personnel onsite indefinitely to run that process partially or fully. Facilities support services, another part of the management services industry has also been on the rise.

Goodman and Steadman find that growth in construction expanded the demand for a variety of types of engineering services; the relative growth of construction employment is evident in recent years in Figure 8.1 (ibid.: 9–10).

Hatch and Clinton (2000: 13) addressed the rapid growth of computer services in the 1990s:

> Computer and data processing services mimicked help supply in its demand for more highly skilled computer professionals. Even though employment growth remained strong during the decade, recession included, there were signs of slowing very late in the decade. Colleges and university could not produce graduates with computer degrees fast enough, as firms scrambled to cure the Y2K bug and design chips and software for computers and other consumer products.

Goodman and Steadman (2002: 10) note that the growth of computer services was predominantly due to business demands (73 percent of sales were to business, 23 percent to government, and only 2 percent to households): 'The upward trend of employment in computer services is the result of two main factors: first, the continuing development of computer technology, and second, a shift in client companies' business models to include more outsourcing of technological services'. They also discuss the advent of the internet, changes in the functionality of computer equipment, and the adoption of industry standards as forces leading to expanded demand for computer services. They note that the increased use of computing services also fuels the demand for management consulting to help implement technologies in firms. These changes also fuel demands for engineering services. They note the slow growth in accounting services, in part due to the use by businesses of spreadsheets and other computer software allowing businesses to do their own accounting (ibid.: 10–11).

Regarding the growth in consumer services, Goodman and Steadman as well as Hatch and Clinton note that it was led by healthcare. Hatch and Clinton (2000: 14) made the following comments about trends in the 1990s:

> Health services, while growing less than half as fast as business services during the 1990's, still contributed more than 2.5 million jobs to nonfarm payrolls. The growth rate slowed from that of the previous decade. The growing popularity of HMO's and the implementation of the perspective payment plan by Congress led to decreased health care expenditures. Not all health service industries experienced the slower growth phenomena. Home health care services grew the fastest of all the industries, and also made the list of the top 20 in terms of number of jobs gained. Several factors contributed to this above-average growth. First, medicare expanded benefits to make more people eligible for home health care coverage, the cost associated with care at home was relatively less costly compared to that at hospitals, and technological advancements provided people the option to receive medical treatment in the comfort of their own home.

Goodman and Steadman (2002: 12) reach similar conclusions regarding the growth in health services: 'While increases in the elderly population and the invention of new treatments and diagnostic tools have added to demand, government and private efforts to control healthcare costs have prevented greater growth than otherwise would have occurred'. They note an increase in spending on daycare, and on assisted living. Also there has been a tendency for hospitals to outsource some functions that were previously done internally. Engel also notes a slowdown in health service employment growth rates, fueled by a desire to contain costs. She concludes that structural changes in the industry will contain employment growth rates and change composition (towards more generalists), but that healthcare will likely still be a major source of new jobs (Engel, 1999).

Both Goodman and Steadman, and Hatch and Clinton, also note the relatively strong growth of employment in amusements and recreation, membership organizations (mostly churches), motion pictures, and museums, zoos and botanical gardens. They argue that growth here was due to higher levels of disposable income that encourages travel to consume these services, although they do not specifically address gambling as an activity that has had strong employment growth (Hatch and Clinton, 2000: 14; Goodman and Steadman, 2002: 12). Goodman and Steadman (p. 12) note that international trade in services also grew, with motion pictures, and engineering and architectural services being singled out as industries with strong growth in foreign exports.

This subsection has summarized some forces associated with the relative growth of some segments of the service economy in the United States. Innovation in services has been facilitated by changes in IT, and by shifting patterns of demand on the part of businesses, government and household consumers.

Studies of regional trends in service activity

Regional trends in service activity have been described in a number of studies over the past several decades in the United States. Various regionalization schemes have been used to document these trends, including the use of metropolitan areas, states, and the Bureau of Economic Analysis (BEA) functional economic areas.

Beyers (1979) used data supplied by BEA to evaluate trends in the BEA functional economic areas over the 1965–75 period. This system of regions, which has been redefined several times since their first definition, divides the territory of the United States into a set of regions with metropolitan areas at their core, and nonmetropolitan counties in peripheral segments of BEA regions. BEA uses commuting and newspaper readership data to define the boundaries of these regions (Johnson, 1995). It should be noted that not every BEA region has a metropolitan core, and some BEA regions do not have nonmetropolitan territory. Beyers developed shift-share and minimum requirements models to describe regional trends and changes in the economic base of communities. This analysis also included analyses of changes in personal income, including earnings by sector and nonearnings income (transfer payments, dividends, pensions, royalties and rents).

Beyers found strong growth in nonearnings income over the 1965–75 period, especially in the South, and found a strong relationship between the growth of nonearnings income and the services sector. He argued that the spending of this expanded nonearnings income stimulated local service industries (Beyers, 1979: 41–2). He also found an uneven pattern of regional growth, with about 20 percent of growth associated with the competitive component in shift-share analyses. The competitive component is the difference between the actual and expected change in employment or earnings, after considering expected overall and sectoral growth rates.[2] Beyers also found rapid growth in trade, communications, business and professional services, and state and local government services. His analysis associated a part of the growth of these services with interregional trade, and he noted that large northeastern BEA regions would have had much larger negative competitive shifts than they did experience, if they had not had this growth in advanced services (ibid.: 40). This analysis also highlighted the strong growth in the Sunbelt and some western BEA regions.

A decade later Beyers again used the BEA economic areas to document regional trends in employment over the 1974–85 period (Beyers, 1991, 1992). Using US County Business Patterns (CBP) data, he employed methods similar to the analyses described for the 1965–75 period. However, the emphasis in the 1974–85 analysis was on the role of producer services in the regional development process. By the time that this project was undertaken, the rapid growth rate in the producer services was widely recognized, and it had become clear from case studies that there was a traded component within the producer services (Beyers and Alvine, 1985; Porterfield and Pulver, 1991). The shift-share analysis undertaken as a part of this study found even stronger redistributive tendencies than were found in the 1965–75 period, with the competitive shift component amounting to 27.5 percent of overall change (Beyers, 1991). This study also noted the very uneven spatial distribution within the producer services, with only about one-sixth of the BEA economic areas having a concentration of producer services at or above the national average share of employment. While the places with the strongest producer services concentrations were the nation's largest BEA economic areas, it was also found that there was some tendency towards deconcentration of these services (Beyers, 1992: 139).

A widely cited monograph by Noyelle and Stanback (1983) used data for the 140 largest metropolitan areas to document the economic transformation of American cities. Their analysis spanned the 1959–76 period, and focused on tendencies towards economic specialization in metropolitan areas, emphasizing the growing role of services in the structure of urban economies. They emphasized the growing importance of the 'complex of corporate activities' – producer services and corporate headquarters – and their strong tendency to be concentrated in the largest places. They found little deconcentration of these activities. They also found that down the urban hierarchy there tended to be more functional specialization in metropolitan structure, with those tied to manufacturing tending to fare relatively poorly compared to those tied to military and resort-retirement activities. They also found strong changes within metropolitan areas in employment mix, with many regions losing significant quantities of manufacturing jobs that were often more than offset by growth in service employment (ibid.: 5). An interesting aspect of Noyelle and Stanback's analysis was the use of cluster analysis to group the structure of metropolitan statistical areas into a functional typology that they used to examine trends in different types of metropolitan regions. This approach is used later in this chapter to group the structure of BEA economic areas.

Stanback has recently written a sequel to his work with Noyelle, focused on the 1974–97 period (Stanback and Grove, 2002). He begins with the year 1974 because he argues that it marked the beginning of an era of real-wage stagnation, greater inequality and deindustrialization. His analysis is broken into two periods: 1974–90 and 1990–97. He makes this break because after 1990 he notes that the economy is on a trajectory of 'rising productivity and vigorous prosperity that continued through the early months of the twenty-first century' (p. 3). He extends his analysis to all metropolitan regions, and includes in his analysis unearned income.

Stanback finds a similar classification of metropolitan area structure as in his earlier work, and he finds only modest changes in the bases of classification (for example, specialization in particular sectors) over his study period. He also finds: 'that the rapid growth of employment in a number of service categories – along with a decline in the importance of goods production as a source of jobs – has brought about major shifts in the industrial composition of employment across a broad spectrum of metropolitan economies' (ibid.: 113).

Stanback also found relatively high earnings in the large metropolitan areas most specialized in producer services. He wrestles with the question of how places historically dependent upon manufacturing and government/military have been able to sustain any job growth, given the declines in these sectors in many communities. He reasons that import substitution has taken place as the service economy has expanded in many of these places:

> Certainly, a greater proportion of sophisticated medical services was performed in local hospitals in 1997 than in 1974. Similarly, no doubt, the percentages of post-high school courses offered locally increased, and a larger share of a variety of unsophisticated business and professional services was performed within the local metropolitan economy. Yet, there appears to be little reason to suspect that the volume of imports diminished or that increases in import substitution could have been sufficient to sustain the weaker metropolitan economies in the face of declining goods production. (Ibid.: 115)

Regarding unearned income, Stanback notes its rise in all metropolitan areas, but the tendency towards strong reliance on this type of income in particular places with concentrations of senior citizens or people with personal wealth. While he does not interpret concentrations of this type of income as a part of the economic base of communities, he does recognize that the consequence of spending this type of income is to support the service economy (ibid.: 115).

In addition to research covering regions for the entire country, or all metropolitan areas, there have been many case studies of particular industries and particular communities. Space does not permit a review of this work, but note Glasmeier and Howland's (1995) analysis of rural counties in the United States, including their emphasis on the role of services. They are not optimistic about the rapidly growing producer services deconcentrating into rural America, but they do argue that it is important to bring IT infrastructure to rural communities, so that they can be players in an age where this type of capital is at the center of development efforts (ibid.: 221–30).

Trade in services

Regions such as the BEA economic areas, or the metropolitan areas analyzed by Stanback, are embedded in a system of interregional and international trade. Early research on central place services showed hierarchical markets, and exports of services from high-order centers to customers located in lower-order peripheral centers (Berry, 1967). Clearly, transportation and wholesale distributive services play a role in the economic base of regional economies. But what about trade in the broad divisions of finance, insurance and real estate, and of services (with major subdivisions of producer, health and consumer services)? There are no statistics on such trade gathered by statistical agencies in the United States. Models of trade such as the minimum requirements approach assign a share of service employment to the traded sector (Ullman and Dacey, 1960). Beyers (2003) has used this approach to estimate the recent contribution of services to the growth of the economic base in the BEA economic areas, and found that all of the increase in export jobs came in the services over the 1995–2000 period. However, this approach with secondary data was shown years ago by Tiebout (1962) to underestimate actual export shares.

Thus far we have selected case studies documenting the geography of interregional and international trade in producer services, but almost no evidence for health and consumer services. Thus, while service employment growth has dominated the US employment growth for some decades, as indicated in Figures 8.1–3, we do not have a strong understanding of the geographical flows of funds associated with these service sectors (and related nonearnings income).

This section has documented the ongoing division of labor within the US service economy, and has reviewed some arguments as to why there has been structural evolution in the services in recent decades. It has also reviewed some studies emphasizing the geography of this process of service-led development, and has argued that services have been a growing force in the economic base of regional economies in the United States.

Recent regional trends in service employment

Let us now turn to a description of regional trends in service employment. First, the development of the database used for this chapter will be described. Then, employment trends will be presented.

Database development

The US has a wealth of regional statistics available from the US Department of Commerce. For the purposes of this chapter, I have utilized data from several sources. I started with data for 1985 and 2000 from US County Business patterns. While the US BEA has an online system for downloading county-level (and BEA region-level) employment and earnings statistics, the employment statistics do not allow a decomposition of the service division into health, producer and consumer services. Therefore, CBP data were used to develop this decomposition at the geographical level of counties (3141 county units) (see Appendix 8A).

Employment trends

Over the 15-year period from 1985 to 2000, employment in the United States expanded by 44.6 million jobs, an increase of 37 percent, as shown in Table 8.1. This table documents the contraction of goods producing employment over this period, and the strong growth of a number of lines of service employment, including health services, producer services, educational services, retail trade, consumer services and non-farm proprietors. As documented in Figure 8.1, the construction sector enjoyed strong growth, reflecting the need for capital investment to support population growth and the strong expansion of production in the economy. The relatively slow growth of wholesale trade reflects the logistical revolution that has downsized inventories in the channel of distribution (Berman, 2004: 72). Reductions in federal employment were dominated by downsizing in the military, while state and local government employment growth was large in absolute terms.

The geographical pattern of employment change was analyzed through the use of shift-share analysis, using the sector definitions included in Table 8.1. Table 8.2 presents an overview of the results of this analysis. Three measures of shift are presented in Table 8.2. The net shift is the difference between actual change and the level of change expected if a region grew at the national growth rate. The industry mix shift is essentially a correction of the expected national growth rate, adjusting expected growth in individual sectors by the difference between the industry growth rate and the overall national growth rate. Thus, for example, the industry mix component in wholesaling would be negative, as

Table 8.1 US employment, 1985–2000 (thousands of jobs)

Sector	1985	2000	Change	Change (%)	Total change (%)
Farm	3,466	3,113	−353	−10.2	−0.8
Agricultural services, forestry, fishing	379	183	−196	−51.7	−0.4
Mining	780	388	−392	−50.2	−0.9
Construction	4,433	6,558	2,124	47.9	4.8
Manufacturing	18,277	16,474	−1,803	−9.9	−4.0
Transportation, communications, utilities	4,615	4,815	200	4.3	0.4
Wholesale trade	5,285	6,109	825	15.6	1.8
Retail trade	16,001	22,953	6,951	43.4	15.6
Finance, insurance, real estate	5,933	7,705	1,773	29.9	4.0
Producer services	9,478	20,110	10,633	112.2	23.9
Health services	6,254	14,108	7,854	125.6	17.6
Educational services	1,504	2,532	1,028	68.4	2.3
Consumer services	8,205	11,633	3,428	41.8	7.7
Federal military	2,746	2,075	−671	−24.4	−1.5
Federal civilian	3,008	2,892	−116	−3.9	−0.3
State & local government	13,503	17,977	4,474	33.1	10.0
Non-farm proprietors	16,722	25,537	8,815	52.7	19.8
Total	120,589	165,162	44,574	37.0	100.0

Sources: US County Business Patterns and US BEA Local Area Personal Income.

Table 8.2 Shift-share model results overview

Type of shift measure	Overall change (%)	Job shift (000)
Net shift	+/−17.2	+/− 7,643
Industry mix shift	+/−4.9	+/− 2,183
Competitive shift	+/−18.6	+/− 8,305

Table 8.3 Leading contributors to positive and negative competitive shifts

BEA region	Positive shift (%)	Historic position	BEA region	Negative shift (%)	Historic position
Sacramento	2.47	3	Buffalo	2.07	1
San Diego	2.48	3	St. Louis	2.79	2
Raleigh-Durham-Chapel Hill	2.51	4	Syracuse	2.80	4
			Pittsburgh	2.81	1
Charlotte	2.62	4	Cleveland	2.84	1
Nashville	3.02	4	Detroit	3.15	1
Portland, Oregon	3.07	4	Chicago	3.34	1
Denver	3.18	1	Philadelphia	6.37	1
Dallas-Fort Worth	3.24	1	Boston	10.51	5
Salt Lake City	3.68	4	New York	39.56	1
Orlando	3.75	3			
Seattle	5.03	3			
Phoenix	5.31	1			
Las Vegas	5.78	4			
Atlanta	8.51	1			
Total	54.67			76.25	

Note: Historic key position
1. In both 1965–75 and 1974–85 analyses.
2. In 1965–75, but not 1974–85 analysis.
3. In 1974–85 but not 1965–75 analysis.
4. In neither 1965–75 nor 1974–85 analysis.
5. Negative 1965–75, but positive 1974–85 analysis.

wholesaling had lower than average expansion. Summing across sectors produces the industry mix shift measure, and it is evident that this 'correction' is relatively modest when compared to the net shift measure. The third measure of shift is the competitive shift, which is the difference between what actually took place in the way of employment change and that expected on an industry by industry basis. This third measure of shift indicates most robustly how regional performance varies from national trends. As with the analyses reported above for 1965–75 and 1974–85, the competitive shift measure outstrips the net and industry mix shift measures.

The geography of the competitive shifts is portrayed in Figure 8.1, and summarized in Tables 8.3 and 8.4. Figure 8.4 depicts the large and small contributors to the positive and negative competitive shifts. There is a clear concentration of negative shifts in the northeast and Midwest, and of positive shifts in the West and South. Table 8.3 identifies the largest

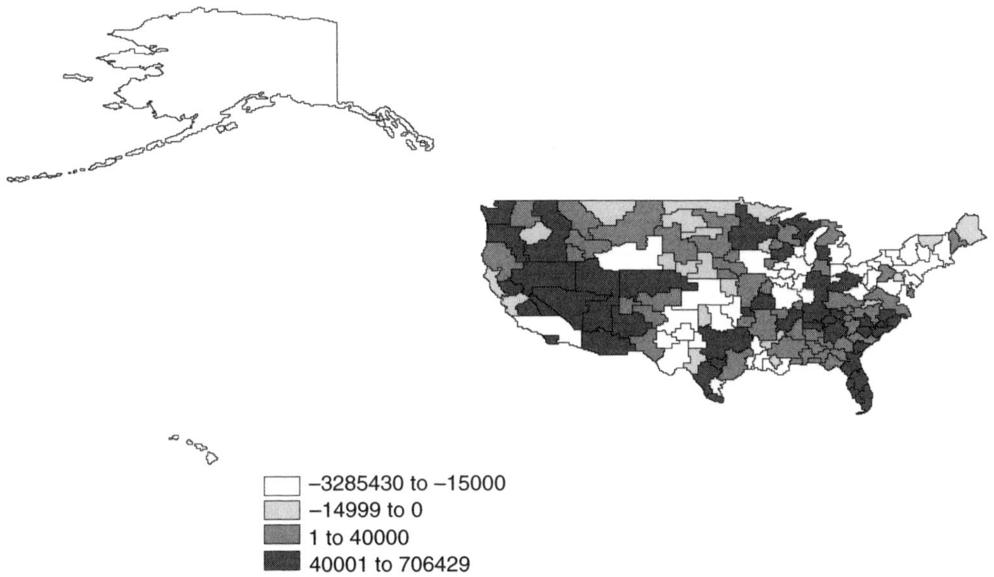

Source: BEA (2000).

Figure 8.4 Competitive shift, 1985–2000

contributors to the positive and negative competitive shifts, and also indicates their position in the author's analyses of the 1965–75 and 1974–85 periods. Addressing the negative shifts, it is clear that most of these regions have been persistently in the large negative shift column, and New York has consistently accounted for the largest percentage of the negative competitive shift.

The places accounting for the largest percentage of the positive competitive shift include a number that were not in the list of regions with large positive shifts in the 1965–75 analyses, but grew to have large positive shifts in the 1974–85 analysis. It also includes a number that are newcomers to the list of fast-growing places, places that might be regarded as 'second-tier cities' (Markusen et al., 1999). No one place in the large positive competitive shift group accounts for nearly as much of the overall positive shift as is the case with the negative competitive shift group, reflecting a more spatially dispersed pattern of positive competitive shifts. Overall, 106 BEA economic areas had a positive competitive shift, while 66 BEA economic areas had a negative competitive shift, another indicator of the relatively widespread spatial trend of growth outpacing the national rate of growth.

Boston and Los Angeles are two major metropolitan regions that have had interesting trajectories. In the 1965–75 analysis, Los Angeles was among the largest negative competitive shifts, but in 1974–85 it was among the largest positive competitive shifts. In the current analysis, Los Angeles had a small negative competitive shift. Boston was in the largest negative competitive shifts in the 1965–75 analysis, but shifted into the top positive competitive shift in 1974–85, and then fell back into the large negative competitive shift group in the current analysis. Washington, DC, Miami, Tampa, and Houston were all in the strong positive competitive shift group in the 1965–75 and 1974–85 analyses, but had weaker performance in the current analysis. San Francisco and Anchorage had strong

Table 8.4 Key sectoral contributors to competitive shift

Large positive shift	Large Negative Shift
Sacramento: Producer services, non-farm proprietors, state & local government	Buffalo: Manufacturing, non-farm proprietors
San Diego: Non-farm proprietors, producer services	St. Louis: Non-farm proprietors, producer services
Raleigh-Durham: Producer services, non-farm proprietors	Syracuse: Manufacturing, non-farm proprietors
Charlotte: Producer services, retail	Pittsburgh: Producer services, retail
Nashville: Non-farm proprietors, manufacturing	Cleveland: Health services, state & local government
Portland, OR: Producer services, manufacturing	Detroit: Health services, state & local government
Denver: Producer services, consumer services	Philadelphia: Manufacturing, producer services
Dallas: Producer services, state & local government	Boston: Manufacturing, producer services
Salt Lake City: Producer services, non-farm proprietors	New York City: Producer services, manufacturing
Orlando: Producer services, consumer services	
Seattle: Producer services, manufacturing	
Phoenix: Producer services, non-farm proprietors	
Las Vegas: Consumer services, non-farm proprietors	
Atlanta: Producer services, retail	

positive competitive shifts in 1974–85, but both moved into the negative competitive shift category in the current analysis. Hartford, St. Louis, and Syracuse were among the large negative competitive shift groups in the 1965–75 or the 1974–85 analyses, but in the current analysis Hartford and Syracuse had small negative competitive shifts, while St. Louis continued to have a strong negative competitive shift.

The key sectoral contributors to the large positive and negative competitive shifts are identified in Table 8.4. This table clearly documents the very strong leading role of producer services in most of the regions with strong positive competitive shifts. Exceptions to this trend include Las Vegas with gambling and entertainment-related consumer services as the leading sector, and the strong role of non-farm proprietors in Nashville and San Diego. Manufacturing appears as a secondary force in Seattle, Portland OR, and Nashville. Places with strong negative competitive shifts had manufacturing and producer services most frequently playing a key role, but it is interesting to see the poor performance of health services as the leading sector in Detroit and Cleveland, and the weakness in the non-farm proprietors sector leading in St. Louis. In the present analysis manufacturing plays a more muted role than in Beyers's 1974–85 analysis, a reflection of the dominant role that service employment growth has played in both rapidly growing places and those experiencing slower growth over the 1985–2000 period (Beyers, 1991).

Another perspective on the spatial distribution of service industries is provided in Table 8.5, which presents coefficients of industrial concentration for 1985 and 2000. This

Table 8.5 Coefficients of industrial concentration

	1985	2000	Change
Farm	0.695	0.650	−0.045
Agricultural services, forestry, fishing	0.339	0.878	0.539
Mining	1.165	1.067	−0.099
Construction	0.260	0.155	−0.106
Manufacturing	0.263	0.299	0.036
Transportation, communications, utilities	0.163	0.187	0.024
Wholesale trade	0.161	0.184	0.023
Retail trade	0.064	0.070	0.006
Finance, insurance, real estate	0.216	0.203	−0.014
Producer services	0.300	0.238	−0.062
Health services	0.181	0.151	−0.030
Educational services	0.450	0.384	−0.067
Consumer services	0.112	0.127	0.016
Federal military	0.654	0.716	0.062
Federal civilian	0.494	0.421	−0.073
State & local government	0.153	0.157	0.004
Non-farm proprietors	0.136	0.130	−0.006

index is constructed by calculating the sum of the difference in the absolute percentage of a sector's employment in a region and the region's overall share of national employment, across all 172 BEA economic areas. The lower the index the more evenly distributed the sector; a value of zero would mean that the sector was distributed among the BEA economic areas exactly like the distribution of total employment. There are several key trends revealed in Table 8.5. The two most rapidly growing services – producer and health services – have declines in their indices between 1985 and 2000, suggesting decentralization of employment in these sectors. The indices for all of the service sectors except the relatively small educational service sector, are all relatively low. These low indices mean that employment growth in these sectors was widely dispersed among the BEA economic areas. This finding may seem at first blush to be at odds with the shift-share analysis, but it actually complements the shift-share results. That analysis highlighted the importance of manufacturing and producer services – two of the more unevenly distributed sectors, one growing and the other declining – in the fate of regions. The data in Table 8.5 reveal that the shrinking manufacturing sector became more unevenly distributed, while at the same time the rapidly growing producer service sector was becoming more evenly distributed. Three sectors that were important sources of job generation – retail, state and local government, and non-farm proprietors – showed little change in their already relatively even distribution among the BEA economic areas. The broad conclusion to be drawn from Table 8.5 is that the dramatic growth of the US service economy from 1985 to 2000 was shared widely among the BEA economic areas.

While the coefficients of industrial concentration indicate that services propelled the growth of most BEA economic areas, they do not indicate the structural bases that distinguish the economy of individual regions. Mirroring the work of Noyelle and Stanback (1983), and Stanback (Stanback and Grove, 2002), a cluster analysis was undertaken of location quotients for the industries identified in Table 8.6 across the BEA economic

Table 8.6 Cluster analysis regionalization of BEA economic areas

	Agriculture		
16	Staunton, VA-WV	110	Grand Forks, ND-MN
45	Johnson City-Kingsport-Bristol, TN-VA	113	Fargo-Moorhead, ND-MN
68	Champaign-Urbana, IL	114	Aberdeen, SD
75	Tupelo, MS-AL-TN	115	Rapid City, SD-MT-NE-ND
76	Greenville, MS	116	Sioux Falls, SD-IA-MN-NE
92	Fayetteville-Springdale-Rogers, AR-MO-OK	117	Sioux City, IA-NE-SD
93	Joplin, MO-KS-OK	118	Omaha, NE-IA-MO
94	Springfield, MO	119	Lincoln, NE
95	Jonesboro, AR-MO	120	Grand Island, NE
97	Springfield, IL-MO	121	North Platte, NE-CO
98	Columbia, MO	123	Topeka, KS
99	Kansas City, MO-KS	142	Scottsbluff, NE-WY
100	Des Moines, IA-IL-MO	145	Great Falls, MT
101	Peoria-Pekin, IL	148	Idaho Falls, ID-WY
103	Cedar Rapids, IA	149	Twin Falls, ID
16	Staunton, VA-WV	162	Fresno, CA
104	Madison, WI-IL-IA	168	Pendleton, OR-WA
105	La Crosse, WI-MN	169	Richland-Kennewick-Pasco, WA
106	Rochester, MN-IA-WI		
107	Minneapolis-St. Paul, MN-WI-IA		
108	Wausau, WI		
	Agriculture – government		
77	Jackson, MS-AL-LA	89	Monroe, LA
79	Montgomery, AL	90	Little Rock-North Little Rock, AR
	Agriculture – mining		
38	Macon, GA	165	Redding, CA-OR
146	Missoula, MT		
	Agriculture, mining, military		
112	Bismarck, ND-MT-SD	129	San Angelo, TX
125	Oklahoma City, OK	132	Corpus Christi, TX
126	Western Oklahoma, OK	144	Billings, MT-WY
128	Abilene, TX		
	Diverse		
3	Boston-Worcester-Lawrence-Lowell-Brockton, MA-NH-RI-VT	63	Milwaukee-Racine, WI
4	Burlington, VT-NY	64	Chicago-Gary-Kenosha, IL-IN-WI
5	Albany-Schenectady-Troy, NY	67	Indianapolis, IN-IL
6	Syracuse, NY-PA	70	Louisville, KY-IN
7	Rochester, NY-PA	71	Nashville, TN-KY
10	New York-Northern New Jersey-Long Island, NY-NJ-CT-PA-MA-VT	73	Memphis, TN-AR-MS-KY
11	Harrisburg-Lebanon-Carlisle, PA	80	Mobile, AL
12	Philadelphia-Wilmington-Atlantic City, PA-NJ-DE-MD	83	New Orleans, LA-MS
14	Salisbury, MD-DE-VA	96	St. Louis, MO-IL
19	Raleigh-Durham-Chapel Hill, NC	127	Dallas-Fort Worth, TX-AR-OK

Table 8.6 (continued)

23	Charlotte-Gastonia-Rock Hill, NC-SC	130	Austin-San Marcos, TX
25	Wilmington, NC-SC	131	Houston-Galveston-Brazoria, TX
33	Sarasota-Bradenton, FL	133	McAllen-Edinburg-Mission, TX
34	Tampa-St. Petersburg-Clearwater, FL	139	Santa Fe, NM
40	Atlanta, GA-AL-NC	141	Denver-Boulder-Greeley, CO-KS-NE
41	Greenville-Spartanburg-Anderson, SC-NC	147	Spokane, WA-ID
44	Knoxville, TN	150	Boise City, ID-OR
49	Cincinnati-Hamilton, OH-KY-IN	152	Salt Lake City-Ogden, UT-ID
51	Columbus, OH	158	Phoenix-Mesa, AZ-NM
53	Pittsburgh, PA-WV	160	Los Angeles-Riverside-Orange County, CA-AZ
54	Erie, PA	163	San Francisco-Oakland-San Jose, CA
55	Cleveland-Akron, OH-PA	167	Portland-Salem, OR-WA
57	Detroit-Ann Arbor-Flint, MI	170	Seattle-Tacoma-Bremerton, WA
	Forestry & fishing		
2	Portland, ME	166	Eugene-Springfield, OR-CA
	Government		
13	Washington-Baltimore, DC-MD-VA-WV-PA	157	El Paso, TX-NM
15	Richmond-Petersburg, VA	159	Tucson, AZ
134	San Antonio, TX	164	Sacramento-Yolo, CA
156	Albuquerque, NM-AZ		
	Government – agriculture		
1	Bangor, ME	36	Dothan, AL-FL-GA
27	Augusta-Aiken, GA-SC	37	Albany, GA
35	Tallahassee, FL-GA	86	Lake Charles, LA
	Government – construction		
84	Baton Rouge, LA-MS		
	Government – military		
20	Norfolk-Virginia Beach-Newport News, VA-NC	29	Jacksonville, FL-GA
21	Greenville, NC	39	Columbus, GA-AL
22	Fayetteville, NC	81	Pensacola, FL
24	Columbia, SC	82	Biloxi-Gulfport-Pascagoula, MS
26	Charleston-North Charleston, SC	161	San Diego, CA
28	Savannah, GA-SC	172	Honolulu, HI
	Government military, mining, agriculture		*Government – mining*
111	Minot, ND	154	Flagstaff, AZ-UT
	Manufacturing		
8	Buffalo-Niagara Falls, NY-PA	56	Toledo, OH
17	Roanoke, VA-NC-WV	60	Appleton-Oshkosh-Neenah, WI
18	Greensboro-Winston-Salem-High Point, NC-VA	62	Grand Rapids-Muskegon-Holland, MI
42	Asheville, NC	65	Elkhart-Goshen, IN-MI
43	Chattanooga, TN-GA	66	Fort Wayne, IN
46	Hickory-Morganton, NC-TN	74	Huntsville, AL-TN
50	Dayton-Springfield, OH	102	Davenport-Moline-Rock Island, IA-IL

Table 8.6 (continued)

Mining	
48 Charleston, WV-KY-OH	135 Odessa-Midland, TX
72 Paducah, KY-IL	137 Lubbock, TX
85 Lafayette, LA	138 Amarillo, TX-NM
87 Beaumont-Port Arthur, TX	140 Pueblo, CO-NM
91 Fort Smith, AR-OK	143 Casper, WY-ID-UT
122 Wichita, KS-OK	155 Farmington, NM-CO
124 Tulsa, OK-KS	
Mining – agriculture – military	
88 Shreveport-Bossier City, LA-AR	
Mining – education	
9 State College, PA	52 Wheeling, WV-OH
Mining – government	
47 Lexington, KY-TN-VA-WV	109 Duluth-Superior, MN-WI
58 Northern Michigan, MI	171 Anchorage, AK
Mining – manufacturing	
59 Green Bay, WI-MI	78 Birmingham, AL
61 Traverse City, MI	
Mining – services	
151 Reno, NV-CA	
Services	
30 Orlando, FL	32 Fort Myers-Cape Coral, FL
31 Miami-Fort Lauderdale, FL	153 Las Vegas, NV-AZ-UT

areas.[3] Location quotients are index numbers that describe the concentration of employment in a region compared to a benchmark; in this case the US as a whole was considered to be the benchmark.

The results of this cluster analysis are reported in Table 8.6. The cluster analysis was interpreted by observing regions grouped together in a dendogram produced as a part of the results of the cluster analysis, and noting the values of the location quotients that were similar for members of individual clusters. What is immediately evident in the result of this cluster analysis is that most BEA economic areas are not structurally associated with the relatively ubiquitously distributed services sectors. Instead, it is their dependence on agriculture, manufacturing, mining and government that becomes the basis for their cluster membership. The clear exception to this result is the group of places considered 'diverse', which tend to be the largest of the BEA economic areas.

The performance of different cluster groups, as measured by employment growth, is reported in Table 8.7. This table documents the relatively strong performance of the diverse and government-oriented BEA economic areas, and the relatively poor performance of those whose industrial structure is demarcated by goods production (agriculture, manufacturing, mining). The four regions associated most strongly with services exhibit extremely strong average growth, a result strongly influenced by Las Vegas. Thus, structure does matter. Most of the regions with large positive or negative competitive

Table 8.7 Growth rates of employment by cluster group

Cluster group	Number of BEA economic areas	Mean growth 1985–2000
Agriculture	50	32.7
Diverse	48	44.4
Forestry/fishing	2	42.8
Government	28	42.1
Manufacturing	14	34.2
Mining	26	31.7
Services	4	94.2
Nation	172	37.0

shifts are in the diverse structure group, where local forces associated with key sectors in the local economy (Table 8.4) led relative economic performance.

Discussion and summary

Services have defined the economic trajectory of regions in the US economy in recent decades. The ongoing division of labor in the service sector has been related to processes of innovation and shifting patterns of demand for services. Various studies have documented the uneven pattern of regional development, driven by this long-run shift to the services. Although data are scarce, it is clear that this structural change has been driven by a growing level of trade interregionally and internationally in services. This flowering of the service economy has occurred in an environment in which IT has advanced rapidly, allowing continuing innovation and shifts in client demands for ever-changing supplies of services.

This chapter has documented not only the long-run shift of employment to the services in the United States, but the ongoing changing division of labor within services. It was argued that this process of growth and development was associated with innovations in types of goods needed to produce services, and in shifting demands for final and intermediate services over time. In recent decades, growth has been led by producer services, health services, non-farm proprietors (most of whom are engaged in service activity) and retailing.

At the regional scale, this chapter has focused on trends over the 1985–2000 period. Over this period, the United States gained 44.6 million jobs, almost all of which were in the services. From a geographic standpoint, this pattern of growth was somewhat uneven, with almost 20 percent of employment change not located in proportion to the distribution of employment in 1985. A handful of large metropolitan regions account for the majority of the places with relatively fast or slow growth. A number of urban regions in the old American Industrial Belt persistently had experienced relatively slow growth, while a set of urban regions in the South and West have experienced relatively rapid growth. Services have played a key role in all the urban areas with relatively rapid growth, while manufacturing was a key factor pulling down urban regions with slow growth. The fastest-growing sectors all show a trend towards a more dispersed pattern of employment.

The geographic patterns observed in this analysis mirror those reported earlier by this author, and by Noyelle and Stanback (Beyers, 1989, 1991, 1992; Noyelle and Stanback, 1983). Most of the places with slow growth have been in this position for decades, a reflection in most cases of the long-term downsizing of manufacturing activity, and specifically the decentralization of producer and financial services from the New York metropolitan area. The rapidly growing places include more 'newcomers', places such as Las Vegas, Nashville, Charlotte and Orlando, where consumer services (entertainment), producer services, and non-farm proprietors are sectors driving development.

The results of the cluster analysis presented in this chapter remind us of the importance of goods production as a defining structural basis for many regional economies in the United States, even if these regions have also gained stronger service sectors. The regions classified as diverse had strong service sectors, as did most of those classified as government, and both categories exhibited relatively strong employment growth. Regions whose defining basis for classification in the cluster analysis was based on goods production in general have exhibited slower growth. These results reinforce the findings from the shift-share analysis, and raise the question of why some regions have gained a strong service sector that is leading development, while other regions have been left behind. BLS forecasts suggest that this process of service-led development will continue for the foreseeable future (Berman, 2004). BLS does not forecast proprietors' employment, but its estimates of wage and salary employment in the 2002–2012 period project continued declines in farming, mining and manufacturing, and continued growth in construction and services. Strongest growth is forecast to continue in producer and health services, but state and local government, retailing and consumer services are also forecast to have strong expansions.

A long-run view of change has been taken in this chapter, reaching back to analyses undertaken for over three decades on a spatial basis, and for a century on a structural basis. The actual trajectories of development are mediated by business cycles, which have not been addressed in this chapter. The US economy has just been through a mild recession, and job growth coming out of this recession has been lackluster. Uncertainties about the future are rampant, as producers and clients may be rearranging how and where they produce services. The current debate in the United States over outsourcing of producer services is indicative of these uncertainties (Brookings Institution, 2004). In my view the continuing stream of innovations in goods that underpin the production of services will continue to spawn innovations in services (and vice versa), leading us into unforecastable new divisions of labor. The current rapid evolution in wireless technology is a good example, allowing mass markets to emerge for equipment, as well as niche markets for content. The burst of demand for consumer electronics related to music and video may also be leading to increased demand for live performances, stimulating more travel, with related multiplier effects in accommodation, restaurants and online booking agents. Thus, structural and spatial trends discussed in this chapter will probably unfold in new and unpredictable ways in the years to come.

Notes

1. The sources used to construct this figure include the census of the United States, economic census data, and data from the US Bureau of Economic Analysis. The data series used are not entirely comparable. Early years are based on census data, which are self-reported sources of work. Later years are based on the ES-202 data gathered by the US Bureau of Labor Statistics. In this figure the recent statistics are based on wage and salary employment, excluding proprietors. If proprietors were included, the share of service employment would be larger than shown in Figure 8.1.
2. For a good discussion of shift-share methodology, see Stevens and Moore (1980).
3. Ward's hierarchical algorithm was used in this cluster analysis.

APPENDIX 8.1

County-level estimates for all categories of private non-farm employment included in the CBP files were estimated according to the sectoring scheme in Table 8.1. This was done on a state by state basis for both time periods, because CBP does not reveal employment estimates in cases where there are too few business establishments, and replaces the employment statistic with a letter code indicating the size range of employment in the industry in the county. Using total county employment and total industry employment by state, a biproportional matrix adjustment method was used to estimate the value of the suppressed employment (Bacharach, 1970). The estimates of suppressed employment were then integrated with the published county statistics. Once this procedure was completed for all states, these data were then aggregated into the 172 BEA economic areas currently defined by BEA. In the year 2000, 1.26 percent of total employment in CBP was estimated to be suppressed, so the overall impact this tedious estimation process was not enormous.

CBP omits three important categories of employment: agriculture, government and proprietors. BEA does provide estimates of farm employment (farm workers and proprietors) and government aggregated to the BEA economic area level. These data were added to the database. BEA reports employment data by industry, inclusive of wage and salary employees, and non-farm proprietors. CBP estimates of employment by industry are only for wage and salary employment. Table 8A.1 indicates the importance of non-farm proprietors within various sectors, ranging from a low of 8.7 percent within the services division, to 91 percent in agricultural services, forestry and fishing; nationally about 18 percent of employment in the private non-farm categories contained in the table is accounted for by proprietors. Because BEA does not provide estimates of employment within the services division at the level of detail wanted for this analysis, I chose to report wage and salary employment by industry, and a summary statistic for non-farm proprietorships. The last column of the table shows the share of this employment by industry, with slightly over 71 percent being located within the various services divisions. This is a slightly smaller share than the share of non-farm private wage and salary employment in services (79 percent). However, in interpreting results of the analyses presented in this chapter, it should be kept in mind that most of the non-farm proprietors' employment is in service industries.

The database developed for this chapter was based on two systems of industrial classification. The 1985 CBP data were defined using the Standard Industrial Classification (SIC) system, while the 2000 CBP data were defined in the North American Industry Classification System (NAICS) adopted by the US Census Bureau in 1997. These two systems are only partially compatible. In some broad industry groups there is complete matching between the two systems, but in other cases industrial activity was dispersed from the SIC system into a set of new industrial categories. For example, computer services was under the SIC system a part of business services. Under the NAICS system it was dispersed to publishing; information; professional, scientific and technical services; retail; and other services. In the process of developing the year 2000 database, an attempt was made to have it approximate as closely as possible the SIC definitions.

In the SIC system, each industry division had employment reported for operating as well as administrative units. The administrative units were referred to as 'auxiliaries', and were typically headquarters-type establishments. The concept of auxiliaries was eliminated with

Table 8.A1 Non-farm proprietors' distributions

Sector	Proprietors' share of sectoral employment (%)	Total non-farm proprietors (%)
Agricultural services, forestry	91.4	7.1
Mining	50.5	1.5
Construction	30.6	10.6
Manufacturing	13.8	9.7
Transportation, communications, utilities	41.6	12.6
Wholesale trade	19.4	5.4
Retail trade	15.7	15.7
Finance, insurance, real estate	41.6	20.2
Services	8.7	17.0
Total (rounded)		100.0

Sources: Calculated by author from BEA Local Area Personal Income and CBP.

the adoption of the NAICS system. Approximately 75 percent of employment in auxiliaries was considered to be in a new NAICS category, administration. When the 1985 CBP files were estimated, estimates of auxiliary employment were made for each division. In the process of aggregating data for this chapter, this auxiliary employment was considered to be a part of producer services. The new administration category in NAICS was also considered to be in producer services. Thus, the sectoral employment estimates used for 1985 are net of auxiliary employment (except for producer services which includes total employment in this category across all divisions).

The various estimation procedures just described have led to a database with total employment that is similar, but not identical in magnitude, to BEA's estimated total employment for 1985 and the year 2000. It was felt that this 15-year period would be long enough to portray clearly contemporary sectoral and regional trends in employment in the United States.

9 Service industries, global city formation and new policy discourses within the Asia-Pacific

T.A. Hutton

Introduction: the ascendancy of service industries

The record of scholarship on service industries within the Asia-Pacific domain reflects an incipient stage of inquiry within the broader tradition of development studies in the region, and occupies a commensurately modest niche within the service industries' research genre. This incipiency is associated in part with the recent provenance of 'take-off' growth in services among many of the constituent regions and economies, as well as the persistence of intellectual attachment on the part of development scholars to the familiar ontologies of the *industrialisation* paradigm. The research community remains resolutely committed to studies of the 'factory world' of production, labour and industrial development regimes within the Asia-Pacific, together with its defining territorial and social manifestations.

This enduring attachment to the workings of industrial production regimes within the Asia-Pacific is to a large extent justified, of course, in the light of the historically exceptional record of growth in manufacturing capacity over the past four decades. Manufacturing, typically fostered by assertive state development policies, has been central to the growth of every leading Asia-Pacific economy since the 1950s, a structural process which included the formation of world-scale industrial metropoles, notably Tokyo, Nagoya, Shanghai, Seoul, Taipei and Hong Kong, among others. But there is now an exigent need to investigate emerging regional development trajectories in the Asia-Pacific which incorporate more prominent (as opposed to merely ancillary) roles for specialised service industries, as well as for advanced-technology manufacturing. To illustrate, invoking the lexicon of 'postindustrialism' to describe the contemporary development phase of Taiwan, South Korea, Hong Kong and Singapore may be problematic in a number of respects, but that the descriptor of 'newly industrialising' for any of these four economies is now decades out of date is surely incontestable.

That said, there is now a burgeoning scholarship on the developmental role of services within the Asia-Pacific region. Lines of inquiry include the retheorisation of Asian development to encompass larger roles for service industries and labour (Yeung and Lin, 2003; Yang and Lin, 2004); explications of the role of 'producer' or intermediate services in the globalisation experiences of Asia-Pacific cities (O'Connor and Hutton, 1998; Daniels and O'Connor, 2000); studies of the social implications of advanced services and allied labour formation for exemplary Asia-Pacific cities (see Baum (1999) and Ho (2005) on social implications of occupational 'professionalisation' in Singapore); Kwok (1999) on the reconstruction of social identity in Hong Kong, and within the 'South China Triangle' (2002); case studies of key service industry groups situated in Asia-Pacific cities and regions (as opposed to sector studies *per se*), such as financial services (Hsu and Chen, 2004), transportation and communications (Rimmer, 1996) and business services (Muller,

2002); and the periodisation of planning responses to urban services growth and development, including taxonomies of exemplary policy models, within the region (Hutton, 2004a). There are also important case studies which demonstrate the pertinence of service industries to the formation of distinctive models of urban growth and change in the Asia-Pacific. We can cite as one of the earliest contributions Bruce Taylor and Reginald Kwok's narrative on intersections of policy and tertiarisation processes in the internationalisation of Hong Kong (Taylor and Kwok, 1989), and Graham Johnson's continuing research on the sociology of industrial (and postindustrial) transformations within Hong Kong's New Territories and the larger economic spaces of Guangdong province (Johnson, 1993, 1996).[1]

Service industry development: conditions, culture and contingency

A governing principle of scholarship in this realm is the need to contextualise Asia-Pacific service development within the specificities of place and the evolving discourses of Asian development theory at national and regional levels (Fan, 1997; Lin, 2002). These conditions subvert any idea of transferring without major modification analytical templates derived from experiences distilled from the dominant 'service world' of Europe and much of North America. The multiple realities of development within the Asia-Pacific are likely to confound efforts to produce transcendent, universalising theory along the lines of the seminal Western models of transformative urban change.[2]

There is an extensive literature which emphasises the need to acknowledge interdependencies between culture and development in the shaping of distinctive regional forms of capitalism in East Asia (in this connection, see Redding, 1990; Brook and Luong, 1997), including monographs which articulate the more specific connections between culture and cities in the region (Kim et al., 1997a). These treatments include distinctions between 'heterogenetic' urban centres such as Singapore, established in the colonial period and reflective of a multicultural heritage and orientation, 'in marked contrast to the older capital cities of the region that functioned as orthogenetic centres perpetuating the cultural heritage of the nations' (Ho, 1997: 214, after Redfield and Singer, 1954), such as Beijing, Tokyo and Hanoi. While Singapore presents features of singularity in this realm, as in others, the Asia-Pacific encompasses other cities of an essentially heterogenetic nature, including Hong Kong, Melbourne, Los Angeles and Vancouver. These cities are defined in large part by their transnational populations and social order, and diverse (and in some ways 'plastic') cultural bases. These qualities tend to impart higher levels of entrepreneurship, collaborative capacity and international connectivity to the urban economy (Hiebert, 2004). Heterogenetic cities within the Asia-Pacific are increasingly reconstructed as sites of inter- and multi-cultural fusion, expression and transmission, which generate both production and social value for their respective communities. At the same time, the old orthogenetic cities have in some cases recovered a sense of the unique resonances of national cultural assets and roles. An appreciation of these historic assets and values finds a place both in metropolitan planning and in economic development strategies, presenting a contrast to the industrial production roles assigned to them in earlier state development policies (Beijing represents an important example: see Mao and Jin, 1996).

We can also identify more specific traditions of development culture which have shaped in part urban service roles and functions. Examples here might include the long-established mercantile and trading culture of Canton (Guangzhou), the legacy of international banking and commerce that underpins a significant element of Shanghai's development, and the emergence of trading centres associated with colonialism and empire (Malacca, Singapore, Rangoon, Jakarta, Sydney, Victoria). The external trading role developed over several centuries in Canton was never entirely extinguished during the period of communist industrialisation (c. 1949–78), and was quickly reinvigorated once Deng Xiaoping's reforms were introduced, providing Guangzhou with a 'head start' over other Chinese cities in the new competitive era of globalisation and service-led development (Cartier, 2001; Johnson, 2002). Then there is the well-known case of Commodore Perry's 'opening up' of the Tokyo Bay ports (1854) as a particularly aggressive imposition of an external trading orientation on a heretofore semi-autarkic economy. While Pacific Asia contains numerous historic regional trading and service centres which have developed more or less organically over a number of centuries (for example, Pulo Prabang and Amoy), there is also a sustained record of exogenous development to consider, as well as the more recent experience of policy-induced (or accelerated) tertiarisation and internationalisation.

The growing centrality of service industries to the transformation of Asia-Pacific cities, economies and societies offers quite extraordinarily rich opportunities for fresh conceptualisation. But researchers seeking to construct new theory must acknowledge the persistence of exceptionalism in the region, and the implications of extreme contrasts in underlying economic, political and social conditions: consider, for example, that both North Korea and Japan are notionally 'East Asian' nations (at least in terms of regional geography), and that Singapore, Cambodia and Burma (Myanmar) are 'Southeast Asian'. There is also the definitional problem of whether to include 'Pacific America' and Australasia within the Asia-Pacific for the purposes of research on the developmental role of services within the region. I have elected to include these areas within the Asia-Pacific for the purposes of this discussion, although this approach may exacerbate problems of heterogeneity in development conditions, as well as stretching to its practical limits the concept of 'regional space'.[3]

Chapter agenda: global city formation and policy experimentation

I propose in this chapter to address a set of salient themes associated with the expansion of services within the Asia-Pacific, including both substantive and symbolic markers of change, and emphasising the critical role of cities as the basing points of tertiarisation within the region. This treatment will be informed by the emerging Asian service literature and related Asian urban studies scholarship, and will be structured by the following questions. First, what roles do service industries play in the transformation of Asia-Pacific cities and city-regions? Second, can we identify within the region manifestations of emerging service trajectories observed among advanced urban economies and societies? Third, how are services reconfiguring global city formation within the Asia-Pacific region; and can we construct alternative models of global cities which incorporate, but transcend, the conventional measures of corporate projection and primacy in intermediate sector banking and finance? Finally, to what extent are these larger constructions of the twenty-first century service economy and its development potential expressed in state and local policy innovation in the region, and in the changing iconography of progress, modernisation and globalisation?

Services and dimensions of urban change

Over the past two decades cities and regions within the broadly defined Asia-Pacific sphere have in many cases experienced high rates of growth in service industries and employment, including specialised intermediate or 'producer' services, as well as a more diverse range of public and consumer (or final demand) services. In the most advanced cities, notably Hong Kong and Singapore in Pacific Asia, and the major city-regions of Australasia and Pacific North America, service industries have clearly supplanted manufacturing as lead sectors of urban growth and change, following in some respects the familiar lineaments of the postindustrial vocation or trajectory.[4]

At one level, these experiences of service growth within much of the Asia-Pacific may appear to replicate the development path of the mature Atlantic domain, albeit in a far more temporally compressed manner. This historical development progression in the 'West' took the form of: (i) a long pre-industrial period of agrarianism, basic staples processing and fabrication, and local service provision; followed by (ii) sequences of increasingly advanced industrial production commencing in England and other technologically innovative societies in the mid-eighteenth century; building toward (iii) the apogee of the 'industrial city' typified by the expansion of Fordist manufacturing and employment over the first half of the twentieth century; and leading to (iv) the emergence of a 'postindustrial society' (Bell, 1973) and 'service economy' (Daniels, 1985) over the last four decades of the twentieth century. While the more euphoric (or apocalyptic) visions of a dematerialised economy never came to pass, Bell's axial principles extolling the primacy of scientific knowledge and the central role of a specialised services workforce offered a cogent interpretation of development within leading capitalist societies.[5] Within Europe and North America, these transformations took place over two and a half centuries, while in the most spectacular Asia-Pacific cases this multi-stage progression has consumed only a half-century or so, an unprecedented compression of regional development sequences.

But there are defining attributes of service industry development within the Asia-Pacific which stand in marked contrast to the earlier transformations within the mature societies of the Atlantic sphere. First, in some important cases the growth of services is coincident with continuing industrialisation, manifested in the sustained development of world-scale manufacturing capacity and labour (McGee and Lin, 1993). Thus in Shanghai and other important examples the urban–regional development trajectory includes a sublation of increasingly advanced industrialisation (Fan and Scott, 2003), including the distribution of manufacturing more extensively throughout the Lower Yangzi Delta (Marton, 1998) *and* accelerated tertiarisation processes within the central city especially. This co-presence of buoyant industrial and service sectors obviates the need for sterile debates concerning the primacy (or autonomy) of services and manufacturing that typified much of the polemical writing in the early years of the postindustrial era (see, for example, Gershuny, 1978). Specialised services and increasingly technology-intensive manufacturing industries are *co-dependent* elements of advanced production systems. As the Asia-Pacific experience demonstrates, however, the balance of firms and employment between each of these principal sectors, and the divisions of labour within these sectors, is subject to change over time, and generally favours service-type occupations (such as management, engineering and design, information technology (IT) workers and technical staff, and sales occupations) both in manufacturing and in service production (including tertiary, and more especially, quaternary sectors).[6] Manufacturing continues to decentralise from the leading metropolitan city-regions of the region to lower-cost jurisdictions (Kim et al., 1997a). It is also the case that global city status among city-regions within Pacific Asia is increasingly defined by the presence of major service industries, corporations, institutions and specialised labour, rather than by the manufacturing industries which characterised the region's industrial metropoles of the 1970s and 1980s. But apart from developmental outliers (notably Singapore, Hong Kong, and perhaps Fukuoka), there are few examples of Asian cities that are truly 'postindustrial' in the sense of the Atlantic core cities, which have in most cases suffered enormous contractions of manufacturing capacity and employment since the 1970s. Even on the eastern and southern margins of the Asia-Pacific, there are metropolitan cities (such as Los Angeles, Seattle and Melbourne) with very substantial manufacturing sectors.

Second, among the mega-cities of Southeast Asia such as Jakarta and Manila (and even to an extent among East Asian conurbations like Taipei and Seoul), the central high-rise office complexes generic to the rapid tertiarisation experience are juxtaposed amid traditional landscapes of informal sector activity, including slums and squatter settlements. These conditions present a far more sharply dichotomous profile of growth and development than in most Western cities. As Michael Leaf has observed, this persistent dualism within the urban landscapes of transitional societies in Southeast Asia suggests a syndrome of 'redevelopment before development', with attendant dislocations, polarisation, and growing disparities of welfare and opportunity (Leaf, 1996).

Third, following four (and in some cases five) decades of state-directed industrialisation, a growing roster of national, regional and urban governments within the Asia-Pacific are pursuing policies designed to promote accelerated tertiarisation. This developmental policy posture towards services stands in marked contrast to the essentially regulatory tradition of local planning and policy established to manage service growth in European and North American cities throughout much of the late twentieth century.[7] The Asia-Pacific tertiarisation experience includes programmatic commitments to fostering services growth in support of globalisation (Shanghai and other coastal Chinese city-regions), modernisation (Vietnam), regional competitive advantage (Singapore) and new phases of advanced industrialisation (Japan). The sectoral focus has tended to privilege corporate control functions and intermediate banking and finance, seen widely as measures of global city status. This is observed in an evolving iconography of progress and development, expressed in ever-higher point towers inscribed on the central landscapes of Tokyo, Hong Kong, Shanghai, Kuala Lumpur and Taipei, among other cities, recalling the initial 'skyscraper rivalry' between Chicago and New York in the late nineteenth century. But service industry policies within Asia-Pacific cities and regions now include programmes for culture and creative industries, knowledge-based industries and higher education, following the continuing evolution of the service sector, and emerging policy discourses among leading urban societies.

Services and multidimensional–multiscalar urban change

The impacts of tertiarisation for cities and urban communities within the Asia-Pacific are both complex and highly varied, reflecting marked contrasts in stages of regional development, local growth conditions, and the contingent features of state and local policy systems. We can identify five principal domains of urban growth and change associated with the expansion of the urban services sector in the Asia-Pacific, as follows:

1. a set of propulsive impacts of tertiarisation on the urban industrial structure, economic base and employment formation, in which service industries (particularly

specialised, knowledge-based and traded services) are assigned leading roles in the strategic repositioning of cities within global and regional hierarchies, and within urban and national development trajectories (Daniels, 2005);

2. the role of service industries in the spatial reconfiguration of the metropolis, comprising (a) at the broader city-region level, specialised service industries as key 'platform' or infrastructural elements (international airports, seaports and other 'gateway' installations; major universities and science parks) of extended metropolitan regions (EMRs) (after McGee, 1991, and following Gottmann's earlier concept of the service-driven 'megalopolis' phenomenon, 1961; see also Fujita, 1992, for the Tokyo Metropolitan Region case study) and (b) within the metropolitan area, the increasing centrality of service industries to generative processes of growth and change, encompassing a relayering of investment capital and the redevelopment of the 'internal production spaces of the metropolis' (Scott, 1988a), which drives (i) the reconfiguration of urban structure and land use (from monocentric to a polycentric urban structure, incorporating suburban and exurban development; see Sit, 1996; Lin and Wei, 2002; and Webster, 2002), (ii) the restructuring of the metropolitan space-economy to incorporate a proliferation of service industry clusters (see, for example, Yan et al., 1996, and Wu and Yeh, 1999, for analyses of the experience in Guangzhou; Wang, 1996, for the influence of commercial development on spatial change in Beijing; Park, 1993, for services and the changing spatial division of labour in Seoul; and Morshidi, 1996 and 2000, for the Kuala Lumpur case), and (iii) the reconstruction of built form to accommodate new landscapes of services production and consumption (Hutton, 2004a);
3. the influence of the rise of services on the reformation of urban class and social morphology, including shifts in social values, cultural practices, and political identity, and exhibiting, variously, elements of the 'professionalisation' and 'polarisation' hypotheses linked to service-led urban development among global cities (Ley, 1996; Baum, 1999; Ho, 2005);
4. the implications of rapid tertiarisation for experiences of everyday life in the spaces and places of the metropolis, including the relational sociologies and geographies of work, amenity and recreation, and commuting, as well as experiences of dislocation, alienation and social tension (Chua, 1989, 1991; Leaf, 2005); and
5. services and the comprehensive re-imaging of the restructured city-region, observed both at the metropolitan level, in discourses of the global, restructured city with its connotations of exclusion and polarisation (Soja, 2000); and manifested at the more localised scale in the state or corporate reconstruction of place (Chang, 1995; Pratiwo, 2000), impelled by service industry investments, redevelopment and the introduction of new policy visions.

These aggregated categories of change suggest at least the broad contours of tertiarisation and its contribution to multiscalar urban transformation within the Asia-Pacific metropolis. There is now a critical need to explore the more specific dimensions of impact among cities within the region, to identify features of commonality, as well as the contingent factors (including urban scale, urban structure, human capital, governance and policy) underpinning experiences of exceptionalism. Critical observers continue to decry the homogenising effects of globalisation and industrial restructuring, cultural as well as economic, which extend to some widely observed features of service growth. These include the office complexes of the central business district (CBD), and the proliferation of retail malls replete with the ubiquitous accoutrements of consumption, for example Starbucks, Benetton and Kentucky Fried Chicken. But there are varied and locally textured experiences of tertiarisation within the Asia-Pacific, embedded within distinctive local and regional models of society, governance and development (see Leaf, 1999 for the Hanoi case), which locate service industries as key markers of urban change in the region.

Emerging trajectories of the urban service economy

The next decade and beyond will see the continued expansion of services along the current pathways within Asia-Pacific cities and city-regions, but will also manifest important new (or significantly reconfigured) trajectories. As observed and documented in the advanced service economies of the mature Atlantic core, service industries within the Asia-Pacific will be reshaped by the relentless application of new production and telecommunications technologies; by the convergence of services, IT and manufacturing in advanced production systems; and by the competitive pressures of globalisation (see Beyers, 2000). These processes will in turn be mediated by state and local policy interventions, and by the distinctive structures of regional development culture.

The exact contours (and theoretical significance) of these inchoate service industry pathways are somewhat 'fuzzy' or evanescent. This condition is associated with contrasts in analytical emphases (for example, on institutional factors, the distinctive nature of production regimes, agglomerative processes and clustering propensity), variation in restructuring experiences from place to place, and episodes of industrial volatility (such as the rise and fall of the dot.coms in 'new media districts'; see Indergaard, 2003) which tend to inhibit adventurous retheorisation. What follows, therefore, is a discussion of the changing mix of factors likely to shape new service industry trajectories in the Asia-Pacific, together with some examples of shifts in service industry organisation and production models, and in service product orientations; as well as connections to larger processes of economic innovation among advanced societies.

Changing development factors and interdependencies Capital will continue to be important to the development of service industries within the Asia-Pacific. The region is a major global theatre of capital accumulation, reflecting in part the extraordinary growth of industrial production (in all sectors) and corporate profits, while the perception of even greater potential and prospects for favourable returns on investment will stimulate new flows of capital (although not without episodes of volatility, as we have seen recurrently over the past decade). Local and regional cultural practices and assets will become increasingly central to the formation of information industries and the knowledge-intensive workforce. In this regard Kim et al. recall Murakami's forecast that the production of 'consummatory' information (knowledge, art and language communication) may ultimately supplant 'instrumental' information (Murakami, 1992), and 'in this event, a city's spiritual and cultural life will have a profound influence on its future development' (Kim et al., 1997b: 10). Second, service production within leading economies of the Asia-Pacific will become more 'social' (Thrift and Olds, 1996), reflecting not only the emphasis on collaboration in complex, highly transactional service enterprises (such as in research, design and marketing), but also the intimate relations between knowledge-intensive production, consumption and amenity. Third, institutional factors will become critical to innovative service industry practice, a reality already acknowledged among leading economies such as Japan and Singapore. This institutional element of advanced service economies includes not only tertiary sector units (universities and colleges), but also special-purpose institutions of various kinds (industry associations, industry–university liaison offices, training agencies), and community-based organisations (CBOs). These institutions facilitate the development of human capital, the generation and transmission of knowledge, and the extension of opportunities for local area residents and workers.

Services–manufacturing co-dependency in advanced industrial production The producer service subsector will expand within Asia-Pacific cities, to meet the growing demand for intermediate services in advanced industrial production regimes throughout the region, and mimicking to a degree the classic shifts in divisions of production labour in leading economies favouring service occupations and task specialisations over 'operatives'. These tasks include production management, IT and technical services, the engineering and design of higher value-added industrial products (capital and consumer goods), sales and marketing. This larger role for specialised services in the progression of advanced industrial systems has been a feature of the Japanese economy for some time, and will be replicated with local variations in other jurisdictions. Shen, for example, has written about the growth of comprehensive service complexes (including producer, as well as consumer, services) established in Shanghai's large and rapidly growing automobile sector (Shen, 2004). Here, we observe a fundamental shift towards increasing services–manufacturing co-dependency and co-production within the Asia-Pacific (intra- and inter-firm, as well as inter-industry), a process in evidence both in 'late capitalist' systems and 'socialist market' economies in transition (Daniels and Bryson, 2002).

'Localising' producer service enterprises Over time, the ratio of foreign producer service suppliers to domestic enterprises within the Asia-Pacific is likely to change in favour of the latter. Urban centres within the region are developing mainstream producer service industries (such as advertising, marketing and accounting) which borrow initially from practices and protocols of leading international professional service companies, but are increasingly 'locally generative'; that is, derived from local business culture, and increasingly oriented to local service needs. Larissa Muller (2002) has demonstrated the feasibility of nurturing successful producer service industries in Thailand and other Southeast Asian states, combining foreign capital and expertise with local business acumen, creativity and knowledge. We can cite as another example the growth of advertising industries in China (Fowler, 2003). The development mode of producer service sectors within individual states and localities of the Asia-Pacific will become less 'generic', and, instead, will embody indigenous practices, cultures and norms. At the same time, service enterprises with advanced core competencies which seek deeper penetration of international markets can form partnerships with local firms. This form of international service collaboration is likely to form a larger part of the new service landscape in the Asia-Pacific in the twenty-first century, and will include higher education and other public enterprises, as well as business and industry.

The rise of the 'new urban cultural economy' The synthesis of foreign capital and local creativity points to another emerging trajectory of urban economic development, in the form of the 'new urban cultural economy' (after Scott, 1997; see also Zukin, 1994). The creative sector (and allied 'creative class', after Florida, 2002) comprises a diverse industrial and occupational structure, but includes (i) *creative design services* (for example, architecture, graphic artists and designers, fashion design and other consumer goods design); (ii) *creative production services* (computer-aided design services, model display and rendering, film and video production and postproduction services, commercial artists and photographers); and (iii) *industrial design services* (automotive, aerospace, naval and marine design, environmental systems design, engineering design) (Hutton, 2000).

These creative industries operate in some ways similar to those of mainstream business or producer services, but embody different divisions of labour, and are characterised by a much more intimate interface with goods production.[8] The creative industry workforce also tends to congregate in distinctive industrial clusters, with a strong connection to service consumption and amenities, notably (but not exclusively) within inner-city districts. The creative sector is acknowledged as an ascendant feature of advanced Western economies, but is now well represented within the Asia-Pacific. Well-known creative districts within the West Coast of North America include the Yaletown district in Vancouver, and the South Park–South of Market Area (SOMA) in San Francisco; but there are also important examples in Pacific Asia, including Singapore (Telok Ayer, situated within Singapore's Chinatown heritage district, immediately adjacent to the CBD, encompasses a 'spontaneous' creative cluster, while the adjacent Far East Square/China Square exemplifies an 'induced' creative/new economy site, shaped by corporate investment and state policy), and in central wards of Tokyo (for example, clusters situated near Shibuya and Shinjuku stations) (Hutton, 2004b).

Implications of the 'new economy' The idea of the new economy is in some respects elusive, in its defining industrial structure, organisation and behavioural characteristics and operating 'mechanics', and indeed there is a literature which refutes the concept of a new economy as an alternative construct to the advanced industrial (or postindustrial) economy.[9] There is also evidence of shifting grounds of conjecture and contestation. The new economy models propounded in the late twentieth century, influenced by the euphoria and hype associated with the 'tech boom' and the rise of the so-called 'dot.coms', insisted on a dominant 'hard technology' foundational idea, with innovation in information and communication technology (ICT) seen as the defining imperative of transformative change. In the wake of the technology sector crash of 2000, there has been a renewed interest in social, cultural, institutional and environmental factors, although a technological deepening of both the production and consumption sectors constitutes a legacy of the initial new economy phase of the 1990s. Here, the new economy is constructed as one in which 'information' is the critical input, 'knowledge' the key output, and with technology, social capital, progressive policy and institutional support comprising the chief motive factors of production.

Within the Asia-Pacific, there has been a powerful state attachment to the idea of the technology-driven new economy which has been manifested in a sequence of strategic (and in some cases grandiose) projects and schemes. Over the past quarter of a century, there has been a sequence of advanced-technology programmes in the Asia-Pacific, starting with Japan, the most advanced economy in Asia, and progressing down the national hierarchy to Taiwan, Malaysia and Vietnam, among other countries in the region. There are some leading examples of new economy ensembles within the internal spaces of the metropolis: Sam Park and Ji Sun Choi have written about the propulsive IT service cluster in the district of Gangnam, south of the Han River in Seoul, which has produced a new core area for the Seoul metropolitan region (Park and Choi, 2005). But the emphasis has been on large, stand-alone capital projects which in some ways mimic the intent and form of the large US science parks and research and development regions, and which are designed to accelerate state developmental and modernisation aspirations.

This developmental concept is exemplified by: the Japanese designation of technology development roles for cities (Edgington, 1989; Hayashi, 2004) and its mutation into the 'technolopolis' idea for Japanese urban areas and (putatively) as a model for other Asia-Pacific cities; the well-known case of the Hsinchu Science Park as a strategic developmental foundation of Taiwan's new economy; and the state promotion of the Multimedia Super Corridor (MSC) regional mega-project. The Malaysian MSC encompasses Putrajaya (the site of 'electronic government') and the 'smart city' of Cyberjaya, as well as a new international airport at Sepang. The massive investments committed to the realisation of this new high-technology vision for Malaysia were justified by political expressions of progress and modernisation (Corey, 1998, 2000), but also projected a state-imposed re-imaging experience with selective tendencies of privilege and exclusion (Bunnell, 2002a, 2002b). In Vietnam, the strategic plan for 'Saigon South', a 3300 hectare project on the southern perimeter of Ho Chi Minh City, encompasses high-cost and high-amenity residential development as well as science parks and branch operations of foreign universities. Citing the emphasis on the lead roles to be played by foreign direct investment (FDI) and skilled foreign workers, Leaf describes Saigon South as 'a mini-Singapore contained within the national territory of Vietnam, and the spatial expression of regional policy emulation for the new economy' (Leaf, 2004: 7). As another variant, regions within the Asia-Pacific are experimenting with the concept of the 'learning region' (Edgington, 1991), with its emphasis on education, human capital, and institutional 'thickness', as a pathway to the new economy.

Services and global city formation: primacy and contestation

Globalisation is often construed as a recent process, with the critical accelerative period encompassing the consequential episodes of privatisation, financial deregulation and market liberalisation in the 1980s. But even the modern history of globalisation takes in the expansion of European colonial empires in the nineteenth century, and the rapid growth of international banking and finance in the first decade of the twentieth century, while the experience of the Venetian, Dutch, Spanish and Portuguese empires points to an earlier provenance of the long-running globalisation project. The Asia-Pacific has become increasingly constructed as a salient theatre of globalisation, as evidenced in the importance of Asia-Pacific production territories and labour markets in the 'new international division of labour' (see, for example, Ho, 1991). Asia-Pacific economies are increasingly integrated within extended trading networks, capital flows and property markets, although intra-regional trading linkages continue to be important.

Cities have constituted essential elements of this extended sequence of globalisation processes and episodes, the theoretical significance of which was acknowledged initially by Peter Hall in his volume on 'world cities' (1966). These world (or global) cities function as centres of finance, control and administration, and incorporate in some cases entrepôt trade and industrial production. Over time, these urban centres developed the critical infrastructures and capital stocks required to manage extended financial and trading systems. These assets include the key multinational corporations, skilled personnel, buildings, institutions, governing bodies and social networks typically situated within central city complexes, established in international centres such as Venice, Milan, Amsterdam, Antwerp, Paris, New York and, above all, London. The changing fortunes of national economies in the twentieth century (and 'gaps' or niches in the market projection of the first-tier global cities) have also given rise to a 'second generation' of global cities which perform important international and national banking, finance and corporate control functions, a cohort which includes Frankfurt, Zurich, Chicago, Boston, San Francisco and Toronto, as well as a 'third generation' of emergent Asia-Pacific world or global cities.

Global cities within the Asia-Pacific region

Set against this extended periodisation of development within the Atlantic and Mediterranean realms, global city formation within the Asia-Pacific has a more recent character, reflecting *inter alia* the strength of regional patterns of trade, the subordinating effects of colonisation, and the historically inward scope of governance among major nation states, with Japan and China as chief exemplars. The postwar emergence of Asia-Pacific cities within the upper echelons of global cities has been influenced by the historical importance of urban primacy as a condition of national corporate and financial hegemony (for example, Bangkok); by the growth of financial and commercial sectors as underpinnings of accelerated industrialisation (Tokyo, Seoul); by endowments of critical infrastructures and institutional expertise accruing from colonial administration (Hong Kong); and by the state-directed expansion of global capacity (finance, business services, technology and higher education) in response to the perceived developmental limitations of regional entrepôt trade (Singapore). Asia-Pacific cities therefore comprise important additions to the roster of global cities (Hutton, 2001). Engagement in global service markets comprises an important dimension of the trajectories of tertiarisation within the region, although it must be acknowledged that nations within the region still experience major deficits in the balance of service trade (including Japan, the leading national economy in Pacific Asia; Ström, 2004). This penetration of Asia-Pacific service markets by external suppliers is evidenced by the profusion of foreign consultants in Chinese cities (Dolven, 2002).

Globalisation implies notions of competitive advantage and hierarchy, although these are by no means entirely immutable conditions. The representation of Asia-Pacific cities within hierarchies of world cities conventionally includes Tokyo as a member of a triumvirate of first-order global cities which includes London and New York, endorsed by Saskia Sassen (Sassen, 1991) and others. This ranking approach tends to heavily favour the global projection of corporate power and major banking and financial institutions and industries as measures of hierarchical status, with CBD office floorspace, producer service labour, and international air connections as ancillary indices of primacy and status.

The designation of Tokyo, London and New York suggests a convenient ordering of primacy for each of the leading continental aggregates within the global economy: Asia, Europe and North America, respectively. Despite implied notions of approximate equivalence in global primacy, however, these three cities exhibit quite significant elements of asymmetry and differentiation. Nor is it invariably the case that the fortunes of the three first-order global cities are linked by covariance: Tokyo, for example, was seriously affected by the so-called 'Asian' crises, but New York and London were relatively insulated from this shock (Doel and Beaverstock, 1999), underscoring the notion that financial markets are 'regional' as well as 'global'. London continues to enjoy long-established primacy in certain highly specialised global financial markets at national and global levels, notably foreign exchange and derivatives, acts as 'the global economy's bourse', and 'has a vital arbitrage role to play between Asia and North America' (Clark and Wójcik, 2001: 124).[10] New York is the dominant city of the world's largest national economy, and performs high-level global financial functions (such as investment banking, securities and stock exchanges), and ranks first in the volume of traded assets among the world's leading financial centres. For both London and New York, the centrality of highly specialised global city functions within the metropolitan economy is underscored by a broader development context of postindustrialism, following the massive contraction of Fordist manufacturing and ancillary industries and labour over the 1960s, 1970s and 1980s (see, for example, Hamnett (2003) for a perspective on postindustrialism in London, and Abu-Lughod (1999) for an analysis of New York's postindustrial trajectory).

In contrast, the Tokyo region still possesses a huge industrial base of advanced manufacturing in both the consumer and capital goods sectors, despite a significant 'hollowing-out' of capacity and employment over the last two decades. Tokyo's claim to membership within the highest echelon of the global city hierarchy is tied in no small measure to the banking and commercial requirements of Japan's industrial economy. The giant financial and industrial corporations arising from this world-scale manufacturing power underpinned in large part the global projection of market reach for Tokyo over the last four decades of the twentieth century. That said, higher-order services are clearly central to Tokyo's global status and national primacy, and to the continuing industrial restructuring of the Tokyo Metropolitan Region (Machimura, 1992).

A combination of generally high-growth performance, the expansion of trade in services as well as goods, and the (selective) liberalisation of markets has underpinned the development of Asia-Pacific metropolitan areas within the second tier of global cities, while other urban centres perform specialised service functions at the international level (Hutton, 2005). The global status of Osaka, Shanghai, Hong Kong, Singapore, Sydney, Los Angeles and San Francisco is defined increasingly by their specialised service sectors and employment, notably in banking and finance, property management, higher education, and gateway and producer services, rather than by manufacturing capacity, although these cities tend to have larger and more buoyant industrial production sectors than those of the old Atlantic core city-regions. Then there are cohorts of medium-size cities in the region which are highly tertiarised and 'global' in terms of international trade dependency, (in some cases) immigration flows and ethnicity, and a range of specialised service industries and institutions. These include cities such as Vancouver, San Diego, Melbourne, Brisbane, Auckland and Fukuoka, some of which (notably Seattle, with Microsoft) have truly global, propulsive-scale corporations. The urban hierarchy of the Asia-Pacific also contains a network of strategic ports, such as Pusan, Kaohsiung, Dalien, Vladivostok, Haiphong, Oakland, Long Beach and Tacoma. As a final category of international service specialisations, the Asia-Pacific comprises numerous travel and tourism centres that serve global markets, which include for the purposes of example

Honolulu, Kona, Gold Coast, Macao, Sapporo, Denpasar and Whistler (summarised from Hutton, 2004a).

Dynamics of contestation and destabilisation

Over the last decade or so the status of cities within the higher levels of the global urban hierarchy, including those situated within the Asia-Pacific, have been subject to recurrent challenge and crisis (Douglass, 2000). There have also been a series of shocks and stresses on the emergent service sectors of Asia-Pacific cities that have constituted a significant check to their growth trajectories. The pathways of service industry development within the Asia-Pacific have been subject to periodic disruption attributed to the rigours of global competition, domestic economic conditions, exogenous events (such as major disease vectors and natural disasters), and major shifts in policy, among other factors.

At the peak of the Asia-Pacific's urban hierarchy, Tokyo's control, banking and financial functions have been affected both by the stress of the long-running stagnation of the national economy, and by the shock of the 1997 Asian economic crisis. Principal Japanese property and integrated development corporations have experienced a deep downturn in their financial positions dating from the collapse of property markets of the early 1990s. Many of the major Japanese banks and financial corporations with headquarters in Tokyo have suffered huge capital losses and liquidity problems ensuing from this property crisis and more general malaise in the national economy. The large, integrated construction companies situated in Tokyo have been deeply affected by the collapse in demand for new buildings in most sectors, and especially in commercial development. Cancellation of major projects in the Tokyo region and elsewhere have also had an impact on prefectural and municipal governments, both in terms of forgone tax revenues from anticipated development, as well as the deferral of projects proposed for city-owned lands. The effects of these several episodes and processes should not be exaggerated, as Tokyo remains the dominant city-region in Pacific Asia. An investment-led recovery in Japan's economic fortunes (and Tokyo's, with it) may be in progress (*The Economist*, 2004).

But the diminution of bank liquidity and high levels of national and regional dependence exposed over the last decade or so might provoke a reconsideration of whether Tokyo can legitimately be placed with London and New York at the peak of the global city hierarchy.[11] Slippage in Tokyo's position in the key intermediate banking and financial sectors, coupled with the growth in the global projection of Los Angeles, may imply that Tokyo's status is now conditionally '1A', more or less co-equal with Los Angeles as the dominant global city of the Asia-Pacific region. Relative to London and New York, too, both Tokyo and Los Angeles have larger manufacturing sectors, including major clusters of high-technology industry, within the extended regional territory.[12] Each exhibits global capacity in the 'new cultural economy' (after Scott, 2000a), including film, video and music production, as well as a varied menu of cultural consumption activities, including Disneyland and other mega-scale attractions. In this scenario we can propose that the global city network of the Asia-Pacific is to an extent bipolar, with Tokyo and Los Angeles occupying the commanding heights of the urban hierarchy within the western and eastern littorals of the Pacific Rim, respectively.

This syndrome of global contestation and instability is not, however, confined to London, New York and Tokyo. Competition is related in part to the aspirations (and pressures) of rapid growth and transformative change, linked in important cases to aggressive development policy programmes, influenced by both domestic and international events and trends. Problems afflicting Tokyo in certain key market sectors have encouraged major regional centres, notably Shanghai, Seoul, Hong Kong and Singapore, to strive for larger shares of regional and international markets for banking, investment, gateway services, business travel and tourism, and higher education, both to augment market 'reach', and also to replace losses in capacity and employment among industries and firms in declining sectors. Each city is endeavouring to establish (or strengthen) competitive advantage in regional and global markets, by means of the standard policy mix of infrastructure investment (international airports, investments in digital connections and enhanced broadband capacity), fiscal measures enacted to attract inward investment, and global marketing; and also by investments in human and social capital (Douglass, 1991).

As a feature of the discourse of globalisation within the Asia-Pacific, cities assert primacy in areas in which they believe they enjoy a demonstrable measure of competitive advantage, and service industries and functions are ineluctably central to this exercise. To illustrate, Shanghai's representatives draw attention to the astonishing growth in world-scale commercial infrastructure situated in the Pudong project, and the putative advantages of comprehensive urban re-imaging associated with this urban mega-project; while Hong Kong tends to underscore its regional competitive advantage in human capital, and more particularly its highly educated, internationally savvy, and largely bilingual workforce. Fukuoka, a highly tertiarised city in Kyushu, proclaims its regional advantages in interconnectivity ('Global Reach') and specialised services, including consumption as well as production industries (with a complementary postindustrial lifestyle), in contrast to the somewhat grittier, obsolescent industrial identity of its neighbouring city, Kitakyushu. Within Southeast Asia, Kuala Lumpur's officials assign great value to both the substantive and symbolic representation of its new commercial infrastructure, notably the Petronas Towers, which represents the 'current phase' of service industry development; while Singapore, the region's most advanced service centre, underscores its leading-edge status in new policy discourses which emphasise higher education (including joint ventures with major foreign universities; see Olds and Thrift, 2005) and creative and cultural industries, which exemplify the 'next phase' of tertiarisation within the Asia-Pacific.

Limits to the 'global city vision' in the Asia-Pacific?

This pervasive emphasis on competitive advantage as a means of maintaining (or enhancing) global positioning in finance and corporate control serves the interest of some constituencies, and success in this domain is likely to produce benefits to the broader public, although this will largely depend on the strength of regional inter-industry linkages, wage levels of constituent industries, and the nature of taxation regimes and redistributive policies. Further, the growth of Asia-Pacific economies will generate continuing demand for specialised, intermediate services, offering significant new potential for the region's major business centres.

There are, however, significant limitations to a single-minded commitment to this strategy of privileging global-level corporate control and finance, including issues of competition, costs and conceptualisation. From the perspective of competition, the experience of corporate mergers and takeovers among the Western economies since the 1980s, in addition to the impact of technology on middle managers and clerical workers, has produced a legacy of job-shedding in many cities, as well as a reconcentration of corporate power in first-order world centres and primate national cities, often to the detriment of second- and third-order cities. While the higher-order service market within the Asia-Pacific presents considerable opportunity for growth, the 'big players' like Tokyo, Shanghai and Hong Kong have made such enormous commitments that smaller centres will have problems competing effectively for shares of this market. At the same time, these second- and third-order cities can compete in international niche-level service markets (sometimes in collaboration with larger enterprises), and can benefit from the localisation of producer services, as described in the preceding section.[13] These smaller (and generally less costly, in terms of staffing and premises) business centres may also be candidates for the growing market in back offices and call centres associated with globalisation processes, as evidenced in China, Southeast Asia and India.

A related problem of unconstrained global city competition within the Asia-Pacific structured narrowly on the lines of the corporate control and international banking sector lies in the area of associated costs (environmental and social, as well as financial). Property markets in Asia-Pacific cities are strewn with the legacies of grandiose visions of corporate control and global projection, with the MM 21 development site in Yokohama constituting a vivid example. There is also a record of reckless expenditure on associated gateway service infrastructure to acknowledge, as exemplified by the proliferation of airports in the Pearl River Delta, which has compromised agricultural land resources and green spaces, as well as overextending public budgets (and displacing other public expenditure priorities). Negative externalities can take the form of inflated land prices and displacement effects, including the dislocation of vulnerable residential communities, local labour market mismatches, and the classic features of social polarisation and class conflict which Saskia Sassen identifies as hallmarks of the global city phenomenon (Sassen, 1999).

There are also conceptual problems associated with the narrowly structured idea of the 'corporate' global city in the Asia-Pacific, relating to scope, scale and structure. First, as K.C. Ho has observed, head-office functions within Asian cities are not in most cases principally concerned with global corporate control, but are largely directed to the management of intra-regional enterprise, trade and investment (Ho, 1998). These are important service functions, to be sure, and confer a range of benefits upon host cities with respect to employment, incomes and revenues, but these firms are in many cases only selectively engaged in markets beyond the Asia-Pacific.

Second, corporate power within the region is not in all respects physically embedded within the CBDs of specific cities, with respect to the locus of entrepreneurship, control, decision making and the exchange of critical business knowledge and signals, but is, rather, more spatially diffused within inter-city business networks defined by kinship, ethnicity and personal association (see Yeung, 2002). This is especially the case for actors operating within the 'Greater China' economic sphere. As an example of the spatial fluidity of 'Sino-capitalism', Koon (1997) has described the operating characteristics of Robert Kuok's empire of service industry corporations, which include commodity trading firms, financial services (especially insurance and securities brokers), hotel ownership and management (including the luxury Shangri-La chain), property development, shipping, retail sales, media and entertainment. Kuok's management centres include Singapore and Kuala Lumpur, but the channels of international connectivity and important business relations extend to Paris, Vancouver and Santiago, among other cities.[14] In another well-known example, Kris Olds has written of the importance of Li Ka-Shing's corporate and business networks, situated in 'transnational cultures' (Olds, 2001: 178), in the globalisation of inner-city spaces in Shanghai (Lijiazui Central Finance District) and in Vancouver (Concord Pacific Place). Olds stresses that these specific experiences have been shaped by the contingency of place and individual human agency, and by the complex interaction of global and local forces, rather than by some distanciated and mechanistic process of capital accumulation set out in the more abstract treatments of globalisation. In other cases, the locus of entrepreneurship and control exhibits a place-specific mélange of 'embedded' and 'transnational' attributes (see Yeung and Li, 2000 for case studies of the Shanghai experience). These examples demonstrate the locationally 'slippery' concept of corporate control and investment within the Asia-Pacific, which is to a significant extent situated within diffuse personal networks, and shaped by the 'global space of flows', as opposed to being fixed immutably in specific cities.

As a final comment on the narrowly corporatist vision of the global city, the international role of city-regions is not confined to head offices and the higher levels of banking and finance, which are in any case restricted to a relatively limited range of urban centres; but, rather, comprises a far more extensive suite of service industries and institutions. These include, for the purposes of illustration: producer services, administration and international agencies (including social agencies and non-governmental organizations), tourism, advanced-technology services, creative services and applied design, education and the knowledge sector, and cultural production and heritage (after Hutton, 2004a: 9). As George Lin observes, too, the expansion of more general-purpose, locally serving business and consumer services will be an important feature of development for the region's high-growth cities and transitional urban economies, such as Guangzhou (Lin, 2005). Over the longer term, an urban development model which incorporates policies for a more balanced set of service industries is likely to yield a commensurately broader set of benefits for the urban community as a whole.

Conclusion: emerging policy agendas and research orientations

The purpose of this chapter has been to present a profile of service industry development trajectories within the Asia-Pacific, including both broader developmental contours, as well as examples of more nuanced and place-specific aspects. Drawing on service industry research, Asian urban scholarship, and an emerging literature which effectively synthesises experiences of tertiarisation and urbanisation within the Asia-Pacific, the narrative and analysis has addressed three salient, related themes: first, interdependencies between the expansion of services and contemporary processes of urban change within the Asia-Pacific; second, a critique of services and global city formation within the region, including an acknowledgement of the costs and limitations of the 'global city vision'; and, third, as adumbrated in each of these sections, evidence of new discourses of policy and planning for service development. In each of these thematic areas, the aim has been to suggest some features of innovation in the ways that these processes and issues are constructed in this increasingly important theatre of urban transformation.

First, the review of new scholarship on services and urban and regional development within the Asia-Pacific demonstrates the powerful roles service industries play in multiscalar processes of structural change within the region. At one level, the signs of urban tertiarisation are readily discerned in the formation of central corporate complexes, in the expansion of gateway infrastructure and systems, and in the growth of service sector labour and related social groups. Outwardly at least the experience of service development within Asia-Pacific cities mimics the earlier examples of established 'service cities' like Chicago, Toronto and Boston, although even here there are significant departures in terms of the scale and pace of service-led development.

But beyond these familiar parameters of urban transformation lies a far more complex landscape of causality and outcome, shaped by local social conditions, governance and policy systems, and the coincidence of service growth with ongoing processes of industrial urbanism. Our survey of innovation in service industry formation within the Asia-Pacific also discloses evidence of new service development trajectories, including creative, cultural and technology-intensive 'new economy' formations among the lead city-regions, as well as the convergence of advanced services, IT and manufacturing in advanced industrial production systems. The differentiation of recent experiences of tertiarisation from place to place, and the complexities of emergent service trajectories, serve to compromise the idea of deploying postindustrialism as a master narrative of development throughout much of the Asia-Pacific. There is now an exigent need to establish comparative research projects on urban services development within the region, to more fully depict aspects of exceptionalism and contingency, and to explore new theoretical possibilities, contructed upon a foundation of more intensive and richly contextuated cases studies of service industry formation.

Second, the last decade or so has seen the emergence of a 'third generation' of global cities within the Asia-Pacific, driven by the dynamism of regional economies and the trading system as a whole, the expansion of service industries (which are more closely linked to cities than is the case for manufacturing industries), the emergence of the Asia-Pacific as a leading sphere of globalisation, and by particularly energetic state and local policy commitments. The salient features of this process include the emergence of Tokyo and Los Angeles as cities at the peak of a bipolar Asia-Pacific urban hierarchy; the ascendancy of Seoul, Shanghai, Hong Kong, Singapore and Sydney as 'world cities', defined increasingly by advanced services (rather than manufacturing capacity); and the global aspirations of a much larger roster of cities in the region. Given the continuing expansion of the Asia-Pacific region as a whole, and the relative stagnation of many of the mature economies and cities of the Atlantic core, there is considerable potential for growth in the global status and function of Asia-Pacific cities. This global capacity may be constructed from generative growth processes within the region, as well as from the competitive advantage of some Asia-Pacific cities which enables them to wrest larger shares of global markets in intermediate finance, corporate control functions and other higher-order, high-value services. But this 'global potential' is not unlimited – corporate mergers and communications technology can produce centralising outcomes – and striving towards more exalted levels of the global corporate hierarchy for many cities tends to incur progressively higher costs, in terms of capital expenditures and overdistended budgets, as well as social and environmental costs.

Finally, this critical perspective on complex services-led development trajectories and globalisation aspirations characteristic of many Asia-Pacific cities leads naturally to a consideration of policy futures in the region. To date, especially in Pacific Asia, the service development model has echoed the heroic scale and orientation of the preceding industrialisation development paradigm, with huge financial commitments, a dominant export-trade orientation, and an implicit discounting of opportunity, social and environmental costs. Although governance cultures and policy systems vary considerably among the Asia-Pacific's states and city-regions, there is now a clear need to explore innovative, integrative policy models which incorporate more progressive regulatory and distributive elements. Global city initiatives, expressed in the imagery of urban mega-projects, ultra high-rise point towers, and 'stand-alone' exurban new economy spaces should be complemented by endogenous development measures. These innovative and forward-looking policy ventures will acknowledge the critical developmental roles played by human capital, the quality of education, access to amenity, housing market access and quality of life factors characteristic of the most advanced service economies and cities.

Notes

1. For a more extensive synthesis and presentation of research on services and cities in the Asia-Pacific, see Daniels et al. (eds) (2005).
2. Here I refer to the trilogy of models advanced to explain the generative forces of urban transformation and implications for the economy and social morphology of the city over the last three decades of the twentieth century: postindustrialism, post-Fordism and postmodernism. Each of these theoretical constructs was vigorously contested from a number of ideological and disciplinary vantage points. But they served, individually and collectively, to re-orient urban research and to provide a set of theories against which to test the contemporary trajectories of cities and urban communities.
3. Dense, multi-channel linkages and flows connect the cities and urban societies of Pacific Asia, North America and Australasia, including those of ethnicity, kinship and culture, underpinned by international migration, and the flows of information and capital (including investment and remittances), as well as by increasing trade, travel and tourism. The strength of these flows and linkages, and their implications for international interdependency, and intersections with broader industrial restructuring processes, support an affirmative response to the question of spatial scope, inclusivity and definition, as posed here. As another dimension of linkage, service industries comprise dynamic forces for urban growth and transformative change among cities situated along the western, southern and eastern margins of the Pacific Rim, in contrast to the generally more lethargic performance of cities within the Atlantic domain, in which service sectors have attained a state of maturity. Finally, a generously inclusive approach to the spatiality of the Asia-Pacific enables comparison of cities separated by vast tracts of global space, but which exhibit defining commonalities in trajectories of service development: the examples of such cities as Hong Kong, Singapore, Osaka, Fukuoka, Sydney, Melbourne, Brisbane, Seattle, San Diego, San Francisco and Vancouver come to mind. In each case, advanced, specialised service industries and employment occupy a more exalted position within the urban economic base and labour force than is the case in proximate regions and hinterland areas. (See in this regard O'Connor et al., 2001 for a discussion of the Australian case.)
4. The effects of postindustrialism were observed throughout the metropolis among advanced societies, but the most intense (and in many ways defining) experiences were felt in the metropolitan core, comprising the CBD, CBD fringe and inner city. A restatement of the transformational processes and conditions of the postindustrial core included (i) processes of industrial restructuring, comprising the collapse of Fordist manufacturing in the inner city and the rapid growth of a new specialised service economy, accompanied by the internationalisation of the core's property market, and market (re)reorientation of CBD service enterprises increasingly in favour of export, rather than domestic, markets; (ii) an asymmetrical respatialisation of the postindustrial metropolitan core, with investment skewed towards the corporate office complex of the CBD, and accompanied by disinvestment, decline and social polarisation in much of the CBD fringe and inner city; (iii) production of a dominant modernist urban form, represented by the growth of the high-rise office complex of the CBD, the 'supreme expression of the functionalist "machine city" of advanced capitalism'; (iv) a comprehensively reordered division of production labour in the metropolitan core, comprising the rapid expansion of employment in the intermediate (producer) service industries, incorporating a highly occupationally segmented office labour force including executive, managerial, professional, technical, sales and clerical labour; and (v) the ascendancy of a postindustrial social class, largely along the lines predicted by Daniel Bell (and elaborated in the later work on urban social class change by Neil Smith, Chris Hamnett, David Ley and others) (adapted from T.A. Hutton, 'Post-industrialism, post-modernism and the reproduction of Vancouver's Central Area: retheorising the 21st century city', *Urban Studies*, 2004: **41**(10): 1953–82.
5. The force of employment change and implications for urban social class over the past three decades has tended to strongly endorse the defining postulates of Bell's postindustrial society model. The changing dimensions of the urban labour force have incontestably favoured service employment (including service-type occupations within the manufacturing sector) among advanced, restructured metropolitan

cities. Chris Hamnett observes that in London, once one of the world's leading industrial cities, only about 10 per cent of the employment is in manufacturing, as conventionally measured. Arguably, of course, service workers, especially those in the production sector, are part of the 'industrial labour force' in a broader sense. But the skill sets, task orientations, social behaviours and housing demand between most service workers and 'industrial workers' in manufacturing are sufficiently differentiated as to support a distinctive social class designation.

6. Jean Gottmann introduced the concept of the quaternary sector in the 1970s as a means of distinguishing the advanced, informational and 'transactional' service industries and occupations from the more 'routinised' tertiary services, such as most retail and personal services. In the 1980s the conceptual division of services into 'producer' (intermediate sector) and 'consumer' (final demand) industries was established as an analytical convention for service industry research, but Gottmann's idea of the quaternary sector represents a benchmark in the evolution of service scholarship.
7. For a discussion of typologies of service sector/industry policy approaches, including regulatory and developmental models, see Daniels et al. (1991).
8. For further discussion of this defining feature of the design-based services, see Hutton (2000) and Bryson et al. (2004a).
9. A number of scholars have asserted the 'novelty' of the new economy with respect to differentiated attributes of industrial regimes (see, for example, Brynjolfson and Kahin (2000), and the role of IT in reshaping markets and the structure of business organisations (for example, Shapiro and Varian, 1999), while others are more sceptical about the ostensibly revolutionary nature of the new economy (see, for example, Mowery, 1997; Gordon, 2000; and Slater, 2001).
10. Gordon Clark and Darius Wójcik (2001) track the pessimistic response of the London financial markets to the Asian crises through the columns of Barry Riley of the Financial Times (FT), relative to the more buoyant response of the *Wall Street Journal*. This may be associated with the contrasting temperaments and reporting styles of the business press in London and New York, or broader national psychologies. But less than a year after the publication of Clark and Wójcik's article in the *Journal of Economic Geography* (January 2001), the 9/11 World Trade Center attackers struck a serious blow against New York and its financial and commercial sector, compromising significant elements of the City's human capital, and demolishing an area of floor space equivalent to that of the CBD of many mid-size cities, as well as generating enormous personal tragedy. The IRA (Irish Republican Army) attacks on London in the 1970s and 1980s underscore the particular allure of high-profile city commercial centres for those seeking to influence the political agenda by undermining the broader public confidence and sense of security.
11. Taylor (2004) identifies a taxonomy of 'leading world cities' which includes producer services, listings of multinational corporations, 'cultural globalization', 'political globalization' and 'social globalization', as well as the conventional measures of primacy in global banking and finance. As might be expected, rankings of cities within each of these categories varies, but Taylor concludes that 'clearly above all others, there are London and New York . . . they emerge here as the most important "all-round" global contributors' (Taylor, 2004: 5).
12. I am indebted to my colleague John Friedmann for reminding me that manufacturing capacity was an element of his global city nomenclature for his seminal 1986 article on the 'global city hypothesis', along with other measures of global city status which included banking and finance, head offices, business services and population. Given the immensity of contraction in manufacturing among many European and North American city-regions, it may be that Asian cities such as Tokyo, Seoul and Shanghai now provide a better 'fit' for Friedmann's 1986 taxonomy than most of the mature 'Atlantic core' cities.
13. To illustrate, Vancouver has 'lost' most of its corporate control functions in the resource sector through a series of mergers, takeovers and acquisitions, while Seattle recently suffered the relocation of Boeing's head office to Chicago, a higher-order business centre (although Seattle still has the global headquarters of Microsoft, Weyerhaeuser and Starbucks, as well as a significant component of Boeing's administrative, engineering and manufacturing divisions). At the same time, both Vancouver and Seattle have achieved significant export platforms in producer services (see Beyers et al., 1985 and Beyers, 2002a for Seattle; Davis and Hutton, 1991 for Vancouver).
14. As Koon observes, Robert Kuok's business orientation towards luxury hotels, securities brokerage, communications and supermarket retailing 'reflects his confidence that Eastern Asia's rapidly growing middle class . . . would offer unprecedented opportunities in consumer service industries' (1997: 167). Further, Kuok's shift into securities brokerage 'exemplifies an innovative application of Chinese culture as a business input' (ibid.), as it mainly includes relations with enterprises owned by his partners in business and 'friends in the Chinese business network' (ibid.).

10 Service development in transition economies: achievements and missing links

*Metka Stare**

Introduction

Since 1980, service activities in developed countries have had to accommodate to the pervasive trends of technological change and globalisation. In addition, transition economies had to face the gap in economic development, which was particularly evident in the poorly developed service sector. Catching up a moving target presents difficult and challenging tasks for transition economies, bearing in mind the legacies of past developments.

Before the start of the reform process, the socio-economic system of transition economies was characterised by state ownership, which hindered private initiative. The central planning system added further to suppressing entrepreneurship and innovation, which foster efficiency and growth. Enterprises were isolated from international markets, and foreign trade was carried out through state trading companies. Thus the behaviour of enterprises was not driven by competition, but by the implementation of the central plan. State planning authorities imposed an excessive degree of specialisation in production and an artificial division of labour.[1] Manufacturing was favoured over other economic activities in line with a 'material concept' of production. Consequently, the supply of services was deficient. Intermediate services were provided in-house by large manufacturing enterprises (for example, transport, some elementary business services) or by centralised state enterprises (distribution, financial services). Providers of services were not exposed to competition from local or foreign suppliers, hence the quality of services was poor. The range of consumer services was also limited.

Market-oriented reforms introduced as part of a broader socio-political transformation initiated the process of fast structural changes that were long restrained. Privatisation, regulatory reforms, liberalisation and the introduction of competition were the major drivers of systemic change. Gradually, mechanisms of economic coordination shifted from state intervention to market allocation and the private sector became dominant. Nevertheless, the process of establishing a fully functioning market economy that is capable of sustainable growth was weighed down with difficulties and its dynamics differed between transition economies. To some extent this process also depended on the speed of integration of transition economies to international relations. The Central and Eastern European Countries[2] (CEECs) took the lead in that regard. They embarked on the process of gradual approach to European Union (EU) membership, along with market-oriented reforms that gave impetus to regulatory reforms and institutional changes. At the beginning of the 1990s some of the CEECs concluded the Europe Agreements with the EU, which provided for non-reciprocal free trade in favour of the CEECs. The process of negotiations for full EU membership later supplemented these agreements. During this process the CEECs harmonised legislation with that of the EU and to a large extent accomplished structural and institutional reforms towards fully fledged market economies. They increased significantly their overall openness to trade and attracted large inflows of foreign direct investment (FDI). In May 2004, eight CEECs took a historic step and became new EU members while Romania and Bulgaria still have to complete structural and institutional reforms. Through integration with the EU, the CEECs are becoming a part of the developed world in which services play an essential role in driving competitiveness and growth.

Transition reforms had a major impact on the growth of services in transition economies. There are few areas where the changes in the past 10–15 years have been as rapid and intensive as the transformation of services in such economies. New services, not available in the past, were introduced by local or foreign suppliers, and some traditional services were externalised from large manufacturing enterprises. As a result, the dynamics of firm growth was the highest in services. Since the beginning of the 1990s the service sector in transition economies has made a big leap forward in terms of value added and employment, although the experience of individual countries differs greatly. Notwithstanding the progress achieved with regard to service development, there remain important drawbacks which undermine the efficiency and competitiveness of transition economies in an increasingly globalised world economy.

The trends of service development in developed countries in the 1990s also point to dynamic changes, which are attributable to different driving forces. The dynamic is reflected not so much in the growing share of services in GDP, although that is still increasing, but much more in the rapid growth of knowledge-intensive services and in increased interlinkages between services and other sectors of the economy (Peneder et al., 2001: 9). The growth of services goes hand in hand with a focus on the search for solutions to problems made possible through the convergence of goods and service production (Bannon, 2002: 122). The outsourcing of services is gaining ground, strengthening the competition and consequently improving the quality of services. In addition, advances in information and communication technology (ICT) have revolutionised the production process in services, significantly improving their efficiency, enabling the introduction of new business models and delivery channels. Some services are being outsourced globally or provided from shared service centres in low-cost locations elsewhere in the world, which poses challenges to employment in both home and host countries.

The rising importance of services and of their linkages with goods production is also seen at the firm level. Large manufacturing enterprises use an increasing number of different services in their business processes. On the other hand, most of their turnover is accounted for by the sales of services. The service sector is increasingly investing in research and development (R&D). Innovation in services is growing as well, providing a strong impetus to competition at the national and international levels. During the 1990s services increased their share in international trade, but even more impressive was the internationalisation of service activities through FDI. Finally, with the introduction of the General Agreement of Trade in Services (GATS) in 1995 services were, for the first time in history, integrated into multilateral regulatory and institutional frameworks.

How can the progress of transition economies in services be assessed and aligned with the major trends of service development in the developed world? The aim of this chapter is to provide some elementary explanation in that regard, concentrating on the recent experience of the CEECs. However, it cannot capture all the specific and diverse features of service sector transformation in individual countries. In the first section, theoretical concepts are addressed that explain the role of services in development and particularly those concepts most relevant for the development of services in transition economies. The analysis of structural changes regarding value added and employment in the CEECs in the 1990s serves to illustrate the rapid shift towards services. Also, we explore the main driving forces underpinning the accelerated growth of services in the CEECs since the beginning of the 1990s. The chapter focuses on key delays and deficiencies representing the missing links of service development in the CEECs, considered from the perspective of the dominant trends in the world. We address the drawbacks in the development of knowledge-intensive services against the background of the main determinants of these services' development. It will be argued that, notwithstanding the success achieved in service sector restructuring in the CEECs, historical patterns and soft elements embedded in the previous socio-economic system are slowing down their ability to successfully follow global trends in service development. The chapter concludes with a discussion of the future focus on service sector development in transition economies and of relevant policy responses.

Emerging service sector: from past to present

Overindustrialisation was the main feature of the past economic system in the transition economies, hence the service sector was largely neglected. Services were not considered important in terms of growth, competitiveness or development. Based on an ideological concept of the non-productive character of services, they were assigned a residual role in all aspects of economic considerations. The disregard of services was reflected in the lack of data and analysis, a poor understanding of their role in development and an absence of policies aimed at service development.

The reason why the service sector was underdeveloped and inefficient has to be sought primarily in the lack of economic conditions conducive to service development within the past economic system. This has to do with the very essence of the former pattern of economic growth and development and the corresponding mechanisms to implement and manage it, which inhibited the development of market forces. The division of labour emerging in this context did not favour market relations and the consequent comprehensive system of inter- and intra-sectoral interlinkages, which characterises a market economy. In the absence of market forces and market relations and in a highly centralised economy, lacking entrepreneurship and innovation, and isolated from external markets, there was no room for the development of service activities (Ghibutiu, 2000: 307–8). Only after market forces were unleashed in transition economies could the process of structural changes towards an increased role for the service sector start. For a proper understanding of the peculiarities of service sector development in the CEECs during transition, some remarks need to be made about the theoretical framework.

Theoretical concepts relevant for service sector development

In the past, services in transition economies were treated in line with Marxist theory, which stressed the dominance of 'material production' in generating value and surplus value. The latter was seen as the key element determining the productivity of material production. On the other hand, services were considered unproductive, except for some categories such as transportation and maintenance. This was reflected by the 'material production system' of accounts adopted by centrally planned economies, which divided the economy into two spheres of activity: productive (or material) and unproductive. The unproductive sphere encompassed the so-called 'non-material services' (for example, finance and banking, insurance, legal and advisory services, tourism and recreation, most professional services, education, health, public administration and defence). Most of these activities were assigned a low priority by the governments of centrally planned economies, given the belief that they did not generate national income (UNCTAD, 1994: 30). The concept of unproductive services could be traced back to Adam Smith to whom services were synonymous with unproductive consumption (Delaunay and Gadrey, 1992: 11–14).

The above theoretical concepts had a decisive impact on producing a negative perception of services in transition economies and influenced economic policy formulation. Due to the low level of economic and cultural ties of these countries with the developed world, this perception has not been affected by the evolution of the theoretical concepts related to service understanding or by the increasing role of services in developed market economies. After the introduction of political changes in the late 1980s, the concepts of material production and of unproductive sphere were quickly abandoned in formal institutional systems; however, they continue to cast a long shadow over efforts to understand the role of services in transition economies.

At the beginning of the transition process, the development of services was still perceived in line with the Allan G.B. Fisher (1935) and Colin Clark (1940) [1951] concept of a stages approach to shifts in employment across economic sectors. Accordingly, it was expected that the weight of the tertiary sector in employment would increase spontaneously and in parallel with income growth and changes in consumer preferences.[3] Economic policy was in general shaped along the principles of the neoclassical theory of market economy, meaning that no specific incentives were provided in favour of service sector development, not even for highly backward services. Apart from that, the poor level of market functioning and institutional set-up in transition economies could not create an environment supportive of the development of services. Debate about the drivers of economic growth and competitiveness in transition economies paid little or no attention to the role of services in that regard. After the introduction of market reforms, services grew more dynamically than income, which hardly fits into the stages approach to service development. Already in the 1980s, it had become increasingly evident in developed economies that economic growth is not about growth or decline of three vertically separated economic sectors (primary, secondary and tertiary) but about their horizontal interlinkages and integration (Giarini and Stahel, 1993: 27). Due to the lack of understanding of the different interlinkages of services and of their effects on growth and development, the discussion in transition economies easily subscribed to deindustrialisation delusion.

Indeed, the decline of employment in manufacturing was often interpreted as harmful deindustrialisation undermining economic strength, due to the low productivity of services. Such attitudes and reactions illustrate the invisible power and perseverance of old ideological concepts concerning the unproductive character of services. They were probably the consequence of rapid changes in economic structure that could not quickly be adopted and assimilated into the mindset of policy makers, managers or researchers who were educated in a different socio-economic environment and were still susceptible to placing an emphasis on the 'material elements' of production and economy.

Notwithstanding the rapid tertiarisation in transition economies, the perception of services at the policy level failed to recognise the increasing interlinkages between economic sectors of the economy and the heterogeneous character of services. Consequently, the rise in intermediate demand for services as an important accelerator of service growth was overlooked. According to Momigliano and Siniscalco, the growth of employment in services is increasingly driven by the demand of industry for intermediate services (1982: 298). Also, little attention was paid in transition economies to the fact that industrial production is being changed radically and that services dominate goods production (Gershuny, 1987: 112). Services are industries that play a key and dynamic role in the economy and accelerate growth in other sectors (Riddle, 1986: 79). With the growing interdependence of industry and services their production processes converge, and this is becoming the key element of growth (Miles and Wyatt, 1991: 15). There is substantial evidence now that services are not only central to production, transportation and consumption of goods, but they also serve as engines of economic growth in their own right (Bryson et al., 2004b: 243).

The complementarity of goods and service production is gradually being understood and comprehended in transition economies even though to a much lesser extent by economic policy actors than by advanced businesses. We argue that the lack of awareness of the interlinkage that exists between services and manufacturing in transition economies, especially the role of knowledge-intensive services, is one of the causes of drawbacks and deficiencies in service development that affect the efficiency of the whole economy. This is elaborated in the following sections.

The transformation of the service sector in the 1990s: trends and underlying factors

Transition economies share many characteristics related to service sector development in the past and during the transition period. A distinctive feature of the pre-transition period was a low level of economic activity in services. The share of services in GDP and employment was small compared to both developed countries and economies at similar levels of development (Illeris, 1996: 162–3). Apart from the low levels of market services in the centrally planned systems, their character was entirely different from that in market economies. It is claimed that transition from a centralised to a market economy has to do with the transformation of the old service sector into a market-oriented one (Keren and Ofer, 2002: 16). Transition economies were faced with the need, on the one hand, to adapt and modernise existing services, and on the other, to adopt and assimilate new services that did not exist under the previous political and institutional system.

In the late 1980s, the CEECs[4] embarked on a process of market-oriented reforms that resulted in huge socio-economic changes. Increasing tertiarisation was one of the consequences, displacing manufacturing, which was for many decades the dominant sector of their economies. With the introduction of the reform process, the institutional and business environment began to change and to adapt gradually to the standards of market economies. In some areas, services compensated for the void left by the collapse of central planning (Facchini and Segnana, 2003: 840). Liberalisation strengthened external competition, while deregulation encouraged local competition and put pressure on existing suppliers. Privatisation and the establishment of a number of small and medium-sized enterprises (SMEs) created a new ownership and size structure of enterprises, and the role of SMEs was important in the shift from industry to services. In addition new services or new forms of their provision emerged (Pietras, 2002: 146).

As a result, the most dynamic changes in CEECs were related to the increased role of services bearing heavily on shifts in GDP and employment structure. These changes took place in parallel with a strong economic downturn in the first half of the 1990s, while the recovery followed only in the second half of the decade. By 1999, GDP levels in most CEECs, except in Poland, were still lagging behind, or were close to, 1989 levels (UNECE, 2000: 225). Structural changes in the CEECs brought about by the transition were rather dramatic owing to the neglect of services in these countries in the past. In the 1988–99 period, the share of services in GDP increased substantially in all CEECs due also to radical changes in relative prices. In 1988 the average share of services in GDP in these countries was 36.9 per cent, but by 1999 this had increased to 61.2 per cent; the respective shares for the EU were 66 and 71.6 per cent. This indicates that in the 1990s the CEECs were broadly catching up with the EU (Facchini and Segnana, 2003: 840). The rise in the share of services in employment was less radical but still high.[5] In the 1990–2002 period, the share of service employment in the CEECs increased between 4 percentage points in Romania and 13.5 percentage points in the Slovak Republic (WIIW, 2003: 102–12). Slower growth of employment in relation to growth of value added in services can partly be explained by the fact that surplus workers who had been laid off from industry or agriculture could not be absorbed easily by service activities. On one hand, the size of companies in manufacturing differs from that in the service sector while on the other, skills mismatch also has an impact.[6]

The shift in employment from industry to services was characteristic for all CEECs, however the intensity of change in the 1990s differed depending on the level of employment in services at the beginning of the period and on trends in agriculture employment. This is confirmed by the comparison of patterns in individual countries (Figure 10.1). In Hungary where services already occupied a dominant share of employment in 1992, the shift towards service employment was rapid only up to 1995. In the Czech Republic the share of service employment increased dynamically throughout the 1990s on account of

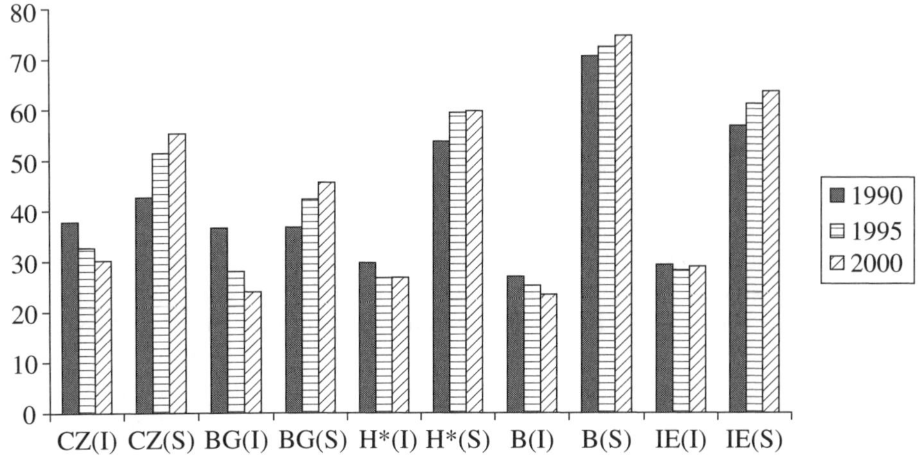

Notes: CZ – Czech Republic, BG – Bulgaria, H – Hungary, B – Belgium, IE – Ireland.
* Data for 1992 instead of 1990.

Sources: WIIW (2003) and Eurostat, NewCronos database (2003).

Figure 10.1 Shift in employment in industry (I) and services (S), 1990, 1995 and 2000 (%)

diminishing shares of employment in both manufacturing and agriculture. On the other hand, the steep decline in employment in industry in Bulgaria was compensated not only by shifts towards service employment but also by rising employment in agriculture. Contrary to the patterns in the CEEC, the EU countries experienced much slower growth of the share of service employment in the 1990s given the fact that it had been increasing gradually during the post- Second World War period.

The overall growth of the service sector in the CEECs since the 1990s can be attributed to the combination of the following major factors:

- market-oriented reforms (privatisation, regulatory reform, liberalisation) required new services not available in the previous economic system. This stimulated the establishment of a number of private enterprises in services (for example, asset valuation, auditing, management consultancy, language schools and so on);
- the need to adjust industrial production and business processes to technological modernisation (the introduction of ICT and other technologies) necessitated specialised services (for example, computer aided manufacturing, computer aided design, introduction of the EAN code (European Article Numbering System – barcodes, introduction of quality standards);
- organisational change towards the externalisation of non-core services from big companies to newly established small enterprises, due to the dissolution and downsizing of large industrial conglomerates (for example, security and cleaning services, catering, transport services);
- increased demand for services (marketing, advertising, public relations) resulting from strengthened competition and the need to improve the efficiency and competitiveness of manufacturing and service enterprises;
- the establishment of new institutions furthered the demand for services, mainly in public administration, related to implementation of the market economy and to the process of accession to the EU and other international organisations (for example, legal services related to the harmonisation of the *acquis communautaire*, veterinary inspection services);
- consumer demand for services increased substantially, reflecting considerable shortages in this field in the past (Vidovic, 2002: 15), but also increased disposable incomes in the CEECs in the second part of the 1990s;
- last but not least, the CEECs' trade in services increased following the opening of their domestic markets to foreign service providers due to liberalisation of service transactions both in the regional (Europe Agreements) and the multilateral (GATS) contexts.

At the beginning of the transition, modest supply capacities in the CEECs could not meet the increased demand for services. FDI played an important role in strengthening the service sector, particularly in some countries (Hungary, the Czech Republic, Estonia). FDI was first directed at manufacturing, although the suppliers of some business services (for example, management consultancy, auditing, advertising) were quick to follow and to provide their partners in home countries with the same quality and range of services in the CEECs. The privatisation process in the CEECs increased the interest of foreign investors in services. By the end of the 1990s, foreign investors became more attracted by service activities in the CEECs and they invested heavily in financial services, trade, telecommunications and business services. In 2000, services accounted for 54 per cent of the FDI stock on average in these countries, that is, one-third more than in 1997 (Statistics in Focus, 2003b). In 2002 the share of services in total FDI stock of the CEECs increased to 56 per cent (UNCTAD, 2004a).

By and large, FDI encouraged the development of the service sector in the CEECs and increased the supply of services. It is being argued that the main benefits from FDI in the service sector of transition economies relate to improved skills, know-how, upgraded service quality (Kostecki and Pietras, 1996: 55), tacit knowledge which is disseminated through a learning-by-doing process (Keren and Ofer, 2002: 19), a broader range of services and a contribution to an overall increase in efficiency as a result of inter-industry linkages (Stare, 2001: 31). On the other hand, the CEECs have started to engage in outward FDI in services, largely exploiting the advantages in the nearby transition economies. Nevertheless, outward FDI by the CEECs has so far been influenced more by the external environment than by investors' firm-specific advantages (Svetličič, 2003: 15).

Considering the relatively underdeveloped service sectors inherited from the past, the performance of the CEECs in rapidly developing and modernising service industries has been remarkable. As a result of the above processes, the gap of these countries in terms of service development in relation to the EU narrowed even though the paths of structural change in individual countries are different. Some countries were more successful in closing the service development gap *vis-à-vis* the EU, while others still have a long way to go (Ghibutiu, 1999: 5).

The missing links in service development: qualitative dimensions

The growth of the service sector in the CEECs during the 1990s was accompanied by the emergence of a large number of local and foreign suppliers of services. While competition evolved slowly it nevertheless contributed to an improved supply of services for intermediate and final consumption as well as to a broader range of services. Despite the progress achieved since 1990, the rather late withdrawal of the CEECs from the industry-led growth and a resource-intensive economy held back a smooth and fast development of the service sector. The changes implied major quantitative shifts in GDP and employment; however, they could not be absorbed rapidly in terms of the efficiency of the service sector, quality of services or the availability of knowledge-intensive services. Further shortcomings concern insufficient competition, a low degree of internationalisation and poor innovation in services. Overall, improvements in service development are much more evident in quantitative rather than in qualitative terms. While the shifts between major economic sectors were relatively fast and radical, this was much less obvious in the case of shifts within the service sector, where change was more gradual and reflected drawbacks from the past.

Public services have historically been at a relatively high level in most CEECs and, during the transition, the proportion of these services in employment and in value added increased even further in the majority of the CEECs (Vidovic, 2002: 21). Data for 2002, however, point to big differences among the CEECs (Table 10.1). Hungary, Poland and Slovenia are almost aligned with the level of public services' share in value added in the EU15, while Romania lags far behind. Due to historical legacies, the development level of market services in the CEECs, as illustrated by their shares in value added, is inferior to that of the EU15. This is mainly the result of the CEECs' gap in knowledge-intensive market services.

Table 10.1 Share of service activities in gross value added in the CEECs, 2002 (%)

	Services	Traditional market services**	Knowledge-intensive market services***	Public services
Bulgaria	59.7	24.1	20.4	15.2
Czech Republic	57.9	25.8	16.6	15.5
Hungary*	64.4	21.6	21.3	21.5
Estonia	65.3	31.5	15.8	18.0
Lithuania	70.6	35.7	15.7	19.2
Latvia	62.2	33.3	10.5	18.4
Poland	66.5	30.0	16.0	20.6
Romania*	48.7	24.0	14.7	10.0
Slovak Republic	63.6	26.8	21.1	15.7
Slovenia	61.8	21.2	20.0	20.6
EU15	71.0	21.5	27.3	22.2

Notes:
* Data for 2001.
** Traditional market services include trade, hotels and restaurants, transportation and communications.
*** Knowledge-intensive market services refer to business and financial services.

Sources: Own calculations based on Statistics in Focus (2003a); for Hungary and Romania: Eurostat (2003); for Slovenia: SORS (2003).

However, some CEECs have achieved remarkable progress since the 1990s and they have caught up with the least-developed EU15 members as revealed below. The lagging behind the EU is of particular concern in some CEECs given the fact that market services currently account for the bulk of labour productivity growth in the OECD area. It is reported that this is linked to an increased use of ICT, greater exposure to international competition and a growing role of R&D. Also, the manufacturing sector requires more services to be competitive, partly due to an increase in the outsourcing of services that were previously produced in-house (OECD, 2003c: 15).

The following subsections identify and explore some of the missing links in service development in the CEECs, particularly with regard to knowledge-intensive services.

The lag in knowledge-intensive services

During the period of domination of industrial production in the CEECs, among the few services that were recognised as useful for distributing goods within the production system were transportation and trade. They were, however, subordinate to industrial production and mostly organised in-house by large manufacturing enterprises or closely related to goods-producing enterprises. Accordingly, these traditional services were not exposed to the market competition likely to provide incentives for improvements in quality and efficiency. Even after the introduction of market-oriented reforms, the models in distribution and trade remained archaic for quite some time (Kostecki and Fehervary, 1996: 250). In the early 1990s, traditional services such as transport, distribution and catering accounted for the largest share of value added in services (Stare and Vanyai, 1995: 345–7) and this has not changed significantly as the growth of traditional services has maintained its dynamic. Table 10.1 shows that in 2002 these services accounted for between 21 and

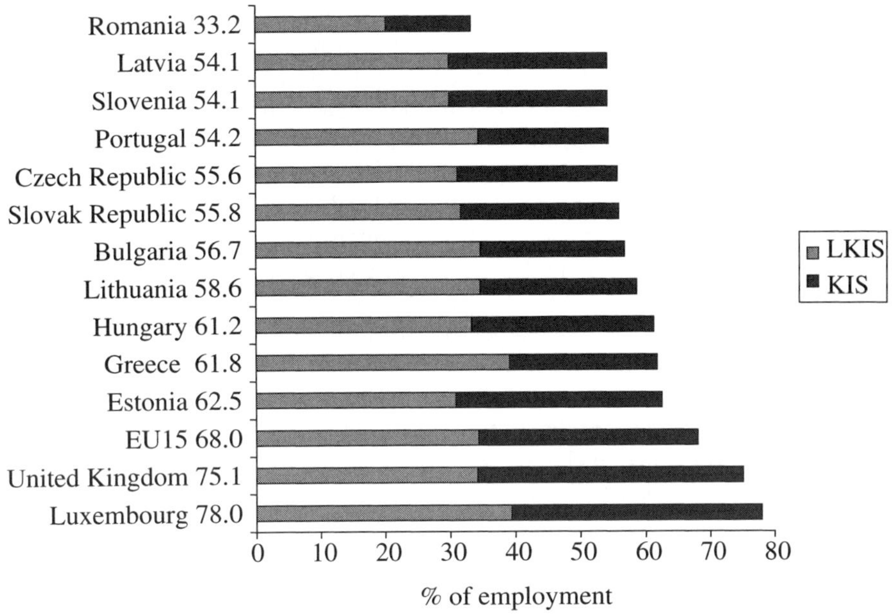

Source: Statistics in Focus (2004).

Figure 10.2 Employment in LKIS and KIS in the CEECs and in the EU15, 2003 (%)

35.7 per cent of total value added. Their weight is exceptionally high in the Baltic states. Knowledge-intensive market services that generate high value added per employee represent a modest share of value added in almost all CEECs, in spite of their rapid growth in the 1990s. In 2002, their share ranged from 10.5 to 21.3 per cent of total value added. This points to a substantial gap, particularly of some CEECs, behind the EU where knowledge-intensive market services accounted for 27.3 per cent (Table 10.1). These services were assessed as the motive power for the restructuring of the transition economies and as critical determinants for the successful conclusion of market-oriented reforms (Kostecki and Fehervary, 1996: 249). They are considered as important vehicles for establishing linkages between the three main domains of systemic transformation: macroeconomic stabilisation, real structural adjustment and institution building (Ghibutiu, 1998: 1).

The comparison of shares of individual service groups in value added might be affected by distortions in relative prices in different sectors. Hence, the share of services in total employment is compared with the EU15 average. Knowledge-intensive services (KIS) are distinguished from less knowledge-intensive services (LKIS).[7] Data for 2003 in Figure 10.2 show that the share of services in employment in some CEECs deviates substantially from the EU15 average. Nevertheless, there are also large differences among the EU15 members and among the CEECs concerning the share of services in employment.[8] The CEECs lag behind the EU15 average share in employment in both KIS and LKIS, however the deviation of CEECs from the EU15 employment pattern is most significant in KIS.[9] Estonia is the only CEEC where the distribution of employment between LKIS and KIS is quite balanced, similar to the EU15 average, while in other CEECs fewer KIS prevail in service employment. The EU15 average also hides a large diversity between member countries. Luxembourg and the United Kingdom are far ahead of the CEECs in terms of KIS employment; however, Greece and Portugal at the lower end of the EU15 lag far behind the EU15 and also behind some CEECs.

Over the 1990s, the CEECs have seen quite rapid expansion of some services, notably of financial and business services, partly due to low levels at the beginning of transition. The data on trends in employment in knowledge-intensive services for the 1997–2002 period are not as encouraging for the CEECs. The average annual employment growth rate in KIS amounted to 3.1 per cent in the EU15, which was matched only by Slovenia among the CEECs. Other CEECs lagged behind substantially. A lack of dynamism in the CEECs is even more obvious in high-tech services,[10] where the EU15 recorded a 5.6 per cent annual employment growth rate while the CEECs were left far behind. In four CEECs (namely in the Czech Republic, Estonia, Lithuania and Romania) employment in high-tech services even declined during this period (Statistics in Focus, 2003c: 4). The poor score of the CEECs might also reflect low levels of service outsourcing in general and in particular in high-tech services.

The divide between the CEECs and the EU is also large with respect to service productivity. In 1998, the CEECs,[11] on average, attained 69 per cent of the EU productivity level in trade, transport and communication services and 66 per cent of the EU level in financial and business services. Nevertheless, the achievement of these countries was much worse in manufacturing where they reached only 41 per cent of EU productivity (Statistics in Focus, 2001: 3–6). This suggests that the restructuring of manufacturing towards high technologies has been too slow, innovation activity modest, and the reorganisation of business processes deficient. Given the fact that intermediate producer services increase the productivity of manufacturing, it could be argued that the lag in manufacturing productivity in the CEECs is partly the result of insufficient utilisation of these services. Also, the reluctance to outsource non-core activities to a larger extent hampers the improvement in the efficiency of manufacturing. The role of services and in particular of KIS is not yet properly understood and their links with other parts of the economy are not fully accounted for.[12] The problem of structural change and putting competitiveness on a wider base is still not sufficiently addressed (Tübke, 2003: 200). This is in line with the conclusions drawn from the discussion of theoretical concepts related to the role of services in the development of transition economies (see above).

The KIS lag is further reflected in the structure of service trade when compared with that of the developed economies.[13] Notwithstanding improvements in the past decade in the CEECs, these services are still characterised by lower quality compared to developed countries. This is confirmed by the poor export performance of the CEECs in knowledge-intensive services. Their experience shows considerable disadvantages in most producer-oriented services, which build on capital, high-skilled labour, knowledge and experience (Römisch, 2001: 36). In the 1993–2000, period, the share of 'other services'[14] in total exports of services from the CEECs declined from 43.8 to 29.4 per cent, while a clear shift in the opposite direction was seen in the EU; exports of these services increased from 42.5 to 47.3 per cent of total service exports (Stare, 2003: 33). On the other hand, the CEECs' imports of other services increased rapidly, revealing insufficient and inadequate domestic supply. High shares of FDI in business and financial services in CEECs further demonstrate the high demand and profitability of these services (Keren and Ofer, 2002: 36).

Determinants of KIS development

It is evident that the demand for financial and business services in the CEECs is constantly growing and that it is not met by the capacity of these countries to supply an adequate quantity and quality of these services. There is strong reason to believe that building a competitive KIS sector takes much longer than a decade and that it requires more than simply the introduction of market reforms and institutional change. The experience of the developed countries indicates that the main determinants of development of these services are the availability of advanced knowledge and skills, intensive use of ICT and competitive markets, which together provide an enhancing environment. We briefly deal with these determinants in the context of the CEECs.

1. *Knowledge and skills* While the general education level and formal learning are at quite high levels in the CEECs, the share of population with tertiary education ranges between 10 and 15 per cent (with the exception of the Baltic states). In the OECD and the EU15 countries it accounts for 25 and 21 per cent, respectively (OECD, 2003b: 49). Apart from educational attainment, the availability of market skills proves to be crucial for competitive KIS. In the past, socialist countries had a technically well-educated labour force but with poor organisational and innovative skills (Illeris, 1996: 186). Human capital inherited from the socialist era is also characterised by low market skills (Keren and Ofer, 2002: 30). These include managerial, organisational and marketing skills that are of utmost importance for the provision of financial and business services. In addition to this, flexibility, creativity, project management skills and communication skills at different levels are the main requirements of the labour force in KIS. Strategic and integrative thinking aimed at problem solving is also underdeveloped (EC, 2002: 70).

   In the old, central planning system these skills were not appreciated as the system was overwhelmed with rigidity, poor communication and cooperation, lack of incentives and no attention paid to consumers' needs. The poor availability of market-related skills also reflects the deficiencies in an entrepreneurial environment not conducive to risk taking (Bučar, 2002: 76). In spite of the improvements since the 1990s, the CEECs still experience a shortage of managerial, organisational and marketing skills. The changes in the education system have contributed towards narrowing the gap to a certain extent and the acquisition of specific knowledge is supplemented by on the job training and learning. However, a highly competitive environment that encourages learning by doing is only gradually being established in the CEECs.
2. *Use of ICTs* One of the dominant characteristics of knowledge-intensive services is their high information intensity; hence the influence of ICTs on the development of these services is of crucial importance. ICTs improve the efficiency and quality of services, change distribution channels, modernise traditional services, generate new services and increase the tradability of services. The use of ICTs in the CEECs is much lower than in the EU, measured by per capita expenditure on information technology, internet use or the density of personal computers (PCs) per 100 inhabitants.[15]

E-commerce is only slowly taking off[16] as companies are not fully aware of the advantages and benefits of services delivered electronically, either from the point of view of costs, or from the point of view of marketing and the distribution of services. Also, limited use of PCs, insufficient and expensive access to infrastructure, and security-related issues hamper faster uptake of e-commerce. In addition, the size of service enterprises (SMEs prevail) hinders the rapid introduction of e-commerce. As mentioned above, investment in ICTs increases labour productivity; however, its full potential can only be realised with complementary investment in education and training (OECD, 2003c: 11). The efficient introduction of ICTs in enterprises' processes requires not only technical skills, but also organisational and managerial skills, which are deficient in the CEECs. In particular, the managers lack ICT skills and the ICT experts have insufficient knowledge of business issues (Bučar, 2001: 224). This partly explains why the CEECs do not utilise ICTs to a greater extent. Finally, lower levels of ICT use in the CEECs' economies makes it more difficult to outsource some services and exploit efficiency gains.

3. *Competitive markets* increase the supply and efficiency of knowledge-intensive market services. Notwithstanding the progress achieved in deregulation and privatisation of financial and telecommunication services, the CEECs still lag behind (Tübke, 2003: 198). Implementation and enforcement of regulation is hesitant, which hinders the establishment of competitive markets for financial services and telecommunications and weakens competitive pressures. In addition, the poor administrative capacity and capabilities of human resources in the CEECs for responding adequately to the political, market and technological changes prevents efficient regulation of markets (EC, 2002: 71). In business services, non-recognition of professional qualifications for some professions imposes formal and informal barriers to market access and decreases competition in the supply of services.

Gaps in knowledge-intensive market service development in the CEECs are important not only because of the direct contribution these services make to growth and employment but much more due to their potential to indirectly increase the efficiency and competitiveness of the total economy via knowledge transfer and progressive specialisation (Rubalcaba-Bermejo, 1999: 136). Failing to recognise the significant interlinkages of services and, in particular, of knowledge-intensive services, with other parts of the economy in the CEECs threatens their capacity to speed up growth and to catch up with the EU15.

Innovation gap in services

Innovation in services is a complex issue given the multi-dimensionality of service sector innovations. The service sector creates innovations, services are themselves major users of innovations enabled by manufacturing, predominantly by the ICTs, and some services are facilitators and catalysts of innovation processes throughout the economy and society. Knowledge-intensive business services are deemed essential to innovation activity. They generate knowledge, process it, and diffuse it within the innovation systems (Miles, 2001: 27, 2000a; Muller and Zenker, 2001: 1514). Compared to manufacturing, service innovation is characterised by much more emphasis on organisational dimensions of innovation (new service concepts, new client interface and new service delivery systems) relative to the technological options (Van Ark et al., 2003: 5).

The CEECs are facing large shortages of innovation capacity in services. Although existing empirical evidence on innovation in services is scarce and deficient, it still points to a lower level of innovative activity by comparison with either the EU15 or innovative activity in manufacturing in the CEECs (European Commission, 2003: 28). The low level of innovativeness in these countries reflects the status of the service sector as such and the poor awareness of innovations in services, but also other barriers that affect innovation in general. The latter range from attitudinal, cultural and institutional impediments, knowledge and skills deficiencies, and lack of finance to policy barriers. The perception of services in transition countries as unproductive labour also contributed to the neglect of innovation in services. The understanding of innovation in these countries is still biased in favour of technical innovation in products while improvements in business processes, organisational methods or change in business culture are usually not deemed to be as instrumental to increasing the competitiveness of enterprises as technical innovation. Innovation policy is typically thought of as R&D policy and consequently, the scope for innovation is narrowed in terms of the activity and actors involved (Stare and Bučar, 2002: 7). In this way it is overlooked that innovation extends far beyond technological R&D and that it can be involved in different functions and activities.

In spite of the progress achieved in the 1990s, the CEECs lack sufficiently competitive markets in individual services to provide for the pressure on companies to innovate. Also, the modest availability of knowledge-intensive services hampers innovation. These services prove to be critical for innovation processes not only as generators of innovation but even more so as facilitators of innovation in other sectors of the economy. The fact that the introduction of ICTs is critical for innovation in services and that CEECs tend to introduce ICTs much more slowly than developed countries also holds back innovation in these countries.

The researchers and analysts of innovation in services in the developed economies are increasingly aware of the need to conceptualise and implement policy measures aimed at innovation in services. In the CEECs, however, the awareness building regarding the critical power of innovations in spurring growth and competitiveness seems to be a very slow and evolutionary process. However, these countries should not repeat the pattern of EU countries that dwelt on innovation in manufacturing for too long, failing to recognise the potential of innovation in services. If the CEECs are to be fully integrated into the EU and also contribute to building the most competitive region in the world by 2010, it is of the utmost priority that the EU-funded programmes in these countries also pay more attention to innovation in services. It has to be borne in mind that EU-funded projects could contribute not only to the awareness building concerning innovation in services in the accession countries but also to revealing and transmitting some of the best practices and mechanisms. Nevertheless, the CEECs have to adapt the policies and instruments related to the innovation in services to the specificities of their own political, socio-economic and cultural environment (ibid.: 17).

Future focus

The discussion of recent developments of the service sector in the CEECs and particularly of its drawbacks seems to fit well into Tomer's argument (2002) about hard and soft elements of socio-economic systems. He claims that the hard elements relate to legal, financial and political relationships and to organisational structures, while the soft elements are mostly intangible. Hard elements change relatively quickly with the establishment of a new socio-economic system while soft elements are embedded in attitudes, values and culture and may consequently be longlasting. Accordingly, the soft part of capitalism is associated with risk taking, innovation, adventure and discovery (ibid.: 422).

Since the beginning of the 1990s, the service sector in the CEECs has made a big leap forward and narrowed the gap in relation to the EU average. Nevertheless, individual CEECs experienced different dynamics of the service sector transformation. The most-advanced CEECs have surpassed the performance of some EU15 member states regarding service sector development, blurring the line between the old and the new EU members. The progress of the CEECs in terms of growth and of an improved range of services was enabled by privatisation, regulatory reform, liberalisation, and institutional, technological and organisational change. Although these hard elements of the service sector transformation are not yet fully completed, they have, however, changed relatively rapidly since the establishment of new socio-economic systems. The changes implied major quantitative shifts in value added and employment distribution, but these could not be absorbed rapidly enough in terms of the efficiency of the service sector, quality of services, service culture and tradition, the availability of knowledge-intensive services or innovation capacity in services. These dimensions depend rather on soft elements (knowledge and market skills, risk taking, attitude), which need more time to accommodate to the new situation. They are deeply rooted in the mindset of entrepreneurs, policy makers and academic circles and accordingly change gradually over a long period of time. The resistance of soft elements to rapid changes is to some extent also reflected in the still prevailing shortage of data, analysis and research on service topics in the CEECs. Particularly neglected are issues of service sector interlinkages with other sectors, service impact on overall economic productivity, the specific role of knowledge-intensive services and innovation capacity in services.[17]

The dichotomy between hard and soft elements of service sector development prevented deeper transformation of the sector, which is in line with the observation that radical structural changes towards the increased role of services were not followed by rapid qualitative changes. The passive policy approach of the CEECs towards services development, based essentially on developed countries' experience of a gradual trajectory from an industry- to a services-dominated economy might well be a main reason for this. Ireland, which deviates from the pattern of most developed countries with regard to service development, underwent rapid transformation of its service sector, owing largely to a successful policy support (Bannon, 2002: 112).

Service sector development in the CEECs has so far mostly been driven by market reforms (privatisation, regulatory reform, opening to foreign investment and trade). In general, the policies in place did not target the progressive development of services even though there are examples of promoting individual service activities. Nevertheless, they were too fragmented and scarce to counteract the long-term bias of policy instruments in favour of manufacturing. Whatever view is taken about the appropriateness of past policies, it is necessary to acknowledge that after more than a decade of passiveness the CEECs need a proactive policy approach, attentive to the critical role of services for the efficient functioning of a modern economy (Kovacs, 2002: 86). This implies not only horizontal measures to strengthen their capabilities to provide high-value-added services (increased investment in education and training, in ICT, telecommunications infrastructure, in R&D

and implementation of regulatory reforms) but also measures oriented towards specific service activities.

Even though the level of services and in particular of KIS development in the EU15 is on average higher than in the CEECs, the European Commission has recently reinvigorated efforts and policy actions to further strengthen the competitiveness of services and their contribution to the performance of enterprises in all economic sectors.[18] This led to the development by the European Commission of an Action Plan for services in 2005 and a Services Directive in 2006 (Commission of the European Communities, 2003: 23–9). It is hoped that the new members of the enlarged EU will be swiftly integrated into this plan and that they will exploit the policy push towards KIS development. The benefits of the accession of the eight CEEC (the Czech Republic, Estonia, Hungary, Latvia, Lithuania, Poland, Slovakia and Slovenia) to the EU with regard to KIS development might also be expected from stronger competition in services and from attracting foreign investors to CEECs' service sectors. FDI not only improves the supply and quality of services but also brings tacit knowledge, skills and know-how of modern management and organisational techniques, which are deficient in the CEECs.

There is emerging evidence of KIS enterprises from the CEECs that have successfully managed to overcome the difficulties of a non-stimulative environment due to strong leadership, innovation activity and sometimes also to coincidence. However, for the CEECs to catch up and to keep abreast of modern tendencies of service development in the world, the accession to the EU, FDI and isolated success stories cannot substitute for a decisive effort at the policy level. Partnership of private and public stakeholders is equally important and has to be oriented towards joint actions to overcome the deficiencies of service sector development and to build an environment conducive to the fast progress of knowledge-intensive services. Some CEECs might choose the accelerated development of other service activities due to their geographical location or endowment with specific factors. Nevertheless, these countries have to improve their capacity in knowledge-intensive services owing to their potential to indirectly increase the efficiency and competitiveness of the total economy via knowledge transfer, innovation diffusion and progressive specialisation. Not recognising the significant interlinkages of services and particularly of knowledge-intensive services with other parts of the economy might jeopardise the progress of the CEECs.

Our discussion of the achievements and missing links of the service sector development in the CEECs points to a high degree of overlapping and interdependence between the gap in KIS development, deficiencies of market skills, imperfections of market competition and poor innovation capacity in services. These create a vicious circle. If the CEECs want to move forward in KIS development they will have to address other related issues, which exceed by far the area of services. Likewise, the improvement of efficiency in manufacturing and in overall competitiveness of the CEECs calls for the acceleration of KIS development. To disentangle this vicious circle, the CEECs need a holistic view of service sector development and a coordinated and synchronised approach towards streamlining knowledge and market skills, advancing innovation and entrepreneurship capabilities and efficient implementation of competition. The private sector is bound to exploit the opportunities.

These conclusions come from the experience of the CEECs; however, most of them are valid for transition economies in general. There is much scope for the supplementing of these conclusions, for further substantiation and argumentation and above all there is a great need for theoretical and empirical analysis of service development issues in transition economies.

Notes

* The author is indebted to Agnes Ghibutiu, John Bryson and Peter Daniels for their valuable comments and suggestions on an earlier version of the text. The research is a part of a wider project 'Possibilities and Opportunities of Slovenia and its Actors in the EU' financed by the Slovenian Ministry of Education, Science and Sport (No. P5-0177).

1. Slovenia was an exception in many regards. It had a unique system of so-called 'social ownership' and a combination of a planning system with elements of a market system. As a part of former Yugoslavia, Slovenia was quite well integrated into international trade and enterprises could directly engage in foreign trade. Since the late 1960s, foreign investors were allowed to invest in the country and form joint ventures with local enterprises.
2. The group of 10 CEECs is very heterogeneous. Some countries (for example, the Baltic states: Estonia, Latvia and Lithuania) were formerly part of the Soviet Union. Other CEECs belonged to the economic integration of centrally planned economies – the Council of Mutual Economic Assistance (CMEA) (for example, Hungary, the Czech Republic and the Slovak Republic, Poland, Romania, Bulgaria) while Slovenia, being a part of Yugoslavia had a specific socio-economic system, with no institutionalised links to CMEA countries. Further differences among the CEECs exist regarding the level of economic development, the level of integration to the European Union, history, culture and location.
3. Even before the transition the growth of the service sector in transition economies was primarily seen as a demand-induced phenomenon. This is why services have been considered as an exclusive attribute of developed countries and were seen as a threat to the development process. Such a perception was related to Engel's theory or deriving from it (for example, see Fourastié (1949), Bell (1973)).
4. This subsection deals with the experience of CEECs that can to a large extent be generalised to other transition economies as well.
5. The extraordinary growth of services in the transition economies is partly due to the statistical realignment of some service activities. In the past, large industrial and agricultural conglomerates integrated under the main activity, as did the departments for transport, distribution, catering, maintenance and other services. Value added and employment in these activities were statistically registered according to the dominant activity of the company. With market-oriented reforms, many of these service activities were organised as independent companies (process of externalisation) and statistically registered as service activities. Accordingly, the growth of value added and employment in services was to a certain extent the result of methodological changes.
6. Service companies tend to be much smaller than those in industry. The closing down or the restructuring of industrial companies resulted in large numbers of (usually low-qualified) workers being laid off, while service enterprises required fewer employees but higher qualifications and skills.
7. KIS include market services (water and air transport, communication services, financial and business services) and public services (education, health and social work, recreational, cultural and sporting activities), LKIS include wholesale and retail trade, hotels and restaurants, road, railway, pipeline and auxiliary transport, public administration, community and personal services (Statistics in Focus, 2004).
8. Data are shown for the CEECs, for the EU15 average and for two EU15 members with the highest and with the lowest share of services in total employment.
9. Deviation is also quite high if we consider market services. However, the results obtained by Raiser et al. (2003: 36) indicate that the share of employment in market services in the CEECs in 2000 and in market economies at comparable income levels was quite similar. It is questionable, however, whether benchmarking of the CEECs with market economies on the basis of income levels is appropriate as it compares economic structures of countries in periods of different technological and institutional contexts. At present, the economic structures of countries and particularly the weight of their service sector is deeply affected by the ICT and outsourcing possibilities, deregulation and internationalisation of services, which was not the case for market economies 30 years ago.
10. High-tech services relate to post and telecommunications, computer and related activities, and R&D (Statistics in Focus, 2003c: 7).
11. CEECs plus Turkey.
12. Interlinkages at the level of an individual economy concern relations between the sectors or subsectors (for example, service inputs to manufacturing). At the firm level, interlinkages concern both the relations between sectors and relations between different functions (for example, contribution of marketing function to sales function). Although both types of interlinkages are important for the efficiency of an economy we address only interlinkages between sectors.

13. The low level of internationalisation of service is also a missing link of service development in transition economies, which needs to be further explored and addressed. This relates to traditional and new modes of service transactions (trade in services, foreign-affiliate trade in services), to new means of service delivery via telecommunication networks (e-enabled trade in service), as well as to innovative ways of organising service supply from shared service centres in low-cost locations.
14. The category 'other services', according to balance of payments classification, is used as a proxy for KIS. It refers to services other than travel and transport.
15. The Czech Republic, Slovenia and Estonia are exceptions to that in some indicators (Statistics in Focus, 2002).
16. Data on the use of ICT by service sectors is very deficient in the CEECs, though anecdotal evidence suggests that commercial banks and public sector organisations are the biggest ICT users (EC, 2002: 21).
17. The observation is based on the author's experience in preparing annual literature surveys on Slovenia for the RESER (Space and Services European Network, www.reser.net/gb/index.html).
18. This includes the Commission Communication on an Internal Market Strategy for Services (December 2000) and Communication on the Competitiveness of Business-related Services and their Contribution to the Performance of European Enterprises (December 2003).

11 Whither global cities: the analytics and the debates

*Saskia Sassen**

Introduction

The aim of this chapter is to specify the analytic locus of the producer services in the global city model, and to address several key critiques of the model we find in the literature. The global city is an analytic construct, not a description of an actual city. What typifies this type of city is a particular capability that can be conceived of as a production function. I posit that global cities have both an economic and a political production function. Along with top-level headquarter functions, the producer services, especially the advanced corporate services, are at the heart of the economic production function. Global cities have emerged as a major scale in the dynamics that constitute the global corporate economy but also in the formation of a new type of political space and subjectivity.[1] Key features of this scaling entail an overriding of older categories for analysis and of older hierarchies of scale. This overriding has brought with it the need for theoretical and methodological innovations and hence, inevitably, a lively debate. The decade of the 1990s saw a multiplication of debates and a launch of a whole new research agenda around questions of cities and the variety of substantive issues they encompass. The 1990s also saw a whole new research literature focused on cities and globalization which has contributed greatly to our understanding of this subject.

Many of the new directions in the scholarship on the subject and many of the debates about the global-city model do not necessarily address the producer services, the focus of this volume. Yet in so far as this sector is at the heart of the global-city model, that literature is often indirectly teasing out one or another implication of the growth and characteristics of producer services in these cities. In this chapter I specify the producer services as a capability that becomes operative (or performative) in the complex environment represented by global cities. Today's network of about 40 global cities evinces considerable variability in the empirical features of that capability – that is to say, the empirical features of producer services across different cities, and, more generally, of the economic production function of the global city.

Generally, the data for the 1990s show an amplification of the trends I first detected, often dimly, in the 1980s. These trends are now much clearer, partly because we know what we are looking for. When I was working on these issues in the 1980s, there was no clear picture, no formulated trends that could aid me in seeing what was taking place. I remember often being in doubt or puzzled by the multiple stories that the data were telling. It took some courage, or lack of prudence, to formulate some of the trends in such forceful language. Researching the 1990s for the new edition of my book (1991 [2001]) was both worrisome and exciting – would my analysis remain useful? I have discussed the major issues in the new edition, chapter by chapter, including completely new sections warranted by the developments of the 1990s.

When it comes to the debates, these are addressed throughout the new edition. There I have mentioned only some of the critical literature, both negative and constructive. It would be impossible for me to do justice to this literature in the frame of a book, let alone in a short chapter. This critical literature is considerable, comes from different disciplines, is in several languages I know and in many I do not. Here I simply focus on some of the questions of substance they raise.

The analytic locus of producer services in the global city model

The bundle of specialized corporate services and top-level corporate headquarter functions is the critical component of the economic production function of the global city. One of the main dynamics specifying this production function is that the more globalized the operations of markets and firms, the greater the need for a diversity of specialized corporate services. A second key dynamic is that the more headquarters actually buy some of their corporate functions from the specialized service sector rather than producing them in-house, the greater their locational options become, including moving out of global cities. What distinguishes the global city in my analysis is not the number of large corporate headquarters of the biggest firms in the world, as is often suggested, but rather the specialized capability to handle the global operations of firms and markets, a capability increasingly centered in the specialized producer service sector. A third key dynamic is that the more large corporate clients buy components of their top-level headquarter functions, the higher the sensitivity to agglomeration economies in the highly specialized corporate service sector in order to be a state of the art, highly networked sector capable of producing a global service, and of absorbing the growing uncertainty and risks that come with global operations.

An important background structural trend evident in all reasonably working economies is the growing service intensity in the organization of all economic sectors, including rather standardized and often non-globalized sectors. From mining and agriculture through manufacturing to service industries such as transport and health, all evince growing purchases of producer services. Some of this translates into a growing demand for producer services in global cities, but much of it translates into a demand for such services from regional centers. The growth in the demand for producer services is then, in my analysis, a structural feature of advanced market economies. What globalization brings to this trend is a sharp increase in the demand for complexity and diversity of professional knowledge. It is this qualitative fact that produces the utility of spatial agglomeration in global cities. Thus what is often interpreted in the scholarship as a departure of producer services from global cities, is actually in good part the result of growth of these services through national economies. The lower growth rates evident in global cities compared with other cities should not necessarily be interpreted as losses for the former, but rather as the latter entering this new structural phase of market economies. I return to this later.

There are seven core hypotheses through which we can organize the data and the theorization of the global-city model (Sassen, 2001). In each of these the producer services are a factor, sometimes directly and others indirectly. There follows a brief discussion of each as a way of specifying the analytic locus of these services in the global-city model.

First, the geographic dispersal of economic activities that marks globalization, along with the simultaneous integration of such geographically dispersed activities, is a key factor feeding the growth and importance of central corporate functions. The more dispersed a firm's operations across different countries, the more complex and strategic its central functions – that is, the work of managing, coordinating, servicing and financing a firm's network of operations.

Second, these central functions become so complex that increasingly the headquarters of large global firms subcontract them: they buy a share of their central functions from highly specialized service firms: accounting, legal, public relations, programming, telecommunications and other such services. Thus while 20 years ago the key site for the production of these central functions was the headquarters of a firm, today there is a second key site: the specialized service firms contracted by headquarters to produce some of these central functions or components of them. This is especially the case with firms involved in global markets and non-routine operations. But increasingly the headquarters of all large firms are buying more of such inputs rather than producing them in-house.

Third, those specialized service firms engaged in the most complex and globalized markets are subject to agglomeration economies. The complexity of the services they need to produce, the uncertainty of the markets they are involved with either directly or through the headquarters for which they are producing the services, and the growing importance of speed in all these transactions, is a mix of conditions that constitutes a new agglomeration dynamic. The mix of firms, talents, expertise and global experience from a broad range of specialized fields makes a certain type of urban environment function as an information center. Being in a global city becomes synonymous with being in an extremely intense and dense information loop. Producer services in more routinized sectors evince weaker agglomeration economies.

A fourth hypothesis, derived from the preceding one, is that the more headquarters outsource their most complex, unstandardized functions, particularly those subject to uncertain and changing markets and to speed, the freer they are to opt for any location because the more the work actually done in the headquarters is not subject to agglomeration economies. This further underlines that the key sector specifying the distinctive production advantages of global cities is the highly specialized and networked service sector. In developing this hypothesis I was responding to the common notion in the scholarship that the number of headquarters is what specifies a global city. Empirically it may still be the case in many countries that the leading business center is also the leading concentration of headquarters, but this may well result from an absence of alternative locational options. In countries with a well-developed infrastructure outside the leading business center, there are likely to be multiple locational options for such headquarters. The variety of inertias built into the spatial organization of economies will tend to slow down this process: the empirics lag behind the theoretical inference.

Fifth, these specialized service firms need to provide a global service which has meant a global network of affiliates, or some other form of decentralized partnerships, that contributes to the strengthening of crossborder city-to-city transactions and networks. At the limit this may well be the beginning of the formation of transnational urban systems. The growth of global markets for finance and specialized services, the need for transnational servicing networks due to sharp increases in international investment, the reduced role of the government in the regulation of international economic activity and the corresponding ascendance of other institutional arenas, notably global markets and corporate headquarters, all point to the existence of a series of transnational networks articulating diverse groupings of cities.

One implication of the strengthening of cross-border urban transactions, and a related hypothesis for research, is that the economic fortunes of these cities can become increasingly disconnected from their broader hinterlands or even their national economies.[2] We can see here the formation, at least incipient, of transnational urban systems. To a large extent it seems to me that the major business centers in the world today draw their importance from these transnational networks. There is no such entity as a single global city – and in this sense there is a sharp contrast with the erstwhile capitals of empires.

A sixth hypothesis is that the growing number of high-level professionals and high-profit-making specialized service firms in global cities has the effect of raising the degree of spatial and socio-economic inequality evident in these cities. The strategic role of these specialized services as inputs raises the value of top-level professionals and their numbers. Further, the structure of rewards is subject to rapid increases at the top of the scale because it is not just that talent matters enormously for the quality of these strategic outputs, but that the importance of speed makes proven talent an added value. Thus, raiding proven talent from each other is the norm and has the effect of sharply raising the salaries of the top layers of professionals – a sort of winner-take-all market. Types of activities and of workers in the city that lack these attributes, whether in manufacturing, industrial services or standardized white-collar sectors, are likely to get caught in the opposite cycle.

A seventh hypothesis is that partly as a result of the dynamics described in hypothesis six, we see the growing informalizing of a range of economic activities whose effective demand is in these cities but whose profit rates prevent them from competing for needed space and other necessary resources with expanding high-profit sectors. Informalizing part or all of their production, servicing and distribution activities, is one way of surviving under these conditions.

In the first four hypotheses, the effort was to qualify what was emerging in the 1980s as a dominant discourse on globalization, technology and cities which posited the end of cities as important economic units or scales. One tendency in that account was to take the existence of a global economic system as a given, a function of the power of transnational corporations and global communications.

My counter-argument was that the capabilities for global operation, coordination and control contained in the new information technologies and in the power of transnational corporations need to be produced, serviced, designed and 'debugged' through specialized cultural work. By focusing on the production of these capabilities we add a neglected dimension to the familiar issue of the power of large corporations and the capacity of the new technologies to neutralize distance and place. Such a focus shifts the emphasis to the *practices* that constitute what we call economic globalization and global control. In addition, while the new information technologies do indeed facilitate geographic dispersal of economic activities without losing system integration, they have also had the effect of strengthening the importance of central coordination and control functions for firms and for markets; further, organizational complexity allows users to maximize the benefits they can derive from using these technologies. Global cities have massive concentrations of state-of-the-art resources and various types of organizational complexity (for example, global firms and financial exchanges) that contribute to maximizing the benefits of telecommunications and to implementing the new conditions for operating globally.

A focus on practices also draws the categories of place and work process into the analysis of economic globalization. These are two categories easily overlooked in accounts centered on the hypermobility of capital and the power of transnational firms. Developing categories such as place and work process does not negate the centrality of hypermobility and power. Rather, it brings to the fore the fact that many of the resources necessary for global economic activities are not hypermobile and are, indeed, deeply embedded in place, notably places such as global cities, global-city regions and export processing zones.

This entails a whole infrastructure of activities, firms and jobs, necessary to run the advanced corporate economy. These industries are typically conceptualized in terms of the hypermobility of their outputs and the high levels of expertise of their professionals rather than in terms of the production or work process involved and the requisite infrastructure of facilities and non-expert jobs that are also part of these industries. Focusing on the work process brings with it a consideration of economic and spatial polarization because of the disproportionate concentration of very high- and very low-income jobs in these major global-city sectors. Emphasizing place, infrastructure and non-expert jobs matters precisely because so much of the focus has been on the neutralization of geography and place made possible by the new technologies, and on the high-level professional component of the work process.

Global cities provide the mix of resources and the social connectivity which allow a firm or market to maximize the benefits of its technical connectivity. There is a type of information that requires a complicated mixture of elements, not only technical but also social networks – what we could think of as the social infrastructure for global connectivity. It is this type of social infrastructure that gives global cities a strategic role. In principle, the technical infrastructure for connectivity can be reproduced anywhere, but not the social connectivity. When the more-complex forms of information and expertise needed to execute major international deals cannot be found in existing databases and a firm's workforce, no matter what one can pay, then one needs the social information loop and the associated de facto interpretations and inferences that come with bouncing off information among talented, informed people.[3] The process of making inferences/interpretations into 'information' takes quite a mix of talents and resources.

Recapturing the geography of places involved in globalization allows us to recapture people, workers, communities and, more specifically, the many different work cultures, besides the corporate culture, involved in the work of globalization. It also brings with it an enormous research agenda, one that goes beyond the by now familiar focus on cross-border flows of goods, capital and information.

Finally, by emphasizing the fact that global processes are at least partly embedded in national territories, such a focus introduces new variables in current conceptions about economic globalization and the shrinking regulatory role of the state. That is to say, the space economy for major new transnational economic processes diverges in significant ways from the duality global/national presupposed in much analysis of the global economy. The duality national versus global suggests two mutually exclusive spaces – where one begins the other ends. One of the outcomes of a global-city analysis is that it makes evident that the global materializes by necessity in specific places and institutional arrangements a good number of which, if not most, are located in national territories. In the case of specialized corporate services there is often a significant set of national regulations at work, even in the most globalized sectors.

The main debates

The literature on the subject of cities and globalization is broad and encompasses several disciplines. Here I focus on the numerous critiques addressed to the first edition (Sassen, 1991) and examine how the data for the 1990s stand up against these critiques. This is one way of illuminating the multiple issues that this new type of conceptual architecture evokes. Hopefully, it is also a way of addressing the many queries I have received from all over the world from researchers and those struggling to advance the theorization of these issues. The debate has also been nurtured by a large number of studies done by scholars in many disciplines and countries that have contributed to strengthen the global city model. I also want to allude to some of these contributions. Finally, it is also an occasion for me to address some of the critiques that set up a straw man or are rested on an understanding of the global-city model which was faulty, partial or completely wrong.

There are, in my reading, six sets of debates: (i) concerns the construct or the model of the global city, its validity, its explanatory power, its 'ontological' status, and the questions of measurement it generates; (ii) concerns the financial industry, its weight in global cities, its spatial organization, notably the extent to which the increasingly digitized markets are articulated at all with global cities; (iii) concerns producer services, particularly their role as indicators of global-city status, their articulation with or dependence on manufacturing, and their spatial organization; (iv) concerns the relations among cities, including the question of competition, hierarchies and networks; (v) concerns the question of inequality in global cities, including earnings inequality and spatial forms of polarization; and (vi) concerns the question as to whether we see in global cities the emergence of a new spatial order. I have grouped the discussion of these debates into four subsections, to which I now turn.

The global-city model

The debate around the validity and nature of the construct itself raised a number of conceptual, methodological and empirical questions. Some of these questions directly or indirectly intersect with the centrality of producer services in the global city, a subject I return to subsequently. Several types of criticisms are based on a conception of the global-city model that is faulty and even flat wrong, while others are, in my reading, correct and yet others are constructive in the sense that they have added questions or actual empirical and theoretical elements to the research literature on the subject.

Globalization and homogenization A first group of critiques of the concept centered on questions linked to globalization and the associated homogenization it is supposed to bring about. One version of this critique is the assertion that in the global-city model, globalization is conceived of as a force coming from outside and homogenizing cities. The standardizing of producer services is one component of this homogenizing, whose dominant form is an instance of Americanization. This type of critique is fundamentally flawed in that the global-city model is precisely an analytic strategy to correct the common assumption in economic approaches to globalization that the global is that which crosses borders and comes from the outside, as in international trade and investment.

The global city represents a strategic space where (a) global processes materialize in national territories and global dynamics run through national institutional arrangements, and (b) national or endogenous capabilities are, in variable extents, denationalized and thereby become constitutive of globalization. In this sense the model overrides the zero-sum notion about the global economy and the national economy as mutually exclusive, and it overrides the notion that global forces come exclusively from the outside. A key purpose of the model is to conceive of economic globalization not just as capital flows, but as the work of coordinating, managing and servicing these flows and the work of servicing the multiple activities of firms and markets operating in more than one country. These forms of work enable us to recover space, notably urban space.

This means that globalization is not simply something that is exogenous. It comes partly from the inside of national corporate structures and elites, and from often long and deep urban histories that have led to particular types of specialized capabilities being prominent in a city. For instance, Chicago's history as an agro-industrial center has led to specialized service capabilities in law, accounting and finance that emerge from the specifics of this history and contrast, for instance with New York, a city always more centered on media and on finance. There are sites where global processes are indeed experienced as an invasion, as coming from the outside, but the global city is precisely the site where global processes can get activated inside a country with the participation of some of its national actors. The global city represents the endogenizing of both particular national and foreign dynamics and conditionalities of the global economy.

Methodologically it enables us to study globalization through detailed sociological and anthropological examinations of these processes as they take place in cities. For me this has meant going all the way from the top to the bottom levels of the social system in an effort to capture the variety of work processes, work cultures, infrastructures and so on, that are part of the global control capabilities concentrated in cities, and are one of the features of the global economic system. Producer services that are part of the globalized sectors are both top-level specialized corporate services and typically low-wage and non-professional industrial services.[4]

Furthermore, I unpack the 'global economy' into a variety of highly specialized cross-border circuits corresponding to specific industries, more precisely, those components of industries which are operating across borders. Among these are a variety of financial sub-sectors, accounting, legal, advertising, construction, engineering, architecture, telecommunication services and so on. Each of these may have its own specific geography of networks, even though there will tend to be strong overlap in the case of some of these, notably finance and its sister industries. This also means that these networks may run through distinct sets of global cities. The global circuits for gold will be different from those for oil, and those for the futures markets may be different from the major currency trading networks. Thus some cities which are part of these circuits may have highly specialized global-city functions and be located on specialized networks that connect them with the leading global cities even though they themselves are not necessarily global cities. Kuala Lumpur is significant as a futures market and Singapore is significant for currency trading, which gives each of these cities specific global-city functions; it also puts each of them on different global specialized financial circuits. The specialized services sector both negotiates the specifics of a particular city and enables its firms and markets to operate globally. The leading global cities in the world tend to have a very large number of these specialized circuits running through them, but even these cities do not involve all specialized components of the global economy. Leading global cities will tend to be highly specialized for the servicing of a particular set of global markets and global firms.[5] Far from positing that all cities become the same, my analysis brings out the deep economic histories of a city.

Further, many of the critiques along the homogenization notion are centered on an incorrect understanding of the type of convergence the model specifies. The content given to this notion is often that, according to the global-city model, the various global cities around the world will become alike, and particularly, that they will resemble New York City. Put that way, I would agree with the critique: why should Paris and Tokyo become like New York? The weight of their institutional, political and cultural histories, the inertia of the built environment, the different roles played by the state in each city will diverge and have its own rich specific history. But that is not the point of convergence in the global-city model: it is the development and partial importation of a set of specialized functions and the direct and indirect effects this may have on the larger city.

While the development of global-city functions in different cities across the world does indeed signal convergence of something, it is not the type of convergence posited in a common critique of the model. It is a highly specialized and institutionally specific process, to be distinguished from the kind of homogenization/convergence we see in consumer markets and the global entertainment industry. Already in the first edition of my book (Sassen, 1991), I found a division of functions among the major global cities rather than simply competition as was and is commonly asserted. But this is not a division of labor *à la* Ricardo, with the ideal of mutually exclusive specializations; that was a model of comparative national advantage. This is a model of cross-border systems, each by necessity installed in multiple different national locations.

Methodologically this underlines the difference between studying a set of cities from a classical comparative approach and from a global approach. The issue of comparability in the latter is not standardizing in order to compare. It is, rather, tracking a given system or dynamic (for example, a particular type of financial market) and its distinct incarnations (operations, institutional setting, accommodation with national laws and regulations and so on) in different countries. Though there is some overlap with comparative analyses, a global approach entails different analytic categories, research techniques and interpretation standards from those of classical comparative methods. There is work to be done on the methods front, an effort that I am currently engaged in.

The above conditions signal that there is no such entity as a single global city. This is one important difference with the capitals of earlier empires or particular world cities in earlier periods. The global city is a function of a cross-border network of strategic sites. In my reading there is no fixed number of global cities, because it depends on countries deregulating their economies, privatizing public sectors (to have something to offer to international investors), and the extent to which national and foreign firms and markets make a particular city (usually an established business center of sorts) a basing point for their operations. What we have seen since the early 1990s is a growing number of countries opting for or being pressured into the new rules of the game and hence a rapid expansion of the network of cities which are global or have global-city functions – a somewhat fuzzy distinction that I find useful in my research.[6] The global-city network is the operational scaffolding of that other fuzzy notion, the global economy.

In brief, the global economy in my analysis is not a vast exogenous homogenizing force. It is constituted through global systems that are multi-sited and hence produce standardized capabilities; for example, accounting and financial reporting standards, growing autonomy of central banks, rising power of ministries of finance in setting national policy to ensure the requirements for having a global capital market and so on. Because this process is filtered through the specifics of each national setting, the result is a partial and highly specialized denationalizing of the particular national components involved. The latter continue to be represented as national. Yet they are no longer national as historically constructed – they just look national but are in fact institutional homes for global agendas (See Sassen, 2005 for a fuller development).

Distinguishing constructs A second major set of issues comes out of the existence of several similar concepts, most notably the 'world-city' concept in both its older and more current meaning as formulated by Friedmann and Goetz (1982). The difference between the classic concept of the world city and the global-city model is one of level of generality and historical specificity. The world-city concept has a certain kind of timelessness attached to it while the global-city concept marks a specific socio-spatial historical phase. A key differentiating element between Friedmann and Goetz's formulation and mine is my emphasis on the production of the global economic system and the production of global control capacities.

A focus on the work behind command functions, on the actual production process in the finance and service complex, and on global marketplaces has the effect of incorporating the material facilities underlying globalization and the whole range of jobs typically not marked as belonging to the corporate sector of the economy. What emerges from such an analysis is an economic configuration that differs sharply from that suggested by the concept information economy. We recover the material conditions, production sites, and place-boundedness that are also part of globalization and the information economy.

Another differentiation is with Castells's (1996) argument about the space of flows and the notion that the global city is not a place but a network. While I already argued (Sassen, 1991) that the global city is a function of a network, I insisted that it is also a place. I briefly touch on my conception of the global city as a network in the above discussion on the unpacking of the global economy in terms of multiple specialized circuits. In the new edition (1991 [2001]: ch. 5) there is a discussion of, among other aspects, the network of transactions among global cities as a space of centrality that is partly deterritorialized operating largely in digital networks and partly re-territorialized in the set of cities that constitute the network.

The 'place-ness' of the global city is a crucial theoretical and methodological issue in my work. Theoretically it captures Harvey's notion of capital fixity as necessary for hypermobility. A key issue for me has been to introduce into our notions of globalization the fact that capital even if dematerialized is not simply hypermobile, or that trade, investment and information flows are not only about flows. Further, place-ness also signals embeddedness in what has been constructed as the 'national', as in national economy and national territory. This brings with it a consideration of political issues and theorizations about the role of the state in the global economy excluded in more conventional accounts about the global economy. Part of the place-ness of the global city is that it is a function of a network – a condition particularly evident in certain sectors. I do not quite agree with the opposition space of flows versus place – these two apparent opposites can evince complex imbrications. Global cities are places but they are so in terms of their functions in specific, often highly specialized networks.

A third concept is that of global-city region. As a category for analysis it shares key propositions with the global-city concept when it comes to economic globalization. But these two concepts overlap only partly when it comes to the features they each capture. The focus on a region introduces a set of different variables. Because of the latter, I find this an enormously useful concept, and hence will return to a more detailed discussion in a later subsection.

A different kind of distinction is that between the global-city construct and the city in general. Quite a few of the negative but also positive critiques fail to understand that I make a distinction between what is encompassed by the global-city model and the larger urban entity called New York, London, Tokyo and so on. This confusion may partly be due to the fact that in Part Three of the book I did examine the larger city. What may not have been stated with adequate clarity in the first edition is that the effort in Part Three was to understand the impact of the global-city function on the larger city, to see whether this impact is beneficial for a large sector of the population or not. My assumption was not that all of the empirical conditions described are necessarily part of the global-city function. Every city has its own larger materiality, polity, sociality, each often part of old lineages. The development of global-city functions, the endogenizing of the dynamics and conditionalities of economic globalization in the space of the city, is a strategic but not all-encompassing event. An important methodological implication is that one can actually study the global-city function without having to study the whole city. One methodological issue raised by this way of conceiving matters, is the boundary question, to which I also return below.

Another distinction is the notion of cities with global-city functions to identify a particular case, that of a city which fulfills a fairly limited and highly specialized set of functions in the management and servicing of the global economy, rather than the multiplicity of functions evident in major global cities. I used the case of Miami as an example as it has emerged with a growing role for European, North American and Asian firms which have operations in Latin America and the Caribbean. This is not necessarily a static function: it may disappear in a way that would be much less likely for London or New York, or it may evolve into the more complex and multifaceted condition of a global city. A certain level of complexity in global-city functions has its own impact on these functions; it can ratchet them upwards into top-level capabilities. For instance, the sophistication of domestic investors in the US pushed the US financial services firms into becoming a state-of-the-art sector which in turn gave it its advantage in global markets.

Finally, there is the distinction between international cities, such as Florence or Venice, and global cities. I agree completely with this differentiation and find it useful. It helps to strengthen the case for a tighter analytic conception of the global city.

Comparing the global city and the global-city region The concept of the global-city region adds a whole new dimension to questions of territory and globalization. Here I want to confine myself to examining the differences between the two concepts. A first difference concerns the question of scale. The territorial scale of the region is far more likely to include a cross-section of a country's economic activities than the scale of the city. It is likely, for instance, to include as key variables manufacturing and basic infrastructure. This, in turn, brings with it a more benign focus on globalization. The concept of the global city introduces a far stronger emphasis on strategic components of the global economy, and hence on questions of power and inequality. Second, the concept of the global city will tend to have a stronger emphasis on the networked economy because of the nature of the industries that tend to be located there: finance, media and other specialized services. And, third, it will tend to have more of an emphasis on economic and spatial polarization because of the disproportionate demand for very high- and very-low-income jobs in the city compared with what would be the case for the region which would have far more middle-range firms and workers.

Overall, the concept of the global city is more attuned to questions of power and inequality. The concept of the global-city region is more attuned to questions about the nature and specifics of broad urbanization patterns, a more encompassing economic base, more middle sectors of both households and firms, and hence to the possibility of having a more even distribution of economic benefits under globalization. In this regard, it could be said that the concept of the global-city region allows us to see the possibilities for a more distributed kind of growth, a wider spread of the benefits associated with the growth dynamics of globalization.

Both concepts have a problem with boundaries of at least two sorts, the boundary of the territorial scale as such and the boundary of the spread of globalization in the organizational structure of industries, institutional orders, places and so on. In the case of the global city I have opted for an analytic strategy that emphasizes core dynamics rather than the unit of the city as a container – the latter being one that requires territorial boundary specification. Emphasizing core dynamics and their spatialization (in both actual and digital space) does not completely solve the boundary problem, but it does allow for a fairly clear trade-off between emphasizing the core or center of these dynamics and their spread institutionally and spatially. In my work I have sought to deal with both sides of this trade-off: by emphasizing, on the one side of the trade-off the most advanced and globalized industries, such as finance, and, on the other side, how the informal economy in major global cities is articulated with some of the leading industries. In the case of the global-city region, it is not clear to me how Scott (2002) specifies the boundary question both in its territorial sense and in terms of its organization and spread.

A second difference is the emphasis on competition and competitiveness, much stronger in the global-city-region construct. In my reading, the nature itself of the leading industries in global cities strengthens the importance of cross-border networks and specialized division of functions among cities in different countries and/or regions rather than international competition *per se*. In the case of global finance and the leading specialized services catering to global firms and markets – law, accounting, credit rating, telecommunications – it is clear that we are dealing with a cross-border system, one that is embedded in a series of cities, each possibly part of a different country. It is a *de facto* global system.

The industries that are likely to dominate global-city regions, on the other hand, are less likely to be networked in this way. For instance, in the case of large manufacturing complexes, and of final and intermediate consumption complexes, the identification with the national is stronger and the often stronger orientation to consumer markets brings to the fore the question of quality, prices and the possibility of substitution. Hence competition and competitiveness are likely to be far more prominent. Further, even when there is significant offshoring of production and in this regard an international division of production, as in the auto industry, for instance, this type of internationalization tends to be in the form of the chain of production internal to a given firm. In so far as most firms still have their central headquarters associated with a specific region and country, the competition question is likely to be prominent and, very importantly, sited – that is, it is the US versus the Japanese auto manufacturers.

Finally, the question of the competitiveness of a region is deeply centered in its infrastructure. To some extent this is also a crucial variable in the case of global cities, but it is a far more specialized type of infrastructure. The regional scale brings to the fore questions of public transport, highway construction and kindred aspects in a way that the focus on global cities does not. Again, it reveals to what extent a focus on the region produces a more benevolent representation of the global economy. A focus on the regional infrastructure is far more likely to include strong consideration of middle-class needs in this regard. In contrast, a focus on the global city will tend to bring to the fore the growing inequalities between highly provisioned and profoundly disadvantaged sectors and spaces of the city, and hence questions of power and inequality.

A third difference, connected to the preceding one, is that a focus on networked cross-border dynamics among global cities also allows us to capture more readily the growing intensity of such transactions in other domains – political, cultural, social and criminal. We now have evidence of greater cross-border transactions among immigrant communities and communities of origin and a greater intensity in the use of these networks once they become established, including for economic activities that had been unlikely until now. We also have evidence of greater cross-border networks for cultural purposes, as in the growth of international markets for art and a transnational class of curators; and for non-formal political purposes, as in the growth of transnational networks of activists around environmental causes, human rights and so on. These are largely city-to-city cross-border networks, or, at least, it appears at this time to be simpler to capture the existence and modalities of these networks at the city level. The same can be said for the new cross-border criminal networks. Dealing with the regional scale does not necessarily facilitate recognizing the existence of such networks from one region to the other. It is far more likely to be from one specific community in a region to another specific community in another region, thereby neutralizing the meaning of the region as such.

What is new? Perhaps deserving separate treatment although it is yet another instance of differentiation, is the assertion that using the notion of 'global city' to describe cities such as London is unwarranted since they were far more international in an earlier era than they are today. At its most extreme, this type of critique rejects the specificity of the concept, arguing either that there is no such entity as a global city or that nothing is new, that London and New York have been international centers for a long time and, if anything, are less international today than they were in the past.

The clearest case of this is London, which can indeed be represented as having much less global influence in the 1990s than it had in the era of the British Empire. My response to this critique is to emphasize the intervening period, when the national state gained ascendance and cross-border economic flows took place within the framework of the inter-state system. It is against this phase, one of variable length for different types of countries, that the emergence of global cities needs to be understood. I do not argue that this is the first time or the most acute instance of this development of intense cross-border networks among cities (see Sassen, 2005). My point is rather, that the formation of a global economic system that follows a phase of national and interstate governance of economies needs to be specified theoretically and empirically and cannot be seen simply as a renewal of older forms. The global-city network is one of the marking features of the organizational architecture of the current phase.

Identification and measurement When it comes to identification and measurement of the variables we can use to specify or understand what makes a city global, we enter a somewhat fuzzy domain. This is partly due to the fact that existing categories, datasets, and research techniques tend to be based on certain notions of closure and scale. The city is a difficult scale for precise empirical measures. The best datasets are at the national scale.[7] Further, closure is a key feature of many datasets, including those at the urban scale. Thus attempting to measure a unit that is characterized by lack of closure brings additional problems, and when this is at the urban scale the problems escalate accordingly. One result has been a series of rather poor indicators of global-city status.

Global-city functions are a specific set of processes taking place in a city. But they are not the whole urban economy, even though they have large shadow effects. Nor can these functions simply be reduced to the whole producer services sector of a city. This is a recurrent confusion when it comes to measures. I discuss these issues in greater detail in the subsection on producer services, below.

Finally, one confusion in some of the literature is the failure to distinguish between the particular role that a global city or a city with global-city functions may have in the global economy and the impact of that role on the city itself. The former may be very significant without the latter being so. The reverse case is rare. The key point regarding the research literature is that an urban economy might be largely domestic – most urban economies probably are – yet play a strategic role in multiple specialized circuits of the global economy. There tends to be a threshold effect whereby global-city functions reach a certain level before a city is particularly significant in the global economy. But this is to some extent an empirical question. We need more studies to specify this.

The outcomes that we capture in the concept of the global city are a result of multiple processes. Different time periods, different contents, different scales, each shape the various processes involved. All of these variables in turn feed the distinction between the significance of global-city functions to a particular city's economy and to the organization of the global economy itself.

The financial order

The analysis of the financial sector in the first edition brought a number of issues on the table that had not been part of the standard accounts and representations. One of the most important of these was my insistence on emphasizing financial centers rather than financial markets and individual financial institutions. This was a crucial part of my global-city model in that it underlined the embeddedness of financial flows in complex organizational structures. A second one was an emphasis on division of functions rather than competition.

Centers versus firms and markets A focus on centers introduces a broad range of conditions and inputs that are excluded from consideration if we focus on firms or markets. Most important perhaps is the fact that this type of interpretation was a response to what I considered an overemphasis on the dematerialized and hence hypermobile outputs of the industry and its increasingly digitized markets. This was then also partly a response to the notion that the industry can locate anywhere. I argued that a financial center cannot be reduced to its financial exchange(s). Since then a small but growing number of scholars have begun to develop ethnographies about financial markets and firms, and shown to what extent these are embedded in a variety of conditions that are usually not taken into account when we focus on markets or firms, for instance, systems of trust (for example, Zaloom, 2005). More generally, introducing the notion of financial centers rather than simply firms and markets, allows us to understand the existence of a space within which a new subculture could be created and enacted (Sassen, 1991 [2001]: chs 5 and 7). I consider this new subculture important in facilitating the successful circulation of innovations evident in the 1980s and 1990s, many of which went against the older conventional forms of banking that had dominated the sector.

In retrospect I would say that the emphasis on financial centers rather than markets and institutions was a good distinction to make at a time when this was not evident. In my current research I have added yet another variable to explain the importance of centers and their distinct role. It is the fact that organizational complexity is an important condition for firms and markets to be able to maximize the benefits they can derive from the new digital technologies. I develop this in Chapter 5 of the new edition. The vast new economic topography that is being implemented through electronic space is one moment, one fragment, of an even vaster economic chain that is in good part embedded in non-electronic spaces. There is no fully dematerialized firm or industry. Even the most advanced information industries, such as finance, are installed only partly in electronic space. And so are industries that produce digital products, such as software designers. The growing digitization of economic activities has not eliminated the need for major international business and financial centers and all the material resources they concentrate, from state-of-the-art telematics infrastructure to brain talent. The new strategic alliances among financial markets in different cities or the project of the New York Exchange of going global are enhanced by the fact that they take place through a network of specific financial centers with distinct advantages. The project is not to eliminate these diverse financial centers but on the contrary to maximize the advantages of a network of centers each with specific strengths and weaknesses.

The emphasis on centers also intersects with the renewed interest in the 1990s in activity clusters and, generally, localized spatial growth evident in a broad range of disciplines. The coincidence between spatial industrial clustering and regional specialization which underlies the proposition of increasing returns to scale in urban and regional economic analysis, may also be at work in the dynamics of financial centers. But what is straightforward in the case of the manufacturing and standardized service sectors which are the focus of these studies, is much more complex and requires making endogenous a series of new variables in the case of highly specialized services and finance. This is especially so for firms geared to the world markets given added complexity and pressures of speed in these industries. Yet the particular interpretation of financial centers developed in the first edition and discussed at greater length in new sections (1991 [2001]: chs 5 and 7), can be seen as yet another instance of such activity clusters.

Competition versus division of functions A second major theme was my argument that global cities, particularly their financial centers, do not simply compete with each other, a subject I already discussed in the section on the concept of the global city. There is, besides competition, also a division of functions. I already saw that in the relationship among New York, London and Tokyo in the late 1980s. It has become even more evident over the last few years. In developing and underlining this feature I was responding to the notions of competition and hierarchy that prevailed at the time and continue to dominate the analysis of financial centers. Thinking in terms of competition leads to an emphasis on position and hence an interpretation of gain or loss depending on that position. It also entails an ongoing state-centric perspective on a sector that is increasingly not embedded in the inter-state system, certainly not in the ways it used to be. As I have already discussed in the preceding subsection, emphasizing competition at the international scale brings with it the optic of conventional comparative studies. My effort was not to deny the validity of this optic for certain purposes, but to add a different optic. Thinking in terms of a division of functions introduces other variables into the analysis. First, emphasizing such features as networks of affiliates or the flows of financial instruments among specific sets of financial centers, brings to the fore the networked nature of much of the global economy. This is quite different from the earlier competition among towns for manufacturing plants – a condition that resembled a zero-sum situation. Second, it brings to the fore that global firms and global markets need more than one city and hence do not necessarily operate as if these cities were competing with one another, but rather as forming a cross-border network for their operations. Such firms and markets need to ensure state-of-the-art infrastructure and resources in a network of cities, not in a single city. The issues I discussed in the preceding subsection on the multiple specialized circuits that constitute the global economic system are also pertinent here. I would say that the competition is predominantly among firms rather than among cities. The recent proliferation of strategic alliances among financial markets in different cities (ibid.) is a good illustration.

Introducing the notion of a division of functions among financial centers also recasts the question of the spatial organization of the industry. Focusing on a cross-border network of financial centers and conceiving of it as an integrated system rather than a series of individual centers in competition with one another radically alters our representation of the spatial organization of the industry. The key locational features of the global financial sector are, in my reading, a cross-border division of functions, and the embeddedness of firms, markets and operations in tight territorial concentrations combined with far-flung global digital networks and markets. With a few rare exceptions, which I discuss in Chapters 5 and 7, there still is not much research on the spatial organization of the global financial industry. The state-of-the-art image is that the globalization of the industry entails its digitization and shift to electronic markets, thereby reducing if not eliminating the role of financial centers. There is no doubt that the role and functions of financial centers have changed profoundly, but they have gained a whole new strategic importance as crucial sites in complex networks.

Global finance and the state A third major theme that has since become central to my work but remained underdeveloped in the first edition was the question about the influence of finance and the global capital market on the state. This was one of the forms assumed by the more general critique about the absence of politics in the global-city model. I have to agree fully with both the particular formulation about global finance and the more general one about the role of the state. Indeed it led me to start a major new multi-year project on the role of the state in globalization and the impact of the latter in altering the logic explaining whose claims become legitimate (1996, 2005). The new edition still does not do justice to this important set of issues. It is such a complex matter that it seemed quite difficult to insert into the organization of the book which is still shaped by the first edition. My response would be that the role of the state in the case of global cities and finance is introduced indirectly through the domain of policy (1991 [2001]: ch. 4). But this is clearly an insufficient treatment of the issues.

The substantive nature of the industry There are a whole range of issues concerning the financial industry and financial firms coming out of my proposition that finance is not simply a service industry. One of the impacts of globalization has been to develop and strengthen those features of the industry that are precisely not confined to servicing other sectors. The formation of new markets and the numbers and types of innovations produced in the 1980s and 1990s increasingly delinked finance from its role as servicing the 'real' economy. This is not the first time this has happened in recent Western history. Clearly the financial markets of the turn of the nineteenth century and the 1930s shared many features with the current phase. But in my reading there are distinctive features that differentiate the current phase from the earlier phase. This was the object of many a criticism. In Chapter 4 (ibid.), I elaborate on what I had presented in the first edition. This is also a response to critiques that assert that there is nothing new in today's market.

The producer services

Here I want to focus on the producer services narrowly. The key issues in the debates around this subject have centered on questions of measurement and use of indicators. Many authors consider the share of producer service employment as an indicator of global-city status; so a small share or a declining share or a share that is growing faster in other, usually smaller cities gets interpreted as an indicator of global-city status decline. Often the decline or a low share of producer services is interpreted as signaling that the city in question is not a global city. A variant on this indicator is the share a city has of national employment in producer services and whether it has grown or fallen. The notion here is that if a city such as New York or London loses share of national employment in producer services, it loses power. Even more problematic is the case of authors who use the measure of total service employment and its growth as an indicator of global-city status. None of these measures in itself is an indicator of global-city status. It requires a far more detailed and disaggregated analysis of producer services.

The key indicator of global-city status is whether a city contains the capabilities for servicing, managing and financing the global operations of firms and markets. In order to establish whether the variety of producer services likely to be present in any major city include this capability, we need a far more disaggregated analysis of the producer service sector and, to a variable degree, we also need qualitative information. This can be operationalized in a variety of ways: do the firms in the various specialized producer services have global networks of affiliates, does the city in question have significant exports of producer services, are foreign firms locating significant headquarter functions in the city in question, does the city have institutions that can finance cross-border operations, does it have global markets, and is it part of the global property market? The producer services are a crucial factor in all of these variables but they cannot simply be used in toto.

This then brings me to the next misunderstanding, one very common in the literature. It is largely a question of interpretation. The fact that cities that are not global are registering higher growth rates of producer services is interpreted as signaling the decline of the global city (cities) in question. I developed a different interpretation, one which addresses the issue of the spatial organization of these services: the high growth rates of producer services in smaller cities as compared with global cities is not necessarily a function of relocations from global cities to better-priced locations, as a microeconomic explanation would have it. It is a function of the growing demand by firms in all sectors for producer services. When these services are for global firms and markets their complexity is such that global cities are the best production sites. But when the demand is for fairly routine producer services, cities at various levels of the urban system can be adequate production sites. The current spatial organization of the producer services reflects this spreading demand across economic sectors rather than the loss of advantage and share of global cities.

In my analysis, what is specific about the shift to services is not merely the growth in service jobs but, most importantly, the growing service intensity in the organization of advanced economies: firms in all industries, from mining to wholesale buy more accounting, legal, advertising, financial and economic forecasting services today than they did 20 years ago. Whether at the global or regional level, urban centers – central cities, edge cities – are adequate and often the best production sites for such specialized services. When it comes to the production of services for the leading globalized sectors, the advantages of location in cities are particularly strong. The rapid growth and disproportionate concentration of such services in cities signals that the latter have re-emerged as significant 'production' sites after losing this role in the period when mass manufacturing was the dominant sector of the economy. Under mass manufacturing and Fordism, the strategic spaces of the economy were the large-scale integrated factory and the government through its Fordist/Keynesian functions.

This in turn carries major implications for urban economic growth. Cities emerge as important production sites for what are key inputs for firms in all industries. I posit that this represents yet another phase in the evolution of cities as economic spaces: with the ascendance of Fordism they lost key production functions; with the ascendance of finance and specialized services they gained new types of production functions.

Another kind of criticism has centered on measures of domestic- versus global-oriented employment. Thus showing that in London's total employment, most jobs are primarily oriented to the domestic economy is then interpreted as a sign that London's status as a global city has been exaggerated. This raises two types of issues in terms of my analysis. One is parallel to the arguments made above for the producer services, particularly that it is not necessary for a city to have a majority of internationally oriented jobs to be a global city. It is rather a matter of a city having the bundle of specialized services and professionals that can handle the needs of global firms and markets. This may not necessarily be a very high share of the city's workforce. Further, some internationally oriented jobs may not have much to do with global-city functions and some domestically oriented jobs may be part of the infrastructure for such global functions. This latter case brings up a second issue here, and that is that there is a range of jobs which are not typically coded as being part of the global-city function but are in fact part of it. Finally, I would posit that measuring value of the global-city sector by employment is increasingly inadequate given the orders of magnitude that can be produced and mobilized by a very small number of professionals, and given that many non-professional jobs are also part of these sectors.

There is a whole series of critiques concerning the weight of different economic sectors as measured by employment. In large cities such as Paris or Tokyo, finance and specialized producer services account for a relatively small share of total employment. This is then used as proof that these are not global cities. Again, this misses the point of the model. The question is whether coordination and specialized servicing of global firms and markets is taking place. And in both cities it is, though mostly for their national firms operating abroad. Yet this has brought with it a growing number of top-level firms, especially from the US and the UK, to handle the specialized servicing. This is in turn making it easier for foreign firms to move into these countries, therewith ratcheting the whole specialized service complex upwards. The critique is correct for the extreme case: if there is no financial and producer service sector in a city, chances are it is not a global city. One caveat here is that high-tech centers such as Silicon Valley and cultural centers such as Berlin may well be akin to global cities in their own specialized domains even though they do not have financial sectors.

A final debate concerned the relation between the producer services and manufacturing. Several authors argue that the producer service sector needs manufacturing in order to grow. I agree with this but argue that the location of manufacturing activity is somewhat irrelevant as long as it is part of a corporate firm in that these are likely to use a significant range of producer services. Thus Detroit's factories may relocate to Mexico and elsewhere but this does not preclude that many, and indeed a growing share, of the specialized servicing of auto manufacturing firms continues to be produced in New York City.

Social and spatial polarization

The critiques here centered on questions of earnings inequality and spatial polarization. Many of these criticisms represented my position as one that asserted that the middle class was disappearing, that the city's spatial order had become dualized, and that all of this was due to globalization. This is partly a misrepresentation, but only partly. My central point in the polarization argument is not that inequality is new, the middle class has disappeared, and it is all due to globalization. The point is rather that specific consequences of globalization have the effect not of contributing to the expansion of a middle class, as we saw with Fordism, but towards increasingly valuing top-level professional workers mostly in the corporate sector – it is not just a matter of being a lawyer, but where it is that you are applying these skills – and the devaluing of other types of economic activities and workers. It is difficult to measure these trends, but in my reading there is evidence to show a growth in advantage of top sectors and of disadvantage at the bottom in all of these cities. This does not mean that the middle disappears; not at all. Only that the basic thrust of the growth dynamic is not towards expanding the middle. Whether the middle class will continue to be a significant sector even under conditions of little growth is likely to depend on a range of issues, notably state policy.

My treatment of these issues warranted further elaboration, which I have done in a whole new section in Chapter 8 about earnings dispersion and inequality. Earnings inequality received little interest in the US and other highly developed economies in the postwar decades, partly because it was assumed to be a constant 'like watching grass grow', as one observer put it. But it became an issue in the US in the 1980s and eventually in

Europe in the 1990s when it became evident that there was growing inequality. Today we have a rich literature and considerable consensus on the fact of growing earnings dispersion in most developed economies.

Another critique centered on my focus on low-wage service jobs, rather than unemployment, as a source of poverty in global cities. It is true that most of my concern was with the types of jobs that growth sectors generate, which meant excluding or at least neglecting such conditions as unemployment. I think, and I argue this in the 2001 edition, that both are important sources of low-income status. Yet I continue to privilege low-wage employment theoretically rather than unemployment, since part of the model posits precisely that new growth sectors are one factor promoting a trend towards growth of high- and low-income jobs. My interest is in understanding what types of jobs the new globalized sectors produce.

While globalization has its own specific impacts in producing these outcomes, I would agree with my critics – and said so – that it is not the sole cause and that it is very difficult to establish for how much it accounts. The impact of globalization will also vary across different cities and countries, in good part because of the different role of the state. Yet we can dissect some of its impacts through a detailed examination of a variety of markets and their impacts on social and spatial features of cities. Elsewhere, I have expanded the focus of analysis beyond the narrowly defined cluster of global city functions (Sassen, 2001) and explored the broader impacts, the larger shadow effects of global-city functions.

It is also this material which has created confusion in being understood by some researchers as signaling that a city's overall employment and sector structure is an indicator of global-city status. Or led to assertions that Paris and Tokyo are not like New York because the criminality, decay, poverty and social exclusion we see in the latter are not present in the former, and hence these cannot be global cities. I would agree that these are enormously different cities – how can one not – but add that this does not prove anything about the global-city status of these cities nor does it prove the absence of dualization tendencies – as described above – in cities such as Paris and Tokyo. An additional assertion is that the pressures towards these sharper forms of polarization or differentiation are not there in many of the cities considered global and hence that this characterization is unwarranted. I would respond that it is partly an act of interpretation to assert whether the pressures are or are not there. In my reading they are, and they are so in a range of very different cities, such as Paris and São Paulo, and in an expanding number of cities beginning in the 1990s, notably Dublin and Helsinki. These trends towards growing inequality assume city-specific patterns.

There is also an issue of interpretation when it comes to the results of studies documenting growing inequality and spatial differentiation in cities. What I would interpret as signaling the emergence of new spatial dynamics, for instance, is frequently interpreted in far more prudent terms – as a mere accentuation of one or another feature or the development of a new layering. I do interpret the data I studied both for the first (1991) and the second edition (2001) as signaling that there is a new spatial dynamic at work in global cities, even though this does not mean that everything has changed. How could it, with the inertia of built environments and socio-spatial segregations that characterize cities. As a social scientist I think it is important to attempt to dissect what appears as a mere incremental transformation and dare to theorize it as the possible emergence of a new dynamic. I am persuaded by the evidence and by the enormously rich scholarship in this domain that we are seeing a new spatial order in global cities, albeit one that inhabits only parts of the city and is constituted as a partial, yet strategic new spatiality.

Conclusion: elements for an emergent research agenda

Throughout the text I have pointed to various subjects and questions that require more research in order to attain better empirical specifications of the global-city model. Here I want to focus on elements for a research agenda arising out of particular current conditions. These elements can be grouped into three subjects.

The first is the ongoing utility of spatial agglomeration of specialized producer services in global cities given ongoing technical developments, and the new vulnerabilities of spatial agglomeration in global cities as the latter have become high visibility targets for international organized terrorism. We can see the events of September 11 2001 in New York City as a sort of natural experiment when it comes to the inertia built into the location patterns of firms: the violence of that day was a brutal way of eliminating that inertia. Only that which needs to be in Manhattan, will stay. An examination of the composition of the specialized producer services in Manhattan today and over the next few years allows us a more precise analysis of the utility of spatial agglomeration for these sectors.

The second one concerns the growing importance of risk as a source of profit in the specialized producer services sector of global cities. In the first edition of *The Global City* I argued that in the 1980s debt became a source of new types of profit making for a variety of specialized producer services (most particularly finance, legal and accounting); as of the mid-1990s, we can see risk play a major role. Further, today, it is precisely the intermediate economy constituted by specialized producer services that increasingly absorbs the costs associated with risk as a profit-making option. In contrast, my reading of the 1980s was that the intermediate economy of producer services did not absorb the risks associated with debt as a source of profit making. We need more research on this subject.

The third subject for further research concerns the institutional organization of producer services in the extreme environment represented by global cities. In what ways have the scandals of the 1990s introduced significant changes? The setting up of walls between advising and investment, the new discipline demanded from major accounting firms, the new demands for accountability coming from large institutional investors such as pensions, and other recent developments are contributing to a reorganization of particular institutional features of the intermediate economy.

Notes

* The idea for this chapter came from the editors. I thank them for inviting me to address the debates engendered by this book (see Sassen, 1991 [2001]).

1. In my more recent work I have developed the political production function for the global city (2002, 2004).
2. The growth of networked cross-border dynamics among global cities includes a broad range of domains – political, cultural, social, criminal and so on. There are cross-border transactions among immigrant communities and communities of origin and a greater intensity in the use of these networks once they become established, including for economic activities that would have been unlikely until now. We also see greater cross-border networks for cultural purposes, as in the growth of international markets for art and a transnational class of curators; and for non-formal political purposes, as in the growth of transnational networks of activists around environmental causes, human rights and so on. These are largely city-to-city cross-border networks, or, at least, it appears at this time to be simpler to capture the existence and modalities of these networks at the city level. The same can be said for the new cross-border criminal networks. For an examination of these networks (see Sassen, 2002, 2004).

3. It is the importance for firms and markets of this complex type of 'information' that has given a whole new importance to credit rating agencies, for instance. Part of the rating has to do with interpreting and inferring. When this interpreting becomes 'authoritative', it becomes 'information' available to all.
4. The fact of low-wage and low-profit producer services and the role of immigrant labor in these services is a key part of the labor question in my analysis. Samers (2002) points out that the labor and the immigration questions have been neglected both in the critical discussion of my work and in the subsequent scholarship and research it generated.
5. There is a growing body of evidence on these specialized global geographies (for example, Meyer, 2000; Beaverstock et al., 2000), including a whole new generation of scholars. The website of the Loughborough center directed by Peter Taylor is a good source for a variety of studies from researchers worldwide.
6. In my estimate the network that is a critical infrastructure for the organizational (as distinct from the consumer) side of economic globalization consists of about 40 global cities. Given the multiple specialized circuits that constitute the global economy, there are also specialized rankings of these cities. There are a few cities that concentrate vast numbers of these specialized circuits and are at the top of the system.
7. In recognition of this fact and given the increasing importance of cities for a broad range of socio-scientific issues, the US National Academy of Sciences has launched a major initiative to study ways of raising the quality of urban-level data. We have now completed this multi-year effort (see *Cities in Transformation*, issued by the US National Academy of Sciences, Washington, DC, 2003).

PART III

TRADING SERVICES: FROM LOCAL TO GLOBAL PRODUCTION

12 Transport services and the global economy: towards a seamless market

Thomas R. Leinbach and John T. Bowen

Introduction

The value of both transport infrastructure and services has long been recognized and considered integral to economic development. But over the last decade especially, the role of transport services has become especially critical. As a result of growing efficiencies and falling costs, both passenger but especially freight transport services have been major factors in the increased globalization of the world economy (Janelle and Beuthe, 2002). Various adjustments and enhancements, both subtle and conspicuous, to transport services have made an impact on the sector and its relations with the globalization process. Accommodating new technologies, new markets and new organizational structures has required major changes on the part of providers and consumers, whether individuals or firms. The pressure of competition requires that firms increasingly be focused upon greater efficiency. Essentially this points to the gradual evolution of a 'seamless' transport market. The basic notion suggests an environment in which national and modal boundaries neither delay movements nor hinder the choice of the most efficient route and/or modal combination for the movement required (Willoughby, 2000). The liberalization of many national (and increasingly regional and international) transport markets and the innovation dynamics of technology-driven services strongly influence this drive for seamlessness. This chapter then addresses progress toward a seamless market as well as obstacles and constraints that interfere. The overriding goal is to examine the contributing and contradictory forces that influence transport services. The focus is on service delivery associated with freight movements. Given the prevalence of global production systems joining trans-oceanic supply and demand locations, air and maritime transport operations are paramount in our discussion.

The backcloth for the drive toward seamlessness in transport services is first and foremost the increasing internationalization and arguably, the increasing globalization of economic activities. Transport and communications especially play a fundamental role as enabling mechanisms in this process. While internationalization has been occurring for centuries, the activities associated with this have been affected by critical innovations. One major element in these developments has been the expansion of the transnational corporation and spatially disaggregated production chains. The coordination and regulation as well as the geographical configuration of these networks have immense importance for the profitability and viability of commerce as practiced by enterprises (Dicken, 2003). In a very real way, transport services hold these global production networks together. The nature of transport services and the way they are applied has become an immensely important consideration for firms as they seek to maintain a competitive advantage.

Overview of transport services in the US and global economy

Transport is a service activity whose function in the economy is relatively easy to understand. Basically all forms of transport are intensive in physical capital and require considerable investments in infrastructure but, increasingly, investment costs for transport service operations require technology upgrades to accommodate the dynamics of change in the global economy (Nusbaumer, 1987).

While the contribution of transport to the economy is widely acknowledged, too frequently we ignore or underestimate its value. On a global scale, value added by transport is estimated to account for 3 to 5 percent of gross world product. Public investment in transport typically accounts for between 2.0 and 2.5 percent of gross domestic product (GDP) and may rise as high as 3.5 percent in countries modernizing outdated transport infrastructure or building new transport infrastructure. Transport likewise commonly accounts for 5 to 8 percent of total paid employment. Demand for freight and passenger transport in most developing and transition countries is growing 1.5 to 2.0 times faster than GDP; the bulk of this increase is for road transport. Although demand for freight transport in industrialized countries is growing less rapidly than GDP, in developing and transitional countries the growth rate is closer to that for passenger transport (World Bank, 2003a).

Further detail regarding the size of this sector can be gained through a closer examination of transport statistics from the United States. Over 1.6 billion tons of international merchandise moved to and from the US in 2001, accounting for 10 percent of the 16 billion tons of freight moved on the nation's transportation system. Even though maritime transportation is the predominant mode for moving US international freight (whether measured by weight or value), freight transported by other modes, notably air and truck, has grown faster. While air cargo accounts for less than 1 percent of US merchandise trade tonnage, it accounts for over one-quarter of the value of the trade (it has been estimated that as much as 40 percent of world trade by value now moves by air; Kasarda, 2000). The number of truck crossings into the United States from Canada and Mexico has grown at an average annual rate of 5 percent per year since the passage of the North American Free Trade Agreement (NAFTA) in 1994 and is expected to continue to climb, especially between Mexico and the United States as all NAFTA trucking provisions are fully implemented.

The international merchandise trade data by mode over a recent five-year period for the United States confirms the dominance of waterborne transport, which carried 38 percent of the total value of American trade in 2001 and 78 percent of the weight (Table 12.1). But as noted above, the growth in total trade value by sea is exceeded by all other modes. Especially interesting is the rate of growth in trade value for air, which is just less than the growth in modal share of value exhibited by truck. The increase in the air transport share of international merchandise trade has come in response to the 'speed imperative' (Kasarda, 2000) of the global economy and the trend towards higher value-to-weight ratios concomitant with the greater knowledge content of manufactured components and finished goods moving across global production networks (Leinbach and Bowen, 2004; Henderson et al., 2002).

The pattern of transportation industries' contribution to GDP in the United States over the period from 1960 to 2001 is shown in Table 12.2. Several observations on this data are important. First, it is clear that trucking and rail together account for the

Table 12.1 Value and weight of US international merchandise trade by mode of transportation, 1997 and 2001

	Total trade		Exports		Imports	
Mode	1997	2001	1997	2001	1997	2001
Value			Billions of current US dollars			
Water	626	718	225	199	401	520
Air	433	519	220	251	213	267
Truck	323	395	167	192	157	204
Rail	70	93	19	23	51	69
Pipeline	14	26	0.2	0.5	14	26
Other, unknown, and miscellaneous	92	121	57	65	35	57
Total, all modes	1557	1873	688	731	870	1142
			Modal shares in percent			
Water	40.2	38.4	32.7	27.2	46.1	45.5
Air	27.8	27.7	32.0	34.4	24.5	23.4
Truck	20.8	21.1	24.3	26.3	18.0	17.8
Rail	4.5	4.9	2.7	3.2	5.9	6.1
Pipeline	0.9	1.4	0.04	0.1	1.6	2.3
Other, unknown, and miscellaneous	5.9	6.5	8.3	8.9	4.0	5.0
Total, all modes	100.0	100.0	100.0	100.0	100.0	100.0
Weight			Millions of short tons[1]			
Water	1144	1276	408	361	736	915
Air	6	6	3	3	3	3
Truck	176	180	92	89	85	92
Rail	84	97	22	22	62	75
Pipeline	75	79	3	4	72	75
Other, unknown, and miscellaneous	76	4	27	2	49	2
Total, all modes	1561	1643	554	481	1007	1162
			Modal shares in percent			
Water	73.3	77.7	73.5	75.1	73.1	78.7
Air	0.4	0.4	0.5	0.6	0.3	0.3
Truck	11.3	11.0	16.6	18.5	8.4	7.9

Notes:

1. BTS estimated the export weight for truck, rail, pipeline, and other and unknown based on value-to-weight ratios from the import data. This was necessary because export weights for surface modes are not currently reported. Weight for water and air exports and imports are reported.
   Excludes imports valued at less than $1250. Import value is based on US general imports, customs values basis. Excludes exports valued at less than $2500. Export value is FAS (free alongside ship) and represents the value of exports at the port of export, including the transaction price and the inland freight, insurance and other charges. Due to the way in which US trade data are collected, the modal shares represent single modes in use at US ports of entry or exit even though more than one mode may be used in transporting the goods from point of origin to destination.

Sources: US Department of Transportation, Bureau of Transportation Statistics, May 2002; based on: total, water, and air data – US Department of Commerce, US Census Bureau, Foreign Trade Division, US Exports of Merchandise CD and US Imports of Merchandise CD, December 2001; truck, rail, pipeline, and other and unknown data – US Department of Transportation, Bureau of Transportation Statistics, Transborder Surface Freight Data, 1997 and 2001; and special tabulations.

Table 12.2 *US GDP attributed to for-hire transportation industries (millions of current dollars)*

Industry	1960	1965	1970	1975	1980	1985	1990	1995	1999	2001
GDP	527,380	720,108	1,039,674	1,635,165	2,795,561	4,213,016	5,803,246	7,400,534	9,299,158	10,082,200
Transportation	23,138	29,533	39,881	59,248	102,948	140,431	177,404	233,379	303,418	306,100
Railroad transportation	8400	9069	10,049	12,555	20,752	22,002	19,819	23,594	23,431	25,800
Local and interurban passenger transit	1906	2176	2880	3488	5271	7731	9077	12,439	17,117	19,100
Trucking and warehousing	7518	10,653	15,029	24,154	40,094	56,326	69,428	89,036	116,627	126,000
Water transportation	1818	2190	2855	3987	7180	8317	10,044	11,627	14,395	15,700
Transportation by air	1959	3422	6360	10,179	18,188	27,063	45,341	67,667	94,996	80,200
Pipelines, except natural gas	595	719	1102	1812	5233	7306	5543	5484	6618	6500
Transportation services	942	1304	1606	3074	6230	11,687	18,151	23,532	30,235	32,900

Source: US Department of Commerce, Bureau of Economic Analysis, 'Gross domestic product by industry and the components of gross domestic income', www.bea.doc.gov/bea/dn2.htm, May 2001.

dominant share of transport's contribution to GDP. But this share has fallen from 69 percent in 1960 to 50 percent in 2001. Similarly, local and interurban passenger transport's share has also declined but to a lesser extent: from 8 percent in 1960 to 6 percent in 2001. Part of this declining share reflects the shift in importance of particular modes. In contrast, the share of transport services (for example, travel agencies, tour operators, arrangement of passengers, freight and cargo, rental of railroad cars, packing and crating, and inspection and weighing services for motor vehicles), while still important, has grown much more slowly from 4 to 11 percent from 1960 to 2001. But especially significant was air transport's contribution, which grew from an 8 percent share in 1960 to a 26 percent share in 2001. The latter of course reflects the increased production of services and higher-value goods which may require and are able to withstand the higher cost of this form of transport. Especially important is the increased use of time-definite services by the integrators.

Finally it is clear that the contribution of transport in general to GDP is declining. From a 4.4 percent share of the US economy in 1960, this figure dropped to 3 percent in 2001. Certainly a major factor in this declining contribution is the continued shift to a postindustrial economy where services, which do not have as significant transport components as do manufactured goods, are increasingly important. In addition, since 1995 and the inception of the internet, the growth of electronic commerce has also played a role in the overall decline. But at the same time the contribution of transport to the global economy in terms of international economic integration is more important than ever. Thus, we may interpret this falling share of transport to GDP rather perhaps as a reflection of the lower cost of distance.

Some explanation of these shifts in the contribution of transport to GDP and shifts in modal share as well must come from the competitive pressure set free by the liberalization of transport services. The effect of deregulation enhances competition between privately and publicly owned transport operators. In addition, we must ask whether over time the pricing structure of transport tends more and more to reflect the private cost of providing services rather than the social costs that govern the operating strategy of public monopolies (Nusbaumer, 1987; Daniels, 1993). The evolution of the pure service element in transport, as distinguished from technological progress in transport equipment and supporting physical infrastructure and facilities will continue to be characterized by a high rate of innovation in routing, intermodalism, flexible load management, cargo handling and warehousing.

Coupled with these contributions from the various transport activities, employment in the transport sector is critical. With regard to the US, despite large cutbacks in employment in some modes (most notably railways), overall employment in the transport service sector has grown strongly over the last several decades. As Willoughby (2000: 2) notes, 'This growth has been twice as fast (nearly 40 percent) in the 17 years since deregulation as in the 17 years before it, mainly reflecting new services and new qualities being provided at the same time as productivity was increasing in the basic, traditional services'. This employment growth shows that trucking and warehousing employment accounts for a large share of the total and this has expanded somewhat over the period from 1964 to 1996. Regarding the employment in the other sectors, noteworthy is the growth in that associated with air transport over the same period.

Driving factors in the search for seamlessness

Having identified the quest for a seamless transport market it is important to identify the forces which are driving this quest. First in a general perspective, it is clear that intense competitive pressures require goods- and service-producing firms to manage almost simultaneously multiple inter-organizational information and material flows. The global scale of this task makes it especially daunting. But attaining efficiencies in this complex endeavor allows firms to source, manufacture, and deliver their goods and services better, faster and cheaper. This development has forced a radical rethinking in the architecture of production, the importance of traditional supply chain relationships and the role of logistics.

Logistics has become an integral part of the modern production process. This term encompasses the process of planning, implementing and controlling the efficient, effective flow and storage of goods, services and related information from point of origin to point of consumption for the purpose of conforming to customer requirements. Perhaps more critically, logistics enables companies to get the right goods to the right place at the right time in the right condition and at the right cost. Important changes in technology, markets, institutional structures and management theory have led to new ways of conceptualizing this process and the development of new efficiencies. Recent developments in logistics include the introduction of the notion of 'reverse logistics', which focuses upon the supply chain that flows opposite to the traditional process of order acceptance and fulfillment. For example, reverse logistics includes the handling of customer returns, the disposal of excess inventory and the return journey of empty trucks and freight cars. As part of this and closely related is the notion of 'green logistics', the process of collecting, moving and storing used, damaged or outdated products and/or packaging from end users. In addition, 'lean logistics', which has evolved to the term 'agile logistics', has become important. These two similar concepts in logistics, which have been derived from the Toyota Motor Company, propose a new way of looking at the supply chain and an alternative way of rethinking the logic of value creation. Central to each concept is a detailed understanding of inefficiencies so that radical or incremental improvements may be made through a framework called 'value stream mapping'. Overall, the rationale is to contribute toward the development of more general logistical systems (Greis and Kasarda, 1997; Hines et al., 2001). Evolving this goal further has moved toward the development of integrated logistical systems where manufacturing and logistics are fully integrated. This process will be characterized by a deep enterprise-wide exchange of information that provides for a fast and flexible flow of materials and products (Greis and Kasarda, 1997; Kasarda and Rondinelli, 1998; McKinnon, 2001). It is important to note that logistics in the economy has two dimensions: logistics management in manufacturing and distribution organizations, and logistics organizations providing services to the manufacturing and distribution companies.

Second, one of the most remarkable shifts in corporate strategy and operational activity in recent decades has been the externalization of production so that corporations are now reliant upon external resources. Once centrally located operational activities such as product design and development, services and facilities management, logistics and even manufacturing have been taken over by suppliers. Consequently there has been an increased emphasis on managing the external relations of production and the control of resource flows from source to consumer. These activities have come to be represented by the term 'supply chain management' as a way of analyzing and detailing the flows of products and materials in complex organizational structures (Hall and Braithwaite, 2001: 81).

The search for competitive advantage at a global scale has forced firms to rely heavily on outsourcing, to seek out favorable labor and resource advantages and to attain as far as possible flexibility in resource access regardless of distance. The implications for transport are that longer and more customized linkages must be achieved through alliances across modes and nations. There is in addition a growing need for secure and efficient transactions which obligates the transport industry to apply procedures and equipment which will foster this (Cook, 2003; Russell and Saldanha, 2003).

Third, it is important to recognize that globalization, logistics and supply chain management depend to a considerable extent upon the ways in which separate modal systems can be brought together into intermodal structures (Slack, 2001). A key factor in the development of intermodal structures has been the application of containerization (Hayuth, 1987). The container has entered virtually every ocean shipping market over a wide range of freight types and has revolutionized shipping. While slower to enter other modal systems, containerization using units of varying dimensions is also being applied in the road transport, rail and airline industries. The implications of containerization are vast. For example, application of this innovation has produced a higher capitalization in terminal facilities because of the need for specialized machinery. Containerization has produced traffic concentration and the emergence of load centers where hub/feeder network structures have evolved in order to justify the capital costs of the system (Robinson, 1998; Airriess, 2001a). In addition, the containerization revolution has produced a need for larger site requirements of intermodal terminals, increasingly important as a result of the need for larger and larger capital outlays as restructuring of the container industry is taking place (Airriess, 2001b; Slack, 2001: 148). This process of concentration and restructuring is being widely felt and is not unique to the container industry (Bowen and Leinbach, 2004). The ramifications and further expression of intermodalism and containerization are discussed below.

Fourth, the role of time in global operations has been heightened. The move to just-in-time (JIT) management of production and distribution processes and the attempt to maintain zero inventories to lower costs has become essential. Differentiation between products and services is founded on so called time-based competition (TBC) (Meersman and Van de Voorde, 2001). Basically firms must develop strategies for production and delivery with the purpose of supplying customers with products and services in as little time as possible. Cost, value and speed are not trade-offs but objectives in their own right. The responses from transport must include a greater sensitivity to the timing of connections, arrivals, departures and the capacities of vehicles and storage units. The demand for real-time information access and exchange means that transport operations must expand their reliance on efficient communications and computer networks through electronic data interchange (EDI) for scheduling and tracking. Finally, opportunities for economies of scope (scope economies exist whenever the same investment can support multiple profitable activities less expensively in combination than separately, for example, when it is less expensive to produce two products together than it would be to produce each one separately) and customized production runs require flexibility in modal choice and timing (Janelle and Beuthe, 2002).

The rapidly changing demands of the marketplace now force firms to organize their operations around real-time information about consumer needs and the availability of productive capacity. Traditionally, logistics has been fed information on customer requirements from long-range forecasts that drove the production cycles of firms. Firms now require current and immediate information about the location of productive activities as well as information linking the locations with available transport opportunities. Thus, the need for seamlessness is being driven in the first instance by the challenge of rapid and flexible customer response. One way of capturing the response to this need is through the extended enterprise, a group of strategically aligned companies that focus on specific market opportunities. In this way firms can exploit the collective resources of the entire extended network of suppliers, vendors, buyers and customers (Greis and Kasarda, 1997). Obviously, fitting logistics in an integrated manner to these networks by the selection of appropriate modes and services is crucial (McKinnon, 2001).

Finally, the rise of e-commerce and e-business through the internet has brought important consequences for the transport system and logistics especially. In the US alone, recent information indicates that e-commerce shipments are most dominant in manufacturing where 18.3 percent ($270 billion) of total sales are attributed to such transactions (US Census Bureau, 2003). E-shipments are dominant in five industry groups: transportation equipment, beverage and tobacco, electrical equipment, appliances and components, and computer and electric products. Secondary areas of importance are merchant wholesalers (drugs, motor vehicle parts, professional equipment), retail trade (especially nonstore retailers), and selected service industries (for example, travel arrangements, publishing, brokerage, securities and commodity contracts, computer systems designs). Business-to-business (B2B) e-commerce represents 93 percent of all e-transactions. The rise of e-commerce produces implications for stocks of goods and, in particular, produces the need for transport of smaller batches and the need for attention to reverse logistics. The response by the integrators, firms which provide time-definite services and 'integrate' the air and ground functions performed by airlines, forwarders, and ancillary service providers, to these situations will be detailed below.

New expressions of seamlessness

The elaboration of production networks, both across borders and within countries, since the Second World War has been manifest in, and has depended upon, a corresponding expansion of transport services, over land, in the air and at sea. The critical role played by transport services within the evolving international economy is evident not only in the quantitative growth of such services but also in qualitative changes within this sector: in the speed of transport services, in the degree of integration across transport modes, in the development of information-intensive transport and logistics services, in the increased dominance of large global transport firms and alliances of firms, and in the shifting geography of the networks over which transport services are delivered. It is these changes that are the focus of this section.

Transport technology and time–space compression

The frenetic pace of the contemporary economy is contingent upon the accelerated flow of people and goods at several scales, but especially at the global scale. Changes in transport technology have been critical in this regard. In sea transport, for instance, containerization, which was begun in the United States in the 1950s, reduced the Hong Kong–New York shipment time from 50 days in the 1970s to 17 days by the late 1990s, with most of the time savings coming through the dramatic reduction of handling time in seaports (Pearson, 2001). Approximately 55 percent of international freight (by weight) is now shipped in sea containers, most of which conform to a standard 40 foot length, permitting the formerly labor-intensive process of loading and unloading to be nearly fully automated. A single container, which might hold, for instance, 33,000 pairs of Nike sneakers or 132 500 VHS movie cassettes, can be unloaded from a ship and placed on a waiting truck in fewer than five minutes (Worthen, 2001) and then later transferred to a train in a similarly efficient manner. The development of ever-larger containerships (with greater economies of scale) and of more efficient operations have helped to push down the cost of transport. As an example, to move a twenty-foot container full of whiskey from Britain to Japan cost $1561 in 1991 and $975 in 2000. For the same reason, the cost per pair of tennis shoes of transport from Asia to Britain was less than $0.18 in 2000 (Stopford, 2000).

Similarly, the advance of technology has sharply reduced travel times and travel cost versus those of the early postwar period. A one-way transatlantic flight in the late 1940s cost more than $6500, adjusted for inflation to 2004 dollars, and took 14 hours. The launch of the Boeing 707 jet in 1958 precipitated a jet age in which competing modes, especially rail and ocean, rapidly lost viability in long-distance passenger transport and more recently in the movement of a growing variety of goods (Hugill, 1993). Interestingly, the speed of passenger jets (apart from the commercially almost irrelevant Concorde) has barely changed since the 1950s. Indeed, rising airspace congestion near major airports has caused an attenuation of scheduled flight times. Nevertheless, real flight times have fallen sharply in the last half-century with the introduction of longer-range aircraft capable of operating much greater distances without refueling and the concomitant proliferation of nonstop flights. Long-term, sustained trends in air safety and in costs per passenger-kilometer (and tonne-kilometer for freight) have reinforced the diminution of the friction of distance.

Together, the new technologies of air travel and containerization contributed to a 'fierce round in that process of annihilation of space through time that has always lain at the center of capitalism's dynamic' (Harvey, 1989: 293). In this new era, geographies of production and consumption have become more flexible and ephemeral (Gottdeiner, 2001), freed from some of the constraints of an earlier age. The elaboration of global production networks in the manufacture of clothing (as in Benetton's much-heralded example), electronics, and automobiles has depended upon falling spatial transaction costs (Knox et al., 2003), as has the consumption across much of the world of French cheeses, Polish beers and fresh tuna (Harvey, 1989; Bestor, 2000). But in greatly extending the spatial horizon of firms (in some industries), these same technological advances also weakened the loose balance of 'big business', 'big labor' and 'big government' that had provided the framework for the post-Second World War expansion of incomes in wealthy economies (Knox et al., 2003). Because firms were better able than unions or the state to take advantage of the new transport technology-engendered flexibility of scale, the balance of the past was replaced by an asymmetry evident in, among other things, a wave of deindustrialization beginning in the 1970s that workers and communities were relatively powerless to impede (Bluestone and Harrison, 1982) and a sustained stagnation in real family incomes.

The degree of time–space compression actually attained via these innovations, often illustrated with a series of ever-smaller globes, has been contingent upon a host of locally specific factors, such that the globe does not shrink evenly. In the international airline industry, for instance, variations in national income levels, (de)regulation, and the strength of national carriers have mediated the time–space compressing effects of new aircraft (Bowen, 2002). Further, the above-mentioned flexibility afforded by new transport technologies is entwined paradoxically with the fixity of capital embodied in massive investments in airports, seaports, highways and railroads. Uneven expansion of that infrastructure can alter patterns of accessibility. In air transport, Singapore, Paris and Dallas have thrived in their respective regions in part because of the more rapid expansion of capacity than rival airports. Similarly, the massive demands of containerization for dockside space have intersected with the uneven ability of seaports to expand in a way that has produced shifting patterns of port competitiveness.

Intermodalism

While individual transport modes have been transformed by technological innovations (for example, the jet engine), much of the recent reduction in transport costs (including costs measured in terms of time) has come through measures to reduce the barriers traditionally separating different modes (that is, road, rail, sea, air). The clearest illustration of intermodalism is containerization, through which containers can be relatively easily transferred among ocean, rail and road (truck) transport systems. Interestingly, the Boeing 747 was designed in part to accommodate the same containers, with the width of its fuselage set equal to two such containers and the nose of the aircraft designed to lift in order to facilitate easy front-loading. In practice, sea freight containers are rarely transferred to aircraft due in part to their weight; but there is an important intermodal connection involving lighter air freight containers and truck transport. A final example of intermodalism is the truck-to-rail transfer of trailers.

The success of intermodalism depends upon the more general internationalization of standards that has facilitated globalization. In this regard, the dimensions of a sea freight container can be likened to the technical specifications of the nearly universally available computer operating systems and office software suites that emerged in the 1980s and 1990s (Borrus, 2000). Intermodalism is also contingent upon regulatory changes and greater incorporation of information technology (IT) into transportation systems. With regard to the former, transport has been among the most strictly regulated service sectors in many economies, with different bodies regulating separate modes. To permit goods to be passed easily among modes has required some degree of regulatory harmonization. With regard to the latter, smoothing the connection among modes has been facilitated not only by common standards and specialized equipment (to lift a container from a ship to a waiting truck, for instance), but also by the development of systems permitting the rapid dissemination of information about shipments. We explore the importance of information technology in transport services further below.

Intermodalism is regarded as a particularly important cure for land transport congestion but has contributed to that same problem in some areas. While the expansion of global economic activity has been predicated upon the earlier discussed advances in long-haul transportation, most trips, both for people and for goods, are relatively short-haul. One result has been worsening congestion on highways in densely populated conurbations. Intermodalism offers a partial solution by shifting a portion of interurban trips to rail. But intermodal transfers have exacerbated congestion within certain urban areas, especially those adjacent to major seaports that attract and disgorge a colossal volume of containers daily. In response, Los Angeles, for instance, built the Alameda Corridor, a 32-kilometer, partially below-ground railway linking the port of Los Angeles to the vast rail yards and transcontinental rail lines downtown (Philips, 2002). Completed in 2002 at a cost of US$2.4 billion, the project eliminated dozens of grade crossings and sharply reduced truck traffic on urban highways, and is regarded as a model for other cities. Indeed, it is precisely in the overlapping major hubs of transport modes that the 'speed imperative' (Kasarda, 2000) of the global economy is most threatened.

Information technology, transport and logistics

While virtually no sector of the economy has been untouched by the advent of new ITs, their impact upon transport services has been profound. The use of IT has permitted the development of faster, more reliable, more precisely timed logistics strategies, within which information-intensive transportation services are central. As noted earlier, logistics, broadly defined, refers to the management of the flow of goods (for example, raw materials, components, finished goods) through supply and distribution chains. The internationalization of production networks combined with the heightened attention to time as a factor in competition (Schoenberger, 1994) has made the operation of those chains a far greater concern for firms in a wide range of industries. In a somewhat self-reinforcing fashion, the decline in transport costs has contributed to keener international competition (particularly from China), which in turn has fueled deflation which has placed still greater pressure on firms to reduce costs, an important part of which is the cost of transportation and logistics (Delaney and Wilson, 2003).

Several examples will give some sense of the breadth of applications of IT that have fostered a greater degree of seamlessness in transport and logistics. First, crossdocking is an increasingly pervasive practice in which goods arriving on one vessel (for example, truck, freighter aircraft) at a hub or other central facility are immediately dispatched on another vessel bound for the goods' final destination, obviating the need for any storage time at the intermediate location. Crossdocking depends on IT tools including bar code scanners linked to complex database management systems. Second, the efficiency of many different transport modes has been enhanced through the use of global positioning systems, permitting express firms, for instance, to minimize pickup and delivery times. Third, warehouse management information systems permit the movement of goods within transport hubs and terminals to be largely automated, minimizing both handling costs and errors (although when such systems fail to work well as during the initial teething problems at Hong Kong's Chek Lap Kok Airport in 1998, the result can be near-paralysis).

The use of IT has also enabled firms to more closely track and control the flow of goods so that the time embodied in a production process in not merely speeded up but is also more carefully managed (Schoenberger, 1994). The best-known illustration of this approach to logistics is JIT production (Dicken, 2003), which reduces inventory stocks (and concomitantly the space and staff that must be devoted to this function), enhances quality control by making defective work more immediately apparent, and accelerates time to market. For instance, in 2000, National Semiconductor outsourced its logistics to UPS. From a newly built global distribution center that UPS operated for the chipmaker in Singapore, delivery times to customers in North America and Europe were trimmed from five days to two days; the use of IT in this system enables National Semiconductor and its customers to track the location of shipments at any point in the supply chain (Shah, 2000; Haddad, 2001).

Those gains, however, come at the cost of greater vulnerability to supply chain interruptions. That vulnerability has been exploited by some workers to enhance their bargaining position (Herod, 2000), with perhaps the best example being the strike by dockworkers on the West Coast of the United States in 2002. It is ironic then that the same rapid reduction in transport costs and concomitant elaboration of global production networks which has weakened the power of manufacturing workers in many industries has augmented the power of workers at strategically crucial junctures in the world's supply chains.

More generally, the vulnerability of attenuated supply chains has placed a break on the degree of internationalization in many industries so that localization (evident, for example, in the tendency of auto parts suppliers to locate plants very close to the auto assemblers they feed) is an important trend even in a time of falling transport costs (Dicken, 2003). Indeed, the persistence of spatially clustered production complexes (for example, Silicon Valley) is testament to the fact that falling transport costs is, in many industries, dwarfed by the effect of localization externalities (for example, nontraded interdependencies like the circulation of specialized knowledge among clustered firms) and geographic path dependency (Storper, 2000).

Due in part to localization, more efficient supply chain management, and the deregulation of major transport modes, the cost of transport and logistics is on the decline in the United States and the same trend can be expected in other major world markets. Business logistics cost US firms $910 billion in 2002, or about 8.7 percent of GDP, down from its peak of 16.2 percent in 1981 when high interest rates exacerbated inventory costs and transport deregulation had yet to yield major savings (Saccomano, 2003). Unsurprisingly, an important contributor to the falling share of the economy committed to transport and logistics has been reduced inventories.

The externalization of logistics functions over the past decade (as in the case of National Semiconductor and UPS) has fueled the rapid growth of what is referred to in the industry as third-party logistics (3PL) (Zhu et al., 2002). 3PL firms carry out logistics functions that would once have been performed by either the shipper (that is, the first party) or the recipient (that is, the second party). Much of the burgeoning 3PL business is carried out by major freight forwarders (the traditional intermediary between a shipper and an ocean freight or sea freight carrier). These firms leverage the volume of the shipments they control, their warehouse space (within which they perform value-added functions like minor assembly), their expertise in state-of-the-art logistics practice, and their advanced IT systems to lower the cost of portions of a customer's supply and/or distribution chain. A more recent development is the advent of so-called 4PL services, in which a firm may take over a client's entire transport and logistics operation. The importance both of IT and of externalized logistics is expected to grow with the rapid expansion of B2B and B2C (business-to-consumer) e-commerce.

The rise of global transport firms

As in most service industries, the last decade has been marked by rising market concentration in most transport modes; in modes where continued regulation precludes cross-border ownership, major firms have formed globe-encircling alliances. Larger firms and alliances enjoy economies of scale and scope and can more easily meet the needs of global customers, whether for passenger or goods traffic. In freight forwarding, for example, mergers have created new players (all of which are European, North American or Japanese) whose unprecedented size and scope enables them to easily outcompete smaller, local firms in an industry where the most important shippers (for example, electronics manufacturers) now look for a 'one-stop shop'; that is, a firm with a near-worldwide presence (Bowen and Leinbach, 2004). In containerized shipping, there is, for similar reasons, a small group of global giants among which the prominence of firms from Asian newly industrializing economies (that is, Taiwan, Singapore) is conspicuous.

Among airlines, the emergence of similarly dominant global carriers has been prevented by regulations that continue to limit cross-border ownership. Although there are important exceptions (especially the 2003 merger of Air France and KLM), the world's leading airlines have circumvented those restrictions principally through the formation of global alliances. The most important of those mergers links airlines from each of the world's major markets. The Star Alliance, for instance, had 15 member airlines at the beginning of 2004, including several of the world's largest carriers (for example, United Airlines, Lufthansa, Singapore Airlines and Varig). Via schedule meshing at major hubs, interlinked frequent flyer programs, and other joint marketing measures, such alliances provide another illustration of the seamlessness towards which contemporary transport systems are moving (Fan et al., 2001).

Similarly, strategic alliances and equity partnerships are important in the container shipping industry. The most conspicuous examples are the merger between British-based P&O and the Dutch line Nedlloyd and the acquisition of the US line APL by Neptune Orient Lines of Singapore. Global alliances such as SeaLand–Maersk, the Grand Alliance (Hapag–Lloyd, P&O–Nedlloyd, MISC, Orient Overseas Container Line), the United Alliance (Hanjin, DSR–Senator, Cho Yang), the New World Alliance (Hyundai Merchant Marine (HMM), APL, Mitsui OSK Lines (MOL)) and the groupings of COSCO (China), Yangming and K-Line are conspicuous.

Each of the shipping entities in these alliances is worthy of further discussion and provides some insight into the shipping industry. For example, Royal P&O Nedlloyd NV of the Netherlands is the fourth-largest provider of container shipping services in the world by fleet capacity, and operates a modern fleet of 154 container ships with a total nominal capacity of 416,732 TEU (twenty-foot equivalent unit). P&O Nedlloyd's ships call at 229 ports in 94 countries. Maersk is unusual in that it is a privately owned Danish company which has now merged with Sealand to produce one of the largest liner shipping companies with more than 300 container vessels and 950,000 containers. COSCO, the major shipping company of China, has benefited from the very significant state investments in ships, operations and the remarkable growth in container traffic, as the modernization process has expanded. Hanjing is a product of Korea's economic transformation in the1990s and has aggressively enlarged its fleet, using Korean shipyards and subsidized new buildings. All three lines have benefited from policy decisions made within the companies to expand their status in the world shipping industry (Slack et al., 2002: 74).

It is clear that globalization and competition has made it essential for container shipping companies to extend their market coverage. The costs of providing such global services have been increasing because of the need to deploy ever-larger and more costly vessels. As a result, vessels have been redeployed, service networks have been reconfigured, and ports of call have been adjusted. Such changes have also made an impact on localities (Slack et al.,

2002). While the instability of some of these alliances has been noted (Midoro and Pitto, 2000), there are some positive impacts of this concentration behavior. First, alliances appear to have introduced more uniformity in the industry. Similar service numbers and frequencies, investment patterns in larger vessels, and total number of port calls appear to be evidence of this. In addition this restructuring has produced an intensification of operations. Pooling assets has enabled firms to widen their scope of business, build up services, increase frequencies, deploy larger vessels and serve more ports. Thus it would appear that alliances in the shipping industry are seen as facilitators of service integration and deepening as well as service conformity. While the first of these may be generally interpreted as positive the latter seems to be a negative result (Slack ibid.: 75).

Air express is perhaps the most concentrated transport mode. Four firms – FedEx, UPS, DHL and TNT – control the world's air express traffic. It is this type of traffic that most rewards an integrated transport service in which as many intermediaries as possible (forwarders, customs brokers and truckers) are eliminated. The two largest integrators, FedEx and UPS, have sought to parlay their network and IT advantages into commanding positions in the 3PL market. Their evolution beyond their early concentration on small package and parcel shipments within the US to a far more diversified suite of services available globally is manifest in the UPS advertising slogan, 'What can Brown do for you?' (Delaney and Wilson, 2003).

Although the integrators are important competitors in truck transport, in general that mode is the least affected by the trend towards higher levels of market concentration. In both Europe and North America, for instance, there are literally hundreds of thousands of trucking firms. That fragmentation reflects the continued dominance (sustained in part by the localization of production networks induced by JIT) of short- and medium-haul trips for which small truckers can remain competitive.

Networks and hubs

The unprecedented pace of contemporary transport services, with few cities separated from one another by more than two days of travel, has depended upon the development of huge infrastructure projects, many of which have unfolded over decades. The fixity of those investments is a constraint on the flexibility of major transport networks. For instance, despite the inefficiencies of London-Heathrow and the difficulty of expanding that airport (Gottdeiner, 2001), it remains the single most important international airport in the world. The development of major transport infrastructure facilities has been slowed in part by the strong local resistance to their negative impact (for example, noise in the case of airports).

There are conflicting trends with respect to the dominance of major hubs in sea freight and airline traffic. On the one hand, the development of larger vessels (that is, containerships, aircraft) has helped to concentrate traffic. This is particularly true in containerized shipping where the world's top port (Hong Kong) handled more than four times as much traffic as the number 10 port (Antwerp) in 2002. The introduction of post-Panamax ships in the 1990s carrying more than 6000 TEUs has augmented the importance of regional load centers. Nevertheless, it is expected that future containerships will not be substantially larger than the most recent generation due to weaker economies of scale beyond about 8000 TEUs (Stopford, 2002). Moreover, such large ships may not be compatible with the increased importance attached to flexibility in logistics management.

In the airline industry, the attraction of direct flights and the proliferation of airlines fostered by deregulation have fueled the fragmentation of airline networks with a consequent de-emphasis of very large aircraft. In the transatlantic market, for instance, mid-size (seating about 200–350 passengers) widebody jets like the Boeing 767 and the Airbus 300 displaced the much larger Boeing 747 (seating about 400 passengers) beginning in the 1980s. With the more recent development of very long-range mid-size jets, including, for instance, the Airbus A340, a similar trend is now apparent in the transPacific market. In 2006, the newest Airbus, the A380, will be launched becoming the world's largest commercial aircraft (seating about 550 passengers in initial versions). The launch of this behemoth nearly four decades after the launch of the Boeing 747 is testament to the preference for mid-size twin-engine jets (twinjets), more than half a dozen types of which were launched during that long interval. That bias reflects the preference among travelers (and shippers) not just for lower costs (very large aircraft like very large containerships tend to have the lowest unit costs) but also for the faster travel times attained by more nonstop services among more cities with somewhat smaller aircraft.

One of the striking features in the development of transport networks has been the shift toward the Pacific Basin (Rimmer, 1997; Bowen, 2002). Nearly half of air freight tonne-kilometers, for instance, were recorded on routes to, from, or within Asia in 2002, for instance; and of the 20 busiest air freight hubs, 10 were on the Pacific Rim (Bowen, 2004). The region's improved prosperity and its incorporation into global production networks has made it more important in the flow of both people and goods. Conversely, the poorest parts of the developing world, especially Sub-Saharan Africa, are, in a relative sense, marginalized within the proliferating networks of the world's major transport carriers. Sub-Saharan Africa's isolation, amid the trend towards greater seamlessness elsewhere, is exemplified by the lack of any integrated rail network within the region, so that the cost of sending a seafreight container from Baltimore to the Ivory Coast in 2001 was estimated at \$3000 but to send the same container from Baltimore to the landlocked Central African Republic (CAR), only 25 percent farther away, was US\$13,000 (Hausmann, 2001). The high transport costs imposed on the CAR, and the rest of the 90 percent of Africans who live more than 100 kilometers from the sea, is a significant impediment to development (Mellinger et al., 2000).

The impact of transport networks upon patterns of development is particularly apparent at the urban level. Road and rail networks, canals and seaports have long affected the prosperity of nearby cities. For the past several decades, airports have been especially influential (Kasarda, 2000). Major airports have attracted time-sensitive manufacturing, advanced logistics, corporate headquarters, and advanced producer services. The latter two categories depend upon the ability to dispatch members of the 'global intelligence corps' (Olds, 1995) quickly on a global basis. One result is the rapid development of corridors linking downtowns and major airports. Employment along the 42-kilometer corridor linking Washington-Dulles and Reagan National airports outside Washington DC grew from 50,000 in 1970 to 600,000 in 1996, attracting the headquarters of firms like Cisco Systems and Nextel (Kasarda, 2000).

Transport and terrorism

The great achievement of the transport industries has been to enable ever-more people and an ever-wider diversity of goods to move about the world with unprecedented freedom and ease. But that same freedom and ease have opened transport systems to the threat of politically inspired terror, a threat made manifest with especially horrific consequences on September 11, 2001. Certainly, the political symbolism and thousands of entry points of the air transport system have made the airline industry more important than any other single part of the global economy as a focal point for terrorism (Wallis, 2003). While acts of violence against civil aviation date back at least to the 1930s, it is no coincidence that the beginning of modern airline terrorism is commonly dated to 1970, the same year that Pan Am became the launch customer for the Boeing 747, an aircraft whose huge size helped to force down airfares, democratize air travel, and quite literally made air travel a far more conspicuous transport mode. In September of that year, in a coordinated attack, the Popular Front for the Liberation of Palestine seized four aircraft in Europe, flew them to airfields in the Middle East, and, after letting the passengers and crew safely escape, the terrorists destroyed the four planes, beginning with a Pan Am 747 in Cairo.

Air terror reached a crescendo in the 1980s with two dozen acts of violence against civil aviation claiming more than 2000 lives. The most notorious attack, the bombing of Pan Am 103 over Scotland in 1988, was poignant testimony to the seamlessness afforded by the airline industry: the government of Libya funded a terrorist attack in which plastic explosives packed in a radio cassette player were surreptitiously placed aboard an aircraft in Malta, transferred to a 747 in Frankfurt, transited London, and then exploded high over Scotland, killing 270 people from 21 different countries. Much as the advances in transport have permitted the rescaling of production networks in manufacturing and service industries, those same advances have permitted regional political conflicts to be projected internationally to an unprecedented degree.

The 1990s brought a lull in the scourge of airline terrorism. More successful interdiction efforts and some tentative steps towards peace in the Middle East (the region most associated with air terror) brought some respite from the fear of the preceding decades. Further, the liberalization of air travel weakened the historic political symbolism of the airline industry. By the early 1990s, for instance, both Pan Am and TWA, flag carriers that had been potent symbols of the United States abroad (and the subjects of a disproportionate share of terrorist attacks) had been completely overshadowed abroad by United, American, Delta and Northwest. In other countries, too, the link between the state and the airline industry became more complex and, to some degree, weaker.

But in a single morning, that comparative calm of the twentieth century's close came to a cataclysmic end. The events of September 11, 2001 were unprecedented in many respects – one of which was the manner in which the four aircraft involved were not the principal objective of the terrorists but only tools with which to attack far more powerful symbols and a second was the use of the American domestic airline system as a tool of international terror.

In the wake of September 11 (and to a lesser extent the Spanish train attacks of March 11, 2004), there has been great fear that the myriad international transportation systems could be used again to carry distant conflicts to the world's most affluent (and transport-intensive) states. Because the 2001 attacks involved aircraft, many of the initial efforts to tighten security focused on the airline industry. More recently, containerized shipping, described by one US senator as the 'soft underbelly' of American security, has attracted great attention because only about 11 percent of containers arriving in the US are inspected by customs authorities, up from 2 percent at the time of the September 11 attacks (Edmonson, 2003). Further, the persistence of piracy in the twenty-first century is evidence of the vulnerability to the age-old attack at sea (Langewiesche, 2003). The number of piracy incidents in Southeast Asia has risen sharply since 2001 and there is fear that Asian trade could be crippled by, for instance, an attack against liquefied petroleum gas tankers in the Straits of Malacca (*The Economist*, 2003).

Obstacles to a seamless world

At the outset of our chapter we noted our intent to address progress toward a seamless market as well as obstacles and constraints which interfere. In truth there are both contributing and contradictory forces that surround the quest for seamlessness. While the enhancement of goods flow has been empowered by liberalization, intermodalism and new logistical approaches which have all been enhanced by technology, important constraints exist and it is to this theme that we now turn.

One argument suggests that the main threat to progress is 'choiceless churning' or the inability of the concerned social and political forces to confront visible challenges and increase the choices available to operators and consumers (Willoughby, 2000). The strongest evidence suggests that transport services are best organized in the private sector. In this perspective, it is clear that the liberalization of transport markets which permits easy entry and exit and espouses open competition on the basis of costs that reflect externalities as well as market values, has yielded good results. The progress in this regard has been most effective in the more advanced nations. Yet even here special-interest groups have managed to thwart progress. But in less-advanced nations the process of deregulation and privatization, while admittedly also having some success, has encountered more serious barriers. Providing alternatives to large state-owned transport companies, maintaining competition in the face of well-entrenched operators, and attempting to establish a cost structure which incorporates externalities and removes subsidies has been difficult. An example is the difficulty that Nigeria has faced in deregulating its airline industry (Akpoghomeh, 1999).

Researchers suggest that extending appropriate entry and exit approaches from national markets to the regional and international levels will be a major issue in the coming years. In the air transport field, Australia and New Zealand have created a single aviation market and progress in this sense is also being made in Africa. Lack of common standards throughout a region often adds to the complexity of creating a truly open regional market. But creating such a regional market can be more difficult when nations involved are at differing levels of economic and social development, such as Mexico within NAFTA and the European Union accession countries (Willoughby, 2000). As nations begin to devolve decision making to regional and local authorities, the implications for transportation operations are huge. This is most conspicuous in an economically diverse and spatially fractured nation such as Indonesia (Leinbach, 1989; Alm et al., 2001).

A conspicuous response to the heightened competition in the transport sector is a flurry of mergers, consolidations and alliances. But the creed of liberalization demands that these be scrutinized to determine whether the proposed new structures maintain competition rather than discouraging it. The pressure is thus heightened for public authorities to monitor the pricing behavior of transport service operations and respond accordingly to practices which constrain new competition. In addition, labor unions play a varying role across the globe in the operations of various modes. The role of unions and their quest for the erosion of wage inadequacies in the air transport industry in the US and elsewhere is well known. Union-called work stoppages for airline attendants and pilots have been problematic in the recent past at Com Air, a regional affiliate of Delta and USAIR. In addition, union supported wage concessions have been important in moving United Airlines out of Chapter 11 status.

The uneven progress towards seamlessness affects the manner and degree to which places are incorporated into the global economy. The drive toward seamlessness is manifest in falling transport costs (both in terms of time and money) and in the advent of more sophisticated logistics management services. The former reduces spatial transaction costs while the latter better enables firms to realize the external economies available through outsourcing (Knox et al., 2003); both grant firms greater flexibility to develop more complex, more internationalized production networks. Those networks link places of course but they particularly favor those places where advances in transportation and related communications technologies have been most fully embraced and where the world's leading transport services firms provide state-of-the-art transportation. Such places provide a richer, superior set of local assets with which to attract investment from 'trans-local' firms. Conversely, those places where significant obstacles remain in the drive towards seamlessness are threatened with deeper marginalization, whether those obstacles are technological (for example, the far slower adoption of containerization and new aircraft technology in the poorest economies), regulatory (for example, state subsidization of woefully inefficient public enterprises), or market related (for example, poor, peripheral markets proving too small to attract major service firms with their industry-leading services).

The success of moves towards seamlessness in some places and the failure of such efforts elsewhere largely reinforce the advantages of the world's richest economies. But the new threat to seamlessness posed by the fear of terrorism is geographically more ambiguous. The terrorist attacks of September 11, 2001 highlighted the enormous vulnerability that comes with an increasingly seamless transport system. In the air, at sea and over land, new security precautions, including, for instance, 'smart containers' fitted with electronic devices to detect tampering and immediately warn relevant authorities, are expected to raise the costs of integrating the world's economy (Clayton, 2004). Such new security procedures, through their added expense and added time, erode the hard-won improvements in supply chains upon which firms have increasingly based their competitiveness (Murray, 2004). Finally, while the United States and other rich countries have led the effort to improve the security of international transport, the costs of better security will reach deep into the developing world via the same global production networks and international supply chains made possible by advances in transport and logistics services.

13 Empirical analysis of barriers to international service transactions and the consequences of liberalization*

Alan V. Deardorff and Robert M. Stern

Introduction

Barriers to trade interfere with the ability of firms from one country to compete with firms from another. This is true of trade in goods, where a tariff or nontariff barrier (NTB) typically drives a wedge between the price of the good on the world market and its domestic price. This wedge, or 'tariff equivalent', provides a convenient and often observable measurement of the size of the impediment. In the case of services, however, no such simple measurement is often observable. It remains true, though, that the concept of a tariff equivalent – now thought of as the equivalent tax on foreign suppliers in their competition with domestic suppliers – is a useful way of quantifying a barrier to trade even though it may be much harder to observe. Both the role of barriers to trade in services and the possible meaning of a tariff equivalent can be better understood in the context of each of the standard four 'modes of supply' that arise for traded services and are shown in Table 13.1 for 1997. The four modes of supply are:

- Mode 1 – services that are traded internationally across borders;
- Mode 2 – services that require the consumer to be in the location of the producer;
- Mode 3 – services that require commercial presence in the form of foreign direct investment (FDI); and
- Mode 4 – services that require the temporary cross-border movement of workers.

To clarify further, Mode 1 refers to 'separated' services such as telecommunications, which are traded internationally across borders in a manner similar to cross-border trade

Table 13.1 International services transactions by modes of supply, 1997

Mode of supply[a]	Category	Value ($bn)	Cumulative share (%)
Mode 1	Commercial services (excl. travel)	890	41.0
Mode 2	Travel/tourism	430	19.8
Mode 3	Gross output of foreign affiliates	820	37.8
Mode 4	Compensation of employees	30	1.4
Total		2170	100.0

Note: a. Modes 1, 2 and 4 are derived from balance-of-payments accounts. Mode 3 is derived from data on the operations of foreign affiliates in host countries.

Source: Karsenty (2000a).

in goods. Here, foreign suppliers of a service provide it to domestic buyers through international means of communication and perhaps transportation, with a unit of the service itself often unobservable as it crosses national borders. A French telecoms company, for example, may provide telephone services to a customer in Mexico, in competition with a Mexican-based provider. A trade barrier in this case might consist of Mexican restrictions on the French firm's access to phone lines in Mexico, discriminatory taxes on its operations, or regulations on the ways that Mexican consumers are allowed to access the foreign firm's services. A tariff equivalent of all such impediments would be defined as the tax on the French firm's operations in Mexico that, if it replaced all other impediments, would cause it to operate at the same level and have the same effects on the domestic telecoms providers and consumers within Mexico. As in the case of traded goods, a single tariff equivalent may not capture all of these effects simultaneously, especially if competition is imperfect. And even with perfect competition, such a tariff equivalent is unlikely to be observable as a simple price difference. There is no world price of Mexican telephone services, for example, with which to compare what Mexican firms are charging, since the nature and cost of a service depends in part on the location of the consumer. None the less, a tariff equivalent is a conceptually useful way of quantifying barriers to trade in services as well as goods, and many studies have sought to express their results in this form.

Mode 2 of service trade refers to services that require the consumer to be in the location of the producer, as in the cases of tourism and education. Here again, the service provided is likely to be differentiated by the location or identity of the provider, so that a world price of the service may not be meaningful. It would be meaningless, for example, to try to compare the 'world price' of a visit to the Taj Mahal or an MBA degree from the Wharton School with the prices of these services within, say, Brazil. But it remains the case that Brazilian restrictions on their citizens' travel to India or the US to consume these services will alter the markets for other tourist attractions and educational institutions within Brazil. Such restrictions again can in principle be quantified as equivalent to a tax on Brazilians' visits abroad for these purposes.

Mode 3 of international service provision is arguably the most general and the most important: provision through a commercial presence that is the result of FDI. Almost any service can be provided by firms from one country to consumers in another if the firms are allowed to establish a physical presence there. This is true even of tourism – think of Euro-Disney. In this case there may well be a foreign price with which one could easily compare, but the comparison is unlikely to be meaningful. It would be a mistake to infer a trade barrier from the higher price of admission to Euro-Disney in Paris as compared to Florida, or the absence of a trade barrier from the lower price of a McDonald's hamburger in Argentina than in New York. In all such cases, prices depend on local costs of labor and raw materials as much as they do on trade barriers. However, and once again, foreign service providers may well face impediments, both to their establishment and to their ongoing operations, the effects of which would be similar to a tax if only we could infer what it is.

The final mode of supply, Mode 4, refers to the temporary cross-border movement of workers. Examples are the movement of computer programmers, engineers, management personnel, and lesser-skilled construction workers who are granted temporary visas to work in a host country. Most movement that is actually permitted consists of workers within industries that produce traded goods or that produce services that are primarily thought of as traded through other modes. Thus we do not think of many industries as producing services that are primarily traded through Mode 4. On the other hand, labor itself is a service that could be traded in this way, and occasionally it has been, in the form of guest-worker programs and the like. The fact that Mode 4 service-provision figures appear to be relatively small in the data on services trade in Table 13.1 is therefore symptomatic of the very high barriers that exist for Mode 4, except within industries where it facilitates other kinds of trade. Mode 4 is the one mode in which the tariff equivalent of barriers could most easily be measured, as simply the differences across countries in the real wages of particular kinds of labor.

For all of the modes, then, one objective of empirical measurement is to deduce some sort of tariff equivalent of the barrier to trade in particular services. Since direct price comparisons seldom serve that purpose, however, researchers have pursued other means of inferring the presence and size of barriers to trade. Some of these methods have been quite direct: they simply ask governments or participants in markets what barriers they impose or face. The answers are usually only qualitative, indicating the presence or absence of a particular type of barrier, but not its quantitative size or effect. Such qualitative information takes on a quantitative dimension, however, when it is tabulated by sector, perhaps with subjective weights to indicate severity. The result is a set of 'frequency measures' of barriers to trade, recording what the barriers are and where, and perhaps also the fraction of trade within a sector or country that is subject to them. Frequency measures do not directly imply anything like the tariff equivalents of trade barriers, but in order to use them for quantitative analysis, analysts have often converted them to that form in rather ad hoc ways that we shall indicate below.

Other, more indirect, measurements of trade barriers in service industries have also been used, alone or in combination with frequency measures. These may be divided into two types: measurements that use information about prices and/or costs; and measurements that observe quantities of trade or production and attempt to infer how trade barriers have affected these quantities. In both cases, as we shall discuss, if one can also measure or assume an appropriate elasticity reflecting the response of quantity to price, a measured effect on either can be translated into an effect on the other. Thus both price and quantity measurements are also often converted into, and reported as, tariff equivalents.

In what follows, we begin with a conceptual framework for understanding international service transactions and the barriers that may affect them. We then turn to a discussion of the characteristics of service barriers, and we provide some examples of barriers for the banking sector and for FDI in service sectors. This is followed with a discussion of methods of measurement of service barriers, including frequency measures and indexes of restrictiveness, price- and quantity-effect measurements, gravity-model estimates and financial-based measurements. In each case, we provide information and examples of how the measurements are constructed and an evaluation of their merits and limitations. We then consider how the various measurements can be used in assessing the economic consequences of the liberalization of service barriers, before concluding with a presentation of guideline principles and recommended procedures for measuring service barriers and assessing the consequences of their liberalization.

Conceptual framework

Demand-and-supply analysis can be used to show how the introduction of a service barrier will affect the domestic price of a service, the quantity demanded and the quantity supplied by domestic and foreign firms. Using three case examples, diagrammatic analysis shows how the service barrier can be measured as a tariff equivalent. In case 1, domestic and foreign firms are highly competitive and their services are highly substitutable (Figure 13.1). For case 2, the services of the domestic and foreign firms are not readily substitutable and have distinctive prices (Figure 13.2). Finally, in case 3 there is a single domestic firm with monopoly power and the entry of foreign firms is restricted (Figure 13.3). The effects of a service barrier, and thus the tariff equivalent, in these various cases will depend on the competitiveness of domestic and foreign firms and the degree of substitution between the services that they provide.

Case 1

The functioning of a domestic market for a service when there are domestic and foreign suppliers present is shown in Figure 13.1. It is assumed that the suppliers are highly competitive and that their services are readily substitutable. Other cases will be considered below. The foreign suppliers may be serving the domestic market through any of the four modes of supply already discussed, although the degree of substitution between the foreign and domestic services may vary for the different modes.

The horizontal axis measures the quantity of the service supplied to and demanded by domestic purchasers. This could include amounts purchased abroad, as in the case of Mode 2, which are none the less regarded here as competing with domestic supplies. The demand schedule for the service is downward sloping with respect to the price, *P*, which is the same for all suppliers. The supply schedules for the two sets of suppliers, domestic

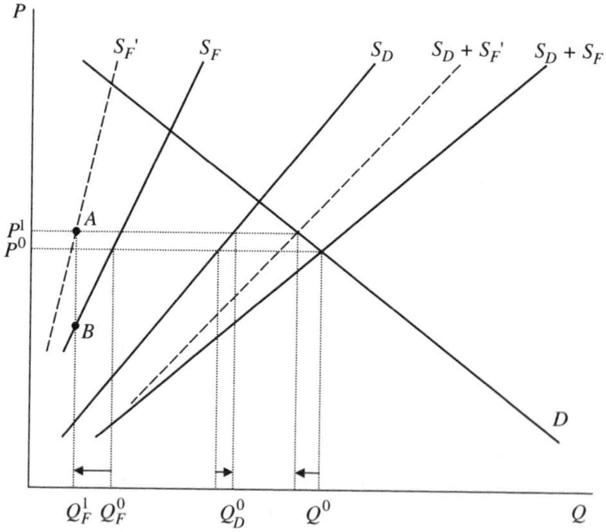

Figure 13.1 Perfect competition and perfect substitution between domestic and foreign services firms

and foreign, are upward sloping and shown by S_D for domestic firms and S_F for foreign firms.[1] In the absence of any impediments to trade, the relevant total supply schedule in this market is the horizontal sum, labeled $S_D + S_F$. Price is determined where the total supply schedule intersects the demand schedule at P^0, with the quantity Q^0 divided between domestic firms, Q_D^0, and foreign firms, Q_F^0.

Let us suppose that a barrier is introduced that inhibits the ability of the foreign firms to serve this market. This may raise foreign firms' costs, shifting their supply schedule upward, or it may reduce or constrain the quantity that they supply, shifting the schedule to the left. Either way, S_F is shifted up and to the left, as is the total supply schedule, $S_D + S_F$, to the positions shown as S_F'' and $S_D + S_F'$. The effect is to raise the price of the service to P^1, reduce the total quantity purchased, and increase the quantity sold by domestic firms. Sales by the foreign firms fall from Q_F^0 to Q_F^1, which is the decline in imports of the service due to the barrier.

The tariff equivalent of this barrier may be defined as the *ad valorem* tax on foreign service providers that would have caused the same effects as this barrier. Such a tax, by increasing the cost of sales by foreign firms, would cause their supply schedule to shift up by the amount of the tax. Therefore, a tax that shifts S_F up so as to pass through point *A* is the tariff equivalent. That is, the tariff equivalent is the percentage by which point *A* lies above point *B*. What should be noted in the case of Figure 13.1 is that the tariff equivalent is not measurable from any observable price or price change. That is, the increase in the price of the service on the domestic market is considerably smaller than the tariff equivalent of the barrier that caused it.

There is, however, one special case in which the tariff equivalent would equal the price change. This occurs when the foreign supply schedule is horizontal (that is, infinitely elastic) at some price P^0 so that the effect of the barrier is to raise foreign firms' cost to P^1. Then the two foreign supply schedules are horizontal at these prices, and the tariff equivalent would be just the amount by which they are shifted upward. To the extent that empirical measurements of tariff equivalents are based on observed prices, a horizontal foreign supply schedule will represent a special case that may exist for a small country that faces a given world price for the service.

Case 2

A case in which the services provided by domestic and foreign firms are not readily substitutable and can therefore have different prices is shown in Figure 13.2. We must consider markets for the two services separately, as is done in the two panels of the figure, and we must also allow for the two services being imperfect substitutes. This is done by having each of the two demand schedules depend on the price in the other market, as indicated. Once again, the figure shows supply and demand schedules, quantities, and prices without any trade barrier with superscript 0, and those in the presence of a trade barrier with superscript 1. The introduction of a barrier shifts the foreign supply schedule to the left and up, as before, to S_F^1 and leads to higher prices in both markets, P_F^1 and P_D^1, which now cause both demand schedules to shift somewhat to the right. As in the case of Figure 13.1, with close substitution of the services, the domestic quantity supplied increases while the foreign quantity supplied declines. And here again, the tariff equivalent can be observed in the figure as the percentage by which S_F^1 lies above S_F^0, that is, the percentage by which point *A* is above point *B*.

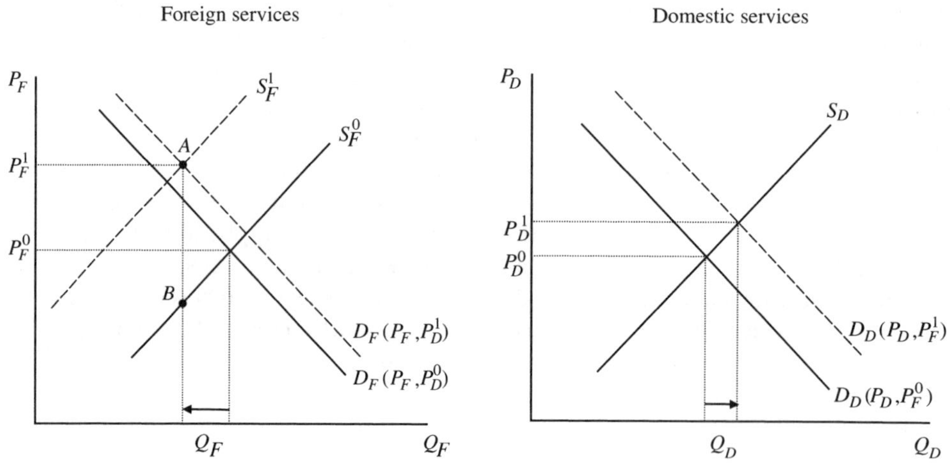

Figure 13.2 Imperfect competition and substitution between domestic and foreign service firms

Case 3

So far we have assumed that markets are highly competitive. But this is clearly inappropriate in many service markets where an incumbent domestic firm may have a monopoly or only a very limited number of competitors. In such markets, a barrier to service trade may be a limit on entry by new firms that, though not explicitly discriminatory, favors the domestic incumbent firm and implicitly limits trade more than domestic supply. We therefore examine the case in which there is a single domestic incumbent firm together with competing foreign suppliers (Figure 13.3). If there is unimpeded entry of firms, the market price will be P^0. In this case, the single domestic firm whose costs are increasing along MC will produce Q_D^0. Total sales are Q^0, and the foreign firms will sell $Q_F^0 = Q^0 - Q_D^0$ in the domestic market. Let us now suppose that a barrier is introduced that raises the cost of the foreign firms when they sell in the domestic market. This would cause the domestic firm's sales to rise along MC and foreign sales to decline. If the foreign cost rises above P^a (the intersection of domestic MC and demand), however, then foreign sales will fall to zero. The domestic firm can thus charge a price that just barely undercuts the foreign cost, so that the domestic firm will be able to monopolize the market. The tariff equivalent of the barrier in the case of Figure 13.3 is therefore the amount by which it increases foreign cost, up to the limit of $P^m - P^0$. However, if the foreign supply schedule were instead upward sloping rather than horizontal, then both the analysis and the identification of the tariff equivalent would be accordingly more difficult to measure. But the general conclusion is that the tariff equivalent of an entry restriction will be measured by the excess of the monopoly price over the competitive price that would have obtained if both trade and entry were free.

Cases 1–3 clearly do not exhaust all of the possible cases. The real world is bound to involve further mixtures of imperfect substitution between the products of domestic and foreign services firms and the degree of competition between these firms that have not been considered here. Also, many service industries have numerous special features,

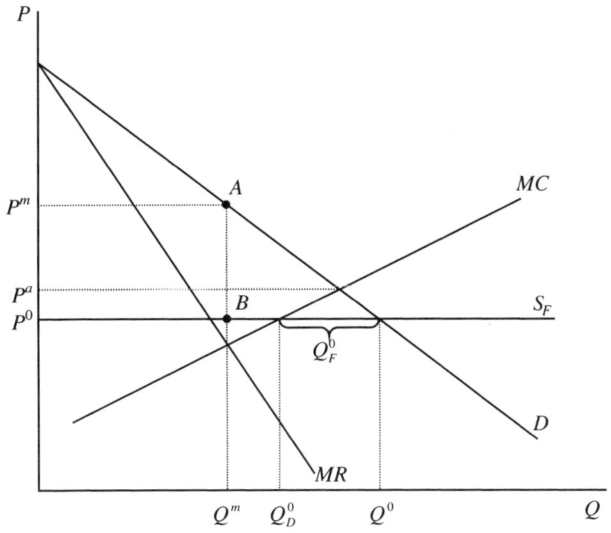

Figure 13.3 Domestic services firm with monopoly power and restrictions on foreign firms

both in the ways that they operate and in their amenability to measurement. Simple theoretical models do not take these factors into account. Empirical work is therefore essential to address the measurement of the various services barriers that impede international services transactions. In what follows, we review and summarize many of the studies that have been undertaken.

Characteristics of services barriers

As noted by Hoekman and Primo Braga (1997: 288), border measures such as tariffs are generally difficult to apply to services because customs agents cannot readily observe services as they cross the border. It is also the case, as discussed above, that many services are provided in the country of consumption rather than cross-border. Typically, therefore, service restrictions are designed in the form of government regulations applied to the different modes of service transactions. Thus, for example, regulations may affect the entry and operations of both domestic and foreign suppliers of services and in turn increase the price or the cost of the services involved. Service barriers are therefore more akin to NTBs than to tariffs, and their impact will depend on how the government regulation is designed and administered.

These regulations can take many forms, and are usually specific to the type of service being regulated. Therefore, since services themselves are so diverse, service barriers are also diverse, making them somewhat difficult to classify in general terms. There are, however, two distinctions that tend to apply across many types of services and service barriers: regulations that apply to entry or establishment of firms versus their operations; and regulations that are nondiscriminatory versus discriminatory.[2] That is, most barriers to trade in services can be placed in one of the four cells of the following simple 2×2 classification:

	Entry/establishment	Operations
Nondiscriminatory		
Discriminatory		

For example, a limit on the number of firms that may be licensed without regard to their nationality would fall into the upper left cell, while such a limit that favors domestically owned firms would be in the lower left. Likewise, a regulation that requires all service providers in an industry to perform certain extra tasks would raise costs or operations in a nondiscriminatory fashion and lie in the upper right cell, while a regulation that requires special performance by foreign providers that is not expected of domestic firms would be in the lower right. Of course a policy could in principle be discriminatory in favor of foreign firms rather than against them, but that would not be typical.

In terms of the conceptual framework posited earlier, the entry versus operations distinction may be thought of as determining whether the regulation shifts the supply schedules of services to the left or up. That is, regulations that restrict or impede the establishment of service providers within a market will usually reduce their number and therefore the quantity supplied at any given price. Regulations of ongoing operations, on the other hand, may not reduce the number of suppliers, but they will increase their costs, causing them to supply a given quantity only at a higher price. This distinction is not perfect, however, and in any case it does not need to be, since as long as the supply schedules are upward sloping, shifts to the left and up have the same qualitative effects, as we have seen. The distinction is useful mainly for classifying different types of barriers.

Likewise, the nondiscriminatory versus discriminatory distinction determines whether a regulation shifts the supply curve of only foreign service providers (when it is discriminatory), or instead raises costs and shifts supply for both foreign and domestic suppliers. As noted earlier, however, a regulation that impedes establishment of all new service providers, in spite of being nondiscriminatory, can none the less limit trade and competition by favoring a domestic incumbent. It is also important to note that some regulations may be designed to achieve certain social objectives, such as health and safety or environmental requirements, and may not be protectionist in intent. Of course, actual regulations differ greatly across service industries and are often based on characteristics of the particular service being provided.

To illustrate, we use the case of banking services based on a study by McGuire and Schuele (2000) done under the auspices of the Australian Productivity Commission. Table 13.2 lists groupings of restrictions that apply especially to Modes 3 and 4 of international banking services transactions. These restrictions relate to commercial presence and 'other restrictions' applied to banking services, together with a brief indication of what these restrictions represent and how an index of them has been constructed.[3] As McGuire and Schuele note (p. 206):

> The commercial presence grouping covers restrictions on licensing, direct investment, joint venture arrangements, and the movement of people. The 'other restrictions' grouping covers restrictions on raising funds, lending funds, providing other lines of business (insurance and securities services), expanding banking outlets, the composition of the board of directors and the temporary movement of people.

Table 13.2 Restriction categories for banking services

Restriction category	Relevant for foreign index	Total weight	Relevant for domestic index	Total weight
Restrictions on commercial presence				
Licensing of banks	Yes	0.200	Yes	0.190
Based inversely on the maximum number of new banking licenses issued with only prudential requirements				
Direct investment	Yes	0.200	Yes	0.190
Based inversely on the maximum equity participation permitted in an existing domestic bank				
Joint venture arrangements	Yes	0.100	No	n.a.
New bank entry only through joint venture with a domestic bank				
Movement of people	Yes	0.020	No	n.a.
Based inversely on years that executives, specialists and/or senior managers can stay				
Other restrictions				
Raising funds by banks	Yes	0.100	Yes	0.143
Banks are restricted from accepting deposits from the public and/or raising funds from domestic capital markets				
Lending funds by banks	Yes	0.100	Yes	0.143
Banks are restricted in types or sizes of loans and/or are directed to lend to housing and small business				
Other business of banks – insurance and securities services	Yes	0.200	Yes	0.095
Banks are excluded from insurance and/or securities services				
Expanding the number of banking outlets	Yes	0.050	Yes	0.048
Based inversely on the number of outlets permitted				
Composition of the board of directors	Yes	0.020	No	n.a.
Based inversely on the percentage of the board that can comprise foreigners				
Temporary movement of people	Yes	0.010	No	n.a.
Based inversely on the number of days temporary entry permitted to executives, specialists and/or senior managers				
Total weighting or highest possible score		1.000		0.808

Source: McGuire and Schuele (2000, Tables 12.1 and 12.3: 204–5, 208).

Thus, the top half of Table 13.2 corresponds roughly to regulations of entry/establishment in Figure 13.4 (see below), while the bottom half corresponds roughly to regulations of operations. For each type of restriction, separate columns also indicate whether they apply to foreign and domestic firms, hence being discriminatory if they apply only to the former. An indication of the restrictiveness of these regulations is also provided in Table 13.2 and will be discussed below.

Just as different subclassifications may be needed for different types of services, so too may the appropriate classification depend on the purpose for which the classification will be used. This point is made especially by Hardin and Holmes (1997) in their discussion of barriers affecting FDI (Mode 3). Focusing, in effect, on the establishment of a commercial presence in many sectors in host countries, they define (p. 24) an FDI barrier as 'any government policy measure which distorts decisions about where to invest and in what form'. In considering ways of classifying such FDI barriers, they note (pp. 33–4):[4]

> The appropriate classification system may vary, depending on the purpose of the exercise. For example, if the purpose is to check and monitor compliance with some policy commitment, then the categories should reflect the key element of the commitment. . . . If the primary interest is instead the resource allocation implications of the barriers, some additional or different information may be useful.
>
> Barriers to FDI may distort international patterns and modes of . . . trade. They may also distort allocation of capital between different economies, between foreign and domestic investment, between different sectors, and between portfolio and direct investment . . . the classification system . . . should highlight the key characteristics of the barriers that will determine their size and impact. Market access and national treatment are . . . relevant categories from a resource allocation perspective. . . national treatment is generally taken to refer to measures affecting firms after establishment. A . . . way to classify barriers is therefore . . . according to what aspect of the investment they most affect: establishment, ownership and control; or operations. In addition . . . some further information may be useful . . . on distinctions . . . between direct versus indirect restrictions on foreign controlled firms; and rules versus case-by-case decisions.[5]

The main types of FDI barriers that have been identified by UNCTAD (1996) are noted in Table 13.3, which divides barriers into three groups, the first of which concerns entry and the last operations. The middle group – ownership and control restrictions – illustrates the weakness of any simple classification system since it seems to include elements of both. Further information on the barriers most commonly used to restrict FDI especially in the APEC (Asia-Pacific Economic Cooperation) economies is provided in Hardin and Holmes (1997, esp. pp. 37–40 and 45–55). As they note (p. 40), some common characteristics appear to be:[6]

> application of some form of screening or registration process involving various degrees of burden for the foreign investor; restrictions on the level or share of foreign ownership, particularly in some service sectors, and often in the context of privatisations; widespread use of case-by-case judgments, often based on national interest criteria; widespread use of restrictions on ownership and control (e.g., restrictions on board membership), particularly in sectors such as telecommunications, broadcasting, banking; and relatively limited use of performance requirements on input controls in services sectors.

It is evident from the foregoing discussion that service barriers exist in a variety of forms, depending on the types of services involved, the country imposing the barriers, and the sectors to which the barriers are applied. To help further the understanding of the

Table 13.3 Barriers to FDI

Restrictions on market entry	Bans on foreign investment in certain sectors Quantitative restrictions (e.g., limit of 25 per cent foreign ownership in a sector) Screening and approval (sometimes involving national interest or net economic benefits tests) Restrictions on the legal form of the foreign entity Minimum capital requirements Conditions on subsequent investment Conditions on location Admission taxes
Ownership and control restrictions	Compulsory joint ventures with domestic investors Limits on the number of foreign board members Government appointed board members Government approval required for certain decisions Restrictions on foreign shareholders' rights Mandatory transfer of some ownership to locals within a specified time (e.g., 15 years)
Operational restrictions	Performance requirements (e.g., export requirements) Local content restrictions Restrictions on imports of labor, capital and raw materials Operational permits or licences Ceilings on royalties Restrictions on repatriation of capital and profits

Source: UNCTAD (1996).

different service barriers, it would be useful accordingly to organize the available information by country and sector, according to the four modes of international service transactions and whether or not they are protectionist in intent. As already noted, these modes cover: cross-border services (Mode 1); consumption abroad (Mode 2); FDI (Mode 3); and the temporary movement of workers (Mode 4). Using this information, the next and difficult step will be to devise methods of measurement of the various barriers and to integrate these measures within a framework designed to assess their economic effects.

It should be emphasized, finally, that not all regulations of services should be viewed as protectionist, even when they do serve to reduce service imports. Many regulations serve legitimate purposes, such as protecting health and safety or preventing fraud and other misconduct. Such a regulation, if applied in a nondiscriminatory manner, is not protectionist and should not be viewed as a barrier to service trade, even though it may maintain a higher standard than prevails abroad and thus reduce imports compared to what they would be without the regulation. On the other hand, nondiscrimination is not by itself enough to absolve a regulation from being protectionist if, say, it enforces a standard that has no legitimate purpose but happens to be met by domestic providers and not by foreign ones. Distinguishing legitimate from illegitimate regulations may not be easy, especially since it usually requires the sort of detailed knowledge of the industry that can only be obtained from industry insiders who are unlikely to be disinterested.

Methods of measurement of service barriers

Measurements of trade barriers, in markets for both goods and services, can be either direct or indirect. Direct measurements start from the observation of an explicit policy or practice, such as an import quota or a regulation of a foreign provider of services, and then attempt in some fashion to measure its economic importance. Indirect measurements try instead to infer the existence of barriers using observed discrepancies between actual economic performance and what would be expected if trade were free. Direct measurements have the advantage that one knows what one is measuring, and the disadvantage that they can only include those barriers that are in fact explicit and recognized. Indirect measurements have the advantage that their quantitative importance is known, at least in the dimension used to identify them, but the disadvantage that they may incorporate unrecognized frictions other than the policy impediments that one seeks to identify.

In the case of trade in goods, direct measurements of NTBs typically take the form of inventories of identified trade restrictions, such as those compiled in the United Nations Conference on Trade and Development (UNCTAD) TRade Analysis and INformation System (TRAINS).[7] Since NTBs usually cover only some industries or products, a first step in quantifying them is often to measure the fraction of trade that they cover in different sectors and countries. These fractions may then be used directly in empirical work, even though they do not themselves say anything about how effective the NTBs have been in restricting trade.[8] Indirect measurements, on the other hand, can be fairly straightforward in the case of goods, based either on their observed prices before and after they cross an international border or on the quantities that cross it. For example, one can often infer both the presence of an import barrier and its effect on price by simply comparing the price of a good inside a country to that outside, since in the absence of any barrier one would expect competitive market forces to cause these prices to be the same. Indirect measurements based on quantities are more difficult, since they depend on a theoretical benchmark for comparability that is likely to be much less certain. None the less, as we note in the following discussion, such quantity-based measurements of NTBs have been used with some success.

For trade in services, direct measurements must be carefully executed, since regulation in service industries is so prevalent that merely to document its presence would not be informative. A common approach is therefore to complement the documentation of regulations by incorporating information about the restrictiveness of the regulations, and then use this information to construct an index of restrictiveness that can be compared across countries. Indirect measurements of restrictiveness are also possible with traded services, although simple price comparisons are seldom of much use. This is because many services are differentiated by location in a way that renders comparison of their prices inside and outside of a country meaningless. For example, the cost of providing telephone service to consumers on the Texas side of the US–Mexican border need bear no particular relationship to the cost, for the same firm, of providing it across the border in Mexico, where wages are much lower but costs of infrastructure may be much higher. So even if trade in the service were completely unimpeded, we would not expect these prices to be the same, and therefore we cannot infer a trade barrier in either direction from the fact that prices are not the same. Similar arguments can be made about most traded services.

Indirect measurements of barriers to trade in services are therefore less common than for trade in goods, although they do exist. There has been some success using the so-called 'gravity model' as a benchmark for quantities of trade in services, and the results of these models have therefore been the basis for indirect measurement of barriers in the quantity dimension. Financial data have also been the basis for inferring barriers from differences in the markups of price over cost.

With indirect measurements of the presence of service barriers less common, however, there is therefore the need for some other approach to quantifying the effects of barriers that have been identified. In this connection, indexes of restrictiveness can be constructed that are typically measured on a scale of zero to one, and they do not purport to say how much a barrier either raises price or reduces quantity. To get such information, another step is needed. Commonly, this step involves using econometric analysis to relate an index of restrictiveness to observed prices or quantities, thus translating the measures of the presence of barriers into an estimate of their economic effect in particular service markets.

In what follows, then, we first discuss the construction of measures of the presence of barriers, commonly referred to as frequency-based measurements, and the use of these measurements to construct indexes of restrictiveness. This is followed by a discussion of how the effects on prices and quantities can be derived. We then turn to methods that attempt to infer the presence of service barriers indirectly, first from a gravity model of the quantities of trade, and second from financial data within service firms.

Frequency studies and indexes of restrictiveness
Studies of frequency-based measures start by identifying the kinds of restriction that apply to a particular service industry or to services in general. For particular industries, this requires considerable industry-specific knowledge, since each industry has, at a minimum, its own terminology, and often also its own distinctive reasons for regulatory concern. Regulations often serve an ostensibly valid purpose – protecting health and safety, for example – and knowledge of the industry is also necessary to distinguish such valid regulations from those that primarily offer protection. Thus, a frequency study is best carried out by an industry specialist, or it must draw upon documents that have been prepared by such specialists. Industry studies therefore often build upon the documentation provided by industry trade groups, such as the International Telecommunications Union in the case of telecoms, bilateral air service arrangements in the case of passenger air travel, or the TradePort website in the case of maritime services.

For broader studies of restrictions in services, covering multiple industries, some source must be found that incorporates such expertise across sectors. An early approach to doing this was in the studies by PECC (1995) and Hoekman (1995 [1996]). These studies used information that countries had submitted to the General Agreement on Trade in Services (GATS) to be used as the basis for commitments to be made for service liberalization in the Uruguay Round negotiations. Such measures are therefore not ideally suited for documenting trade barriers. Better information requires that someone deliberately collects the details of actual barriers and regulatory practices, as in the data collected by APEC and used by Hardin and Holmes (1997), whose study we also discuss below. In all cases, the goal is not just to assemble a complete list of barriers, but also to know the restrictiveness of these barriers in terms such as the number of firms or countries to which they apply and other characteristics. This latter information is then used to construct an Index of Restrictiveness. Typically, each barrier is assigned a score between zero and one, with a score of one being the most restrictive and a score of zero being the least restrictive. These scores are then averaged using weights that are intended to reflect the relative importance of each type of barrier.

There are several ways in which the weights on different barriers in a restrictiveness index may be assigned. Most commonly, these reflect the judgments of knowledgeable investigators as to the importance of each type of barrier. This may well be the best approach if the investigator really is knowledgeable, as in the case when an index is being constructed for a specific, narrowly defined industry. An alternative that has been used by Nicoletti et al. (2000) and subsequently by Doove et al. (2001) is to apply factor analysis to the data once they are assembled. This enables them to distinguish those barriers that vary most independently among their data, and then to apply the largest weights to them. This is a purely statistical technique that is not, in our view, necessarily an improvement on the use of judgmental weights.

A third approach is not to construct an index at all, but rather to use the scores or proxy measures for each barrier separately in an empirical analysis. The difficulty here is that these scores may be interrelated, so that their independent influence on any variable of interest may be impossible to ascertain using standard statistical methods. If this can be done, however, the advantage is that it allows for the fact that barriers may differ in their importance for different aspects of economic performance, and this approach allows these differences to make themselves known. Ideally, one would prefer an approach that allows the weights in an index of restrictiveness to be estimated simultaneously with the importance of that index for a particular economic outcome. Thus the construction of the index would be interlinked with its use for estimating, for example, effects on prices and quantities. Before examining this, we discuss a few of the main studies that have constructed frequency measurements and indexes of restrictiveness.

PECC and Hoekman

PECC (1995) and Hoekman (1995 [1996]) use information contained in the country schedules of the GATS, referring to all four modes of supply of services, to construct frequency ratios that measure the extent of liberalization promised by countries in their commitments to the GATS, as part of the Uruguay Round negotiations completed in 1993–94. The frequency ratios are constructed based on the number of commitments that were scheduled by individual countries designating sectors or subsectors as unrestricted or partially restricted. The ratios that are calculated equal the number of actual commitments in relation to the maximum possible number of commitments.[9] Hoekman focused on commitments relating to market access and national treatment. As he notes (1996: 101), there were 155 sectors and subsectors and four modes of supply specified in the GATS. This yields $620 \times 2 = 1440$ total commitments on market access and national treatment for each of 97 countries.[10] The frequency ratio for a country or a sector is then defined as the fraction of these possible commitments that were in fact made, implying an index of trade restrictiveness equal to one minus this fraction.

There are some important limitations to these calculations that are worth mentioning. Thus, as Holmes and Hardin (2000: 58–9) note, Hoekman's method may be misleading or biased because it assumes that the absence of positive country commitments in the GATS schedules can be interpreted as indicating the presence of restrictions, which may not be the case in fact. Also, the different types of restrictions are given equal weight.[11]

Table 13.4 Components of an index of FDI restrictions

Type of restriction	Weight
Foreign equity limits on all firms	
No foreign equity permitted	1.000
Less than 50 per cent foreign equity permitted	0.500
More than 50 per cent and less than 100 per cent foreign equity permitted	0.250
Foreign equity limits on existing firms, none on greenfield	
No foreign equity permitted	0.500
Less than 50 per cent foreign equity permitted	0.250
More than 50 per cent and less than 100 per cent foreign equity permitted	0.125
Screening and approval	
Investor required to demonstrate net economic benefits	0.100
Approval unless contrary to national interest	0.075
Notification (pre or post)	0.050
Control and management restrictions	
All firms	0.200
Existing firms, none for greenfield	0.100
Input and operational restrictions	
All firms	0.200
Existing firms, none for greenfield	0.100

Source: Holmes and Hardin (2000: 62).

Hardin and Holmes (1997) and Holmes and Hardin (2000) have attempted to build on and improve Hoekman's methodology, though focusing only on restrictions on FDI in services (Mode 3). In particular, they use information on the actual FDI restrictions taken from APEC, rather than just the GATS commitments. Rather than treating all restrictions equally, they devise a judgmental system of weighting that is designed, as in the case of the banking restrictions noted in Table 13.2, to reflect the efficiency costs of the different barriers. The components of their index and the weights assigned to the different subcategories are given in Table 13.4. It can be seen, for example, that foreign equity limits are given greater weights than the other barriers noted. Their results for 15 APEC countries for the 1996–98 period are summarized in Table 13.5.[12] It is evident that communications and financial services are most subject to FDI restrictions, while business, distribution, environmental and recreational services are the least restricted. Korea, Indonesia, China, Thailand and the Philippines have relatively high restrictiveness indexes, while the United States and Hong Kong have the lowest indexes.

McGuire and Schuele

Table 13.2 indicated the restriction categories and weights applied to banking services in the study by McGuire and Schuele (2000) which is based on a variety of data sources (pp. 202–3), including the GATS schedules of commitments and a number of other reports and documentation pertaining to actual financial-sector restrictions in 38 economies for the 1995–98 period. McGuire and Schuele (pp. 204–5) have assigned scores for different degrees of restriction, ranging between 0 (least restrictive) and 1 (most restrictive). The various categories are weighted judgmentally in terms of how great the costs involved are assumed to

Table 13.5 FDI restrictiveness indexes for selected APEC economies and selected sectors, 1996–98 (%)

Sectors	Australia	Canada	China	Hong Kong	Indonesia	Japan	Korea	Malaysia
Business	0.183	0.225	0.360	0.015	0.560	0.062	0.565	0.316
Communications	0.443	0.514	0.819	0.350	0.644	0.350	0.685	0.416
Postal	1.000	1.000	1.000	1.000	1.000	1.000	1.000	1.000
Courier	0.175	0.200	0.275	0.000	0.525	0.050	0.550	0.075
Telecommunications	0.300	0.325	1.000	0.200	0.525	0.100	0.550	0.375
Audiovisual	0.295	0.530	1.000	0.200	0.525	0.250	0.640	0.215
Construction	0.175	0.200	0.400	0.000	0.525	0.050	0.750	0.775
Distribution	0.175	0.200	0.275	0.050	0.525	0.050	0.625	0.075
Education	0.175	0.200	0.525	0.000	0.525	0.200	0.550	0.075
Environmental	0.175	0.200	0.275	0.000	0.525	0.117	0.700	0.075
Financial	0.450	0.375	0.450	0.233	0.550	0.358	0.875	0.608
Insurance and related	0.275	0.425	0.475	0.400	0.575	0.450	0.838	0.600
Banking and other	0.625	0.325	0.425	0.067	0.525	0.267	0.913	0.617
Health	0.175	0.200	0.275	0.000	0.525	0.050	0.550	0.317
Tourism	0.175	0.200	0.283	0.000	0.525	0.050	0.617	0.542
Recreation	0.175	0.200	0.275	0.000	0.525	0.050	0.550	0.175
Transport	0.204	0.235	0.455	0.093	0.525	0.114	0.573	0.122

	Mexico	New Zealand	Papua New Guinea	Philippines	Singapore	Thailand	USA
Business	0.289	0.086	0.300	0.479	0.261	0.775	0.005
Communications	0.739	0.434	0.475	0.758	0.518	0.838	0.345
Postal	1.000	1.000	1.000	1.000	1.000	1.000	1.000
Courier	0.775	0.075	0.300	0.475	0.250	0.775	0.000
Telecommunications	0.705	0.425	0.300	0.975	0.571	0.804	0.200
Audiovisual	0.475	0.235	0.300	0.580	0.250	0.775	0.180
Construction	0.450	0.075	0.300	0.475	0.250	0.775	0.000
Distribution	0.325	0.075	0.300	0.475	0.250	0.775	0.000

Education	0.450	0.075	0.300	0.475	0.250	0.775	0.000
Environmental	0.075	0.075	0.300	0.475	0.250	0.775	0.000
Financial	0.554	0.200	0.300	0.954	0.378	0.875	0.200
Insurance and related	0.575	0.125	0.300	0.975	0.250	0.775	0.000
Banking and other	0.533	0.275	0.300	0.933	0.506	0.975	0.400
Health	0.408	0.075	0.300	0.475	0.250	0.775	0.000
Tourism	0.275	0.075	0.300	0.808	0.317	0.775	0.000
Recreational	0.075	0.075	0.300	0.475	0.250	0.775	0.000
Transport	0.283	0.131	0.300	0.975	0.250	0.780	0.025

Note: The higher the score, the greater the degree to which an industry is restricted. The maximum score is 100%. Because of data constraints on the value of output by sector, the indexes shown are based on simple averages of the subsectors involved in the individual countries.

Source: Adapted from Holmes and Hardin (2000: 63–4).

be with respect to the effect on economic efficiency. Thus, it can be seen in Table 13.2 that restrictions on the licensing of banks are taken to be more burdensome than restrictions on the movement of people. Also, the scores are given separately for the restrictions applicable only to foreign banks and the 'domestic' restrictions applicable to all banks. The differences between the foreign and domestic measures can then be interpreted as indicating the discrimination imposed on foreign banks. Finally, it will be noted that the foreign scores sum to a maximum of 1 and the domestic scores to a maximum of 0.808, because some of the restrictions noted apply only to foreign banks and not to domestic banks.

Based on detailed information available, the scores for banking restrictions in individual countries can be constructed. Using the category weights in Table 13.2, it is then possible to calculate 'indexes of restrictiveness' of the foreign and domestic regulations by country. These indexes are depicted graphically for selected Asia-Pacific countries, South Africa and Turkey (Figure 13.4) and for western hemisphere countries (Figure 13.5). India, Indonesia, Malaysia and the Philippines can be seen to have relatively high foreign index scores, Korea, Singapore, Thailand and Turkey have moderate foreign index scores, and Australia, Hong Kong, Japan, New Zealand and South Africa have the lowest foreign index scores. The domestic index scores are indicative of the restrictions applied to both domestic and foreign banks, and it appears that the domestic index scores are highest for Japan, Korea, Malaysia and the Philippines.

While the absolute values of the foreign and domestic index scores are not reported, the differences in the scores can be interpreted visually as a measurement of the discrimination applied to foreign banks. Thus, India, Indonesia, Korea, Malaysia, the Philippines,

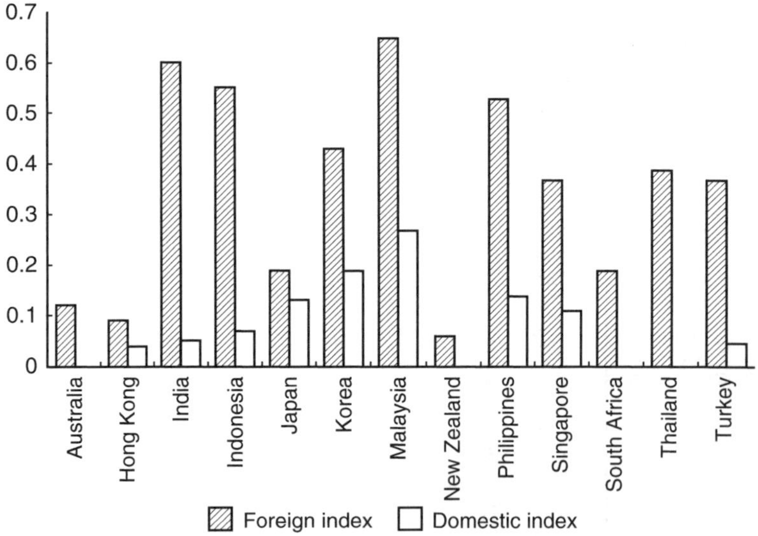

Note: The higher the score the more restrictive an economy; scores range from 0 to 1.

Source: McGuire and Schuele (2000: 211).

Figure 13.4 Restrictiveness indexes for selected Asia-Pacific economies, South Africa and Turkey

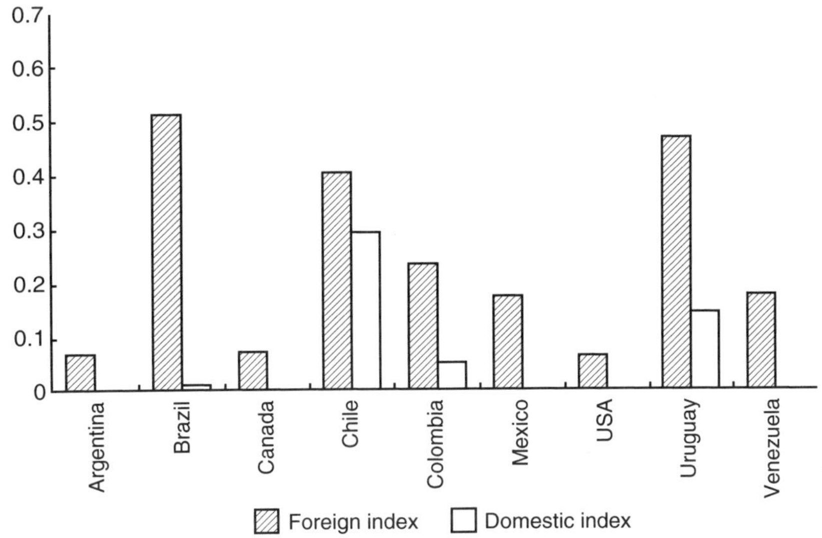

Note: The higher the score the more restrictive an economy; scores range from 0 to 1.

Source: Mcguire and Schuele (2000: 211).

Figure 13.5 Restrictiveness indexes for selected western hemisphere economies

Singapore, Thailand and Turkey appear to have the highest discrimination against foreign banks (Figure 13.4). Brazil, Chile and Uruguay have the highest foreign index scores, Colombia, Mexico and Venezuela have moderate scores, and Argentina, Canada and the United States have the lowest scores (Figure 13.5). Chile and Uruguay have the highest domestic index scores, while Argentina, Canada, Mexico, the United States and Venezuela have domestic index scores of zero. Brazil, Colombia, and Uruguay have the most discriminatory regimes against foreign banks.[13] McGuire and Schuele (2000: 212–13) further found that countries with less restricted banking sectors tended to have higher GNP per capita.

The frequency measures and indexes of restriction that we have discussed thus far are especially useful in identifying the types of barriers and the relative degrees of protection afforded to particular service sectors across countries.[14] It is evident that there exists a considerable amount of information on barriers covering a wide variety of service sectors, including financial services, telecommunications, accountancy, distribution, air transport and electricity supply. As such, the compilation of such measurements and construction of such indexes are important first steps that can provide the basis for the next step, which involves using available methodologies to assess the economic effects of maintaining or eliminating the barriers.

Price-impact measurements[15]

As already noted, the nature of services tends to prevent the use of price and quantity differences across borders to measure their presence or size. Therefore, in order to construct measurements of the price and/or quantity effects of barriers to trade in services, some other approach is needed.

The simplest is just to make an informed guess. For example, having constructed a frequency ratio for offers to liberalize service trade in the GATS as discussed above, Hoekman (1995 [1996]) then assumed that failure to liberalize in a sector would be equivalent to some particular tariff level that he selected using knowledge of the sector. These maximum tariff equivalents ranged from a high of 200 per cent for sectors in which market access was essentially prohibited in most countries (for example, maritime cabotage, air transport, postal services, voice telecommunications and life insurance) to 20–50 percent for sectors in which market access was less constrained. He then applied his frequency-ratio measurements of liberalization to these maximum tariffs to construct tariff equivalents that differed by country based on their offers in the GATS. Thus, for example, assuming a benchmark tariff equivalent of, say, 200 per cent for postal services, and a frequency ratio of 40 per cent to reflect a country's scheduled market access commitments, the tariff equivalent for that sector and country is set at 200 – 0.4(200) = 120 per cent.

Using the value of output by sector for a representative industrialized country, it is then possible to construct weighted average measurements by sector and country. Weighted-average tariff equivalent 'guesstimates' for 1-digit International Standard Industrial Classification (ISIC) sectors for selected countries can then be produced (Table 13.6). It can be seen that the tariff equivalents are highest for ISIC 7 (transportation, storage & communications), reflecting the significant constraints applied within this sector. There is

Table 13.6 Constructed ad valorem *tariff equivalent 'guesstimates' by 1-digit ISIC services sectors for selected countries (%)*

Country	ISIC 5 Construction	ISIC 6 Wholesale & retail distribution	ISIC 7 Transport, storage & communications	ISIC 8 Business & financial services	ISIC 9 Social & personal services
Australia	12.0	7.4	183.4	24.8	25.4
Austria	5.0	4.6	98.7	20.1	13.9
Canada	6.0	9.0	117.7	25.9	40.2
Chile	40.0	34.4	182.2	45.2	42.9
EU	10.0	10.0	182.0	27.2	23.6
Finland	19.0	14.6	181.0	23.8	31.7
Hong Kong	32.0	31.5	149.8	39.0	42.9
Japan	5.0	4.6	142.0	28.9	32.3
Korea	16.0	21.4	164.9	36.3	40.7
Mexico	24.0	21.3	152.3	40.9	29.8
New Zealand	5.0	13.4	181.5	30.5	36.1
Norway	5.0	13.4	122.2	25.7	24.0
Singapore	12.0	34.4	138.8	35.9	33.7
Sweden	12.0	13.4	184.2	22.5	26.9
Switzerland	5.0	8.0	178.1	27.7	32.3
Turkey	5.0	34.4	31.6	35.4	35.9
USA	5.0	4.6	111.4	21.7	31.7

Source: Hoekman (1995: 355–6).

also considerable variation within the individual sectors for the relatively highly industrialized countries listed in Table 13.6. It should be emphasized that Hoekman's measurements are designed to indicate only the *relative* degree of restriction. We refer to them as 'guesstimates', which are not to be taken literally as indicators of absolute *ad valorem* tariff equivalents. That is, the tariff equivalent benchmarks are just judgmental and are not distinguished according to their economic impact. Further, the benchmarks include only market access restrictions and cover all of the different modes of service delivery.

An improved approach that has been used in more recent studies is to combine other data together with an index or proxy measures of restrictiveness in order to estimate econometrically the effects of barriers. For example, suppose that an index of restrictiveness has been constructed for a group of countries, and that price data are also available for the services involved in this same group. Using knowledge and data on the economic determinants of these prices, an econometric model can be formulated to explain them. Then, if the restrictiveness index and/or proxy measures of restrictiveness are included in this equation as additional explanatory variables, the estimated coefficient(s) will measure the effect of the trade restrictions on prices, controlling for the other determinants of prices that have been included in the model. Use of this method of course requires data on more than just the barriers themselves, including prices and other relevant determinants of prices. However, these additional data may be needed for only a subset of the countries for which the restrictiveness measures have been constructed, so long as one can assume that the effects of restrictions may be common across countries.

The coefficients relating restrictiveness to prices can be estimated for a subset of countries for which the requisite data are available, and the estimated coefficients can then be applied to the other countries as well. An example of this approach may be found in the study of the international air passenger transport industry by Doove et al. (2001: ch. 2). Their indexes of bilateral restrictions on international air passenger transport referred to 35 economies in the Asia-Pacific, Americas and European regions. Focusing on the discount segment of the air passenger market, they implement a procedure for estimating the price effects of the applicable restrictions, using fare data primarily for the end years of the 1990s. The results indicated that the higher price effects range from 12 to 22 percent in the Asia-Pacific economies, 9–18 percent in the Americas, and generally below 10 percent in the European economies (Table 13.7). The price impacts for business and economy airfares were considerably higher but should be interpreted tentatively due to data constraints. Doove et al. built on work by Gonenc and Nicoletti (2001), who had constructed an index of restrictiveness for this industry in the manner already discussed, and who had also used an econometric model to estimate the effects of restrictiveness for a group of 13 OECD countries. They also extended the index of restrictiveness to a larger set of 35 OECD and non-OECD countries and applied this estimated coefficient to calculate price effects.

The estimating equation used for this was the following:

$$p = \alpha + \beta BRI + \gamma E + \varepsilon, \qquad (13.1)$$

where p represents the price of air travel over a particular route, BRI is the index of restrictiveness for that route, and E is a vector of variables for the determinants of prices, including indexes of market structure both for the route and at the route ends, measurements of airport conditions, government control and propensity for air travel. The coefficients, α, β and γ are to be estimated econometrically, while ε is the disturbance term. The price variable $\dot{p}$ in this equation is of some interest, since it demonstrates the not uncommon need to model particular features of a service industry. It is based on a separate analysis of international airfares, relating them to distance and to other route-specific variables. The price that is entered in equation (13.1) is then the percentage that the actual airfare lies above the price predicted from this analysis.

Thus, holding this predicted price constant as unaffected by a particular trade restriction, the estimated coefficient β measures the percentage by which the price – air fare in this case – is increased by a restrictiveness of one, compared to the price at a restrictiveness of zero. Applying this estimated coefficient to the values of the index of restrictiveness for the larger set of countries, Doove et al. produced the price-effect estimates reported in Table 13.7. As can be seen, these tend to be largest for developing economies and for business travel.

Other studies have been done using variations on this technique. These variations include the use of separate indexes of restrictiveness or proxy measures for different types of trade barriers, including individual modes of supply. These studies cover several sectors, including international air services, wholesale and retail food distributors, banks, maritime services, engineering services, telecommunications and industrial electricity supply in both developed and developing countries.[16] These various sectors are evidently distinctive in terms of their economic characteristics and the regulatory measures that affect their operations. Specialized knowledge of the sectors is thus essential in designing the conceptual framework and adapting the available data to calculate the price impacts of the regulatory measures involved.

Quantity-impact measurements

Another approach, appropriate for some service industries, is to model the determination of quantity rather than price, and then to include the trade restrictiveness index in a quantity equation. The result, analogous to that for prices above, is an estimate of effects of trade barriers on quantities. This can in turn be converted into an effect on prices by use of an assumed or an estimated price elasticity of demand.[17]

For example, Warren (2000b) has assessed the quantitative impact of barriers in telecommunications services, chiefly mobile telephony and fixed network services, for 136 countries. For this purpose he estimated equations such as the following, which was for mobile telephony:

$$Q_i^m = \alpha + \beta_1 Y_i + \beta_2 Y_i^2 + \beta_3 PD_i + \beta_4 [P_i^m] + \varepsilon_i \tag{13.2}$$

Here, for each country i, Q_i^m is the number of cellular telephone subscribers per 100 inhabitants, Y_i is GDP per capita, and PD_i is population density. $[P_i^m]$ is a policy variable, which for mobile telephony took two forms: an index of market access for investment in the industry based on number of competitors, privatization, and policies towards competition; and a broader average of several trade and investment-related indexes.

Combining these quantitative estimates of the effects of removing existing barriers with an estimate of the price elasticity of demand for the telecommunications services involved, tariff equivalents in the form of price wedges were calculated. The tariff equivalents for

Table 13.7 International air passenger transport: bilateral restriction indexes and price impacts

	Number of agreements/routes	Bilateral restriction index[a]	Price impacts[b]		
			Business	Economy	Discount
Asia-Pacific economies					
Australia	24	0.62	146.0	54.8	14.6
India	20	0.77	164.4	81.3	21.8
Indonesia	16	0.73	139.7	53.0	20.4
Japan	29	0.73	121.1	41.4	18.1
Korea	18	0.72	181.5	89.9	20.4
Malaysia	22	0.71	199.1	95.6	18.4
New Zealand	15	0.39	82.1	66.8	11.7
Philippines	20	0.79	207.5	70.1	20.9
Singapore	30	0.70	141.5	57.5	16.8
Thailand	25	0.68	124.5	71.3	16.2
Americas economies					
Argentina	12	0.74	161.7	62.0	17.5
Brazil	19	0.70	195.5	63.9	15.5
Canada	29	0.60	114.5	56.9	11.4
Chile	17	0.61	125.2	49.5	12.9
Mexico	19	0.82	224.7	92.2	18.4
Uruguay	32	0.52	96.9	38.5	12.3
USA	32	0.40	52.9	33.2	8.9
European economies					
Austria	28	0.32	47.2	20.6	6.1
Belgium	31	0.36	63.3	22.0	6.9
Denmark	30	0.34	53.1	21.1	7.0
Finland	22	0.23	33.6	11.5	3.8
France	32	0.35	57.0	20.8	8.3
Germany	32	0.37	56.5	20.3	8.1
Greece	26	0.31	72.1	24.9	7.2
Ireland	23	0.21	32.2	20.1	4.5
Italy	25	0.29	49.9	18.5	6.4
Luxembourg	23	0.24	36.9	15.0	4.2
Netherlands	31	0.39	104.0	20.0	10.0
Norway	28	0.32	62.1	16.4	4.4
Portugal	21	0.14	45.5	20.3	6.1
Spain	31	0.36	68.0	25.4	8.9
Sweden	29	0.32	45.5	20.3	6.1
Switzerland	32	0.75	102.5	42.6	13.8
Turkey	20	0.56	98.8	32.2	10.7
UK	32	0.30	46.3	21.5	7.6

Notes:

a. Unweighted average of the route-level bilateral restriction indexes for each economy based on the number of agreements/routes shown in the preceding column. Ranges from 0 to 0.97, with a higher score indicating more restrictions.

b. Percentage increase in airfares compared to the benchmark regime.

Source: Doove et al. (2001: 39).

Table 13.8 Tariff equivalents of barriers to telecommunication services in major nations (%)

	Domestic	Foreign
Australia	0.31	0.31
Austria	0.85	0.85
Belgium	0.65	1.31
Brazil	3.81	5.68
Canada	1.07	3.37
Chile	1.68	1.68
Hong Kong	1.26	1.26
Colombia	10.55	24.27
Denmark	0.20	0.20
Finland	0.00	0.00
France	0.34	1.43
Germany	0.32	0.32
Ireland	1.46	2.67
Italy	1.00	1.00
Japan	0.26	0.26
Korea	4.30	8.43
Mexico	6.24	14.43
Netherlands	0.20	0.20
New Zealand	0.27	0.27
Singapore	2.10	2.72
Spain	2.03	3.93
Sweden	0.65	0.65
Switzerland	1.23	1.23
Turkey	19.59	33.53
UK	0.00	0.00
USA	0.20	0.20

Source: Adapted from Warren (2000b).

domestic and for foreign providers of telecommunication services in the major nations show estimates for the advanced industrialized countries that are relatively low in comparison to the much higher estimates for the newly industrializing countries (Table 13.8). There are cases of developing countries (not shown except Columbia) that in some cases have very large tariff equivalents, including some with several hundred percent, for example, China (804 and 1000 percent), Colombia (11 and 24 percent), India (861 and 1000 percent), Indonesia (71 and 128 percent), South Africa (14 and 21 percent) and Venezuela (10 and 15 percent).

Gravity-model estimates

Because the modeling of prices that is needed to estimate a price effect above is necessarily very sector specific, the techniques described so far have limited use for quantifying barriers across sectors. Likewise, they are not useful for comparing the overall levels of service trade barriers across countries. For that, one needs a more general model of trade to use as a benchmark, and the natural choice is the so-called 'gravity model'. This model

Table 13.9 Estimated tariff equivalents in traded services: gravity-model-based regression method (%)

Countries/regions	Business/financial services	Construction
North America[b]	8.2	9.8
Western Europe	8.5	18.3
Australia and New Zealand	6.9	24.4
Japan	19.7	29.7
China	18.8	40.9
Taiwan	2.6	5.3
Other newly industrialized countries	2.1	10.3
Indonesia	6.8	9.6
Other South East Asia	5.0	17.7
India	13.1	61.6
Other South Asia[a]	20.4	46.3
Brazil	35.7	57.2
Other Latin America	4.7	26.0
Turkey[b]	20.4	46.3
Other Middle East and North Africa	4.0	9.5
CEECs & Russia	18.4	51.9
South Africa	15.7	42.1
Other Sub-Saharan Africa	0.3	11.1
Rest of World (ROW)	20.4	46.3

Notes:
a. Turkey and Other South Asia are not available, separately, in the US data, and have been assigned estimated ROW values.
b. North America values involve assigning Canada/Mexico numbers to the United States.

Source: Francois (1999).

relates bilateral trade volumes positively to the incomes of both trading partners, and also negatively to the distance between them.[18] It has become a very popular tool in recent years for eliciting the effects of a wide variety of policy and structural influences on trade in a manner that controls for the obvious importance of income and distance.

Francois (1999) has fitted a gravity model to bilateral services trade for the United States and its major trading partners, taking Hong Kong and Singapore to be free trade benchmarks. The independent variables, in addition to distance between trading partners, included per capita income, gross domestic product (GDP), and a western hemisphere dummy variable. The differences between actual and predicted imports were taken to be indicative of trade barriers and were then normalized relative to the free trade benchmarks for Hong Kong and Singapore. Combining this with an assumed demand elasticity of 4, tariff equivalents can be estimated. The results for business/financial services and for construction show that Brazil has the highest estimated tariff equivalent for business/financial services (35.7 percent), followed by Japan, China, Other South Asia and Turkey at about 20 percent (Table 13.9). The estimated tariff equivalents are considerably higher for construction services, in the 40–60 percent range for China, South Asia, Brazil, Turkey, Central Europe, Russia and South Africa, and in the 10–30 percent range for the industrialized countries.

Financial-based measurements

Hoekman (2000) has suggested that financial data on gross operating margins calculated by sector and country may provide information about the effects of government policies on firm entry and conditions of competition.[19] As he notes (p. 36):

> In general, a large number of factors will determine the ability of firms to generate high margins, including market size (number of firms), the business cycle, the state of competition, policy enforcement, the substitutability of products, fixed costs, etc. Notwithstanding the impossibility of inferring that high margins are due to high barriers, there should be a correlation between the two across countries for any given sector. Data on operating margins provide some sense of the relative profitability of activities, and therefore, the relative magnitude (restrictiveness) of barriers to entry/exit that may exist.

The country-region results of Hoekman's analysis, averaged over firms and sectors for 1994–96, are indicated for agriculture, manufacturing and services in Table 13.10. Sectoral results for services only are given in Table 13.11. Service margins are generally higher than manufacturing margins by 10–15 percentage points, and the service margins vary considerably across countries. Australia, Hong Kong and Singapore have the lowest service margins – in the neighborhood of 20 percent – while Chile, China, Indonesia, the Philippines, Taiwan, Thailand and the United States have service margins in excess of 40 percent. The sectoral results indicate that the margins for hotels and financial services are relatively high, and those for wholesale and retail trade are lower. The margins for several

Table 13.10 Average gross operating margins of firms listed on national stock exchanges, 1994–96 by country/region (%)

Country/region	Agriculture	Manufacturing	Services
Australia	8.4	15.5	16.6
Canada	32.1	22.6	32.9
Chile	39.1	40.8	44.0
China	30.6	28.1	49.5
European Union	22.9	23.8	31.6
Hong Kong	25.9	12.8	18.1
Indonesia	41.8	34.3	41.3
Japan	38.4	26.4	28.7
Republic of Korea	11.2	25.7	25.8
Malaysia	22.6	6.0	21.6
Mexico	38.4	39.3	37.2
New Zealand	33.3	16.6	26.8
Philippines	18.1	28.6	42.3
Singapore	0.0	11.1	22.0
Taiwan	19.6	25.1	41.3
Thailand	38.2	27.3	52.6
United States	36.6	21.2	42.3
Rest of Cairns Group[a]	36.3	31.1	39.0

Note: a. Includes Argentina, Brazil and Colombia.

Source: Hoekman (2000). Based on calculations using Disclosure (1998) data.

Table 13.11 Average gross operating margins of services firms listed on national stock exchanges, 1994–96, by country/region and by sector (%)

Country/region	Recreation	Business services	Construction	Consulting	Finance	Health	Hotels	Retail trade	Wholesale	Transport/ utilities
Australia	17.9	13.8	15.3	7.0	41.0	b	27.3	7.9	9.1	c
Canada	60.1	51.7	14.4	19.2	44.5	2.3	67.8	12.0	16.0	36.5
Chile	b	b	68.7	b	55.2	b	b	21.3	27.9	46.8
China	b	b	45.9	67.1	34.0	b	77.5	24.4	25.5	46.9
EU	42.5	32.1	19.3	22.1	51.6	22.3	23.7	23.6	19.9	32.6
Hong Kong	b	6.5	12.9	11.5	25.4	b	31.3	10.1	6.9	31.0
Indonesia	b	81.1	22.9	25.3	53.6	b	68.2	26.4	24.8	45.3
Japan	28.1	31.6	14.2	28.6	40.5	40.1	27.2	32.9	15.6	20.6
Republic of Korea	b	41.2	15.3	b	b	b	b	26.7	14.9	31.2
Malaysia	13.3	c	18.3	14.7	28.3	24.3	38.7	11.2	10.8	30.7
Mexico	19.6	b	25.7	37.3	33.3	b	49.6	28.4	25.0	51.0
New Zealand	b	b	13.8	b	57.6	b	26.9	6.6	19.7	35.6
Philippines	19.9	b	40.2	b	53.9	b	55.8	43.9	40.3	42.3
Singapore	46.7	8.6	10.6	7.7	46.3	29.2	28.2	5.4	7.9	28.0
Taiwan	79.9	36.3	21.6	11.1	64.8	b	74.5	21.5	23.2	38.9
Thailand	85.4	35.8	38.1	c	60.3	40.6	55.5	44.2	25.6	56.7
USA	46.8	56.2	20.2	c	56.3	37.0	48.5	34.6	27.0	43.4
Other Cairns[a]	b	b	28.9	26.2	69.8	29.3	64.6	24.2	22.9	52.4

Notes:
a. Includes Argentina, Brazil and Colombia.
b. Data not available.
c. Reflects negative gross operating margin.

Source: Hoekman (2000). Based on calculations using Disclosure (1998) data.

developing countries appear to be relatively high in a number of sectors. Overall, as Hoekman suggests (p. 39): 'business services, consultancy, and distribution do not appear to be among the most protected sectors. . . . barriers to competition are higher in transportation, finance, and telecommunications. These are also basic "backbone" imports that are crucial for the ability of enterprises to compete internationally'.

Measuring the economic consequences of liberalizing service barriers

While the various measurements of service barriers that we have reviewed are of interest in themselves, they need to be incorporated into an explicit economic modeling framework in order to determine how the existence or removal of the barriers will affect conditions of competition, productivity, the allocation of resources, and economic welfare within or between sectors and countries. In this regard, a modeling framework can be devised for individual sectors or on an economy-wide basis using computable general equilibrium (CGE) modeling.

Sectoral modeling

An example of sectoral modeling is provided by Fink et al. (2003), who analyze the impact of policy reform on sectoral performance in basic telecommunications. Their data cover 86 developing countries globally for the 1985–99 period. They address three questions, covering the impact of: (i) policy changes relating to ownership, competition and regulation; (ii) any one policy reform coupled with the implementation of complementary reforms; and (iii) the sequencing of reforms. Their findings are: first, privatization and the introduction of competition significantly increase labor productivity and the density of telecommunication mainlines; second, privatization and competition work best through their interactions; and third, there are more favorable effects from introducing competition before privatization. They further conclude that autonomous technological progress outweighs the effects of policy reforms in increasing the growth of teledensity.

What is especially noteworthy about this type of study is its focus on both the policy and market structure of the sector and the econometric framework that is designed to measure the determinants of teledensity and telecommunications productivity. The assessment of particular service barriers may therefore be most effectively addressed when incorporated into a sectoral modeling framework.[20]

CGE modeling

In contrast to sectoral modeling, CGE modeling provides a framework for multi-sectoral and multi-country analysis of the economic effects of service barriers and related policies. Most CGE modeling research to date has been focused on barriers to international trade in goods rather than trade in services and FDI. The reasons for this stem in large part from the lack of comprehensive data on cross-border services trade and FDI and the associated barriers, together with the difficult conceptual problems of modeling that are encountered. Some indication of pertinent CGE modeling work relating to services is provided in Hardin and Holmes (1997: 85), Brown and Stern (2001: 272–4) and Stern (2002: 254–6). The approaches to modeling can be divided as follows: (i) analysis of cross-border services trade liberalization in response to reductions in service barriers; (ii) modeling in which FDI is assumed to result from trade liberalization or other exogenous changes that generate international capital flows in the form of FDI in response to changes in rates of return; and (iii) modeling of links between multinational corporations' (MNCs) parents and affiliates and distinctions between foreign and domestic firms in a given country/region.

The third type of CGE modeling study just noted comes closest to capturing the important role played especially by MNCs and their foreign affiliates in providing Mode 3-type services. This, for example, is the focus of the study by Brown and Stern (2001) who analyze the effects of removal of services barriers under alternative conditions of international capital mobility and changes in the world capital stock due to increased investment. Their results suggest that the welfare effects of removing service barriers are sizable and vary across countries depending on how international capital movements and changes in domestic investment respond to changes in rates of return. The largest potential benefits are realized for all of the major developed and developing countries when allowance is made for changes in investment that augment the stock of capital.

Some principles and procedures for measuring service barriers and for assessing the consequences of their liberalization

The methodologies for measuring service barriers and using these measurements to assess the consequences of liberalization in services may be summarized as a set of principles and procedures.

Principles

1. Most barriers to trade and investment in services take the form of domestic regulations, rather than measures at the border.
2. No single methodology is sufficient for documenting and measuring barriers to trade in services. Instead, investigators need to draw upon all available information, including both direct observation of particular barriers and indirect inference of barriers using data on prices and quantities.
3. Because of the special role of incumbent firms in many service industries, regulations do not need to be explicitly discriminatory against foreign firms in order to have discriminatory effects.

Procedures

1. Collect the details of domestic regulations and related policies affecting service firms in the countries and/or sectors being examined, including the manner in which they apply to foreign versus domestic firms, plus quantitative details of their application, such as any percentage or dollar limits that they impose.
2. Ideally, this information should be collected by systematic surveys of governments and/or firms. However, it may also be possible to infer it less directly from documents prepared for other purposes, such as the commitments that governments made to the GATS in the Uruguay Round and subsequent negotiations.
3. For each type of regulation or policy, define degrees of restrictiveness and assign scores to each, ranging from zero for least restrictive to one for most restrictive.
4. Construct a measure of restrictiveness by: weighting the scores from step 3 based on judgments of the relative importance of each policy; using a statistical methodology

such as factor analysis that will serve to identify the weights; or designing proxy measures, such as dummy variables, to represent particular restrictions. The resulting measures can then be used directly for reporting the presence and importance of barriers across industries and countries, as well as for providing an input to subsequent analysis.

5. Convert the measures of restrictiveness from step 4 into a set of tariff equivalents by one or more of the following methods. Depending on the quality of information that goes into their construction, these tariff equivalents may be superior to the measures themselves for reporting about barriers and analyzing their effects:
   a. Assign judgmental tariff-equivalent values to each of the component measures, representing the percentage taxes on foreign suppliers to which each component is thought to correspond at their most restrictive levels (index = 1).
   b. Use data on prices and their determinants as the basis for a regression model that includes an index or other measures of restrictiveness and that estimates the effect on prices.
   c. Use data on quantities produced or traded as the basis for a regression model that includes an index or other measures of restrictiveness and that estimates the effect on quantities. This estimate can then be converted to tariff equivalents using an assumed or estimated price elasticity of demand.
6. Use an index or other measures of restrictiveness or the tariff equivalents constructed above as inputs into a model of production and trade in order to ascertain the effects of changes in the barriers to which they correspond. The appropriate model for this purpose depends on whether sectoral or economy-wide policy changes are to be analyzed. For economy-wide policy changes, the model should be a general equilibrium one, incorporating the full effects of barriers across sectors and countries. Ideally, too, the model should be designed to capture the effects of service regulations in the form that they have been observed and quantified as above.

Conclusion

As should be clear from the foregoing, studies of service barriers have used a wide variety of approaches. This is not surprising given the wide variety of the service industries themselves and the variation across them in the data that may be available. By way of conclusion, the steps that seem to have been most commonly used and/or successful in the largest number of studies have been summarized. It very much remains the case that research on service barriers must often make do with whatever information may be available. This may require creative exploitation of seemingly heroic assumptions in order to extract any information at all.

Notes

* This chapter has been adapted from a longer version prepared under World Bank auspices and included here with their permission.

1. Domestic supply is shown as further to the right (larger quantity for given price) than foreign supply, but this is not needed for any of the implications of the analysis.
2. These distinctions are suggested by the Australian Productivity Commission, whose website can be consulted for more details (www.pc.gov.au/research/memoranda/servicesrestriction/index.html). See also Hoekman and Primo Braga (1997: 288), who classify and provide examples of service barriers as follows: (i) quotas, local content and prohibitions; (ii) price-based instruments; (iii) standards, licensing and procurement; and (iv) discriminatory access to distribution networks.

3. See the Productivity Commission website for detailed listings by country of the categories of domestic and foreign restrictions on establishment and ongoing operations for some selected service sectors, including: accountancy, architectural and engineering services; banking; distribution; and maritime services.
4. See also Holmes and Hardin (2000).
5. Direct restrictions include limitations on the total size or share of investment in a sector and requirements on inputs used (for example, local content). Indirect restrictions include net benefit or national interest criteria and limitations on membership of company boards. The distinction between rules and case-by-case decisions relates to issues of clarity in specification and transparency as compared to the exercise of administrative discretion.
6. Hardin and Holmes (pp. 40–43) also provide information on investment incentives, which are widely used and for the most part are not subject to multilateral disciplines.
7. TRAINS is available on-line at www.unctad.org.
8. In fact, they are somewhat perverse for this purpose, since the more restrictive an NTB, the less will be the trade that it permits.
9. In counting commitments, the commitment for a sector or subsector to be unrestricted is counted as one, whereas a listing of the restrictions that will continue to apply, so that the commitment to liberalization is only partial, is counted as one-half.
10. As noted in Hardin and Holmes (1997: 70), the GATS commitments are based on a 'positive list' approach and therefore do not take into account sectors and restrictions that are unscheduled. In PECC (1995), it is assumed that all unscheduled sectors and commitments are unrestricted, which will then significantly raise the calculated frequency ratios compared to Hoekman (1996), who treats unscheduled sectors as fully restricted.
11. More information is needed accordingly on the restrictions that may apply to both scheduled and unscheduled service sectors in order to obtain a comprehensive measure of all existing restrictions.
12. Details on the construction of the indexes and their sensitivity to variations in the restrictiveness weights are discussed in Hardin and Holmes (1997, esp. 103–11).
13. The detailed scores for the components of the domestic and foreign banking restrictions are broken down by individual countries and are available on the Productivity Commission website.
14. Some other studies using frequency measures and indexes of restrictions include: Marko (1998); Mattoo (1998); McGuire (1998); Colecchia (2000); Kalirajan (2000); Kemp (2000); McGuire et al. (2000); Nguyen-Hong (2000); Warren (2000a and b); and Doove et al.(2001).
15. See Bosworth et al. (2000) for a useful methodological discussion of the construction and interpretation of price-impact measurements of impediments to service trade.
16. See: Johnson et al. (2000); Kalirajan (2000); Kalirajan et al. (2000); Kang (2000); Nguyen-Hong (2000); Trewin (2000); Doove et al. (2000); and Fink et al. (2002).
17. That is, having estimated that barriers reduce the quantity of a service by some percentage, this is divided by the elasticity of demand to obtain the percentage price increase to which it corresponds.
18. Typically, the log of the volume of total bilateral trade between two countries is regressed on the logs of their national income, the log of distance between them, and other variables such as per capita income and dummy variables to reflect a common border, common language and so on.
19. Gross operating margins are defined as total sales revenue minus total average costs divided by total average costs.
20. See also Fink et al. (2002) for a summary of the importance of restrictive trade policies and private anti-competitive practices relating to international maritime services.

14 Multinational service firms and global strategy

Peter Enderwick

Introduction

While other chapters in this volume have highlighted the significance of services in national output and employment, the continuing internationalisation of services in recent years means that they now play a significant role in the global economy. A number of measures highlight this growing significance. Trade in services were worth US$1.4 trillion, about 20 per cent of total world exports at the turn of the millennium (WTO, 2001), service firms were involved in 60 per cent of cross-border mergers and acquisitions in 1999 (UNCTAD, 2000), while the overseas sales of US affiliates in services increased by 383 per cent in the years 1990–99, compared with an increase of 198 per cent for all US multinational enterprises (MNEs). Services represented around half of the total stock of FDI in the mid-1990s (Mallampally and Zimny, 2000).

The growing internationalisation of service activity, and the ways in which these operations are managed, is the subject of this chapter. In doing this we bring together two major areas of research – those of international business and strategic management – which provide insights into the key questions of why firms internationalise (the domain of international business theory), and how operations are managed (addressed in strategic management). While these two disciplines have developed somewhat independently, there is considerable overlap which has become increasingly evident with the globalisation of business activity.

In applying these concepts to international service firms we highlight the growing convergence between the strategies of manufacturing and service firms and the declining influence of the distinct characteristics of services as explanatory variables in understanding the internationalisation of service firms. Growing deregulation and liberalisation, the pervasive role of technological change, particularly information and communication technology (ICT), global competitive pressure, and increasing knowledge intensity across all sectors, have reduced the idiosyncrasy of multinational service firms. This is not to suggest that the particular characteristics of services no longer matter; rather they may matter less.

Types of service multinationals

It is useful to clarify exactly what is meant by 'service multinationals'. Much of the literature, and the focus of our discussion, concerns parent firms based in service industries which expand overseas in the same or other service industries. While this defines service multinationals in simple and straightforward industry terms, it is somewhat restrictive. For example, firms based in the primary and manufacturing sectors may place in-house services overseas in specialist units. Similarly, specialist services in finance and shipping may be attracted to overseas locations for tax or regulatory reasons. The incentives offered by such locations apply to a range of parent companies, not just service-based producers. At the same time a number of manufacturing multinationals have begun to diversify into services. For example, between 1990 and 1998 General Electric increased the share of its total turnover from services from less than a fifth to two-thirds (Slater, 1999), yet would still be classified as primarily a manufacturing firm. Data limitations mean that at best we can only estimate the relative importance of the different types of international service firms. Available information on US-based MNEs suggests that the narrow definition picks up only about half of the stock of service foreign direct investment (FDI). A very significant amount of service FDI in the areas of trading and financial services is made by petroleum and manufacturing firms (ibid. 2000). However, our definition does encompass some of the most interesting and dynamic service industries, particularly the rapidly internationalizing business service sector.

Challenges of understanding multinational service firms

The internationalisation of services takes a variety of forms, including exports, foreign investment, knowledge agreements and strategic alliances. Because of the traditional difficulties of exporting many services as well as extensive industry regulation, FDI has been the most important overseas market servicing mode for services. This is still the case. While service exports are valued at \$1.4 trillion, if we assume that the service sector share of MNE affiliate sales corresponds to their share of total FDI stock (at 50 per cent), then affiliate sales in 2002 were \$8.5 trillion, some six times greater than exports (UNCTAD, 2003a). The same MNEs were also involved in exporting; about one-third of world trade comprises intra-firm trade. Knowledge agreements – in the forms of franchising and management contracts – are widespread in the fast-food and hotel industries. This means that theories of international production will need to be able to explain this diversity of modes.

At the same time, measurement problems are considerable. The true growth rate of service internationalisation may be overstated where 'externalisation' of business services previously performed in-house, occurs. The growth of specialist business service firms made possible by developments in ICT allows such firms to achieve considerable economies of scale and scope and to offer their services at very competitive rates. On the other hand, undervaluation of service internationalisation could occur when a service provider works very closely with a client firm. In the extreme case the service may be provided through the client firm's organisational infrastructure, negating the need for traditional forms of supplier internationalisation. This happens in industries such as management consultancy and training.

Conceptualising the internationalisation of services is also fraught with difficulties. While research has offered a number of distinct classifications of services (Clark et al., 1996; Lovelock and Yip, 1996; Patterson and Cicic, 1995; Roberts, 1998), most of these have been developed within a marketing perspective and do not correspond readily with international business analyses of overseas market entry modes. Classifications based on tangibility (Patterson and Cicic, 1995) or operational processes (Lovelock and Yip, 1996) are amenable to internationalisation in a variety of forms. Classifications organised around tradability (Roberts, 1998) are more helpful, but suffer from two weaknesses. The first is that ease of tradability changes over time. Electronic commerce, for example, has made possible the international trade of services traditionally thought of as locational-bound. Second, tradability does not explain the precise form of such trade, whether it occurs as an export or some type of knowledge agreement. The focus of our discussion is multinational service firms and such firms are typically involved in trade, FDI and the transfer of knowledge, often simultaneously.

Understanding the service internationalisation process is also made more difficult by the considerable fragmentation that has occurred within the value chain of many services. The separation of back- and front-office activities has altered the extent of 'internalisation' within service multinationals and increased the management demands for effective integration of activities. This, in turn, has affected organisational structures and the growth of specialist (offshore) suppliers.

Structure of the chapter

In addressing the interplay between multinationalisation of service firms and the corporate strategies they adopt, this chapter will examine two questions: first, where does the firm compete (markets, products and activities) and second, how does it compete (form of competitive advantage, type of strategy and organisational structure)? The following section provides a brief overview of what we might term 'traditional approaches' to explaining multinational service firms. This early work, in applying concepts originally developed for manufacturing firms, emphasised the distinctiveness of services and their limited tradability. However, the changing business environment (third section) means that such distinctiveness may be less important than previously believed. In the light of this, the fourth section examines the changing strategies of service firms. We reconsider the distinctiveness of services in the fifth section and examine the case for possible convergence between services and manufacturing. Final conclusions are offered in the last section.

Traditional approaches to explaining multinational service firms (MSFs)

Academic study of MSFs is fairly recent and when we refer to 'traditional' approaches we are referring to work that emerged in the 1980s (Boddewyn et al., 1986; Enderwick, 1988; Dunning, 1989). The early research was distinctive in five principal ways. First, understanding of MSFs was sought through the application of existing conceptualisations of the MNE, initially developed to explain the emergence of primary and manufacturing multinationals. The best known of these was the eclectic or OLI (ownership – location – internationalisation) framework (Dunning, 1979). Second, it was argued that existing tools could provide an understanding of service multinationals, but some adaptation was necessary to accommodate the distinctive characteristics of service industries. Much of the conceptualisation focused on identifying the nature of ownership, location and internalisation advantages of service firms (Enderwick, 1988; Dunning, 1989). Third, the early research developed within an environment characterised by considerable impediments to the internationalisation of service firms. The principal impediments arose from pervasive regulation of service industries in many countries (Aronson and Cowhey, 1984) and high transactions costs associated with the international exchange of intangibles (Teece, 1986). Fourth, the research emphasis was narrow and focused on service firms based in and expanding within, the same or other, service industries. Although it was accepted that many service investments were made by non-service industry firms (Dunning, 1989) such enterprises received little research attention. Fifth, the emphasis of understanding of work at this time was the internationalisation process, that is, the international market entry methods chosen by service firms. There was very little consideration of the strategy choices of such firms.

Table 14.1 provides a summary of the traditional and more recent re-conceptualisations of multinational service firms. This table highlights the ways in which academic research has developed over the past 15 years and the implications for understanding MSFs.

Table 14.1 Traditional and recent conceptualisations of multinational service firms

	Traditional conceptualisations	Recent re-conceptualisations
Sources of competitive advantage	Economies of scale and scope	Economies of scale, scope and expertise
Economies of scale	Leveraging market position and development of capabilities Important. Achieved largely through internal growth	Competence and learning Important in driving industry structure Achieved through internal and external growth
Economies of scope	Modest importance Focus on product/market relatedness Early onset of conglomerate diseconomies	Central importance Related diversification built on internal capabilities
Degree of vertical integration	High, pursuit of economies of scale, consistent quality, common branding Consumer education	Increased outsourcing of back-office functions Rapid growth of offshore specialist suppliers
Role of clusters	Acknowledged but not well understood Emphasis on labour supply	Significant as source of externalities and learning
Alliances and networks	Limited importance	Great importance in industries with high fixed costs, demand variability and rapid changes in technology
Use of constellations	Embryonic. Used to provide legitimacy	Very widespread. Stable and unstable. Customer and production orientation
Importance of innovation	Modest importance Largely 'imported'	High importance. Increasingly 'internalised' as routines or business models
Importance of knowledge	High Focus on problems of transfer	Central Focus on role in competitive advantage Problems of managing knowledge Driver of industry structure
Role of branding	Primarily for quality assurance	Primarily for market development and IP protection
Strategy types	Primarily multi-domestic Focus on cultural adaptation	Central importance in global economy Growth of global strategies Increase in standardisation
Strategy determinants	Market positioning	Inimitability of processes and routines Network position
Benefits of an international structure	Market development Risk diversification	Major source of learning and competitive advantage

Compared with the traditional approaches we now have new conceptual tools (knowledge-based model of the firm, network analysis) and far more research data on the operation of service multinationals (methods of market servicing, reliance on clustering, strategy choice) which greatly enriches understanding.

Current work differs from traditional conceptions in a number of ways. First, the distinctive characteristics of the service sector are recognised, but are not seen as sufficient to invalidate more general approaches to understanding business behaviour. In part this is because of a perception of growing convergence between service and non-service firms. The growth of competitive pressure, emergence of knowledge as a key resource, increased importance of economies of scale, preference for alliance and network structures and increased reliance on sophisticated ICT are common to most international firms. Liberalisation of service industries has facilitated the rapid internationalisation of this sector. Developments in ICT have increased the tradability and manageability of international service activities.

Second, widespread changes in the international business environment have dramatically changed the strategic choices available to service firms. Opportunities in terms of industry and market access, costs of managing international service transactions and the forms of competitive advantage displayed by service firms have all changed significantly. To understand the emerging strategies of MSFs it is necessary to overview this changing environment.

The changing business environment and MSFs

Because other chapters in this book provide detailed analysis of many of the topics considered in this section, our discussion is brief. We identify five key factors which have dramatically changed the business environment for service firms: liberalisation; globalisation, knowledge intensity, the blurring of industry boundaries and developments in ICT.

Liberalisation and the promotion of FDI

Trade and investment liberalisation has continued over the past decade with the effect of both facilitating international trade and investment in services, and markedly increasing competition within service industries. The Uruguay Trade Round brought services trade within the remit of multilateral rules. Since that time, the growth of international investment agreements that protect and facilitate internationalisation of business has been significant (UNCTAD, 2003a).

Liberalisation manifests itself as reductions in tariff and nontariff barriers, the growth of regional trade areas and increased deregulation and privatisation of service industries including telecommunications, financial services and transportation. Restrictions to international exchange of services typically take the form of nontariff barriers and raise concerns regarding market access, non-discriminatory treatment of foreign investors and protection and compensation in the event of expropriation. For example, the incidence of performance requirements – stipulations imposed on foreign investors to behave in ways thought to be beneficial to the host economy – have declined (UNCTAD, 2003b). Increasingly, governments now use other strategic trade, investment and competition policies to achieve such objectives. A complexity of non-tariff regulations is that they may be imposed for policy purposes other than simply trade restriction, for example, because of safety concerns in the case of health services or for cultural reasons in education and the media. Similarly, the nature of international business in services – involving trade, investment, the movement of staff, consumers and data – means that a wide range of policies potentially impact on the ease of international service transactions (Samiee, 1999). Generally, developing countries are more restrictive and discriminatory than developed countries (OECD, 2003).

In many economies liberalisation has evolved into a more generic form with the adoption of 'market-friendly policies' encompassing robust macroeconomic management, non-discriminatory business rules, promotion of competition and supportive investments in innovation and education. At the same time, these have been coupled with aggressive FDI attraction strategies based on incentives.

Continuing liberalisation of services may be expected to affect the strategies of MSFs in several ways. First, the opening up of service industries has undoubtedly increased international competition in these industries. As suggested above, trade and FDI in services are both growing faster than in non-service industries. New markets, particularly the emerging economies, have become significant players in global services. Second, this competitive pressure has triggered successive rounds of corporate and industry restructuring, in many cases in the form of cross-border mergers and acquisitions. In 1999, three of the top 10 MNEs concluding the largest cross-border deals were in the telecommunications industry. Global concentration in telecommunications, insurance and banking have all increased in recent years as a result of cross-border mergers and acquisitions (UNCTAD, 2000). Third, the likely impact of liberalisation on market entry choices is unclear. On the one hand, liberalisation might be expected to increase both trade and FDI in services. In this sense, trade and FDI in services may be complementary. On the other hand, services are still subject to far more restrictions than other sectors, discouraging these forms of market entry. Indeed, there is some suggestion that liberalisation may be associated with higher levels of industry-specific administrative regulations, raising compliance costs for business (Nicoletti, 2003). In such cases we might expect an increasing return to local knowledge and the adoption of cooperative arrangements such as joint ventures. Fourth, entry into emerging markets is likely to be more sensitive to restrictions as such countries are characterised by higher levels of both restrictions and discrimination. Banking services in Brazil, India and Indonesia are characterised by some of the most restrictive and discriminatory regulations in the world. This suggests a continuing idiosyncrasy in strategy selection in such markets.

Globalisation

Globalisation refers to the stage of evolution of the world economy distinctive in terms of both internationalisation and interdependency. The global era, the period since 1989, is also characterised by the primacy of economic competition and private sector, generally multinational, business activity. The service sector is a critical part of this global economy. Indeed, factors pushing globalisation of services are no different from those driving globalisation more generally. In common with manufacturing and extractive firms, MSFs are both a cause of, and a response to, globalisation. And like their manufacturing counterparts, the nature of service firms has changed in the global era as increasingly they become centres for the creation, processing and application of knowledge (Aharoni and Nachum, 2000). Information-based advantages are increasingly sourced from throughout the subsidiary network, elevating the importance of knowledge transfer and management skills Nachum, 1999; Kogut, 2002).

In strategy terms, the MSF faces tensions similar to those encountered by any global competitor; in particular the balance between standardisation and local responsiveness. The globalisation of client firms has encouraged providers in a range of service industries including aircraft maintenance (Seng and Enderwick, 2000), air travel (Seristo, 2000) and courier services (Kostecki, 2000) to develop matching strategies. Where standardisation of client strategy brings increased standardisation of service supplier strategy, there may be considerable cost savings. In addition, standardisation may enhance quality control and a perception that the firm is both competent and committed to client needs. This can be a significant form of advantage in industries where reputation is used as an indicator of potential performance (Aharoni, 2000). On the other hand, the nature of much service business, particularly within professional service firms, means that little standardisation may be achievable. Rather, the firm is forced to pursue a multi-domestic strategy and display a marked 'polycentric' orientation (Lowendahl, 2000). In a number of cases this has encouraged the development of novel operating forms such as the international partnership structure, the widespread use of alliance arrangements and the combination of a standardised core product with customised supplementary services.

Knowledge intensity

Rapid technological change and significant structural shifts in economic activity have brought higher levels of knowledge intensity to most industries, including services. Differential capability in knowledge acquisition, accumulation, utilisation and dissemination provides opportunity for differentiation and the creation of advantage (Grant, 1996). Knowledge-intensive services are characterised by the importance of tacit or intangible knowledge and hence, reliance on key human resources. The customised nature of such services means that interactions with client firms and the effective transfer of experience and learning are key sources of competitive advantage.

The particular economics of knowledge affects strategy in a number of ways. They encourage the pursuit of economies of scale, scope and learning, specialisation and the integration of stages of value adding, as well as first-mover advantages (Enderwick, 1988). They suggest the value of network forms of organisation, structured in ways that encourage cross-border learning (Bartlett and Ghoshal, 1989), the devolution of autonomy to subsidiaries and effective knowledge management systems. Internally, it is apparent that structures such as liaisons, teams and meetings encourage knowledge sharing (Eisenhardt and Santos, 2002). However, the quality of interaction between the knowledge-intensive service supplier and the client firms also depends upon the absorptive capability of the client (Cohen and Levinthal, 1990).

Blurring of industry boundaries

Technological change in a number of areas is diminishing the traditional boundaries that existed between industries. The growing convergence between telecommunications, entertainment and education is one example. Service firms have been at the forefront of capitalising on these trends. As suggested above, service firms invest into both related service and non-service industries; while manufacturing firms are regular investors in the service sector. Evidence on cross-border mergers and acquisitions shows that during the 1990s wholesale and retail trade and business services sold twice as much in assets as they purchased (UNCTAD, 2000: 125). The evidence strongly suggests that service firms have been more successful when following a strategy of concentric diversification rather than conglomerate operations (Roberts, 1998). Diversification greatly increases the complexity of the management task and may trigger a shift in organisational form, typically from a unitary or functional (U-form), to a multidivisional (M-form) structure. There are two key drivers of related diversification; to exploit economies of scope in operations and economies of scope in intangible assets. In the former case the firm may pursue related diversification to spread the fixed costs of ICT investments, to exploit client bases and international networks. This type of cross-referral business is found in the accounting/auditing/consulting and market research/advertising/customer service interfaces. In the second case, relatedness from a resource perspective, the primary source of value creation stems from the application of resources across different industries. Such capabilities result from a number of sources (Markides and Williamson, 1996).

Developments in ICT

Since the implications for services of the rapid development of ICTs are covered extensively elsewhere in this volume, here the focus is on how they impact on the internationalisation process and the management of MSFs. First, the service sector has long been a developer or early adopter of new technologies. In cases like computer reservation systems (CRS) these have become valued competitive advantages. Second, ICT has changed the nature of economies of scale and scope within international services, on balance facilitating the attainment of both of these. Third, while ICT has in some cases increased the tradability of services, it has been just as significant in facilitating the management of international service operations (Bancel-Charensol, 1999). It thus has implications for the pattern of service internationalisation. To the extent that trade and FDI in services are complementary, and the simultaneous growth of both might suggest that this is the case, ICT is an important contributor to service globalisation. If, on the other hand, ICT facilitates tradability of services which substitutes for former service investments, the pattern of internationalisation becomes less clear (Mallampally and Zimny, 2000).

Fourth, ICT is changing the basic business model within many service industries. For industries such as banking, music and publishing the change is radical with novel new ways of doing business or protecting property rights emerging (Wymbs, 2000). More generally, ICT has facilitated a more rational international division of labour and the adoption of international production models long favoured in the manufacturing sector. These involve a splitting of the production process (with back-door operations increasingly sourced 'offshore') (ibid.) and the emergence of specialist service suppliers based in lower-cost emerging markets. ICT also facilitates the effective management and control of deeply integrated production systems (Bancel-Charensol, 1999).

Finally, ICT has also changed the nature of organisational structures within the service sector. While enabling more network structures (Quinn and Paquette, 1990), they have also substantially altered the nature of supplier–client interaction, markedly increasing client participation and responsibility. Successful locking in of clients and deep mining of client-related data may create a considerable barrier to potential competitors.

Internationalisation strategies of MSFs

In this section we shall examine the two questions raised in the introduction: the drivers of multinationality and the strategies followed by MSFs. The first question, multinationality, addresses issues such as the motives for internationalisation, entry modes adopted by MSFs, and the benefits of multinationality to the firm.

Drivers of multinationality

Motives for internationalisation The international business literature identifies four primary motives for firm internationalisation: market seeking; cost oriented; efficiency seeking; and creative asset seeking. The internationalisation behaviour of service firms can be analysed using these concepts. Like most firms pursuing internationalisation, there is evidence that service firms build out from a successful domestic base (Edvardsson et al., 1993). Domestic success facilitates the development of competitive advantage and client confidence. There is wide acceptance of the belief that following clients overseas is a primary driver of service firm internationalisation (Roberts, 1998; Nachum, 1999). This is particularly true of smaller service providers who face considerable entry barriers in international markets (O'Farrell and Wood, 1994). The nature of many services, requiring close interaction between supplier and client, may necessitate this following. Oligopolistic reaction, where competitors follow one another into overseas markets, has been observed for larger service firms (Li and Guisinger, 1992). Evidence that service investment is responsive to market size (ibid.) suggests that beyond simply client following, MSFs may then seek wider opportunities in the host market (Mallampally and Zimny, 2000).

While cost may not have been a prime motive for the internationalisation of service firms (Roberts, 1998), this may be changing with the growth of offshore sourcing of services (see below). More widespread is the pursuit of economies of scale and scope in utilising corporate resources across more than one market. The competitive resources possessed by service firms typically relate to professional staff, extensive customer databases, capital-intensive information and communications systems, and investments in knowledge.

The significance of cross-border mergers and high rates of acquisition of smaller, domestic service firms suggests that strategic asset seeking investment may be of increasing importance within service industries. The widespread availability of low-cost skilled and creative labour, particularly within emerging markets, coupled with the increased tradability of services is encouraging this type of investment (Mallampally and Zimny, 2000). Survey studies of leading service multinationals support this expectation (Dunning and McKaig-Berliner, 2002).

Modes of international market entry The forms that service multinationals adopt when entering overseas markets has been subject to considerable research attention (Erramilli and Rao, 1990, 1993; Fladmoe-Lindquist and Jacque, 1995). The focus of this work has been on understanding how the distinctive characteristics of services affect modal choice. In comparison with manufacturing firms, international service firms are generally smaller in size and internationalise at an earlier stage in their life cycle. However, as a sector, service internationalisation has occurred later, encouraging the use of mergers and acquisitions (Roberts, 1998; Segal-Horn and Faulkner, 1999).

The considerable impediments to trade in services resulting from the intangibility and inseparability of many services, the need for ongoing client contact and cultural adaptation, a desire to protect reputation and pervasive regulation, have been used to explain the high propensity for FDI within the service sector (Roberts, 1998). Sales of foreign affiliates of service multinationals far exceed exports of services (Mallampally and Zimny, 2000). These impediments also help to explain the incidence of FDI in services. Knowledge- and skill-intensive service firms in particular benefit from internalising transactions subject to high market costs. Close client–supplier relations and the need to maintain such closeness, may encourage international expansion through FDI. International variations in culture and regulatory controls raise the value of local knowledge and the benefits of a local presence. Internalisation may also facilitate quality control, service customisation and the achievement of economies of scale, particularly in capital-intensive services such as telecommunications and shipping (Enderwick, 1988; Dunning, 1989; Roberts, 1998).

While the pressures for internalisation appear to be formidable within services, many service industries are characterised by the widespread use of knowledge agreements, including franchising (Fladmoe-Lindquist, 2000), management contracts (Contractor and Kundu, 2000) and alliances (Seristo, 2000). Knowledge agreements are attractive when knowledge can be codified and transferred via contracts, where risks must be shared, local knowledge is vital, investors are too small or resource constrained, and where complementary assets are sought.

Irrespective of the entry mode selected, MSFs display high levels of adaptability. Service products generally require more adaptation for local markets than goods. Adaptation is achieved in a variety of ways including strong parental direction, the cultivation of close client–supplier relations (Lindsay et al., 2003) and, in the case of knowledge-intensive firms, the co-production of new knowledge (Windrum and Tomlinson, 1999). The diversity of operating conditions faced by service firms means that they operate in a variety of modes; this variety is evident even with the same industry or enterprise (Roberts, 1998).

Developments in ICTs have significantly affected modal choice. While increasing the tradability of many services, and hence the ability to export, ICT has also greatly enhanced the ability to manage and control international service operations. Increasingly, it is possible for global service providers to disintegrate value chains and to take advantage of differences in comparative advantage. However, available evidence, while now somewhat dated, suggests that there is little multinational service investment with the intention to re-export (Kravis and Lipsey, 1988). As suggested earlier, the precise impact depends on the extent to which service exports and FDI are seen as substitutes or complements (Mallampally and Zimny, 2000). Regardless of the particular mode, ICT has changed the nature of customer–supplier interaction, greatly increasing the demands on clients as well as their involvement in the production process. Supplier personnel have moved towards greater involvement by exception, usually where the customer experiences difficulties. The greater availability of client information has enabled more focused customisation and marketing (Bancel-Charensol, 1999).

The importance of adaptation within service multinationals does not appear to be reflected in changes in operating modes which remain rare, certainly within smaller firms (O'Farrell et al., 1998). There is some evidence of evolutionary development in choice of operating mode within service firms. This evolution appears to differ from that of manufacturing firms with stages being shorter and more variable (Roberts, 1998, 1999), not necessarily involving greater resource commitment (O'Farrell et al., 1998), but reflected in a more global orientation (Edvardsson et al., 1993). The trigger point, in particular from exports to FDI, may occur earlier for service firms because the fixed costs of investment are lower; most MSFs need to make only modest office establishment investments, their principal cost being internationally mobile professional staff.

Benefits of multinationality Much of the international business literature is based on the assumption that an existing competitive advantage enables the firm to internationalise operations. Much of the research on service firms is based on the same assumption (Enderwick, 1988; Dunning, 1989). More recently, there has been a growing recognition that the relationship may be two-way; with multinationality reinforcing competitiveness (Dunning and McKaig-Berliner, 2002; Mallampally and Zimny, 2000). MSFs appear to be reducing dependence on their home countries for created advantages (Nachum, 2000) with advantages based on relational skills, specialised labour, and linkages with outside bodies, increasingly sourced from foreign affiliates (Dunning and McKaig-Berliner, 2002). The transfer of knowledge across affiliates and between the firms and partner organisations may now be the key competitive advantage of the service multinational, reinforcing the view of the firm as primarily a knowledge creation, processing and transfer entity (Kogut and Zander, 1993). Lowendahl (2000) proposes an extreme version of this view for business service firms, suggesting that internationalisation is driven by the desire to acquire knowledge from a diversity of projects rather than simply following multinational clients. Aharoni (2000) highlights the interaction between reputation and multinationality with a global presence contributing to the credibility of the firm as an indicator of capability and client commitment. Growth within service providers based on knowledge acquisition from diverse operations suggests a process dissimilar to the 'asset deepening' characteristic of manufacturing firms (Segal-Horn and Faulkner, 1999).

The strategies of MSFs

Turning to the competitive strategies pursued by MSFs we focus on four key aspects: the forms of competitive advantage possessed; the use of variety types; the growing fragmentation of service production through offshore sourcing; and the linkages between strategy and structure.

Competitive advantages of service multinationals The sources of ownership-specific or competitive advantages within service multinationals are diverse. Traditionally, the focus has been on economies of scale and scope, market structure, branding and technology (Enderwick, 1988; Dunning, 1989; Roberts, 1998). While these remain important sources of advantages, more recent thinking has considerably augmented understanding. Consistent with more general developments within the field of strategic management, the conceptualisation of competitive advantage within service firms has shifted from a primarily static and structural position to a more dynamic and behavioural one (Venkatraman and Subramaniam, 2002) with an increasing emphasis on the resources of the firm rather than a fortuitous market structure (Cool et al., 2002). At the same time, new sources of advantage with the service firm have been examined, including client and market knowledge and relationships (Grosse, 2000; Seng and Enderwick, 2000; Lindsay et al., 2003), economies of scale in knowledge management (Moore and Birkinshaw, 1998; Lowendahl, 2000), reputation and firm-specificity of advantages (Aharoni, 2000; Mallampally and Zimny, 2000), organisational skills and routines (Aharoni and Nachum, 2000), network position and externalities (Katz and Shapiro, 1994), economies of scope in resource use (Grant, 2002) and economies of expertise (Venkatraman and Subramaniam, 2002). More generally, it is now recognised that achieving sustainable competitive advantage is dependent, in the long term, on the investment strategy of the firm. Recent work, while still at an early stage, has begun to focus on the firm as a generator of future options as opposed to simply a nexus of contracts (Jensen, 2000).

Choice of competitive strategy The existence of competitive advantage and a commitment to internationalisation, then, requires the service firm to make critical choices regarding the type of strategy to be pursued. While research has identified a variety of strategy choices (Porter, 1980; Bartlett and Ghoshal, 1989), for most service multinationals the choice is between multi-domestic and global strategy (Lovelock and Yip, 1996). The attractions of a global strategy – which focuses on cost reduction through standardisation – are in the scale and cost advantages it can yield. However, this may be at the expense of local responsiveness, the primary benefit of a multi-domestic strategy which emphasises adaptation to local market conditions. Frameworks developed to explain the drive towards global strategy within manufacturing have been applied to services with minor modification (ibid.). It is frequently argued that radical changes in competitive strategy are infeasible within marketing industries characterised by deeply embedded service delivery programmes and cultures. Because of this, we might expect to see more gradual evolution in service strategy.

Perhaps as a result of this, strategic thinking in services has drawn distinctions between core and supplementary services and front- and back-office activities. These distinctions allow for differentiation in strategy focus along the value chain. For example, it may be possible to achieve a high level of standardisation and cost reduction in core services, while simultaneously enhancing responsiveness through the development of supplementary services. Standardisation is likely to not only lower cost, it may also increase consistency. Standardisation may be achieved through the substitution of capital for labour, such as automated bank teller machines, or by the establishment of routines and processes for labour, such as self-service and billing supermarkets. Standardisation has reached a very high level in hotel services where codification of designs, procedures and systems is well advanced (Contractor and Kundu, 2000).

Where core services are standardised it becomes possible to source them from specialist outside suppliers who benefit from large scale, lower costs and extensive experience. India, for example, has a number of highly competitive software houses such as Tata and Wipro that provide solutions for businesses in many parts of the world. Differentiation can be achieved through the provision of customised supplementary services. In the extreme case supplementary services are almost bespoke, ensuring a very high level of responsiveness to customer needs. DHL Worldwide Express adopts such a strategy (Kostecki, 2000). The ability to standardise varies among service industries and is much harder to achieve in professional business services (Aharoni, 2000) or in consumer services requiring cultural adaptation.

The distinction between front- and back-office activities relates to the degree of client interaction. Interaction is high for front-office activities but low or even non-existent for back-office functions. For this reason, standardisation generally focuses on back-office tasks. For example, while Kentucky Fried Chicken has standardised to a considerable degree its R&D activity, layout design and some promotion, it still offers over 400 different menu items. Technology is facilitating this separation (and subsequent reintegration), of activities for a range of services in terms of trade, foreign investment and electronic delivery. Outsourcing is now starting to occur within front-office activities such as customer service systems which are operated remotely (Lovelock and Yip, 1996).

In an increasing number of industries, firms are under pressure not simply to choose between cost reduction (global strategy) and local responsiveness (multi-domestic strategy), but to achieve these two things simultaneously. This is described in terms of a transnational strategy (Bartlett and Ghoshal, 1989; Campbell and Verbeke, 1994). Relatively few service sector multinationals could accurately be described as pursuing a true transnational strategy. Campbell and Verbeke (1994) discuss the constraints that service firms face in separating functions such as research and marketing. For most firms, the likely strategic shift is from a multi-domestic to a global strategy. The pressures on service firms to make this shift are, perhaps, not as powerful as those faced by manufacturing firms. The very high incidence of repeat business, for professional business service firms perhaps 80 per cent of all work, means that reputation, referrals and past performance may be more important considerations than cost (Aharoni, 2000). Multi-domestic strategies, and considerable price dispersion, may also persist because of the difficulty of trading services across disparate markets (Lovelock and Yip, 1994). Lovelock (1999) argues that within the service sector many so-called global strategies are, in reality, basically multi-domestic. Caution is required in generalising in this way about all service industries. The relative importance of cost and responsiveness pressures clearly differs across industries and a much more disaggregated approach to the study of strategy choice within service industries is required.

Outsourcing and the service value chain As competitive pressures have increased within service industries, firms have responded with a growth of offshore sourcing. Services appear to be mirroring, somewhat later, manufacturing industries in the development of integrated international production systems (UNCTAD, 1993). Standardised, back-office activities are relocated to developing countries where the stock of service sector FDI has increased dramatically (Mallampally and Zimny, 2000). Such a development is also consistent with increasing levels of intra-firm trade in services. This pattern of 'disintegration' (Feenstra, 1998) or service unbundling is not straightforward. At the same time that standardised service tasks (efficiency tasks in Maister's 1986 typology) are being sourced offshore, the same MSFs are integrating other transactions, particularly those in intangibles, under common governance. Within financial and business services, firms are pursuing growth and consolidation in the pursuit of economies of scale and scope. Developments in ICT have created conditions where it is now feasible to manage more complex, but more flexible service value chains.

The growth of service outsourcing is linked to created-asset-seeking investments. In this case these assets are accessed through outsourcing rather than being acquired through acquisition. Furthermore, externalisation also facilitates a concentration on core business activities. In the case of SAS, a desire to rationalise the business encouraged the sale of its catering business and the acquisition of a partner (Radisson) in its hotel division. These developments have interesting implications for understanding the operations of MSFs. Traditionally, it has been argued that the distinctive characteristics of services encourage internalisation; outsourcing suggests benefits accrue not from markets, but from network relations (Aharoni and Nachum, 2000).

Organisation structures As strategies change, we would expect to see concomitant changes in organisation structures (Chandler, 1962). The management demands of a large international service multinational suggest that global MSFs will have moved beyond simple unitary or functional structures (U-forms). Diversification encourages the shift to multidivisional (M-form) structures. Where effective knowledge sharing becomes the primary goal of the firm we might see a move towards CM forms where the involvement of the corporate centre increases (Hill and Hoskisson, 1987). More recent research has recognised that the knowledge firm is involved in more than simply sharing knowledge; it is concerned with the creation, processing, application and dissemination of knowledge. This work introduces the concept of the 'network' or N-form business (Hedlund, 1994).

As the motives determining organisational structure evolve, so does organisational form. In parallel with manufacturing, MSFs have evolved beyond simple hierarchies to elaborate network structures. Internal and external networks have become central to the knowledge management process (Gulati et al., 2000). In the case of professional business services, constellations – multiple partner alliances – have become commonplace (Jones et al., 1998). In each of these cases the interaction of the parties is paramount and the boundaries of individual firms become blurred.

Paralleling these external organisational changes are significant internal developments. On the one hand, globalisation encourages further integration as firms pursue the cost benefits of economies of scale and scope. On the other hand, the need for close links with clients and service customisation drive the decentralisation of decision making. In professional business services adopting a partnership structure and the absence of common ownership inhibits integration. The result is likely to be higher degrees of affiliate independence than are found within manufacturing firms (Nachum, 2000).

The centrality of professionals in service firms means that the effective management of staff is likely to be a key determinant of firm competitiveness. MSFs are at the experimental edge in devising effective processes and systems for maximising staff contributions. These include training, work assignment, an assurance of competent colleagues, opportunities for continuous learning (Lowendahl, 2000), team working (Grosse, 2000) and centres of excellence (Moore and Birkinshaw, 1998).

International services and manufacturing: convergence or divergence?

The discussion above highlights a number of areas of apparent convergence, and some divergence, between service and manufacturing multinationals. The key trends are summarised in Table 14.2.

The table identifies four principal areas of convergence between the two sectors. The first is with regard to the impact of ICT. While its impact has been pervasive, affecting the entire economy, the impact on the service sector has been particularly significant, changing the strategic options available to firms (for example, the tradability of services), costs,

Table 14.2 Convergence and divergence: service and manufacturing multinationals

Convergence	Divergence
Impact of ICT	*Characteristics of MSFs*
Pervasive, changing options, costs, control and management process	Supplier/client interaction along the value chain Evolution of international market servicing modes Lower levels of resource commitment for FDI Lower degree of locational substitutability home/host countries Asset deepening versus asset accretion
Strategy drivers	*Operational differences*
Globalisation drivers Sources/forms of competitive advantage Economies of scope in resource utilisation Centrality of knowledge Strategy determines structure	Challenges of achieving standardisation
Value chain structure	*Organisational differences*
Disintegration of global value chain Growing importance of locational factors Increasing corporate integration of activities	Novel organisational forms, e.g., peer group professional partnerships
Operational management	
Non-traditional internationalisation path similar to 'Born Globals' Growing importance of created-asset seeking investment Growing importance of M&As Devolution of innovative capacity Role of subsidiaries from passive to active Move to network structures	

customer involvement, control and management processes. The net effect has been an attenuation of some of the traditional impediments to service internationalisation resulting from the distinctive traits of services.

Second, the strategy drivers affecting services are increasingly similar to those shaping manufacturing. Market liberalisation and industry deregulation are greatly facilitating the penetration of both advanced and emerging markets. At the same time, the sources of competitive advantage underpinning internationalisation for all sectors are increasingly dynamic, behavioural and knowledge based. Service firms also appear to follow the dictum that strategy determines structure.

Third, service value chains are being reconfigured as ICT and the dispersion of created assets enables global disaggregation along efficiency lines. More back-office activities are being relocated offshore in the same way that simple labour-intensive manufacturing jobs in clothing, textiles, footwear, toys and sports goods migrated in the 1980s. As created asset-seeking investment becomes more important, locational factors including education, training, innovation and appropriate supporting policies exercise a greater influence on the placement of service activities. Fragmentation is also accompanied by increasing integration at the strategy level as managements seek to optimise the contribution and effectiveness of each stage of the chain.

The fourth area of apparent convergence is in the area of operational management. We note a general trend for MSFs to move along non-traditional internationalisation paths, skipping or truncating stages in ways similar to the manufacturing 'Born Global' firm (Knight and Cavusgil, 1996). The increasing importance of created asset-seeking as a motive for FDI is encouraging cross-border mergers and acquisitions (M&As) as well as the devolution of innovative capacity to the level of the individual affiliate. Subsidiaries take on a more active role as the firm increasingly adopts a network type structure. These changes are all mirrored within leading manufacturing multinationals.

At the same time there are still areas of clear divergence between services and manufacturing. The distinct characteristics of services still matter. They result in high levels of client/supplier interaction at almost all stages of the value chain and influence the evolution of international commitment, for example, allowing service firms with lower fixed establishment costs to commit to FDI at an earlier stage in the life cycle. The growth strategies of the two sectors may also differ, with manufacturing firms more likely to pursue a strategy of asset deepening (through economies of scale) while service firms follow asset-accretion strategies (economies of scope), melding resources across different markets and sectors. Service firms are likely to display lower degrees of locational substitutability between home- and host-country affiliates where much of their investment is client following or market seeking. However, the increased tradability of services means that we might expect to see in the future, marked increases in levels of intra-firm service trade and, hence, substitutability. This is at the centre of the current US concern with offshore sourcing of business services such as software.

Operational and organisational differences also exist. The nature of many services, particularly business services, makes standardisation of offerings extremely difficult. While we have argued that standardisation is occurring with back-office activities, service design and delivery still entails significant client involvement. We also observe novel organisational forms within the service sector, the professional partnership being perhaps the most widespread. On balance, we believe that the forces of convergence between service and manufacturing multinationals outweigh those of divergence.

Conclusions

This chapter has examined the two related issues of multinationality and strategy choice within international service firms. While internationalisation is achieved on the basis of the overseas application of firm-specific competitive advantage, management also has to make decisions regarding the strategy to be pursued. For MSFs the most common choices are between multi-domestic and global strategies. Our examination of developments in these areas suggests a number of conclusions.

First, our discussion supports the idea that services are becoming increasingly global. The growth of international trade, FDI and knowledge agreements within the service sector is consistent with globalisation. Competitive pressure and fundamental changes in the international business environment are encouraging the pursuit of dynamic, behavioural forms of sustainable advantage, typically based around knowledge and embodied in key personnel. Service value chains are increasingly disintegrated, with standardised back-office activities relocated to low-cost specialist providers in emerging markets. The growth of global strategy within MSFs is accompanied by new organisational forms, often network based. While domestic service industries remain fragmented and populated by a myriad small firms, international service markets are becoming increasingly concentrated through acquisition and rationalisation strategies.

Second, these trends are not unique to services, and lend support to the view that convergence between the various sectors of the advanced economies is under way. This convergence does not mean that the distinctive characteristics of services, long the subject of academic analysis, no longer matter; rather we suggest that they matter less in terms of international business activity. Developments in ICT have created vast new opportunities for the international exchange of services long considered location bound. Interestingly, the convergence appears to be driven more from the manufacturing than from the service side. We would argue that it is the increasing knowledge and service content of goods that is propelling convergence.

Third, our discussion, and the belief that convergence is occurring, suggests the value of further academic research on the underlying issues of MSFs. One implication may be the benefits of shifting the research focus beyond the characteristics of services to examine the utility of applying new ideas and concepts pioneered in the fields of strategic management and industrial economics to a sector which has long been treated as both 'different' and 'residual'. Interesting opportunities arise from recent conceptions of the firm as a knowledge centre (Grant, 1996; Eisenhardt and Santos, 2002), as a set of routines (Nelson and Winter, 1982), a repository of property rights (Hart and Moore, 1990) and as a collection of complementary competences (Dosi and Teece, 1998). Similarly, the implications of the pursuit of economies of expertise (Venkatraman and Subramaniam, 2002) are barely understood. Within the field of international business, the growing acceptance of interaction between multinationality and competitive advantage suggests the need for more work on the benefits that accrue to MSFs from various forms of multinational involvement.

Finally, we need to note the potential dangers of overgeneralisation within our discussion. Caution is necessary in two areas. The first is in grouping together all service industries. Such a grouping suppresses the very considerable heterogeneity that exists in the service sector. Within the banking industry, finance and strategies of risk management are key strategy drivers. Consistency is the paramount consideration for international audit firms. For personal services such as healthcare, the idiosyncratic nature of encounters encourages the standardisation of policies, procedures and performance assessment. These distinctive characteristics exist *within* the service sector as much as *between* sectors. Similarly, it may be misleading to generalise across nationality differences. While it is widely accepted that the US and UK contain world-class MSFs, this also seems to be true of a country such as Germany (Ochel, 2002). Again, further disaggregated work would be of value.

PART IV

SERVICES, TECHNOLOGY AND INNOVATION

15 Knowledge-intensive services and innovation

Ian Miles

Introduction

This chapter examines the role of knowledge-intensive services in innovation processes. These services apply high levels of expert knowledge to their activities – this can be roughly assessed by the proportion of highly qualified staff in their workforce. They can themselves be the focus of innovation – innovation in their own services, or in the production and other processes that support the design, generation and delivery of the services. But some of these services also play a role in innovation in other firms too, since some knowledge-intensive services (especially KIBS – knowledge-intensive business services) contribute to the choice and use of new technologies or organisational practices among their clients. So a knowledge-intensive financial service firm may innovate itself in terms of, say, its back-office computer systems, its use of communication technologies to communicate with clients, the creation of new types of financial service product and so on. A knowledge-intensive consultancy firm may also undertake such innovations for itself. But it can also provide clients – perhaps the financial services firm – with advice on choice and implementation of new technologies, ways of restructuring its business (such as outsourcing its call centres and communications networks), training of staff in the new systems and so on.

This chapter examines both types of linkage to innovation processes. Its focus will tend to be on technological innovation, which has received rather more attention than organisational and other forms of innovation. It begins by considering what sorts of service firm can be described as being most knowledge intensive. Then it moves on to consider innovation within these firms, and finally their contribution to innovation in their clients (and more generally).

Knowledge-intensive services

All economic activities are based on some knowledge, of course. All employees and managers deploy knowledge in their work. All societies are knowledge-based societies, and to talk of our current era as *the* knowledge economy implies that we are paying special attention to the types of knowledge being used, how they are produced and applied, and so on. For example, we may be focusing on the role of scientific and technological knowledge (and thinking about our increased reliance on a series of new technologies), on the importance of research and development (R&D) and innovation in economic competition and growth, and so on. There may also be some reference to the idea of the 'learning society', the notion that skills and practices are becoming more rapidly obsolescent (largely as a result of innovation), and that lifelong learning and organisational flexibility will need to become the norm.

When people talk of knowledge intensity, they are usually referring to highly specialised knowledge. The emphasis is on so-called 'codified knowledge', on understanding of principles and methods that can be generalised across numerous specific situations and problems. Such knowledge ('know-why') is contrasted with 'know-how' and 'know-whom', forms of knowledge that are tied to very particular tasks and places. These last forms of knowledge can be quite difficult to assess. Fortunately, if we are concerned with know-why, knowledge intensity can be related to training and the acquisition of qualifications. Convenient indicators can be derived from statistics and other data concerning educational credentials. Especially relevant will be information concerning higher and non-vocational qualifications, that should in principle be about more generalisable knowledge. Of course, such indicators are bound to be limited – indicators are by definition limited. In no way is the use of such indicators meant to devalue the very substantial knowledge that can be gained by means other than taking university courses or undergoing other forms of high-level training. Other sorts of data on the possession or application of high-level knowledge – such as the classification of jobs in the USA according to the complexity with which they deal with data or devices – should also be explored.

Much of the literature on knowledge intensity and services has concentrated on KIBS, knowledge-intensive *business* services. Research into these sectors has repeatedly noted that there are two broad classes of specialised knowledge involved in KIBS. First is the social and institutional knowledge involved in many traditional professional services. Second is the knowledge that has risen to the fore in recent years, which is more focused on science and technology.

Some recent studies have used survey data concerning the prevalence of people with higher educational qualifications in different industries. A recent case is the work of Tether and Swann (2003) using the UK's CIS3 data. (CIS3 is the third CIS, Community Innovation Survey.) This survey is applied across the EU, and covers a wide spectrum of firms – though not most personal and public services. The CIS3 data provide information on how far the firms sampled are reliant on graduate staff. This is an indicator of the use of professional knowledge, up to graduate level. It obviously captures neither postgraduate training, nor the quality of on-the-job and other professional training – some of these issues could be addressed from employee-level data such as the Labour Force Survey. The data differentiate between S&E – science (including social science) and engineering – graduates, on the one hand, and other graduates (including arts and humanities and so on) on the other (we can label these latter OGs).

Figure 15.1 displays results from the UK CIS3, comparing manufacturing and other sectors with the services covered in the survey. The results give several insights into the knowledge-intensive service sectors. First, in terms of the share of graduate employees, it is service sectors that tend to be particularly knowledge intensive compared with other economic sectors. A number of services – for example, TRS (transport), WHS (wholesale) and IT2 (telecommunications) – do have a fairly low proportion of staff that are graduates, and relatively unqualified operatives, compared to other services, at least.

Three distinct groups of service sectors employ high shares of graduates:

1. *Heavy employers of S&E graduates only*: this consists of the one category of technology-based knowledge-intensive services: Technical Services 2 (R&D and testing services).
2. *Heavy employers of other graduates only*: mainly professional services, and more knowledge-intensive parts of finance and transport services: Financial Services 1, all types of Professional Services, and Transport Services 3 (that is, 'other transport services').

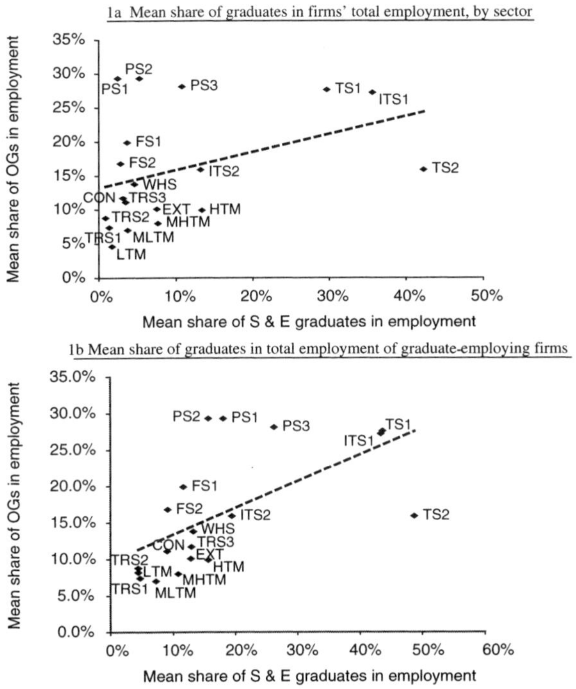

Codes

	Service sectors		Non-services
FS1	Banks, Insurance, etc	CON	Construction
FS2	Renting & Leasing	EXT	Extractive industries (mining etc)
IT1	Computer Services		
IT2	Telecommunications & Other	Manufacturing Sectors (OECD classification)	
PS1	Legal & Accounting	HTM	High Tech Manufacturing
PS2	Informational Services	MHTM	Medium High Tech Manufacturing
PS3	Managerial Services	MLTM	Medium Low Tech Manufacturing
TR1	Passenger Transport	LTM	Low Tech Manufacturing
TR2	Freight & Storage		
TR3	Other Transport Services		
TS1	Architecture & Engineering		
TS2	R&D & Tech. Testing		
WS	Wholesale		

Note: Data are unweighted.

Source: Based on results calculated by Tether and Swann (2003).

Figure 15.1 Employment of graduates: UK CIS3 Data

3. *Heavy employers of both types of graduate*: this consists of the other categories of technology-based knowledge-intensive services, mainly IT services: both types of InfoTech Services, plus Technical Services 1 (architecture and engineering).

We are liable to find some exceptional firms in all sectors – some firms with many graduates are to be found in sectors that generally employ few, and vice versa. But a high proportion (more than two-thirds) of firms in the three groups of knowledge-intensive service sectors noted above, do employ graduates. Further, employers of graduates in these sectors tend to employ a greater share of graduates than do employers of graduates in other sectors. Technical services and computer services tend to have an especially high proportion of graduates in their total workforce.

So this identifies knowledge-intensive services. What lies behind the statistical patterns? Services can be seen as problem solvers. Some problems are highly specific and/or complex ones, demanding highly specialised solutions. Others are common problems requiring relatively routine solutions. The presence of many people with higher education and professional qualifications in a service sector suggests that these services provide for the first set of problems and solutions. A large share of the effort of the workforce in non-knowledge-intensive services is being expended in much more routine ways. (This is not to suggest that everything that is done in services such as transport and logistics, mass entertainment, or post and telecommunications is routine: but the preponderance of efforts is oriented in this way – at least, at present.)

The group of traditional professional services is typically dealing with problems associated with social systems and institutions, especially administrative rules and regulations (for example, legal and accountancy services). Many marketing and consultancy services also deal with problems concerning social groups and interests, or interorganisational activities (such as supply-chain management).

The more S&T (science and technology) intensive services are more concerned with artefacts and the physical world. Thus, for example, there are engineering services concerned with aircraft, construction, oil and transport infrastructure. Laboratory testing and research services are concerned with testing or transforming materials and artefacts (and sometimes biological organisms or samples). IT services of various kinds are concerned with symbol processing or with the configuration and integration of discrete items of hardware and software, and the data that these systems process.

There are services that combine these different classes of knowledge. Architectural and design services combine aesthetic creativity with knowledge of technological possibilities, often using new technologies in their activities. Some services with a professional service orientation or history have come to play substantial technology-related functions for clients. Thus some accounting and management consultancy firms supply information technology (IT) consulting for their clients, some lawyers specialise in intellectual property rights concerning IT or environmental regulations concerning other technologies, and so on. Exactly where they fall in terms of surveys and statistics can be quite contingent on history, convention and happenstance.

Knowledge-intensive services as users of technology and sites of innovation

Knowledge-intensive services are major users of new technologies. This is especially true of new IT, where financial services and the sets of business services mentioned above have typically been among the earliest and most intensive users of the new technology. Evidence for this comes from many sources, including survey and input–output analyses.[1]

Moving away from a focus on IT, more recent analyses of European Community Innovation Surveys (CIS2 in this case, from the mid-1990s) confirm that knowledge-intensive services, especially technology-related ones, are among the most active innovators in the economy. The CIS2 survey has been used to classify firms as innovative or non-innovative. Figure 15.2 presents such data aggregated from information gathered in

14 EU countries (Spain was alone in the then EU15, in not providing data). Patterns in the individual countries are more or less similar to those depicted here.

Service sectors on average lag slightly behind manufacturing in terms of reported innovation. Overall, 51 per cent of manufacturing enterprises and 40 per cent of services were classified as innovative from these survey analyses. Smaller firms tend to be less often classified as innovative than larger ones, but this is not the explanation of the sectoral differences. As Figure 15.2 suggests, the differences persist even when controlling for the tendency for service firms to be smaller.[2] In contrast to the typical picture for services, the knowledge-intensive services do have high levels of innovation. The proportions classified as innovative were: 54 per cent of financial services; 55 per cent of technical services; 64 per cent of telecommunications; and 68 per cent of computer services.

The CIS survey enquires as to the reasons for innovation, providing a little more information about the why and how of innovation. These reasons were remarkably similar across the different sectors examined. The most widespread aim of innovation was improving the quality of the services offered. Other aims that were reported to be very important objectives of their innovation activities were extending service range and opening new markets.

Although it was asserted not long ago that services do not conduct R&D, almost half of the innovating service enterprises examined in CIS2 did report engaging in R&D, and about half of these did so on a continuous basis. But innovating service enterprises are less likely to engage in R&D than innovating manufacturers (almost 70 per cent of these conducted R&D). Larger service firms report more, and more continuous R&D – though there is still more such activity in comparable manufacturers. For instance, a third of the large innovating service enterprises engaged in R&D on a continuous basis, as compared to more than two-thirds of large innovating manufacturers. In-house R&D was most

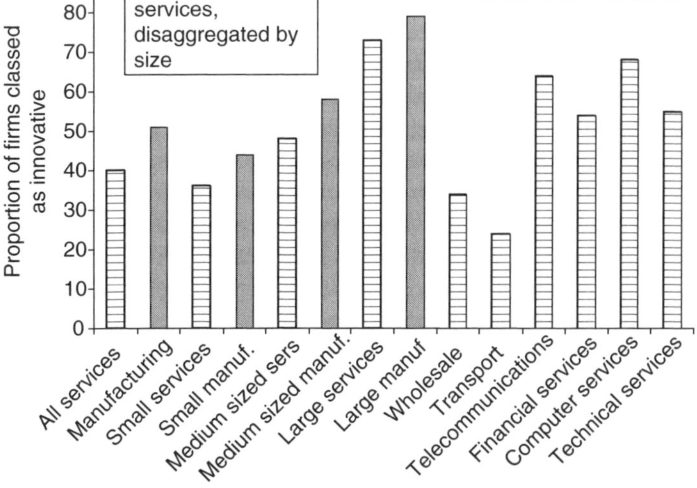

Source: From Table 3.2.5 in Tether et al. (2000).

Figure 15.2 Proportions of innovative firms in various sectors, EU countries, mid-1990s

important for innovation for those services that were technology related: telecommunications, computer services and technical services. Forty-five per cent of the innovating computer service enterprises engaged in R&D on a continuous basis, as did 33 per cent of the innovating technical service enterprises. Only 18 per cent of financial service enterprises did so, in contrast. The less knowledge-intensive wholesale sector was close to financial services, while a mere 4 per cent of transport services undertook continuous R&D.

The firms in the more technologically oriented sectors typically spent more on innovation-related activities than those in the other service sectors. But there was high variation in expenditure from firm to firm, within all sectors. The most widely undertaken innovation-related activities were the acquisition of machinery and equipment, the acquisition of other external technology (including software), and training of staff. Each of these activities was undertaken by about half the innovating service enterprises in 1996. Even though the more technologically oriented sectors were more likely to engage in intra-mural R&D, enterprises in these sectors also placed stress on acquiring machinery, equipment or other external technologies for innovation. The proportion of innovation expenditure on these purchases is lower, and of course, that on R&D is higher, in these sectors.

So, we see that knowledge-intensive services are often quite innovative sectors, though their innovation strategies tend to be less oriented round R&D than is the case for manufacturing industry. Analyses of innovation processes that are derived from studies of manufacturing industry may fail to capture much of what happens in services. For example, the importance of innovation in the delivery of services may be especially important – but surveys such as the CIS only examine the conventional product versus process innovation dichotomy.

The CIS data, and case-study work, tend to support another argument – service sectors are generally less well linked into innovation systems and networks that provide support for innovation than are manufacturing firms (IOIR, 2003). Thus there are relatively few research associations and research centres in the public sector that cater to service industries. But as usual, there are exceptions to any generalisation about services. Some knowledge-intensive services play extremely important roles in innovation systems.

Knowledge-intensive services: impact on innovation across the economy

Here we shall focus on KIBS, whose role is to solve problems for their clients in business and public services. KIBS are *business* services not because they exclusively service businesses, but because they deal with *business processes*. Sometimes the problem solution involves the client in little change – the service firm takes on the task of preparing their accounts, reporting on their markets, monitoring or disposing of their waste, auditing their establishments and running their building or IT facilities. But often the solutions do require change on the part of the client organisations, and these changes may involve technological or other innovations.

Technology-related KIBS, employing (as we have seen) high levels of S&E graduates, have important roles to play in innovation processes (see Miles et al., 1995 and Bilderbeek et al., 1998). They may:

- Conduct R&D into new technologies – R&D services, by the turn of the millennium, were accounting for 10 per cent of business R&D in the UK. Some high-tech sectors of the economy – for instance, chemical and pharmaceutical firms – make extensive use of such services.[3]

- Perform testing of various sorts – to see that the products or operations of their clients conform to health and safety, environmental or technical standards, for example.
- Other service firms provide support for product design. Sometimes this is more like R&D (providing ideas as to how to create usable products). Sometimes this function resembles testing, examining whether and how far products are functionally and ergonomically effective – rapid prototyping and related services actually manufacture model products to test their designs or proposed production process.
- As well as services to help improve the client's product,[4] other technology support services help clients requiring knowledge for using new technology in their production, office, marketing and other activities. Examples include web and internet, software and computer services.[5] Equivalent services have emerged in the biotechnology sphere, and around environmental technologies.
- Rental of equipment also counts as a service activity. Often rental is not a particularly knowledge-intensive service activity – equipment is supplied, but there is little high-level application of knowledge. But specialised firms here may also be in the business of supplying technology advice – as well as permitting users to adopt new technologies earlier and faster than would otherwise be the case.[6]
- Training of staff to make use of new systems is also an important function (and one where there has been a great deal of innovation in terms of developing training technologies). Other services effectively 'loan' implant knowledge to the client, rather than trying to cultivate it among existing staff. Some specialised personnel services help clients deal with changing conditions (such as a product launch or entry to new markets, or a merger or demerger) by offering knowledge-intensive temporary work services (for example, contract management services), locating and sometimes training and supporting the new staff.
- Consultancy and strategic advice as to the choice and implementation of new process technologies is a very important service activity.[7] 'Systems integrators' – which may be firms that statistically hail from manufacturing or service sectors – are in the business of sourcing, integrating and configuring hardware and software – and skills and business practices – to perform the tasks that clients need to have done.
- Facilities management services actively handle the task of using the new technologies for the client – managing a 'smart building', running a call centre or outsourced computer network and so on. The KIBS implements the solution to the problem, providing the client with a capability to which it is reluctant to devote its own staff and management time.

The technology-related KIBS will typically propose technological solutions to their clients, and thus tend to promote technological innovation. We shall examine this in more depth shortly.

But other KIBS may also be active in promoting organisational or other forms of innovation. Management consultancy and staff training activities, for example, may establish awareness in the client of how other organisations are tackling problems (for example, best practice analysis), or even develop new ways of solving them (for example, creativity workshops). Some services actually focus on engendering creativity among clients, while others support team building and other human relations functions that might facilitate innovation and/or adaptation to change. For example, a chemicals firm that needed to rapidly develop alternatives to ozone-depleting CFCs, halved its normal product development time by creating a new cross-disciplinary team. Services supported the consolidation and effective functioning of the group though team-building exercises (such as orienteering) and counselling support (Miles and Green, 1996).[8]

It is also not uncommon to find firms that were initially based in professional service sectors to begin offering technology advice or support – based on their own experience – to other firms in their sector or to clients. Thus there has been a great deal of activity around software and similar tools for accountancy, architecture, publishing and the like. Other services offer specialised information about, for example, environmental regulations bearing on new products or processes.

As problem solvers, KIBS focus their knowledge on the problems faced by their clients, and potential solutions to these problems. KIBS may effect solutions themselves, provide clients with the tools and skills to do this themselves, or provide clients with resources that will enable them to better understand their problems and develop means to overcome them.

We can label these roles, and provide some examples, as follows:

- *Informative*: providing information on features of the companies environment, from which the client will itself define its problems and strategic responses. Such KIBS produce or locate information using research and so on, and process it for clients, usually with a service product involving reports or presentations. Such information may be about the organisation itself, about its environment, or about its position relative to its environment (for example, how do its practices compare to those of competitors, what are its levels of emission of pollutants). Many KIBS firms provide financial analyses, market intelligence, digests of regulatory and similar issues for their clients. These range from rather standardised newsletters to bespoke analyses such as environmental scanning for single clients. (Contrast conventional publishing, which is a manufacturing activity in standard statistics, and involves a large labour force in printing and distribution activities – though online publishing may change this.)
- *Diagnostic*: helping the client define and understand the nature of a problem. An environmental monitoring service may point to specific emissions from a factory chimney; an auditing service may detect fraud in the accounts coming from a branch of a firm; a market research organisation may point to a problem with the image of a company's products. (It is hard to think of non-KIBS equivalents of diagnostic services, apart from areas like consumer and public-oriented health, education and counselling.)
- *Advisory*: suggesting and evaluating possible solutions for a client. Such KIBS may be active in prioritising, recommending choices, and similar activities, for practically any of the topics of knowledge discussed above. This typically involves active dialogue with the organisation. It may require a mediating role where different views and objectives are held by different members or branches of the organisation – and

sometimes this is precisely why KIBS are employed to recommend and promote courses of action already favoured by some parties in the firm. Eco-design services can help firms select between alternative energy systems for reduced environmental footprint, computer services can advise on systems and combinations of systems and services to acquire, financial specialists and brokers suggest insurance and investment options. (Again there are consumer-oriented advisory services, from kitchen design to mortgage brokers – though these are often involved in other service functions as well.)

- *Facilitative*: helping the client with elements of implementing solutions. Training services provide skills required to operate the firms' systems, and may be required even where there are no technological innovations – for example, to provide linguistic or cultural training for new markets, or to train a new workforce in the event of expansion or staff turnover. Training may involve preparation of documentation and other material for client employees to undertake specific tasks and use specific technologies (increasingly this involves tools such as CD-ROM learning aids). Face-to-face training is often employed where more generalised knowledge needs to be developed, to help staff members develop skills and capabilities (and sometimes motivation) required for their job. A very different sort of facilitative service is provided by rapid prototyping firms, who have the capability of quickly producing full-size or scale model products from the client's designs, allowing for testing to see whether the designs are internally consistent, meet required standards, are aesthetically satisfying and so on.
- *Turnkey*: effectively creating (or acquiring) and installing the means to achieve the solution for the client, and providing the necessary know-how to continue to use (and possibly even to upgrade) it. Systems integrators, for example, are able to combine and configure elements of existing and new IT hardware and software to provide the operating facilities that the client requires. Many manufacturing companies supply turnkey solutions, too, and when a client is first acquiring a system, at least, there is liable to be a good deal of KIBS-like service provision in such circumstances. (One non-KIBS equivalent of this may be having basic maintenance of equipment and plant performed by an outside contractor.)
- *Managerial*: effecting the solution for the client, on a one-off, irregular or routine basis. Advanced waste disposal services (not just taking garbage away to deposit it in a pit!), facilities management services, building management, and outsourced computer and telecommunications services are examples of KIBS here.

Table 15.1 sets out some of the implications of these distinct service functions for innovation, both in the KIBS firms and in their clients. (Note that knowledge management methods could be applied in all of the cells – and potentially in the linkages between KIBS and their clients.) The distinct service roles may seem rather exaggerated, since many firms supply a bundle of such services as a package – and there may be economies in so doing, since the service interaction requires learning a great deal about the client, at least where a non-standardised service is being supplied. But in some KIBS branches – perhaps relating to the evolution of the market and of knowledge about the problems it is addressing – the services are fairly well demarcated across different suppliers. (We found this for different environmental services in the UK in the mid-1990s, for example: Miles, 2000a.)

Table 15.1 KIBS roles in services and innovation (examples)

KIBS role	Innovation in KIBS	KIBS-related innovation in client
Informative	New methods of searching for, synthesising, and presenting relevant information. (Examples: use of patent analysis and bibliometric methods in technology watch type of environmental scanning, use of visualisation techniques to represent such results)	Service may alert clients to scientific and technological possibilities or trajectories – for example, from analysis of underpinning literature, of competitor strategies, of regulatory developments
Diagnostic	New methods of monitoring and analysing data, and presenting relevant information. (Examples: new sensors in monitoring environmental impacts, computer models for modelling such impacts, internet-based communications for accessing data from and delivering results to client, and use of various means for reporting to clients.) Interaction with client in problem definition provides opportunities for mutual learning and even co-production of innovations	By clarifying nature of the problem, client's innovative strategies can be focused more effectively on search for solutions. Interaction with KIBS in problem definition provides opportunities for mutual learning and even co-production of innovations
Advisory	As informative and diagnostic services	Reduce risks of adopting innovations by using service's superior knowledge of alternative possibilities, prior experience, best practice, etc.
Facilitative	Innovation in KIBS services and production processes. E.g. training services have extended the range of subjects and types of skill they tackle; they have innovated in the use of multimedia and in face-to-face instructional settings. Rapid prototyping services are using computer links to exchange designs and results with clients, and new equipment to construct their models	Reduce risks of implementing innovations by reducing need for (or accelerating process of) learning by doing. Opportunities to learn from a wider knowledge base than provided in-house, and sometimes to experience solutions tried out elsewhere
Turnkey	Innovation in the elements of systems being combined together, and in the applications to which these capabilities may be applied. Opportunities to learn from doing in concrete circumstances	As facilitative

Table 15.1 (continued)

KIBS role	Innovation in KIBS	KIBS-related innovation in client
Managerial	Specialisation on the service can allow for learning from diverse applications, for specialised innovative efforts; knowledge-intensive elements may evolve out of relatively routine services as more knowledge of strategic application of services to client functions, beyond the immediate problem, is acquired	Reduces need for detailed knowledge of service, freeing resources to concentrate on core competences (though sufficient knowledge to ensure appropriateness of service provision is still required). Increases opportunities to benefit from scale economies and KIBS's innovation

KIBS can focus on solving problems of many sorts. They can help clients orient themselves to just about any feature of their external and internal environments – market development, employee relations, changes in relevant technologies and regulations, and so on. There are even consultancies which provide services to help firms reduce their reliance on consultancies! There is little literature that systematically addresses the question of how different types of KIBS operate, and little that focuses on how the technology- and innovation-related KIBS go about their work. This is a matter that requires more attention.

One relevant analysis of distinctive approaches adopted in specific KIBS–client relations was introduced in studies of professional services by Tordoir (1996), who differentiated between 'jobbing' relations (where the service supplier provides a relatively standardised service), and 'sparring' ones (where the supplier and client negotiate the details of what service is to be provided, and how). Focusing on innovation-related services, Tordoir's distinction bears on the question of how far the service supplier actively promotes innovation in the client. Does the KIBS propose new solutions? Or, in contrast, how far is the KIBS simply supporting solutions that the client has already identified? How far does the KIBS supply knowledge from outside the firm that can challenge established practice based on what is familiar to the client?

One study has used (German) survey data to examine a closely related issue: how far services provide standardised solutions, as opposed to ones that are specially produced or adapted to specific clients. Hipp et al. (2000) examine firms' responses to a question about how far their activities were standardised, as opposed to being customised to the requirements of specific clients. Notably, technology-related KIBS were more likely than other firms to produce specialised service outputs. Twenty-seven per cent of technical services, and 18 per cent of software firms, reported that a third or more of their output was specialised – as opposed to 4 per cent for banking and insurance (but 18 per cent for 'other financial services'), 5 per cent for trade, 2 per cent for transport and communication, 10 per cent for 'other business services' and 4 per cent for a 'residual' category.

The more specialised services can be expected to require greater exchange of knowledge between service firm and client. This creates opportunities for mutual learning, in which clients may gain new understanding of their problems (and thus be empowered to generate

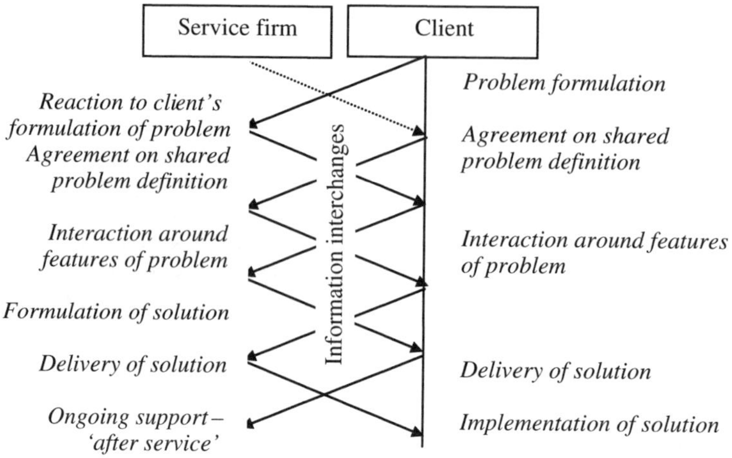

Figure 15.3 Interactions between service firms and their clients

their own innovative solutions), as well as being provided with solutions by the KIBS. The study reports that the specialised firms were much more likely to report that their services had an important impact on their clients' performance and/or productivity – though we do not know what the clients themselves think!

Figure 15.3 portrays a stylised picture of the relationship between clients and KIBS. In the 'jobbing' relationship, the client defines the problems for the service firm, and more or less thoroughly sets out the solution it wants implementing. In the 'sparring' relationship there is much more negotiation as to the nature of the problem, and thus of the service that will be provided. The service firm then plays a diagnostic role, supplying knowledge as to what the problem is that underlies the difficulties being experienced by the client.

The interactions between the KIBS and the client reflect the different types of knowledge that have to be fused together to produce the service. The client firm has its own knowledge of the processes and markets it engages with, and the difficulties it is experiencing. The KIBS has to access and understand this 'local knowledge'. It also brings to bear its more 'generic knowledge' – based on an understanding of the technologies or organisational elements that are or could be applied to the problem. Finally, it can draw on experience with dealing with similar problems (perhaps with firms of the same type and/or in the same sector as the client). These classes of knowledge are typically combined as the KIBS comes to develop its solution to the business problem.

Thus Strambach (2001) sees KIBS as integrating different types of knowledge for particular clients, as adapting or elaborating its generic knowledge to their demands and requirements. KIBS sometimes engage in research independent of specific client commissions, and may develop new knowledge in this way. Sometimes they even generate innovations or the ideas for innovations that they will seek partners in manufacturing or other services to bring to market. But practically all KIBS develop knowledge through their problem-solving interactions with clients. This may sometimes be best thought of as a *co-production* of knowledge, when both parties are learning about the problem, and about potential solutions to it, through their interactions. The KIBS may turn this knowledge into information that can be communicated and routines that can be applied more generally – and the KIBS can then use this in new client relationships.

This raises the question of why clients are prepared to allow KIBS to gain knowledge of their internal operations. They are prepared to entrust KIBS with strategic information because this is necessary for achieving the right solution to their problems. They contribute to, but can also draw directly or indirectly upon, the KIBS's stock of knowledge about clients' experiences and problems.

When a KIBS firm provides a highly specialised service, it is in effect generating a new product, a new way of solving a problem or of applying a solution to a problem. A successful KIBS firm should be able to generalise from such creativity. It can, in principle, learn from producing such a new product, so that it can supply better services – and use better processes for producing them – in the future. How far KIBS firms have elaborated 'knowledge management' tools and practices for such organisational learning is a question that requires more analysis. Reimus (1997) found that about 75 per cent of the US management consultancies he surveyed had instituted processes for capturing best practices, sharing information from one project to another and documenting innovative new ways of solving client problems. But these were largely informal initiatives, sharing innovative knowledge from the staff through spontaneous meetings and so on. But Hansen et al. (1999: 108), looking at larger firms, argue that 'because knowledge is the core asset of consultancies, they were among the first businesses to pay attention to and make heavy investments in the management of knowledge'.

Hansen et al. (1999) examined use of IT-based knowledge management systems in knowledge-intensive services in the US (including large healthcare services and especially consultancies). Two main successful use strategies were identified. In practice a mixture of the two was common (the authors suggest that it is important to make one the core orientation, while devoting say 20 per cent of resources to the other approach). The two strategies are:

- *Codification* Here, the main aim is to enable rapid and frequent reuse of information resources developed by staff, such as presentations, templates or algorithms. This allows for rapid minor customisation of fairly standardised solutions to common problems by relatively junior staff. Because professionals often prefer to retain their own information resources, incentive structures need to reward contributions to the general pool.
- *Personalisation* Here, the aim is to facilitate communication among service workers, so that appropriate expertise can be located and consulted; incentive structures need to reward contributions to others' problem solving. This sort of system is employed where client problems are complex and variable, requiring bespoke or highly customised solutions, with high levels of input from senior staff (who will typically be working at high profit margins rather than focusing on volume of business).

It would be interesting to examine further how far these strategies support different kinds of innovation. For instance, the codified strategy should lead to more rapid internal diffusion of innovations in the KIBS – but excessive reuse of earlier work might reduce search for new types of solution. Personalised systems may be less efficient in enabling rapid reuse of material, but allow for more creative exchanges among key professionals – though codification might free up senior staff to be more creative. Dawson (2000) argues that professional KIBS often need to develop strategies *not* to standardise their products, but to engage in more sophisticated knowledge sharing with clients, adding value to the KIBS–client relationship.

Figure 15.3 also draws our attention to what is happening on the client side of the relationship. Most social and economic research suggests that KIBS do benefit their clients – though there are also many more anecdotal stories of failed relationships. There have been several studies suggesting that KIBS do benefit their clients, based on macro data of one type or another.[9] But there has been much less analysis of what happens at the interface of individual firms. Studies of technological innovation have demonstrated that the benefits of using new technologies are at least as much a matter of user strategy as of the technologies themselves. The user has to develop and apply knowledge of how to use the technology to best effect. It is highly plausible that, similarly, the capacity to effectively interface with KIBS will strongly shape the impacts of their use. Inadequate capacity to use the services can mean that solutions to business problems are applied poorly. Industry criticism of consultants – which is not infrequently encountered! – may not only mean that some service firms offer poor-quality products. Some services probably do, but there are also cases where clients have difficulties in using service inputs in an informed way.

Clients thus require capabilities to make effective use of KIBS. They also need to be able to choose among and combine different service suppliers (and to combine these with in-house skills), and they will need to be able to negotiate the definition of problems and solutions in sparring relationships, and so on. Sjøholt (2001) examined transnational consultancy firms and their clients in Norway. Along with other case-study analysts (for example, Wood, 2002a) he concludes that more sophisticated clients make better use of business services. The 'best' client has already accumulated knowledge that can be used to 'absorb' KIBS inputs, and has capabilities to formulate and reformulate problems in the course of the interaction. Often the more knowledgeable clients seek to establish long-term sparring relations with their suppliers to maintain their competitive advantages. Glückler (1999) likewise argues that clients who contract consultants in order to improve on certain operations are by no means necessarily the weaker firms in their sectors.

In Sjøholt's study, clients did see some of the less successful experiences as a result of their own lack of focus and for underutilisation of the KIBS's competence. Not surprisingly, they were often prone to blame the consultants for any problems that did emerge. Sjøholt relates this to the knowledge-transfer mechanisms employed. One of the most common ways of interacting in knowledge transfer was by formation of team structures. But these were sometimes far from ideally composed, for instance drawing on professionals with a generalist problem approach, rather than setting up teams with an explicitly transdisciplinary approach. Sjøholt suggests that the latter type of team is increasingly necessitated by the nature of contemporary organisational and strategic problems. Some tasks can, of course, be satisfactorily solved by the general practitioner, others (as in Tordoir's 'sales' relationships) by the more specialised professional adviser. Well-defined and controllable tasks of a more systemic learning nature are generally positively evaluated by the clients Sjøholt studied. The broader, more intangible strategic consultancy assignments received more ambiguous assessments in terms of provision of value for money.

Other work on client roles has appeared in recent years. Thus, Hislop (2002) examines the role played by client firms in shaping their relations with consultants. This study drew on case studies of four organisations implementing similar technological innovations. The client firms were found to play a key role in shaping their consultancy relations. Furthermore, the character of the consultancy relations thus formed was found to influence the innovation processes in substantial ways. The diversity of client behaviour found in this study was interpreted by Hislop in terms of the social networks and organisational cultures within which staff in the client firm were embedded. Mason and Wagner (1999) suggest that there are cross-national differences in KIBS use, to further complicate the picture – the implication is that in some countries (and industries?) the services are in much more of a subordinate role, in other cases they are treated as highly knowledgeable partners.

One of the most thorough discussions of client roles and strategies is provided by Camal Gallouj (1997), who draws on the contributions of several earlier scholars to analyse how clients select and evaluate business services. A four-step model (derived from O'Farrell and Moffat (1991) is derived, and for each step, a large number of methods that may be used by the client are identified:

- *Search for general information on suppliers* This may be accomplished on the basis of past contacts, knowledge within the organisation, examination of publications and conference presentations, and so on. Gallouj suggests that since search costs can be high, the client will tend to look for a satisfactory solution, rather than making exhaustive efforts to find the 'optimal supplier'.
- *Evaluation of potential suppliers and the call for tender* This may be accomplished on the basis of applying selection criteria (KIBS qualifications, the nature of the problem and so on) to a list of potential suppliers.
- *Evaluation of tenders and shortlisting* This may be based on the candidates having displayed understanding of the problem, proposed a valid and viable approach to solving it, and demonstrated availability of appropriate experience and a competent team. The client will arrive at a small set of consultants (typically two to five) who will be invited to present their proposals.
- *Presentations by the selected consultancies and the final choice* This is based upon a more detailed application of the criteria employed in earlier steps. More attention will be paid to such issues as: the precise methodology and variations in it, the control of the project and scope for delivery of results on time, the process of interaction that is feasible between KIBS and client, and so on.

Gallouj explores the client's use of signals of quality that can help reduce uncertainty in the selection and evaluation of the service provider (that is, to limit the informational asymmetries). Such signals include certification (qualifications, membership of professional associations and so on), reputation (for example, brand name, comments in the trade press), and various indicators of quality. The client may also seek to impose contractual guarantees, and/or contingency clauses (payment by results, penalties for late delivery and so on) to ensure that the consultant delivers the service required. It may not be possible to establish best practice in the use of such mechanisms, across the wide variety of relationships that can exist in the use of KIBS, but this sort of detailed analysis serves as a guide to case studies and management practice alike. It also underlines the importance of establishing trust in KIBS–client relationships – and demonstrates that trust is liable to involve more elements than just rapport in interpersonal relations! The latter is termed 'process-based trust', as opposed to 'character based' or other sources of evidence as to trustworthiness.

What about the KIBS workforce? The staff of KIBS are instrumental in generating novel solutions to the problems of the client firms, and novel processes within the KIBS itself. They act as the interfaces with clients, so that KIBS become intermediary agents in innovation systems. Their skills have to be severalfold. They typically carry some generic knowledge that is represented in their expertise. They have to be able to apply this and perhaps develop it further in order to meet the requirements and solve the problems of the client (eliciting and organising client-specific knowledge, fusing this local and the more generic knowledge into a solution). Thus they require skills in interpersonal communication, presentation of materials, 'impression management', and the like. These are fairly rare capabilities, and their combination is rarer still: for this reason labour costs and wages are high in most KIBS.

Tomlinson suggests that KIBS staff may be in many ways exemplars of 'lifelong learning' (Tomlinson and Miles, 1999). He examined UK survey data, concluding that – despite concerns about job instability and pressured work lives – these workers are more likely to learn new things, to receive training, work with computers, and to move between different types of work. Tomlinson argues that KIBS provide an alternative route to promoting labour mobility as a means for diffusing knowledge around the economy. People are the carriers of knowledge: they can bring new knowledge into organisations. The stress on labour mobility assumes that this happens by way of employees changing jobs. A KIBS perspective indicates that it can also happen through the interface between service and client. Learning may take place in both parties.

This confirms the importance of the human resources that embody and carry this knowledge. Policies need to be directed towards developing workforce skills appropriate to KIBS. Training systems will need to adapt in order to equip people for the volatile new career structures of the twenty-first century, and the particular demands of KIBS. This involves equipping people with skills to search for work and create it themselves, and, in addition to technical and cognitive skills, to possess the sorts of social, interpersonal and self-organisational skills required for effective KIBS (see Toivonen, 2001). Traditional disciplinary structures are probably inadequate to this challenge. Vocational systems will need to develop much better intelligence as to the changing skill demands of KIBS.

KIBS firms need systems of governance that can increase the quality of human resources, rather than the control of the workforce. (This may involve, for example, more professionalisation of some of the newer forms of expertise; it may require more use of semi-professionals in service production and delivery.) It is liable to push knowledge management systems in new ways that can accommodate the concerns and highly complex characteristics of knowledge professionals, and that can interface the systems of KIBS themselves with their clients. And the need for clients to be informed as to good practice in recruiting and using KIBS is important, if their use is to contribute to innovation and dynamism more generally. These are activities that (parts of) the private sector have awareness of, and, sometimes, take responsibility for. But support from public policy may prove helpful to smaller firms (KIBS and KIBS's potential clients) and peripheral regions (where access to KIBS may be a crucial developmental resource). The rise of KIBS means that important knowledge-producing and -using activities are being effected outside of the long-established structures that have governed the quality of science and the integrity of professions. These structures are of course themselves evolving in the knowledge-based economy. But the rise of KIBS means that action may also be required to support the professionalism of some types of expert – who may come under particularly heavy financial or moral pressure in their work. This is a general issue of corporate governance, but may have implications for innovation both directly (poor advice on systems to acquire, for example) and indirectly (diverting resources and destabilising the economic environment).

Conclusions

In this chapter, first we examined just what services can be reasonably described as knowledge intensive. Second, we outlined recent results dealing with the nature of innovation in knowledge-intensive services. While there is much about the innovation processes and outcomes in these services that is familiar to innovation researchers, it also emerges that there are distinctive features of the organisation of innovation in these firms. Such features may be becoming more important generally, with the rise in knowledge-intensity and service elements in production processes across the economy. Third, we reviewed some approaches that appear promising in enabling us to better understand the (changing) roles of KIBS in innovation processes. The rise of KIBS is associated with the increased variety of technological and administrative knowledge, and the complexity of the combinations of knowledge, required by contemporary firms. KIBS are agents for creating, integrating and bearing knowledge.

An understanding of these roles and processes is essential if we are to get a grasp on what is really new about the 'knowledge-based economies' that industrial – or postindustrial – societies are supposedly becoming. The literature reviewed here demonstrates that systematic research into these topics is now being taken up in numerous countries and research groups. We can hope for considerable progress in exploring the nature of innovation in knowledge-intensive services in the next few years.

Notes

1. For an early overview, see OECD (ICCP) 1993.
2. Note that some service sectors, like finance, actually tend to feature larger firms than is typical for manufacturing, though most services tend to be dominated by smaller enterprises.
3. A recent study has identified clusters of economic sectors that make very distinctive use of different types of business services. Sectors that are intensive users of external R&D services in OECD countries (proportional to the output of the user sectors) were: chemicals; pharmaceuticals; secondary raw materials; trade, maintenance and repair of motor vehicles and motorcycles; retail sale of automotive fuel; wholesale and retail trade; repairs; wholesale trade and commission trade services, except of motor vehicles and motor cycles; retail trade services (some); repair services of personal and household goods; recreational, cultural and sporting services; and 'other services'. These results are produced by ECORYS (2004) on the basis of input–output analyses.
4. Marketing and advertising services may also have specialised roles to play in establishing markets for new products.
5. ECORYS (2004) reports that the most intensive users of IT services are: supporting and auxiliary transport services; electricity, gas and water supply; travel agency services; post and telecommunication services; financial intermediation services (except insurance and pension funding services); finance, insurance; insurance and pension funding services (except compulsory social security services); and services auxiliary to financial intermediation.
6. Sectors reported by ECORYS to be intensive users of renting of machinery and equipment services were: coal and lignite; peat; mining and quarrying; other mining and quarrying products; aircraft and spacecraft; construction; land transport; transport via pipeline services; transport and storage; water transport services.
7. The OECD's studies found that across 21 OECD countries, 'strategic business services' – close to our

concept of KIBS – had a turnover of some $1.5 trillion in 1999 (Murphy and Vickery, 1999, and more recent information from OECD website). They employed around 11 million workers (about 3 per cent of total employment). Business organisation services were largest in terms of employment (over 4 million) – this will include all sorts of management consultancy, not just technology-related activities. Computer, and R&D and technical services together reached about the same total (4 million; around a million were employed in marketing, and a small fraction of this in human resources development, including training). These strategic business services grew rapidly over the 1990s – about 10 per cent per annum in terms of turnover. (An extended European analysis is provided in Rubalcabo-Bermejo, 1999.)

8. The CFC case also saw an interesting use of a KIBS for testing innovative products. A number of chemical firms speeded up the approval process for their new compounds by collectively commissioning a service firm to run simultaneous tests on these products, avoiding the need for the rivals to share confidential information about specific products' composition and production.
9. For instance, European Commission (2000); Muller (2001); Tomlinson (2000).

16 Small and medium-sized enterprises and the consumption of traded (producer service expertise) versus untraded knowledge and expertise

*John R. Bryson and Peter W. Daniels**

> We take trade magazines, there are 4 in our business which are pretty essential and give us a good overview of what is happening in advertising in general. They produce a lot of potential new business leads, and there are other books and reference manuals that are published that we can buy into for information. You've also got electronic information – Reuter's databank. We get all sorts of information on what clients are doing and about personnel changes in advertising. So we've got no problems sourcing information and *then there's the jungle drums in the village itself* [localised agglomeration]. There are the formal gatherings and then there's the casual bit in the pub. (Interview, London Advertising Company, our italics)

Introduction

One of the most important questions concerning the relationship between entrepreneurship and regional development is the ways in which organisations as well as individuals acquire access to knowledge and expertise. The relationship between an entrepreneur and the regional economy is structured around formal and informal relationships between people and institutions. This interpretation builds on the well-known sociological concept of 'embeddedness' of Granovetter (1985), Giddens (1991) and Boden (1994). To Boden, society and its structures are the result of many local interactions. At the heart of these interactions is the development of a common language that structures individuals' understanding and forces them to adopt a particular way of understanding. Such languages can be heavily localised as well as being specific to a particular industry. There are two ways of conceptualising a regional flow of knowledge. First, a micro or agency approach places the emphasis on the everyday actions of individuals, but this ignores the ways in which such actions are partly determined by external structures. Second, a macro or structural approach highlights the role of regional institutions in creating and distributing knowledge, but underplays the complex ways in which the everyday actions of individuals result in the creation and reproduction of institutions (Bailey and Bryson, 2006).

These different ways of conceptualising regional knowledge flows come together in the revival of interest in the regional economy and territorial specialism, and in Storper's suggestion that 'the theoretical status of the region is as a nexus of untraded interdependencies' (1995: 211). Untraded interdependencies are formal or informal linkages between companies and individuals. The concept draws on the work of Francois Perroux, who considered that the economy consisted of organisations linked together by common types of knowledge, machines or ways of organisation (Perroux, 1950). The important point is that these linkages between companies are untraded and can produce regional advantages for a group of companies. The concept of untraded interdependencies is related to the notion that the boundaries of the organisation are becoming increasingly blurred; ideas and innovations are increasingly transferred between internal and external labour markets. Firms become dependent on decisions made by other companies and organisations. To Storper, untraded interdependencies 'generate region-specific material and non-material assets in production' (1995: 192) which are scarce resources and are hence vital for regional competitiveness. The region is thus considered as important in underpinning untraded interdependencies. It is necessary not to overstate the importance of regionally localised traded and untraded interdependencies (Bryson, 2000). Many untraded interdependencies form from or around traded relationships and these interactions between people as well as firms frequently go well beyond the confines of a regional economy. An apparent untraded relationship may hide the fact that the impetus behind the relationship was formed via an earlier traded exchange. Rusten et al. (2005) note that close friendships form in places and these friendships are then split apart as people relocate; however, in many cases the relationship will continue and traded and untraded interactions will still occur.

The blurring of organisational boundaries is partially explained by the dramatic growth that has occurred in the advanced economies in employment in business service activities, those companies which supply expertise and knowledge that are considered to add value to the output and competitiveness of their clients (Bryson, 1996; Bryson et al., 2004b). The growth in business service firms is considered by many commentators to be symptomatic of the development of a knowledge-based economy (Castells, 1996; Lash and Urry, 1994; Bryson et al., 2004b). It is important to remember that the economy operates as an integrated whole. This is to highlight relationships that exist between different economic sectors. Business service firms should not be considered in isolation from their clients as they play an important role in stimulating development and innovations among client companies (Bailly et al., 1987; Ley and Hutton, 1987; Bryson, 1997a; Rusten et al., 2005).

Despite a significant recent body of research into the operational dynamics of small business service firms (Keeble et al., 1991; Bryson et al., 1993a and b; Birley and Westhead, 1994; Kirby, 1997; O'Farrell et al., 1998), few studies have been undertaken into client use of external business service expertise (Bryson, 1997a; Bennett and Robson, 1999a; Rusten et al., 2005). Business service expertise needs to be understood in relationship to the management strengths and weaknesses of client companies as the knowledge supplied by an external provider has to be managed and consumed internally by the client company. The growing significance of business service expertise for client companies suggests that more research needs to be undertaken into small and medium-sized enterprises (SMEs) and their use of external expertise. The relationship between SME owner-managers and external expertise is especially important given the dependence of large companies on SMEs in their supply chain, and the limited management resources of the majority of SME owner-managers.

This chapter identifies the management strengths and weaknesses of a sample of SMEs in the UK, before exploring their consumption of external business service knowledge and expertise provided through the agency of Business Link, the UK's 'one-stop-shop' government-funded advice initiative for SMEs (Bryson, 1997b; Bennett and Robson, 1999b), or direct from the private sector. The reasons for employing outside expertise and the relationship between the internal and external environments of SMEs are explored. Business service expertise is, however, only one form of knowledge and expertise available to SMEs, and it is a traded form. Business service expertise may not be as important as other forms of untraded knowledge and expertise transfer (Storper, 1995, 1997).

Interviews with SMEs highlight the importance of 'the jungle drums in the village' as a valuable source of advice and expertise. 'The village' in this quotation refers to a localised agglomeration or business community (Saxenian, 1996), but it also applies to industries with social networks that function nationally and internationally. An agglomeration does not have to consist of a cluster of interdependent businesses (Scott, 1988b), but can consist of a knowledge community in which best practice, general information and knowledge is shared between companies, many of which may not even be competitors or be part of the same commodity chain.

The findings presented in this chapter are derived from an ESRC-funded project exploring the relationships between SMEs and their use of externally provided knowledge and expertise. A two-stage methodology was employed. First, extensive research involving a postal survey of a representative sample of SMEs in England was undertaken during 1996 and 1997. The survey covered independent manufacturing, business, professional and technical service enterprises, exploring their characteristics, strengths and weaknesses and use of a whole series of both public and private sector external advisers. Companies in the sample are independently owned, employing between 10 and 250 employees (Table 16.1). Respondents to the survey had a median employment size in 1996 of 32 full-time employees (see Bryson and Daniels, 1998a, for details of this methodology). Second, intensive research was undertaken in the form of detailed face-to-face interviews with a sample of 60 SMEs (34 manufacturing and 26 service companies) equally divided among London, the West Midlands and Cumbria. These interviews provide an understanding of the ways in which different types of SME utilise external information in different operating environments. This stage also involved face-to-face interviews with private sector management consultants and representatives of Business Link consulted by each of the SMEs in the interview survey.

Table 16.1 Characteristics of the firms in the survey

	No.	%
a) Employment size		
1–10	15	10
11–20	39	25
21–40	38	24
41–80	28	18
81–150	15	10
>150	17	11
Missing cases	4	3
b) Sector		
Manufacturing	72	47
Transport, storage and communications	15	10
Renting of equipment	9	6
Computer and related activities	6	4
Research and development	4	3
Other business services	46	30
Total	152	100
Missing cases	4	

Traded service expertise versus untraded tacit knowledge

There are two different and frequently unrelated approaches in the literature to explain the growing importance of knowledge in economic activity. The first literature has its roots in Alan Scott's innovative work on new industrial spaces (1988b). In the complex set of literatures and debates that have developed from this work, regional economies have come to be conceptualised as consisting of networks of untraded interdependencies (Storper, 1995, 1997; Scott, 2000a). Much of this work has concentrated on the identification of distinctive clusters of economic activity that have developed into 'neo-Marshallian nodes in global networks' (Amin and Thrift, 1992: 571). More recent conceptualisations of clusters have emphasised the 'innovative milieux' or 'learning region' as crucial for the innovativeness of clusters and regions (Asheim and Cooke, 1999; Keeble, 2000). The collective learning processes that occur in such regions are the consequence of intensive and frequent inter-firm informal and personal contacts and the exchange of tacit knowledge and embodied expertise. The emphasis in much of this literature is on the exchange of tacit knowledge between companies operating in the same industrial sector (Nachum and Keeble, 1999). However, such an exchange of tacit knowledge is not restricted to companies linked together as part of a commodity chain, but also occurs between unrelated companies as a consequence of personal contacts.

The second literature identifies the growth of knowledge-intensive business service firms as being implicated in the increased need for companies to obtain access to knowledge that does not exist inside their company or even local economy as well as to sources of global information and knowledge. This literature emphasises the growth of management consultants and other forms of external advice as creators and distributors of knowledge at both a local as well as global level (Beyers and Lindahl, 1997; Bennett and Robson, 1999a; Bryson et al., 2004b; Rusten et al., 2005; Bryson and Rusten, 2006). Both literatures explore issues connected to the competitiveness of companies and regional economies, but the emphasis placed on traded as against untraded knowledge is different. We argue that these literatures need to be combined in order to develop a more complete understanding of the operation of regional economies. A business enterprise may be part of a neo-Marshallian cluster and be drawing upon business service expertise, but it must be noted that the majority of firms are not located in such clusters but are still able to access forms of collective knowledge (Rusten et al., 2005).

The transformation of the economy away from employment in manufacturing-related activities to service activities has important implications for town and cities, as well as reflecting alterations in the organisation of economic activities. Both Mulgan (1991) and Lash and Urry suggest that towns and cities should be increasingly considered as 'centres for the switching of information, knowledge, images and symbols' (1994: 220). Concentration of professional capital in key urban centres has important implications for the range, availability and quality of professional expertise in peripheral locations (Bryson and Daniels, 2007). Such concentrations may result in differential access to a whole series of strategic business service activities. The concentration of business service companies in 'service spaces' (Bryson, 1997a) generates new knowledge and expertise which can be consumed by any client, no matter where they are located, as long as the client possesses the capability to identify, access and utilise such service expertise effectively (Rusten et al., 2005). Such information-rich environments also offer opportunities for individuals to create a reputation for a particular type of service expertise which may become of national or even global significance (Bryson and Rusten, 2005). Service spaces contain information-intensive companies functioning as innovation, information and expertise transfer agents. Effectively they operate as pivotal information nodes in the global economic system (Castells, 1996; Bryson and Daniels, 2007).

Large companies have both the ability and resources to search for the right types of external expertise irrespective of the location of the business service supplier (Bryson, 1997a). They are able to maintain contacts with centres of business service excellence acquiring access to the latest management and technological innovations. In contrast, SMEs have limited management time and resources to search for external expertise. They also employ very few external business service firms, and thus have limited opportunities to develop expertise and experience of choosing business service companies, and of managing the relationship with outside suppliers of external expertise.

Part of the transformation in the ways in which organisations are structured reflects differences between the relationship of core and support activities. Firms have been transformed into 'extended' or flexible firms in which the boundaries between externalised and internalised management expertise have become increasingly blurred. Management and other forms of expertise do not necessarily have to be contained within the confines of an organisation, but can exist in a state of symbiosis. Organisations with blurred boundaries can develop a just-in-time approach to expertise and knowledge, but the management of symbiotic relationships demands both management time and expertise. Much work has been undertaken into the concentration by large firms on core activities, and the impact this has on the externalisation of support and management functions (Perry, 1990; Goe, 1991; Beyers and Lindahl, 1997). Comparatively little work, however, has explored the blurring of the SME management boundary (Hitchens et al., 1994; Hitchens, 1997).

The most effective way to obtain, interpret and implement new information and knowledge is by co-present interaction (Boden and Molotch, 1994). Such interaction is much more complex than face-to-face interaction as it includes the advantages that may accrue to a company from a location surrounded by similar companies or business service firms. Untraded interdependencies may develop which produce innovations as a consequence of tacit knowledge and expertise transfer (Marshall, 1909; Storper, 1995). Co-present interaction thus includes 'inadvertent' meetings that 'occur when people of the same ilk frequent the same spaces' (Boden and Molotch, 1994). Such interaction creates trust, and results in the transfer of knowledge and information (Granovetter, 1985). The co-presence of business service firms with some of their clients 'shapes the possibilities of trust between them' (Friedland and Boden, 1994; Friedland and Palmer, 1994). It also determines the extent to which client firms develop strategies and structures to cope with market uncertainty (Beck, 1992).

Notions of untraded interdependencies (Storper, 1995, 1997) and co-presence raise serious questions concerning the role of business service expertise – traded expertise – relative to other sources of advice, knowledge and information. Capitalist production is controlled by the articulation of information into knowledge to create expertise. Information and expertise is required to identify suitable sources of capital and raw materials, manage the labour force, and manipulate the transformation of the finished commodity into capital. The overemphasis in business service research on one type of traded knowledge and expertise, that supplied by business service enterprises and professionals, obscures the numerous different types of information and knowledge which flow into client organisations via other sources and routes. SMEs should be conceptualised as being situated in a knowledge web (Figure 16.1). This web consists of two types of knowledge flow: formal traded business service knowledge and less formal/informal untraded knowledge; and two types of knowledge: management versus product related. There are many ways in which an organisation acquires new types of knowledge: a new managing director; boardroom linkages; the recruitment of a new manager; publications and other forms of media; scrutiny of competitors' products; external training; interim management; takeover activity; movement of knowledge down the supply chain and various forms of untraded interdependency, such as membership of a trade association, discussions in pubs, golf clubs and other forms of social interaction (Figure 16.1). We want to return to the ideas of the Cambridge economist Alfred Marshall. Writing in 1909 (pp. 152–3) about agglomeration economies he noted:

> The mysteries of [a] trade become no mysteries; but are as it were in the air, and children learn many of them unconsciously. Good work is rightly appreciated; inventions and improvements in machinery, in processes and the general organization of the business have their merits promptly discussed; if one man [sic] starts a new idea it is taken up by others and combined with suggestions of their own, and thus becomes the source of further ideas.

Thus, the secrets of industry are *partly* in the air and not necessarily in the hands of the nearest management consultant or business adviser. Companies acquire information about new management practices, machines and potential employees from combining information, expertise and knowledge that is obtained via traded and untraded interactions which are driven by social relationships that have developed from some type of co-present interaction. It is worth emphasising that some of these relationships may have been established in one place, but now operate across space as the parties to the relationship may no longer be co-located.

Management strengths and weaknesses of SMEs

One of the questions that needs to be addressed is whether untraded knowledge occurs more frequently or has a greater impact than traded business service knowledge. This chapter can only go so far in addressing this issue, but one part of the answer comes from exploring the strengths and weaknesses of the management teams of SMEs. As part of this research the managers of our sample of SMEs were asked to identify their management strengths and weaknesses (Table 16.2). This list, which is in rank order from the weakest to the strongest elements of management, can be interpreted by dividing it into three sections.

First, SMEs are weakest in management areas which involve liaison with external organisations and individuals. The weakest element is the use and management of external expertise. To avoid wasting money, a company employing an outside expert has to invest a considerable amount of internal management time in the formulation of the project brief, and the management of the relationship with the external adviser. Without this internal expertise SME owner-managers are sold packages which are inappropriate, or being encouraged to implement ideas that are not suitable for the size, culture and organisation of their company. Consultancy projects will have a higher risk of failure as the owner-manager will not possess the skills required to manage the external provider of expertise. In one of our case studies a consultant had taken over the running of the company from the managing director rather than acting as an adviser (Bryson et al.,

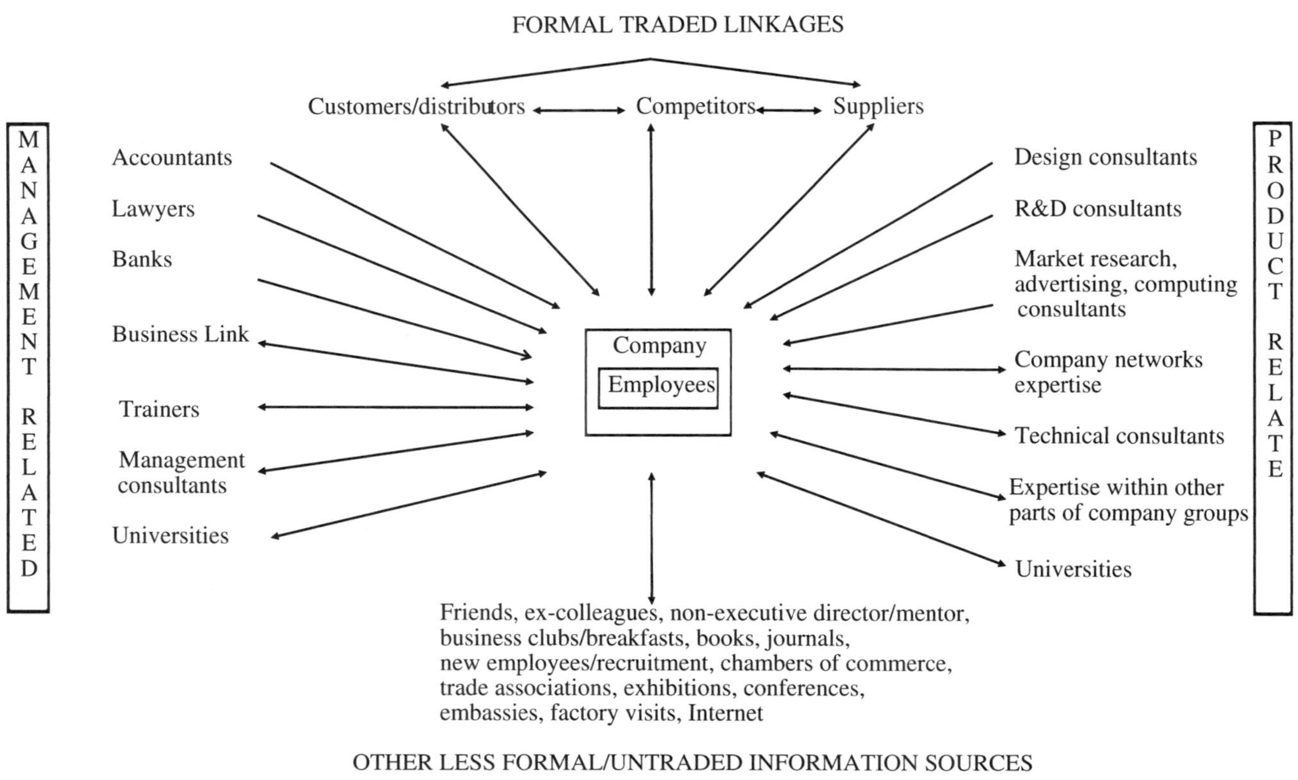

Figure 16.1 SME traded and untraded information flows

Table 16.2 Strengths and weaknesses in particular management areas (scale of 1 to 5 with 1 as weakest)

Management area	Mean
1. Use of external advisers	2.89
2. Use of advertising and promotional methods	2.89
3. Innovation and R&D	3.14
4. Recruitment	3.22
5. Identifying and fulfilling the training needs of staff	3.25
6. Use of management concepts and techniques	3.34
7. Use of business information	3.37
8. Personnel management	3.39
9. Development of a company culture	3.55
10. Business planning	3.62
11. Experience in management	3.75
12. Financial management	3.91
13. Relationships with creditors and suppliers	4.09
14. Other (practical knowledge, customer relations, creativity, sales)	4.27

1999). In another case, the consultant had become a permanent addition to the management term, being engaged for the past three years, for one day a week, for general advice, rather than for a specific project.

Second, elements 4, 5, 8 and 9 (Table 16.2) are weaknesses based around personnel management. Inability to engage in successful employee management and development will have important implications for the future prosperity of the company. These weaknesses suggest that organisations like Business Link need to explore ways in which SME owner-managers can develop their recruitment and personnel management skills. This is especially important in a service-driven environment in which the success of a client customer relationship is increasingly dependent on the service or employee component of the interaction (Hochschild, 1983).

Third, the strongest management areas are those which either are experienced daily, or are routine business practices. Thus, relationships with customers, creditors and suppliers are regular occurrences providing opportunities for SME management to develop a good working relationship based around trust. Business planning and financial management have become accepted features of SME management, as banks will not lend without evidence of a company's future profitability and of the existence of acceptable financial management controls. These routine interactions provide opportunities for the untraded exchange of information, knowledge and innovation that may be more important than the periodic flow of information that occurs with the employment of an external consultant.

These finding have important policy implications. They suggest that SME management teams have more expertise in sourcing knowledge by drawing upon untraded rather than traded sources of expertise. Internal and external diseconomies may result from SMEs' inability to manage the relationship with outside suppliers of expertise. The implementation of policies designed to improve, and/or subsidise SME access to external business service expertise (for example, the Business Link initiative in the UK) will be undermined unless resources are directed to overcoming this management deficiency.

SMEs and traded interdependencies

The inability of many SMEs to manage the relationship with external suppliers of business service expertise does not appear to prevent the majority of SMEs from employing external advisers. A total of 84 per cent of respondents had employed either public or private sector advisers. One third (51) of firms had employed only private sector advisers, and 29 firms had not used external advisers. Nearly one-third (31 per cent) of private sector consultants employed by SMEs were small firms, 24 per cent were sole practitioners, 17 per cent specialist computer consultancies and 11 per cent large multifunctional consultancy companies. Those companies that had not employed advisers considered them either unnecessary or too expensive. Some companies noted that they did not employ external expertise because they had no knowledge of what was available.

The most utilised public sector advice agencies were the training and enterprise councils (TECs) (37 per cent), followed by Business Link (33 per cent) (Table 16.3a). SMEs consulted public sector advice agencies predominantly because of the availability of grants, subsidised consultancy and value for money (37 per cent) and because they were good sources of general information and advice (33 per cent) (Table 16.3b). Fifteen per cent stated that the services were good value for money, or just inexpensive. Private sector consultants were most frequently employed for their specialist knowledge and skill (37 per cent) and for an independent impartial analysis of a problem (Bryson and Daniels, 1998a: 271). External advisers are able to examine the operation of an SME without the constraints imposed by day-to-day management responsibilities. Just under one-fifth (18 per cent) of SMEs employed an external adviser because they required intensive help for a short period, and 12 per cent, because there was insufficient time to develop the required skills or expertise internally.

Consultants provided specialist technical advice to clients (25 per cent), or undertook elements of a specific project (13 per cent). Sometimes they offered basic management advice in the areas of human resource management (7 per cent) and market research (7 per cent). In comparison to large companies, the SME client/consultant relationship is unbalanced with the majority of consultants not working in partnership with internal staff. A survey of the use of consultants by large companies found that 43 per cent (Bryson, 1997a) worked closely with the internal staff. This type of interaction occurred in only 13 per cent of SMEs and is another indication of a serious SME problem related to the management of the relationship with external advisers. In 12 per cent of cases the consultant provided a 'blueprint for change', with clients expecting their in-house staff to implement the proposal. Such a strategy will work only if the internal staff have been actively involved in the construction of the 'blueprint'.

Of those companies not using public sector advice agencies, 57 per cent stated that it was because such advice was not required, and surprisingly, given the marketing of the Business Link initiative, 13 per cent were not aware of public sector advice agencies. Twenty-three per cent considered that such agencies were too idealistic, not practical and that they had no confidence in them, their services or employees. There appears to be a significant problem over the ways in which a small proportion of SMEs are interpreting the quality and usefulness of the advice available via government-funded agencies (Table 16.3b).

Overall, the choice of consultants depended heavily on three related characteristics (Table 16.4). First, the perception held by business friends and acquaintances of the reputation of a consultancy company and individual consultant. The decision to employ a

Table 16.3 Type consulted and reasons for using public sector advice services

a) Type consulted

	No.	%
Business Link	38	33
Enterprise initiative	29	25
Local council economic development services	6	5
Training and enterprise councils	42	37
Total	115	

b) Reasons for using or not using public sector advice agencies

Reasons for use	No.	%	Reasons for non-use	No.	%
For information and advice	31	33	Not required	27	57
Grants and finance for consultancy available	21	22	No confidence in them/people/services	11	23
Free, cheap, value for money	14	15	Unaware of what is available	6	13
Training courses	9	10	Requires specialist expertise	3	6
Company appraisal/quality systems	9	10			
Other	10	11			
Total	94		Total	47	

Table 16.4 Ways in which private sector advisers were identified

	No.	%
Networking	40	38
Previous use	18	17
Via DTI, TEC, chambers of commerce, Business Link	15	14
Mailshot/cold call	13	12
Sought specialist skills	8	8
Via accountant, bank, solicitor	6	6
Via Business Link	5	5
Total	105	

particular consultancy company is thus strongly influenced by untraded interdependencies, or in other words 'the jungle drums in the village'. Second, previous client experience of working with the consultancy; in most cases this will reflect experience of working with a particular consultant rather than a company. Third, a recommendation made by a public agency, for example, Business Link or Chamber of Commerce. The SME search strategy for a consultant is locationally restricted or forged around extant social relationships that can stretch over space (Rusten et al., 2004b, 2005). There is thus a double geography at work here. First, local relationships that are explained by notions of co-presence

Table 16.5 Proportion of SMEs using private sector external advisers for particular types of advice

	%
Information technology and computerised systems	35
Marketing (advertising and public relations)	29
Legal issues	28
Personnel management/ recruitment	28
Finance and administrative systems	28
Business planning	27
Market research and intelligence	24
Organisational change and development	19
Financial management	16
Environmental issues	9

and embeddedness (Bryson and Daniels, 1998a: 272–3) and, second, dislocation in which social relationships formed in one place continue to be effective as people relocate and substitute place- with space-based relationships (Rusten et al., 2005).

Surveyed firms were asked about their use of private sector external firms and expertise in 10 areas, ranging from information technology to environmental issues (Table 16.5). By far the highest reported use of external experts was for information technology and computerised systems (35 per cent). This is not surprising given the growth in specialised software packages targeted at the SME sector, and attempts by commercial internet service providers to persuade SMEs that they require a presence on the internet, nor is the position of marketing as the next most highly used group of external advisers. It is significant that advertising and promotional methods have already been identified as a key SME management weakness; the significance and need for marketing consultancy advice is a recurrent theme in most surveys of SME performance (Small Business Research Centre, 1992). Well over one-quarter of firms had employed outside legal advisers, but this represents expertise which cannot be developed and retained inside a small company.

The consideration of a firm's future growth objectives and business strategy is an important area in which a proportion of SMEs are seeking external advice. Thus, 27 per cent of firms had employed independent business planning advisers, almost certainly management consultants. Just under a quarter of companies had also sought external market research advice, which would support either a marketing initiative, or technological innovation. Overall then, it is in the areas of information technology, marketing, legal issues, personnel management, finance and business planning, that SMEs seek help most frequently.

The least frequent use of external advice was in the areas of 'environmental issues' (9 per cent) and financial management (16 per cent). Many SMEs are too small, or too concerned with everyday management issues, to give much attention to environmental issues. SMEs, however, can no longer ignore environmental legislation. Uncertainty over this legislation is one of the most difficult problems facing the SME manufacturing company. SMEs generally have poorly developed systems for keeping up to date with environmental legislation. Most SMEs learn about new regulations from technical journals, trade associations and from the Health and Safety Executive. Some of the banks have also begun to attempt to raise business awareness of environmental issues.

One of the most surprising aspects of Table 16.5 is the low proportion of SMEs consulting external experts for advice over financial management. This is a difficult finding to interpret. Most SMEs will consult an accountant who will also provide them with advice over aspects of financial management. Perhaps small firms consider that they are unable to afford this type of expertise, or that they are able to obtain this advice from the public sector.

The secrets of industry are in the air or 'on the jungle drums in the village'

The concentration of research on management consultancy and business support agencies has encouraged policy makers to ignore the role of untraded interdependencies or formal and informal linkages which exist between companies and individuals. It is commonly assumed that SME owner-managers are too preoccupied with the day-to-day running of their companies to search for information or knowledge which may impact on company performance (Bryson and Daniels, 1998a; Ram, 1994). However, the economy consists of organisations which are linked together by common types of knowledge, machines and modes of organisation. Knowledge flows tacitly and explicitly between companies as soon as individuals meet or a rival's product is purchased for examination or viewed in the trade press or at a trade exhibition. SMEs are engaged in a continuous process of interactive and collective learning that is not just related to the employment of an external adviser (Bryson, 1997b). SMEs learn from their own internal experiences, but also from a variety of external sources: competitors, suppliers, customers, universities and many other types of individual and organisation (Figure 16.1). Firms learn from their competitors through both informal and formal linkages (von Hippel, 1987; Foray, 1991).

Informal linkages or untraded interdependencies may involve the recruitment of staff trained by a competitor, hiring the same business service firms and equipment suppliers or the transfer of knowledge through friendships and acquaintances. Thus, the intensification of competition in the chocolate industry in the 1970s led to increased secrecy between competing manufacturers in the UK. Visits of Cadbury's managers to the Rowntree-Mackintosh plant, for example, were now things of the past. Cadbury then had to rely on the recruitment of staff from competitors and technology transfer and knowledge from equipment suppliers. According to Kleinknecht and Reijnen (1992) and Cohen and Levinthal (1989) internal research and development (R&D) departments are conducive to the generation of internal knowledge, but also serve 'as an observatory that enhances a firm's capability to exploit external sources of knowledge' (Kleinknecht and Reijnen, 1992: 357). Such exploitation relates to untraded interdependencies between companies in the same sector as well as to the operation of social networks between members of R&D departments.

Some of the most important untraded interdependencies are the result of the creation of relations of trust based on personal reputation. The importance of trust in binding individuals together is well known in traditional economic theory. Marshall noted that the chief difficulty in obtaining capital is overcome by:

> Co-operators who have firstly a high order of business ability and probity, and secondly the 'personal capital' of a great reputation among their fellows for these qualities, will have no difficulty in getting the command of enough material capital for a considerable undertaking: the real difficulty is to convince a sufficient number of those around that [they possess] these rare qualities. (Marshall, 1932: 173–4)

The creation of trust during a number of successful traded exchanges may establish the necessary conditions to produce trust based on reputation which will lead to the establishment of untraded interactions between individuals. In this case, the argument is that the ties that bind industry together are based on the establishment of trust between individuals, and that this trust is articulated through social networks. The important point is that an individual will treat knowledge obtained from a relationship of trust as superior to that obtained from an unknown, unproven and untrusted source. This explains the failure of many attempts to persuade SMEs to use information or consultancy services provided by government. A reputation takes a long time to establish and is easily destroyed. The owner of a small West Midlands (UK) subcontracting engineering company noted that a Business Link manufacturing consultant 'had wonderful theories in this room [the MD's office] but when we went out on the shopfloor he couldn't cope with the environment' (Interview). The apparent inability of the consultant to deal with a real situation has turned this company away from using the services of Business Link. Organisations attempting to provide SMEs with advice need to be extremely careful in the way in which they establish and maintain their contact with the management team.

Consultants and Business Link are a comparatively minor mechanism employed by SMEs to acquire information. They nevertheless have an important impact because they are consulted at irregular intervals, and outsiders are frequently considered to have superior expertise to in-house staff. In many cases this advice is ignored as being inappropriate or too expensive or impossible to implement. Figure 16.2 provides in ranked numeric order the types of information source consulted by the 60 case-study companies. During in-depth face-to-face interviews, managers were requested to provide details of all types and forms of formal and informal information/knowledge. Subsequently the interviews were transcribed and this information coded to produce the ranked list. The face-to-face interviews identified that customers were the most important sources of information being used by 65 per cent of SMEs (Figure 16.2). This can take the form of learning about export procedures, new production methodologies, or machines. One company noted that: 'you can do so much on the phone, so much by fax, but there is nothing like visiting customers, you pick up a lot more just by talking to individuals that you would never do by talking on the phone' (Interview). It is worth highlighting that the important role customers play as a source of ideas and innovations represents a blurring of the division between untraded and traded information flows. The knowledge or information obtained from customers may be untraded, but it is combined with a traded relationship. A good example of customer-related information flows is the relationship that exists between a large company and its supply chain. Knowledge and information flows are informal and valued as they are founded upon a long-term established reputation and importantly a traded relationship.

Journals and magazines were consulted by 58 per cent of companies, with owners noting that it was the best way to keep up with current management fashions. Books may be an initial source of ideas, but 'if it is not on the shelf . . . I will just pick up the phone and ask someone' (Interview). Books, however, can be dangerous in that ideas which are more suited to a different business sector or size of company may be discovered and implemented. One of the partners of a London advertising company reads business and management books avidly. According to the managing director of this company:

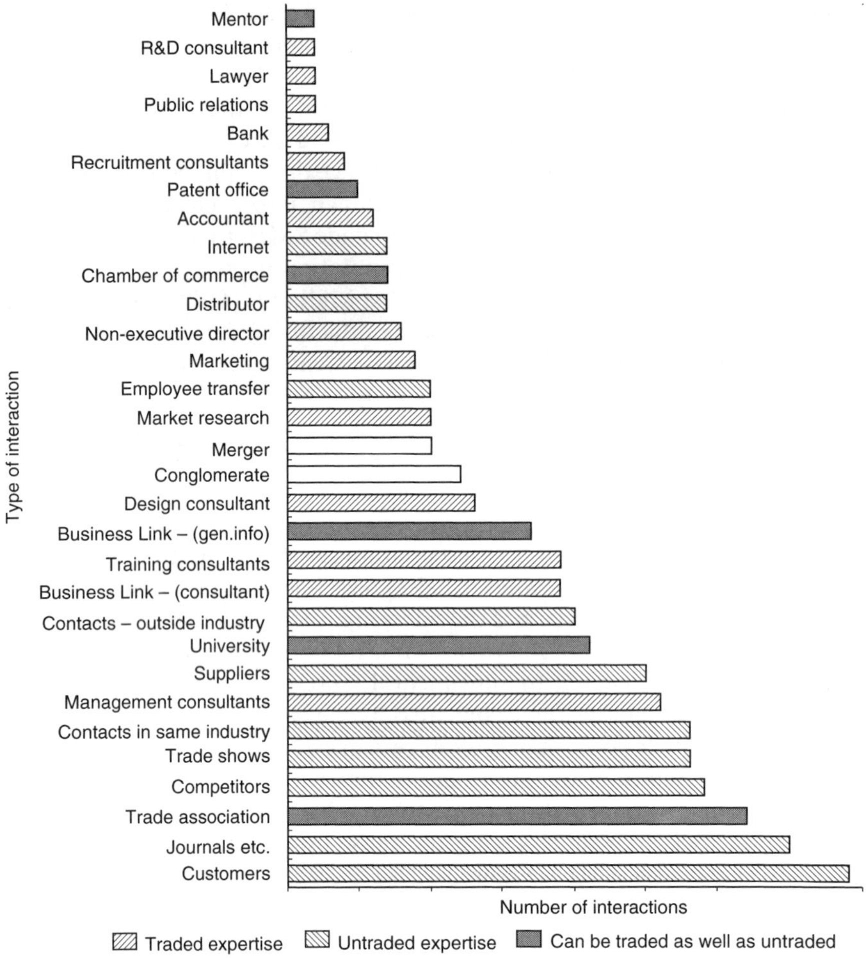

Figure 16.2 Sources of traded and untraded information and expertise used by 60 SMEs in the UK

> [H]e would have been better off going down the pub and listening to people. There are some useful ideas in them and some extremely good tips and hints, but they don't provide a model for running a business. Business is about 90 per cent expediency and 10 per cent business theory, because you are dealing with people. (Interview)

The partner worried the managing director about the lack of management method in the company and forced the company to employ a large consultancy company to undertake a review of the business. The consultant's report noted that the company was: 'chaos, it's total chaos, but it's a chaos that works, we don't know why it works, but all we know is that you shouldn't change it' (Interview). Related to this source of information is the importance of trade associations, which were consulted by 53 per cent of companies. Trade associations frequently convert densely written government and European Union documents into easy to read guides and trade magazines, as well as providing a forum for the discussion of common problems (Bennett, 1998). The social networking aspect of trade associations as well as breakfast and luncheon clubs must not be underestimated. A director of a manufacturing company based in the West Midlands noted that:

> Yesterday, I went to a meeting of the British Sports and Allied Industries Federation on exports to Denmark, which is a small but important market of ours and there I met somebody who exports cloth, and someone who exports chocolate bars and somebody who exports fishing equipment. None of these are remotely related to our industry, but all have a tale to tell: 'Which shipping line do you use? How do you fly there? Where do you get the best priced air fares? Is it better to have distributors in xxxx and Copenhagen or just in Copenhagen?'. They are not consultants with their own agenda, but people who are earning at the sharp end and their experience is very practical and is formed by the most important question of all: how do you make money out of this market? You form allies, you develop business contacts and acquaintances and most people are very helpful, and staggeringly open, especially once they know you are not a competitor. (Interview)

Nearly 50 per cent (48 per cent) of companies noted that competitors are a valuable source of information. For example, both quarry owners in Cumbria and Savile Row tailors in London talk to competitors in an attempt to promote their respective industries. The managing director of an engineering company based in Coventry noted that one of the partners: 'was very well plugged into the engineering Mafia' (Interview). Companies visit trade exhibitions in the UK and Europe predominantly to learn about rival products, but also to provide an opportunity to talk to competitors. In one case, a manufacturer of hotel towel rails attended a German exhibition because the company wanted to develop a bathroom range for the general public. They identified a design which they have altered and are now manufacturing and selling in the UK. Informal information exchange may occur between SMEs located in different countries. Thus, a Cumbria-based training provider shares information with a company based in Portugal, and another in Germany.

The diversity of information flows into and between SMEs is highlighted in Figure 16.2. The most effective flows of advice are those that are obtained from a relationship of trust or from an apparently successful competitor. It is impossible to determine the importance of these 'secrets of industry which are in the air' in relation to traded sources of advice. It does seem, however, that one of the best ways to alter SME business behaviour is by the dissemination of advice through an informal network of social contacts rather than via management consultants and Business Link companies. The formal mechanisms have their place, but they may be much less important than other sources of information and expertise. It is also important to note that the informal untraded knowledge and expertise flows identified in Figure 16.2 largely occur between companies that are not part of the same commodity chain. Industrial districts and the process of collective learning do not have to occur between companies engaged in the same or related business activity, but are common and very important among all business enterprises.

Conclusion

The operation of both large and small private and public sector organisations consists of a complex interplay between in-house and external expertise and knowledge. Increasing business environment complexity, competition, internationalisation, technological change as well as the operation of government policies designed to encourage SMEs to consult outside advisers have all contributed to a recent growth in demand from SMEs for outside expertise and knowledge. The relationship between an SME and outside flows of knowledge and expertise is much more complex than just flows of knowledge from private sector consultants and organisations like Business Link. Most studies highlight the role of accountants, bank managers, trade associations and friends and acquaintances (Wheelock, 1992; Bryson and Daniels, 1998a), but very few explore the complex web of information, knowledge and advice within which SMEs are situated. Management consultants and other forms of business adviser may be of limited significance relative to customers, competitors and the business media. The problem is how to devise measures for determining the significance of different forms of information and expertise flows into and between SMEs. Without these types of measures, policy makers will discount the importance of these types of expertise flow. Without them any attempt to assess the impact and significance of expertise flows will fail, given the complexity and heterogeneity of the client/knowledge provider relationship. The important point is that all companies are embedded into a regional economy, and more specifically into a web of dynamic social relationships.

The success of SME business support policies would be substantially improved and access to these services widened if organisations like Business Link were able to access informal support networks. The problem is, however, that this type of activity will not contribute directly to the earning stream of a Business Link company, or be suitable for evaluation in any formal manner. The 'jungle drums in the village' will always be one of the most successful means for obtaining and disseminating information as the social relationships in such a 'village community' will be founded on established reputations and social relationships.

Note

* The research on which this article is based was supported by a research grant from the Economic and Social Science Research Council (ESRC) (R000236366) and by the NatWest Group Charitable Trust. Any views expressed do not necessarily reflect those of the sponsoring organisations.

17 Understanding the relationship between information and communication technology and the behaviour of firms located in regional clusters

Grete Rusten and John R. Bryson

Introduction

The growth of information and communication technologies (ICTs) and their application in the economy has played an important role in the ways in which firms are organised and orientated in the marketplace. Boundaries between organisations are becoming increasingly blurred as new forms of organising production develop, facilitated and enabled by ICT. Organisations 'are becoming increasingly integrated into dynamic networks connected by time–space compressing information and communication technologies' (Grimshaw et al., 2005: 1). ICT enables firms to be part of distributed networks of relationships with other firms and resource providers. In an increasingly competitive business environment, organisational survival is partially dependent on the quality and strength of a firm's connections or relationships with other firms and institutions.

Cairncross (1997) argues that the digital revolution is associated with the death of distance as new technologies increase accessibility. Nevertheless, many economic activities remain geographically concentrated and some co-located firms are part of a fully functioning localised cluster. According to Porter (2000) a cluster is defined as a relatively concentrated agglomeration of firms and organisations that are integrated through business transactions, collaboration, rivalry and knowledge transfer. Firms located in a cluster benefit from being geographically and socially close to one another as well as being able to exploit locally developed cluster-supporting infrastructure (local institutions, for example training establishments, local supply networks, access to raw materials) and access to a well-trained workforce.

All firms are embedded in a complex matrix of external relationships with suppliers, customers and other companies; these relationships do not have to be concentrated in a particular locality. The literature on new industrial districts and clusters suggests that the ideal environment for doing business is in an industrial cluster in which firms benefit from agglomeration economies, proximity and the availability of information, expertise, skilled labour, technology and finance (Asheim, 1992). It is unsurprising that in other settings, in which local networks and a concentration of local resources has failed to develop, firms either draw upon their own resources or use expertise/knowledge from outside their home region (Birley and Westhead, 1990; Hitchens et al., 1994). This division between local and non-local resources is artificial as firms blend different forms and sources of external resource together. The academic literature on clusters tends to overemphasise local and regional linkages at the expense of national and international relationships (Amin and Cohendet, 2000; Maskell et al., 1998). Most firms are situated in a complex evolving matrix of local, regional, national and sometimes international linkages (Coe, 1998; Simmie, 2002; Keeble and Nachum, 2002). The geographical extent of these linkages has important implications for the identification of a cluster's boundary. The cluster metaphor restricts the focus of academic attention to the relationship between firms and their local environments. From the perspective of the individual firm it might be more useful to draw upon Thompson's (1967) concept of the 'task environment' of the firm. This concept refers to the whole range of relationships in which any one firm is situated and, more importantly, the 'task environment' depends on the actors involved and the nature of each business project. In this perspective, organisational success is dependent on the effective management of a firm's task environment, which includes task interdependencies that lie behind a firm's core work activities.

The task environment is a traditional conception of the firm that focuses on the role of market resources and competition in determining organisational behaviour and outcomes. The institutional perspective on organisational environments represents a radical departure from the task environment perspective of the firm as it draws attention to the role played by a firm's institutional environment in influencing, shaping and sometimes controlling firm behaviour (DiMaggio and Powell, 1983; Oliver, 1997). DiMaggio and Powell (1983) highlight the social forces that lead to the copying of organisational practices between firms. These two perspectives on the firm are not mutually exclusive, but can be used to inform each other. The task environment approach highlights the networks within which firms operate while the institutional approach draws attention to the ways in which these networks influence firm behaviour. The distinction between these approaches is methodological as well as conceptual.

We want to argue that the literature on clusters has been too preoccupied with identifying clusters and in either exploring the task environments of clustered firms or in applying an institutional informed perspective to firm behaviour. What is absent from much of this literature is an analysis of the role played by ICT either in extending the geography of a firm's task environment or in reinforcing a local agglomeration. In the latter case, ICT does not undermine the importance of geographical proximity. A strict definition of a cluster that highlights intra-cluster rather than inter-firm/inter-cluster relationships should not exclude the contribution that ICT makes to the way firms interact with one another. ICT facilitates communication between firms regardless of distance. The nature of the interaction differs depending on the quality of the relationship that exists between participants and the type of information that is being transmitted (confidential or intended for all). ICT is also used for other purposes apart from communication. It may be used to collect information that informs a decision-making process. In a competitive marketplace, ICT also enables firms to customise products for individual clients and to identify and adjust to the changing needs of their target customers.

The adoption of an ICT system by a firm, supply chain or even by a cluster of firms may represent a form of DiMaggio and Powell's isomorphism in which firms are forced or encouraged to copy the behaviour of others. Three types of isomorphism have been identified – coercive, normative and mimetic. *Coercive isomorphism* results from relationships in an industrial sector between the 'totality of actors' (suppliers, producers, consumers, regulators) and their relational networks. The organisational field produces coercive isomorphism by tacitly or explicitly imposing upon individual companies a set of organisational practices and regulatory structures. Second, *mimetic isomorphism* results from uncertainty that encourages organisations to model themselves on others. Copying is an inexpensive strategy in comparison to the development of novel solutions.

Models are traded either formally or informally via untraded interdependencies and they are obtained via employee transfers, management consultancy firms, trade associations or in published form in both the business press and in management textbooks (Guillen, 1994). Third, *normative isomorphism* results from increasing professionalism. Professional associations impose upon their members a limited range of expertise and knowledge that defines the nature of their work. ICT may be adopted by a firm as a result of all three types of isomorphism. In a supply chain, ICT adoption may be the result of coercion as a firm may have to adopt a common ICT platform. In this case, the dominant firm determines the ICT investment decisions of other firms involved in the supply chain.

In this chapter we explore the role that ICT plays in contributing to the factors that have been identified as being important for the foundation and functioning of industrial clusters. The discussion also explores the wider role that ICT plays within a cluster. It is a common misconception that ICT implies the end of geography or the importance of space as it has the ability to overcome the constraints imposed by distance (Cairncross, 1997). ICT removes some of the advantages that are attributed to a location in a cluster but it can also be used to bind clustered firms closer together or even to create local agglomerations. A further question concerns the relationship between a location in a cluster and the implementation and use by firms of ICT. Clustered firms may have different adoption experiences compared to firms located in other geographical settings. This chapter explores the characteristics of clusters and the role that ICT plays in relation to different dimensions of the value chain. The following sections provide a framework for exploring the relationship between ICT adoption and cluster performance and behaviour. The chapter is based on a series of case studies that have been developed from in-depth interviews with small and medium-sized enterprises (SMEs) located in Norway. The research methodology is not designed to test the exact quantitative relationship between ICT adoption and cluster behaviour, but rather to identify some dimensions of the relationship.

Clusters, geography and ICT

Firms located in dynamic industrial clusters are supposed to be more innovative and have lower transaction costs compared to firms located in other geographic settings (Scott, 1988a). Clustering is associated with a series of complementarities including developed infrastructure, arenas of competence and the availability of trained labour. These resources are supposed to provide clustered firms with enhanced competitive advantage compared with more isolated enterprises. Clustering can also encourage innovation as a close relationship with local customers may result in improvements to products and processes. Suppliers may receive advice on how to upgrade delivery systems and incentives (positive and coercive) ensure that they respond to such demands. Firms located in a cluster also benefit from exchanges of competences that come with the movement of staff between firms (Reve and Jakobsen, 2001). Firms located in the cluster can also further the business activities of co-located companies by recommending them to their own customers and suppliers. This type of promotional activity on behalf of co-located firms is one indicator that a business community is functioning as an agglomeration.

The formation of clusters can, among other things, be related to the development of specialised and flexible organisational forms. Access to co-located resources may partially overcome SMEs' limited ability to develop internal economies of scale; ICT can enable the development of local and even non-local economies of scale. It is important to remember that as a communication and distribution technology, ICT is utilised when actors are located close to one another (even in the next room), as well as far apart. There are three ways in which ICT adds value to the activities of firms. First, technology may enhance organisational efficiency in all parts of the value chain including those parts that reach beyond the boundaries of the firm. ICT makes it easier to exchange information, to cooperate and to coordinate production between individuals, units and organisations. ICT is useful for collecting information about innovations, markets and regulations. The whole process of searching for suitable suppliers, comparing prices and quality, is far simpler when facilitated by ICT, and suppliers can be more aware of clients' requirements through the development of customer profiles. In practical terms, a firm's supply chain will consist of a blending of firms located in different places; every firm relies on a distinctive combination of local, regional, national and even international relationships. Each of these spatial relationships will be supported and facilitated by a combination of technologies ranging from face-to-face relationships to various types of technologically enabled remote presence (phone, fax, e-mail, shared computer programs).

Second, ICT alters the relationship between customers and firms; the relationship can be more interactive even to the extent of permitting the development of customised products and services. Clients and suppliers are able to invest in shared integrated ICT systems that enable real-time exchanges of information about stock levels, logistics, design detailing, and alterations to the technological detailing or function of a product. The last is especially important where firms are part of a complex production system in which they are contributing elements of a much more complex product. In such cases, it is essential that all parties to the supply chain are integrated together by the adoption of a shared ICT platform. The incorporation of ICT into a supply chain enhances information flows and contributes to the development of long-term relationships. It also locks firms in to as well as out of a supply chain. Firms within the supply chain have access to information that is denied to other firms; the time and cost required to adopt a specified ICT platform may restrict new entrants to the supply chain. Lock-in may initially be beneficial, but may also result in pressure to reduce the cost of parts supplied by any one member of the supply chain.

Third, ICT is part of the tool-kit that a firm can deploy to project itself as an attractive company. Websites are part of a firm's branding and marketing strategy. This way of presenting the business may also be one way of projecting a firm's power/position in the marketplace that can be read by potential business partners as well as investors. The firm may, for instance, highlight the global nature of its activities by providing information on its website about exports, overseas offices and key customers. Corporate websites often contain photographs of buildings that symbolise size and modernity or highlight the firm's location in a cluster and/or national setting. This type of marketing activity concentrates on highlighting the positive aspects of a firm's image.

The adoption of ICT among Norwegian firms

Before 1990, Norwegian firms used information technology (IT) in a very restricted manner. At this time, many firms considered IT to be a cost rather than a tool that presented firms with new markets and ways of organisation. During this period, ICT was not really used as a communication tool, but by the end of the 1990s, IT had been transformed into ICT and was now associated with e-business or e-commerce. ICT now emerged as an important tool for product and process development, management, logistics and for serving customers.

The Nordic countries are among the most successful countries in the Institute for Management Development (IMD) ranking of nations as measured by computers per capita (IMD, 2002). The USA holds the top place in this table having 639 computers per 1000 capita followed by Sweden (626), Finland (614) and Norway (610). The UK is ranked at 13 with 492 computers per 1000 capita. These countries have a relatively well-developed ICT economy and, for a variety of reasons, have high levels of access to new technologies. These countries are relatively small, have high living standards and education levels. Telecommunication systems are advanced with a high coverage of ISDN (Integrated Services Digital Network) even in rural areas and usage costs are low especially in relation to salary levels. An additional explanation for the high number of users is perhaps explained by second-mover advantage and the benefits that are associated with being 'rapid followers'. The Nordic countries avoided the costs associated with pioneering a new technology; these costs were borne by larger industrialised countries, for example, the US and France (OECD, 1999b). Measurements of access are, however, very different from those that show e-commerce adoption levels. The use of e-commerce in Norway is at a similar high level to that of the UK (Table 17.1). Over half of Norwegian firms have their own website, but overall a low proportion of firms sell their services or products via e-commerce. Only 10 per cent of Norwegian firms are engaged in e-commerce sales. Other countries have been more successful in the adoption of ICT as a tool that enables sales transactions.

We have been unable to identify any data on ICT adoption and use that is entirely restricted to firms located in a cluster. This is not surprising; we therefore explore more general data concerning Norwegian firms' use of ICT. Infrastructure investments and access to digital technology are the foundation stones of the ICT-enabled economy and, in these terms, the Nordic countries compare favourably with other nations (Rusten and Cornford, 2003). Between 1998 and 2003, Norwegian firms increased their use of a wide range of ICT (Table 17.2). Over this period, the Nordic economy was becoming increasingly enabled by the adoption of new technologies especially with firms having access to the internet and to Webpage technology. There was also a significant escalation in the use of more advanced forms of ICT, for example extranet and e-commerce, but it is worth noting that this was from a low base.

Table 17.1 The adoption of e-commerce by SMEs, 2001

Percentage of SMEs	Denmark	Finland	Sweden	Spain	Germany	UK	Norway
Using ICT	95	98	96	91	96	92	93
Having web access	86	91	90	66	82	62	73
Having its own website	62	58	67	6	65	49	47
Engaged in e-commerce purchasing	36	34	31	9	35	32	43
Engaged in e-commerce sales	27	13	11	6	29	16	10

Source: Benchmarking National and Regional e-business Policies, Enterprise IDG.

Table 17.2 Use of ICT by Norwegian firms with 10 or more employees, 1998–2003 (%)

	1998	1999	2000	2001	2003
Firms with internet access	40	66	74	82	87
Firms with web page	22	36	48	55	64
Firms with intranet	4	3	11	19	28
Firms with extranet	1	1	4	9	14
Firms engaged in e-commerce from own websites	4	6	8	10	11

These statistics provide an indication of the general adoption trend, but reveal nothing about the ways in which firms incorporate ICT into their day-to-day business activities. The most important aspect of ICT is the impact it has on the performance of an individual firm and the ways in which ICT alters a firm's relationship with the world beyond its boundaries. There is an important difference between access to ICT compared to actual use that improves a firm's competitive position. There are also indications that firms begin initially by adopting a primitive or a least-cost form of new technology. In 2001, a study of SMEs' use of ICT found that 80 per cent of firms had developed their own web pages for marketing, while few had actually introduced systems that could manage financial transactions. The main conclusion of this study was that firms were not particularly advanced and innovative in their use of ICT. Some regional differences in real access among firms were identified but these can be partly explained by size and sector rather than by geography (Pilskog et al., 2002).

Similarly, a study of ICT usage among SMEs in Norway and the UK revealed a considerable range both in actual use and the ways in which ICT was integrated in firms' strategies and business models. The range of adoption forms was more extensive than could be explained by sector or region. One of the more important factors related to the adoption of ICT is the formal educational backgrounds and interests of the management team. There are many different ways in which individual firms incorporate ICT into their business activities. The use of ICT also depends on external conditions such as the actions of other firms in the locality (forms of isomorphism), and whether they receive information or encouragement from customers, trade organisations, development agencies, the ICT industry or others (Rusten and Cornford, 2003). It is also important to highlight joint projects designed to improve access and ICT usage, for example, the development of community broadband or joint web-portal initiatives. These activities are also found in many clusters and are also part of cluster policy tool-kits that have evolved to try to enable the development of localised clusters.

According to Porter (2001) the absence of a carefully considered ICT strategy is an important part of the explanation for why no obvious positive impacts have been identified that are linked to the adoption of ICT by firms. Some firms invest in ICT only because they are copying the behaviour of others and, in many instances, such firms will not have considered the ways in which ICT should be integrated into their business operations. A good indicator that a firm is trying to use ICT to improve competitiveness is when ICT is integrated into a firm's strategy rather than only as a form of supporting architecture. For some companies, ICT not only involves technical investment and related training, but is also associated with organisational restructuring, sometimes involving a shift from team to project work. New ways of organising enhance flexibility developed around telephone conferences and other ways of virtual working. On the one hand, the geographical location of the firm may become increasingly irrelevant but, on the other, a division of labour based on geography may be one of the reasons driving the collaboration. For example, Nordic-based consultancy firms have developed strategic partnership networks across Scandinavia that are enabled by ICT. These partnerships permit collaborating firms to develop and project a Nordic business image that enables them to compete for business in Norway, Sweden, Finland and Denmark (Bryson and Rusten, 2005).

ICT also increases flexibility in terms of where and when each individual is able to work. The ability to travel with a laptop replaces the requirement for fixed office space – the employee's office becomes the home, train and plane – any space in which a laptop can be used effectively. Nevertheless, individuals still need to socialise as part of a process of face-to-face interaction that creates loyalty and trust. In reality, face-to-face communication supports and is supported by ICT rather than ICT replacing the need for personal contact (Rusten and Cornford, 2003). The importance of face-to-face communication is illustrated by the role played by the photocopier or water cooler in the office; these are places in which gossip is exchanged as well as potential business opportunities developed or discussed. Water-cooler-style meetings facilitate other forms of office-based communications. This type of combination or blending of communication forms (ICT, telephone, face-to-face) also characterises the relationship that exists between firms located in an industrial cluster.

ICT and project type

The traditional organisational form based on the internal organisation of tasks, stable employment contracts, hierarchy and stable or clearly defined boundaries to the firm, are more than ever under pressure. An important part of this pressure is the development of complex divisions of activities between businesses that are part of large complex supply networks. Efficiency in all aspects of the organisation is prioritised. Enhanced competition makes it increasingly important to run the business efficiently. The need to be up to date and to have access to new expertise and competencies can be fulfilled by making greater use of external resources. Additionally, outsourcing is one way of externalising part of the risk in an ever-changing market; firms can often obtain goods and services from co-located firms.

Fordism founded on large-scale rigid mass production systems has to some extent been replaced by order-based, just-in-time and small-scale production systems. The flexibility required for this type of production system can often be obtained by drawing upon a well-developed resource base that is found in a cluster. Post-Fordist production systems may be extremely flexible as production volumes and product characteristics can be altered relatively simply. Using suppliers on demand rather than retaining high stock levels is far more efficient than retaining all production capacity in-house. Being close to a broad group of suppliers is an important characteristic of a cluster. Much of the ordering and coordination of activities can take place online. ICT is an important tool for searching for suitable suppliers, but more importantly for coordinating the different activities that are required to create a product or service.

Many firms with ICT-enabled business models match production to incoming online orders. This creates new challenges as customers expect a rapid response irrespective of other pressures that a firm may be experiencing. The deployment of temporary staff, multi-skilling or the use of a call centre are some of the solutions to this problem. One of the advantages a firm may obtain from a location in a cluster is access to a much broader spectrum of skills and expertise, both codified and tacit.

ICT may increase a firm's internal flexibility, but can also enhance external flexibility. It improves the way a firm interacts with suppliers and collaborators (Rusten, 1997). In both cases, ICT plays a substantial role in the coordination of individuals, activities and businesses. Flexible production systems in one or other variant are common, especially among firms in design or craft-intensive sectors (for example, furniture and textiles); high-tech firms (for example, electronic/mechanical industry) and a broad spectrum of business services (for example, technical services, auditing and accountancy, temporary employment agencies, research institutes and so on). Increased international competition, rapid change and complex and individualised products have resulted in increased and enhanced collaboration between organisations. Just-in-time production systems based on customised orders must be based in places that can receive regular deliveries. A location in a local production complex with access to suppliers (manufacturers as well as business and professional services), skilled labour and collaborators is a competitive advantage. Norwegian clusters such as Bømlo (maritime equipment), Kongsberg (defence and offshore industry), Horten (electronics), Ulsteinvik (wharf), Sykkylven (furniture) and Leksvik (electronic and mechanical industry) all contain firms that are organised in this way.

In clusters and in other types of business locations, different communication forms, including ICT, telephone, documents and face-to-face interaction, supplement one another depending on what is the most suitable form, as well as on the degree of formality that exists in the relationship. ICT is used as part of routine business activity or to facilitate more specialist or unusual interactions between people and firms. A whole range of relationship forms and settings are described in Figure 17.1. The arrows reflect the intensity of the relationship; the base of the arrow representing, for example, numbers of participants, frequency of communication or cost. A complex non-routine relationship between a firm and a project team that is being organised by external consultants will, for example, occur over a relatively long period, involve a number of individuals/firms in the

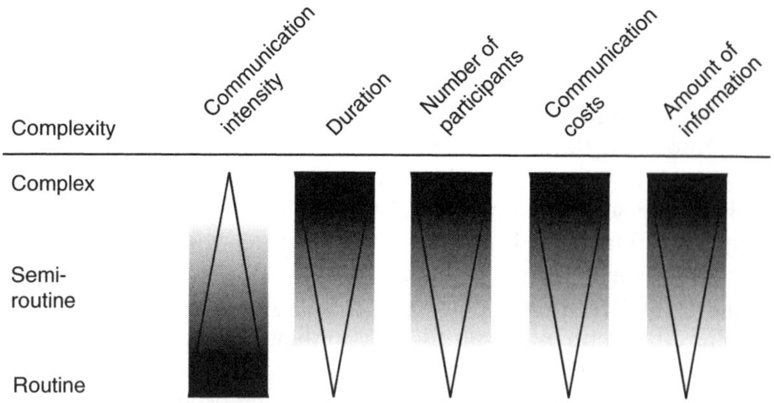

Figure 17.1 Types of project and variations in the characteristics of communication

relationship and a transfer of complex knowledge that will be expensive to communicate between the client and the project team. In contrast, simple e-commerce transactions will involve many individual customers, but each contact between customer and provider will occur rapidly, involve very few people, limited quantities of information and be associated with low communication costs.

The first generation of communication technology was used predominantly for exchanging routine information, while more complex exchanges required face-to-face interaction. More sophisticated ICT and new ways of organising production have, however, revolutionised the process of information exchange. What is occurring is an interaction between different modes in which information is exchanged – from face-to-face to various levels of cyber exchange.

ICT and supply-chain relationships: the Royal Marines, Norway

The extensive use of ICT has permitted the dispersion of some supply-chain relationships. It is important to explore whether the development of knowledge-intensive production processes has enhanced the importance of local agglomerations (Leamer et al., 2001). To explore this issue it is useful to consider a special case – the relationship between the Norwegian navy and its supply base. The relationship between the civilian maritime cluster (suppliers) and the Royal Marines (the client) in Bergen, Norway, is based around complex inspections, testing and the coordination of innovative activities and fundamental to this integration is the development of long-term relationships. This represents a complex series of interactions that exhibits all the characteristics identified in Figure 17.1. Client and customer need to meet regularly to inspect the equipment together. Much of this equipment is not standardised and available off the shelf, but expensive bespoke parts either have to be repaired or spare parts manufactured on demand. This type of production process has to be efficient as it is essential that ships are not out of service for long periods. The time factor in this relationship is another reason why the parties need to be located close to one another so that they can easily meet and inspect ships' engines when required. A representative of one of the major companies in this sector described the supplier recruitment process as an exercise in gathering companies together which they already trusted. He noted:

> These are the ones [people] we go fishing with. Besides they have the necessary licences and we know they are capable and will do their very best to deliver as requested. Being firms located in this town also means that they can be reached and can meet us at very short notice.

Companies involved in this complex production system have a shared background which goes well beyond the contact involved to deliver the Royal Marine project (Rusten et al., 2004a). It is worth emphasising that these relationships are based on trust and experience. This trust is established during face-to-face interaction and, once established, much of the standard exchange of information takes place through ICT as part of a shared extranet.

The development of mutual trust and understanding leads to successful projects with low transaction costs and projects in which the unexpected can be overcome by the co-location of collaborators and by the trust that exists between them. The Royal Marines project highlights the processes through which a group of firms have to pass through in

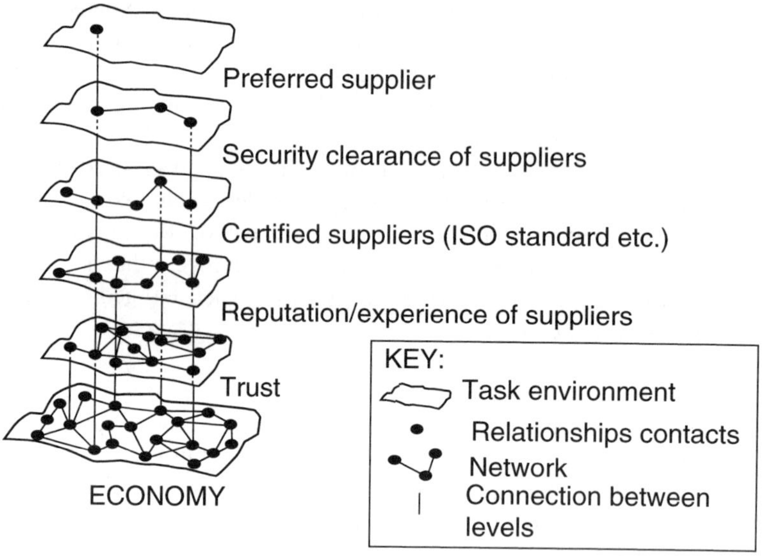

Figure 17.2 The process by which client firms identify suppliers

order to identify a preferred supplier (Figure 17.2). Potentially, all firms that have the capability to provide the part or the service are included in the search and selection process. Only some firms are included in the search process as they are known to the potential customer or they have established reputations. From this group, the main supplier is only able to transact business with firms that have the right level of certification and security clearance. This process reduces the field of available partners to such an extent that perhaps only one company is identified.

We have so far explored flexible organisational forms related to locations in clusters, and the ways in which ICT can enhance the efficiency of a firm's activities. There are other examples of how ICT represents the foundations of a new business model that also has cluster implications. Some firms use ICT to distribute market surveys, develop projects and provide online travel services. These were formerly in-house activities or based on face-to-face meetings between the customer and service provider. Some firms subcontract the search process to identify suitable suppliers to a third party or broker. A broker is a business management adviser who deals with suppliers on behalf of several client firms. The brokers not only have a better opportunity to obtain current information on a specific topic but can also negotiate a better deal on behalf of several clients. ICT is an important tool in organising, collecting and distributing these services.

Transferring responsibility for the choice of suppliers to brokers often means that traditional local trading relationships break down and are replaced by transactions with non-local firms negotiated via the broker's network. Searching for good suppliers using ICT may increase competition, especially where local players compete with non-local providers. Brokering is, therefore, an example of an institutional structure that might weaken the position of a cluster as a local market space. In some circumstances, public policy in Norway has developed initiatives that are designed to establish relationships between local/regional suppliers. Such policies are intended to develop a cluster or to strengthen an existing cluster.

Virtual clusters or virtual firms and ICT

Another organisational form that is totally reliant on ICT is the 'virtual cluster' or network of independent firms, for example, sole practitioners providing management services. Virtual firms consist of temporary networks of independent companies established to share expertise, reputations and provide opportunities to acquire contracts which would be too complex, large or of too great a spatial extent for any one small company or sole practitioner. Virtual business service firms are engaged in the joint production of expertise and competence to meet specific clients' needs. In this context, the use of the term 'cluster' indicates that the social dynamics that support or drive a localised cluster can stretch over space – in other words, the social relationships that create and support the development of a virtual firm may operate beyond a local area. For the virtual firm, the cluster is defined as the geographic extent of the network, or more correctly via a project team mapping exercise that would identify the most active parts of the network. Many independent small firms and individuals use ICT to combine their individual portfolios and contact networks to form virtual consortia. In some cases, each member pays an annual fee and in return becomes an equal shareholder. Experience is exchanged and project teams are formed according to the type of expertise and capacity required by a client. The members of Norwegian virtual consultancy networks may be dispersed over Norway. The virtual firm provides each member of the network with the possibility of working with clients beyond their home region as well as with access to the social and business networks of other members of the virtual firm. Virtual clusters/firms may also develop their own brands and a website. In the cases we have studied this was organised as an extranet service where dedicated customers could log in and obtain up-to-date information about their projects. In one case, customers also received an electronic newsletter six times per year that covered different management topics. A virtual firm's website and legal identity as an independent firm provides the members of the network with a formal presence or existence.

Interviews with client firms revealed that some clients prefer to use consultants that are working with others rather than employ a sole practitioner. They considered that a virtual firm ensured the delivery of a project and reduced the risks associated with relying on a single individual. Consultants that are part of a virtual cluster work individually as well as with members of the virtual firm and much of the communication takes place online. From time to time, members of the virtual firm meet in person. Seminars are arranged regularly throughout the year as one important mechanism for ensuring that the vitality of the network is maintained. The virtual cluster is a way of organising business around the use of ICT that leads to production efficiency, customer efficiency, attraction and trust. It also overcomes many of the problems that must be overcome by sole practitioners – loneliness, isolation and capacity problems.

One advantage of a virtual cluster is the reduction in expenditure on office space. Many consultants operate from home, which gives higher flexibility in the way the consultants organise their time and fewer resources (time and money) are spent on commuting. Being online or operating individually through the use of a laptop does in reality enable the consultant to work anywhere at anytime. It is the outputs and keeping to deadlines that are more important than having regular hours of work. Some of the customers also appreciated the absence of expensive office premises as this is taken as a sign of a down-to-earth attitude to business with a focus on delivering services as efficiently as possible (Rusten et al., 2005). Some virtual companies do, however, find it necessary to have some office space available so that from time to time, partners are able to work together. Virtual clusters are relatively easy to form, reorganise and dissolve. Customers can obtain some degree of stability in business relations as they can employ an individual consultant irrespective of their employer or location. ICT-enabled virtual clusters are relatively dislocated from a specific location (Bryson et al., 2004b; Rusten et al., 2005). Virtual clusters can be based anywhere and be formed around firms that are located near or far apart from each other. Sometimes these networks cross national borders. Virtual clusters are therefore not necessarily geographically concentrated; the operation and activities of the virtual firm provides dispersed members with some of the advantages that are associated with a location in a defined cluster – sharing of information and co-production. These advantages are constructed around face-to-face interactions and are also facilitated and enabled by ICT.

ICT and the ability of a firm to utilise a cluster's resource base

ICT enables efficient adjustments to be made to business activities including the rationalisation of a firm's supply chain, and access to up-to-date information about holdings and markets. An enhanced information flow in all parts of the value chain, by itself, improves the ability of a firm to function more effectively. ICT, in combination with new organisational forms and management systems, may produce more efficient firms as well as opening up opportunities for the formation of new business opportunities. Firms can act individually, or in collaboration through the use of ICT, to develop new products or services. They can gather and distribute information over the internet and they can use the internet for promotion, ordering, distribution, after-sales service and payment.

The use of ICT in business can take place in all types of geographical settings. There are certain limitations as firms may lack the necessary expertise to utilise fully the benefits that are associated with ICT. Access to competent staff is usually highlighted as an advantage possessed by clusters, but there may be local competition for high-quality employees and employee turnover in firms located in a cluster may be relatively high. A location in a cluster may encourage a firm to adopt strategies that have enhanced the competitiveness of other firms. This type of *mimetic isomorphism* may eventually undermine or reduce the competitiveness of a firm or group of firms as they begin to operate in the same manner.

The advantages of being located in a cluster are sector specific and depend on the type of activity being undertaken by firms. For instance, it is vital that shipbuilders base their products on the needs and experiences of their customers. A close dialogue must occur between suppliers and customers and several adjustments may have to be made during the construction process to ensure that a ship meets client expectations. The maritime cluster in western Norway has many of the conditions required for the effective construction of a ship, as most suppliers are located in the area. In all parts of the value chain there is a considerable need for communication based on trust and informal dialogue. Equipment must be tested and the exchange of tacit knowledge that cannot be codified in writing means that the partners in the production process must meet face-to-face. Other types of information can be exchanged by telephone, through documents as well as via ICT.

In some situations, for instance when a firm is developing a business idea, it may be important to limit information flows with external firms to protect the ideas from others. In this situation, an intranet can be developed that limits access to a project team. Clusters are by no means a hindrance for communication across industrial sectors. The shipping industry in Bergen has become more receptive to developing contacts with firms working in other sectors of the economy. Collaboration across traditional sectors is recognised as being less sensitive compared with developing contacts or exchanging information with same-sector competitor firms. Untraditional contacts can lead to the exchange of useful knowledge that the firm does not already possess. Informal and social settings represent important arenas for the exchange of information. A manager of a foreign company located in the oil cluster in Stavanger highlighted the importance of being able to visit neighbouring firms and arrange informal lunches; in this way important contacts are maintained. The geographic concentration and the informal business climate that characterises the Norwegian economy make it relatively easy to maintain contacts in this way. These contacts are not only an important information source but are also crucial for developing mutual understanding and trust – elements which are important in face-to-face as well as ICT communication.

There are many different types of communication arena in these networks ranging from informal to formal, for example, active participation in a variety of clubs linked to sport, music, church or hobbies may be useful sources for developing and maintaining business contacts. Local preferences can sometimes be important when choosing suppliers. Employing a local firm reduces the time and cost spent in trying to identify suitable suppliers. Additionally, some managers have an ethical position that favours supporting their local business community. A combination of these factors lies behind one firm's decision to employ a neighbouring firm as their ICT supplier. The manager noted: 'We know what we can expect from them, and they can come and help us at very short notice'.

ICT and the reduction of a firm's dependency on local resources

We have so far explored the role of local resources in clusters. The adoption of ICT may enhance information flows and increase access to products and services, but also, through improved transportation systems and other conditions that ease the flow of goods and services across national borders, make it easier for firms to identify the best co-located or remotely located suppliers. In this way, firms that traditionally served the local market are forced to increase their competitiveness in terms of price and/or quality as existing clients are able to use ICT to compare their products and services with those produced by other companies. Firms located in a cluster are now exposed to intensified price-based competition as ICT has enabled competition from firms located outside the cluster. It has become much easier to identify the right supplier, and also to check references and creditability. Not only does this reduce the risk of making the wrong decision but it also makes it easer to become involved in new business relationships. Firms are no longer dependent on their regional economy for the supply of goods and services and, in this sense, ICT may be weakening elements of the advantages associated with a location in a cluster. ICT may be a tool used to advertise and organise a competitive bidding process. A web portal can contain the documents and details required to compete for a contract and ICT also enables networks of firms located in different places to combine their expertise and strengths in order to compete for complex or large contracts that might otherwise go to larger firms.

ICT and the enhancement of links that exist between actors located in clusters

ICT can make firms more efficient in communicating with other co-located and geographically distant companies and actors. ICT may increase a firm's locational decisions as different units can be based in different locations but still be able to work together in real time. The possibilities for enhancing the spatial division of labour are utilised by firms that choose to locate in certain industrial areas for strategic reasons. For example, a firm may locate part of its production system so that it is close to expertise and knowledge that exists in a particular area (Ellison and Glaeser, 1997). This is one of the factors behind the locational decision of oil-related FDI entering Norway (Rusten et al., 1999).

International competition requires, in some cases, that firms use suppliers from all over the world, and this clearly puts some pressure on existing business partners to become more efficient. Some clients or suppliers prefer bundled deliveries rather than single products. Both trends relate to purchasing supplies which will usually favour larger companies. Over the last few years, regulations and the ability to transfer capital across national borders have also become far easier. ICT may eventually mean that competition to win contracts becomes ever-more international. The answer for some firms is to be able to meet these challenges by joining various networks. This can be one way of strengthening competencies as well as being able to deliver the bundle of products and services that is required by a customer. There are examples of this way of cooperating among firms delivering equipment for shipping and similar suppliers targeting the marine sector. Some firms have also chosen to join portals where they are presented as being part of a larger product/service catalogue. In some cases, firms that collaborate have complementary products. Clusters may represent an arena for the development of these types of collaborative activities, but they may also involve actors in other locations.

Some instances of ICT adoption are connected to the management and coordination of collaborating parties. A manager of a shipbuilding firm based in western Norway noted:

> For us what counts is to get five–six different software programs belonging to our business partners to function together. That is systems that measure stability, strength, pipe dimensions and engine power. These systems require substantial hard-disc capacity. In addition, we need assistance from others when these programs are to be repaired, upgraded or expanded. These systems also require that our partners based on the wharfs have the same programs.

Different ICT systems, combined with the fact that they are costly to purchase and install and also have associated training costs, can prevent collaboration from occurring. This example also draws attention to the fact that the preparation required before communication can take place can be considerable; systems have to be compatible. Specialised competence is also needed to implement as well as use these systems. Some of these competences can be found in-house but other types of expertise will have to be purchased from external suppliers.

Some large companies, for example in the oil industry, prefer long-term contracts. This strategy ensures that products are delivered to an agreed quality and also provides higher volumes on orders and thereby an enhanced ability to negotiate on price. Bryson et al. (2004b) have noted that some large companies insist on suppliers being integrated into an ICT-enabled supply chain. This is also the case for some oil companies in western Norway (Rusten and Cornford, 2003). What is interesting is that the initiative sometimes comes from the supplier. In one case, a small technology firm, through its business relations with a large oil company, established an electronic system for exchanging documentation. The selection of the software was based on the requirements of the larger firm (ibid.). ICT, in this case, was vital for the internal efficiency of both firms as well as enabling rapid and clear communication between customer and supplier. This may not reduce production times, but it does enable the process to be documented or reduce administration costs.

ICT and other forms of communication

In some areas, ICT minimises the disadvantages of distance, but not necessarily social or cultural distance. In complex projects, involving high risk and a requirement for rapid decision making, it is advantageous that the parties to the transaction know each other. It is also extremely useful to meet face-to-face to discuss different options before a final decision is made. An informal setting, by itself or combined with geographical proximity, will in many cases provide the right conditions for an exchange of information. Such an exchange can take place online, via documentation or through direct face-to-face contact.

In relation to informal communication, it is often convenient for the parties to meet. The use of ICT will implicitly require some degree of formalisation, but this may vary and depend on the type of system or information, the identities of the parties and the nature of their relationship. E-mail can be a relatively informal method of communication. The transmission of more complex and formalised documents, for example constructional drawings, requires more preparation and usually a formal agreement between the parties. A joint software installation may be required. These examples illustrate the range of information that can be exchanged electronically.

E-mail communication is based on standardised technology that is available to all. A considerable proportion of e-mail communication (not counting spam) is between parties that know each other and are co-located. It is likely that this type of communication will take place internally as well as with firms that are part of a company's contact network. Table 17.2 showed how access to e-mail communications has increased dramatically in the private business sector over the last five years, and has become a very popular communication form within and between businesses. Some managers consider that it would be useful to restrict the amount of e-mail sent and what was transacted by e-mail (ibid.). The overall experience then and now is that e-mail supplements rather than entirely replaces other forms of communication. The manager of a firm producing electronic equipment noted:

> To some degree we use e-mail to spread information here in our building. At other times when everyone is to be reached, it can be more efficient to bring the people together in a short meeting. E-mail can, however, be useful when arranging the meeting. It is, however, a great problem if the number of e-mails gets out of hand. Too many e-mails may reduce productivity.

A Norwegian journalist has recently estimated that Norwegian office workers receive so many e-mails during their holiday period that they spend, on average, half the first working day back at the office dealing with the backlog. The majority of these e-mails will be spam and the national productivity loss is estimated at around €70 million.

Concentrated industrial clusters may be an important meeting arena in which different projects can be developed. Efficient communication requires trust and the parties must know each other. One manager stated:

> ICT will perhaps give us some more freedom and we can choose other locations but we will still be part of the Norwegian oil cluster. The most important thing for us is to be placed where we can get qualified staff. It is no doubt that there is a lot of communication between the firms located at this site, also employees can meet socially. The communication that takes place between firms is based on the fact that individuals know each other. It is also to our advantage that we share some of the transport to our customers. This is not only convenient to us, but also to our customers who receive deliveries that have been assembled together.

ICT and the development or projection of a shared identity

A cluster of related firms may have a shared identity, vision and strategy. Businesses located in a cluster can collaborate on projects that are designed to improve competitive ability. These initiatives may lower transaction costs within the cluster or network of partner firms. Through interviews with managers at firms located at the Ågotnes oil base in western Norway we have found that these firms obtain several advantages from being part of a cluster. These and other clusters are defined as industrial technology hot-spots that receive attention from the market and political arena. A location in a cluster may provide opportunities to share expertise or to develop local infrastructure and supporting institutions, but it can also be a mechanism for projecting a shared or group identity. Annual reports and visible projects can be a useful method designed to attract new investors. To be entered on an online list of producers is a further example of the way these firms may collaborate in marketing their business activities. Larger numbers of co-located firms may attract potential skilled and unskilled employees to the area. During an interview, one company noted: 'after we moved here [into the established cluster] it has become easier for customers to find us. We are now considered as a more serious player in the market'. Another company stated: 'I was a bit worried about moving to this [industrial] park that I would get lost among all the other firms. However, I have experienced the opposite as all the people here act as my agents. We recommend our neighbours to external businesses all the time'.

A location in a recognised cluster with an established reputation is an indicator that a firm is part of a larger business community. A cluster can operate informally or the participants can decide to project and capitalise on the development of a cluster brand; branding can be something that glues the parties in the cluster together. A shared geographical identity can be one way in which a firm can establish their brand or marketing strategy. For example, firms based in western Norway emphasise their location in the oil cluster. One manager suggested: 'To be able to present the business as a supplier of some of the larger oil companies is an important signal to the market that you are part of the game'.

The internet provides firms with one way of presenting themselves to the world and place-based associations or geographical labels play an important part in the construction of some company brands. These labels, at the same time, help customers that wish to navigate or sort out the information they receive over the internet. Businesses can be associated together via web-enabled linkages that permit them to build portals that suit the needs of customers. Methlie and Pedersen (1999) explore car dealerships that have established links with insurance companies, banks and car registration authorities. These clusters may represent real geographical concentrations or can just be virtual clusters of businesses geographically separated but linked via ICT.

Some of the interviewed firms argued that culture may limit the development of a global marketplace. A good example is firms that base their business relationships on a

Table 17.3 Languages used in the websites of Norwegian firms, 2003

Sector	Norwegian	Foreign	Norwegian+ combinations	Population
Manufacturing	42	6	17	886
Construction	40	1	2	407
Trade	37	1	7	1071
Hotels and restaurants	22	0	22	248
Transport, telecom and business and private services (excluding finance)	39	5	18	1024
Bank and finance	52	2	20	81
All sectors	38	3	12	3717

limited network of larger customers founded upon trust, informal and stable agreements rather than written contracts. Language can also act as a barrier, but several of the larger Norwegian firms have adopted English as their business language; the oil and shipping sectors transact their business through English. Many foreign-owned firms also transact business via English. In 2003, Statistics Norway undertook a survey to explore the ICT performance of 3707 firms. The survey included questions on the language in which business was performed and on the language(s) used on a firm's web pages. There are important differences in the use or non-use of English by sector (Table 17.3). Hotels and restaurants, banking and finance and manufacturing sectors of the economy are more likely to transact their business in Norwegian as well as a foreign language. Furthermore, compared to SMEs (250 > 5) larger firms are more likely to use an international language rather than only Norwegian.

Not all web pages are designed for the general public. In some cases, the pages are meant for dedicated customers or collaborating parties. The language of the website is used as a strategic tool to enable the creation of a Nordic intranet; compared to English websites those only in Norwegian limit the geographic reach of a firm. In some instances, the selection of Norwegian is the result of capacity constraints while, in others, it is a deliberate strategy to avoid customers located outside the Nordic countries.

Some firms restrict access to all or certain parts of their website through the use of passwords. In some cases, the information supports existing business relationships, such as access to production catalogues, track and trace systems and technical specifications. Information access may be differentiated and with an extranet involved companies can log in and receive or leave information that directly concerns them, for example regarding sales figures or the status of deliveries.

Table 17.2 showed that 14 per cent of firms in the sample had established an extranet. In some cases, the extranet strengthens already existing links within a cluster or other network. A manager put it this way: 'To be a supplier and have password access to a large oil company shows dedication and that the relationship will exist for a while'. Another manager claimed:

> We will show who we are through what is written on our web pages, also in relation to our products. The customer has the ability to check on us in advance, and this saves them from asking us about these things. This means that the web pages are continuously updated, so that customers find the information needed. They should not need to ask much afterwards.

Another manager stated:

> Some of the customers will have their own pin-code, and this enables them to log in and check the status of their order, the date of delivery, delays and so forth. At the same time, we wish to establish online service reports. All this will save us paperwork. Our network will mostly be made up of dedicated suppliers.

E-commerce in the oil and gas sector is part of the sharing of information and documents, remote control of operations, virtual project rooms, exchange of seismic information, license trade via electronic marketplaces, and energy product trading. Electronic marketplaces span industrial sectors and may also vary according to the location of the companies involved. The joint rationale for both buyer and seller is the possibility of reducing transaction costs (the time spent searching for customers, suppliers, agreements, products, time and costs related to the transaction of goods or services including payment).

Conclusion

We have explored some ways in which ICT strengthens the relationships that already exist in clusters. ICT simplifies the possibilities of coordination and makes firms and clusters more visible and thereby attractive towards the outside world. At the same time, this extensive exposition encourages increased competition that challenges a cluster's characteristics, pushes the requirement to reduce transaction costs and triggers innovations. The combination of formal and informal, the planned and spontaneous, the digitalised and more personal relations connected to knowledge transfer, implies companies/individuals that are geographically close will have more options for the exchange of information compared to firms/individuals that are far apart and seldom meet.

The development of new technology challenges the ways in which organisations handle information and communications. New technology and specifically developments in ICT can enhance production rates, reduce distance gaps and alter decision-making hierarchies. The borders within and between organisations are changing vertically, horizontally, externally, geographically and temporally. Mutual understanding and trust are necessary for cooperation to occur between firms and to reduce confusion. The development of a contractual or working framework that the parties can agree upon will often require face-to-face contact. This is essential in ensuring that those participating are able to work together efficiently, but also important given humans' natural requirement for social contact.

It is still not clear if ICT has reduced the number of business-related journeys, since many firms have enlarged the geographical extent of their activities. The use of ICT intensifies the need for individuals to be available at all times. ICT reduces transaction costs for those situations where the parties can communicate online rather than meet, but there are still a substantial number of situations where goods or people have to be transported. In some cases, the use of ICT has reduced the response time. One reason is that information can now be mailed electronically. There is also an obvious saving obtained when orders, invoices and payments are transferred and processed electronically. ICT can also lead to the creation of new organisational forms that are much more flexible in controlling stock and production volumes. Rather than keeping all capacity in-house it is, in many instances, easier to employ external suppliers whenever they are required. A location in a cluster is a favourable geographical strategy for this type of flexibility.

While some authors have claimed the death of distance (Cairncross, 1997), our main argument is that geography, both the consequences of being co-located as well as far apart, is still important. Clustered locations reduce some transaction costs measured by the time spent in searching for suppliers as well as reducing risks since the parties usually know one another. Some of the preparations required for an interaction have already been completed. There are many ways in which geography still matters; exports of several products and goods are still controlled by tariff and nontariff regulations. Disadvantages related to distance will, in some cases, mean that co-located suppliers and clients will possess advantages that cannot be held by firms located elsewhere.

Many transactions are founded on trust and on established working or social/friendship relationships. A location in a cluster increases in value with the communication intensiveness of the interactions that take place between the parties involved in a transaction (Figure 17.1). In addition, the cluster may be an important learning arena for new organisational models and technologies; one firm's successful e-commerce activities may inspire other firms. Firms located in the cluster may also have access to co-located service suppliers that can be engaged to undertake the organisational and technological preparations that are required for the introduction of new ICT systems and other forms of new technology. Trading partners and customers force firms to keep up to date and to use compatible computer programs.

In policy terms, a cluster is a strong symbolic statement. The identification of a cluster in a regional economy highlights the presence of a significant number of competitive companies. The cluster concept has received much attention from academics as well as policy makers. Clusters receive public project support, attract private capital and also act as a symbol of regional and even national economic power. It may sometimes be important for Norwegian firms to show the outside world that they are part of an industrial milieu. This can be achieved by being listed in product catalogues, portals or by listing important customers and projects on their websites. The actual strength of the links within a cluster may be relatively unimportant. What counts is the presentation or symbols that are associated with the right address. The use of ICT may, in fact, be a way of strengthening a cluster's image. It can highlight the fact that the cluster has a considerable number of actors within a wide spectrum of activities related to the requirements of a particular sector.

Well-developed and implemented ICT solutions are increasingly critical for operational cost efficiency. To be able to utilise the potential provided by this technology requires the ability to identify and select between different potential technological solutions. ICT reduces production costs, the costs of searching for the best suppliers and it also opens up new markets and provides new ways of interacting with customers irrespective of location. For this to occur, several other factors must be present. Well-organised transportation systems as well as technical competence are crucial business factors supporting and enabling the development of the new economy. ICT can supplement rather than replace other forms of communication. The new economy has, therefore, not eliminated the need for face-to-face meetings, but rather widened the range of contacts available to firms.

The basis for business success depends on the development of a relatively unique concept and/or product. ICT can make it easier for firms to identify customers, develop new solutions and serve customers in different ways. ICT is, however, not the solution to all business difficulties, and many firms will have to reconsider their wider strategies. Cost-efficient production solutions are to a large extent based upon flexibility in which rapid delivery and price efficient solutions can be critical. ICT lowers transaction costs in all parts of the value chain and may enhance internal productivity. This represents a benefit to an individual firm, but unfortunately it is one that is also available to competitors.

18 Services and the internet

Andrew Murphy

Introduction

In 10 years the internet[1] has grown from the preserve of geeks and guns, of selected American universities and defence researchers, to a mass communication and consumption system. How did this happen, and how were and are services implicated in this? This chapter explores how services were instrumental in the growth and maintenance of the internet and e-commerce as we know it today, and were themselves transformed by it. It considers which service industries are most at risk of substantial change triggered by or enacted through the internet, and those which may be relatively immune, and which service industries are at the forefront in promulgating these very changes.

The meteoric rise and apparent ubiquity[2] of the internet and electronic commerce lead to some interesting questions about the interplay of technology, service provision, and our understanding of how 'the economy' is constructed and operates. Can an e-commerce transaction be conceived as a service if there is no direct human involvement?[3] Does e-commerce herald a new form of economic organisation, a 'new economy' (Beyers, 2002b; Christensen and Maskell, 2003; Daniels, 2003); or does it build upon and rely on pre-existing catalogue, telephonic or televisual-based transaction systems (such as the Sears catalogue, ATMs (automated teller machines) and shopping channels)?

This chapter does not endeavour to provide final answers to these questions. It seeks to address them through the organising framework of the notion of 'disruptive innovation': a change in technological capabilities and attributes that undermines the basis upon which products, companies or industries are organised and add value. First, the history of the internet is reviewed, detailing in brief the service functions that were important in its development. The notion of disruptive innovation, and how it has been theorised, is then investigated. This is followed with an exploration of how the internet has created a constellation of technologies and practices that are simultaneously disruptive to other technologies, practices and industries, and is in turn disrupted. The chapter concludes with a number of case examples of how services and the internet are connected and the extent to which innovative disruption is made manifest.

The internet: a (brief) history

The story of the birth and growth of the internet has been extensively examined (see, for example, Hicks, 1998; Abbate, 1999; Naughton, 1999; Castells, 2000, 2001; Cassidy, 2002), but an overview that emphasises the involvement of services is enlightening. The internet has its origins in 1969 in the United States Defense Department's ARPANET (Advanced Research Projects Agency Network), which linked the mainframes used by researchers at key university sites in the United States (the Stanford Research Institute; the University of Utah; the University of California at Los Angeles (UCLA) and UC Santa Barbara). The concept of packet switching, the core technology that underlies the flexibility of the internet, was based on the idea of building a distributed telecommunications network capable of withstanding a nuclear attack targeted on military communications systems; this was not the core mission for ARPANET (Castells, 2001). The network's physical infrastructure, or 'backbone', was constructed by a private computer engineering firm, Bolt, Beranek and Newman, largely staffed by computer scientists and engineers from Harvard and the Massachusetts Institute of Technology (MIT). The software to run the distributed interconnected network was derived from American universities, with the key software (TCP, or Transmission Control Protocol, which determines how data is divided into deliverable packets at the source and recombined at the destination; and IP, or Inter-network Protocol, which controls how the data packets are sent around the internet) written by Vint Cerf and colleagues at Stanford, UCLA and USC (University of Southern Carolina) in 1973 and updated in 1978. This was later combined with File Transfer Protocol (FTP) to control the transfer of whole documents or programs.

E-mail was designed in the early 1980s by MIT scientists, and with it came (academic) community mail-lists. In 1983 ARPANET was split into educational and military parts, and in 1985 the educational part was merged with a newly created rival from the National Science Foundation (CSNET) to create NSFNET, and made available to all US educational institutions. The NSF, with IBM, had also founded a second non-science educational network, BITNET; although independently managed, BITNET was also reliant on APRANET's 'backbone', and in the US became part of NSFNET (Castells, 2000). Offshoots arose elsewhere, such as in Britain (the Joint Academic Network, or JANet was initiated in 1983), although University College London had been directly linked to ARPANET since 1973 (Cassidy, 2002; THOCP, 2002). Localised private networks increasingly sought links with the broader NSFNET, typically through a connection at a university 'node' (Castells, 2001). In 1985 the domain name system ('.com', '.edu' and '.uk') became operational, thus paving the way for independent commercial operations.

Commercial exploitation of the internet was slow to start, because of two significant barriers: an 'acceptable use policy' that reserved the NSF-funded internet for academic and research use only; and the myriad software programs that were required for accessing another computer, navigating within that computer to find the file of interest, and in utilising that file once retrieved (via FTP). As noted by Castells (2001) there were several missed opportunities for early corporate involvement in building and managing the internet. Attempts to privatise ARPANET in the early 1970s, and NSFNET in 1990, had to be abandoned when telecommunications companies such as AT&T showed no interest, in part because of the costly investment required to bring analog telephone networks up to digital standard. The UK had a chance to build a national communications system for computers several years before America: the National Physical Laboratory had developed two computer networks in the 1960s based on rival packet-switching research. The Post Office was approached to build out the network, but declined until 1977, whereupon it used Telenet (a US firm) to construct a TCP/IP-based network (ibid.: 22–3).

First commercial use in the US began in 1974 through Telenet, which built a data network using TCP/IP technologies, but most non-research use continued to rely on direct computer-to-computer links that used the telephone network via modems, rather than the nascent internet. Modulator–demodulator (modem) programs and devices, popularised in the 1983 movie 'War Games', were developed in 1978 by two Chicago students. Modems helped popularise online bulletin board communities such as USENET News (from 1979) and FIDONET (from 1983) (Castells, 2000; Cassidy, 2002).[4] Now commonplace technological applications, such as Multi-User Domains (multi-player games in virtual environments, first developed in 1979) and Internet Relay Chat (now known as instant messenger software, in 1988) also became popular before the internet found its commercial purpose, primarily among the students who were designing and using the nascent network of networks.

By 1991 the first commercialisation barrier began to crumble when the NSF proposed handing over the funding and construction of the internet to a variety of private enterprises (including US telecommunications companies MCI and Sprint, and former not-for-profit regional networks such as PSI Net (Cassidy, 2002). Commercialising the administration of the internet meant removal of the acceptable use policy, since the internet would become a series of connected private networks, with the divisions and connections invisible to the user; this transformation was completed in 1995. At the same time, the other handicap to commercialisation was overcome: a simple system of programs to render the anarchy of the internet in useable form had been devised by Tim Berners-Lee of the European Centre for Particle Physics (CERN, Geneva): HyperText Markup Language (HTML, which formatted text with actionable 'tags'), HyperText Transfer Protocol (HTTP, which allowed these actionable tags to send and retrieve data which could then be rendered into HTML text and graphics) and the Universal Resource Locator (URL, which tells HTTP where text and graphics documents can be found). These had been posted on the world's first website (with the HTML document 'index.html' located at the URL http://www.info.cern.ch/index.html) in 1991 (Castells, 2000; THOCP, 2002).

Computer developers were greatly interested in the publicly available World Wide Web technologies, and during 1992 released many software applications (or 'browsers') to access and utilise Berners-Lee's hypertext system (Castells, 2001). In January 1993, Marc Andreeson and colleagues at the National Center for Supercomputing Applications at the University of Illinois released (via Usenet) a user-friendly browser named Mosaic for navigating the World Wide Web (WWW). This technology was commercialised two years later in Netscape's Navigator, the first product of one of the first – and most important – internet startups). In April 1993, CERN made the WWW software royalty free (Cassidy, 2002). The gold rush was under way, albeit slowly. It took two more years before HTML-based data packets (the language of the World Wide Web) overtook FTP packets in traffic counts to become the most ubiquitous use of the internet (THOCP, 2002).

Control over domain names was held by a single non-commercial register from 1992 to 1998, run by Network Solutions (operating InterNIC.net) and supervised by the US-based Internet Assigned Numbers Authority. In 1998 this was transferred to a commercial structure, overseen by the Internet Corporation for Assigned Names and Numbers (ICANN) and licensed to a plethora of commercial operations including Network Solutions, which still controlled the overarching registrant database. The transfer itself was very lucrative: Network Solutions was purchased by VeriSign (which operates a 'trust' verification service for websites) for $20 billion in March 2000 (just before the end of the dot-com boom).

*Internet history in (*post-hoc*) context*

While the above might sound like a linear, non-disrupting story, the reality was far from it. The internet has been profoundly disruptive to established and anticipated telecommunications and computing technologies. Until the release of Mosaic and Netscape

Navigator, many media pundits were predicting that commercial success would come through interactive television. US cable and telecommunications companies were investing large sums in set-top boxes and upgrading the 'local loop' to enable interactivity, initiatives that are only now bearing fruit. Private and independent online service providers, such as CompuServe, America Online (AOL), and Prodigy, operating through direct dial-up, had been established for some time (1969, 1982 and 1990, respectively), but did not allow connection to the wider internet until 1995, for a simple reason: their rapidly growing revenues were dependent on subscription income in return for proprietary information, which was threatened by the free-for-all of the World Wide Web. AOL did in fact capitalise on the connection by introducing a largely computer- and internet-phobic population to the plethora of information and communication possibilities afforded by internet connectivity. This popularity eventually enabled the company to acquire Netscape in 1999, once the company had been undercut by Microsoft's (allegedly monopolistic) bundling of Internet Explorer with its Windows desktop,[5] and was a significant factor behind the 2001 takeover by AOL of Time Warner, one of the largest American media conglomerates. This acquisition was based on the synergies seen between Time Warner's 'content' and 'cables' and AOL's digital 'portal':

> At last count, AOL had 29 million subscribers who purchased $20 billion worth of goods and services through the online service last year, according to the company. That formidable membership will now be exposed to all manner of promotions from Time Warner's global empire of magazines, cable service and entertainment studios. (Hu, 2001)

Less than a year later, Ted Turner, formerly CEO of the offline Time Warner, was speculating that the 'AOL' moniker in AOL Time Warner was acting as a negative externality on the value of the merged company's stock, and called for its removal, along with the inherited executives from AOL. By 2003, AOL Time Warner was reporting an annual loss of almost $100 billion, the AOL division was losing customers (a first in its history) and it was being investigated for accounting fraud.

Content providers were not the only companies suffering from the dot-com bust. The attempt to create a network of networks spawned numerous competing communications and information-processing technological standards. The adaptability of the freely available TCP/IP and HTTP/URL software architectures allowed these competing standards to interoperate, but this required inputs by countless computer programmers, mostly employed at national research institutions and funded through investments by public services such as the National Science Foundation. By the 1990s this effort for the public good had been privatised; the task of funding and building the backbone infrastructure of the internet was passed to myriad telecommunications and cable companies such as Qwest, GlobalCrossing, MCI Worldcom, Alcatel, Verizon, Nortel Networks and JDSUniphase. The transfer was not entirely successful; in 2000 alone, these telecommunications carrier companies invested US$117 billion in internet capacity, mostly in fibre-optic backbone intercontinental pipes (Schonfeld, 2001), but within two years, the first three in the list were bankrupt, and the rest heavily indebted. In May 2004 it was estimated that only 11 per cent of existing undersea cables were 'lit' (being actively used); this (temporary?) vast overcapacity led to crashing prices, and forecasts of further consolidation among carriers (Belson, 2004).

The internet as we know it in the twenty-first century is therefore a product of decades of research and innovation, false starts, dashed hopes and wealthless worth (fame for the technologies and technologists, but little by way of fortune). This can be seen as hugely disruptive to the profitability or even survivability of companies central to the effort of building the infrastructure and hosting the vast stores of information on the internet. Each burst of technological innovation, planned or spontaneous, was accompanied by a range of services: initially mostly in the public sector, but increasingly replaced by private sector consultants and companies. Quite how disruptive these technologies were, in theory and in practice, is examined in the next section.

Disruptive innovations

The most acclaimed writer on the notion of 'disruptive technologies' is Clayton Christensen, a management scientist at Harvard's Business School and previously a consultant with Boston Consulting Group. In his highly cited 1997 monograph *The Innovator's Dilemma*, Christensen explored the circumstances in which 'new technologies cause great firms to fail'. With this agenda, Christensen builds on a stream of business-related research into innovation processes and industrial change, stretching back to Schumpeter's (1979: 83) 'creative destruction' of capitalist processes, where the 'fundamental impulse that sets and keeps the capitalist engine in motion comes from the new consumers' goods, the new methods of production and transportation, the new markets, the new forms of industrial organisation that capitalist enterprise creates'. Similar and important ideas can be found in Michael Porter's (1985, 1990) work on the 'competitive advantage' of firms and nations, Drucker's (1985) *Innovation and Entrepreneurship*, and Peters and Waterman's (1982) *In Search of Excellence*.

According to Christensen (1997), rational, competent decisions made by corporate managers which lead to short-run success can also result in the long-run loss of a position of innovation leadership when facing 'disruptive technologies'. These often exhibit:

> worse product performance, at least in the near-term . . . [but] bring to a market a very different value proposition than had been available previously. Generally, disruptive technologies underperform established products in mainstream markets. But they have other features that a few fringe (and generally new) customers value. Products based on disruptive technologies are typically cheaper, simpler, smaller, and frequently, more convenient to use. (Ibid.: xv)

These are in contrast to 'sustaining' technological advances which 'improve the performance of established products, along the dimensions of performance that mainstream customers in major markets have historically valued' (p. xv; Figure 18.1). While sustaining technologies can be radically different, they can be coped with using known management methods, and are allegedly not the source of cultural crises of interest to Schoenberger (1997); this role belongs to disruptive technologies. Christensen offers a smorgasbord of 'rules . . . that managers can use to judge when the widely accepted principles of good management should be followed and when alternative principles [which he conveniently supplies] are appropriate' (1997: xii–xiii). Among his solutions to this dilemma are to match the size of the organisation to the size of the market, since:

> a disruptive technology in a small, emerging market is very unlikely to be considered essential to success in a large company; small markets don't solve the growth problems of big companies . . . large companies should seek to embed the project in an organization that is small enough to be motivated by the opportunity offered by a disruptive technology in its early years. (Ibid.: 138–9)

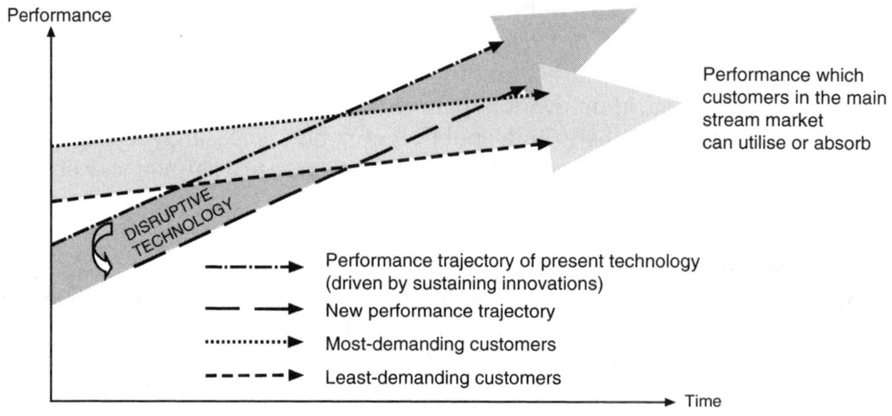

Source: After Christensen et al. (2000: 6).

Figure 18.1 Disruptive and sustaining innovations

This insight was seized upon by management consultants and business leaders in the late 1990s to recommend and justify the establishment of 'spin-off' subsidiary companies to handle the emerging 'digital economy' (Coyle, 1997; Tapscott, 1996).

Traditional tools of market research, such as listening to customers and other external stakeholders, are not appropriate for disruptive technologies, since: 'Markets that do not exist cannot be analyzed: Suppliers and customers must discover them together. Not only are the market applications for disruptive technologies *unknown* at the time of their development, they are *unknowable*' (Christensen, 1997: 147, emphasis in original).

Companies grappling with disruptive innovations should therefore expect – and plan for – failure:

> Guessing the right strategy at the outset isn't nearly as important to success as conserving enough resources (or having the relationships with trusting backers or investors) so that new business initiatives get a second or third stab at getting it right. Those that run out of resources or credibility before they can iterate toward a viable strategy are the ones that fail. (Ibid.: 159)

However, this is very difficult to incorporate into corporate practice, since it goes against instincts for managerial self-preservation and enhancing managerial social capital:

> Middle managers – acting in both their own and the company's interest – tend to back those projects for which market demand seems most assured. They then work to package the proposals for their chosen projects in ways geared to win senior management approval. As such, while senior managers may think they're making the resource allocation decisions, many of the really critical resource allocation decisions have actually been made long before senior management gets involved: Middle managers have made their decisions about which projects they'll back and carry to senior management – and which they will allow to languish. (Ibid.: 82–3)

Christensen and Tedlow (2000) and Christensen et al. (2000) updated this analysis to the retailing sector and electronic commerce (a potentially disruptive technology that was absent in his earlier study). However, in the meantime, other researchers such as Hagel and Armstrong (1997) had promoted the importance of 'first-mover advantage' in electronic commerce: the necessity to 'get ahead [and stay ahead] of the curve' for disruptive technologies. 'Once the market really begins to take off, it will become increasingly difficult (and expensive) to catch up with market leaders. But we're also mindful of the various levels of uncertainty that substantially increase risk for those who move quickly' (ibid.: 6–7).

The disruptive potential of the internet

The commercialisation of the infrastructure of the internet, and thus access to it, paved the way for companies to advertise their goods and services through the internet. Until the mid-1990s, bulletin boards (such as Usenet News) had explicit policies of barring and removing commercially oriented messages and references. With the development of the World Wide Web, and the subsequent democratising of information provision, the flood of commercialism was overwhelming. Within a very short space of time the potential for advertising or transacting products and services via the internet was coupled with the interest of venture capitalists and public investors in the companies involved. As noted earlier, the stellar success of the 1995 initial public offering (IPO) of Netscape Communications is often credited as the start of the 'dot-com boom'. In actual fact the volume of IPO activity did not accelerate until late 1998, when a series of spectacular internet offerings began with the online auction company eBay. In 1999 internet IPOs accounted for 46 per cent of all offerings in the year, and almost 20 per cent of the capital raised, up from 3 and 1.6 per cent, respectively in 1997 (Figure 18.2). The capital frenzy was short-lived, however, with both number of offers and capital obtained declining sharply from early 2001.

Accompanying the stock market's irrational exuberance (Shiller, 2001) came a veritable 'rhetorical flourish' (Thrift, 2001) of stock market punditry. The arguments seemed compelling, and investors were duly compelled. As one such analyst and reporter put it,

> As long as that cheap financing existed, no companies were safe. For example, I sold my supermarket stocks because I figured that every online delivery service that wanted to would get a billion dollars to destroy America's supermarket business. . . . I figured they could borrow a page from Amazon and lose money on everything they sold until they wiped out the existing supermarkets. Seemed plausible. Who knows how long a financing fad is going to last? It didn't last long enough. Now it is time for the bricks-and-mortar companies to strike back. And they will. . . . I had seen so many people bet against Amazon and go out of business doing so . . . You just didn't know when the people would run out of an appetite for startups. . . . Sure was goofy while it lasted. (Cramer, 2000)

The line of argument suggests that service organisations, and particularly those offering 'middleman' information and connection functions such as retailers, were expected to be significantly transformed by the 'disruptive technology' that is the internet (Christensen, 1997; Christensen and Tedlow, 2000). Transformation can be positive (improving productivity) as well as negative (reducing or eliminating competitiveness and profitability). Positively 'transformed' organisations are often seen as the top of an ascending ladder of impact of information and communication technologies (ICTs). Figure 18.3 shows the UK Department of Trade and Industry's depiction of the process of e-commerce adoption by small firms, as if changes of this sort are progressive, cumulative and inevitable.

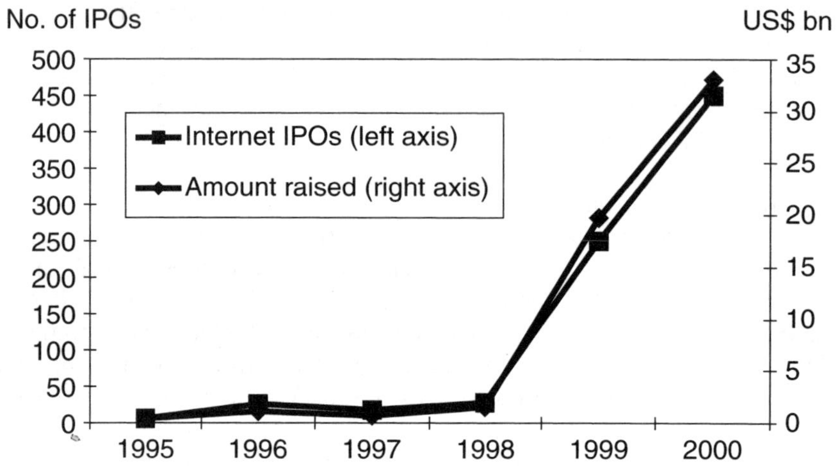

Source: Data from *Industry Standard*, 21 June 1999.

Figure 18.2 Internet initial public offerings, 1995–2000

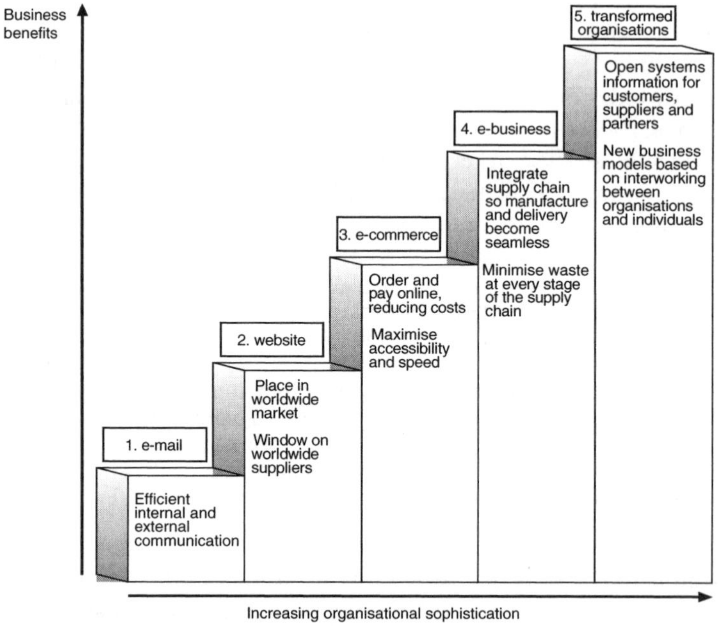

Source: After Taylor and Murphy (2004: 321), based on Martin and Matlay (2001).

Figure 18.3 Transformative power of the internet: the ladder metaphor

Jens Christensen (2003: 213) gives more detail on how these stages are enacted by corporations, along with associated dates of general accomplishment (Table 18.1). Leading the way (or at least providing the signposting) in this evolutionary endeavour are a number of service functions. Given the purportively disruptive nature of the internet, coupled

Table 18.1 The evolution of corporate use of internet technologies

Stages in corporate use of the internet	Stage 1: External communication (1994/95)	Stage 2: Internal communication (1995/96)	Stage 3: e-commerce (1997/98)	Stage 4: Off/online business alignment (1998/99)	Stage 5: Corporate system integration (1999)
Focus	E-mail and web-based promotion	Administrative information and support systems	Online order processing	Re-design of business procedures	Technical functionality/ integration
Perception	A new communication and promotion medium	Tool for internal information exchange/ control	A new transaction medium	A support for corporate objectives	Connecting internal and external stakeholders
Key business functions involved	PR, media and marketing departments	IT and marketing departments	Sales/ distribution/ e-business departments	Most business functions	Most business functions

Source: After Christensen (2003: 213).

with its uncertain level of commitment and required skill base, it is unsurprising to discover that many of these functions are outsourced to specialist ('new economy') internet agencies, or to ('old economy') management consultants adopting new expertise. These internet service providers have themselves evolved over time, as 'a bunch of unkempt 22-year olds' (Christensen et al., 2000) in a startup, or a spin-off from an existing service firm, grew, learned and prospered.

First on the scene were web agencies, specialising in creating and managing 'home pages' and other simple (external) communication tools. As e-commerce tools and requirements became increasingly sophisticated, information technology (IT) specialist agencies and firms (such as SAP, EDS and IBM) took on system development and integration roles, and management consultants expanded their in-house IT expertise (Figure 18.4).

Underlying these conceptions of change, however, is the presumption of 'sequential and progressive' engagement with technology, in an adoption ladder (Taylor and Murphy, 2004; Figure 18.3). An alternative conception recognises the inherent diversity in rates and capabilities of change (Taylor and Murphy, 2004; Figure 18.5). Here, rather than a linear progression toward greater levels of sophisticated technology use across all functions, firms are instead seen as *potentially* utilising technology in greater depth in a variety of activity areas (including logistics, purchasing and marketing), at different rates in different areas, along with new synergies that might emerge in truly transformed organisations.

In this rather more messy view of technological change the possibilities for synergistic transformations of business practices improve as ICTs penetrate more deeply into organisational functions. In particular, it is in the automation of these functions that services are most implicated. By replacing routine, labour-intensive, poorly paid activities such as invoicing or call centres with automated, customer-centred processes at the technology-leading margin, whole service functions face the threat of outright closure. Technologically

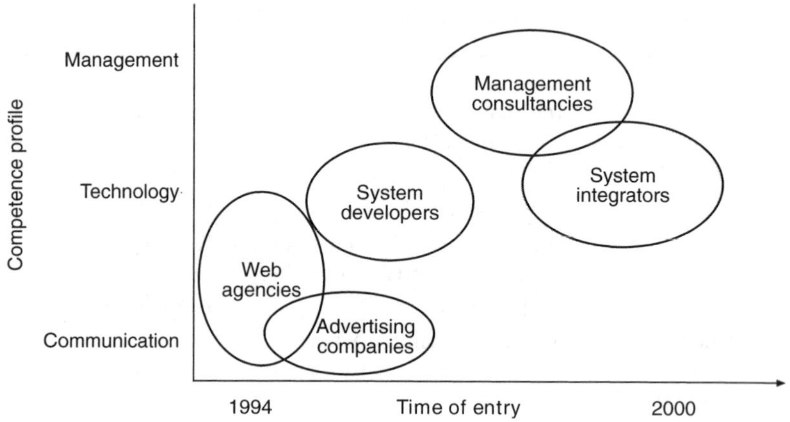

Source: After Christensen and Maskell (2003: 215).

Figure 18.4 Strategic groupings of internet services

laggard companies which must compete with the innovative leaders might instead outsource these functions to India and other countries with the combination of lower labour costs and an educated workforce. At the other end of the spectrum, new classes of service activities are required: to program, install, maintain and update these automated, system-critical functions.[6] These service activities are knowledge intensive, scarce and expensive, and themselves rely on somewhat routine, labour-intensive and (relatively) poorly paid functions (such as building security).

High-level automation may not necessarily produce cost and efficiency savings, as numerous government IT initiatives (the UK's National Health Service (NHS) patient booking portal; Air Traffic Control upgrades in the UK and US; and police and homeland security computer integration projects) have demonstrated. The private sector is not immune: witness J Sainsbury's notable loss in 2004, mostly caused by expensively and incompetently automated warehouse systems. Clayton Christensen has an answer for this: disruptive technologies such as the internet (and IT automation more generally) help drive a continually changing basis of competition (Figure 18.6).

As Figure 18.1 showed, Christensen et al. (2000) claim that a new product[7] undergoes a rising 'performance trajectory' in design and features that inevitably eventually exceeds the desire or capability of 'mainstream' customers to absorb it. Once this happens, the basis of competition changes from adding new features to improving reliability. Once these needs are saturated, competition switches to measures of convenience, and finally to price. As Christensen et al. (ibid.: 24) put it,

> price-based competition – which we'll define as the inability to achieve price or margin premiums by virtue of improving the product – only occurs when performance has overshot what customers can utilize on the functionality, reliability and convenience dimensions. The factor that drives the transition from one basis of competition to the next is oversupply. . . . Many Internet-based companies that are struggling to sustain viability suffer from this problem – they prematurely leapt to a convenience- or price-based competitive model in markets that are not yet overserved on the prior basis of competition.

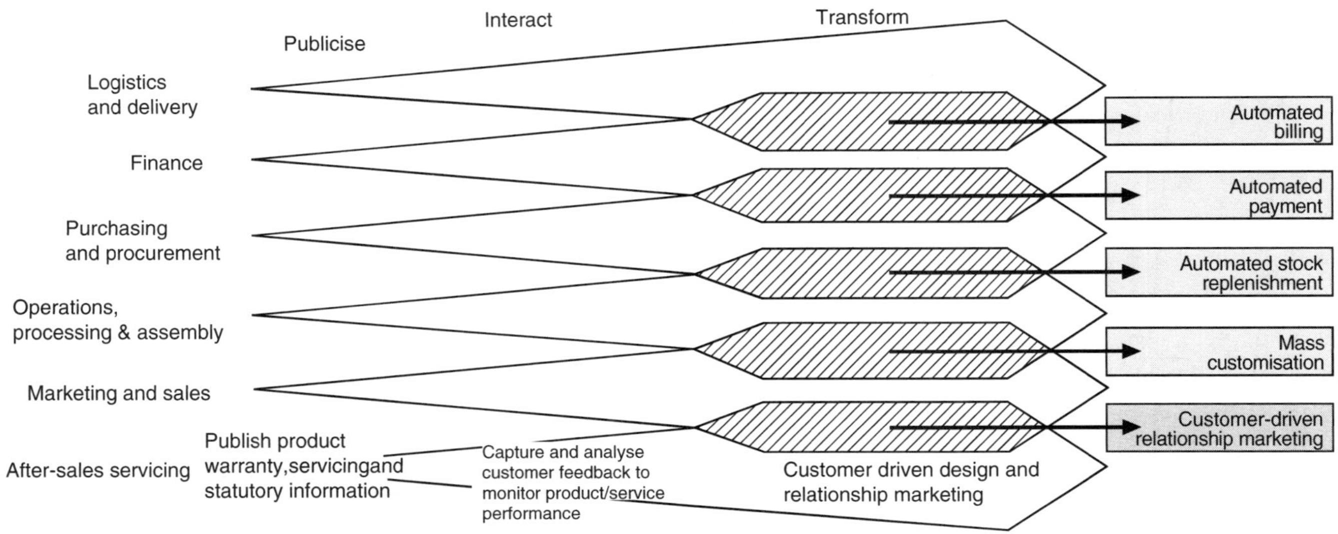

Source: After Taylor and Murphy (2004: 322), based on Foley and Ram (2002).

Figure 18.5 ICT adoption in businesses

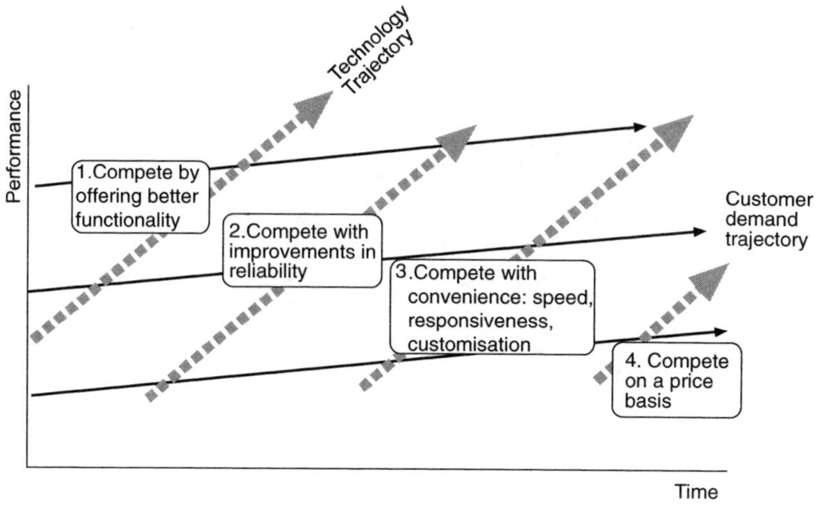

Source: After Christensen et al. (2000: 22).

Figure 18.6 Changing basis of competition

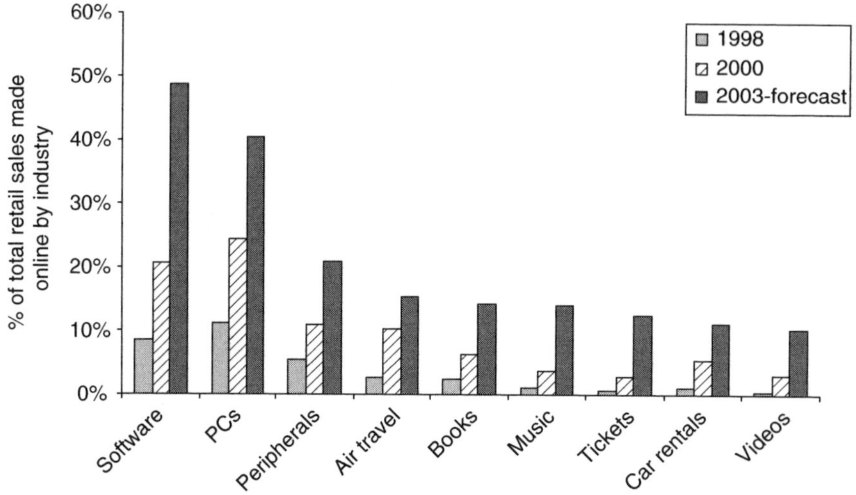

Source: Based on data in Christensen et al. (2000: 30).

Figure 18.7 Penetration of e-commerce by industry, US, 1998, 2000 and 2003

Many e-commerce organisations have stressed the value of convenience, and for some industries this has led to the rapid diffusion of the internet into everyday consumption practices. This in turn has resulted in a rapid (expected) increase in retail sales conducted through business-to-consumer (B2C) e-commerce channels for selected industries (Figure 18.7, with 2003 figures forecast in 2000). Taken as a whole, however, e-commerce has remained a bit-player in retail sales (Figure 18.8), although commercial data tell a

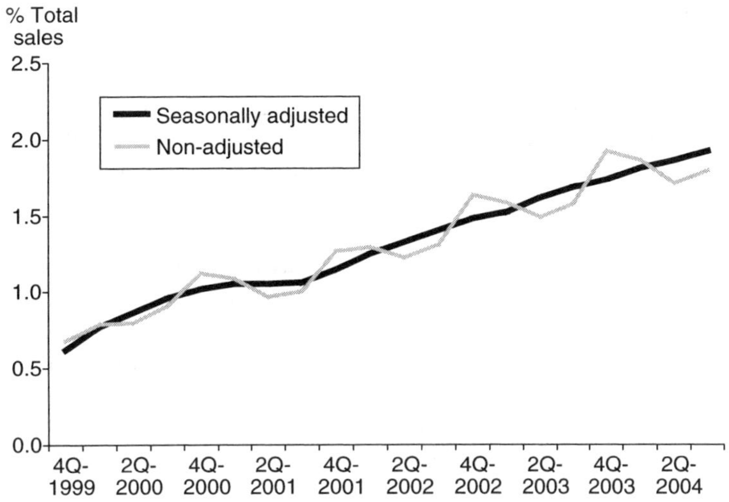

Source: Data from US Census Bureau Quarterly Retail Trade Survey.

Figure 18.8 US e-commerce sales as per cent of total retail sales, 1999–2004

somewhat different story, with e-commerce reputed to comprise approximately 5.8 per cent of total retail sales in the UK in 2003, compared to 5.7 per cent in the US (*The Economist*, 2004).

Services that created and transformed the internet

As the brief history above indicates, there are a number of established services that were and are integral to the establishment and promulgation of the internet and the World Wide Web. First, the internet is nothing without the networks themselves. While initially funded by governments and their educational research bodies, the majority of the internet backbone was constructed by telecommunications companies, such as AT&T, Global Crossing and MCI Worldcom in the United States. As commercial use of the internet increased, and the construction and maintenance of it was deregulated in the United States (beginning in 1995 for the physical infrastructure and 1998 for the domain naming system that controls it), the number of telecommunications firms involved, and the total wealth expended on the expansion exploded. Telecoms firms laid millions of kilometres of fibre-optic cable and put up satellites, such as the doomed Iridium project, and manufactured and installed the millions of routers and switches needed to manage the flow of information through and around these complex interconnected private networks. While the manufacturing component of this activity captured the headlines:

> The big money in the Internet economy is behind the scenes, in the companies building the networks, software and computers over which information flows, a University of Texas study finds. Though the largest number of jobs and about one-third of the revenue are in the commerce sector, the engineers of the Internet are the kingpins – at least for now. So-called infrastructure companies – including networking companies, telecommunications giants, Internet providers and PC makers – rack up average revenue of [US]$308,708 per employee. By contrast, commerce companies average $211,401 per worker, the study says. Networking and hardware companies

are growing faster because businesses are spending billions of dollars to get traditional companies online. (Levy and Rosenbush, 1999: 22)

The services aspect of these operations – the laying and lighting of the fibre-optic, the maintenance of the equipment, and the (re)programming of their functions – was incredibly costly, but also difficult to differentiate from the total equipment expenditure. In addition to the teams of electrical engineers and trench diggers required to build the physical infrastructure, as discussed by Graham (1998, 2004; Graham and Marvin, 2001), a veritable 'knowledge army' is required: computer engineers, repair technicians and call centre operators to maintain the 99.999 per cent reliability of software and hardware that seems to elude university network administrators and Microsoft; plus others to design, maintain and use the computer systems that the network enables. Companies providing these services, including the Ross Poirot spin-off EDS; database manufacturers Oracle (San Francisco) and SAP (Germany), routing hardware and software manufacturers Cisco Systems and Nortel, Lucent and JDS Uniphase, became the stars of the 'telecoms' stock-price boom in the United States from 1998 to 2001, and generally maintained their inflated value for longer than the B2C e-commerce startups. More importantly, the internet has spawned new categories of service employment: network consultants who install and support home and small business computers and networks, and administrators who manage those of larger businesses; anti-virus and anti-spam programmers who battle outbreaks of computer viruses, worms and trojans, along with unwanted solicitations for male organ extensions; and computer technicians who attempt to repair the after-effects of the former.

Services created or (potentially) transformed by the internet

Management consultants, investment bankers and lawyers did very well out of the US dot-com boom. IPOs seemed to require extensive specialist knowledge-intensive business service provision, with investment roadshows touring the United States. Lawyers continued to do well in the subsequent bust, with the accompanying accounting discrepancies, securities fraud and anti-monopoly investigations. The US Justice Department's lawsuit against Microsoft's bundling of Internet Explorer into its Windows suite took more than 7 years to reach a stalemate (the finding of monopolist abuse stood, but the remedy, which threatened to split Microsoft into two, was overturned), and cost the company more than US$2 billion in settlements. A separate lawsuit by the European Commission against the bundling of Media Player into Windows lasted several years, with the settlement requiring Microsoft to allow fair access to internet media software from Real Networks or Apple's Quicktime. A future lawsuit may come with the bundling of a web search service into Windows, competing against Google and other independent search engines. In each of these cases the allegation is the same: Microsoft is unfairly leveraging its control of 90 per cent of computer desktops to limit the ability of competing internet services to establish their product as a standard. Because of their initial popularity, Netscape, Real Networks and Google were too expensive for Microsoft to purchase outright (its favoured method of 'innovation', as with MSDOS, Excel and Hotmail, for example), but were also offering too popular a service to ignore. By bundling competing products into Windows system software, Microsoft can ensure that its standard prevails – and coincidentally sell more server software (streaming servers, for example) to run them, and promote other

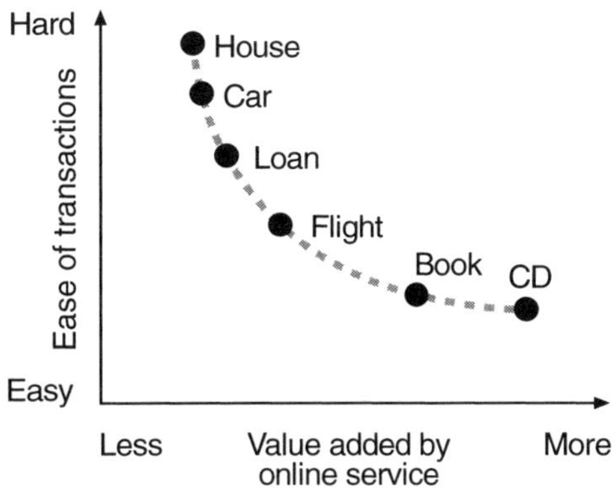

Source: *The Economist* (Anon) (1997: 7).

Figure 18.9 Industries at risk of disruption

Microsoft services (such as the .Net strategy). Should this strategy continue to be successful, the list of technologies and associated companies vulnerable to Microsoft's dominance looks set to increase. The company's strategic turnaround from 1995, when Bill Gates was openly dismissive of the nascent commercial internet, is astonishing, and offers a (not unproblematic) counterpoint to the 'inevitable technological disruption' argument.

During the dot-com boom, the list of industries said to be vulnerable to disruption from the internet was large. Among those typically mentioned were banking, education, the media, mail services, market research, music and film, and books. *The Economist* (Anon) (1997), in one of its earliest surveys of e-commerce, indicated some industries that were expected to be heavily affected by the nascent technology (Figure 18.9). According to this categorisation, industries which offer products or services which place informational demands on their customers are vulnerable to websites which simplify these demands (such as locating a low-rate mortgage through comparison sites). Such websites do not need to add much value to the goods or services concerned because of the reduction of the 'hassle' factor. By comparison, for websites to successfully sell products with properties well understood by consumers (such as books), considerable value must be added to the service, such as consumer reviews or other features not found in a typical bricks and mortar bookstore.

As noted in the same *Economist* survey, banking had already been transformed by self-service ICT in the form of ATMs, telephone banking and the widespread diffusion of debit and credit cards and electronic data interchange between banks. As *The Economist* (ibid.: 5) put it:

> All these are forms of electronic commerce, and all have changed their own markets in sometimes radical ways. So why single out the Internet? Because it alone has the potential to deliver what the notion of electronic commerce had always implied. Computerised financial markets gave brokers equal and instant access to information and let them act on it there and then. The Internet promises to do the same for everyone from the individual investor to the casual shopper. Credit cards spurred home shopping by creating a virtual payment system that transcended national borders. The Internet extends this beyond the transaction itself to everything that comes before and after, from marketing and product display to order-tracking and sometimes even delivery.

> And unlike the commercial online services [such as AOL at that point], which reserve their services for their subscribers and selected merchants, the Internet is open to everyone.

Education was seen as being vulnerable to the internet through pervasive distance learning. Printed media, in particular daily newspapers and regular magazines, could be threatened by the ability of websites to rapidly reproduce 'breaking news' and to provide access to story archives. Mail services could see volumes drop as letters and bills are replaced by e-mail (but conversely could be at risk of a boom of home delivery, requiring expensive storage of undelivered parcels or even more costly repeated deliveries). Market research could see data collection computerised via website entry, as demonstrated by web surveys such as the UK's YouGov, threatening the jobs of data entry and basic processing staff. Finally, music, film and books were all seen as vulnerable to digitisation, and thus the replacement of 'atom'-based supply chains by 'bit'-based digital distribution (Leyshon, 2001, 2003; Currah, 2003; Leyshon et al., 2005).

Computer-assisted retailing suffers from high costs associated with expensive ICT support. REI, a US-based outdoor recreation equipment store, discovered early on that supporting its online operations was labour intensive and costly:

> 'Technical people are a lot more expensive than part-time salesclerks,' he said. Now, for example, REI's flagship store in Seattle employs roughly 300 people, while all of rei.com has but 60. Yet Hyde says the payrolls for that store and for rei.com come out to about the same. Soon, he says, the balance will tilt toward the Web site, as the cost of the site's payroll rises steadily. . . . It is true that the average REI store costs $6 million, including everything from building costs to new fixtures, and is remodeled every 5 to 10 years. Rei.com, in contrast, spent $500,000 for its original opening, including all machinery and programming. But the rei.com upgrades have never ceased – and probably never will. (Kaufman, 1999)

The processes of digitisation, innovation and disruption are by no means complete, and these expensive internet service jobs may indeed be lost (or at least relocated) as tasks become increasingly computer mediated. However the extent to which the internet may be the medium for future B2C commerce is still largely within the bounds of speculation, with Figure 18.7 indicating the extent to which product categories have been (and might be) transformed into e-commerce 'category killers'. Not featuring in this list at all is the product group that comprises the bulk of consumer discretionary spending each week: groceries.

Services largely untouched (as of yet) by the internet

The many industries not included in Figure 18.7 might give some indication of the extent to which the internet remains disruptive only to particular service niches. Many services have had minor facets of their operations assisted or changed by the internet, but some have to a great extent remained largely unaffected. Returning to the ladder and interlocking metaphors of Figures 18.3 and 18.5, it is evident that a number of industries are experiencing only initial (low-rung or dagger-point) adoption of e-commerce and the internet into most operations, primarily in the form of advertising, information serving and public relations and branding (from the supply side) and web searches and e-mail (from the demand side).

Prime among the non-transformed services are 'face-to-face' (performed) services such as live entertainment and higher education (earlier comments on distance learning notwithstanding). This is not to suggest that the internet has no place in these sectors: streamed and archived radio shows and interactive television clearly point to the incremental convergence of broadcast entertainment and narrowcast computer-based interaction. The integration of WebCT and other web-based 'learning facilitation software' likewise shows that the internet can augment (rather than effectively supplant) human-led teaching and learning. Moreover, while streamed live theatre has not become a large market, several services required by the theatre for proper functioning have been affected – if not transformed – by the internet: notably ticket sales, promotions and reviews.

Government services have also been slow in the transformation stakes. While many governments and state agencies have spent substantial sums commissioning large-scale e-government projects, these have for the most part sought to automate existing government-to-consumer (G2C) interactions and processes. The e-filing of tax returns is a case in point: these systems simplify data entry for tax agencies by passing that function to taxpayers, but the complexity of the service prevents a transformation of the process from the vantage point of the taxpayer. Perhaps because of distrust of security issues or the 'long arm of the state', or because of the multitude of incompatible computer systems, these projects are a long way from truly transformed processes, whereby tax returns are generated automatically through interlinked corporate-employer, charity, banking and investment, property and local government systems. High-profile examples of UK government IT project failures, such as the spiralling costs and delayed completion of the NHS computerised GP booking system, and the abandonment of the government's Office of the E-Envoy strategy for 'portalising' G2C transactions, highlight how problematic, and expensive, these projects can be, requiring ever more ICT service expertise. None the less, e-government initiatives are high on the funding priorities of many national governments, and facilitating e-government features as one of the core funding initiatives of the European Union's 'Framework 6' research programme.

Services and the internet: some case examples

Building on the discussion above, it is useful to consider some case examples of how services and the internet have become intermingled, disrupted or transformed. For simplicity, I organise them in scale, from the smallest and most local to the largest and most global; and conversely, from the largest product to the smallest.

The Cooperative Auto Network, Vancouver Canada

The Cooperative Auto Network (CAN) is a not-for-profit car-sharing organisation. It owns a fleet of cars which are shared by members of the cooperative on an hourly or daily basis through a system of communal keys, and paid for use by the hour and the mile. While similar in principle to a localised car rental agency, the organisation has two prime goals: to improve accessibility to private transportation, and to alleviate the need for (primarily urban dwelling) members to own their own cars. CAN operates on the basis that cars should be utilised for as many hours of the day as possible, and thus relies on a sophisticated booking system that matches members to the nearest compatible car. Operating since 1996, CAN initially used a paper-based booking and invoicing system; over time this became computerised through the use of part-time computer consultants. As its membership grew, however, CAN needed a more flexible reservation system that would allow members to view their bookings and usage, and to make new or alter existing bookings through automated systems. Naturally enough CAN turned to the web.

Like many small organisations CAN could not afford to engage the services of large management consultants. It instead employed a sole programmer to revamp the entire back-end computerised reservation and invoicing system, and create the front-end web-based interface. In common with many computer projects, large and small, the anticipated timeframe to completion was wildly optimistic, with the project requiring four times the original time budget as additional features were conceived and integrated. As long as the wider internet and the local intranet remain stable, the internet booking system is an efficient way of managing the volume of calls about bookings, car locations, troubleshooting the common key system, and invoices, enabling the organisation to expand without a dramatic increase in (marginal) support costs.

In principle, placing the booking system on the web also enables the cooperative to expand beyond its Vancouver base. With intelligent programming, it would make little difference to members or the organisation if the service expanded to other Canadian cities or internationally, or even franchised its computer system to other organisations, as long as there were support people on the ground to maintain and chase broken down or lost cars. This could also be done through telephone support only, but the costs of doing so increase in line with volume. However, the internet is not as unproblematic a panacea as perhaps first thought: the internet or webserver system can be intermittently unstable, particularly with the ADSL network that connects the back-end servers to the front-end web interface and internet, effectively severing CAN from the e-commerce world. Members may also be insufficiently computer literate, and require hand-holding to make or change reservations. In these situations the volume of calls can increase substantially, particularly at times of widespread virus attacks; or rumours of security breaches at other e-commerce sites, or when the front-end interface changes. CAN therefore frequently acts as a computer helpdesk and occasionally a counselling service for its customers.

The organisation must keep up to date with the latest security patches, and employ or contract computer technicians who keep abreast of the latest virus information and firewalls to prevent mischievous internet traffic from overloading the system. It must also manage the process of maintaining the front-end (web and application) servers, and introducing improvements to the system without losing time (and thus bookings) or records (only held digitally), or member trust. In other words, CAN must act as much as a computer company as a car sharing cooperative.

Woolworths Supermarkets, New Zealand

Supermarkets have run home-delivery operations for much of their existence, but these were mostly small-scale and ad hoc prior to e-commerce (Murphy, 2002, 2003). It is only with the widespread diffusion of the internet that grocers have paid serious attention to and invested significant cash in the distribution of food to the home. Woolworths Supermarkets of New Zealand[8] began online operations in 1996 via CD-ROM-based catalogues, and web-based operations in 1998. The internet is vital to grocery home-delivery operations for a number of reasons: it substantially reduces the costs of processing orders, and can improve stock control and prediction, particularly if the orders database is linked to a store or warehouse inventory system (Murphy, 2003). It attracts customers who like the 'hi-tech' nature of the service, and/or who prefer to place orders using predefined lists (such as past orders, or geodemographic 'typical user' purchase profiles), and is thus potentially gaining market share from less technologically progressive competitors.[9]

Existing grocery chains have a longstanding programme of computerisation, including point-of-sale scanning equipment and inventory control, and increasingly sophisticated supply-chain management (through integrated regional distribution centres) and customer relationship management systems (managing loyalty cards, for example). Online supermarkets therefore tend to have well-established in-house IT departments that are used to operating on medium-term implementation planning cycles. Introducing a web-based operation requires a whole new skillset, however: new programming languages (html, xml, cascading style sheets and java); a customer focus as opposed to the supply chain; and a much compressed timeframe between idea conception and implementation. For these and other reasons, online grocers often outsource the development of the front-end to specialist web agencies or system developers. Woolworths initially contracted an American web development company to do this, on the urging of its then Hong Kong-based parent company Dairy Farm International, which wanted to use the same consultant across its subsidiary companies and headquarters. This parent–subcontractor relationship proved impossible for Woolworths, as the subcontractor had its priorities elsewhere:

> They weren't supermarket people, they weren't retailers, they were young [programmers] fresh out of school. They don't understand how you need to operate a business and how you need to be managing for customers. . . . As soon as we got it going here, our parent company said 'great, we've got New Zealand going, let's get it up to Hong Kong real quick'. So they all went over to Hong Kong, and we were left with a whole lot of stuff that was just wrong. (Woolworths E-Commerce manager, March 2000, as quoted in Murphy, 2002: 54–5)

The New Zealand company eventually purchased the source code for its web interface from the US developer, and contracted a small, local company to provide the ongoing development work. Over time, more of this was brought in-house, as the pace of innovation increased, the skill base of the IT department improved, and senior management became more committed to the online operation. Like CAN, the retailer began to talk like, and resemble in business practice, a software company: it referred to website updates as 'releases', and incomplete release verification as 'beta-testing'.

In sum, while a much larger organisation than CAN, Woolworths faced similar pressures with its online operation: managing the process of innovation, through which the online service could become in turn more powerful, more reliable, more convenient, and lower cost (Christensen et al.'s changing bases of competition, as shown in Figure 18.6). Woolworths' key problem was coordinating the subcontractors' work on the front-end with internal and subcontracted development of the back-end inventory systems, which were also undergoing a significant period of investment and change (primarily through systems integration contractors). These processes have been quite disruptive to the retailer's customary IT development cycle. Until the advent of internet shopping, a grocery retailer's strategy could follow a predictable path of development: larger stores, a more centralised distribution system, strengthening retailer control over goods distribution, pricing and promotion, and progressive shifts towards customer self-service (Murphy, 2002: 57–8). With home delivery, it is the retailer that does all the work of picking, packing and carrying for the consumer. This is a substantial and potentially disruptive shift in the value

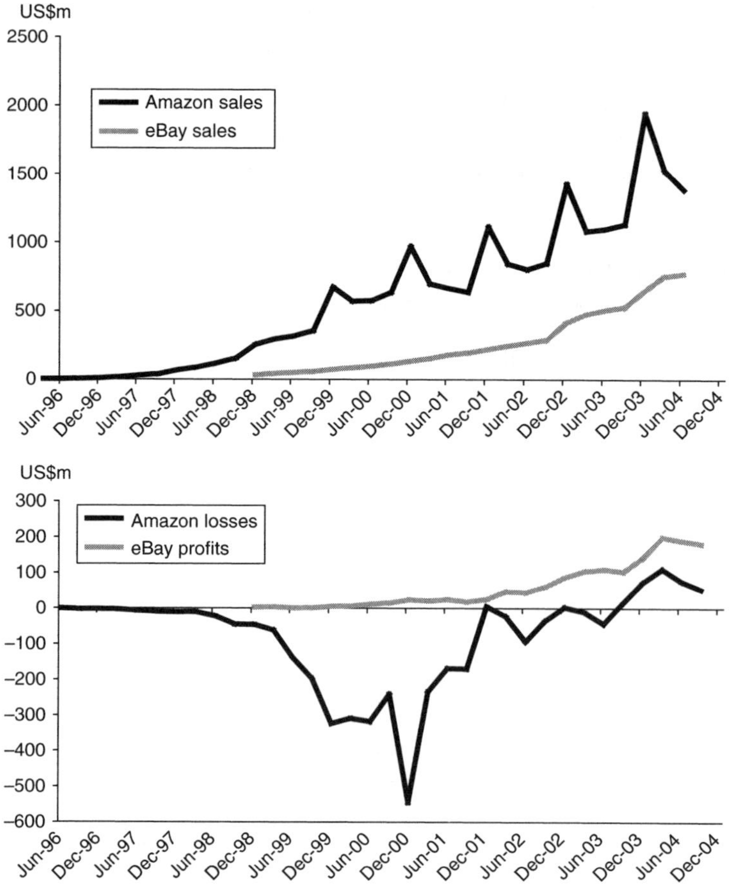

Source: Company quarterly reports, 1996–2004.

Figure 18.10 Quarterly sales and profits/losses: eBay and Amazon

chain, and may form a new basis of competition within the grocery industry. Tesco of the UK has used this disruption to its competitors as part of a strategy to increase its global market share, and has established internet home delivery operations in the UK, Ireland, South Korea and the United States. While it is problematic to untangle the potential cross-subsidisation from other parts of its increasingly eclectic business, Tesco claims that its Tesco.com operation is both growing fast (sales up 29 per cent from 2002 to 2003 and now exceeding US$1 billion, accounting for nearly 2 per cent of its total sales), and profitable (the 2004 Annual Report indicates US$36 million, which exceeds Amazon's profits in the same year) (Figure 18.10).

eBay

The online auction site eBay is one of the few e-commerce success stories, if measured by profits. eBay has been profitable since initiating quarterly reports in December 1998. In the six years to 2004, eBay recorded sales of over US$6 billion (over $2 billion in 2003

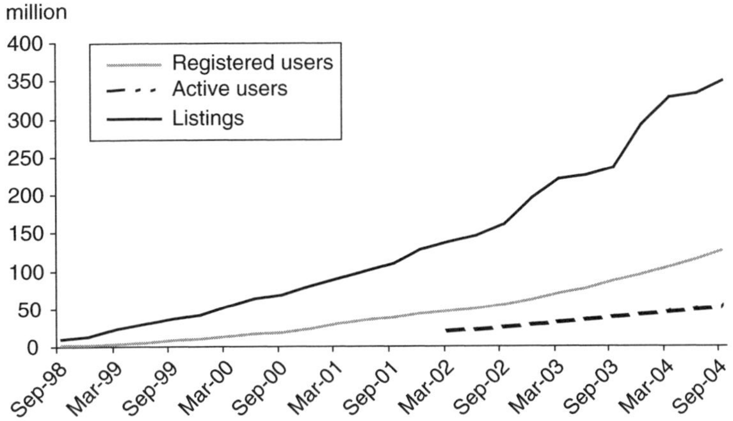

Source: Company quarterly reports, 1996–2004.

Figure 18.11 eBay's quarterly listings and users

alone), and cumulative profits of more than $1 billion ($460 million in 2003 alone). In comparison, the other 'poster child' of e-commerce, Amazon.com, recorded sales of almost $20 billion (1998–2004, $5.2 billion in 2003) but losses of $2.6 billion (profit of $35 million for 2003) (Figure 18.10).

eBay has been so successful to date by acting as an 'infomediary', an information intermediary between buying and selling consumers (C2C e-commerce) and taking a commission in the process. More recently, it has branched into hosting more B2C and even business-to-business (B2B) transactions through its 'buy it now' fixed-price button, which mostly appeals to established retail outlets and companies. The ability of consumers and businesses to find extraordinary miscellany (eBay first became notable for exchanging collections of Pez candy dispensers; while the London Underground was reportedly using the service to find spare parts for its obsolete Intel 8086 processors that power the signals and other vital equipment) has proved the size of the market. More than $24 billion worth of goods was sold through its website in 2003 by its 52 million active users, up from 37 million the year before, trading as many as 10 million items at any one point in time (348 million listings were recorded in the July to September 2004 quarter; Figure 18.11). eBay's ubiquity in auctions has caused significant trouble for some industries, however: CNET News.com reported that airlines were attempting to halt auctions for frequent flyer reward vouchers, for fear of excessive cashing in of otherwise unrealised liabilities (Sandoval, 2002).

Mass auctions of products, new and old, mass market and obscure, have become well embedded in contemporary business and consumer practice and imagination. The Christmas period in 2004 was notable for the visibility of eBay in charity auctions and in providing an indicator of the lasting value of products and of personalities (such as for signed books or radio prizes). eBay has also become in part a 'social service', used by commentators and activists to highlight matters of social concern: the offering of universities for 'sale' during the UK's higher education tuition fees debate in 2004, and reports of students offering to auction their virginity or their souls in order to pay fees.

Conclusions

This chapter has attempted to portray how services are bound up in the processes of innovation that comprise the internet – past, present and future. From its foundation of the 'network of networks' as a research forum in the 1960s to its commercialisation in the 1990s to its current near ubiquity, the internet has relied on public good investments in infrastructure, open source gifting of intellectual property to the user community, and the cycling of billions of speculative dollars by venture capitalists and the public into new ventures. The companies and services these investments created have been quite disruptive to existing products, companies and business practices. The process is far from complete, and the internet may yet transform more completely government services and performed services. The process of transforming organisations and their interactions within and without goes beyond the need for infrastructure and funds, however; for many services and organisations it is the reimagining of business practice and strategy that matters as much, if not more, than the technologies themselves.

Many internet services are costly to provide but contribute little obvious revenue streams, at least in the short run. This includes the fan and information sites dedicated to television, movies and music. For example, Paramount Pictures' Star Trek 'portal' website (www.startrek.com) provides a plethora of pages on the ships, planets, species, characters, actors and storylines that run throughout the 10 movies and five shows, put together by the show makers. Links are provided to the DVDs of the shows and movies, and so the website presumably intends to satisfy the knowledge and acquisition requirements of loyal fans (thus preventing an independent effort perhaps linking to pirated copies of the movies or shows). The Internet Movie Database (www.imdb.com) uses the opposite strategy, providing a forum for fans to enter the details and reviews of their favourite movies and actors in a 'bottom-up' process. This collective database demonstrates the power of 'network effects' and 'lock-in' (Liebowitz, 2002), whereby a resource or program becomes more valuable as it becomes more widely adopted; once established as a standard, there is little incentive for users and providers to switch to something different, until an obviously superior alternative comes along. The IMDb is a resource of first choice for users wishing to recall who played character X in movie Y, or where they have seen that actor before, or find user reviews, or the status of movies in production. The database also provides a second 'professional' for-fee layer of information to those in the industry, hidden from those accessing the freely available database information. In a similar position is cddb, a website (now hosted by Gracenote) which encouraged users to enter music liner notes for CDs into a public database. Once acquired by Gracenote, the strategy changed to encouraging other companies (such as the music library program iTunes) to pay to access the service, an activity that is seamless to users of Apple Computer's program.

There is growing evidence that B2C e-commerce services have not only survived the dot-com downturn, but are becoming increasingly profitable. While this trajectory may not equate with the levels anticipated during the boom, companies such as eBay and Tesco are proving that the internet can be a lucrative business channel. Yet it is more than just a means of transacting: the internet presents a seemingly limitless store of information for businesses and customers, governments and citizens that is indispensable, distracting and dangerous. The tsunami events in the Indian Ocean on Boxing Day 2004 demonstrated how important the internet can be as a communications tool and as a reference manual for tectonic plate and wave mechanics. Meanwhile on discussion boards, fans continue to discuss the 'philosophy of Star Trek', and elsewhere hackers attempt to release yet another trojan or virus disguised as a helpful message from the bank. Its usefulness and potential threat to the functioning of the state is also becoming clear. The internet was heavily utilised in the 2003 US presidential election to help raise funds, mobilise supporters, and to counter statements from the rival camp (most obviously in the furore over the national guard service record of George W. Bush, led by weblogs). At the same time, legal cases demonstrate how the global reach of the internet complicates the functioning of state law. In Australia, a judge has ruled that all websites must remove any information pertaining to a case before the courts, in case potential jurors use the internet to inform themselves ahead of time. How this would be enforced for websites operating outside the nation's jurisdiction remains to be seen. Elsewhere the American manager of eBay's Indian subsidiary Baazee was arrested for not preventing the sale of videotapes showing underage sexual activity, while in France, Yahoo! was prosecuted for allowing French web surfers to view Nazi memorabilia on its American auction websites, something that contravenes French racial hatred incitement laws. The implications go further than the legal liability of information provided through internet services, as cross-border digital interactions and trade raise other questions regarding protection of intellectual property rights (such as patents and copyright) given differences in national standards, and the consumer and seller protection laws that apply. As *The Economist* puts it:

> Consumer groups want local laws to apply to consumers who buy things online, on the grounds that they cannot be expected to understand how laws might vary from place to place. But companies that wish to do business online do not want to get involved with myriad sets of regulations either. They would prefer to be able to impose 'click-through' agreements on their websites, requiring customers to agree that transactions will be subject to the laws of the country in which the company is based. (*The Economist*, 2001: 67)

It is clear that as a forum for discourse, entertainment and information the internet is now firmly established. The popularity of downloaded music, promulgated initially through Napster but consolidated through the rapid adoption of Apple's iPod and iTunes, the increasing penetration of the internet into other media such as television shows and films via BitTorrent, and the overwhelming popularity of auction sites such as eBay has shown that consumers are unafraid to transact online for a growing variety of goods and services. Air, bus and rail travel and accommodation bookings have flourished online, although these can at times be frustrating experiences due to complex timetables, booking codes or alteration restrictions. Online banking has been widely adopted, though it is a sector heavily targeted by fraudsters and malicious computer code. In these areas, and still others, the internet has exerted a powerful disruptive influence on former (profitable) ways of doing business. For many the impact has been as deflationary as it is revolutionary, as internet users have become accustomed to accessing services at no charge, and service providers (such as online grocers, news organisations, banks and software companies) have struggled to find ways to encourage consumers to pay for the service offered. If and when they do, the digital economy – and accompanying digital society – will have truly arrived.

Notes

1. In this chapter I refer to the 'internet' in lower case, implying that the aggregation of information and communications technologies, services and actors necessary for its construction and maintenance is no more coherent and unimorphological than the 'telephone', 'railway' or 'television'.

2. The 'ubiquity' of internet accessibility does not universally apply, as the many reports on digital divides attest (NTIA, 1995, 1999, 2000; James, 2003; Taylor and Murphy, 2004).
3. This is not a new question: see Gershuny and Miles (1983) on 'self-service'. It should be noted that any internet-enabled transaction relies on a pre-existing infrastructure of hardware and software, which were themselves created through human involvement. This point will be addressed later in the chapter.
4. FIDONET later spread worldwide and continued as an internet service provider after the dot-com boom. USENET newsgroup discussions are still available (such as 'alt.tv.amazing-race', on the TV show), and are archived through Google groups, though they now play a much less important role in providing news and advice.
5. AOL had earlier attempted to invest in Netscape (before its 1995 initial public offering), but had been rebuffed.
6. Of course, new service functions have accompanied the 'computer revolution' from the beginning, including computer programmers and systems analysts.
7. Christensen et al. (2000) generally mean a tangible product (a 'good', such as a music player), but the same principle applies to software and to packaged services, such as a banking product.
8. Woolworths NZ is a national grocery chain that in 2002 became one of several fascia of the Australian-owned but New Zealand-based Progressive Enterprises.
9. Ironically, Progressive Enterprises had long proclaimed it was not interested in the costly diversion that was internet-based home shopping, and required Woolworths management to justify keeping the service operating. The organisation now offers home shopping services under two of its grocery fascia: Woolworths and Foodtown.

19 Knowledge creation in a Japanese convenience store chain: the case of Seven-Eleven Japan

Ikujiro Nonaka, Vesa Peltokorpi and Dai Senoo

Introduction

Markets evolve through progressive steps initiated by innovative entrepreneurs and changing environment. The innovation processes and market evolution can be interpreted through the positivist or phenomenological philosophies. Theories influenced by the three schools of positivism (nineteenth-century positivism, logical positivism and logical empiricism) explain the process through linear changes in which agents act as passive information processors. In contrast, phenomenology, starting with the internal world of embedded actors, enables one to describe innovation from the actor's subjective point of view. The reality lies between the objective and subjective worlds, as retail innovations are based on constant subjective anticipation of changing customer needs through constantly absorbing, processing and systemizing internal and external information/knowledge. An essential part of the process is knowledge creation, not information and knowledge *per se* (Nonaka, 1991, 1994; Nonaka and Takeuchi, 1995).

While innovations and retail evolution are dialectic processes, they are frequently explained through linear causalities. Some scholars have departed from dualistic dichotomies by explaining innovative retail evolution through Hegelian dialectics (Gist, 1968). Albeit providing a dynamic perspective, dialectic frameworks mainly focus on holistic change, placing little emphasis on purposive and interest-driven behavior and/or the nexus between internal and external change. The interaction among embedded actors is a crucial part of the innovation processes in franchising relationships, which is the focus of this chapter. We describe retail innovation using the dialectic knowledge-based view, taking into account tacit knowledge and agent-structure dynamics (Nonaka, 1991, 1994; Nonaka and Takeuchi, 1995; Nonaka and Toyama, 2002, 2003; Nonaka et al., 2005). Dialectic is a model of both agent-environment change and knowledge creation as these processes are closely intertwined. By processing and embracing the external world, agents create knowledge and consequently restructure the retail environment.

The conceptual discussion is applied to the Japanese convenience store chain Seven-Eleven Japan ('SEJ') for three reasons. First, having a network of more than 10,000 stores, SEJ has evolved as Japan's biggest convenience store chain in co-evolution with the environment. A steady stream of innovations is made possible by the supporting components of our framework: knowledge vision, driving objectives, dialogues and creative routines. SEJ has been profitable for 30 years by constantly anticipating changing trends regardless of the severe business environment. Instead of pointing the finger at the harsh business environment, Chairman and CEO Toshifumi Suzuki asserts that badly performing retailers should blame themselves because they do not satisfy the customers' changing needs. Second, the company has utilized multi-layered *ba* (shared context of interaction) and networked knowledge to introduce products and services faster than its main competitors. Third, SEJ has been able to create a balance between supportive information systems (objectivity) and human insight (subjectivity).

This chapter comprises three sections. The first lays out the conceptual framework. The discussion covers the agent–structure interaction, the contradictory nature of the franchising firm in the network economy, the basic components of knowledge creation and the process of knowledge creation. In the second section, we describe the components that reinforce product and service innovations at SEJ. We propose that the main components behind the sustainable profitability of the company are based on (i) the ability to convert knowledge through interlinked *ba*, making innovation a co-creation process; (ii) the dialectics of information and social system that shifts primary attention to the customer interface and enables one to utilize external knowledge in internal knowledge-creating processes; and (iii) creating and managing reinforcing components of knowledge vision, driving objectives, dialogues and creative routines that enable the detection of emerging customer desires and environmental changes. The final section deals with the conclusions, limitations and managerial implications.

Conceptual framework

Corporate innovations are the sources of retail evolution, environmental change and Schumpeterian rents. Innovation is a 'process of industrial mutation . . . that incessantly revolutionizes the economic structure from within' (Schumpeter, 1942: 83). It is conventionally explained as a deterministic process because scholars influenced by the positivist philosophy seek to objectify and categorize the agents and the environment. The goal in these causal theories is to generate universal knowledge to manipulate organizational and environmental variables. For example, the systems perspective categorizes the environment as a set of all objects whose attributes affect both the system, as well as those objects whose attributes are changed by the behavior of the system (Hall and Fagen, 1956). In the field of retail research, the environment is described as consisting of various factors, such as size and spatial distribution of population, consumer preferences, income and income distribution, technology and state regulations (Roth and Klein, 1993). While objectivity is the foundation of causal rationality, it gives little room to describe what the surrounding reality means to the embedded actors.

In the dualistic world of objective agents and environment, contingency theorists and organizational ecologists describe evolutionary change as environmentally deterministic phenomena (Hannan and Freeman, 1977, 1984; Hannan and Carroll, 1992). In its most extreme version, population ecology theory suggested that firms could not change and that the study of populations of firms was the only legitimate application of evolutionary thinking (Hannan and Freeman, 1977). In this reactive world, only environmentally sensitive companies survive like biological species in the Darwinist evolutionary cycles. While adaptation to environment is essential for organizational survival, the passive posture of agents creates a dilemma: 'how do actors change institutions if they are conditioned by the institutions they want to change?'. A part of the dilemma is created by deterministic models with a uniformity assumption and simplistic view of human actors who respond to environmental stimuli through rule-based behavior. We claim that the structural change can be described only by shifting focus to the utilization of agents' tacit knowledge in a specific time–space.

In retail research, a widely popular wheel of retailing theory postulates that new types of retailers usually enter the market as low-status, low-margin and low-price operators (McNair, 1958). The institutional changes occur when the innovators enter the retail arena. Customer services and prices increase once the innovators become established, which results in the emergence of another cycle of retail innovation. Albeit providing a general framework of retail change, the emergence of convenience stores challenges the assumption of low cost as a necessary requirement. The emphasis on price echoes the economic-based conceptualization of human actors. Moreover, the theory lacks discussion about managerial heuristics that lead to market entry. Other cyclical approaches further describe retail evolution as a process of interaction that proceeds through the stages of action, reaction and assimilation (Brown, 1987). Based on Hegelian dialectics, retail change is explained as a succession of steps where each step contrasts with the previous one (thesis and antithesis) before merging into synthesis that starts the process all over again (Gist, 1968). The relative weakness in this approach is the existence of deterministic developments and behavior, neglecting a thorough analysis of the factors underlying these developments.

The transcendental realists (Bhaskar, 1993) and Anthony Giddens (1984) overcome the positivist, subject–object separation by the co-evolutionary process between the human agents and their environment. The critical realists claim that the agents and structures in these views are ontologically inseparable because each enters into the other's constitution (Archer, 2003). The claimed problem is that change cannot be explained without some ontological differences between 'objective' structures and 'subjective' human agents. While the ontological discussion in the structuration theory can be elaborated, Giddens (1984) differentiates agents from structures, arguing that daily action is performed through practical and discursive consciousness. Where the former refers to tacit stocks of knowledge on which humans draw in social activity, the latter describes the conscious level of knowing. Like tacit knowledge, practical consciousness reflects intentional people being an integral part of the life-world. Knowledge creation is consequently context/environment specific on the one hand, while human action is largely constrained by environmental factors, such as norms, resources and so on, on the other.

The knowledge-based view, by embracing internal organizational and environmental complexity, seeks to transgress some of the above-mentioned limitations by explaining the continuous organization–environment dialectic interaction in two ways (Nonaka and Toyama, 2002, 2003; Nonaka et al., 2005). First, the ontological assumption of shared context in motion (*ba*) implies that companies create knowledge in a dialectic interaction between 'subjective' human agents and 'objectified' environment. The environment is conceptualized as a reservoir of knowledge that both enables and constrains agents (Nonaka et al., 2005). As most successful innovations satisfy emerging customer needs, human agents, through knowledge-creation processes, develop a reasonable and accurate view of evolving human nature as well as the changing environment. Second, the epistemological assumption of knowledge conversion implies the process in which human agents seek to objectify their environment. The root of innovative change is the conversion of tacit knowledge into explicit knowledge, and back to tacit knowledge. Although context-specific research is often downplayed in positivist-influenced theories (Blair and Hunt, 1986), we emphasize the role of contextually embedded human agents whose intentional actors initiate knowledge creation.

Dialectic nature of the franchising firm in the network economy

Organizational existence can be interpreted through the positivist 'outsiders' and the phenomenological 'insiders' perspectives. Based on the Cartesian split and Humean event regularity, positivists begin explanations with the external world of nature, viewing humans as rationally acting parts of that nature (see Husserl, 1931). The positivist assumptions enable conceptualizations with great precision at the risk of disregarding some important elements, such as values and choice. In contrast, phenomenological philosophy directs attention to embedded actors embracing human values and subjective knowledge (ibid.; Heidegger, 1962). Contrary to positivism, the phenomenological meaning world is vague and context dependent. We seek to synthesize these contrasting philosophical perspectives, describing organizational ontology as *ba*.

Franchising, from the positivist point of view, is a hybrid form of organization combining markets (manufacturers selling to independent vendors) and firms (company-owned stores). The emphasis in conceptualizations is placed on economic efficiency rather than context-specific creativity. Under the franchising model, entrepreneurs license the chain's business concept: the right to use its brand name and access to its marketing strategies, organizational routines, and context-free operating manuals (Caves and Murphy, 1976). In return, the franchisee pays the franchiser both an initial fee and ongoing royalties, but retains rights to the establishment's earnings. Like other entrepreneurs, franchisees perceive opportunities for wealth creation and risk their own capital pursuing them. Unlike many other entrepreneurs, however, franchisees choose to purchase substantial strategic and operational support from the franchiser. Placing the emphasis on causalities, most economic discussions on franchising focus on monitoring, contracts, fee structures and opportunism (ibid.; Rubin, 1978). The context in which actors are acting in franchising arrangements remains a 'black box'.

Phenomenology enables one to move from the objectified agents and structures to explain contextual phenomena through the eyes of embedded actors (Husserl, 1931; Heidegger, 1962). Intentional and knowledgeable actors construct their realities in a given time–space and view the world through 'life-world' frames (Husserl, 1931). The notions of situational, intransitive, and subjective knowledge enable one to describe change through dialectic knowledge-creation cycles that link objectivity and subjectivity, as well as explicit and tacit knowledge. In contrast to the objective notion of knowledge, the world is in the dialectic process of making due to the primacy of tacit knowledge over prepositional knowledge (Hayek, 1945). Utilization of phenomenology as such in franchising research is challenging because the emphasis is placed more on meaning creation than on economic efficiency. Moreover, the conceptualizations in which objects and subjects are interlinked in time–space has aroused criticism as phenomenological predictions lack the systematic hierarchy of determinations and are too vague for empirical testing (Popper, 1959).

Objective structures and subjective agents are dialectically related; they cannot exist interdependently. The *ba* concept provides a 'middle path' to explain the organizational ontology by synthesizing form/context and rationalism/idealism (Nonaka and Toyama, 2003). The view is based on the assumption that reality is not solely constructed of physical objects, but also based on actors' experiences with the physical world. That is, human agents use environmentally derived knowledge to create a new objective social reality. Instead of adopting the positivist assumption of a fixed set of preferences, we emphasize evolutionary human values and posit that knowledge is created only through context-specific situated action, as actors share and validate their subjective experiences. In addition to the rational cost–benefit calculations, human actors seek to locate, create and utilize knowledge through various social interactions taking place at various organizational and interorganizational levels. Individual action creates tendencies at higher levels of analysis, as individuals as well as organizations are part of a whole. Individuals and organizations do not merely evolve; they co-evolve, both with other entities and with the changing environment.

The notion of organizations as organic entities highlights the importance of networked knowledge in franchising companies. In contrast to handling information asymmetries through contracts (Williamson, 1975), inter-firm cooperation is mainly based on accessing and sharing knowledge (Grant and Baden-Fuller, 2004). The role of dispersed knowledge is recognized in franchising, as franchisees possess decentralized knowledge and consequently make decisions and provide ideas (Minkler, 1992). As tacit knowledge creates imperfections and contractual uncertainty, the monitoring argument in transactive economics does not take into account knowledge as a binding factor among the agents. Also, change creates coordination problems (Hayek, 1945). Due to the role of knowledge in networked relations, we posit that the retail industry is partly an evolving social system featuring a complex set of relationships based on solidarity, open dialogues and knowledge creation. Tacit knowledge forces the dominant company to take a cautious role when exercising power, as domination decreases open knowledge exchange.

In summary, franchising companies are subject to context-free economic efficiency and context-specific creativity. In the light of the franchising and retailing research, managers are facing an apparent paradox because an overemphasis on the efficiency has a detrimental impact on creativity, and vice versa. Instead of choosing between these mutually exclusive theoretical alternatives, franchisers need to synthesize various dualities in order to create a sustainable competitive advantage. As every manager faces these kinds of paradoxes in everyday organizational action, management theorists should create holistic frameworks that take into account contextually embedded actors. The epistemology and ontology of the knowledge-based theory creates a synthesis between objectivity and subjectivity, efficiency and creativity, explicit and tacit knowledge, and forms and context (Nonaka, 1991, 1994; Nonaka and Takeuchi, 1995). Instead of dissecting the franchising relationships into small, objective entities, we claim that the supporting components and dialectic ability to change through knowledge conversion explains the differences between franchising companies.

Basic components of knowledge creation

In the networked arrangements, franchisers possessing superior resources create a web of mechanisms enabling all participants to create value. Cooperation is facilitated by transparency and conferring access to complementary knowledge resources. Symbiotic relationships lead to a sense of identity, implicit roles and shared destiny regardless of a member's apparent strength, because all networked entities need each other to generate rents and survive. The action and coherence in interconnected relationships within and beyond a firm's boundaries can be described through the dynamic interactions of knowledge vision, driving objectives, dialogues and creative practices (Figure 19.1).

Knowledge vision, determining a firm's ideal mission and domain, is rooted in the essential question of 'for what purpose does a company exist?'. As knowledge and truth

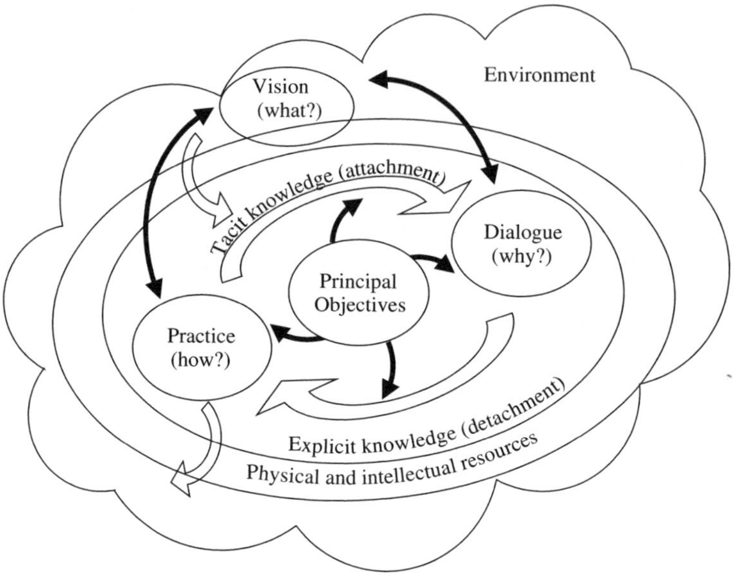

Figure 19.1 Basic mechanisms of the knowledge-based firm

are context dependent, their purpose is to increase reflection and intentionality by freeing agents from the restricting influence of the utilitarian 'I and Other' dichotomy. Instead of living the world of Pareto optimality, the most important dimension of temporality is future because it presents the existential 'potentiality-for-Being' (Heidegger, 1962). The shared future among intertwined entities forms a nexus with the diverse past in the present meaning creation. Thus knowledge vision provides an idealistic goal and benefits to all participants. As organizations exist for different purposes, it is possible to detect large differences among companies due to the level of environmental turbulence and the amount of networked relationships needed for sustainable value creation. For example, the environmental reality of sawmills deviates largely from that of software companies. The rules of the game are influenced by the legal system, government regulations, customer preferences, nature of competition and so on. As a consequence, their knowledge vision and way of competing is bound to be different.

Driving objectives generally appear as practical concepts, numbers and collective discipline. They make it possible to measure the knowledge vision, and energize the interaction between dialogues and creative routines in a dynamic coherence. Acting as a bridge between the structure and context, driving objectives provide guidance for agents on how to conduct business activities in the constantly evolving world. They motivate employees by providing explicit, mid-ranged goals for action linked to incentives. In franchising systems, a franchiser creates and provides a platform of services, tools, manuals and technologies that other entities in the system can use to enhance store performance, as well as to generate profits to the franchiser through ongoing royalties. In fact, franchiser companies in most convenience stores share their franchisees' and suppliers' information and knowledge on customer demand and preferences through information systems and human interaction. In return, stores provide franchiser information and knowledge from the customer interface. This symbiotic information and knowledge exchange provides valuc to customers and enables economic entities to generate profits. In a simplified way, driving objectives have a motivational impact as they increase the feeling of responsibility towards a common organizational goal.

Dialogues (dialectic in thought) enhance co-understanding by linking various actors within and beyond the organizational boundaries (Nonaka et al., 2005). As a process in which deeply held beliefs and assumptions surface (Bohm, 1990), dialogues link rationality/idealism and organization/environment through the dialectic of knowledge and language. Organizations use dialogues to increase collective understanding, knowledge dissemination and diversity, and trust/satisfaction. First, open meaning flow provides a shared space to reflect the functioning of feelings, beliefs, ideas and thought. Social life and organizational reality is never static, and idea exchange through dialogue challenges the status quo and increases reflection. The constant challenging of existing paradigms is essential because the dominant logic filters out ideas and behaviors (Prahalad and Bettis, 1986). Dialogues managed by third persons potentially evolve into trialogues, or dialectics of harmony. Second, dialogues enable the dispersal of knowledge in networks. As management in franchising relationships is often problematic due to different opinions between franchisers and franchisees, dialogues serve to increase transparency among them. Recent research shows that communication is important in reinforcing franchisees' trust and overall satisfaction with the franchise system (Chiou et al., 2004).

Creative routines (dialectic in action) enable human actors to reflect the acquired tacit knowledge and skills based on self-transcending action. A part of action is tacit, creative routines that deviate from organizational routines as the collective capacity to perform recognizable patterns of action (Nelson and Winter, 1982). The concept of creative routines can be equated more with the Japanese practice of *kata*, the ideal style of action and practice composed of the continuous cycle of learning (*shu*) $\Rightarrow$ breaking (*ha*) $\Rightarrow$ creating (*ri*). The dialectic cycles apply, for example, to learning, production, product development, quality control, customer interaction and technology transfer. The ideal form is achieved either by the dialectic of action and reflection through practical involvement, and/or by temporal suspension in action. That is, while some scholars argue that people are able to reflect their doings in the midst of action (Heidegger, 1962; Shön, 1983), others claim that reflexivity occurs after action (Polanyi, 1952). Reflexivity in action is asserted to paralyze action (Polanyi, 1952); action, therefore, is possible to the extent that the actor remains a being in the world, unaware of what makes action possible (Heidegger, 1962). Albeit part of action is always tacit, employees are capable of bringing part of the action-related tacit knowledge to the surface. This implies that humans might be able to know in two ways: one based on experience, the other based on the exercise of reason (Spender, 1996).

Dialectics of subjectivity and objectivity in the SECI (socialization, externalization, combination and internalization) process

As knowledge creation is defined as justifying towards truth (Nonaka, 1994), the focus in this chapter is on the 'justified' rather than the 'true' aspect, because knowledge is relational, dynamic and pluralistic. Indeed, as Alfred North Whitehead stated: 'There are no whole truths; all truths are half-truths' (Price, 1954: 16) Knowledge contains a tacit dimension that is personal, hard to externalize and context specific (Polanyi, 1952), and an explicit dimension that can be expressed, codified and transferred with relative ease.

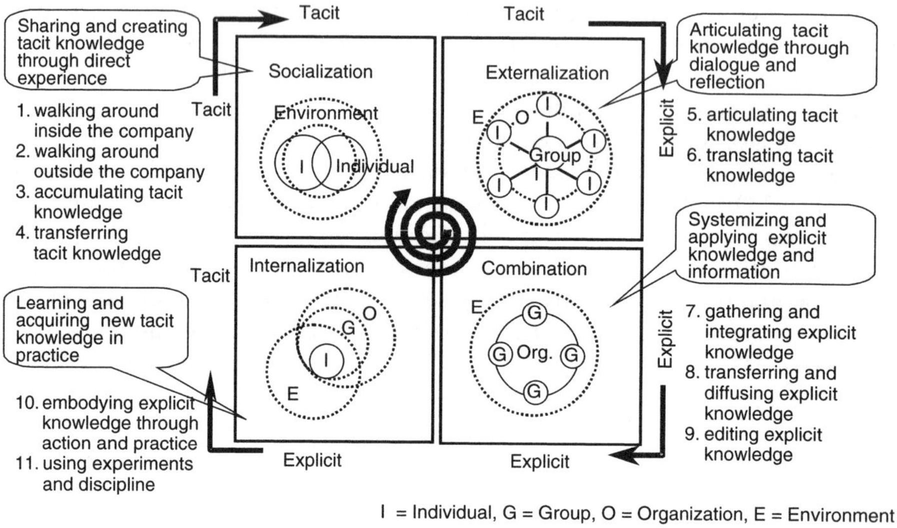

Figure 19.2 SECI model

Tacit knowledge is not only more extensive than explicit knowledge; it has priority over explicit knowledge as well. The two interrelated types of knowledge promote the SECI process (Nonaka, 1991, 1994) (Figure 19.2).

In the socialization phase, tacit knowledge is accumulated through direct and shared experiences. In each environment-related event, individuals create meanings through self-negation, in which feelings play a prominent role (Husserl, 1931; Nishida, 1970). The environment-derived tacit knowledge is raw material and stimuli-enabling knowledge creation, because human thought can be conceptualized either as a process taking place in the private world of the mind, or as a direct reflection of the world realities (Lackoff and Johnson, 1999). By balancing between the inner and outer world, decision makers are able to develop hypotheses to increase the fit between market needs and introduced products and services. The knowledge-creating action, therefore, entails a particular type of human behavior that involves conscious and purposeful departures from being a structurally conditioned passive agent.

The acquired personal knowledge is not much use unless it is externalized through metaphors and dialogues in social space. This phase corresponds to dialogues or dialectic in thought. Exposure of diverse points of view is essential, as every step in innovation is about someone asking about imaginary possibilities, speculating about what would happen if, and reflecting on yet-realized and perhaps unrealizable solutions (Rescher, 2003). A sequential use of the methods of abduction and retroduction is effective to systematize the process in order to externalize deeper layers of personal knowledge (Lawson, 1997). The methods further enable individuals to synthesize the contradictions between one's tacit knowledge and the structure, or contradictions among the tacit knowledge of individuals (Nonaka and Toyama, 2003).

The externalized knowledge combined, systematized and presented in explicit form, can be verified with complementary knowledge within and beyond the firms' boundaries.

Franchisers, for example, translate experience gathered from the customer interface, various meetings and other forms of social interaction, into explicit, shared understanding in manuals, models and systems. The process can be facilitated through the creative use of computerized networks and large-scale databases. It should be noted that knowledge is different from data because knowledge is grounded in values and purposeful action. Knowledge creation, therefore, does not equate setting up computer databases, as new knowledge emerges only through human interaction. From a pragmatic standpoint, the validation process decreases chances for utilization of faulty knowledge.

Organizations help actors to internalize new explicit knowledge through training, reflective practice, simulation and social interaction. The internalization mode describes how the created knowledge becomes a base for new practices, routines and tacit knowledge. This phase corresponds to creative routines or dialectic in action. The created concepts and products, as the end product of knowledge creation, drive profits and shareholder value through profitable growth. The process further enables organizations to accumulate physical and intellectual resources. As a consequence, human intention and a new praxis provide the basis for new, consequent spirals of dialectic knowledge creation, expanding horizontally and vertically as it moves through communities of interaction that transcend sectional, departmental, divisional and even organizational boundaries.

The SECI model is a spiral-like, upward movement of incremental and radical innovations. It takes place due to the ontological differences between human agents and structures, tacit and explicit knowledge, micro and macro, and so on. The prominence of tacit knowledge during the early phases of knowledge creation emphasizes the role of creativity, and the role of explicit knowledge during the latter phases emphasizes the importance of efficiency. In the networked arrangement, knowledge creation can be based on complementary resources. Sorenson and Sorensen (2001) have found that there is a distribution of innovation in franchising networks. The franchisee is more focused on radical innovations, and the franchiser is more focused on incremental innovations due to differentiated roles and resources.

The case of Seven-Eleven Japan[1]

SEJ celebrated the 30th anniversary of its establishment in 2003. The history of the company starts in 1973, when the Southland Corporation (USA) licensed Ito-Yokado Co., Ltd the rights to develop the Seven-Eleven concept and name in Japan. The subsidiary, York-Seven Co., Ltd changed its name to Seven-Eleven Japan Co., Ltd ('SEJ') in 1978. The convenience store concept was an instant success and experienced tremendous growth. Since opening the first store in Tokyo in 1978 and being publicly listed five years later, SEJ has been one of the most profitable companies in Japan. It is currently larger than its parent company Ito-Yokado. Chairman and CEO of SEJ Toshifumi Suzuki is known as the father of the convenience store industry in Japan. He opened the first store, led the drive to computerize operations, and pushed his way to the top of SEJ and Ito-Yokado. The relentless knowledge creation enabled SEJ to reciprocate by buying out the Southland Corporation from bankruptcy in 1991.

SEJ is the leading Japanese convenience store chain with the largest store network and the highest net income. It holds a 31.5 per cent share in sales and 21.7 per cent in the number of stores. SEJ's sales profit ratio exceeded 36 per cent in 2003, while its main competitors, Lawson and Family Mart, showed about 14 and 13 per cent, respectively. The number of outlets passed 10,000 on August 31, 2003, making this the first case of a retailer possessing such a large number of stores within a single country anywhere in the world. The number of stores in Japan is currently 10,303 (February 29, 2004). All member stores, except those under direct management of headquarters, are currently franchise stores run by self-employed managers. SEJ has an overall network of 25,796 stores in 18 countries around the world (December 31, 2003). Total store sales were 2,213,298 million yen, and the operating revenue was 400,664 million yen in fiscal 2003. Average daily sales per store was 656,000 yen, about 100,000 yen more than at other convenience store chains.

SEJ has remained innovative throughout the years by relentlessly seeking to cater to the dynamically evolving customer needs. Business operations change to reflect the constantly evolving environmental reality, because customers are placed at the heart of the corporate philosophy. This forms a dialectic pattern in which employees focus on hypothesizing the ever-changing customer needs, taking action to satisfy them, accessing its success, and then repeating the process. This role is not limited to top management because all employees are encouraged to reflect the practices and tackle new challenges from the customer's point of view. The corporate tenets of 'Modernizing and Revitalizing Small- and Medium-Sized Retail Stores' and 'Coexistence and Co-Prosperity with our Franchisees' further indicate that the product and service innovations are based on networked co-creation. In particular, the extra franchising networks are essential to introduce premium-quality products and to develop production, distribution and marketing systems. The co-prosperity with franchisees and various external partners is based on the interlinking dynamisms of knowledge vision, driving objectives, dialogues and creative routines.

Knowledge vision

The knowledge vision of SEJ is to predict and respond rapidly to the constantly changing customer needs. According to CEO Suzuki, 'our competitors are not other stores but our customers' needs and wants'. The vision is based on absolute value because the company competes solely to satisfy customer needs and wants rather than based on relative market positioning. The future-oriented and context-specific nature of knowledge vision is captured in the two statements of 'adaptation to change' and 'pursuit of fundamentals' as well as CEO Suzuki's simplistic question: 'what does the customer want?'. The future orientation is crucial because past practices need to be challenged, broken and recreated in order to move flexibly to new directions. And the operational context specificity indicates that successful convenience store operations require context sensitivity. This is because CEO Suzuki claims that there is no universal franchising management model. The business operations, since the establishment of the first store, have been geared to meet the changing demand of Japanese society. Each convenience store consequently seeks to reflect and satisfy the specific needs of various local regions in Japan. The only Southland Corporation legacies in the present operations are the logo and some parts of the accounting system.

SEJ is doing business for the future and constantly challenges its employees to reflect how the present operations should be arranged. The answers for future-oriented challenges cannot be found from past successes. Imitation and market positioning, according to CEO Suzuki, are merely processes of the extending past. The dominance of the past successes may impose a paradox of unwanted plenty in the present operations. That occurs when consumers have difficulty in finding what they want even as there is an increasing amount of products available. The imitation and overextending of past successes, therefore, may create a situation in which the offered products/services are not aligned with the emerging customer needs. The result is a downward spiral because the wrong products in shelves decrease customer loyalty and profits, and frequently promote even more frantic imitation. There is, consequently, a clear trend in the convenience store industry that the best-selling products and services are those that offer unique features. Those products and services can only be developed based on embracing and systematizing tacit knowledge from customer interface. The knowledge vision challenges conventional competitive logic because strategic positioning *vis-à-vis* major competitors and imitation are doomed to fail in a dynamic environment with increasingly fast product life cycles. Convenience store chains, according to CEO Suzuki, are successful only by denying the past and constantly reflecting the future to find fundamental solutions.

Most companies are past-oriented because extension of past routines creates stability and continuity. SEJ, in contrast, embraces changes and constant development. As nobody can perfectly predict the future, the focus in knowledge vision on the emergent future in business operations creates a sense of emergency and creative chaos. The operations are developed to an extreme by a collective determination to challenge existing practices and work harder in a relentless attempt to predict and satisfy the ever-changing customer needs. This makes SEJ's convenience store chain an organic system in which all parts reflect the knowledge vision. The networked system is designed and managed to respond to environmental changes quickly to reduce lost sales opportunities. In the dialectic change process, tacit knowledge gained in the customer interface is used as a raw material enabling SEJ to miss fewer emergent opportunities in comparison to the other convenience store chains. SEJ operations, therefore, are created, evaluated, and re-created at the state of creative chaos in which tacit knowledge is shared, processed and systematized in new products and services. Instead of being overly concerned about rival convenience store chains, the biggest concern for SEJ is a decreased ability to respond to the changing customer needs. It can be claimed that the organic system has been highly efficient because SEJ was the first convenience store chain to offer payment acceptance, parcel reception, self-service copying, ticket sales services and meal delivery.

Driving objectives

The driving objective at SEJ is the reduction of lost opportunities through the constant 'hypotheses development and testing' spiral. In a simplistic way, the lost opportunities can be explained as a temporal inability to provide the needed products/services at the right place/time. On the contrary, hypotheses promoting the detection of emerging opportunities enable convenience stores to co-evolve with the changing customer needs. The most important long-term impacts in convenience store operations are the realized opportunities in product and service development, which can range from 100 yen rice balls to the networked establishment of capital-intensive banking services. Due to the environment-reflective driving objectives, the new products and diversification of services reflect customer needs and are readily accepted in the markets. The driving objectives, therefore, explain part of the high profitability and the steady introduction of innovative products/services over the years. This is because the fundamentals for business operations remain the same despite the increasingly harsh retailing environment in Japan.

The driving objectives provide a collective discipline in the convenience store network, because all employees participate to develop business operations through a constant spiral of subjective hypotheses development and their objective testing based on accumulated data. At the shop floor, the process takes place by creating hypotheses in product ordering about the emerging customer demand in a specific local context. In the overall operations, an emphasis is placed on the emerging insights from the lower echelons. According to CEO Suzuki, product ordering is the most important part of the convenience store business because it is based on embracing environmental tacit knowledge. Managers at the upper echelons consequently form hypotheses to develop future operations based on the accumulated data from the stores and subjective insights. Hypotheses are further developed with manufacturers and venders through team merchandizing to create original products. The success of the original products is consequently tested in the convenience stores. This creates a spiral in which the environmental knowledge is processed to create new products/services, which have a changing impact on the environment.

The driving objectives increase individual/collective reflection and knowledge sharing in all parts of the convenience store chain. Employees stay focused and motivated because a great deal of their daily action is based on reflective hypotheses creation and constant questioning of the current practices. It can be claimed to be one contributing reason why SEJ has been able to maintain its highly entrepreneurial climate for the last 30 years. Great imagination on the part of the employees is needed because opportunity losses are difficult to measure quantitatively. They are buried in the psychology and consumer action. This requirement for creativity and intentionality transcends the traditional role and responsibility for part-time employees in convenience stores. Instead of following blindly the orders from manuals, employees are encouraged to think and act based on their subjective insights. The driving objectives further increase shared understanding that the success of future operations is based on dynamic response to changes and relentless pursuit of fundamentals. Despite the increased role of information technology in the convenience store industry, SEJ operations are largely based on the power of human insights and attempt to move to the essence of the prevailing problems in daily activities.

Dialogues

SEJ has put considerable effort into establishing various venues to synthesize diverse subjective views into dynamic coherence. In addition to normal daily interaction, several weekly meetings are held at the headquarters. The sharing of dispersed tacit knowledge from all parts of the franchising network enables the company to modify all operational components to reflect the environmental reality. In addition to a dynamic synthesis of the bottom-up knowledge flows, the meetings enable the top-down flow of information in terms of reinforced knowledge vision and need for constant changes. The amalgam of the 'bottom-up' and the 'top-down' realities linked by operation field counselors (OFCs) enables them to find answers to emerging problems and being caught off-guard by unanticipated environmental occurrences. The collective desire to fulfill customer needs and wants is the basis for dialogues that are connected to real phenomena occurring at customer interface.

Headquarters meetings

SEJ is the only company in Japan that systematically holds weekly meetings with more than 1000 people from all over the country. The most important vehicle of meaning creation is the field counselor meeting every Tuesday at the Tokyo headquarters. The meeting involves OFCs, recruiting field counselors, district managers (OFCs' superiors), zone managers (district managers' superiors), several merchandisers, systems development personnel, and head office executives. In the meetings, retailers and SEJ employees share tacit knowledge to find new ways to provide services. CEO Suzuki participates in the meetings and directly communicates management policies, marketing research findings and prevailing management problems. Reflecting the knowledge vision, he addresses the question of 'what does the customer want?' in every meeting. The direct exposure to various networked agents in shared space and time enables the participants to share their opinions through dialogues and later disseminate the emerging reality throughout the franchising network.

The knowledge sharing is a two-way process as SEJ seeks to objectify part of the emerging subjective knowledge. The information systems development personnel attend the OFC meetings to discuss practical problems and ways to develop the information system. The new ideas and expressed concerns of how to systematize customer needs act as the basis and raw material for systems development. The former head of the SEJ Information Systems Department, Mr Usui, stated that his job was 'to provide solutions to the problems that arise at the convenience store rather than the development of the system itself'. In other words, systems development is conducted according to the knowledge vision through a continuous cycle of subjective attachment and objective detachment to solve practical problems in stores, link the company to manufacturers and suppliers, and aid decision making at various corporate levels. The various components in the information system act as a concrete linkage between the shop-floor reality and objective decision-making tools at the headquarters. When information systems-related issues arise in the meeting, priority is given to quick problem solving. The information system, therefore, develops organically as it is challenged every week. The meetings enable it to closely follow the emerging reality in the convenience stores.

Managers have group meetings every Monday. In the morning they review the performance of the stores for the previous week, and develop strategies in the afternoon. The participants are prepared with the statistical and digital data and ready to make presentations about their field of responsibility. While the data show only the objectified view of the present reality, managers seek to anticipate future trends by reflecting their subjective knowledge through metaphors based on the presentation data. An emphasis in these meetings is placed on reflexivity through objective detachment. It is interesting to note that CEO Suzuki does not visit stores because 'my view will be clouded once I am there'. Important for him as CEO is to penetrate to the essence in order to understand the underlying mechanisms among the various interrelated contexts. Great importance is placed on implementation speed in the meetings. For example, he expects the managers facing problems to leave the meeting so that they can solve those problems immediately, and then return to report on the actions as well as the early results of those actions. The constant 'problem identification ⇒ action ⇒ inspection' cycle enables the franchising network to avoid being blinded by past success and co-evolve with changing customer needs. The conclusions of the meeting are debriefed to OFCs on Tuesday.

While these systematic processes of knowledge exchange and creation reinforce the dynamic coherence of corporate vision, driving objectives, dialogues and creative routines, the gathering of large amounts of people every week in meetings is costly. It has been estimated that SEJ spends more than 18 million dollars annually on traveling, lodging and other related costs. Indirect costs are further present as the employees are prevented from working during the meetings. This is especially the case for field counselors from peripheral areas. The importance of meetings to the franchising network cannot be explained by simplistic economic rationale. The meetings enable dialogues in shared time–space in which a dynamic coherence with the environment is created. A failure to understand and evolve with the changing environment initiates lost opportunities in terms of service/product quality and eventually profits. This focus on emerging human insights differentiates SEJ from other Japanese convenience store chains.

Creative routines

The creative routines at SEJ are created to enforce reflection in action. New employees in convenience stores and headquarters are encouraged to think from the consumers' point of view during the uniform training period. Reflection in the day-to-day process is encouraged during frequent OFC visits. This is because new opportunities are embedded in face-to-face customer interaction. The consequent hypothesis creation is efficient in reflecting the experiences based on abduction and retroduction. The process is systematized by a state-of-the-art information system, which creates a dialectic interaction between the subjective insights and objective verification through the accumulated hypotheses data. Accurately formed hypotheses enable the company to reduce lost opportunities because the customers find the needed products at nearby stores at the right time.

Training

SEJ provides systematic training to ensure that all employees internalize the importance of environmental tacit knowledge in hypotheses creation. The franchisee training process consequently emphasizes practical knowledge accumulated on the shop floor. New franchisees are first trained at the central training center for a month, after which they go through a two-month on-the-job (OTJ) training period in a regular store. The training methods encourage franchisees to think constantly about offered services from the customers' perspective. An emphasis is further placed on the externalization of ideas to find ways to improve service and product quality. The knowledge vision of putting the customers first initiates dialectics between action and reflection, as trainees continuously monitor the changing customer needs by constant questioning and incremental improvements in daily practices.

In addition to management training, all part-time employees are trained in practical skills through observation, guidance and practice in each store. An important part of part-time workers' OTJ is product ordering through a POS (point of sales) information system that ties dialogues, practice and knowledge vision to driving objectives. In the training, employees are encouraged to place orders, thinking first from the perspective of an average customer, second from an average family, and finally from the perspective of close friends. SEJ acknowledges that the reality emerges at the shop floor and seeks to motivate employees by challenges and increasing responsibilities. Store managers are consequently encouraged to let part-time workers take on demanding work tasks and create hypotheses of emerging customer needs because, according to CEO Suzuki, 'Responsibility makes work enjoyable and increases independent thinking'. Individual responsibility is important because all dimensions of store operations cannot be captured in explicit form, and the success of franchising operations depends on constant knowledge flows from the customer interface.

SEJ seeks to reduce boundaries between the headquarters employees and franchisees. In order to acquire tacit knowledge in close customer interaction, the career of all new employees at SEJ is started with extensive OTJ in Seven-Eleven stores. As a part of systematic job rotation, new employees are required first to work at stores in various functions for about two years in order to accumulate experience in dealing directly with customers and managing stores. For this purpose, some stores are run directly by the headquarters. This experience-based tacit knowledge provides the basis for decision making at all organizational echelons. Some of these employees later become OFCs, acting as an important knowledge link between the headquarters and stores.

One unique instrument of SEJ for accumulating and disseminating tacit knowledge at the shop floor and throughout the organization is *burabura shain* ('walking around employees'), whose task is to wander around in the stores and socialize with customers. These young employees working in the Product Planning Department make it possible to bring in new insights, especially from young customers' points of view. The knowledge accumulated by the *burabura shain* is converted to explicit form in company reports.

Operation field counselors

SEJ has about 300 OFCs to give store managers advice on store planning, hypotheses creation, information systems and so on. Each OFC is responsible for seven to eight stores and visits each store twice a week for two to three hours. During the store visits, they share knowledge about new products, and give practical advice to prevent fast-selling products from selling out and to remove slow-selling products. The core of store operations is based on the principles of product assortment, quality, service, cleanliness and value. The close social interaction processes enable OFCs to absorb tacit knowledge about customer preferences in a specific time and context. Moreover, the frequent OFC visits to the headquarters and convenience stores enables the franchising system to detect environmental changes. If an OFC notices an innovative idea in any single store, he/she can quickly disseminate it to other stores and zone managers to whom OFCs report directly. The zone managers, in turn, transfer knowledge to other OFCs, management at the headquarters, and so on through meetings and other face-to-face interactions. As a consequence, OFCs link the bottom-up reality with the top-down reality through intensive social interaction.

Information system

In order to accommodate the rapidly changing customer preferences, SEJ has reformed its information system five times. At a development cost of 60 billion yen, the current, fifth-generation system was introduced in 1999. The current system is the world's largest, connecting convenience stores, distribution centers, manufacturers, headquarters, OFCs and district offices as integrated information networks through satellite telecommunications and an integrated digital network. Convenience stores are provided with multimedia information, such as moving and still pictures, audio, text and numerical data. The information system allows employees to check the latest product information, weather and events, the company's current television commercials and product display methods. SEJ provides information about past order entries, sales records, sold-out stocks, sales trends and new products. Moreover, the information system enables each store to create a database of sales performance figures, and to use voice and handwritten memos for intra-store communication.

In hypotheses creation, the information system creates a link between subjective intuitions and systematized accumulated knowledge at the shop floor. The system maintains past order entry and sales records used when placing order entries. In the system, employees determine order entry volumes based on a hypothesis that he/she formulated. The hypotheses are developed by embracing environmental knowledge (for example, customer interaction, observations and media information) and computerized information (for example, sales records). When placing orders, employees draw partly on their tacit knowledge to hypothesize, for example, that the consumption of beer and fast food will increase tomorrow due to a local festival. The information about local events is often gained through customer interaction. In order to increase the accuracy of the developed hypothesis, employees can check consumption patterns related to previous local festivals before placing an order. As the order is placed, the sales data verify whether the hypothesis was accurate and uses this information for the next order entry. This method is called 'hypothesis and checking' because stores accumulate data based on the dialectics of generated hypotheses and POS data. As the headquarters decides the order entry volume, the responsibility of poorly selling items is shifted to SEJ.

SEJ accumulates data based on created hypotheses and customer transactions. Employees enter into the POS system the purchased items, the time of the purchase (every two hours), the type of customer, and the place where the item was displayed. These four headings give access to 13 pieces of data, such as gender, age and so on. The item-by-item control is considered to be the key point among the four important criteria. The data is collected and analyzed at headquarters three times a day in roughly 20 minutes. The system network allows access to data from every store, district and zone for more detailed analysis. Given the number of customer visits to stores, SEJ analyzed about 9.8 million people's POS data daily in 2003 (about 7 per cent of the Japanese population). The data warehouse accumulates more than one year's worth of sales data per item and supports refined objective analysis for sales forecasting. The detailed information on how many goods were sold to what kind of customers is accumulated and used in future product development.

In addition to constantly accumulating POS data, SEJ collects information on trends (consumer behavior, lifestyles and habits, business trends and so on), market movements (corporate strategies, product life cycles and so on), regional differences (population changes, school events and so on), and weather forecasts. The information is sent in reports through ISDN (Integrated Services Digital Network) to the stores. An interesting detail is weather information that stores used to collect individually and analyze its effect on consumption patterns. The process was systematized in 1996 when SEJ formed a partnership to create an information network that provided regional weather forecasts. Every day, five reports arrive electronically from hundreds of weather centers, each covering a radius of 20 kilometers. This is useful in Japan, where temperatures between towns 40 kilometers apart can vary as much as 5 degrees Celsius. The information system further allows the comparison of daily temperatures. According to Mr Usui, 'the change of 10 Celsius degrees can feel very different depending on whether it was one degree Celsius or 10 degrees Celsius yesterday'. The impact of weather on consumer behavior is taken into account when making hypotheses during product ordering.

Ba and external networks
SEJ cooperates with various external partners on temporary and semi-permanent bases to introduce new products/services as well as to increase operational efficiency. The nature of external cooperation reflects the allocated resources and the kind of task. While the combination of diverse knowledge resources in temporary team merchandizing projects enables the steady introduction of original products, strong and relatively stable relationships are made for the incremental operational improvements. The former relationships are efficient in utilizing diverse knowledge, and the latter in making incremental process improvements. SEJ is efficient at creating a shared context in which diverse knowledge of venders and manufacturing companies is synthesized. It has also taken into account the contextual need for stability and long-term commitment in the distribution system development and capital-intensive arrangements. Both types of collaborative arrangements are based on open exchange and combination of tacit knowledge because they provide benefits to all involved parties. Knowledge exchange is further possible because the knowledge bases tend to remain differentiated.

Team merchandizing SEJ cooperates with venders and manufacturing companies through team merchandizing to create and introduce original products. The systematic knowledge creation is crucial because original products constitute an increasing share of total sales. At SEJ, net sales of original products accounted for about 50 per cent of total sales in 2003. They make a substantial contribution in the gross profit margin because original items have higher gross margins than regular merchandise. The tie-ups are based on win–win relationships, as team merchandizing provides manufacturers with comprehensive, nationwide exposure and knowledge about the market changes. Manufacturers are not responsible for unsold items because SEJ is required to purchase exclusively produced merchandise.

Knowledge creation through team merchandising is a systematized process as about 100 new items are introduced to the market every week. The process starts with determining the market needs and deciding what type of product to introduce. The company identifies market need for new products based on POS data, surveys and tacit knowledge from customer interface. The creative combination of data and subjective, tacit knowledge enables SEJ occasionally to break conventional assumptions. For example, in contrast to the conventional assumption that ice cream is a seasonal product, creative interpretation of POS data revealed that high-priced ice cream sells well throughout the year. SEJ was also the first convenience store chain to develop oven-fresh bread, due to a perceived difference in what consumers were looking for and what national brand bread makers were offering. In most cases the product development process is initiated by a perceived mismatch between offered products and customers' emerging needs.

SEJ simultaneously approaches several manufacturers with new product ideas and seeks their initial feedback on the feasibility and production costs. Manufacturers outline costs in a product sheet by breaking down components to the raw materials. Just as CEO Suzuki acknowledges that value is the most important element to attract customers, manufacturers emphasize the importance of product quality. The cooperation is conducted mostly with large manufacturers because Japanese customers prefer well-established national brands with good reputations. In order to develop the previously mentioned original premium ice cream, SEJ approached five major manufacturers.

Morinaga Milk, Morinaga and Akagi Milk decided to jointly embark on the product development process. The ice cream was a success, selling two to six times more than existing products. In developing the oven-fresh bread, SEJ collaborated with such major food processors as Ajinomoto Co., Inc. (which supplies frozen dough), Itochu Corporation (a general trading company in charge of procuring ingredients and building a nationwide system), and local bread bakeries (which have bread-baking plants near stores). The product played an important role in differentiating Seven-Eleven stores from competitors in the bread market. The ice-cream and bread projects indicate how important it is for franchisers to link various actors with distinctive knowledge in *ba* to create innovative products.

Team merchandizing requires open knowledge fertilization, because only the combination of diverse knowledge leads to superior products. SEJ starts the process by sharing POS data with manufacturers and wholesalers in order to create a clear understanding of the target customer segment for the new products. The responsible product development team at SEJ selects trial products, which are tested for appearance and taste. The most important phase of knowledge sharing takes place at the consequent meetings in which all members share ideas for further improvements. Manufacturers frequently share sample products, recipes and various related know-how to create products to meet market demand. The fine-tuning and product development requires several meetings before a product is ready for final approval. For example, it took one and a half years to develop the right taste for the recently popular fried rice. Production starts after final approval at the officers' meeting. As original products are accounting for an increasing share of sales, SEJ is seeking to further systematize the process by creating 'dream teams' with wide knowledge diversity. The latest noodle project tied in five well-known noodle manufacturers with three soup makers, five content makers, two package makers and six noodle restaurants.

SEJ has also intensified cooperation with non-food producers to attract customers and to differentiate products. For example, SEJ jointly produced with Asahi Soft Drinks Co. a drink called *Tocho Oolongcha* (Oolong Tea) that was initially sold exclusively at Seven-Eleven outlets. Moreover, a new organic beer called *Maroyaka Kobo*, developed with Kirin Brewery Co., became highly successful nationwide. The accelerated introduction of original products requires some innovative solutions due to the limited store space. On average, 190 different drinks are offered in each convenience store with an average area of 100 square meters. Due to the recent regulatory changes, an increasing number of stores sell alcoholic beverages. The large number of drinks prompted the company to install display cases that could be used for either hot or cold items with the flip of a switch. As a consequence, the company was able to introduce about 20 new hot drinks during the winter. Distribution of the *Maroyaka Kobo* beer, which contains live yeast, was made possible by the temperature-controlled distribution chain. SEJ also cooperates internationally with companies such as Wal-Mart, Benetton and Playboy.

Distribution system development Instead of building its own distribution centers, SEJ has established cooperative arrangements with various external partners. As the cooperation links manufacturers and suppliers, the company was early to eliminate wholesalers, or middlemen, who have long symbolized the inefficiency of the Japanese distribution industry. In order to accommodate the dilemma of the increased number of products and limited floor space, SEJ has gone through a series of distribution system innovations to create greater value and satisfaction for the customers. The innovations have enabled SEJ to decrease daily deliveries from 70 in 1970, to 10 in 1998. The average stock turnover time per store was nine days in 2003.

The distribution management is integrated into the information system that connects stores through headquarters to manufacturers and distribution centers. Convenience stores are connected by an online system to almost 300 temperature-separated distribution centers nationwide. The distribution centers are located within easy reach of the stores to allow the arranging of convenient, efficient delivery routes. Distribution centers are connected to almost 300 daily production plants that prepare products for distribution. The food distribution centers are divided based on specialized temperatures into centers for refrigerated items, rice-based items, frozen items, and items with ambient temperature, such as processed foods. High-rotating items, such as lunch boxes and rice balls, are delivered three times a day. The slow-moving items, such as frozen products, are delivered three to seven times per week. Books and magazines are delivered daily from separate distribution centers.

The distribution system's efficiency relies on the information system, knowledge sharing and continuous improvement among all involved parties. The core of the distribution system's improvement is frequent human interaction. In order to increase the efficiency, SEJ holds regular meetings with the heads of combined distribution centers. Moreover, distribution officers from the headquarters pay regular visits to the centers to address any distribution problems that may arise. The knowledge exchange and shared responsibilities make it possible to identify new areas for improvement at the distribution centers and in the supporting information system. The current information system in the integrated supply chain enables quick data processing. For example, orders sent in by 10 am for delivery after 4 pm can be processed electronically in less than seven minutes. In the case of just-in-time products, manufacturers receive the orders and deliver only the required amount to the distribution centers, which then sort for each store.

The distribution system links the entire supply chain for all categories of products. It can be seen as a centrally controlled system with extensive knowledge flows in both directions. Because the innovations reduced delivery time, SEJ was able to eliminate the use of food preservatives and artificial coloring in most fast-food items in 2002. Lawson has also recently banned the use of synthetic seasonings in about 160 processed food items, such as lunch boxes, buns and noodles. Moreover, there is no loss due to excess production and no need to carry large inventories due to the system integration. The distribution innovations can be seen as a reinforcing mechanism of the overall knowledge-creation process, as it allows the creation of new products and services in order to meet the knowledge vision.

Knowledge alliances SEJ has made joint arrangements and established affiliate companies with external business partners to diversify services. The organic expansion of business activities has been facilitated by the information system, regulatory changes, changing consumer preferences and a wide business network. Among the several other expansions in business activities, SEJ has proactively used its know-how and information system to move into electronic commerce. The movement is rational due to the combined customers' uncertainty about ordering goods through the internet, and SEJ's good reputation, large store network, long opening hours, information infrastructure and distribution network.

SEJ has further established itself as a payment point for online transactions, due to the relatively low diffusion of credit cards in Japan. Moreover, SEJ has recently agreed to run joint convenience store/gas station complexes with Exxon Mobil. The first outlets were opened during spring 2004 in Tokyo.

Among the new services, SEJ has been the most committed to e-commerce. In 2000, SEJ established a virtual shopping mall called 7dream in cooperation with several large companies, such as NEC, Nomura Research Institute and Sony. All partners came with distinctive competencies that were combined to create the new entity. For example, NEC contributed to the business with its cutting-edge, internet-related technology. The cooperation was facilitated by the large national presence of SEJ. As CEO Suzuki commented, 'With our large network of stores and distribution base, we are attracting powerful partners'. On the website, products are introduced in six categories: music; travel and leisure; general merchandise; internet products; automotive products; and photographs. The service currently offers over 100,000 items online. The service concept is simple: after placing orders on the Web, the products are delivered to customers or can be picked up at Seven-Eleven stores. Thus, the biggest problem in e-commerce, how to deliver goods bought on the net to customers and how to collect the money, could be solved by the store networks covering the country. Most orders are delivered to stores and processed at SEJ distribution centers.

Motivated by the relative insensitivity to customer demand by Japanese financial institutions, as well as regulatory changes of the financial industry in 1998, Ito-Yokado started to operate its IY Bank venture as the first non-traditional retail bank in 2001. The service linked the needs of the working urban population with SEJ's long operating hours. Automated teller machines (ATMs) in most banks at that time provided services until 5 pm. IY Bank operates solely through ATM terminals located at Seven-Eleven stores, having no other street presence. Since most convenience stores operate 24 hours a day, the ATMs were among the first to allow around-the-clock banking and payment for online services. The services include cash withdrawals, deposits and settlements with IY Bank and affiliated financial institutions. In 2003, 49 financial institutions were associated with IY Bank, which had completed the installation of ATMs at about 6000 stores in 14 prefectures.

The services, similar to original products, are introduced based on the systematic search to identify market needs through embracing customer tacit knowledge, monitoring regulatory changes, and contacting external partners for cooperation. The basis for the diversification, according to CEO Suzuki, is customer needs. However, overstretch of activities is avoided because the introduced services are related to or seek to complement the existing competencies. As Mr Kenichi Yamamoto from SEJ's information department commented, 'At present, these services fill a gap in our over-the-counter services'. It can be claimed that SEJ service innovations over the years have changed customer preferences because they no longer have to commute long distances or be concerned about opening hours. The product/service innovations and the evolutionary changes in consumer preferences, therefore, are dialectically interrelated, constituting constant changes in the the retail environment, for example, in terms of the increased amount of franchising networks in Japan.

Knowledge-creation components

The goal of SEJ is to be flexible with regard to change as well as commitment to its fundamental principle of responding to rapidly changing consumer needs. Headquarters and affiliated stores share the belief that competition arises not through the other companies or stores, but through the consumer and his/her needs and wants. Instead of following daily routines, all employees at SEJ are encouraged to have a future- and customer-oriented mindset. The existential nature of SEJ was shown in the recent advertising campaign by a question: 'what does number seven mean to you?'. The question was formulated by CEO Suzuki to encourage both customers and employees to reflect on the products and services in their neighborhood Seven-Eleven convenience store. Instead of co-evolving with the environment, the neglect of knowledge from customer interface makes many retail companies inward oriented. Only the future-oriented reflection of present activities enables one to utilize past experiences efficiently. That is, the desire to fulfill future consumer needs gives meaning to the past purchase patterns. This ontology gives rise to the detection of opportunities leading to an endless repetition of hypothesizing, execution and inspection in SEJ convenience stores. The process is utilized to some extent in interactions with external partners.

Conclusion

This chapter indicates that innovations and retail evolution are caused by the dialectic agent-environment and knowledge-creating interaction. Instead of describing the phenomena through the positivist cause-and-effect conjunctures, in which parts depend only on wholes, the phenomenology allows support to be given to the emerging nature of knowledge without denying its diachronic emergence from the environment. The knowledge-based view consequently seeks to avoid the naive positivist claims and foggy world of phenomenology in order to synthesize a 'middle path' for knowledge by combining skepticism and hope. In the retail industry, innovations are frequently introduced through networked linkages because knowledge transfer/conversion among diverse sets of entities speeds up the knowledge-creation processes. This factor allows the conceptualization of retail chains partly as social exchange systems with distinctive rules, trust and knowledge-transfer/creation practices. The distinctive mechanisms are evolutionary, reflecting environmental changes and the fluid nature of knowledge.

Dialectic knowledge creation was explained in the case of Seven-Eleven Japan. SEJ is a company that dynamically interlocks dialogue and practice with 'opportunity loss' as the driving objective. Moreover, mutual interactions with the environment seem to be taking place at differing phases between practice and dialogue such as incorporating tacit knowledge embedded in the environment through practice (integration of subject and object) and transcending this tacit knowledge by thorough conceptualization of dialogue (separation of subject and object). This knowledge creation is the everyday way of being at SEJ as employees at the shop floor create hypotheses of consumer behavior, managers change emerging ideas of new products and services, and manufacturers cross-fertilize knowledge through team merchandizing. The ontology of SEJ is future orientation because emerging customer needs drive the operations. The constant focus on customer interface enables employees to utilize the past experiences in the present reality. The epistemology of SEJ takes place through the objectification of subjective insights by hypotheses testing. The process creates a dialectic linkage between humans and machines as store inventory management innovations facilitate employees' order data input, order data transfer and data analysis to accomplish streamlined, just-in-time inventory.

The case study in this chapter is a descriptive and context-specific illustration of how one successful convenience store chain has innovated over time in co-evolution with its environment. Our purpose is not to provide a normative model of evolutionary change, as predicting innovative events in organizations is seldom possible. As SEJ is a distinctive company with evolutionary practices, implication of its processes in a different context will most probably initiate different outcomes. This is because copying a part of leading firms' superior processes of complex systems does not always bring expected results. It can, though, be asserted that all companies create knowledge through dialectic identification, processing and developing processes towards more inclusive totalities. It can be further assumed that knowledge-creating action is founded on the mechanisms of knowledge vision, dialogues and creative practices, as well as on the SECI process. In order to identify the specific mechanisms and differences between companies, future research could be conducted using longitudinal ethnography and case histories.

Note

1. The case is based on prolonged cooperation with SEJ. The interest in interviews over the years has been to identify the main internal and external linkages and organizational mechanisms that explain the innovative processes at SEJ. Most interviews and presentations by SEJ managers were recorded and fully transcribed. The information was supplemented and validated with internal documents.

PART V

SERVICE EMPLOYMENT: EMBODIED AND EMOTIONAL LABOUR

20 Embodied information, actor networks and global value-added services

Barney Warf

Introduction

The purpose of this chapter is to link analyses of globalized services, long dominated by empiricist and neoclassical economic understandings, to insights drawn from contemporary social theory and political economy, particularly actor-network theory. The analysis of services has often been overly sterile, reluctant to engage in questions of power, politics and social relations. Conjoining services and political economy allows for the effective integration of diverse topics under a broad, systematic line of inquiry in line with Harvey's (2001) call for a holistic social science capable of synthesizing diverse aspects of global capitalism in a critical manner rather than offering an endless series of disconnected 'hypotheses'. By invoking several strands of contemporary critical theory, this chapter attempts to demonstrate that the global service economy linked by telecommunications is not some teleological necessity, but the contingent outcome of actors situated in networks.

This chapter takes as its point of departure the question of how and why some forms of service production are concentrated in a small handful of locales while other services freely roam the globe, creating a constantly changing kaleidoscope of new locales. High value-added services, using skilled labor and tacit forms of knowledge, are highly agglomerated in the world's global cities. Such functions tend to be deeply embedded territorially and thus the competitive advantages of established centers are difficult to reproduce. In contrast, relatively low value-added service functions, such as back offices, call centers and offshore banks, are increasingly dispersed to the world's low-wage periphery. These operations, relying upon disembedded, standardized knowledge, are footloose and change locations frequently. These two sets of services represent opposite poles of one continuous process that geographically segregates functions on the basis of their value-added and types of skills and knowledges utilized. Both types of services are embodied in people and embedded in local and international contexts, forming complex mixtures of the local and global. Their locations in space – at the cores and peripheries of the world economy, respectively – are thus differential forms of embodiment, a perspective best seen through the lens of actor-network theory.

The chapter begins with an overview of global services in light of the ascendancy of post-Fordism and neoliberalism. Second, it focuses on the new relations between capital and space these changes generated, including hypermobile capital. Third, it invokes poststructuralist thought to emphasize how services are embodied in actors in different cultural contexts, noting the central role played by tacit and standardized forms of information. Fourth, it utilizes actor-network theory to argue the boundaries between global and local in the study of global services are artificial and misleading; rather, value-added networks form topologies that defy conventional geographic notions such as distance and proximity. Fifth, it examines the production of high-wage, high value-added services in the world's core, the global cities that dominate corporate decision making, noting the critical role of tacit knowledge and face-to-face contact. Sixth, it points to three types of low-wage, low value-added services – back offices, call centers and offshore banks – that comprise different forms of disembedded information reliant upon telecommunications. Finally, the conclusion moves beyond the simple dichotomy of tacit versus standardized knowledge to assert a spectrum of services that constantly changes under the intense pressures of innovation.

Global services, post-Fordism and neoliberalism

Globalization has unquestionably become the defining process of the contemporary world. So extensive has the acceleration in the scope, magnitude and velocity of international transactions become that few analyses of local events and processes can afford to ignore it. International trade, investment and finance form the backdrop to virtually all analyses of economic geography today (Dicken, 2003). While there have been many episodes of globalization in the past, the current round, which began to take shape after the collapse of the Bretton Woods regime and the petrocrises of the 1970s, has been particularly rapid and penetrating. Contemporary globalization also has important political repercussions, including the neoliberalism dogma of deregulation and privatization, which are important to the creation of a global services economy.

The current epoch of globalization has also witnessed enormous technological changes born from the microelectronics revolution, a transition generally typified as the emergence of post-Fordist flexible production systems (Amin, 1994). While most attention has been directed to manufacturing, the regulation theory that informs flexible production is also applicable to services. Indeed, producer services surged in the 1980s and 1990s precisely when flexible production was coming into being. The rise of post-Fordism should therefore be seen not as oppositional to the growth of producer services, but as complementary (Wood, 1991). Commonly, it is argued that the expansion of producer services reflects the widespread vertical disintegration that occurred in the late twentieth century, leading to a steady contracting out of many functions or the emergence of new ones (Coffey and Bailly, 1991; Goe, 1991).

Part and parcel of the current round of globalization has been the construction of a vast and comprehensive worldwide infrastructure of telecommunications networks (Warf, 1995b; Graham and Marvin, 1996; Wheeler et al., 2000). Graham (1999) notes that the skein of fiber lines linking the world constitutes the core of interlinked urban systems today. The investment in these systems, and the digitized 'spatial fix' (Harvey, 1989) that they represent, result from the enormous pressures on firms to transmit vast quantities of information and capital over the planet's surface. Electronic funds transfer systems, in particular, comprise the nervous system of the global service economy, allowing financial institutions to switch vast sums of capital from one place to another instantaneously, in the process arbitraging interest rate differentials, speculating of foreign exchange fluctuations, and investing or disinvesting in a wide variety of instruments in a diverse array of markets (Kurtzman, 1993; Kobrin, 1997; Cohen, 1998; Martin, 1999). As astoundingly large quantities of money flow effortlessly across national borders, national monetary policies to control interest, inflation and exchange rates have become increasingly problematic.

Schiller (1999) refers to this flexible, globalized, post-Fordist system of market relations as 'digital capitalism'. No large corporation today can operate in multiple national markets simultaneously, coordinating the activities of thousands of employees within highly specialized intra-firm divisions of labor, without access to sophisticated communications networks that convey information instantaneously and securely. The collection, transformation and transmission of large volumes of data arguably constitute the core of economic activity in the industrialized world. The vast majority of jobs in industrialized nations, particularly well-paying, white-collar ones, consist of information processing in one form or another, including management, finance, research and design, engineering, marketing and computer services. These functions have increased in importance as computing has dramatically declined in cost and risen exponentially in power, as the production of all goods and services has become markedly more information intensive, technological change accelerated, product cycles shortened, and as a deregulated, worldwide market has increased uncertainty and accelerated the competition among places for investment and jobs.

New global geographies of post-Fordist services

Resulting directly from the rise of networked post-Fordist production systems, a fundamental reworking of the relations between capital and space took place, a change with massive political ramifications. In particular, the enhanced mobility of capital underpinned, accompanied and reinforced the contraction of the Keynesian welfare state and its displacement by global neoliberalism, a massive policy shift evident at the global, national and urban scales (Gaffikin and Warf, 1993; Klak, 1998; MacEwan, 1999). A new geographic flexibility, manifested in an ability of firms to move across local and national borders with ever greater ease, can be readily contrasted with the traditional lack of mobility (as expressed in many textbooks in terms such as 'locational inertia', or a calculus in which transportation costs figure prominently). Freed from many of the technological and political barriers that hampered it, capital has become not merely mobile, but *hypermobile*. As Castells (1996, 1997) famously emphasizes, the 'network' society of contemporary capitalism, dominated by a 'space of flows' rather than a 'space of places', has led to new political formations, forms of identity and spatial associations. Swyngedow (1989) makes a similar argument for the positionality of regions in a volatile, postmodern 'hyperspace'. In climbing out of the crisis of Fordism, capital replaced the Keynesian national 'spatial fix' (Harvey, 1989) with a highly fluid, globalized set of localities. (Although the spatial fix argument reeks of crude functionalism, it does capture the deeply geographical level at which social and political processes are constructed and play out.)

Hidden within this transformation, however, was a fundamental reworking of the relations between capital and place, one that pits hypermobile financial capital against increasingly vulnerable localities. Globalization has heightened competition among places for capital, a process generally manifested in popular calls for a 'good business climate', deregulation, privatization, tax concessions, subsidies, relaxations of environmental controls and reductions in social expenditures. In an age of low productivity and employment growth, many localities vie with one another for ever-greater concessions to attract firms in an auction resembling a zero-sum game. The effects of such a competition are hardly beneficial to those with the least purchasing power and political clout, lowering wages and inhibiting union organization. Economic and political imperatives are interpreted in light of their ability to 'generate jobs' or a 'good business climate'. Thus, globalization has been deeply entwined with the decline of national Keynesianism and the emergence of a new social contract. Under such circumstances, when neoliberal doctrines naturalize inequality, sympathy for the poor, the homeless, and the handicapped melts away under discourses that emphasize self-reliance and 'individual initiative'. Left to auction themselves to the highest corporate bidder, localities find themselves in a 'race to the bottom' in which entrepreneurial governments promote growth – but do not regulate its aftermath – via tax breaks, subsidies, training programs, low-interest loans, infrastructure grants and zoning exemptions.

In public policy terms, the transition to a post-Fordist, hypermobile regime of accumulation has induced a switch from 'managerial' to 'entrepreneurial' planning (Fainstein, 1991). Governments, national and local, have become increasingly less concerned with issues of social redistribution, compensation for negative externalities, provision of public services and so forth, and more enthralled with questions of economic competitiveness. As planners have come to involve themselves more directly in economic development, market rationality and local competitiveness have replaced comprehensiveness and equity as the primary criteria by which planning projects are judged. Thus, long-term capital budgeting, master planning and a concern for the environment have gradually given way to short-term concerns of job generation, looser regulations and tax relief. Planning is hence concerned more with promoting development and less with regulating its aftermath. In short, the emergence of a globalized, post-Fordist production regime has accompanied, and been simultaneously underpinned by, the collapse of the national Keynesian state and its replacement by a series of localities intent on auctioning themselves off regardless of the costs.

In a climate of globalized, hypermobile capital, however, local successes are bound to be transitory and ephemeral. Indeed, if nation states lacked the power to set economic policy in the face of hypermobile capital, localities are sure to fare much worse (Tickell and Peck, 1995). The competition among localities is, at best, one in which a few may benefit but most will find themselves virtually powerless. Such a devaluation of the power of places leads ultimately to the negation of even the strongest places. As Peck and Tickell (1994: 304) note, 'the more vigorously localities compete with one another, the more pronounced their subordination to supralocal forces becomes'.

New approaches for new times: enculturating and embodying services

Concomitant with the changes noted above, geographers have searched for new frames of reference to make sense of the emerging geographies of centrality and peripherality unleashed by global flexible production. Rising in parallel with the focus on globalization, but unfortunately too often detached from it, has been the 'cultural turn' in economic geography (Thrift and Olds, 1996; Schoenberger, 1997; Thrift, 2000). Sensitized to the need to incorporate a more realistic and flexible understanding of human consciousness and actors, economic geographers delved into the detailed mechanics of what makes successful regions work. This line of thought reflected in part a fascination with the obvious success of regions such as Italy's Emilia-Romagna or California's Silicon Valley. Geographical analyses of post-Fordist regionalism have focused largely on dense urban networks of interactions among firms as an older tradition concerned with the theory of the firm was reworked in light of the economics of vertical integration and disintegration, deregulation, subcontracting, corporate downsizing, 'untraded dependencies' and local linkages to the global economy (Storper, 1997). Similarly, in *Postmetropolis*, Soja (2000) advocates an aggressively city-centric view of the world based on what he calls 'synekism', the creative energy that oozes from the close proximity cities offer. However, it became readily apparent that the exploration of such regions requires approaches more nuanced than simply invoking traditional agglomeration economies. Rather, it is necessary to understand the resurgence of regionality in light of the cultural dynamics of contemporary globalization.

The literature on globalization has simultaneously recognized the fact that global capital accommodates to the specifics of individual places and the role of culture in this process. A growing corpus of writings is concerned with the cultural dimensions of globalization, including commodity chains and their relations to globalized consumption (Gereffi and Korzeniewicz, 1994; Dicken et al., 2001), identity and everyday life (Giddens, 2000). By revealing how the global and the local are shot through with one another, or in Swyngedouw's (1997) term, 'glocalized', this literature has contributed mightily to more nuanced understandings of how globalization is manifested differently in different places (Cox, 1997), thus helping to dispel simplistic popular assertions that globalization is synonymous with homogenization devoid of geographic specificity. As the 'cultural turn' in globalization studies has revealed, far from constituting an unstoppable force – a common assertion of teleological interpretations – global processes are in fact contradictory, contingent and contested. Because this issue has been explored in great depth elsewhere (Appadurai, 1996; King, 1997; Featherstone and Lash, 1999; Waters, 2001), a brief synopsis serves the immediate purpose here, that is, to make evident that the cultural and ideological dimensions of capitalism are at least as formidable and significant as the economic and political ones.

Given the cultural turn, it readily became apparent that there was no simple formula to generate propulsive regions such as Silicon Valley or Emilia-Romagna, which typically emerged contingently through fortuitous happenstance. Thus, work pointed to the powerful roles played in regional competitiveness by 'non-economic' factors such as learning, reflexivity, convention, expectations, trust, uncertainty and reputation in the interactions of actors (Amin and Thrift, 1992; Gertler, 1992, 1995). Drawing upon Granovetter's (1985, 1991) famous notion of embeddedness, economic geographers came to emphasize culture as a complex, contingent set of relations every bit as important as putatively 'economic' factors in the structuring of economic landscapes. Such works have abundantly demonstrated that the cultural and ideological dimensions of capitalism are at least as formidable and significant as the economic and political ones. Indeed, the disassociation of culture from political economy is itself a naive and analytically disastrous mode of interpretation.

One step in this analytical sequence is the embodiment (both literally and figuratively) of the space of flows, a project that has forced economic geographers to contend with the importance of identity and the body in the negotiation of economic transactions. This shift has been accompanied by the growing popularity of post-structural perspectives that emphasize the complexity and contingency of identity. In the process, the classical, Cartesian notion of the subject, as a consistent, rational bundle of traits that transcends contexts has given way to views that maintain identity is a multiplicity of different, unstable, context-dependent traits that vary over time and space (Pile and Thrift, 1995; Kirby, 1996). Moreover, identities are power relations that reflect and contest relations of normality and marginality. Identities are constructed through the social production of difference, by defining what they are not: there is always an Other, and othering is a power relation. Finally, identities are both space forming and space formed, that is, inextricably intertwined with geographies in complex and contingent ways. This perspective emerges, for example, in divisions between the public and private, front and back stages, and the phenomenological meanings we attach to places through everyday life. Identities under post-modern, post-Fordist capitalism are rapidly being transformed by the disorienting time–space compression unleashed by telecommunications.

In embodying the space of flows, geographers have irrevocably sutured identity, the body and place together (Duncan, 1996; Schatzki and Natter, 1997; Hubbard et al., 2002). Thus, the unfolding of digital capitalism involves a new appreciation of the role of the body in the reproduction of social relations. While bodies typically appear as 'natural', they are in fact social constructions deeply inscribed with multiple meanings, 'embodiments' of class, gender, ethnic and other relations. The body is the primary vehicle through which prevailing economic and political institutions inscribe the self, producing a bundle of signs that encodes, reproduces and contests hegemonic notions of identity, order and discipline, morality and ethics, sensuality and sexuality. In *The Production of Space*, Lefebvre (1991: 405) goes so far as to argue that 'the whole of (social) space proceeds from the body . . . the passive body (the senses) and the active body (labour) converge in space'. Similarly, Foucault (1978) dwells on what he calls 'biopower' and the 'micropolitics of desire', the specific form of power/knowledge in contemporary societies that produces healthy, secure and productive individuals. The body is the most personalized form of politics; all power is, ultimately, power over the body. Recent feminist perspectives on the body have highlighted the importance of gender, sexuality and the legal dimensions of bodies as the expression of social codes stratified by sex.

In the same vein, digital technology allowed for a far-reaching rescripting of the 'natural' body (Featherstone and Burrows, 1995; Shields, 1996; Kitchin, 1998; Crang et al., 1999), so that simple dichotomies such as 'offline' and 'online' fail to do justice to the depth to which they are shot through with one another (Warf, 2000). Harraway (1991) persuasively argued that in the current age, the simple boundaries between bodies and machines, the natural and the artificial, have become progressively blurred, a notion manifested in her famous use of the term 'cyborgs' (cybernetic organisms), complex articulations of tissue and technologies. Such a trope problematizes dominant conceptions of 'nature' as non-mechanical when our bodies rely heavily, and even incorporate as prosthetics, machines in many forms (Luke, 1997). Thus, the human/machine threshold has shifted over time, and never more so than in the aftermath of the microelectronics revolution of the late twentieth century. Like identity, the social construction of the body is thus part of the contemporary wave of time–space compression, or 'distanciation', to use Giddens's (1984) term for how societies are stretched over time and space.

Actor networks, topologies and embodied services

The latest product of this line of reasoning is actor-network theory (Murdoch, 1995; Law and Hassard, 1999). Inspired by the work of Latour (1993) and Serres (1997; see also Serres and Latour, 1995), actor-network theory incorporates sociological understandings of structuration theory (Giddens, 1984) with a poststructuralist, French, social-constructivist philosophy of science. This view meshes closely both with Castells's (1996) notion of a network society and with the work concerned with flexible production and the roles of networks in the construction of local agglomerative economies (Gertler, 1992, 1995). The essence of actor-network theory is the linkages among different ontological categories, a departure from the Enlightenment focus on pure essences that created dualities such as individual and society, people and nature, human and non-human, western and non-western, urban and rural, micro and macro, local and global. Rather, it takes as its point of departure the linkages among these categories as actors draw upon and combine them in various forms of hybridity (Murdoch, 1997). As Latour (1993: 77) notes, 'How are we to gain access to networks, those beings whose topology is so odd and whose ontology is even more unusual, beings that possess both the capacity to produce both time and space?'.

Networks involve the mobilization of rules, resources and power, including information, in order to accomplish tasks, creating a net of intended and unintended consequences that stretch across the spatio-temporal boundaries of the network. To maintain network functionality, actors must perform by being engaged with one another recursively, interpreting and translating one another's behavior. Actors and networks are thus twin, mutually presupposing aspects of one phenomenon, simultaneously enabling and constraining actions in time and space. Because actor-network theory strives to overcome the artificial boundaries between culture and nature (Latour, 1993), actors in this sociotechnical seamless 'nature–culture' nexus need not be human, but may include inanimate objects such as books, papers or computer systems (Bingham, 1996; Murdoch, 1997), which are necessary to the maintenance and operation of networks.

Networks obviously can and do change over time, sometimes dramatically, and actors may enter and exit networks, but if the network is to achieve the purposes for which it is designed, actors must be able to draw upon its resources and effect the necessary consequences. Thus, it is not simply actors in everyday life who constitute the primary focus here, but their relative positionality and powers within integrated systems of power and information that matter most. For example, Thrift and Leyshon (1994) employed actor-network theory to examine the dynamics of global capital markets as they are structured by firms, nation states, the media and telecommunications, all of which are deployed simultaneously to produce, transmit and consume knowledge about markets and other actors. Such a perspective has helped to humanize even the most abstract of economic processes by revealing them to be the products of agents enmeshed in webs of power and meaning, not disembodied processes that operate independently of the people who create them (Law, 1994). The strategy of embodiment goes a long way toward demythologizing teleological interpretations of globalization, which present it as natural and inevitable, and reveal global processes to be the contingent outcomes of decisions made by human actors tied up in networks that cross multiple spatial scales.

Such a view elides the conventional focus on spatial scale, for networks operate across many scales simultaneously, creating as Latour (1993: 121) puts it, 'an Ariadne's thread that allows us to pass with continuity from the local to the global, from the human to the nonhuman. It is the thread of networks of practices and instruments, of documents and translations'. Likewise, Massey's (1999) well-received notion of power-geometries has called attention to the intertwined scales of the global, national and local, refusing to see these as a simple hierarchy in which the global determines the local; the distinctions among these scales are as misleading as they are enlightening. Smith (1993) argues that scale is produced through and constitutive of social relationships, and Thrift (1995: 33) goes so far as to claim 'There is no such thing as scale'. By forcing us to rethink how time and space are produced – that is, topologically rather than in terms of conventional Cartesian and Kantian views of space that have dominated geography – actor-network theory becomes 'a machine for waging war on Euclideanism' (Law, quoted in Murdoch, 1998: 357).

Actor-network theory and the associated focus on embodiment and topology have yet to be applied to the analysis of global services (see Latham, 2002). However, it is a useful starting point for making sense of the primary division in the world economy, that which separates high-wage, high value-added services from low-wage, low value-added ones, each of which manifests a unique geography. In particular, this view highlights the ways in which actor networks in global cities and in several low valued-added services suture together diverse groups of people and non-human elements (for example, computers, fiber optic lines, information flows) to produce and transcend spatial scales, creating patterns that are simultaneously local and global.

The centralization of high value-added services

The recent round of globalization has witnessed a resurgence of 'global cities' at different levels of the international urban hierarchy (Sassen, 1994). Such places are by definition tied through vast tentacles of investment, trade, migration and telecommunications to clients and markets, suppliers and competitors, consumers and producers around the world. Global cities serve as the home to massive complexes of financial firms, producer services and corporate headquarters, or 'command and control' centers in the world system. Typically, the trio of London, New York and Tokyo is positioned at the top, with cascading layers demarcated by successively smaller roles in the world economy, including cities such as Paris, Frankfurt, Toronto, Los Angeles, Osaka, Hong Kong and Singapore (Markusen and Gwiasda, 1994; Beaverstock et al., 2000; Taylor, 2000). Because there exists a vast literature on this topic, it is not necessary to recite all of their characteristics here. Rather, it is the role of global cities in planetary networks of value added that most concerns us.

The core of such conglomerations – Manhattan or the City of London – allow for dense networks of interaction necessary to the performance of headquarters functions, including: monitoring frequent changes in niche product markets; negotiating with labor unions; keeping abreast of new technologies and government regulations; keeping an eye on the competition; staying attuned to an increasingly complex financial environment; initiating or resisting leveraged buy-outs and hostile takeovers; seeking new investment opportunities, and so forth. Because their *raison d'être* cannot immediately be classified as 'economic', but includes a vast variety of formal and informal cultural and political interactions such as tourism, the media and fashion industries, global cities are more than simply poles for the production of corporate knowledge (Knox, 1995). The crux of global cities' role in the post-Fordist world economy is to serve as arenas of interaction, allowing face-to-face contact, political connections, artistic and cultural activities, and elites to rub shoulders easily (Thrift, 1994; Budd, 1999). At their core, global cities allow the generation of specialized expertise upon which so much of the current producer service economy depends (Howells, 1990). The creation of expertise is no simple task, involving the transformation of information into useful knowledge (Bryson and Daniels, 1998a; Howells, 2000b). Rather than simple structural outcomes of the worldwide division of labor, global cities are contingent social constructs constructed and maintained by actors (Smith, 1998). In this respect, global cities resemble the 'learning regions' that preoccupied geographers in the 1980s and 1990s under the umbrella of post-Fordism (Storper, 1997).

The analysis of the functionality of global cities can draw much from the work of Polanyi (1967), who offered a well-known and highly influential distinction between explicit (or standardized) and tacit knowledge. Explicit knowledge refers to standardized forms of information that are easily transmitted from one person to another, including quantitative data, publicly known rules and standards, and orderly records. Explicit knowledge is designed to be as free as possible from its context and easy to transmit over time and space, and involves operating rules to make it applicable to a wide array of environments, such as blueprints and operating manuals. As such, explicit knowledge is relatively easy to obtain and generates comparatively little in terms of value added.

Tacit knowledge, on the other hand, includes information that is unstandardized, changes rapidly and is often not written down. Tacit knowledge is heavily context dependent and subject to informal rules of organization that make it difficult to transmit from one situation to another, including gossip, oral histories and invisible corporate cultures. Much of tacit knowledge involves the symbolic manipulation of information in ways that lead to corporate learning and innovation, a feature that makes it of great value to firms. It tends to circulate only within narrow social and geographical channels with a limited spatial range, and have a small degree of fungibility, that is, substitutability in different contexts. Expertise of this type takes years to develop and involves the acquisition of highly specialized knowledge from diverse sources. Often such information is collected informally, over lunches, drinks and dinners, in the locker rooms of sports clubs, on golf courses, and through a variety of social and cultural events.

Face-to-face contact is essential to the performance of actors in non-routine functions. The early literature on office contact patterns (Kutay, 1986), for example, revealed how difficult it is to substitute electronic contacts for personal meetings. Despite the enormous ability of telecommunications to transmit information instantaneously over vast distances, face-to-face contact remains the most efficient and effective means of obtaining and conveying irregular forms of information, particularly when it is highly sensitive (or even illegal, as the current wave of corporate malfeasance and insider trading demonstrates). Thus, in the context of face-to-face meetings, actors monitor one another's intentions and behavior through observations of body language, including handshakes and eye contact, which are essential to establishing relations of trust and mutual understanding. Such interactions are simply not substitutable to the digital form required by telecommunications.

Trading among markets and firms is largely managed, for example, by teams of traders rather than individuals, groups of people, computers and buildings that together constitute the interrelated formations that lie at the heart of actor-network theory. Such a line of thought does not negate the importance of regional production systems to the sociopsychology of individuals; on the other hand, as the literatures on flexible production and actor-network theory demonstrate, nor can the functionality of large agglomerative complexes exist without precisely those types of interactions. The stability of such networks allows them to become 'structural' in the sense that they endure over time and space, reproducing the role of these cities in the world economy.

As a sizable body of literature concerned with New York and London has demonstrated (Mollenkopf and Castells, 1991; Budd and Whimster, 1992; Fainstein et al., 1992; Fainstein, 1994; Longcore and Rees, 1996), the elites of global cities rely heavily on interpersonal contacts saturated with trust and reciprocity to 'get things done'. Such assets are very difficult to reproduce in other contexts, an observation that goes far to explain why the primacy of global cities such as Amsterdam, London and New York has changed little over the last 500 years. While Polanyi's distinction has been mapped onto the global economy (Maskell, 1999; Maskell and Malmberg, 1999), such works typically focus on industry and have paid scant attention to the globalization of services. Allen (2000) warns against the simple dichotomy of tacit versus explicit knowledge (a point to which we return later).

As McDowell and Court (1994a, 1994b) have shown, gender is important to the performativity of actors engaged in the provision of financial services. McDowell (1997) illustrates, for example, how banking in London largely hinges on the networks of trust among white businessmen, a process in which the appearance and behavior of actors is critical to the reproduction both of global banking systems and the City's premier position within them. Gender roles thus cemented relations among male actors and worked to marginalize the attempts of women to 'break into the club'.

Similarly, the ethnic dimensions of services have been extensively analyzed, particularly in the context of Chinese business practices. Mitchell (1995), for example, demonstrated how capitalist relations in the Chinese context differed significantly from the North American model, relying heavily upon trust and family networks, indicating there is no single, 'standard' model of capitalist relations, only a diversity of local models. Zhou (1996, 1998, 2000) examined the activities of Chinese-owned producer service firms in Los Angeles. He found that small, privately owned and decentralized Chinese accountants, banks and computer companies located in Los Angeles play a key role in connecting immigrant economic activities with the international circulation of information, goods and capital and especially with their place of origin (see also Li et al., 2002). Such firms facilitated the expansion into the US of Chinese-based corporations. The rapid growth of the Chinese immigrant population, along with investments (particularly during the 1990s as the return of Hong Kong became imminent), played important roles in the success of such establishments. The Chinese community in Los Angeles was thus poised at the threshold of the global and the local, coordinating interactions over long distances and serving as an intermediary between the American and Chinese business communities. Similarly, Mitchell and Olds (2000) studied management practices of Hong Kong property managers with investments in Vancouver, spanning the Pacific Ocean and competitively combining diverse types of knowledges. These examples illustrate actor networks transcending geographic scales.

The continued importance of global cities in the face of a networked space of flows is worth emphasizing. Repeated proclamations that telecommunications would allow everyone to engage in telecommuting, dispersing all functions and spelling the obsolescence of cities (O'Brien, 1992; Cairncross, 1997) and leading to a 'borderless world' (Ohmae, 1990), have fallen flat in the face of the persistence of growth in dense urbanized places. In fact, telecommunications are a notoriously poor substitute for face-to-face meetings, the medium through which sensitive corporate interactions occur, particularly when the information involved is irregular, proprietary and unstandardized in nature. Most managers spend the bulk of their working time engaged in face-to-face contact, such as in meetings, and no electronic technology can yet allow for the subtlety and nuances critical to such encounters. Indeed, financial and business service firms not only pay high rents to be near city centers, and endure the congestion such locations entail, but spend lavishly to fly their executives around the world to meet with their counterparts in person. Even electronic conferencing has been unable to substitute for direct personal contact. For this reason, a century of technological change, from the telephone to fiber optics, has left most high-wage, white-collar, administrative command and control functions clustered in downtown areas. In contrast, telecommunications are ideally suited for the transmission of routinized, standardized forms of data, facilitating the dispersal of functions involved with their processing (that is, back offices) to low-wage regions.

The local contact systems of global cities are, of course, embedded in the diverse space–times located around the globe that are entwined with international financial networks. Global cities thus 'fold' space and time around the world to their advantage; they are simultaneously global and local, as actor-network theory suggests. Murdoch (1998: 362) notes that this view 'directs our attention to the means by which scale becomes defined within particular networks. Spatial scales are marked out and distinguished in line with the priorities for action which prevail within networks'. Thus, the scale of the global is produced by the powerful actor networks centered in London and New York but reaching into every continent.

Jones (2002) offers an insightful critique of the global cities thesis, noting that it tends to oversimplify the nature of corporate command and control functions by privileging physical location over networks, that is, by focusing on the concentration of head offices. Rather, he argues, corporate power is wielded throughout the networks of international firms. He argues (p. 343) that 'to use physical locations as an epistemological framework for theorizing command and control is to a large extent arbitrary and obfuscates the socially constituted complexity of managerial power within the transnational firm'. The corporate decision-making process is deeply embedded in various layers of the firm, including localized forms of knowledge not available at headquarters, and is often a negotiated outcome of groups involved in constant interaction with one another. Thus, by refocusing attention on the social practices that constitute multinational firms, actor-network theory has led the global cities literature to become more sensitive to issues of power and scale. In this light, *all* cities are global cities in that they are all enveloped in worldwide networks of goods, people, capital and information.

The decentralization of low value-added services

Concomitant with the resurgence of global cities over the last three decades has been a widespread decentralization of other types of service into the global periphery. The offshoring of services is similar to the dispersal of forms of unskilled manufacturing in textiles, automobiles and electronics that has taken the form of branch plants, such as Mexico's maquilladoras. Attracting foreign capital has, of course, been a prime prerogative of countries seeking to carve a competitive niche for themselves in a neoliberal world economy, a task greatly facilitated by the use of tax-free export zones. In the case of services, however, this process takes a different form, primarily because the intangible nature of the output allows the use of telecommunications systems.

The decentralization of low-wage, low value-added services to the world's periphery may be demonstrated through three sectoral studies, back offices, call centers and offshore banks, which in many respects are different facets of one phenomenon. Despite the manifold differences among these industries, they share certain characteristics in common: all of them are essentially concerned with the processing of standardized information, to use Polanyi's

(1967) term; they all rely heavily on telecommunications networks, particularly fiber optic lines; all use unskilled labor, particularly women; and all of them have decentralized to low-wage, less-regulated parts of the planet. Low value-added services are both a form of restructuring in the service economy and a novel means of producing and delivering services. Because they necessitate both human actors (for example, data entry operators) and non-human ones (for example, extensive computer equipment), these systems exemplify actor networks, albeit a very different kind from that found in global cities. In contrast to the enduring geographies of high value-added services, in which global cities retain their hegemony for decades or centuries, the geographies of standardized services change at warp speed as global capital pits places against one another in a neoliberal world economy.

Back offices

In contrast to the headquarters functions typically clustered in global cities, back offices involve a variety of routine clerical jobs that revolve largely around data entry. The information entered includes payroll and billing records, bank checks, insurance claims, hospital records, airline tickets and magazine subscriptions. These types of data exemplify Polanyi's (1967) standardized information *par excellence*, with geographic and social context mattering little or not at all. Back-office tasks involve unskilled or semi-skilled labor, primarily women, and typically operate on a 24-hour-per-day basis. Because the inputs are sent directly by the client, often by airplane, back offices have few of the interfirm linkages associated with headquarters activities. In neoclassical terms, they have a paucity of backward linkages, and associated low multiplier effects. The primary locational requirements are reliable electricity, computer facilities, and high capacity telecommunications networks.

Historically, back offices have located adjacent to headquarters activities in downtown areas, often in the same building, a proximity necessary to ensure close management supervision and rapid turnaround of information. However, increasingly freed from this constraint by the introduction of digital communications systems, large service firms – particularly those facing acute competitive pressures under deregulation, such as banks and airlines – began to uncouple their back offices by relocating them to lower-cost locations on the urban periphery, often to avail themselves of pliable suburban female labor forces (Moss and Dunau, 1986; Nelson, 1986). At a broader scale, many American firms began to relocate their back offices out of large metropolitan areas (Warf, 1993), leaving New York, San Francisco and Los Angeles for small towns in the South and Midwest. Phoenix, Atlanta and Kansas City have been recent beneficiaries of this trend.

On an even broader stage, by using satellites and the rapidly expanding network of transoceanic fiber optic lines, back offices have 'gone global' as banks, airlines and insurance companies seek to minimize their production costs by relocating to the developing world. Ireland, for example, has benefited considerably from the relocation of New York-based firms there (McGahey et al., 1990; Grimes, 1997). Airplanes containing documents to be entered into computers are unloaded at Shannon Airport and transported by Federal Express to back offices in small towns employing young, female workers. In the Caribbean, likewise, back offices sprouted up as American Airlines established data-processing centers in Barbados, Jamaica and the Dominican Republic (Warf, 1995a). Similarly, Manila has emerged as a Philipino back-office center (Money, 1992). In each case, the operations involve hybrid mixtures of local and global elements that are so thoroughly intertwined that separating them is impossible. Back offices are 'glocalized', and the actor networks that comprise them cross spatial scales with abandon (see also Latham, 2002).

The role of back offices as exporters of information and generators of jobs should not be taken to mean that the working conditions they generate are produced unproblematically. Mullings (1999) explored how women employed in Jamaican back offices deployed a variety of tactics to cope and resist simultaneously the low wages, oppressive working conditions and lack of occupational mobility they offer. None the less, in the context of neoliberal structural adjustment, these centers are often the most attractive option that desperate workers in impoverished environments can encounter.

Call Centers

A second form of low-wage, low value-added services involves centers of telework, often labeled 'call centers'. Bodin and Dawson (2002: 39) define call centers as 'places where calls are placed, or received, in high volume for the purpose of sales, marketing, customer service, telemarketing, technical support or other specialized business activity' (see also Belt et al., 2000). Call-center functions include telemarketing, customer assistance and phone orders, often with designated 1-800 numbers. They range greatly in size, from as few as five to as many as several thousand employees (Richardson, 2002). Despite their prevalence, call centers have remained in the shadow of other well-known information-dependent industries such as financial services.

Like back offices, call centers are primarily screen based and do not require proximity to clients. The major cost consideration is labor, although the workforce consists primarily of low-skilled women, and high turnover rates are common. They are thus the epitome of a footloose industry, disembedded from their local milieu and highly mobile. There are an estimated 80,000–100,000 call centers within the US, which employ between 3 and 5 percent of the national labor force (Uchitelle, 2002), the majority of which are located in urban or suburban locations. Cities that have recently established competitive niches in this domain include Omaha, Nebraska; San Antonio, Texas; Wilmington, Delaware; Albuquerque, New Mexico; and Columbus, Ohio (Richardson, 1994).

Like back offices, call centers have become increasingly globalized. India, for example, has attracted a significant number of customer service centers near its software capital of Bangalore, where workers are trained to speak with the US dialect of English and are able to gossip with customers about pop culture (Waldman, 2003). Wages there, which average $US2000 per year, are higher than average Indian salaries but are only 10 percent of what equivalent jobs pay in the US.

Call centers likewise form nodes in actor networks that include First World firms, Third World workers, telephone networks, clients and massive, if invisible, information flows, that is, both human and non-human elements without which the systems would not exist and could not function. The Indian example illustrates how blurry the boundaries are between the local and global: a Bangalore operator speaking to a British customer calling for help with an American software program all comprise parts of one integrated topology that erases the convenient closures afforded by conventional geography.

Offshore banking

As Wechsler (2001: 43) notes, 'Thanks to globalization and advances in banking technologies, distant countries are now just a mouse-click away'. Thus, a third instance of the peripheralization of relatively capital-intensive, routinized services is offshore banking (Gorostriaga, 1984; Bowe, 1998; Cobb, 1998; Palan, 1998a, 1998b; Warf, 2002). Roberts (1994) identified five major world clusters of offshore finance, including the Caribbean (for example, the Cayman Islands, Bahamas, Panama); Europe (the Isle of Man, Jersey, and microstates on the Continent); the Middle East (Cyprus, Lebanon, and particularly Bahrain); Southeast Asia (Hong Kong, Singapore); and the south Pacific (Vanuatu, Nauru). Such places provide commercial investment services (that is, loans and advice), foreign currency trades, asset protection (insurance), investment consulting, international tax planning and trade finance (for example, letters of credit). Employment in offshore banking is relatively capital intensive when compared to the labor-intensive headquarters in global cities: for example, in the Cayman Islands, the world's largest center of offshore finance, Roberts (1995) notes that 1000 foreign banks employ only 538 people; most are 'brass plate' or shell banks. The high degree of capital intensity in this case speaks to the hybrid nature of offshore banks, which combine computers, software, buildings and an occasional worker to form actor networks that vary from place to place.

Conventional geographic preoccupations with proximity mean little in this case, for the topologies of global finance are formed and deformed in ways that the language of location theory cannot capture. Rather, it is the political economy of the actor networks in question that are central to the evolving spatial distribution of this segment of the global service economy. Offshore centers are the 'black holes' in the global topography of financial regulation, a status that emanates directly from the enhanced ability of large financial institutions to shift funds electronically to take advantage of lax regulations, freedom from taxes and currency controls, and other restrictions to be found on the periphery of the global financial system. As the technological barriers to moving money have fallen, allowing digital money to circulate at will, legal and regulatory ones have increased in importance. As Harvey (2001) emphasizes, globalization does not eliminate local differences, it accentuates them. Even relatively minor differences in regulations concerning corporate taxes or repatriated profits may attract or repel large quantities of capital to enter, or exit, particular places. Thus, Hudson (2000) argues that the phenomenon of offshore banking is redefining national sovereignty, uncoupling political and financial control from the territories that long held sway over financial institutions.

Offshore banking centers have long suffered from the cloud of suspicion that they constitute little more than havens for tax evasion and money laundering of illicitly obtained funds (Hampton, 1996a; Hampton and Christensen, 1999). As electronic money has come to dominate global finance, the use of offshore banking centers for illegitimate purposes has grown apace. Indeed, just as large corporations can use the internet and fiber optics to move funds from place to place, so can actors in the 'dark side' of the global economy, including tax evaders, drug cartels, arms traffickers, terrorists and corrupt government officials. Given that they often occupy the boundary between 'legitimate' and 'illegitimate' financial activity, a key issue in the success or failure of offshore banking centers is the degree of confidentiality that investors feel they can obtain. Indeed, the quality of offshore banking centers is often judged by the quality of laws protecting the privacy of investors. The use of shell companies, including holding corporations and increasingly, foundations, blurs legal lines of liability, keeping insurance rates low, and protecting assets (both legal and otherwise) from public scrutiny through deliberately impenetrable webs of cross-ownership that typically deflect even the most dogged of auditors. Thus, despite the putatively aspatial nature of electronic money and the extreme fungibility of electronic financial capital, place still matters in the geography of offshore banking in the form of locally embedded local policies.

What do back offices, call centers and offshore banks have in common? Information and services in such places is also embodied in actor networks, but in a very different manner and to a very different degree from that found in global cities. Precisely because such functions rely on standardized, highly fungible sorts of information, or Polanyi's (1967) explicit knowledge, they can be disembedded from local cultures. Such low-wage, unskilled tasks can be switched easily from one locale to another, leaving these places vulnerable to the demands of firms. The labor force of such operations utilizes docile women who are never engaged in contacts with clients or suppliers. Thus, standardized services tend to be vertically integrated. As world-systems advocates have long maintained (Wallerstein, 1979; Shannon, 1996; Chase-Dunn, 1998), one of the key differences between the world's core and periphery is the presence of free versus unfree labor, the former characterized by relatively high wages and better working conditions. In this respect, back offices and call centers represent the plantations of the global service economy. This concept has almost always been invoked with regard to agricultural and industrial labor, yet would seem to be equally applicable to the analysis of services.

Concluding thoughts

For the last 30 years, neoliberalism has ensured that the multitude of places throughout the world will be opened up to capital in an increasingly seamless surface. Unimpeded by national restrictions undone by deregulation, capital roams the globe effortlessly, testimony to the worldwide decline in technological and regulatory barriers. Globalization does not lead automatically to a homogenization of local landscapes, however, as the global and local become entwined in complex, contingent regional formations of capital and labor. Different forms of capital respond to this deregulated, globalized environment in different ways depending upon the specific types of information and skills they require and utilize. From the perspective of actor-network theory, both high and low value-added services reflect constellations of people, skills, information and equipment that combine to form hybrid arrangements with their own topologies. Functions that rely on cognitive manipulation of tacit knowledge tend to be highly embodied in their local context. These locally embodied services – typically skilled, high value-added executive ones – have remained concentrated in the same handful of places that have dominated the global economy for a century, if not more. Thus, globalization has accentuated, not reduced, the role of global cities as centers of managerial and creative control. Conversely, low value-added services – which typically rely on unskilled labor and disembodied information – have become the most fluid and mobile economic activities in the world. The microelectronics and telecommunications revolutions allowed for the dispersal not only of offshore banks, back offices, and call centers, but also telephone operators, graphic designers, internet service providers and readers of MRI (magnetic resonance imaging) records, which can be transmitted easily through the internet.

In short, telecommunications facilitate the simultaneous concentration and deconcentration of economic activities (Moss, 1987), albeit of very different types. It follows that the global division of labor and the simultaneous centralization and decentralization of different types of service constitute two interlinked facets of the worldwide information economy. Actor-network theory and global commodity chains offer insights into the maintenance and reproduction of such systems over time and space. Thus, it is imperative that high value-added services in global cities and low value-added services on the world's periphery be viewed as complementary facets of one worldwide division of labor. This understanding elides the traditional focus on industries as units of empirical measurement in favor of the skills and degree of value added – and thus the degree of embodied versus disembodied information – that different steps in the production process exhibit.

Some years ago, Leontief (1953) suggested a paradox in international trade: while neoclassical theory (that is, the Heckscher–Ohlin model) predicts that labor-intensive functions should migrate to low-wage parts of the world, and capital-intensive ones be retained in developing countries, trade data indicated quite the opposite: as measured by human capital, exports from the developed world tend to be labor intensive, while those in the developing countries tend to be relatively capital intensive. This paradox, it is by now evident, reflects the degree to which the global division of labor relies upon human capital. While the Leontief paradox has been extensively studied in the case of manufacturing and has become a staple of international trade theory (for example, Trefler, 1993), its applicability to services has not been examined.

Finally, it is important to move beyond the simple dichotomy presented here that consists solely of unskilled low value-added and highly skilled high value-added services to include a more nuanced gradation that positions services – and the places that produce them – along a spectrum that includes a mixture of these forms. Even in the most significant of global cities, low-wage back-office jobs are yet to be found; conversely, in emerging sites of disembodied information production, such as Bangalore, Bahrain or the Cayman Islands, one finds hesitant attempts to climb the value-added ladder and move into more skilled functions. The evacuation of computer programmers from Silicon Valley to India, for example, exemplifies the unyielding attempts by capital to free itself from the constraints of locally embodied services by standardizing and globalizing them using time-honored tactics such as capital intensification and Taylorist fragmentation of complex jobs. Maskell and Malmberg (1999: 16), for example, argue that 'when formally tacit knowledge is converted into a fully codified form, a process is initiated which will soon or later – usually sooner – turn it into a ubiquity by making it accessible on the global market'. Thus, in a ceaseless search to lower costs and raise profits, capital challenges the locally embedded nature of knowledge, seeking to standardize and disembody it, all the while generating new forms of innovation. Yet standardizing tacit knowledge and rendering it disembodied tends to lower its profitability, allowing competitors to harness or imitate it to their own ends. The simultaneous processes of standardization and innovation, or movement back and forth across the gradient of different knowledges, points to the restlessness of commodity production in general. The world's service economy is thus in constant flux, creating new forms of knowledge and information, cognition and labor, and ever-changing geographies of centrality and peripherality.

21 Gender divisions of labour: sex, gender, sexuality and embodiment in the service sector

Linda McDowell

Introduction

My focus in this chapter is on the ways in which gender as a social characteristic affects and is affected by the nature and structure of service sector work. I shall explore the ways in which the growth of service sector occupations has had an impact on both the opportunities and labour participation rates of men and women, as well as on changes in the construction of idealised workers in the growing emphasis on an embodied performance at work. There has been a long tradition of work, in the main by feminist scholars, that has both documented and explained women's inequality in the labour market, arguing that not only are the characteristics of masculinity and femininity differentially valued and rewarded in the labour market but also that jobs, occupations and organisations themselves are imbued with gendered characteristics. I shall examine some of these arguments in an assessment of the implications of service sector growth for men and women. Has the growing dominance of the service economy recut and reshaped gender divisions? Are women as a group still concentrated into 'female ghettos' and consequently more poorly rewarded and remunerated? Or have the current patterns of restructuring in the service sector, as well as broader social changes including girls' and women's success in gaining educational and occupational qualifications, altered older patterns of gender discrimination? Certainly women are entering the labour market in unprecedented numbers, as I shall document below, in assessing arguments about the 'feminisation' of employment.

I shall then turn to the definition of service work as interactive and embodied in an economy that increasingly depends on the construction and manipulation of consumer desire. One of the distinctive aspects of service sector employment lies in its very description: it is about providing a service, about servicing the needs of others, whether these needs are goods, ideas, knowledge or personal services such as a massage or a meal. In this exchange between the providers and consumers of a service, there is almost always a close personal exchange or an interaction between the provider and consumer in which the personal characteristics of the service provider take on a far greater significance than in older forms of employment and exchange. Robin Leidner (1993) has argued that in 'interactive' work in the service sector, the bodily attributes of the service provider are an important part of the service provision. Weight, height, looks, accent and demeanour all take on an importance that was by and large irrelevant when the typical form of employment, for men at least, was in the manufacturing sector. Thus in the second substantive section of this chapter, I shall look at the significance of embodiment, suggesting that idealised notions of femininity and masculinity and of docile bodies position men and women differentially and unequally as desirable workers in different service sector occupations. I shall then briefly introduce the expanding literature on gendered organisations and workplace cultures, before turning to case studies to explore the differential impact of embodiment in different types of service sector work. Here I shall suggest that the significance of embodiment works in different ways at the top and bottom ends of the sector. As I shall demonstrate, the significance of conventional or stereotypical attributes of femininity increasingly seem to exclude young working-class men from bottom-end service sector employment in the retail, fast-food and hospitality sectors, for example. Even when men are prepared to accept typically 'female' types of work such as providing secretarial services, their gendered performances challenge structures of authority based on notions of appropriate or suitable work for women and for men and make workplace relations uneasy. At the top end of the service sector the evidence for changing patterns of inequality based on gender and the opportunity for transgressive gender performances is far more ambiguous. As I shall show, in aggregate, women continue to be discriminated against when measured by indicators such as levels of pay, domination of the most powerful positions and pension and other job entitlements. And it may be that forms of discrimination based on the body – verbal and sexual harassment, for example – are becoming increasingly common or, perhaps, less tolerated by women in 'top jobs' who are more prepared to argue for equal treatment than in the past.

Finally, I shall conclude with a brief assessment of the contemporary significance of gender divisions in the workplace. There is no doubt that the old Fordist pattern of employment, based on the male breadwinner/dependent partner model, that relied on an ideology of separate spheres – the public sphere of work for men and the private sphere of the home for women – has changed (McDowell, 1991, 2001) but there is little evidence to support an enthusiastic endorsement of a post-feminist, post-Fordist era of equality. Class and gender continue to segment the labour market in complex, albeit changing, ways as I document in this chapter. Traditional patterns of gender discrimination have not been overturned: indeed far from it. Women in full-time employment in 2002, for example, earned almost 19 per cent less per hour than men in full-time jobs and the gap is much wider when the comparison includes women in part-time employment. Overall, in 2002 women's average gross individual income (including earnings from employment, pensions, benefits, interest and so on) was 51 per cent less than men's (EOC, 2003): clearly, gendered patterns of difference and dependence are still extremely significant in the new economy.

Women's labour market entry: is the service economy feminised?

One of the most marked features associated with rapid service sector employment growth in the late twentieth century was women's entry into waged labour. At the start of the twenty-first century 67 per cent of all women of working age in Great Britain were in employment, compared with about 30 per cent half a century earlier. The gender gap in patterns of participation has clearly diminished over this half-century (see Table 21.1). Currently 79 per cent of men of working age are in waged work which is actually a lower proportion than 50 years earlier (Alcock et al., 2003). The period of most active participation for both men and women is between the ages of 25 and 44 (73 per cent of women compared with 88 per cent of men) which means, of course, that women in the child-bearing and -rearing stage of their life cycle are also the women who are most likely to be in employment. In the last three decades of the twentieth century, the rates of increase in women's labour market participation has been most noticeable among mothers (Gregg and Wadsworth, 1999) and a pattern of continuous employment with shorter and shorter breaks for childbirth and -rearing has become more common. In her research with women employees in the North East of England, for example, Harriet Bradley (1999) found that

Table 21.1 Employment rates by gender, Great Britain

Year	Men	Women	Difference men – women
1975	92.3	59.4	32.9
1981	84.7	59.6	25.1
1987	80.4	63.3	17.1
1990	84.4	68.1	16.3
1998	81.0	69.3	11.7
2002	79.0	67.0	12.0

Note: Employment rate = all men and women aged 16–64 in employment.

Source: Labour Force Survey, Spring Quarter.

the average time spent out of the labour force bringing up children had fallen from just over ten and a half years among the oldest group to only a year among women under 30.

It is now widely accepted that mothers of young children should remain in the labour market, combining their domestic responsibilities with employment, in order to provide for their families. Indeed, the current welfare policies of New Labour represent an overturning of the ideal of domesticity for mothers that lay at the centre of the postwar welfare state (McDowell, 2004b). Increasingly, all adults, whatever their caring responsibilities are 'encouraged' to enter the workforce. The current aim of the government, for example, is to increase the proportion of single mothers who are in waged work. Irwin and Bottero (2000), in an interesting assessment of the changing moral assumptions over the postwar period that structure unpaid caring work in Britain, have argued that the notion of 'good mothering' now encompasses a high level of material provision through financial contributions to children who are dependent for a longer time as well as (or instead of?) time, love and unpaid care. Indeed some commentators of changing social relationships in the late modern era have argued that women's behaviour, both in the family and in the labour market, is now more like men's, based on notions of individualisation. It has been suggested, for example, that modern families are now based on 'negotiated' relationships that are increasingly subject to recall and change (Giddens, 1991, 1992; Beck, 1992; Beck and Beck-Gernsheim, 1995) rather than on a clearly defined gender division of responsibilities.

It seems clear, however, that these assumptions about gender and its declining significance are not supported at present by empirical evidence, at least in the aggregate sense. Women continue to enter the labour market on a different basis from men and in different occupations. Futhermore, many women continue to provide the majority of domestic care and services for their families, resolving the time contradiction between domestic and labour market responsibilities by part-time waged work. While 43 per cent of all employed women in Great Britain are currently employed on a part-time basis, only 9 per cent of all employed men are. Thus, although more women are in waged work at the start of the twenty-first century than in previous decades, in terms of total hours of employment undertaken in the British economy the gender balance has seen less change. Furthermore, women continue to be concentrated in a narrow range of occupations. While there is little doubt of the significance of the expansion of service sector work for women (82 per cent of all women are employed in the service sector and 60 per cent of all men), it is also clear that older patterns of segregation into specific types of work (known as 'horizontal segregation') and into the bottom rungs of job hierarchies ('vertical segregation') have been maintained. A good measure of gender segregation is whether or not co-workers are male or female. In 2002, 69 per cent or more of all administrative and secretarial, personal service and sales and customer service jobs were undertaken by women, whereas 69 per cent or more of all managers and senior officials, skilled trade and process, plant and machine operatives were men, reflecting idealised but stereotypical assumptions about the relative strengths of men and women as employees. Despite women's growing significance as employees, it is clear that they remain confined to the sorts of jobs and levels of responsibility assumed to map onto femininity, including women's supposed deference, empathy with and care for others and an apparent lack of authority or ambition. Therefore, in the next section I shall examine the ways in which desire characterises service-based economies, showing how the correlates of masculinity and femininity are connected to the growth of embodied and emotional labour and to the evident polarisation between skilled and credentialised service occupations and generic 'servicing' jobs (Castells, 2000).

Embodied labour in economies of desire

As well as mapping patterns of gender differences in participation, it is increasingly evident that ideas about gender, sex, sexuality and embodiment have come to assume a central significance in contemporary debates about waged labour and the growth of service sector work. In the new service economy it has become clear that the social characteristics of individual workers have assumed a greater significance both in the allocation of workers to employment categories and in theoretical explanations of these patterns. As earlier chapters have documented, the economies of advanced industrial societies are largely dependent on continued high demand from consumers for innovative products. Thus, in the transition of these economies from mass-society, mass-demand models, producing a limited range of goods for a relatively differentiated market, to economies based on the development of a highly differentiated range of products, including knowledge and information, for niche markets, the significance of advertising and the manipulation of desire has greatly increased. Bauman (1998), for example, has argued that consumer societies are volatile and temporary; objects of desire not only must be instantly available but also must bring instant satisfaction, which quickly wanes: 'Consumers must be constantly exposed to new temptations in order to be kept in a state of constantly seething, never wilting excitation and, indeed, in a state of suspicion and disaffection' (p. 26). He suggests an explicit parallel with sexual desire: 'It is often said that the consumer market seduces its customers. But in order to do so it needs customers who are ready and keen to be seduced. In a properly working consumer society consumers seek actively to be seduced' (p. 26). The providers and sellers of goods and services become agents of seduction in economies 'organised around desire and choice' (p. 29). Thus in growing numbers of service occupations, the interaction between clients and providers has become an exchange based on the manipulation of emotions and desire, a transaction in which the gender, weight, looks, bodily performance and the sexuality of the server is a key part of the exchange/seduction. While Hochschild's (1983) now-classic study of the significance of emotional labour (and see Bryson and Daniels, Chapter 1 in this collection) in occupations as diverse as airline stewarding and debt collection is the forerunner of contemporary work on the service sector, the last decade has been marked by a more self-conscious development of theoretical explorations of the social construction of sex, gender and sexuality: terms which might now usefully be defined.

Thinking theoretically about sex, gender and sexuality

Thinking about the significance of sex, gender and sexuality in the contemporary labour market necessitates some introductory comments about the relationship between the terms. As Rosemary Pringle (1999: 248) has argued, all these terms tend to be used in ways that often conflate their meaning. Furthermore, the terms are often assumed to be gender specific, marking the difference between men and women, but attributing particular characteristics and their significance for social relations and behaviour only to women. Thus while women are marked as sexed bodies, men are not. The Victorians, for example, referred to women as 'the sex'. Women were embodied and inferior, the 'Other', as Simone de Beauvoir (1972) noted, to the masculine disembodied, rational and cerebral 'One'.

For the larger part of the twentieth century, sex was assumed to refer to biological attributes that both distinguished men from women and also mapped onto significant social and psychological differences that were regarded as a natural consequence of these biological distinctions. The differentiation of the term sex from gender, to allow for the socially constructed rather than natural biological differences, awaited the development of second-wave feminist theory in the late 1960s and 1970s that insisted on the variety across time and space as well as the fluidity of gendered identities (Moore, 1988: 199). More recently, a complex debate has developed addressing the interconnections between sex and gender and insisting on the significance of the body in their interconnections (Diprose, 1994; Grosz, 1994).

The term 'sexuality' has a longer and more complex history, emerging in the late nineteenth century, especially in Freudian theory, to capture the diverse patterns of behaviour associated with sexual activities and expression and, as Pringle argues, has now taken on 'broader meanings related to representation, identity and desire' (1999: 249). Sexualised identities came to be seen as socially constructed, deriving from complex interactions between social relations and discourses of representation, instead of an output of a natural sex drive originating outside the social. Thus, as theorists such as Foucault (1978) and Butler (1990, 1993), whose work has been crucial in explorations of gendered performances in the workplace, have argued, sexuality is a socially constructed set of meanings and behaviours. In their theorisation then, sexuality and gendered identities are a set of scripts that have to be learnt and practised, reinforced by powerful social regulations of sexualised behaviour. Foucault (1978) insisted that the body is an inscripted surface, in which self-discipline and normalisation are based on multiple discourses (temporally and culturally specific sets of ideas, images, institutional structures, practices and regulations). These discourses are crucial in the production and maintenance of an approved body at different sites. Butler (1990, 1993) argues that gender is a regulatory fiction, reinforced by the everyday performativity of identity. The relationship of sexuality as a performance to the sexed body, however, remains a contentious area of debate.

Expanding the definition of sexuality from sexual acts *per se* to include representations, everyday interactions and social regulations as well as ideas of fantasy and desire opened up new areas of research about the economy. Investigations of the ways in which notions of desire and pleasure, of acceptable sexualised behaviours in arenas other than the bedroom, have been undertaken, including the performance and regulation of everyday behaviours in the workplace as well as analyses of workplace cultures. These new studies range beyond an earlier focus on sexual harassment or consensual sexual relationships in the workplace and have demonstrated how conventional attributes of hegemonic gender identity and a dominant version of heterosexuality are performed and confirmed in daily and institutional practices in workplaces in ways that benefit (certain) men. Here, Pringle has been a key innovator in drawing on the more recent work on the discursive construction of identity, to explore the relationship between sexuality and workplace identities in theoretical and empirical explorations of several occupations, including secretarial work and medicine (Pringle, 1988, 1998). In the next section I shall look in a little more detail at some of this work on workplace cultures and identities, that might be collected together and broadly be defined as a 'gender and organisation' school.

Gendered organisations and workplace cultures

As economies have changed and as the gendered attributes of employees became recognised as a key explanatory variable by an expanding group of scholars in different disciplines interested in labour market change and economic restructuring, the significance of workplace relations and cultures in perpetuating gendered patterns has become more significant. Perhaps the first challenge to the notion of rational bureaucratic organisations or disembodied non-sexual and non-sexualised (and by default masculine) workers, that dominated economic sociology and other associated disciplines, came in studies now collected under the heading of 'gender and organisations'. In 1990, Joan Acker, building on the feminist research about gender and organisations that was beginning to emerge, challenged the notion that organisations consist of profit-maximising institutions that, through the employment of hierarchies of employees without dependants, achieve market-defined ends. In this view of the world, employees, whose skills and knowledge best fit the goals of the organisation, initially are appointed and then are rewarded and promoted on the basis of an objective evaluation of their performance. Acker argued instead that organisations are seldom rational or objective but that their structures, cultures and everyday practices are riven with essentialist and non-essentialist assumptions about gender and sexuality in ways which consistently benefit certain workers, usually white heterosexual men. The disadvantaged include that usual cast of 'Others': women, people of colour, less physically able workers and people with alternative sexual identities. These Others may be excluded or alternatively constructed as less suitable, or inferior, workers and restricted to a narrow range of jobs and occupations that are congruent with their gendered and sexualised identities. In consequence, the division of labour *per se* and organisations and their practices are deeply gendered. Both conscious and unconscious practices produce and maintain gender inequality in the workplace and the various ways in which the discursive construction of organisational practices produces and maintains patterns of gendered and sexualised behaviour have begun to be documented in a wide range of sites. As Ferree et al. (1999: xxix) noted:

> Not only are there gendered assumptions built into most job descriptions and job assignments, as well as variations in pay scales and occupational ladders/promotion schemes, organisations also sexualise workers – presenting authority and physical labour as testaments to heterosexual masculinity, and good looks, 'service with a smile' and covert sexiness as evidence of heterosexual femininity. These norms and expectations are maintained by open and hidden

harassment and subtle and blunt sanctions by workers of each other and by bosses of workers under them.

In this type of work, there is general agreement that if gender and sexuality are theorised as fluid and mutable, constructed through everyday interactions, then workplace performances are also variable (Adkins and Lury, 1996, 1999). Gender, in other words, is not fixed in place as employees come through the door into the office or the shop but is challenged, reaffirmed or transgressed though the cultural assumptions and daily practices in different occupations and in different workplaces.

Building on Pringle's (1988) pathbreaking work on the secretarial labour process, there are now numerous studies exploring workplace performances in a range of service sector occupations. They illustrate how conventional attributes of hegemonic gender identity and a dominant version of heterosexuality continue to be performed and confirmed in daily and institutional practices in workplaces in ways that benefit (certain) men. Thus studies of, for example, insurance sale forces (Leidner, 1993) and retail banking (Halford et al., 1996) have documented how particular occupations are ring-fenced for men by their association with heroic masculinity or with superior patriarchal knowledge-based notions of an idealised rationality. In each of these examples, the construction of a hegemonic version of masculinity, with concomitant higher financial rewards for men, also proved to be the downfall for male workers as restructuring and cost-cutting drew on an alternative gendered script to recast and feminise both insurance sales and banking. Other studies of female-dominated occupations and workplaces have shown how women workers often draw on alternative, feminised scripts and performances in their discursive construction of identity and in their definition of work roles and relations with co-workers in order to challenge masculinised norms and male domination. They introduce questions about familial obligations, pregnancy and menstruation, for example, in a previously disembodied workplace discourse, but may as a result reconfirm notions of (inferior) femininity (see, for example, Westwood's (1984) fascinating study of a Midlands hosiery firm).

In these studies, and in the new service economy, as I argued above, the concept of an embodied, sexualised performance is key, in which the attributes of a desirable and desiring body play a part. As Iris Young (1990) has argued, in her recasting of a distributive definition of inequality into a group-based definition based on what she terms 'five faces of oppression' (p. 9), the body is a significant dimension of oppression. Ugly, fat, non-white, elderly bodies are inadmissible in the interactive sales/advice-giving industries and occupations that increasingly dominate in advanced industrial societies. In this type of work, as Young argued, 'dynamics of desire and the pulses of attraction and aversion' (p. 9) influence the scope and content of interactions between workers, their peers, superiors, clients and customers. As du Gay (1996) has shown in his study of fashion retail outlets, a scripted exchange, in this case based on an ideal of youthful equality, rather than the heterosexist interactions that Hochschild (1983) had earlier noted in the airline industry, is common in clothes shops aimed at the youth market. Here the conventional distinction between the workers and clients is blurred in interactions that depend increasingly on the similarity of the sales staff and the customers and their participation in a sociable, yet scripted, ritual that is based on a false notion of equality and familiarity. In these exchanges, a groomed, trimmed, tamed and toned, sexually desirable body and the capacity for continual self-discipline is an increasingly significant aspect of the employment relationship, as it increasingly is in many professional occupations. In the retail sector, on the shop floor, casual flirting is a recognised part of the script in which both young men and young women, whether customers or assistants, have learnt to participate, perpetuating a myth of equality between them. But these embodied attributes of gender – the ideal body, the maintenance of a deferential attitude to clients, the ability to seduce clients through looks and (practised) talk – are neither equally distributed nor equally maintained among the service sector workforce, and putative employers also make assumptions about prospective employees that maintain or create patterns of gender and class discrimination. Here I shall return to the earlier argument about the feminisation of the service sector labour market in order to examine the ways in which established associations between masculinity and femininity and different types of work are being transformed and challenged in a service-based economy. I shall do this through the lens of case studies of different forms of work, including fast-food, clerical work and professional employment in banking and the law.

Challenging and entrenching embodied gender difference

Docility and deference: taming the young male body

There has been a long debate in British sociology, social policy and urban studies about young working-class men and their social construction as masculine threats, as folk devils, strutting lads, as a threatening part of the urban mob (Cohen, 1973; Pearson, 1983; McDowell, 2002). As numerous commentators have pointed out, for working-class men part of an acceptable version of masculinity lies in the associations between attributes of embodied physicality and the public arena of the streets, leisure spheres and the workplace. Compared to the highly valued cerebral rationality of middle-class masculinity, working-class men's only advantage in the labour market is their physical strength (Connell, 1995, 2000), as studies of traditional occupations such as mining, fishing and heavy manufacturing industries have made clear. In his now-classic study *Learning to Labour* (1977), Paul Willis demonstrated how the school system in the middle decades of the twentieth century reinforced these associations by socialising working-class boys in ways that both prepared them for and restricted them to manual labour.

By the end of the century, however, the opportunities for young male school leavers, with little educational and social capital, had been transformed by economic restructuring, service sector expansion and manufacturing decline. The young men whose fathers had typically worked in the heavy industries that dominated the economies of many of Britain's northern towns and cities found themselves facing a different set of opportunities when they left school. For low-achieving school leavers in the twenty-first century, labour market opportunities are predominantly in casualised and poorly paid servicing jobs rather than in manufacturing. And for many prospective employers, the stroppy, macho, often awkward young men that they interview when filling vacancies are less appealing prospects than either young women from the same class position or the growing number of older women returning to work as their children go to school, often to make up for the declining incomes of their husbands and partners who are also affected by declining opportunities for men (Alcock et al., 2003). Add to this prospective labour force growing numbers of schoolchildren and, especially, students in higher education, affected by rising fees and inadequate loans, and the position for young, unskilled male school-leavers looks increasingly unpromising.

For many young working-class men masculinity, as it is conventionally constructed and enacted, is now a disadvantage rather than an advantage in the labour market. In the types of servicing work available in shops, restaurants and fast-food outlets, or in office services, young working-class men increasingly find themselves as inappropriately embodied and aggressively sexualised in their search for work. These forms of interactive work require not only a basic minimum education but, more significantly, 'service with a smile', the ability to defer to both clients and superiors, and the presentation of a neat, clean servile body that conforms to conventional norms in terms of weight, height, accent, hirsuteness and decoration. In a study of young minority men in a New York City neighbourhood disadvantaged by the almost complete disappearance of blue-collar jobs, Philippe Bourgois (1995) found that the particular version of a tough, aggressive, sexualised street credibility valorised by young men in that locality disqualified them from the only types of vacancy available in the city. As he noted, these youths 'find themselves propelled headlong into an explosive confrontation between their sense of cultural dignity versus the humiliating interpersonal subordination of service work' (ibid.: 14), as photocopiers or messengers, for example. Their social and cultural capital is inappropriate in white-collar workplaces. Later in the book he argued:

> Their interpersonal social skills are even more inadequate than their limited professional capacities. They do not know how to look at their fellow service workers – let alone their supervisors – without intimidating them. They cannot walk down the hallway to the water fountain without unconsciously swaying their shoulders aggressively as if patrolling their home turf. Gender barriers are an even more culturally charged realm. They are repeatedly reprimanded for offending co-workers with sexually aggressive behaviour. (Ibid.: 142–3)

In a similar study in the UK, I looked at the employment prospects of working-class young men in Cambridge and Sheffield (McDowell, 2003). I also found that the educational and cultural capital of these men largely disqualified them from many of the vacancies on offer, whether by their own choice or because prospective employees refused them. Many young men to whom I talked had clear views about the type of work they were prepared to consider, regarding most routine, casualised service sector work as 'women's work' and so beneath their dignity. Even if they were prepared to consider employment in the shops, clubs and fast-food outlets that were the main source of work for unqualified school leavers in both cities, they often disqualified themselves as potential employees by their appearance (piercings and tattoos as well as inappropriate clothes) and their attitudes during the recruitment process. Employers read the surface signals of bodily demeanour, dress and language as indicators of the underlying qualities they are seeking, or more typically as characteristics they are careful to avoid. If these young men did find work, often their sexualised, aggressive embodied interactions, especially with women co-workers and superiors, disqualified them, as Bourgois found, and many of them found it hard to perform the deferential servility required in the service economy.

But this was not insuperable. Many of the men whom I interviewed were prepared to perform the sort of servile docility required in the service sector, justifying their employment in conventional masculine terms about male identity through work and providing for others. They found themselves, however, involved in a complex negotiation between the sort of respectability required to perform satisfactorily in the workplace and the macho/laddish street credibility that brought them the respect of their peers. In some arenas of employment, this negotiation places difficult demands on young men. For those who work in fast-food outlets, for example, their dismissive treatment by many customers or the expectations of friends that they could expect free food or drink places these men in an awkward contradiction, reducing their sense of independence. As Newman (1999) has argued, based on a study of fast-food employment in New York City, the social characteristics of inner-city male youth culture, especially in its celebration of independence and rejection of deference, constructs young men as singularly unsuited to this form of deferential interactive service work. As one of the young men I interviewed noted: 'They push people around, management does. . . . people often don't last long here. They leave after about two months because they can't handle it. They answer back and that'.

Young women, on the other hand, are often more experienced in presenting a modest demeanour and deferential attitudes to adult authority, as well as more able to defuse difficult situations. In these situations, many young men simply leave and move on into other forms of casualised work. Their future employment prospects seem limited in service economies in which educational credentials, as well as hegemonic forms of embodied capital, are an increasingly dominant requirement of success. But not all men are disadvantaged in bottom-end female-dominated service work, as I explore in the second case study.

Gender pretences: men doing 'female' work

As I noted earlier Pringle's (1988) analysis of secretarial work was crucial in identifying the links between gender and sexuality and in showing how workplace-based social relations are based on discourses of desire and pleasure. In her study she argued that employees are not passive objects but instead active agents, whose identity is not fixed as they enter the workplace but is instead open, negotiable, shifting and ambiguous. Gendered sexualised identities are constructed and challenged through workplace practices in official and unofficial arenas that are saturated by notions about gender and sexuality. Thus organisations are locations and sites for the construction of identity, in which men and women 'do' gender through everyday interactions in dynamic organisations that are themselves embedded within wider social structures, attitudes and assumptions about gender and sexuality. Pringle showed how the relations between secretaries and their bosses in large part depended on gendered interactions and stereotypical associations of a differential set of attributes and talents to men and women. Through interviews in offices, she showed how female secretaries, for example, drew on a number of gendered and/or sexualised discourses, including the office 'mistress' and the office 'wife', to construct particular power relations between them and their male bosses. Flirting and having fun was a common script for male boss/female secretary interaction, as well as the extension of office duties into 'homemaker' tasks (making coffee, arranging food at meetings, buying flowers for the office or gifts for the boss's household for example). In contrast, between women bosses and women secretaries the social relations were both more straightforward and less deferential and typically confined to more strictly defined office-based and work-related activities. I shall draw on a study of men doing secretarial work to show how their gender paradoxically both destabilises and reinforces these commonplace associations between femininity and the definition of secretarial work.

As I documented in the first section, gender segregation is a deep structural attribute of industrial economies. A large number of employees work only with other individuals of the same sex as themselves and as a consequence, as well as because of the mapping of feminine attributes of certain types of work, especially caring and servicing occupations, a whole range of employment opportunities is classified as more appropriate for one sex or the other. This explanation is an important part of studies documenting the ways in which women are made to feel out of place in masculinised occupations and professions such as the police force, the armed services and the legal profession (Cornwall and Lindisfarne, 1994). What is less clear is the way in which men feel out of place in feminised roles such as primary school teachers, nurses, social workers or secretaries. From the limited evidence available, it seems that while men may be seen as 'less manly', in many cases they benefit in terms of rewards and authority by crossing into 'women's work', often quickly achieving promotion into the more prestigious and better-paid positions (Williams, 1989, 1992, 1995). However, in most 'bottom-end' service jobs, secretarial and clerical work included, there is often limited mobility for either men or women. In an interesting study of the performance of masculinity in temporary clerical work carried out in Chicago and Los Angeles, Kevin Hanson and Jackie Rogers (2001) looked at the ways in which men do gender in the types of jobs that require a performance that emphasises femininity, including deference and care-taking behaviours. Believing that they would find the presumed heterosexuality of men who do this type of work called into question, Hanson and Rogers found instead that the male temporary clerical workers were able to 'do masculinity' in ways which reasserted the feminine identification of the job while at the same time successfully rejecting its application to them as individuals, so reproducing rather than challenging the conventional gender order of the office. Clearly a male presence 'disrupted the taken for granted naturalness of workplace gender segregation' (ibid.: 223) but the men who were interviewed found a range of ways to construct themselves as different from and superior to their female co-workers.

As Leidner (1993) found in her study of insurance selling, male employees were able to construct the work as congruent with their gender identity by emphasising particular traits. Thus, the strategies adopted by male clerical workers included renaming and reframing the work as appropriately masculine, through, for example, emphasising the technical competencies required or by borrowing the name and prestige of the employing agency when talking about their work to others. A second strategy was to refuse to 'do deference', a strategy which employers tended to collude with as far fewer men than women were expected to provide deferential services. None of the men in the study, for example, was asked to make coffee, a request many women reported with great irritation. However, like the young men in Bourgois's study and my own research, in some cases, these men's refusal to undertake what they saw as demeaning tasks beneath their masculine dignity did lose them the position. This may penalise individual men but by reconfirming the assumption that men are not suited to secretarial and clerical work, it reproduces the conventional gender order. As Hanson and Rogers conclude 'through their gender strategies, male temporary clerical workers strike a hegemonic bargain, retracing the lines of occupational segregation and reinvigorating hegemonic masculinity and its dominance over women and subaltern men' (p. 236).

Disciplining the female body: harassment in 'top' jobs

My third case study focuses on women in traditionally male occupations, drawing on my own work in merchant banks. While many occupations, but perhaps especially investment banking and the legal profession, have long-established and clear class and gender connotations, their rapid growth throughout the economic booms of the 1980s and 1990s led to a change in both recruitment practices and daily interactions in the banking halls, boardrooms and chambers. A challenge was mounted to that form of 'gentlemanly capitalism' (Auger, 2001) based on trust and established through generations of familial and educational connections that had dominated the City of London for generations. Instead a set of new interactions developed, dubbed in banking the 'Americanisation' of the City (Lewis, 1989) as British-owned banks (now an absence in the twenty-first-century City) recruited a wider range of employees, from non-elite universities for example, more women and foreign nationals. This new, more cosmopolitan workforce with different ways of doing things may have challenged British constraint but it seems that women may not have greatly benefited.

In a study of workplace interactions in three merchant banks in the City of London in the early to mid-1990s (McDowell, 1997), I found that women bank employees were constrained by their construction as a sexualised Other, as out of place in the cerebral world of corporate banking as in the masculinised boys' school/sports club carnivalesque atmosphere of the trading floor, in which the conventional assumptions that dominate white-collar work are discarded. In a range of ways from derogatory comments to outright sexual harassment, women were marked out both as inappropriately sexual and inferior in the different arenas of investment banking. In the more conventional arenas of corporate banking where interaction with business clients is a key part of the work, women tended to be treated with patriarchal courtesy and to be excluded through talk and interactions, based on networks of contacts that depend on 'the old school tie'. Even in this side of banking, however, the body matters, despite its covering by pin-striped tailoring. Male interviewees emphasised the importance of the correct clothes – their (high) quality and (sober) colour – as well as the importance of bodily hygiene and keeping weight within certain limits. In this world a certain relatively youthful, male public school form of embodied performance based on rigorously disciplined body was the dominant appearance of success. Although women, especially younger employees, tried to disguise their femininity with a masculine masquerade, visiting male tailors for striped shirts for example, their pretence was largely unsuccessful, as I show in more detail below. Slenderness and an idealised image of male youthful heterosexuality was the most highly valorised form of embodiment and through recruitment practices largely reproduced from year to year.

While they may have found it hard to conform to the sober performance of pin-striped hegemonic masculinity in the boardrooms and offices of corporate banking, women found themselves at an even greater disadvantage on the trading floor and in the dealing rooms where exaggerated forms of masculinised language and behaviour were commonplace when I undertook my fieldwork in the early and mid-1990s. Horse-play, sexualised banter, loud and aggressive talk and forms of sexual harassment were typical – constructing women as either unwilling arbiters of boundaries or less than willing participants in the sexualised banter. But women in the main were and still are visible on trading floors only by their absence. As one male told the *Independent on Sunday* (8 November 2002) 'as I look around this floor, the only woman I can see is making my tea'. It has been suggested that on the floor, especially in bull markets, this aggressive, hetero-sexualised masculine confidence in their own abilities creates an atmosphere which is not only inimical to many women and to gay men, but which in the now-current bear market, seems also to lead to poor advice. In a recent study, analysts James Montier (*The Observer Business*, 23 February 2003) noted that 'much of the psychology behind markets has to do with the overconfidence of traders and the tendency to exaggerate their own abilities' and so to underestimate the impact of a falling market. Men, according to Theodora Zenek, an asset manager in the City of London, 'are aggressive buyers, but that either gives you staggering out-performance or staggering under-performance', in part because as she noted men have a 'tendency to fall in love with their investments' (quoted in the *Independent on Sunday* 8 November 2002).

I completed my empirical work in the mid-1990s as the City was beginning to boom again and recruitment was high. In this optimistic atmosphere, women may have felt more able to take risks. Even so, women remained a tiny minority in the higher echelons of merchant banks. At the present time, however, the financial sector is once again experiencing redundancies, and although I hesitate to draw a connection between women's experiences of discrimination and tense working conditions, it is noticeable that a number of high-profile cases of harassment and unfair dismissal have recently reached the courts. Most of these cases involve discrimination in salaries, especially in performance-related bonuses, as well as sexist behaviours and practices in the firms, including for example, the hiring of escort girls for company parties. This was the basis of a claim made by Kay Swinburne who was awarded a substantial amount in October 2000 after her boss at Deutsche Bank falsely alleged that she had slept with a client.

In the broadsheets, as well as in the popular press, women in the financial sector often find their claims treated in ways that emphasise their sexual difference and their inappropriate location as embodied women in the spaces of the City. Even Clara Furse, the first woman chief executive of the London Stock Exchange and so the highest-profile woman in the City since 2001, found she was not immune from sexist practices. In early 2003, a report that rumours were circulating the City based on distressing innuendoes about her sexuality hit the papers and other news media (*The Observer Business*, 23 February 2003: 3), even though according to another report in the same paper (ibid.: 21), Furse was described as 'having the prim exterior associated with a geography mistress', 'almost devoid of sex appeal'. Despite this, as Furse herself noted in a speech, 'city news (with some important exceptions) seems to focus on the odd corporate failure, job cuts and, in the case of the London Stock Exchange, merger speculation, the colour of my suits and the cut of my hair' (reported by Treanor, 2003).

Women in other types of City and professional employment have also found themselves the victims of inimical workplace cultures. As in investment banking, women, especially those in junior positions, in City legal firms consider that their femininity places them at a disadvantage. Nearly two-thirds of women lawyers who took part in a survey undertaken by the City of London Law Society in 2002, for example, felt that their gender was a disadvantage when being considered for a partnership. Some of the largest and most prestigious City firms were singled out for particular criticism. Slaughter and May, for example, was criticised for its atmosphere of a gentleman's club for (white, male) Oxbridge lawyers. Barristers' chambers were also criticised for their old-fashioned, patriarchal atmosphere and refusal to implement family-friendly policies. Thus, in professional City occupations, women's sexuality is paradoxically both ignored, as family-friendly policies largely remain unimplemented, and exaggerated in everyday interactions that continue to construct women as inappropriately sexualised bodies and so inappropriately embodied to conform to the idealised model of a serious employee. Until equal opportunities are taken more seriously, both in terms of policies to improve work–life balance and permit both men and women to fulfil their caring responsibilities, but also through challenges to workplace cultures that continue to disadvantage women, it seems unlikely that men's continued dominance of high-status occupations will diminish.

Conclusions: detraditionalisation, gendered inequalities and social change

As I have documented in this chapter, the rise of the service sector has been associated with significant changes in gender divisions of labour and in the significance of gender relations and embodied gendered performances in workplaces. The connections between gender and social class have been recut in ways that may advantage highly skilled and well-educated women. However, as the last case study showed, women in professional and high-status jobs are still too often constructed as inferior and inappropriately sexualised bodies, out of place in still male-dominated organisations. For many working-class men and women, the new economy has reduced their life chances and prospects of secure life-time employment in a reasonable well-paid job. Poor conditions, temporary contracts, casualised work and low pay are the lot of many of the employees, whether male or female, at the bottom end of the service sector. But even here, gender still matters as men apparently feel more insecure than women (Charles and James, 2003). Women are more willing than men to take any job that comes along whereas men feel a continued adherence to the male breadwinner ideology and thus worry about the implications of insecurity. For both men and women, however, the dominance of low-paid, casualised and temporary employment at the bottom end of the service sector is reflected in rising numbers of the working poor (see, for example, Ehrenreich, 2001 and Toynbee, 2003). This is accompanied by growing income inequality in economies such as the UK and the USA at the same time as apparent economic growth and expansion.

While optimistic commentators on the new economy have emphasised the opportunities available in a 'risk society' in which portfolio workers are able to construct mobile careers based on marketing their own skills, so escaping the traditional constraints of class, gender and family, more-grounded analyses of the implications of occupational change and economic restructuring have emphasised the continuing significance of older patterns of inequality in which age, gender and class position continue to structure life chances and earning capacity (Adkins and Lury, 2000; Tannock, 2001). While a minority of highly educated mobile middle-class people may escape the iron hand of structural forms of determination, the majority of British men and women continue to labour and to serve in jobs that not only depend on embodied gender divisions but also reinforce their significance in service economies increasingly based on the manipulation of sexuality and desire.

22 Transnational work: global professional labour markets in professional service accounting firms

*Jonathan V. Beaverstock**

Introduction

In 2001 at Doha, the World Trade Organisation's (WTO) General Agreement on Trade in Services (GATS) highlighted the need for the liberalisation of trade involving the temporary movement of people to supply services across national borders (termed GATS Mode 4):[1]

> GATS Mode 4 only covers movement of people supplying services; there are no parallel WTO rules covering movement of people in other areas such as agriculture or manufacturing. And while in theory Mode 4 covers service suppliers at all skill levels, in practice WTO members' commitments are limited to the higher skilled, usually managers, executives and specialists . . . There are at present no reliable global figures for the size of Mode 4 trade . . . Nonetheless, the very rough estimates we do have suggest that Mode 4, valued at USD 30 billion in 1997, is the smallest of the services supply defined by GATS. (OECD, 2003d: 2)

For developing countries, when it comes to international trade in services, the liberalisation of labour mobility is pressing in areas such as nursing or information technology, as 'sending people abroad to work temporarily is seen as virtually their only export interest in services (ibid.: 1). In developed countries the liberalisation of trade 'via presence of natural persons (GATS Mode 4)' (ibid.: 2) is also vitally important in services, as economic and technological change continues to increase labour market demand for the highly skilled in different temporal and spatial contexts. As GATS Mode 4 is the key to liberalising WTO member state immigration legislation regarding the temporary movement of the highly skilled, for transnational corporations (TNCs) who service markets almost entirely via the export or import of highly skilled staff, GATS Mode 4 provides the meta framework for understanding the production of global professional labour markets in contemporary economy. As we shall now see, in advanced producer or professional services, liberalisation of GATS Mode 4 is crucial to economic development and successful global penetration of markets because TNCs depend increasingly upon exporting or importing highly skilled labour into the international market to meet the requirements of their knowledge-hungry clientele.

Professional services, like architecture, accounting, consultancy and law for example, depend almost entirely upon the embodied knowledge of professional staff to create value, and therefore secure both market share and profitability in the firm (see Greenwood and Lachman, 1996). As Greenwood et al. (1999: 268) suggest,

> The core competence of the professional service firm (PSF) is the expertise and experience of its workforce. The asset base is knowledge and the competitive advantage of the firm is its reputation . . . The importance of reputation is heightened by the inability of existing and potential clients to assess services in advance of consumption. Decisions on which firm to hire are thus

> made partly on the basis of perceived reputation, and partly on the personal rapport established between client and . . . [firm] . . . Knowledge-based organisations are thus deeply reliant upon highly mobile professional workers.

In most, if not all PSFs, the client is 'King' (Maister, 2003). Clients purchase idiosyncratic knowledge, expertise and skills from the firm, where the ability to deliver 'customised' complex business solutions is tightly bound to the professionalism, experience, performance and reputation of the individual (Hanlon, 1994; Morris and Empson, 1998; Greenwood et al., 1999; Thrift, 2000; Lowendahl et al., 2001). Those PSFs which are TNCs seek a foreign presence in an international market to service existing clients and seek new ones (processes which have been discussed in the producer service discourse, see Ascher, 1993; Daniels, 1993; Bagchi-Sen and Sen, 1997; Beaverstock et al., 1999; Aharoni and Nachum, 2000; Warf, 2001). In PSFs, international offices are repositories for professional staff of all nationalities, including local hires, who physically travel to service clients on-site, and simultaneously work with colleagues in back-client office activities (Jones, 2002, 2003). In short, transnational PSFs have globalised their human resources to manage cross-border client relationships (Bartlett and Ghoshal, 1989) as they deliver their services cross-border through professional labour mobility because such knowledge is not easily tradable in virtual form. Labour mobility is an efficient mechanism to deliver sophisticated and customised solutions to clients, while enriching the local office network where tacit knowledge can be transferred (become explicit) through local socialisation (Nonaka and Takeuchi, 1995).

The main argument presented in this chapter is that professional labour markets exist on a global scale in professional services because the physical movement of people intra-firm and between firm and client are key processes which account for the development, management and diffusion of knowledge in cross-border firm–client connections and relationships. The rest of this chapter is divided into four major sections. The first accounts for the existence of global professional labour markets in professional services. It is posited that global professional labour markets are produced by the planned physical movement of professional staff between international offices and clients, alongside the employment of local hires, business travel and virtual communication systems (for example, video conferencing). International mobility is accordingly a key globalisation process of PSFs as they service clients in close proximity with their knowledge- and professional-rich human resources. The next section focuses on the globalisation of professional service accounting firms and explains how they create the conditions for the production of global professional labour markets. The following section analyses research findings that illustrate global professional labour markets in four of the Big-Six accounting firms. The final section discusses the accounting study in relation to the principal conceptual ideas explaining the production of global professional labour markets and several conclusions are reached on the role of international mobility in transnational knowledge management.

Transnational knowledge management and the production of global professional labour markets

Bartlett and Ghoshal (1989) note that one of the key characteristics of worldwide multi-locational firms is the efficient 'diffusion of knowledge' between subsidiaries (whether

Table 22.1 Organisational characteristics of the transnational

Organisational characteristics	Multinational	Global	International	Transnational
Configuration of assets and capabilities	Decentralised and nationally self-sufficient	Centralised and globally scaled	Sources of core competences centralised, others decentralised	Dispersed, interdependent, and specialised
Role of overseas operations	Sensing and exploiting local opportunities and strategies	Implementing parent company competences	Adapting and leveraging parent company	Differentiated contributions by national units to integrated worldwide operations
Development and diffusion of knowledge	Knowledge developed and retained within each unit	Knowledge developed and retained at the centre	Knowledge developed at the centre and transferred to overseas units	Knowledge developed jointly and shared worldwide

Source: Bartlett and Ghoshal (1989: 75).

wholly owned, partnerships or franchises). They suggest that in the 'transnational' firm, knowledge is 'developed and jointly shared on a worldwide basis' (p. 75) (Table 22.1). The key attribute of knowledge development and diffusion in transnational firms is that it is circulated both vertically (up and down from headquarters) and horizontally (laterally between subsidiaries) between all units of the firm. Transnational firms are integrated networks spanning cross-border activities which are sustained by communication and mobility between different subsidiaries and head office (Morgan, 2001; Dicken, 2003). Nohria and Ghoshal (1997) refer to the transnational firm as being a 'differential network' because the organisation is composed of many interrelated linkages and relationships which can be both 'local' (within each national subsidiary) and global (between headquarters and subsidiaries, and subsidiaries themselves).

Global professional labour markets are produced within the transnational firm as an organisational strategy to deliver transnational knowledge management. Firms manage the complexities of knowledge diffusion cross-border in many different ways. One way is increasingly through virtual transfer – e-learning, e-mail communication, information and communication technologies (ICTs) – and another is via residential training, seminars and outsourcing (Thrift, 1997). Firms, however, still engage in moving people around international offices in order to develop and diffuse knowledge and best practice, between both business units and clients (Gupta and Govindarajan, 2000; O'Donnell, 2000; Morgan et al., 2001). In order to unpack the production of global professional labour markets in transnational PSFs, two particular discourses will be examined. First, from PSFs, the role of professional labour in producing and diffusing knowledge; and, second, drawing from international human resource management (IHRM), an analysis of why firms use international assignees (which are still referred to as 'expatriates'; see Schell and Solomon, 1997) in contemporary globalisation.

Global professional labour markets in professional service firms

> In recent years there has been an increased emphasis within the management literature on the role of organisational knowledge as a means of gaining and sustaining competitive advantage in the 'post-industrial' economy . . . which sees employees as embodying the strategic capabilities of the firm, in terms of the knowledge that they possess. (Morris and Empson, 1998: 609)

In PSFs, the strategic resource of the firm is knowledge, embodied in the individual (Skyrme, 1999; Pritchard et al., 2000; Maister, 2003). Firms create wealth and add value in capital accumulation through the successful deployment of professional staff who can meet the intrinsic and idiosyncratic business requirements of the client in co-location (Aharoni, 1993; Beaverstock, 2004). Morris and Empson (1998: 610) use the term PSF in the context of accounting and consultancy to refer to, 'an organisation that trades mainly on the knowledge of its human capital, that is its employees and the producer-owners, to develop and deliver intangible solutions to client problems'. Lowendahl et al. (2001: 912) agree with this interpretation of PSFs in the world economy, but go further and suggest that they, 'represent a growing part of both employment and value creation in western economies' (also see Lowendahl, 1997).

Lowendahl (1997: 20) suggests that PSFs have seven major organisational characteristics, all of which depend upon the knowledge, performance, creativity and reputation of its knowledge-rich workforce. First, PSFs employ very high proportions of highly educated people, who keep abreast with new ideas and innovation through contact with industry-specific research institutes, seminars and scientific meetings. Second, PSFs deliver services which are formulated on professional advice, assessment and diagnosis. Third, PSFs offer clients very high degrees of personalised judgements and in some sectors, professional staff may be held personally liable for such advice. Fourth, PSFs 'customise' services to meet the exact requirements of clients, which results in most work being non-routine or not duplicated to others. Fifth, individuals employed in PSFs are usually trained as members of professional bodies with standardised, certificated qualifications (for example, the Law Society), but they can be untrained and uncertified, relying upon other elements in their individual portfolio of knowledge and skills (for example, creativity in advertising). Finally, and of significant importance, 'delivery involves a high degree of interaction with the client representatives, for diagnosis as well as delivery' (ibid.).

Professional–client interaction is of the utmost importance for knowledge transfer in professional services. Nonaka and Takeuchi (1995) recognise that socialisation is the vector which translates tacit into explicit knowledge through the process of codification. Without interaction, knowledge cannot easily be transferred within PSFs, and between PSFs and clients, because without socialisation, it cannot be embodied or embedded in different spatial contexts (Hedlund and Nonaka, 1993; Nonaka and Konno, 1998). In geographical circles, the process of 'face-to-face' contact is suggested by many as being a factor of production responsible for knowledge sharing (Sassen, 2001). 'Face-to-face' relationships are a key constituent of the world city financial centre (Thrift, 1999, 2000), the homeland of PSFs. Without face-to-face contact with clients, competitors or regulators, PSFs cannot function because professional staff are required to perform in the market and display their credentials over and above their professional qualifications to court clients and be successful (for example, trustworthiness; social graces; coherence; reciprocity – see Goffman, 1967; Nohria and Eccles, 1992; Van Krogh et al., 2000).

Transnational PSFs can deliver intrinsic services to clients only through personal interaction. In international offices, such delivery occurs through the employment of local hires and international staff, who stretch knowledge systems cross-border (Allen, 2000). It is these individuals who produce global professional labour markets in PSFs. In short, but of crucial significance in the production of global professional labour markets, 'the mobility of personnel is widely recognised as a mechanism for distributing tacit knowledge and skills, or human capital across space and time' (Madsen et al., 2002: 164).

International mobility and the firm

Professional staff have always moved within, and between, the international internal labour markets of firms, a process referred to as 'organisational labour migration' (Salt, 1988). But, it is within the realms of management science that such mobility has been scrutinised inter- and intra-firm; synonymous with 'expatriation' (Tung, 1988). Research on expatriation has mushroomed in management science over recent years. American researchers have examined expatriation and international occupational mobility within US firms since the 1960s (1961 saw the publication of the US John Wiley & Co. journal *Human Resource Management*). Since the 1970s, we have witnessed the emergence of the study of IHRM in 'western' management science, and latterly global business school environs (stimulating the birth of new journals devoted to the subject area – for example, the *International Journal of Human Resource Management* was established in 1989; *Human Resource Management Review* in 1990). IHRM research is now intensively investigating all aspects of expatriation (selection, training, adjustment, strategic roles, gender relations, dual-career couples, family, repatriation and career development; see Brewster, 1991; Black et al., 1992; Selmer, 1995), but its greatest asset still remains in explaining why firms need to send professional staff abroad to international subsidiaries.

The organisational strategy to use international assignees (expatriates) rather than local professional staff has always been a great discussion point in IHRM (Schell and Solomon, 1997). Thirty-five years ago, it was Edstrom and Galbraith's (1977a, b) pioneering work on expatriation that set the foundations for explaining why cross-border international transfers were prevalent within multinational corporations (MNCs). They suggested that professional and technical personnel were sent to work in MNC international locations for one or more of three main reasons. First, to fill vacancies that cannot be filled by locally qualified personnel because either they are unavailable or they cannot easily be trained. Second, as a process for developing the international experience of management within the firm because of the necessity to expose junior and middle-ranking staff to international business systems, even if locally qualified staff are in plentiful supply. Third, as a corporate policy to develop the organisation as a whole, where international assignments are used to disseminate corporate policy, decision making and best practice. It is interesting to note, however, that despite many different analyses of expatriation with firms (for example, Black et al., 1992), the IHRM specialists have not made any real quantum leaps into refining the explanation for expatriation as many have retained the 'multinational' mode of knowledge development and dissemination (that is, up and down from headquarters to subsidiaries) rather than taking on board the network relationships of the transnational corporation (Dicken, 2003; Bartlett and Ghoshal, 1989).

Globalisation and professional labour markets in large accountancy firms
Post-Enron and Worldcom, international accounting is dominated by the organisational activities of the 'Big Four': PricewaterhouseCoopers; Deloitte Touche Tohmatsu; KPMG International; and Ernst and Young. By the end of 2002, combined, these firms accumulated a worldwide fee income of $56,261 million (more than three times higher than the aggregated income of the next 16 firms) and operated through extensive office networks, each in over 130+ countries worldwide (Table 22.2; see Figure 22.1). PricewaterhouseCoopers is the largest accountancy network in the world. At financial year end June 2001, it had a staggering worldwide fee income of $22,300 million, almost double that of its nearest rival Deloitte Touche Tohmatsu ($12,400 million), a network of 814 offices in 150 countries and employed 9200 partners and another 135,300 professional staff (excluding administrative employees) (Table 22.2). Since the pioneering work of Daniels, Leyshon and Thrift in the late 1980s (for example, Daniels et al., 1988, 1989), it is still the case that investigating the global organisational strategies of accounting firms is the most fertile approach for explaining the globalisation of accountancy worldwide (see Greenwood et al., 1999); and therefore the production of global accounting professional labour markets (see Beaverstock, 1991; Hanlon, 1999).

Dunning's (1988, 1993) 'eclectic' ownership–location–internationalisation' (OLI) paradigm is one explanatory framework which can be used to understand why business service firms engage in international production. Dunning (1993) notes that such firms go abroad to service the interests of their clients who have already entered foreign markets (client following) and to service new foreign and domestic customers (market seeking) (Erramilli and Rao, 1990). The crux of Dunning's (1993) argument is that the firm will only engage in international production if it has a competitive advantage with respect to ownership, location and internalisation in that particular market (Table 22.3). With respect to the globalisation strategies of international accounting firms, Dunning observes that they will only engage in international activities cross-border if they have specific advantages regarding: ownership (for example, access to transnational clients); location (for example, on-the-spot contact with clients); and internalisation (for example, limited inter-firm linkages). Of great significance in Dunning's (ibid.: 272) use of the OLI paradigm is the form of entry into the market for accounting which is as a partnership or wholly owned subsidiary operating through the office network (see United Nations Center for Transnational Corporations, 1988).

The principal organisational mode for globalisation in professional service accounting firms is though a wholly owned presence represented by the international office (Radebaugh and Gray, 1993; Bagchi-Sen and Sen, 1997). Those accounting firms that have gone global over the last 30 years have done so through combinations of organic start-ups (that is, opening new offices in international markets) and/or aggressive merger and acquisition activity (that is, buying other firms) (Rajan and Fryatt, 1988; Daniels et al., 1989; Beaverstock, 1991). In both instances, the major organisational outcome of the globalisation of accounting has been concentration in the international market. A small group of firms' (the 'Big Six') oligopolies fee income is generated from extensive office networks worldwide because clients expect to be serviced in proximity by professional, highly

Table 22.2 International accountancy networks, 2001/2 (ranked by fee income $m)

Network	UK member firm	Fee income	Countries	Offices	Member firms	Partners	Prof. Staff
PricewaterhouseCoopers	PwC	22,330	150	814	–	9219	135,295
Deloitte Touche Tohatsu	Deloitte & Touche	12,400	140	–	–	–	95,000
KPMG International	KPMG	11,700	152	754	147	6655	72,690
Ernst & Young	Ernst & Young	9,861	130	670		5777	57,645
BDO International	BDO Stoy Hayward	2,203	98	589	88	2168	15,412
Grant Thornton Int'L	Grant Thornton	1790	109	652	–	2270	21,879
RSM International	RSM Rhodes Rhodes	1632	65	565	64	2065	11,547
Horwarth International	Horwarth Clark Whitehill	1447	80	375	–	2161	12,956
Moores Rowland Int'L	Moores Rowland	1380	92	646	170	2118	12,486
Baker Tilly Int'L	Baker Tilly	1208	58	448	106	1651	9623
Nexia International	Smith & Williamson	1189	72	241	99	1312	9821
AGN International	More than one member	933	76	448	182	1205	8657
HLB International	Numerica	875	105	451	183	1346	7797
Moores Stephens Int'L	Moores Stephens	687	82	445	259	1395	8289
Kreston International	More than one member	642	66	349	176	982	5312
IGAF	More than one member	551	64	366	138	969	669
MacIntyre St. Int'L	Haysmacintyre	550	85	235	207	1300	4000
BKR International	BKR Haynes Watts	506	61	288	121	886	5713
CPA Ass., Inc	MacIntyre Hudson	505	45	235	107	610	3660
PKF International	PKF	500	105	282	156	875	7003
Next 10 firms (mean)		309	54	192	111	577	3115

Source: Accountancy (2002).

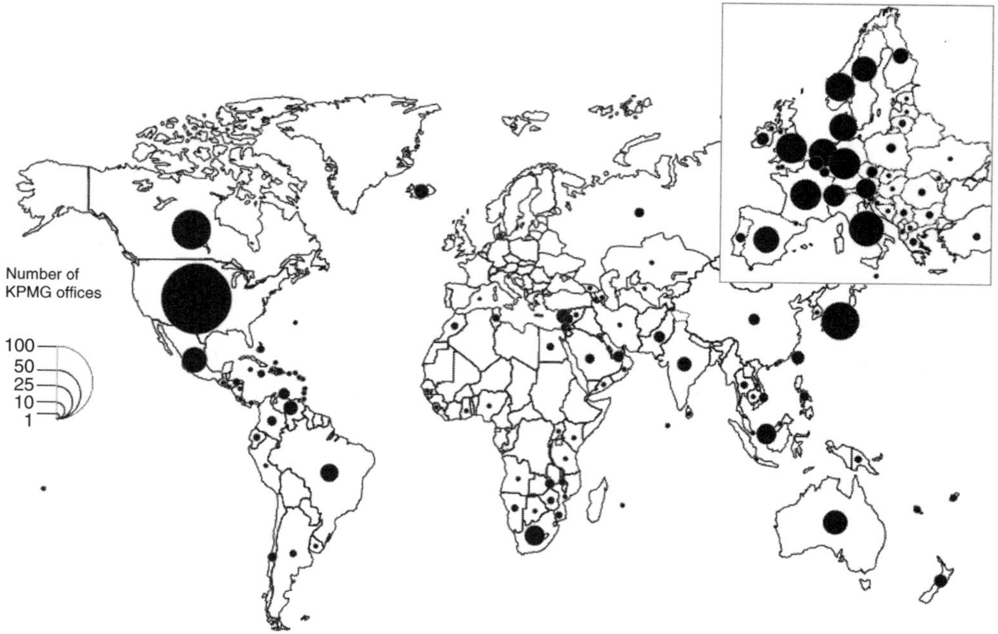

Source: KPMG Office Directory, www.kpmg.com/about/locations.asp, accessed 3 December 2003.

Figure 22.1 The international office network of KPMG, 2003

Table 22.3 Ownership, location and internalisation advantages in transnational accounting/auditing corporations

Ownership (competitive advantages)	Location (configuration advantages)	Internalisation (coordinating advantages)	Organisational form
Access to transnational clients	On-the-spot contact with clients	Limited interfirm linkages	Mostly partnerships or individual proprietorships
Experience of standards required	Accounting tends to be culture sensitive	Quality control over (international) standards	Overseas subsidiaries loosely organised, little centralised control
Brand image of leading accounting firms	Adaptation to local reporting standards and procedures. Oligopolistic interaction	Government insistence on local participation	Few joint ventures, little inter-firm trade

Source: Adapted from Dunning (1993: 272).

qualified personnel either within the confines of the firm, or within their own company infrastructure (normally undertaken by staff on secondment) (Hanlon, 1994; Beaverstock, 1996).

Chartered accountancy is very much a client-focused industry (Hanlon, 1994) as: 'the work is knowledge intensive and requires employment of highly-trained professionals . . . [and] . . . requires that the knowledge professional be located near the client and that he or she practise marketing and service delivery at one and the same time' (Greenwood et al., 1999: 269). Accordingly, transnational accounting firms sell intricate expertise and professionalism in auditing, taxation, financial services, corporate finance and recovery, e-commerce solutions and forensic litigation to other transnational, national and local clients on a global stage (Table 22.4). Each firm's international office acts as a global knowledge resource of professional staff who have the capacity to provide global business solutions to clients at global, national, regional or local scales. For accountancy, the principal factor responsible for its globalisation is the requirement to have professional staff engaging in 'face-to-face' contact with clients or being able to provide generic and intrinsic expertise in non-client-facing projects in the office, but in physical proximity to the client when called upon (Beaverstock, 1996; Grey, 1998). As Greenwood et al. (1999: 269) comment, 'these professionals represent the asset stock of the firm. The firm is dependent upon these workers'. Like with other PSFs (for example, law, see Warf, 2001), accountants need to be in close proximity to the client, supplier or support services (for example, legal firms), accessible and purvey an aura of trust, credibility and sheer competence at all times in all markets. Partners are responsible for managing teams of professional staff (seniors, post-qualified and qualifying), generating fee income and bringing into the firm new clientele – a process which often requires significant networking activities and often cross-border travel (Hanlon, 1994, 1999;

Table 22.4 Main services provided by professional service accounting firms

Service	Descriptor	Mode of delivery
Audit	The analysis of client income/expenditure balance sheets. The mainstay of fee income for accounting firms (37% in 2003)	Client or office
Taxation	Firms advise clients how they can best minimise their tax burden while complying with country tax regulations (29% of fee income in 2003)	Client or office
Corporate finance	Firms provide advice to clients on mergers and acquisitions, corporate restructuring and debt management (8% of fee income in 2003)	Client or office
Insolvency	Firms advise clients' creditors on bankruptcy and business recovery services, and administer bankrupt businesses (accounted for 10% of fee income in 2003)	Client or office
Consulting	Consulting (IT, e-commerce, human resource) business accounted for 9% of income in 2003	Client
Legal	The newest service provided by the leading firms. Firms acquired legal firms in member countries to provide complete professional services and compete with London/New York firms (less than 5% of fee income in 2003)	Client

Source: Adapted from the International Financial Services London (2003).

Beaverstock, 1996, 2002). Seniors, post-qualified and qualifying staff can be both at the client interface or working in project teams away from the direct gaze of the client, but in either case, it is the combined knowledge, expertise, professionalism and competences of the accounting firm's professional staff which build the reputation of the firm, and ultimately determine its growth, profitability and survival in the international market (Morris and Empson, 1998). Once the illegal accounting procedures of Arthur Andersen & Co.'s professional staff in Texas made the global news stands in 2002, the magic qualities of trust, credibility, competence and confidence were instantaneously destroyed, and in a real-time domino effect collapsed worldwide. As Greenwood et al. (1999: 269) lament, 'knowledge workers are mobile assets, and could easily damage the reputation of a firm either by defection of by engaging in inappropriate behaviours (e.g. low quality service) while with the firm'.

The existence of global professional labour markets within large accounting firms (partners and other professional staff – seniors, post-qualified and qualifying, excluding technical support) is, therefore, an essential organisational strategy in their existence as PSFs. Those accounting firms with 'world firm' status in terms of office numbers and geographical representation, and transnational clients (institutions, firms and nation states),

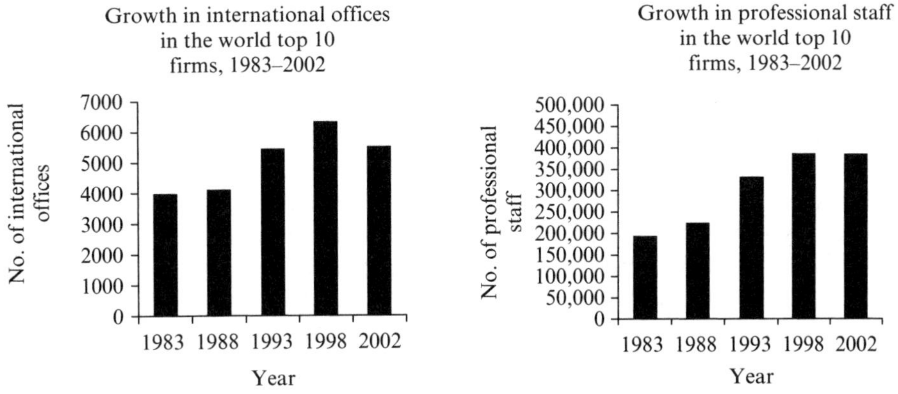

Source: Accountancy (2002); *International Accounting Bulletin* (1983, 1988, 1993).

Figure 22.2 Professional labour market and office change in the world's top 10 accounting firms, 1983–2002

operate organisational structures in partnerships or wholly own subsidiaries which are characterised by homogeneity with respect to business practice, standards and culture across all international boundaries (Hanlon, 1999). An important mechanism with which large accounting firms produce and disseminate knowledge, expertise and competences within their global organisational structure is through the employment of large-scale global professional labour markets, operating out of extensive international office networks (Beaverstock, 1996).

Within large accounting firms there has been continual growth in the professional labour market. In 1983 the top 10 leading global firms employed 191,328 total professional staff worldwide and by 1988 this figure had increased by 17 per cent to 224,461 in 4099 offices (*International Accounting Bulletin*, 1983, 1988; see Figure 22.2). Remarkably, five years on, the top 10 leading firms employed a staggering 331,286 total professional staff in 5446 offices (75 per cent more than in 1983 and 48 per cent more than in 1988, respectively). But, between 1993 and 2002 the market stabilised, and the number of total professional staff employed by the top 10 world firms increased by 16 per cent, from 331,286 to 383,712 (*International Accounting Bulletin*, 1993; Accountancy, 2002). During the same 10-year period, the firms' international office networks increased by only 1 per cent, from 5446 to 5513 (see Figure 22.2). It must be noted, however, that the 2002 data exclude Arthur Andersen & Co. for both total professional staff and office networks.

Both Hanlon (1994, 1999) and Beaverstock (1996) agree that the expansion in the total global professional labour markets for large accounting firms was the key to their success in globalisation during the last quarter of the twentieth century. As firms established new organic starts or acquired offices through merger and acquisition activity, the domination of the global six firms, and more latterly the Big Four, provided the impetus for professional labour markets in accountancy to begin to operate on a global scale through the organisational strategy of international assignments, secondments or transfers within and between the international office networks of the large world firms. Beaverstock (1991, 1996) noted that all the Big Six regularly moved partners, seniors, post-qualified and qualifying staff cross-border for more than one year: to check skill shortages in newly opened or extremely busy offices; to manage departments and or offices; as part of structured career development programmes; to fire-fight and trouble shoot; and as a training device for international staff to circulate between branch offices and the firms' HQ (in London, Amsterdam, New York or Chicago). Hanlon (1999) also noted that during the late 1980s and throughout the 1990s, the Big Six used international migration of professional staff between offices to recruit graduates into the firm and retain post-qualified staff under extremely tight labour market conditions. But, more importantly, Hanlon (ibid.: 206) suggested that all the Big Six used the international migration of professional staff as a means of 'selling themselves as "world firms" to clients'.

Clearly, accountancy as a professional service is dependent upon the professional labour market to produce, disseminate and reproduce generic and specific knowledge, expertise and competences within, and between, international office networks. Of course, such labour market characteristics can be fulfilled by the employment of national domiciles who have the appropriate professionalisation, expertise and competences, at all professional and managerial scales (managing partner, partner, senior, post-qualified, qualified, qualifying), but to have the professionalism, expertise and skills to work for one of the Big Six is another matter (Coffey, 1994; Grey, 1998). In the United Kingdom in 2002 there was an estimated qualified labour supply of 236,000 individuals certified by the professional bodies (International Financial Services London, 2003). What is of great interest in the analysis of qualified membership data for accounting was that 26 per cent of the total qualified members (83,381) worked outside of the United Kingdom in 2002 (Table 22.5). Increasingly, the largest 10 accounting firms have significant percentages of their qualified staff working outside of their country of permanent residence, whose transnational working practices represent an important strategic organisational

Table 22.5 Qualified membership of accounting professional bodies in the UK, 2002

	Location		
Professional body	UK	Outside UK	Total
ICAEW	109,000	14,719	123,719
ICAS	12,950	2079	15,029
ICAI	3000	9000	12,000
ACCA	53,500	41,916	95,416
CIMA	44,500	15,396	59,896
CIPFA	13,200	271	13,471
Total	236,150	83,381	319,531

Notes:
Institute of Chartered Accountants of England and Wales (ICAEW).
Institute of Chartered Accountants of Scotland (ICAS).
Institute of Chartered Accountants of Ireland (ICAI).
Association of Chartered Certified Accountants (ACCA).
Chartered Institute of Management Accountants (CIMA).
Chartered Institute of Public Finance and Accountancy (CIPFA).

Source: International Financial Services London (2003).

device to ensure the firms' continued world status, transnational knowledge management and dissemination and career development (Hanlon, 1999). Accordingly, what is not in dispute is that global professional labour markets within accounting PSFs are reproduced through international migration. But what is of significant importance is to unpack the firm processes which have created the existence of global professional labour markets in accounting PSFs which are now increasingly being characterised by mobility rather than migration, frequent cross-border business travel and transnational embodied and virtual working practices, aided by fast jet travel, information technology and the internet age.

International mobility and global professional labour markets

Case-study research has always been a chief methodology to understand the organisational strategies of service firms in the world economy (Daniels, 1993). But, before the interview survey is reported, the role of global professional labour markets in creating value for networked firm–client relationships are discussed within PricewaterhouseCoopers (PwC).

PricewaterhouseCoopers

On the front cover of PwC's (2003) *Global Annual Review* the strap-line is 'connected thinking'. Samuel A. DiPiazza Jr, the chief executive officer of PwC International Ltd, in his opening address 'Staying connected' makes the observation:

> [H]aving highly skilled people . . . is crucial to providing high-quality service. We remain committed to our people and our values: excellence, teamwork and leadership. Our global connectivity enables our people to consult with one another and to search for better answers across national borders. This is our style, and it's an effective one . . . We believe the term 'Connected Thinking' most clearly describes our unique global network of people, values, services and purposes. (p. 3)

The key message from DiPiazza's statement is that PwC's ability to create trust, value, quality and integrity for clients is built very much around the knowledge and expertise of its global professional staff. It is recognised as a 'truly global organisation with member firm offices in 768 cities in 139 countries' (p. 6) because it is able to offer clients, wherever they are in the world, 'industry knowledge and professional expertise to identify, report, protect, realise and create value' (p. 8). At the fulcrum of this mission statement is the ability to deliver breadth and depth in business solutions to client relationships through the expertise of its global professional workforce (7879 partners; 87,727 client service staff; and 27,214 practice support staff in 2003).

PwC adopts a 'Global Deployment Programme' (GDP) to ensure that the worldwide network of firms 'stay connected', with respect to both corporate philosophy and client expectations. As the PwC network is composed of legally separated and locally owned and managed firms around the globe, the GDP 'creates the organisational glue at every level, from individual client teams to global lines of service and industry groupings' (pp. 24–5). In essence, all of PwCs' professional staff remain connected to the ethos of the international firm network through the GDP which connects individuals and teams virtually through e-learning, industry-specific residential conferences and travel, but more importantly, through the physical mobility of professional staff between international offices (and firms) in the worldwide network.

PwC uses the international mobility of professional staff to 'build understanding of each other's cultures and working environments and sustain the formal and informal networks that connect the . . . [PwC] . . . community worldwide' (p. 25). The worldwide firm supports three types of international deployment streams:

1. long-term assignments of more than one year that are of strategic importance to the worldwide firm;
2. short-term tactical or strategic assignments; and
3. tactical deployment for the purpose of individual professional development.

In 1999/2000, the firm had 5000 professional staff on all three international deployments (almost 5 per cent of its total global professional staff) (Personal Communication, 30 June 1999). The 2003 *Global Annual Review* noted that in total some 2300 partners and professional staff (about 2 per cent of the professional workforce) were involved in international assignments of the three types from six months to five years in 76 countries. Approximately 1040 of these professional staff were involved in 'long-term assignments' to service clients and further cultivate the strength of the PwC worldwide network of firms (see Figure 22.3), where almost a quarter were deployed to the USA (a pattern not out of line with other studies: Beaverstock, 1996). The remaining 2300 were involved in much shorter time-scale 'short-term' or 'tactical' deployments. In 2003 PwC had significantly increased the number of staff who were sent on short-term and tactical assignments to 'give more people the opportunity to build international experience' and for the Fiscal Year 2004, PwC would again increase the mobility of those working on short-term assignments (2003 *Global Annual Review*).

Results from the firm interview survey

The empirical study reported in this part of the chapter was collected from secondary sources and semi-structured interviews with senior partners responsible for international human resources in three of the Big Six accounting PSFs in 1999/2000 (before the collapse of Arthur Andersen & Co.). All firms interviewed were legally organised as international networks composed of separately owned member firms or partnerships in different countries or regions of the globe. Each international network was managed by an international board with elected partners from each member firm or partnership. All human resource partners interviewed were responsible for moving professional people into and out of their member firm or partnership, usually the UK. All firms interviewed, firm-specific official and unofficial sources are anonymised to protect confidentiality. It is the economic geography of these global professional labour markets, produced through the cross-border deployment of international human resources, that will form the basis of the proceeding discussion.

The corporate rationale for producing global professional labour markets

As with PwC, an analysis of the accounting firms' annual reports and World Wide Web sites depict an industry which is constantly projecting the professional expertise, trust, experience and credibility of its partners and professional staff as being the prime resources of the firm in the global accounting business. Of course, this is not a surprising finding as these are knowledge-intensive PSFs where value is created by the competence

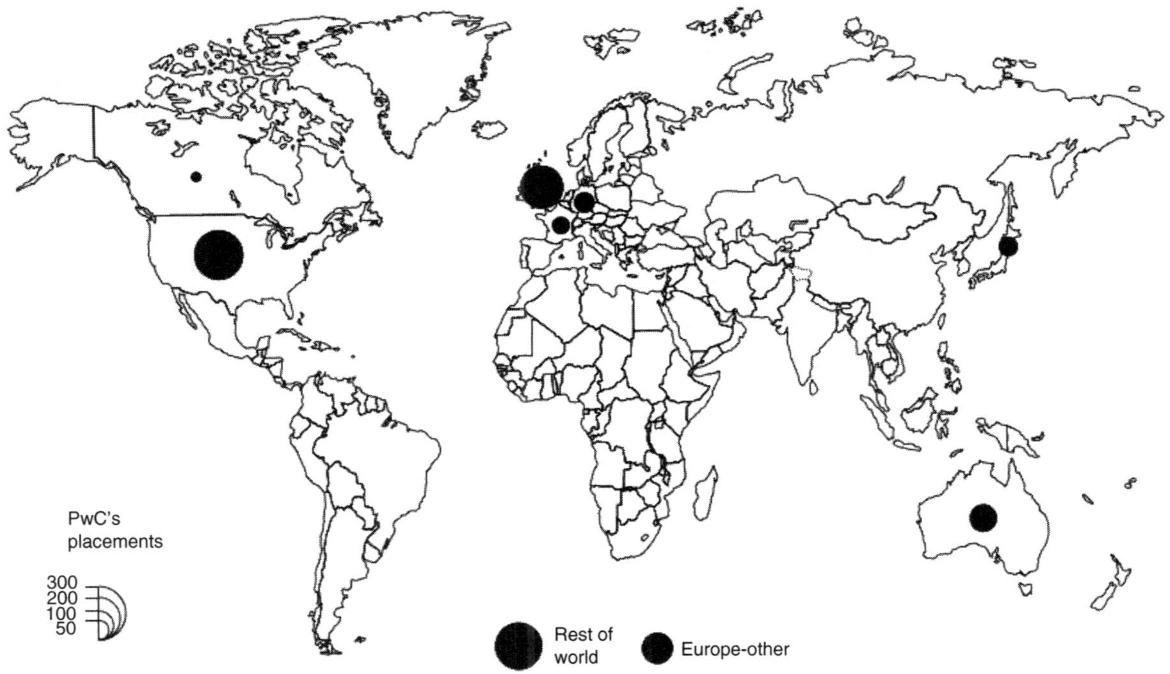

Source: PricewaterhouseCoopers (2003).

Figure 22.3 Distribution of professional staff on long-term assignments in PwC's worldwide network or international member firms, 2003

of the firm's human capital in client networks and trust relationships (Hanlon, 2003). At interview with all firms (A1, A2, A3) the key message was that they all still required professional labour to be assigned to international offices for short (less than one year) or longer (greater than one year) periods, despite the increasing use of business travel, videoconferencing, e-learning and other ICT. As one partner (Firm A2) commented:

> It seems like a paradox in a way because you would think that we've got telecoms, we've got video conferencing facilities, etc., and why do you need to send someone abroad . . . in order to actually make it happen . . . to set it up and do it. The firm wants to globalise and increase its links around the world and you want people to gain international experience.

The firm transfers knowledge, skills and competences embodied in individuals to either its own international offices or to those of other member firms, or to specific clients. Simultaneously, the worldwide firm facilitates international mobility of its professional workforce between member firm offices in order to instil a global cohesion for the execution of corporate policy on the global stage. International mobility is an organisational strategy which promotes the worldwide firm's global reach which cannot be underestimated in projecting the global corporate image of the firm. As Firm A3 noted:

> It is very much seen as an international firm now. They are encouraging global movements, encouraging that we all work together as one big firm, because inevitably as we work together we are going to be a global unit for all our clients. We will have skills and experiences from all over the world that we can offer them.

Within these three Big Six firms, global professional labour markets are produced and reproduced through four major organisational strategies:

1. *Strategic, business-led mobility* Firms post professional accounting staff cross-border within and between member firms of the network in order to bring new or duplicated knowledge, expertise and competences to a particular time–space point of demand. International assignees work for a range of different clients in their specialist area. Partners are usually sent on an international assignment to head up newly established offices or departments in established offices, or to manage project teams in long-term client-based relationships. For example, all of A2's new office start-ups and growth through mergers and acquisitions in Eastern Europe, post-Soviet states, Africa and Latin America, have been managed by partners from its major US offices. In contrast, post-qualified accountants, seniors or managers are sent to international offices within or outside the member firm not to manage or create the office practice, but to bring specific specialist expertise to client-facing and back-client project teams as required. For all firms, this was the major rationale for posting professional staff to international offices. Just as partners are sent to start up new offices or departments, post-qualified staff are sent to the same destination to work alongside locally qualified staff. Equally, post-qualified staff are sent to work in teams managed by host-qualified partners. Sending professional staff to international offices within or between member firms is required because all the firms, 'need to have people who are mobile, people with the right skills . . . it's enhancing the skills and abilities of our people to meet client needs' (Firm A1). For example, each firm assigned audit and

taxation post-qualified staff to meet the labour market demand for these skills in international offices as local regulatory frameworks dictated different accounting 'seasons' for the client end of financial year reporting – a process which accounts for substantial flows of accounting staff in all firms to Australia, New Zealand and North America. As Firm A2 comments, 'we do a lot of moves . . . in the tax division, where different countries have different tax years, the busy season, you move people around the world to cover everybody's tax season'.

2. *Management development programmes* Each firm executed a standard international network-wide international assignment policy for both business strategy and career development. Global-wide international assignment programmes were used as a mechanism to standardise mobility between member firms, regulate unusually high volumes of movement and provide equalised 'expatriate packages' (for example, adjusted salaries; tax harmonisation; subsidised accommodation) within the international network. Firm A1, for example, has the International Mobility Assignment Program (IMAP) directed from its New York office. All international assignments in the firm, except business travel and business commuting, are regulated through IMAP, which is divided into three programmes: international secondments (where staff remain employed by the member firm, even when working for the client); international transfers (where staff are employed by other member-firm offices); and international exchanges (*quid pro quo* exchanges with member and non-member offices used for training and career development for qualifying staff). In a similar vein, Firm A3's 'Global Staffing Policy' is organised into the same three international programmes as Firm A1: career development (transfers within the member firm's international office network); secondments (to clients and other member-firm offices); and exchange (for training). The leading 10 global firms have always sent professional staff on international assignments through the organisational lens of the management development programme (Beaverstock, 1991, 1996; Hanlon, 1999).

3. *Secondments to clients* All three firms have transnational clients who expect the firm's staff to represent their interests worldwide. Firm A3 sends the majority of its assignees outside of the firm to service the cross-border requirements of its clientele, 'we have clients all over the world . . . and we have to send our staff to these places . . . to service our clients'. Firm A2 agrees and noted:

   > [T]here will be a specific requirement for a skill set which is not available locally. It can be because the client is UK based, knows the people that have done work for them here in the UK and wants to move the same people to wherever the other location happens to be.

   In all three firms, accounting staff physically worked in their clients' offices auditing their books or providing taxation or other advice (corporate, insolvency, expatriate). In addition, many consultancy-based projects require specialist staff to be ensconced with the client, but in real-time communication with their home or closest international office.

4. *Cross-border projects, business travel and business commuting* Increasingly the work process in accountancy is client-project based (for one, two or three or six months), involving frequent trans-border circulation of both accounting personnel and management consultants. All firms regularly engaged professional staff in very flexible and time-specific cross-border working activities. Four major types of hyper-international

mobility can be identified. First, is *business travel* between office and client, or client and client. Typically, professional staff would engage in such cross-border activities at least once or twice a month or, for some, on a weekly basis depending on the requirements and location of the client, or strategic labour shortage in any receiving office. All firms had staff moving within Europe (for example, London to Paris; Frankfurt to London; Amsterdam to Paris and so on), but also between London and North American cities and vice versa, especially (Chicago, New York, Boston, Los Angeles). Second, is *business commuting*, characterised by frequent travel back 'home' during an international assignment or project. For example, Firm A3 has US professional staff in London who work in the city three weeks in four and then return 'home' for one week and then return to London for another three weeks and so on (three weeks 'on', one week 'off'). Third, is directly *client led*. These are short-term, frequent assignments to clients which could last from a few days to one week to six months, but are also characterised with business travel and commuting back to the sending office. For example, Firm A2 has a group of staff supporting clients (physically located in their offices), but returning to the sending office at least once a week or month (for a few days) to deal with the client's UK interests. Fourth, is *international hot-desking* in member-firm offices, which occurred within specific pan-regional contexts (for example, within Europe and between Europe and Eastern Europe; between Australia and New Zealand). For example, all firms frequently moved staff between pan-regional international offices to meet very short-term skilled labour market demands as they were identified in specific client relationships and projects. Here, the crucial point is that these personnel were not tied to any one specific client or project like many, but were just brought into the firm–client relationship or project when specific knowledge and expertise was required in high volume, resulting in very, very short-term hyper-mobility between international locations, clients and member offices.

The geography of global professional labour markets

All firms had cadres of internationally mobile professional staff, representing anything between 3 and 6 per cent of the total number of professional staff in the global network (Table 22.6). These data are misleading, however, because they exclude those personnel who move very frequently, especially management consultants, who are not 'classified' as being on an international assignment (the traditional expatriate). All of the 5000 to 6500 staff on international assignment in Firms A1 to A3 were fee-earning staff, liaising directly with clients either in-office or within the client's premises. Given the transnational organisation of these accounting firms, where organisational strategy flowed both horizontally and vertically within the firm's internal international structure (Bartlett and Ghoshal's (1989) transnational model – see Dicken, 2003), in all instances, these staff worked alongside locally qualified professional staff and accountants of other nationalities. In all cases, the global professional labour markets of the major pan-regional offices within these firms were characterised by managing, senior and junior partners, and post-qualified staff and trainees of many nationalities. Exceptions to these office labour market dynamics were where firms had recently opened new offices in Eastern Europe or Asia, and then they were managed by an international assignee in the first instance, who worked alongside local hires.

Specifically, the firms' major world city and capital city offices were the major locations for professional staff numbers and, therefore, international assignees who reproduced the

Table 22.6 International assignments in firm professional labour markets, 1999–2000

Firm	International assignments in	
	Worldwide network	Member firm
A1	1000–1500	75–100
A2	2000–3000	600
A3	2000	600
Total	5000–6500	1275–1300

Note: Data for the member firm are included in the firm's worldwide network, which will include several other member firms in their organisational, partnership structure. Thus Firm A3's 2000 international assignees in its worldwide network, is composed of 600 originating from its European member firm and the remaining 1200 supplied by other world regional member firms (for example, Central and South American).

Source: Fieldwork.

'global' in this labour market group, thus corroborating previous research which indicated that world cities provided the strategic locations for global professional labour markets in PSFs (Beaverstock, 1996, 2002; Hanlon, 1999; Sassen, 2001). As all these firms had their headquarters within the member firm, London in the case of the UK member firms, substantial flows of accounting international assignees flowed from London to the headquarters of other member firms within the international network. Firm A3's comments summarised very succinctly the locational dynamics of this labour market:

> The US used to be just New York but now it is all over, every office, if you are looking at consulting, they are all going to the West coast, if you are looking at financial services, the majority are going to Boston, Chicago, New York, your big financial areas, if you are looking at areas of tax, they go all over. The other big recruiter is Australia, Sydney and Melbourne both being big financial service centres, they are probably our biggest recruiter. New Zealand, Auckland, Wellington, they are quite small offices, so they have quite a big expatriate program in comparison to the size of the office. Europe, we send people to France, Germany, Eastern Europe. Canada is another big recruiter. Then you have got the islands, the financial services big-time recruiters are the islands offshore, so you are looking at Bermuda, British Virgin Islands, Cayman Islands, they are financial service hubs, anybody that you speak to that works in those areas will know what they do best is insurance or banking.

Accordingly, substantial two-way flows of personnel were identified between London and cities in: the United States (for example, Boston, Chicago, New York); Europe (for example, Amsterdam, Paris, Brussels, Frankfurt, Madrid, Stockholm, Copenhagen, Rome); Eastern Europe and beyond (for example, Moscow, Budapest, Prague, Warsaw); the Middle East (for example, Manama); the Indian sub-continent (for example, New Delhi, Bangalore, Mumbai); the Far East (for example, Singapore, Hong Kong, Ho Chi Minh City); and Australasia (for example, Sydney, Auckland). Despite office density and proximities in Western Europe, international assignments are still of importance in this region, as Firm A2 notes: 'we have seen people moving much more across Western European boundaries, borders, Germany to Italy, France to Spain, Switzerland to the UK. Everybody is much more mobile, much more globally aware . . . Borders are not what they once were'.

In most cases, international assignees and other internationally mobile staff circulated between the member firm's largest offices (ranked by fee income and professional staff), which act as the focus point for servicing transnational and national clients in the specific country market. In these offices, international assignees were principally auditors or taxation specialists. In almost all firms, auditors and taxation specialists made up the majority of international assignments which were of an expatriate nature (that is, for more than one year).

Two other important points can be made about the locational dynamics of these global professional labour markets. First, much of the project-based cross-border consultancy work was undertaken directly with the client, which could be located in any city, or elsewhere. However, as many of these firms' transnational clients are also located in world cities, especially those in related financial services, e-commerce, legal for example, these locations are also the most significant destinations for those involved in frequent, very short-term international mobility. Second, given the very high volumes of cross-border business travel and commuting being undertaken between continents and within continents, all firms stressed that their professional staff reached clients wherever their location. Consequently, many situations occurred in all firms where professionals were assigned to an office in one city, but then moved in frequent cross-border business or commuting travel between both offices and clients.

The research findings highlighted an interesting dimension to the operation of these global professional labour markets. In recently opened organic offices or those created through merger and acquisition activity (for example, new ventures in Eastern Europe or East Asia), initial line management would be delegated by an international assignee (managing partner), who hired locals and also hired international assignees (fee-earning professionals) from the member firm. In established offices worldwide, the demarcation between international assignees and other professional staff was more complex and horizontal in scope. International assignees worked alongside local hires and assignees of other nationalities in departments headed by local managing partners and/or international assignees alike. Those professional staff who were seconded directly to clients in their organisations had high degrees of autonomy, but were in constant dialogue with their line manager, the managing partner in the sending office. Those professional staff who were constantly involved in business and commuting travel entered working relationships with clients and local hires and other international assignees. In sum, accounting global professional labour markets: (i) function at different global–local scales; (ii) are hyper-mobile and flexible with respect to location and time-scale; (iii) are composed of combinations of local and international staff; and (iv) include the so-called 'frequent flyers' – business travellers and business commuters, who work alongside locally contracted foreign nationals (as in the case of many European Union citizens working throughout the single market).

Discussion and conclusions

All of the leading accounting firms perpetuate professional labour markets at the global scale through the circulation of partners and qualified staff between international office locations, and the employment of local hires in situ. The global circulation of professional staff is a business system used to transfer knowledge, expertise and professionalism cross-border, or in the words of Bartlett and Ghoshal (1989: 75) for 'the development and diffusion of knowledge . . . worldwide'. Since the accountancy industry is very much a client-focused and -led sector, where many inherent characteristics of PSFs are relevant (Hanlon, 1994; Morris and Empson, 1998; Greenwood et al., 1999; Lowendahl et al., 2001), the existence of global professional labour markets is essential to service clients both locally and in cross-border relationships. In short, fee income in the accountancy industry is sought, created and generated in particular through the knowledge, expertise, professional competences and skills of certified staff. Accordingly, a vital globalisation strategy of accounting firms, like other PSFs, is to reach transnational clients through professional labour markets. Evidence from the firms supports the findings of both the PSF and IHRM specialists, and provides explanations as to why accounting firms reproduce their global professional labour markets worldwide through international assignments and mobility. All firms assigned professional staff to international office networks, within and outside of the member firm, to transfer knowledge, expertise and skills to particular time–space points of demand in the business cycle. International assignments were used to manage offices or departments, add global expertise to local teams or to just simply add numbers of certified staff to meet high-volume demand (for example, taxation busy seasons). Equally, assigning staff between international member firms was used as a mechanism to share best practice and perpetuate the global ethos of the international firm. Moreover, given the relatively high number of international assignees circulating between the international offices of member and non-member firms, all firms regulated these professional labour markets with international management development programmes. Although all movements were dictated by client need, firms moved staff within the regulatory framework of the international network firm to standardise 'expatriate packages' and employment contracts. More interestingly, given that many international assignees moved within well-established office networks (USA, Europe, Australasia and so on), receiving offices were cosmopolitan in both nationality and line management. In contrast, in some emerging markets (for example, Eastern Europe), new starts reflected the traditional 'multinational' operations – offices headed by international assignees and the employment of both international assignees and local hires. In short, this group of accounting firms actively continued to use international assignees in conjunction with local staff and cross-border commuters and business travellers, to add value by servicing clients in close physical proximity either in the office environment or directly liaising with the client. International assignments in accounting remain an organisational strategy of the firm because in many instances capital can only be accumulated through the embodied knowledge, expertise and professional competences of fee-earning staff, especially where the client expects physical onsite servicing or co-location in international financial centres (Table 22.7).

But, perhaps one of the most significant findings from this research is the prevalence of very short-term international assignments and the nomadic modes of international mobility which also constitute global professional labour markets. The research constantly reported on the increasing frequency of short-term assignments of one year or less which were directed specifically at alleviating time–space labour market demands (for example, taxation, audit). Of great significance, however, was the reportage of high incidences of very frequent and very short forms of transnational mobility. Professional staff are now involved in international projects through business travel rather than the traditional assignment, or business commuting involving highly flexible cross-border working

Table 22.7 Dimensions of transfer policies in transnational professional service firms

	Reasons for transfers		
Dimensions	Fill positions	Develop managers	Develop organisation
Relative numbers	Many	Many	Many
Specialities transferred	Fee earning	Fee earning	Fee earning
Location of host	All countries	All countries	All countries
Direction of flow	Between subsidiaries and between HQ and subsidiaries	Between subsidiaries and between HQ office and subsidiaries	Between subsidiaries and between HQ office and subsidiaires
Age of assignee	Throughout career	Young to middle	Throughout career
Frequency	Many moves	Several moves	Many moves
Nationality of assignee	All nationalities	All nationalities	All nationalities
Personnel information system	Extensive lists of candidates monitored by personnel in all offices	Extensive lists of candidates monitored by personnel in all offices	Extensive lists of candidates monitored by personnel in all offices
Power of personnel department	Strong	Strong	Strong
Strategic placement and distribution	Extensive	Extensive	Extensive

Source: Adapted from Edstrom and Galbraith (1977a: 253).

arrangements. Distance is no longer becoming a barrier for working patterns. In a globalised world, where these firms service the business needs of almost all of the Fortune 500 or FTSE 100 companies, the transnational accounting firm is expected to have a transnational, highly mobile, highly professional workforce which can attend cross-border client meetings or provide expertise and advice in-house or with the client to produce global business solutions. Being a professional service transnational firm in the twenty-first century is all about delivering best practice and offering business and diagnostic solutions at the global scale.

In conclusion, I would like to posit that global professional labour markets exist within PSFs, like accounting, to develop, manage and stretch knowledge systems and competences from the core of the firm to subsidiaries, and just as importantly, between all subsidiaries of the firm in a network symmetry. In accounting, many traits of professionalism and certified knowledge are embodied and personal interaction and embedded socialisation play important functions in dissemination to clients. The existence of global professional labour markets is no organisational accident or leftover from the multinational organisation of the world economy. Global professional labour markets, constituted by international staff circulating between office units and local hires dealing with national and international business, are vital actors in the process of stretching knowledge over space. International assignees, or project-based cross-border travellers, or business commuters all culminate together, with local hires, to perform geographies of 'transnational knowledge management' (Bartlett and Ghoshal, 2000) in highly spatialised environments – the world cities (Sassen, 2001). In professional services where knowledge systems cannot easily be traded because 'face-to-face' interaction is required and *expected* by clients to add value and deliver business solutions, sending staff cross-border is an essential business requirement of the firm.

As to the future, PSFs will expect their qualified staff to be not only highly professional and knowledge-rich individuals, but also hyper-mobile, globally flexible and completely client focused. PSFs will also seek GATS Mode 4 to be executed in full, thus providing complete liberalisation of trade involving the temporary movement of highly skilled persons which will allow unrestricted access to service markets throughout WTO member states. Firms will expect their staff to be able to operate in a borderless business environment where global mobility is a given part of being a Big Four professional, but without it, professionals are cast away to find employment with the much smaller firms (Grey, 1998). Transnational firms offering global–local business solutions, whether in taxation advice, mergers and acquisitions, e-commerce or forensic litigation, will be expected by their clients to supply the best-qualified individuals to undertake such tasks irrespective of their point of demand – in cross-border, hyper-mobile and flexible relationships.

Notes

* This project was funded by the UK's Economic and Social Research Council's Transnational Communities Programme (Award L2144252001). The research support of Dr James T. Boardwell was very much appreciated.

Parts of this chapter are revised versions of sections of a chapter published in Bainham et al. (eds) *Sexual Positions: Sexuality and the Law* (Hart, Oxford, 2004). I am grateful to the editors and publishers for permission to use this material.

1. Mode 4 is defined as 'the supply of a service by a supplier of one WTO member, through the presence of natural persons in the territory of another member on a temporary basis . . . Mode 4 service suppliers generally: gain entry for a specific purpose (e.g. to fulfil a service contract); are confined to one sector; and are temporary . . . the time frame . . . on Mode 4 ranges from several weeks up to 3–5 years' (OECD, 2003d: 2).

References

Abbate, J. (1999), *Inventing the Internet*, Cambridge, MA: MIT Press.

Abu-Lughod, J. (1999), *New York, Chicago, Los Angeles: America's Global Cities*, Minneapolis, MN: University of Minnesota Press.

Accountancy (2002), Survey of the top international firms, www.accountancy/surveys/Accfirmsint.htm, 3 December 2005.

Acker, J. (1990), 'Hierarchies, jobs, bodies: a theory of gendered organisations', *Gender and Society*, **4**: 139–58.

Adkins, L. and C. Lury (1996), 'The sexual, the cultural and the gendering of the labour market', in L. Adkins and V. Merchant (eds), *Sexualising the Social: Power and the Organisation of Sexuality*, Basingstoke, Macmillan, pp. 204–23.

Adkins, L. and C. Lury (1999), 'The labour of identity: performing identities, performing economies', *Economy and Society*, **28**, 598–614.

Adkins, L. and C. Lury (2000), 'Making bodies, making people, making work', in L. McKie and N. Watson (eds), *Organizing Bodies: Policy, Institutions and Work*, Basingstoke: Macmillan, pp. 151–66.

Aharoni, Y. (ed.) (1993), *Coalitions and Competition: The Globalization of Professional Business Services*, London: Routledge.

Aharoni, Y. (2000), 'The role of reputation in global professional business services', in Aharoni and Nachum (eds), pp. 125–41.

Aharoni, Y. and L. Nachum (eds) (2000), *Globalization of Services: Some Implications for Theory and Practice*, London: Routledge.

Airriess, C.A. (2001a), 'Regional production, information-communication technology, and the developmental state: the rise of Singapore as a global container hub', *Geoforum*, **32**: 235–54.

Airriess, C.A. (2001b), 'The regionalization of Hutchison Port Holdings in Mainland China', *Journal of Transport Geography*, **9**: 267–78.

Akpoghomeh, Osi S. (1999), 'The development of air transportation in Nigeria', *Journal of Transport Geography*, **7**: 135–46.

Alcock, P., C. Beatty, S. Fothergill, R. Macmillan and S. Yeandle (2003), *Work to Welfare: How Men Become Detached from the Labour Market*, Cambridge: Cambridge University Press.

Alexander, N. and A.M. Doherty (2002), *Relationship Development in International Retail Franchising: Case Study*, Coleraine: University of Ulster, Faculty of Business and Management.

Allen, J. (2000), 'Power/economic knowledge: symbolic and spatial formations', in J.R. Bryson, P.W. Daniels, N. Henry and J. Pollard (eds), *Knowledge, Space, Economy*, London: Routledge, pp. 15–33.

Allen, J. and P. du Gay (1994), 'Industry and the rest: the economic identity of services', *Work, Employment and Society*, **8**(2): 255–71.

Alm, J., R.H. Aten and R. Bahl (2001), 'Can Indonesia decentralise successfully? Plans, problems and prospects', *Bulletin of Indonesian Economic Studies*, **37**(1): 83–102.

Amable, B., R. Barré, R. Boyer (1997), *Les systèmes d'innovation à l'ère de la globalisation*, Economica, Paris.

Amable, B. and P. Petit (2001), 'The diversity of social systems of innovation and production during the 1990s', CEPREMAP Working Paper 2001-15, www.cepremap.cnrs.fr.

Amin, A. (ed.) (1994), *Post-Fordism: A Reader*, Oxford: Blackwell.

Amin, A. and P. Cohendet (2000), 'Organisational learning and governance through embedded practices', *Journal of Management and Governance*, **4**(1–2): 93–116.

Amin, A. and N. Thrift (1992), 'Neo-Marshallian nodes in global networks', *International Journal of Urban and Regional Research*, **16**(4): 571–87.

Amin, A. and N.J. Thrift (1994), *Globalisation, Institutions, and Regional Development in Europe*, Oxford, Oxford University Press.

Anders, G. (1956 [1980]), *Die Antiquiertheit des Menschen*, Muenchen: Beck.

Andersen, B. and J. Howells (2000), 'Intellectual property rights shaping innovation in services', in Andersen et al. (eds), pp. 229–47.

Andersen, B., J. Howells, R. Hull, I. Miles and J. Roberts (eds) (2000), *Knowledge and Innovation in the New Service Economy*, Cheltenham, UK and Northampton, MA, USA: Edward Elgar.

Anderson, R. and N.T. Gallini (eds) (1998), *Competition Policy and Intellectual Property Rights in the Knowledge-based Economy*, Industry Canada Research Series 9, Calgary: University of Calgary Press, pp. 463–70.

Angell, I. (1996), 'Winners and losers in the information age', *Society*, **34**: 81–5.

Anxo, D., L. Flood and Y. Kocoglu (2001), 'Allocation des temps et partage des tâches en France et en Suède', INSEE, Paris, *Premières synthèses*, no. 11.2, March.

Anxo, D. and M. Johanson (1995), 'Les discriminations salariales en Suède', *Les cahiers du MAGE*, 2/95: 23–34.

Anxo, D. and D. Storrie (eds) (2001), *The Job Creation Potential of the Service Sector in Europe*, Luxembourg: Office for Official Publications of the European Communities.

Aoyama, Y. and M. Castells (2002), 'An empirical assessment of the informational society: employment and occupational structures of G-7 countries, 1920–2000', *International Labour Review*, **141**(1–2): 123–59.

Appadurai, A. (1996), *Modernity at Large: Cultural Dimensions of Globalization*, Minneapolis, MN: University of Minnesota Press.

Archer, M.S. (2003), *Structure, Agency and the Internal Conversation*, New York: Cambridge University Press.

Archibugi, D. and J. Michie (1997), *Technology, Globalisation and Economic Performance*, Cambridge: Cambridge University Press.

Arestis, P., M. Baddeley and J. McCombie (eds) (2003), *Globalisation, Regionalisation and Economic Growth*, Cheltenham, UK and Northampton, MA, USA: Edward Elgar.

Arkell, J. (2002), *STATS ON FATS! Statistics on Foreign Affiliates Trade in Services: The New International Statistical Standard*, Washington, DC: Mark Twain Institute.

Aron, R. (1962 [1967]), *18 Lectures on Industrial Society*, London: Weidenfeld & Nicolson.

Aronson, J.D. and P.F. Cowhey (1984), *Trade in Services: A Case for Open Markets*, Washington, DC: American Enterprise Institute for Public Policy Research.

Ascher, B. (1993), 'Business and professional services: competing in a more mobile world', in Aharoni (ed.), pp. 20–31.

Asheim, B.T. (1992), 'Flexible specialisation, industrical district and small firms: a critical appraisal', in H. Ernste and V. Meier (eds), *Regional Development and Contemporary Industrial Response: Extending Flexible Specialisation*, London: Belhaven, pp. 45–63.

Asheim, B.T. and P. Cooke (1999), 'Local learning and interactive innovation networks in a global economy', in E.J. Malecki and P. Oinas (eds), *Making Connections: Technological Learning and Regional Economic Change*, Aldershot: Ashgate, pp. 145–78.

Auger, P. (2001), *The Death of Gentlemanly Capitalism*, London: Penguin.

Bacharach, M. (1970), *Biproportional Matrices and Input–Output Change*, Cambridge: Cambridge University Press.

Bacon, F. (1597 [1924]), *Mediations, Places of Perswasion and Disswasion*, London: Haslewood Books.

Bagchi-Sen, S. and J. Sen (1997), 'The current state of knowledge in international business in producer services', *Environment and Planning A*, **29**: 1153–74.

Bailey, A.R. and J.R. Bryson (2006), 'Stories of suburbia (Bournville, UK): from planning to people tales', *Social and Cultural Geography*, **7**(2): 178–97.

Bailly, A.S., D. Maillat and W.J. Coffey (1987), 'Service activities and regional development: some European examples', *Environment and Planning A*, **19**: 653–68.

Bancel-Charensol, L. (1999), 'Impacts of information and communications technologies on service production systems', *The Service Industries Journal*, **19**(4): 147–58.

Bannon, J.M. (2002), 'The Republic of Ireland's policies in the field of services: lessons for other countries', in E. Kigossy-Schmidt (ed.), *Business Related Services in Central and Eastern Europe*, Wiesbaden Deutscher Universitäts-Verlag, pp. 95–129.

Baran, B. (1985), 'Technological innovation and deregulation: the transformation of the labor process in the insurance industry', *BRIE Working Paper*, Berkeley: University of California.

Barcet, A. (1986), *Les Services dans le système productif – vers une typologie de la production des services*, Lyon: Économie et Humanisme.

Barcet, A. (1987), *La Montée des services: vers une économie de la servuction*, Lyon: Université Lumière.

Barcet, A. and J. Bonamy (1999a), 'Eléments pour une théorie de l'intégration biens/services', *Économie et Société, Série Économie et Gestion des Services*, **1**(5): 197–220.

Barcet, A. and J. Bonamy (1999b), 'Opérationnalité de la notion de service: dilution ou approfondissement?', *Revue d'Économie Industrielle*, **90**: 93–104.

Barnes, B. (1985), *About Science*, Oxford: Blackwell.

Barnett, D. (1998), *London: Hub of the Industrial Revolution: A Revisionary History: 1775–1825*, London: Tauris Academic Studies.

Barras, R. (1986), 'Towards a theory of innovation in services', *Research Policy*, **15**: 161–73.

Barras, R. (1990), 'Interactive innovation in financial and business services: the vanguard of the service revolution', *Research Policy*, **19**: 215–37.

Bartlett, C. and S. Ghoshal (1989), *Managing Across Borders: The Transnational Solution*, Boston, MA: Harvard Business School Press.

Bartlett, C. and S. Ghoshal (2000), *Transnational Management*, 3rd edn, New York: McGraw-Hill.

Baum, S. (1999), 'Social transformations in the global city: Singapore', *Urban Studies*, **36**: 1095–117.

Bauman, Z. (1998), *Work, Consumerism and the New Poor*, Buckingham: Open University Press.

Baumol, W.J. (1967), 'Macroeconomics of unbalanced growth: the anatomy of urban crisis', *American Economic Review*, **57**, June: 415–26.

Baumol, W.J. (1985), 'Productivity policy and the service sector', in P.R. Inman (ed.), *Managing the Service Economy*, Cambridge: Cambridge University Press, pp. 301–17.

Baumol, W.J. (2002), 'Service as leaders and the leader of the services', in Gadrey and Gallouj (eds), pp. 147–63.

Baumol, W.J., S.A.B. Blackman and E.N. Wolff (1989), *Productivity and American Leadership: The Long View*, Cambridge, MA: MIT Press.

Beaverstock, J.V. (1989), 'Highly-skilled professional and managerial labour migration: the case of large chartered accountancy firms', University of Bristol and Service Industries Research Centre, Portsmouth Polytechnic.

Beaverstock, J.V. (1990), 'New international labour markets: the case of managerial labour migration within large chartered accountancy firms', *Area*, **22**: 151–8.

Beaverstock, J.V. (1991), 'Skilled international migration: an analysis of the geography of international secondments within large accountancy firms', *Environment and Planning A*, **23**: 1133–46.

Beaverstock, J.V. (1996), 'Subcontracting the accountant! Professional labour markets, migration and organisational networks in the global accountancy industry', *Environment and Planning A*, **28**: 303–27.

Beaverstock, J.V. (2002), 'Transnational elite communities in global cities: connectivities, flows and networks', in A. Meurer and J. Vogt (eds), *Stadt und Region: Dynamik von Lebenswelten. Tagungsbericht und wissenschaftliche Abhandlungen*, Leipzig: Mayr, Deutsche Gelleschaft für Geographie, pp. 87–97.

Beaverstock, J.V. (2004), 'Managing across borders: transnational knowledge management and expatriation in legal firms', *Journal of Economic Geography*, **4**: 157–79.

Beaverstock, J.V. and J. Smith (1996), 'Lending jobs to global cities: skilled international labour migration, investment banking and the city of London', *Urban Studies*, **33**(8): 1377–94.

Beaverstock, J.V., R. Smith and P.J. Taylor (1999), 'The long arm of the law: the globalization of London's law firms', *Environment and Planning A*, **31**: 1857–76.

Beaverstock, J., R. Smith and P. Taylor (2000), ' "World city network" a new metageography for the future?', *Annals of the Association of American Geographers*, **90**: 123–34.

Beblo, M. (1999), 'How do German couples spend their time? A panel-data analysis', *DIW-Vierteljahrshefte zur Wirtschaftsforschung*, **2**(99): 146–52.

Beck, U. (1992), *Risk Society: Towards New Modernity*, London: Sage.

Beck, U. and E. Beck-Gernsheim (1995), *The Normal Chaos of Love*, Cambridge: Polity.

Behara, R.S. (2000), 'Process innovation in knowledge-intensive services', in J.A. Fitzsimmons and M.J. Fitzsimmons (eds), *New Service Development*, Thousand Oaks, CA: Sage, pp. 138–51.

Bell, Daniel (1968), 'The measurement of knowledge and technology', in Eleanor B. Sheldon and Wilbert E. Moore (eds), *Indicators of Social Change: Concepts and Measurements*, Hartford, CT: Russell Sage Foundation, pp. 145–246.

Bell, Daniel (1973), *The Coming of Post-Industrial Society: A Venture in Social Forecasting*, New York: Basic Books.

Belson, K. (2004), 'New undersea cable projects face some old problems', *New York Times*, May 10.

Belt, V., R. Richardson and J. Weber (2000), 'Women's work in the information economy: the case of telephone call centers', *Information, Communication, Society*, **3**: 3.

Beniger, James R. (1986), *The Control Revolution: Technological and Economic Origins of the Information Society*, Cambridge, MA: Harvard University Press.

Bennett, R.J. (1998), 'Business associations and their potential to contribute to economic development: reexploring an interface between the state and market', *Environment and Planning A*, **30**: 1367–87.

Bennett, R.J. and P.J.A. Robson (1999a), 'Intensity of interaction in supply of business advice and client impact: a comparison of consultancy, business association and government support initiatives for SMEs', *British Journal of Management*, **10**: 351–69.

Bennett, R.J. and P.J.A. Robson (1999b), 'The use of external business advice by SMEs in Britain', *Entrepreneurship and Regional Development*, **11**: 155–80.

Beresford, Q. (2000), *Governments, Markets and Globalisation: Public Policy in Context*, St Leonards, NSW: Allen & Unwin.

Berman, J.M. (2004), 'Industry output and employment projections to 2012', *Monthly Labor Review*, **124**: 58–79.

Berry, B.J.L. (1967), *Geography of Market Centers and Retail Distribution*, Englewood Cliffs, NJ, Prentice-Hall.

Bestor, T. (2000), 'How sushi went global', *Foreign Policy*, **121**, November/December: 54–63.

Bettencourt, L.A., A.L. Ostrom, S.W. Brown and R.J. Roundtree (2002), 'Client co-production in knowledge-intensive business services', *California Management Review*, **44**(4): 100–128.

Beyers, W.B. (1979), 'Contemporary trends in the regional economic development of the United States', *Professional Geographer*, **31**(1): 34–44.

Beyers, W.B. (1989), *The Producer Services and Economic Development in the United States: The Last Decade*, Washington, DC: US Department of Commerce, Economic Development Administration.

Beyers, W.B. (1991), 'Trends in the producer services in the USA: the last decade', in P.W. Daniels (ed.), *Services and Metropolitan Development: International Perspectives*, London: Routledge, pp. 146–72.

Beyers, W.B. (1992), 'Producer services and metropolitan growth and development', in E.S. Mills and J.F. McDonald (eds), *Sources of Metropolitan Growth*, New Brunswick, NJ: Center for Urban Policy Research, pp. 125–46.

Beyers, W.B. (2000), 'Services and the new economy: elements of a research agenda', paper presented to the Global Conference on Economic Geography, National University of Singapore, 5–9 December.

Beyers, W.B. (2002a), 'Service industries and development trajectories in the Seattle Metropolitan Region', paper presented to an Exploratory Workshop on Service Industries and New Models of Urban Change within the Asia-Pacific, Peter Wall Institute for Advanced Studies, University of British Columbia, Vancouver: 26 March.

Beyers, W.B. (2002b), 'Services and the new economy: elements of a research agenda', *Journal of Economic Geography*, **2**: 1–29.

Beyers, W.B. (2003), 'Trade in services and regional development in the United States', paper presented at the 13th International Conference of RESER (European Network Services and Space), Services and Regional Development, Mons, France, 9–10 October.

Beyers, W.B. and M.J. Alvine (1985), 'Export services in postindustrial society', *Papers of the Regional Science Association*, **57**: 33–45.

Beyers, W., M. Alvine and E. Johnsen (1985), *The Service Economy: Export of Services in the Central Puget Sound Region*, Seattle, WA: Central Puget Sound Economic Development District.

Beyers, W.B. and D. Lindahl (1996a), 'Lone eagles and high fliers in rural producer services', *Rural Development Perspectives*, **12**: 2–10.

Beyers, W.B. and D.P. Lindahl (1996b), 'Explaining the demand for producer services: is cost-driven externalization the major factor?', *Papers in Regional Science*, **75**(3): 351–74.

Beyers, W.B. and D.P. Lindahl (1997), 'Strategic behaviour and development sequences in producer service businesses', *Environment and Planning A*, **29**: 887–912.

Beyers, W.B. and D.P. Lindahl (1999), 'Workplace flexibilities in the producer services', *The Service Industries Journal*, **19**(1): 35–60.

Bhaskar, R. (1993), *Dialectic: The Pulse of Freedom*, London: Verso.

Bilderbeek, R., P. den Hertog, G. Marklund and I. Miles (1998), 'Services in Innovation: Knowledge Intensive Business Services (KIBS) as co-producers of innovation', Report of WP 5 and 6 of SI4S project, PREST mimeo, University of Manchester: available at SI4S website, www.step.no.

Bingham, N. (1996), 'Object-ions: from technological determinism towards geographies of relations', *Environment and Planning D: Society and Space*, **14**: 635–57.

Birley, S. and P. Westhead (1990), ' "North–south" contrasts in the characteristics and performance of small firms', *Entrepreneurship and Regional Development*, **2**: 27–48.

Birley, S. and P. Westhead (1994), 'New producer service businesses: are they any different from the new manufacturing ventures?', *The Service Industries Journal*, **14**: 455–81.

Black, J., H.B. Gregersen and M.E. Mendenhall (1992), *Global Assignments: Successfully Expatriating and Repatriating International Managers*, San Francisco, CA: Jossey-Bass.

Blair, J.D. and J.G. Hunt (1986), 'Getting inside the head of the management researcher one more time: context-free and context-specific orientations in research', *Journal of Management*, **12**: 147–66.

Blind, K., J. Elder, U. Schlock, B. Andersen, J. Howells, I. Miles, J. Roberts, C. Hipp and R. Evangelista (2003), 'Patents in the Service Sector', Final Report to Directorate General for Research, Commission of the European Communities, Brussels.

Block, F. (1985), 'Post-industrial development and the obsolescence of economic categories', *Politics and Society*, **14**(1): 71–104.

Block, F. and L. Hirschhorn (1979), 'New productive forces and the contradictions of contemporary capitalism', *Theory and Society*, **17**, 363–95.

Bluestone, B. and B. Harrison (1982), *The Deindustrialization of America: Plant Closings, Community Abandonment, and the Dismantling of Basic Industry*, New York: Basic Books.

Boddewyn, J.J., M.B. Halbrich and A.C. Perry (1986), 'Service multinationals: conceptualization, measurement and theory', *Journal of International Business Studies*, **17**(3): 41–57.

Boden, D. (1994), *The Business of Talk: Organisations in Action*, Cambridge: Polity Press.
Boden, D. and H.L. Molotch (1994), 'The compulsion of proximity', in R. Friedland and D. Boden (eds), *Space, Time and Modernity*, Berkeley, CA: University of California Press, pp. 257–86.
Bodin, M. and K. Dawson (2002), *The Call Center Dictionary: The Complete Guide to Call Center and Customer Support Technology Solutions*, New York: CMP Books.
Bohm, D. (1990), *David Bohm: On Dialogue*, Ojai: David Bohm Seminars.
Bonamy, J. and P.W. Daniels (1993), 'Firm organisation and spatial dynamics', in P.W. Daniels, S. Illeris, J. Bonamy and J. Philippe (eds), *The Geography of Services*, London: Routledge, pp. 69–76.
Bonke, J. and E. Koch-Weser (2001), 'The welfare state and time allocation', Working paper 9/2001, Danish Institute of Social Research, Copenhagen.
Boone, T. (2000), 'Exploring the link between product and process innovation in services', in J.A. Fitzsimmons and M.J. Fitzsimmons (eds), *New Service Development*, Thousand Oaks, CA: Sage: pp. 92–110.
Borgmann, A. (1999), *Holding on to Reality: The Nature of Information at the Turn of the Millennium*, Chicago: University of Chicago Press.
Borrus, M. (2000), 'The resurgence of US electronics: Asian production networks and the rise of Wintelism', in M. Borrus, D. Ernst and S. Haggard (eds), *International Production Networks in Asia: Rivalry or Riches?*, London: Routledge, pp. 57–79.
Bosch, G. and S. Lehndorff (2001), 'New forms of employment and working time in the service economy', Report for the TSER programme of the European Commission, Brussels.
Boskin, M.J., G.R. Dulberger, Z. Griliches and D. Jorgenson (1996), 'Towards a more accurate measure of the cost of living', final report to the Senate Finance Committee, 4 December.
Bosworth, M., C. Findlay, R. Trewin and T. Warren (2000), 'Price-impact measures of impediments to services trade', in Findlay and Warren (eds), pp. 42–551.
Bourdieu, P. (1979 [1984]), *Distinction*, Cambridge, MA: Harvard University Press.
Bourgois, P. (1995), *In Search of Respect: Selling Crack in El Barrio*, Cambridge: Cambridge University Press.
Bowden, R. (2003), *Globalisation: The Impact on Our Lives*, London: Hodder Wayland.
Bowe, M. (ed.) (1998), *Banking and Finance in Islands and Small States*, London and Washington, DC: Pinter.
Bowen, J. (2002), 'Network change, deregulation, and access in the global airline industry', *Economic Geography*, **78**(4): 425–39.
Bowen, J. (2004), 'The geography of freighter aircraft operations in the Pacific Basin', *Journal of Transport Geography*, **12**(1): 1–11.
Bowen, J. and T.R. Leinbach (2004), 'Market concentration in the air freight forwarding industry', *Tijdschift voor Economische en Sociale Geografie*, **95**(2): 174–88.
Bradley, H. (1999), *Gender and Power in the Workplace: Analysing the Impact of Economic Change*, Basingstoke: Macmillan.
Brewer, Ann M., K. Button and D.A Hensher (eds) (2001), *Handbook of Logistics and Supply Chain Management*, London: Pergamon.
Brewster, C. (1991), *The Management of Expatriates*, London: Kogan Page.

Bridges.org (2001), *Spanning the Digital Divide: Understanding and Tackling the Issues*, Washington, DC: Bridges.org.

Bristow, G., M. Munday and P. Gripaios (2000), 'Call centre growth and location: corporate strategy and the spatial division of labour', *Environment and Planning A*, **32**: 519–38.

Brook, T. and H. Luong (eds) (1997), *Culture and Development: The Shaping of Capitalism in Eastern Asia*, Ann Arbor, MI: University of Michigan Press.

Brookings Institution (2004), 'Services offshoring: what do the data tell us?', www.brook.edu/pge/20040622_offshoring.htm.

Broussole, D. (2000), 'La distinction biens-services est-elle encore utile?', in *Conférence Internationale Économie et Socio-Économie des Services*, I, 22–23 June, Lille-Roubaix, pp. 3–16.

Brown, D. and R.M. Stern (2001), 'Measurement and modeling of the economic effects of trade and investment barriers in services', *Review of International Economics*, **9**: 262–86.

Brown, S. (1987), 'Institutional change in retailing: a review and synthesis', *European Journal of Marketing*, **21**(6): 5–29.

Browning, H.C. and J. Singelmann (1975), *The Emergence of a Service Society*, Springfield, UA: National Technical Information Service.

Brunn, S.D. and T.R. Leinbach (2000), 'Nokia as a regional information technology fountainhead', in Wheeler et al. (eds), pp. 130–41.

Brynjolfson, E. and B. Kahin (2000), *Understanding the Digital Economy*, Cambridge, MA: MIT Press.

Brynjolfsson, E. and L.M. Hitt (2000), 'Beyond computation: information technology, organizational transformation and business performance', *Journal of Economic Perspectives*, **14**(4), Fall: 23–48.

Bryson, J.R. (1996), 'Small business service firms and the 1990s recession in the United Kingdom: implications for local economic development', *Local Economy Journal*, **11**: 221–36.

Bryson, J.R. (1997a), 'Business service firms, service space and the management of change', *Entrepreneurship and Regional Development*, **9**: 93–111.

Bryson, J.R. (1997b), 'Small and medium-sized enterprises, business link and the new knowledge workers', *Policy Studies*, **18**(1): 67–80.

Bryson, J.R. (2000), 'Spreading the message: management consultants and the shaping of economic geographies in time and space', in J.R. Bryson, P.W. Daniels, N. Henry and J. Pollard (eds), *Knowledge Space, Economy*, London: Routledge, pp. 157–75.

Bryson, J.R. and P.W. Daniels (1998a), 'Business links, strong ties, and the walls of silence: small and medium-sized enterprises and external business-service expertise', *Environment and Planning C: Government and Policy*, **16**: 265–80.

Bryson, J.R. and P.W. Daniels (1998b), *Service Industries in the Global Economy:* vol 1: *Service Theories and Service Employment*; vol 2: *Services, Globalization and Economic Development*, Cheltenham, UK and Northampton, MA, USA: Edward Elgar.

Bryson, J.R. and P.W. Daniels (1999), 'The contribution that producer service firms make to manufacturing enterprises: some evidence from the UK', *Policy Studies*, **20**: 95–105.

Bryson, J.R. and P.W. Daniels (2007), 'A segmentation approach to understanding business and professional services in city-regions: shifting the horizon beyond global cities', in L. Rubalcaba-Bermejo, H. Kok and P. Baker (eds), *Business Services in European Economic Growth*, London: Palgrave Macmillan.

Bryson, J.R., P.W. Daniels and D.R. Ingram (1999), 'Methodological problems and economic geography: the case of business services', *The Service Industries Journal*, **19**(4): 1–17.

Bryson, J.R., P.W. Daniels and G. Rusten (2004a), 'The design workshop of the world'? Producing and consuming industrial design services in the United Kingdom', paper presented to the IGU Commission Residential Conference, Birmingham, 9–13 August.

Bryson, J.R., P.W. Daniels and B. Warf (2004b), *Service Worlds: People, Organisations, Technologies*, London: Routledge.

Bryson, J.R., D. Keeble and P.A. Wood (1993a), 'The creation, location and growth of small business service firms in the United Kingdom', *The Service Industries Journal*, **13**(2): 118–31.

Bryson, J.R., D. Keeble and P.A. Wood (1993b), 'Business networks, small firm flexibility and regional development in UK business services', *Entrepreneurship and Regional Development*, **5**: 265–77.

Bryson, J.R. and M.C. Monnoyer (2004), 'Understanding the relationship between services and innovation: the RESER review of the European service literature on innovation, 2002', *The Service Industries Journal*, **24**: 205–22.

Bryson, J.R. and G. Rusten (2005), 'Spatial divisions of expertise: knowledge intensive business service firms and regional development in Norway', *The Services Industries Journal*, **25**(8): 959–77.

Bryson, J.R. and G. Rusten (2006), 'Spatial divisions of expertise and transnational "service" firms: aerospace and management consultancy', in J.W. Harrington and P.W. Daniels (eds), *Knowledge-based Services and Internationalisation*, Aldershot: Ashgate, pp. 79–100.

Bučar, M. (2001), *Razvojno dohitevanje z informacijsko tehnologijo? Knjižna zbirka Pravo in gospodarstvo*, Ljubljana: Fakulteta za druûbene vede.

Bučar, M. (2002), 'Catching-up with information technology: a viable option for transition economies?', *Emergo* (Cracow), **9**(3): 66–82.

Budd, L. (1999), 'Globalisation and the crisis of territorial embeddedness of international financial markets', in R. Martin (ed.), *Money and the Space Economy*, Chichester: Wiley, pp. 115–37.

Budd, L. and S. Whimster (1992), *Global Finance and Urban Living: A Study of Metropolitan Change*, London: Routledge.

Bunnell, T. (2002a) '(Re)positioning Malaysia: high-tech networks and the multicultural rescripting of national identity', *Political Geography*, **21**: 105–24.

Bunnell, T. (2002b) 'Multimedia Utopia? A geographical critique of high tech development in Malaysia's supercorridor', *Antipode*, **34**: 265–95.

Burton-Jones, A. (1999), *Knowledge Capitalism: Business, Work, and Learning in the New Economy*, Oxford: Oxford University Press.

Butler, J. (1990), *Gender Trouble*, London: Routledge.

Butler, J. (1993), *Bodies that Matter*, London: Routledge.

Cairncross, F. (1997), *The Death of Distance*, Boston, MA: Harvard Business School Press and Cambridge: Cambridge University Press.

Cairncross, F. (2001), *The Death of Distance: How the Communications Revolution will Change our Lives*, London: Texere.

Cameron, N.I. (2002), *The History of Ashleigh Road – Solihull*, Studley: Brewin Books.

Campbell, A.J. and A. Verbeke (1994), 'The globalisation of service multinationals', *Long Range Planning*, **27**(2): 95–102.
Capling, A. and K.R. Nossal (2000), *Death of Distance or Tyranny of Distance? The Internet, Deterritorialisation, and the Anti-globalisation Movement in Australia*, Canberra: Research School of Pacific and Asian Studies, Australian National University.
Cartier, C. (2001), *Globalizing South China*, Oxford: Blackwell.
Cassidy, J. (2002), *Dot.con: The Greatest Story Ever Sold*, London: Penguin.
Castells, M. (1996), *The Information Age, volume I: The Rise of the Network Society*, Oxford: Blackwell.
Castells, M. (1997), *The Information Age, volume II: The Power of Identity*, Cambridge: Blackwell.
Castells, M. (2000), 'Materials for an exploratory theory of the network society', *British Journal of Sociology*, **51**: 5–24.
Castells, M. (2001), *The Internet Galaxy*, Oxford: Oxford University Press.
Castells, M. and Y. Aoyama (1994), 'Paths towards the informational society: employment structures in G-7 countries', *International Labour Review, 1920–1990*, **133**(1): 6–33.
Caves, R.E. and W.F. Murphy (1976), 'Franchising: firms, markets, and intangible assets', *Southern Economic Journal*, **42**: 572–86.
Chanda, R. (2002), *Globalization of Services: India's Opportunities and Constraints*, Oxford, New Delhi and New York: Oxford University Press.
Chandler, A.D. (1962), *Strategy and Structure: Chapters in the History of the Industrial Enterprise*, Cambridge, MA: MIT Press.
Chang, H.-J. (2003), *Globalisation, Economic Development, and the Role of the State*, London: Zed Books.
Chang, T. (1995), 'The expatriatisation of Holland Village', in B. Yeoh and L. Kong (eds), *Portraits of Places: History, Community and Identity in Singapore*, Singapore: Times Edition, pp. 140–57.
Charles, N. and E. James (2003), 'The gender dimensions of job insecurity in a local labour market', *Work, Employment and Society*, **17**: 531–52.
Chase-Dunn, C. (1998), *Global Formation: Structures of the World-Economy*, 2nd edn, Lanham, MD: Rowman & Littlefield.
Chiou, J., C. Hsieh and C. Yang (2004), 'The effect of franchisors' communication, service assistance, and competitive advantage on franchisees' intentions to remain in the franchise system', *Journal of Small Business Management*, **42**(1): 19–36.
Christensen, C. (1997), *The Innovator's Dilemma: When New Technologies Cause Great Firms to Fail*, Boston, MA: Harvard Business School Press.
Christensen, C., C. Johnston, M. Overdorf and A. Barragee (2000), *After the Gold Rush: Patterns of Success and Failure on the Internet*, Belmont, MA: Innosight.
Christensen, C. and R. Tedlow (2000), 'Patterns of disruption in retailing', *Harvard Business Review*, January–February, 42–5.
Christensen, J.F. (2003), 'Innovation and industrial dynamics in internet services', in J.F. Christensen and P. Maskell (eds), *The Industrial Dynamics of the New Digital Economy*, Cheltenham, UK and Northampton, MA, USA: Edward Elgar.
Christensen, J.F. and P. Maskell (eds) (2003), *The Industrial Dynamics of the New Digital Economy*, Cheltenham, UK and Northampton, MA, USA: Edward Elgar.

Chua, B.-H. (1989), 'The business of living', in K. Sandhu and P. Wheatley (eds), *Management of Successes: Moulding of Modern Singapore*, Singapore: Institute of Southeast Asian Studies, pp. 1003–21.

Chua, B.-H. (1991), 'Modernism and the vernacular: transformation of public spaces and social life in Singapore', *Journal of Architectural and Planning Research*, **8**: 203–21.

Chung, C. (1998), *Globalisation and the Environment: Perspectives from OECD and Dynamic Non-member Economies*, Paris: Organisation for Economic Cooperation and Development.

City of London Corporation (2005), 'The competitive position of London as a global financial centre', London: City of London Economic Development Research Programme.

Clark, C. (1940 [1951]), *The Conditions of Economic Progress*, London: Macmillan.

Clark, G. and D. Wójcik (2001), 'The City of London in the Asian crisis', *Journal of Economic Geography*, **1**(1): 107–30.

Clark, T., D. Rajaratnam and T. Smith (1996), 'Toward a theory of international services: marketing intangibles in a world of nations', *Journal of International Marketing*, **4**(2): 9–29.

Clayton, Mark (2004), 'Can technology plug the gap?', *The Christian Science Monitor*, January, 12: 11.

Cobb, S. (1998), 'Global finance and the growth of offshore financial centers: the Manx experience', *Geoforum*, **29**: 7–21.

Coe, N. (1998), 'Exploring uneven development in producer service sectors: detailed evidence from the British computer services industry', *Environment and Planning A*, **30**: 2041–68.

Coe, N.M. (2000), 'The externalisation of producer services debate: the UK computer services sector', *The Service Industries Journal*, **20**(2): 64–81.

Coffey, A. (1994), 'Timing is everything: graduate accountants, time and organisational commitment', *Sociology*, **28**: 943–56.

Coffey, W. and A. Bailly (1991), 'Producer services and flexible production: an exploratory analysis', *Growth and Change*, **22**: 95–117.

Coffey, W.J. and M. Polèse (1989), 'Producer services and regional development: a policy oriented perspective', *Papers of the Regional Science Association*, **67**: 13–27.

Cohen, B. (1998), *The Geography of Money*, Ithaca, NY: Cornell University Press.

Cohen, S. (1973), *Folk Devils and Moral Panics*, St Albans: Paladin.

Cohen, W. and D. Levinthal (1989), 'Innovation and learning: the two faces of R&D', *Economic Journal*, **99**: 569–96.

Cohen, W.M. and D.A. Levinthal (1990), 'Absorptive capacity: a new perspective on learning and innovation', *Administrative Science Quarterly*, **35**: 128–52.

Colecchia, A. (2000), 'Measuring barriers to market access for services: a pilot study on accountancy services', in Findlay and Warren (eds), pp. 245–66.

Collier, D.A. (1983), 'The service sector revolution: the automation of services', *Long Range Planning*, **16**: 10–20.

Commission of the European Communities (2003), *The Competitiveness of Business-Related Services and their Contribution to the Performance of European Enterprises*, Communication from the Commission to the Council, European Parliament, the European Economic and Social Committee and the Committee of the Regions, COM (2003) 747 final, Commission of the European Communities, Brussels.

Commission on Intellectual Property Rights (2002), 'Integrating intellectual property rights and development policy', Report of the Commission on Intellectual Property Rights, London.

Connell, R.W. (1995), *Masculinities*, Cambridge: Polity.

Connell, R.W. (2000), *The Men and the Boys*, Cambridge: Polity.

Contractor, F.J. and S.K. Kundu (2000), 'Globalization of hotel services: an examination of ownership and alliance patterns in a maturing service sector', in Y. Aharoni and L. Nachum (eds), *Globalization of Services: Some Implications for Theory and Practice*, London: Routledge, pp. 296–319.

Cook, Thomas A. (2003), 'A new security mandate', *Supply Chain Management Review*, **7**(5): 11–13.

Cool, K., Costa, L.A. and I. Dierickx (2002), 'Constructing competitive advantage', in A. Pettigrew, H. Thomas and R. Whittington (eds), *Handbook of Strategy and Management*, London: Sage, pp. 55–71.

Corey, K. (1998), 'Information technology and telecommunications policies in Southeast Asian development: cases in vision and leadership', in V. Savage, L. Kong and W. Neville (eds), *The Naga Awakens: Growth and Change in Southeast Asia*, Singapore: Times Academic Press, pp. 145–201.

Corey, K. (2000), 'Intelligent corridors: outcomes of electronic space policies', *Journal of Urban Technology*, **7**: 1–22.

Cornish, S.L. (1996), 'Marketing software products: the importance of "being there" and the implications for business service exports', *Environment and Planning A*, **28**: 1661–82.

Cornwall, A. and N. Lindisfarne (eds) (1994), *Dislocating Masculinity: Comparative Ethnographies*, London: Routledge.

Cox, K (ed.) (1997), *Spaces of Globalization: Reasserting the Power of the Local*, New York: Guilford.

Coyle, D. (1997), *The Weightless World: Strategies for Managing the Digital Economy*, Oxford: Capstone.

Cramer, J.J. (2000), 'Door slams shut on dot-coms', *The Street.com*, May 15, http://abcnews.go.com/sections/business/TheStreet/cramer 000515.html.

Crang, M., P. Crang, P. and J. May (1999), *Virtual Geographies: Bodies, Space and Relations*, London: Routledge.

Cuadrado-Roura, J.R., L. Rubalcaba-Bermejo and J.R. Bryson (eds) (2002), *Trading Services in the Global Economy*, Cheltenham, UK and Northampton, MA, USA: Edward Elgar.

Currah, A. (2003), 'Digital effects in the spatial economy of film: towards a research agenda', *Area*, **35**(1): 64–73.

Daniels, P.W. (1983), 'Service industries: supporting role or centre stage?', *Area*, **15**: 301–9.

Daniels, P.W. (1985), *Service Industries: A Geographical Appraisal*, London: Methuen.

Daniels, P.W. (1993), *Service Industries in the World Economy*, Oxford: Blackwell.

Daniels, P.W. (2000), 'Exports of services or servicing exports?', *Geografiska Annaler*, **82**(B): 1–15.

Daniels, P.W. (2003), ' "Old" economy, "new" economy and services', Working Papers in the Service Sector, 11, School of Geography, Earth and Environmental Science, University of Birmingham.

Daniels, P.W. (2005), 'Services, globalization and the Asia-Pacific region', in Daniels et al. (eds), pp. 21–51.
Daniels, P.W. and J.R. Bryson (2002), 'Manufacturing services and servicing manufacturing: changing forms of production in advanced capitalist economies', *Urban Studies*, **39**(5–6): 977–91.
Daniels, P.W., T. Hutton and K. O'Connor (1991), 'The planning response to urban service sector growth', *Growth and Change*, **22**: 3–26.
Daniels, P.W., K.C. Ho and T. Hutton (eds) (2005), *Service Industries and Asia-Pacific Cities: New Development Trajectories*, London: Routledge.
Daniels, P.W., A. Leyshon and N. Thrift (1988), 'Large accountancy firms in the UK: operational adaptation and spatial development', *The Service Industries Journal*, **8**: 317–46.
Daniels, P.W. and K. O'Connor (2000), 'Globalization, producer services, and the Asian City', paper presented to the Global Conference on Economic Geography, National University of Singapore, Singapore, 6–8 December 2000.
Daniels, P.W., N. Thrift and A. Leyshon (1989), 'Internationalization of Professional Producer Services: Accountancy Conglomerates', in P. Enderwick (ed.), *Multinational Service Firms*, London: Routledge, pp. 79–106.
Darnton, Robert (2000), 'An early information society: news and the media in nineteenth-century Paris', *American Historical Review*, **105**: 1–17.
Dasgupta, Partha S. and P.A. David (1994), 'Toward a new economics of science', *Research Policy*, **23**: 487–521.
Davis, C. and T. Hutton (1991), 'An empirical analysis of producer service exports from the Vancouver region', *Canadian Journal of Regional Science*, **14**: 375–94.
Dawson, R. (2000), *Developing Knowledge-Based Client Relationships*, London: Butterworth-Heinemann.
de Bandt, J. (1994), 'La notion de marché est-elle transposable dans le domaine des services informationnels aux entreprises?', in J. de Bandt and J. Gadrey (eds), *Relations de service, marchés de services*, Paris: CNRS, pp. 217–40.
de Bandt, J. (1995), *Services aux entreprise*, Paris: Economica.
de Bandt, J. and L. Dibiaggio (2002), 'Informational activities as co-production of knowledge and values', in Gadrey and Gallouj (eds), pp. 54–75.
De Beauvoir, S. (1972) (in French 1949), *The Second Sex*, Harmondsworth: Penguin.
Deane, P. and W. Cole (1962), *British Economic Growth 1688–1959*, Cambridge: Cambridge University Press.
Delaney, R.V. and R. Wilson (2003), 'The case for reconfiguration', 14th annual 'State of Logistics Report', Speech delivered at Washington, DC, June 2, Copy available at www.cassinfo.com.
Delaunay, J.-C. and J. Gadrey (1987), *Les Enjeux de la société de service*, Paris: Presses de la Fondation Nationale des Sciences Politiques.
Delaunay, Jean-Claude and J. Gadrey (1992), *Services in Economic Thought: Three Centuries of Debate*, Boston, MA: Kluwer Academic.
Den Hertog, P. (2000), 'Knowledge intensive business services as co-producers of innovation', *International Journal of Innovation Management*, **4**: 91–528.
Den Hertog, P., R. Bilderbeek and S. Maltha (1997), 'Intangibles: the soft side of innovation', *Futures*, **29**: 33–45.

Department of Trade and Industry (DTI) (2003), *Services and Offshoring: The Impact of Increasing International Competition in Services (A Consultation Document)*, London: Department of Trade and Industry.
Department of Trade and Industry (DTI) (2004), *The UK Contact Centre Industry: A Study*, London: Department of Trade and Industry.
Dicken, P. (2003), *Global Shift: The Internationalization of Economic Activity*, 4th edn, New York: Guilford Press.
Dicken, P., P. Kelly, K. Olds and H. Yeung (2001), 'Chains and networks, territories and scales: towards an analytical framework for the global economy', *Global Networks*, **1**: 89–112.
DiMaggio, P.J. and W.W. Powell (1983), 'The iron cage revisited: institutional isomorphism and collective rationality in organisational fields', *American Sociological Review*, **48**: 147–60.
Diprose, R. (1994), *The Bodies of Women: Ethics, Embodiment and Sexual Difference*, London: Routledge.
Disclosure (1998), *Global Researcher: Worldscope Database*, Bethesda, MD: Disclosure.
Dizard, Wilson P.J. (1997), *Meganet. How Global Communications Network will connect Everyone on Earth*, Boulder, CO: Westview Press.
Djellal, F. and F. Gallouj (2001), 'Patterns of innovation organisation in service firms: postal survey results and theoretical models', *Science and Public Policy*, **28**: 57–67.
Doel, M. and J. Beaverstock (1999), 'London's and New York's response to the Asian financial crisis', paper presented to the 95th Annual Meeting of the Association of American Geographers, Honolulu, HI, 23–27 March.
Dolfsma, W. and C. Dannreuther (2003), *Globalisation, Social Capital, and Inequality: Contested Concepts, Contested Experiences*, Cheltenham, UK and Northampton, MA, USA: Edward Elgar.
Dolven, B. (2002), 'The great consulting pile-up', *Far Eastern Economic Review*, 16 May, pp. 26–9.
Doove, S., O. Gabbitas, D. Nguyen-Hong and J. Owen (2001), 'Price effects of regulation: telecommunications, air passenger transport and electricity supply', Productivity Commission Staff Research Paper, AusInfo, Canberra (October).
Dosi, G. (ed.) (1996), *Organization and Strategy in the Evolution of the Enterprise*, Basingstoke: Macmillan.
Dosi, G. and D.J. Teece (1998), 'Organizational competencies and the boundaries of the firm', in R. Arena and C. Longhi (eds), *Markets and Organizations*, New York: Springer, pp. 282–302.
Douglass, M. (1991), 'Transnational capital and the social reconstruction of comparative advantage in Southeast Asia', *Southeast Asia Journal of Social Science*, **19**(1–2): 14–43.
Drinkwater, S., P. Levine, E. Lotti and J. Pearlman (2002), 'The Economic Impact of Migration: A Survey', Second Workshop of the Fifth Framework Project on European Enlargement, The Impact of East–West Migration on Growth and Employment, Vienna.
Drucker P.F. (1985), *Innovation and Entrepreneurship: Practice and Principles*, London: Heinemann.
Drucker, Peter (1969), *The Age of Discontinuity: Guidelines to our Changing Society*, New York: Harper & Row.
Du Gay, P. (1996), *Consumption and Identity at Work*, London: Sage.

Ducatel, K. (1999), 'Information technologies in non-knowledge services: innovations on the margin?', in J.S. Metcalfe and I. Miles (eds), *Innovation Systems in the Services Economy: Measurement and Case Study Analysis*, Norwell, MA: Kluwer, pp. 221–45.

Duncan, N. (ed.) (1996), *BodySpace*, London: Routledge.

Dunning, J.H. (1979), 'Explaining changing patterns of international production: in defence of the eclectic theory', *Oxford Bulletin of Economics and Statistics*, **41**(4): 269–95.

Dunning, J. (1988), *Explaining International Production*, London: Unwin Hyman.

Dunning, J.H. (1989), 'Multinational enterprises and the growth of services: some conceptual and theoretical issues', *The Service Industries Journal*, **9**(1): 5–39.

Dunning, J. (1993), *The Globalization of Business: The Challenge of the 1990s*, London: Routledge.

Dunning, J.H. and A. McKaig-Berliner (2002), 'The geographical sources of competitiveness: the professional business service industry', *Transnational Corporations*, **11**: 1–38.

Economist, The (2003), 'Peril at sea', 4 October: 57–8.

Economist, The (2004), 'Hokkaido: Japan's coddled frontier', 11–17 December: 40.

Economist, The (Anon) (1997), 'In search of the perfect market', 10 May: 78–82.

Economist, The (Anon) (2001), 'Regulating the internet: tied up in knots', 9 June: 67.

Economist, The (Anon) (2004), 'Windows shopping', 22 January.

ECORYS (2004), 'EU2004 REACH, The impact of REACH: Overview over 36 studies: ECORYS and OpdenKamp Adviesgroep', preparation document for the REACH Impact Assessment, 25–27 October 2004, The Hague, Netherlands.

Edgington, D. (1989), 'New strategies for technology development in Japanese cities and regions', *Town Planning Review*, **60**(1): 1–27.

Edgington, D. (1991), 'Economic restructuring in Yokohama: from gateway port to international core city', *Asian Geographer*, **10**: 62–78.

Edmonson, R.G. (2003), 'Lines welcome increased box inspections', *Journal of Commerce Online*, June 9.

Edstrom, A. and J. Galbraith (1977a), 'Transfer of managers as a coordination and control strategy in multinational corporations', *Administrative Science Quarterly*, **22**: 248–63.

Edstrom, A. and J. Galbraith (1977b), 'Alternative policies for international transfers of managers', *Management International Review*, **17**: 11–22.

Edvardsson, B., L. Edvisson and H. Nystrom (1993), 'Internationalisation in service companies', *The Service Industries Journal*, **13**(1): 80–97.

Ehrenreich, B. (2002), *Nickel and Dimed: On (Not) Getting by in America*, New York: Metropolitan Books.

Eiglier, P. and E. Langeard (1987), *Le marketing des services*, Paris: McGraw-Hill.

Eisenhardt, K.M. and F.M. Santos (2002), 'Knowledge-based view: a new theory of strategy', in A. Pettigrew, H. Thomas and R. Whittington (eds), *Handbook of Strategy and Management*, London: Sage, pp. 139–64.

Elfring, T. (1992), 'An international comparison of service sector employment growth', in *United Nations Commission for Europe, Personal and Collective Services: an International Perspective*, Discussion paper, **2**(1): 1–13.

Ellison, G. and E.L. Glaeser (1997), 'Geographical concentration in US manufacturing industries: a dartboard approach', *Journal of Political Economy*, **107**: 207–23.

Enderwick, P. (1988), 'Some economics of service sector multinationals', in P. Enderwick (ed.), *Multinational Service Firms*, London: Routledge, pp. 3–24.

Engel, C. (1999), 'Health services industry: still a job machine?', *Monthly Labor Review*, **122**, March: 3–14.
Equal Opportunities Commission (EOC) (2003), *Men and Women in the Labour Market*, Manchester: EOC.
Erramilli, M.K. and C.P. Rao (1990), 'Choice of foreign market entry modes by service firms: role of market knowledge', *Management International Review*, **30**(2): 135–50.
Erramilli, M.K. and C.P. Rao (1993), 'Service firms' international entry mode choice: a modified transaction cost analysis approach', *Journal of Marketing*, **57**: 19–38.
Esping-Andersen, G. (1990), *The Three Worlds of Welfare Capitalism*, Princeton, NJ: Princeton University Press.
European Commission (EC) (2000), *European Competitiveness Report, 2000*, Brussels.
European Commission (EC) (2002), *Information and Communication Technologies, Enlargement*, Futures Report Series 05, Joint Research Centre (JRC), Institute for Prospective Technological Studies, Brussels.
European Commission (EC) (2004), 'Business-related services: a key driver of European competitiveness – an enhanced economic analysis', Enterprise DG Working Paper, Enterprise Directorate General, Brussels, December.
European Commission (EIS) (2003), European Innovation Scoreboard, Commission Staff Working Paper, SEC(2003) 1255, Commission of the European Communities.
Eurostat (2003), *NewCronos database, Theme 2, Economy and Finance*, europa.eu.int/newcronos, 13 November 2003.
Evangelista, R. (2000), 'Sectoral patterns of technological change in services', *Economics of Innovation and New Technology*, **9**: 183–221.
Evangelista, R. and M. Savona (2003), 'Innovation, employment and skills in services. Firm and sectoral evidence', *Structural Change and Economic Dynamics*, **14**: 449–74.
Evangelista, R. and G. Sirilli (1995), 'Measuring innovation in services', *Research Evaluation*, **5**(3): 207–15.
Facchini, G. and M.L. Segnana (2003), 'Growth at the EU periphery: the next enlargement', *Quarterly Review of Economics and Finance*, **43**(5): 827–62.
Fainstein, S. (1991), 'Promoting economic development: urban planning in the United States and Great Britain', *Journal of the American Planning Association*, **57**: 22–33.
Fainstein, S. (1994), *The City Builders: Property, Politics, and Planning in London and New York*, Oxford: Blackwell.
Fainstein, S., I. Gordon and M. Harloe (1992), *Divided Cities: New York and London in the Contemporary World*, Oxford: Blackwell.
Fan, C. (1997), 'Uneven development and beyond: regional development theory in post-Mao China', *International Journal of Urban and Regional Research*, **21**: 620–39.
Fan, C. and A. Scott (2003), 'Industrial agglomeration and development: a survey of spatial economic issues in East Asia and a statistical analysis of Chinese regions', *Economic Geography*, **79**(3): 295–319.
Fan, T., J. Bosler, J. Wilmking, L. Vigeant-Langlois and C. Geissler (2001), 'Evolution of global strategic airline alliance and consolidation in the twenty-first century', *Journal of Air Transport Management*, **7**(6): 349–60.
Featherstone, M. and R. Burrows (eds) (1995), *Cyberspace, Cyberbodies, Cyberpunk: Cultures of Technological Embodiment*, London: Sage.
Featherstone, M. and S. Lash (eds) (1999), *Spaces of Culture*, London: Sage.

Federal Reserve Bank of Boston (2004), 'Understanding the "job-loss recovery" ', Public Policy Briefs No. 04-1, Federal Reserve Bank of Boston, Boston.
Feenstra, R. (1998), 'Integration of trade and disintegration of production in the global economy', *Journal of Economic Perspectives*, **12**(4): 31–50.
Feketekuty, G. (1988), *International Trade in Services*, New York: Ballinger.
Fernandez, M.T.F. (2001), 'Performance of business services multinationals in host countries: contrasting different patterns of behaviour between foreign affiliates and national enterprises', *The Service Industries Journal*, **21**(1): 5–18.
Ferree, M.M., J. Lorber and B.B. Hess (eds) (1999), *Revisioning Gender*, London: Sage.
Findlay, Christopher and Tony Warren (eds) (2000), *Impediments to Trade in Services: Measurement and Policy Implications*, London and New York: Routledge.
Fink, Carsten, Aaditya Mattoo and Ileana Cristina Neagu (2002), 'Trade in international maritime services: how much does policy matter?', *World Bank Economic Review*, **16**: 81–108.
Fink, Carsten, Aaditya Mattoo and Randeep Rathindran (2003), 'An assessment of telecommunications reform in developing countries', *Information Economics and Policy*, **15**: 443–66.
Fisher, A.G.B. (1935), *The Clash of Progress and Security*, London: Macmillan.
Fisher, A.G.B. (1939), 'Production, primary, secondary and tertiary', *Economic Record*, **15**, June, 24–38.
Fladmoe-Linquist, K. (2000), 'International franchising: a network approach to FDI', in Aharoni and Nachum (eds), pp. 197–216.
Fladmoe-Lindquist, K. and L.L. Jacque (1995), 'Control modes in international service operations: the propensity to franchise', *Management Science*, **41**(7): 1238–49.
Florida, R. (2002), *The Rise of the Creative Class: And How It's Transforming Work, Leisure, Community and Everyday Life*, New York: Basic Books.
Foley, P. and M. Ram (2002), 'The use of online technology by ethnic minority businesses: a comparative study of the West Midlands and UK', De Montfort University monograph, Leicester, available from author.
Foray, D. (1991), 'The secrets of industry are in the air: industrial cooperation and the organizational dynamics of the innovative firm', *Research Policy*, **20**: 393–405.
Forfás (2005), *Review 2005 and Outlook 2006*, Forfás, Dublin, report, www.forfas.ie/publications/forfas060131/index.html, 1 February 2006.
Foucault, M. (1978), *The History of Sexuality. Volume 1: An Introduction*, London: Allen Lane.
Fourastié, J. (1949), *Le Grand Espoir du XXe siècle*, Paris: Presses Universitaires de France.
Fowler, G. (2003), 'Commercial break: the art of selling' ('China creative: global ads from a brand new source'), *Far Eastern Economic Review*, 30 October, pp. 30–33.
Francois, Joseph (1999), 'Estimates of barriers to trade in services', Erasmus University, Rotterdam, unpublished manuscript.
Fraunhofer Institute of Systems and Innovation Research (ISI) (2000), *Surveying Organisational Innovation on a European Level: Challenges and Options*, Karlsruhe: Fraunhofer ISI.
Freund, C. and D. Weinhold (2002), 'The internet and international trade in services', *American Economic Review*, **92**(2): 236–40.

Friedland, R. and D. Boden (1994), 'NowHere: an introduction to space, time and modernity', in R. Friedland and D. Boden (eds), *Space, Time and Modernity*, Berkeley, CA: University of California Press, pp. 1–60.
Friedland, R. and D. Palmer (1994), 'Space, corporation, and class: towards a grounded theory', in R. Friedland and D. Boden (eds), *Space, Time and Modernity*, Berkeley, CA: University of California Press, pp. 87–334.
Friedmann, J. (1986), 'The world city hypothesis', *Development and Change*, **17**: 69–83.
Friedmann, J. and W. Goetz (1982), 'World city formation: an agenda for research and action', *International Journal of Urban and Regional Research*, **6**: 309–44.
Fuchs, V.R. (1968), *The Service Economy*, New York: National Bureau of Economic Research.
Fujita, K. (1992), 'A world city and flexible specialization: restructuring of the Tokyo Metropolis', *International Journal of Urban and Regional Research*, **15**: 269–84.
G8 (2001), *Digital Opportunities for All: Meeting the Challenge*, Washington, DC: G8.
Gadrey, J. (1994), 'Relations, contrats et conventions de service', in J. de Bandt and J. Gadrey (eds), *Relations de service, marchés de services*, Paris: CNRS: pp. 123–51.
Gadrey, J. (1996), *Services: la productivité en question*, Paris: Desclée de Brouwer.
Gadrey, J. (2000), 'The characterization of goods and services: an alternative approach', *Review of Income and Wealth*, **46**(3): 369–87.
Gadrey, J. (2002), 'The misuse of productivity concepts in services: lessons from a comparison between France and the United States', in Gadrey and Gallouj (eds), pp. 26–53.
Gadrey, J. and F. Gallouj (1998), 'The provider-customer interface in business and professional services', *The Service Industries Journal*, **18**: 1–15.
Gadrey J. and F. Gallouj (eds) (2002), *Productivity, Innovation and Knowledge in Services*, Cheltenham, UK and Northampton, MA, USA: Edward Elgar.
Gaffikin, F. and A. Nickson (1984), *Jobs Crisis and the Multi-Nationals*, Birmingham: Birmingham Trade Union Group for World Development.
Gaffikin, F. and B. Warf (1993), 'Urban policy and the Post-Keynesian state in the United Kingdom and the United States', *International Journal of Urban and Regional Research*, **17**: 67–84.
Gallouj, C. (1997), 'Asymmetry of information and the service relationship: selection and evaluation of the service provider', *International Journal of Service Industry Management*, **8**(1): 42–64.
Gallouj, F. (2002), *Innovation in the Service Economy: The New Wealth of Nations*, Cheltenham, UK and Northampton, MA, USA: Edward Elgar.
Gallouj, F. and O. Weinstein (1997), 'Innovation in services', *Research Policy*, **26**: 537–56.
Gallunc, D.C. and S. Rodan (1998), 'Resource recombinations in the firm: knowledge structures and the potential for Schumpeterian innovation', *Strategic Management Journal*, **19**: 1193–201.
Gereffi, G. and M. Kornzeniewicz (eds) (1994), *Commodity Chains and Global Capitalism*, Westport, CI: Greenwood Press.
Gershuny, J. (1978), *After Industrial Society? The Emerging Self-Service Economy*, London: Macmillan.
Gershuny, J. (1987), 'The future of service employment', in O. Giarini (ed.), *The Emerging Service Economy*, New York: Praeger, pp. 105–23.

Gershuny J. and I. Miles (1983), *The New Service Economy: The Transformation of Employment in Industrial Societies*, London: Pinter.
Gertler, M. (1992), 'Flexibility revisited: districts, nation-states, and the forces of production', *Transactions of the Institute of British Geographers*, **17**: 259–78.
Gertler, M. (1995), ' "Being there": proximity, organisation, and culture in the development and adoption of advanced manufacturing technologies', *Economic Geography*, **71**: 1–26.
Ghibutiu, Agnes (1998), 'Business services and the Romanian integration into Western markets', paper presented at the 14 PROGRES Seminar, Geneva, 11–12 September.
Ghibutiu, Agnes (1999), 'Considering the contribution of services to economic growth and development in emerging market economies: the case of Romania', paper presented at the World Services Congress, Atlanta, 1–3 November.
Ghibutiu, Agnes (2000), *Serviciile si dezvoltarea. De la prejudecati la noi orizonturi* (Services and development. From prejudices towards new insights), Bucharest: Editura Expert.
Giarini, O. (2001), 'Basic features of services and some fundamentals of the (new) service economy', *Progress*, **33**: 20–28.
Giarini, O. (2002), 'The globalization of services in economic theory and economic practice: some conceptual issues', in Cuadrado-Roura et al. (eds), pp. 58–77.
Giarini, O. and Walter R. Stahel (1993), *The Limits to Certainty: International Studies on the Service Economy*, Boston, MA: Kluwer Academic.
Giddens, A. (1984), *The Constitution of Society: Outline of the Theory of Structuration*, Berkeley, CA: University of California Press.
Giddens, A. (1991), *Modernity and Self-identity: Self and Society in the Late Modern Age*, Cambridge: Polity.
Giddens, A. (1992), *The Transformation of Intimacy: Sexuality, Love and Eroticism in Modern Societies*, Cambridge: Polity.
Giddens, A. (2000), *Runaway World: How Globalisation is Reshaping our Lives*, New York: Routledge.
Gist, R.R. (1968), *Retailing: Concepts and Decisions*, New York: John Wiley & Sons.
Glasmeier, A.K. and M. Howland (1995), *From Combines to Computers. Rural Services and Development in the Age of Information Technology*, Albany, NY: State University of New York Press.
Glückler, J. (1999), 'Management consulting – structure and growth of a knowledge intensive business service market in Europe', Institut für Wirtschafts- und Sozialgeographie, Department of Economic and Social Geography Johann Wolfgang Goethe-Universität Frankfurt, IWSG Working Papers 12-1999.
Goe, R. (1991), 'The growth of producer services industries: sorting through the externalization debate', *Growth and Change*, **22**(4): 118–41.
Goffman, E. (1967), *Interaction Ritual: Essays on Face to Face Behaviour*, New York: Doubleday.
Gonenc, R. and G. Nicoletti (2001), 'Regulation, Market Structure and Performance in Air Passenger Transportation', OECD Economic Studies, No. 32, OECD, Paris.
Goodman, B. and R. Steadman (2002), 'Services: business demand rivals consumer demand in driving job growth', *Monthly Labor Review*, **125**, April: 3–16.
Goodwin, J.S. and J.L. Neal (1990), 'Global trade in business services: exploiting competitive opportunity and advantages', Graduate School of Business Administration, University of Virginia.

Gordon, R. (2000), 'Does the "New Economy" measure up to the great inventions of the past?', *Journal of Economic Perspectives*, **14**: 49–74.
Gorostriaga, X. (1984), *The Role of the International Financial Centers in Underdeveloped Countries*, New York: St. Martin's Press.
Goto, J. (2000), 'International migration and trade liberalization', Economic and Business Administration Working Papers 109, Kobe University Research Institute for Economic and Business Adminsitration, Kobe.
Gottdeiner, M. (2001), *Life in the Air: Surviving the New Culture of Air Travel*, Boulder, CO: Rowman & Littlefield.
Gottmann, J. (1961), *Megalopolis: The Urbanized Northeastern Seaboard of the United States*, New York: Twentieth Century Fund.
Graham, S. (1998), 'The end of geography or the explosion of place? Conceptualizing space, place and information technology', *Progress in Human Geography*, **22**(2): 165–85.
Graham, S. (1999), 'Global grids of glass: on global cities, telecommunications and planetary urban networks', *Urban Studies*, 36(5–6): 929–49.
Graham, S. (2004), 'The software-sorted city: rethinking the "digital divide"', in S. Graham and S. Marvin (eds), *The Cybercities Reader*, London: Routledge, pp. 324–32.
Graham, S. and S. Marvin (1996), *Telecommunications and the City: Electronic Spaces, Urban Places*, London: Routledge.
Graham, S. and S. Marvin (2001), *Splintering Urbanism: Networked Infrastructures, Technological Mobilities and the Urban Condition*, London: Routledge.
Granovetter, M. (1985), 'Economic action and social structure: the problem of embeddedness', *American Journal of Sociology*, **91**: 481–510.
Granovetter, M. (1991), 'The social construction of economic institutions', in N. Nohria and R. Eccles (eds), *Networks and Organisations: Structure, Form and Action*, Cambridge, MA: Harvard Business School Press.
Grant, R.M. (1996), 'Towards a knowledge-based theory of the firm', *Strategic Management Journal*, **17**: 109–22.
Grant, R.M. (2002), 'Corporate strategy: managing scope and strategy content', in A. Pettigrew, H. Thomas and R. Whittington (eds), *Handbook of Strategy and Management*, London: Sage, pp. 72–97.
Grant, R.M. and C. Baden-Fuller (2004), 'A knowledge accessing theory of strategic alliances', *Journal of Management Studies*, **41**(1): 61–84.
Greenan, N., J. Mairesse and A. Topiol-Bensaid (2001), 'Information technology and research and development impacts on productivity and skills: looking for correlations on French firm-level data', NBER Working Paper 8075, Cambridge, MA: National Bureau of Economic Research.
Greenfield, H.I. (1966), *Manpower and the Growth of Producer Services*, New York: Columbia University Press.
Greenwood, R. and R. Lachman (1996), 'Change as an underlying thing in professional service organisations: an introduction', *Organisation Studies*, **17**: 563–72.
Greenwood, R., T. Rose, J. Brown, D. Cooper and B. Hinings (1999), 'The global management of professional services: the example of accounting', in S.R. Clegg, E. Ibarra-Colado and L. Bueno-Rodriquez (eds), *Global Management*, London: Sage, pp. 265–9.
Gregg, P. and J. Wadsworth (eds) (1999), *The State of Working Britain*, Manchester: Manchester University Press.

Greis, N.P. and J.D. Kasarda (1997), 'Enterprise logistics in the information era', *California Management Review*, **39**: 55–78.

Grey, C. (1998), 'On being a professional in a Big Six professional firm', *Accounting, Organizations and Society*, **23**: 569–87.

Griliches, Z. (1994), 'Productivity, R&D, and the data constraint', *American Economic Review*, **84**(1): 1–23.

Grimes, S. (1997), 'Attracting information technology investment to Ireland's branch plant economy', in E. Roche and H. Bakis (eds), *Developments in Telecommunications: Between Global and Local*, Aldershot, UK and Brookfield, VT: Ashgate, pp. 209–332.

Grimshaw, D., M. Marchington, J. Rubery and H. Willmot (2005), 'Fragmenting work across organizational boundaries', in M. Marchington, D. Grimshaw, J. Rubery and H. Willmot (eds), *Fragmenting Work: Blurring Organizational Boundaries and Disordering Hierarchies*, Oxford: Oxford University Press, pp. 1–31.

Grint, K. and S. Woolgar (1997), *The Machine at Work: Technology, Work and Organisation*, Oxford: Polity.

Grosse, R. (2000), 'Knowledge creation and transfer in global service firms', in Aharoni and Nachum (eds), pp. 217–32.

Grosz, E. (1994), *Volatile Bodies: Toward a Corporeal Feminism*, Bloomington, IN: Indiana University Press.

Grundmann, R. and N. Stehr (2000), 'Social science and the absence of nature', *Social Science Information*, **39**: 155–79.

Grünfeld, L.A. and A. Moxnes (2003), *The Intangible Globalization : Explaining the Patterns of International Trade in Services*, Oslo: Norsk Utenrikspolitisk Institutt.

Guile, B.R. and J.B. Quinn (eds) (1988a), *Managing Innovation: Cases from the Services Industries*, Washington, DC: National Academy Press.

Guile, B.R. and J.B. Quinn (eds) (1988b), *Technology in Services: Policies for Growth, Trade, and Employment*, Washington, DC: National Academy Press.

Guillen, M.F. (1994), Models of Management: Work, Authority and Organization in a Comparative Perspective, Chicago: University of Chicago Press.

Gulati, R., N. Nohria and A. Zaheer (2000), 'Strategic networks', *Strategic Management Journal*, **21**: 203–16.

Gupta, A.K. and V. Govindarajan (2000), 'Knowledge flows within multinational corporations', *Strategic Management Journal*, **21**: 473–96.

Haddad, Charles (2001), 'Ground wars: UPS's rapid ascent leaves FedEx scrambling', *Business Week*, May, **21**: 64.

Hagel, J. and A.G. Armstrong (1997), *Net Gain: Expanding Markets Through Virtual Communities*, New York: Harvard Business School.

Haggert, P., A.D. Cliff and A.E. Frey (1977), *Locational Analysis in Human Geography*, London: Edward Arnold.

Halford, S.M., A. Savage and A. Witz (1996), *Gender, Careers and Organisations*, Basingstoke: Macmillan.

Hall, A.D. and R.E. Fagen (1956), 'Definition of system', in *General Systems Yearbook*, **1**, 18–28.

Hall, D. and A. Braithwaite (2001), 'The development of thinking in supply chain and logistics management', in Brewer et al. (eds), pp. 81–98.

Hall, P. (1966), *The World Cities*, London: Weidenfeld & Nicolson.

Hamnett, C. (2003), *Unequal City: London in the Global Arena*, London: Routledge.
Hampton, M. (1996a), 'Exploring the offshore interface: the relationship between tax havens, tax evasion, corruption and economic development', *Crime Law and Social Change*, **24**: 293–317.
Hampton, M. (1996b), *The Offshore Interface: Tax Havens in the Global Economy*, New York: St Martin's Press.
Hampton, M. and J. Christensen (1999), 'Treasure Island revisited: Jersey's offshore finance centre crisis: implications for other small island economies', *Environment and Planning A*, **31**: 1619–37.
Hanlon, G. (1994), *The Commercialisation of Accountancy: Flexible Accumulation and the Transformation of the Service Class*, London: Macmillan.
Hanlon, G. (1999), 'International professional labour markets and the narratives of accountants', *Critical Perspectives on Accounting*, **10**: 199–221.
Hanlon, G. (2003), 'Institutional forms and organisational structures: homology, trust and reputational capital in professional service firms', *Organization*, **11**(2): 187–210.
Hannan, M.T. and G. Carroll (1992), *Dynamics of Organizational Populations*, New York: Oxford University Press.
Hannan, M.T. and J.H. Freeman (1977), 'The population ecology of organizations', *American Journal of Sociology*, **82**: 929–64.
Hannan, M.T. and J. Freeman (1984), 'Structural inertia and organizational change', *American Sociological Review*, **49**: 149–64.
Hansen, M.T., N. Nokria and T. Tierney (1999), 'What's your strategy for managing knowledge?', *Harvard Business Review*, March–April: 106–16.
Hanson, K. and J. Rogers (2001), ' "Why Marcia you've changed!" Male clerical temporary workers doing masculinity in a feminized occupation', *Gender and Society*, **15**: 218–38.
Haqqani, A.B. (2003), *The Role of Information and Communications Technology in Global Development: Analyses and Recommendations*, UN ICT Task Force Series, No. 3, New York: United Nations.
Hardin, A. and L. Holmes (1997), *Services Trade and Foreign Direct Investment*, Staff Research Paper, Industry Commission, Canberra: Australian Government Publishing Services.
Harraway, D. (1991), *Simians, Cyborgs and Women: The Reinvention of Nature*, New York: Routledge.
Hart, O. and J. Moore (1990), 'Property rights and the nature of the firm', *Journal of Political Economy*, **98**(6): 1119–58.
Hart, S.J. and L.M. Service (1993), 'Cross-functional integration in the new product introduction process: an application of action science in services', *International Journal of Service Industry Management*, **4**: 50–66.
Harvey, D. (1989), *The Condition of Postmodernity*, Oxford: Basil Blackwell.
Harvey, D. (2001), *Spaces of Capital: Towards a Critical Geography*, New York: Routledge.
Hatch, J. and A. Clinton (2000), 'Job growth in the 1990s: a retrospect', *Monthly Labor Review*, December, **123**: 3–18.
Hatchuel, A. (1994), 'Modèles de service et activité industrielle: La place de la prescription', in J. de Bandt and J. Gadrey (eds), *Relations de service, marchés de services*, Paris: CNRS, pp. 63–84.

Hausmann, R. (2001), 'Prisoners of geography', *Foreign Policy*, **122**, January/February: 44–53.

Hayashi, N. (2004), 'Location patterns of information technology services in Japan', paper presented to the IGU Commission Residential Conference, Birmingham, UK, 9–13 August.

Hayek, F.A. (1945), 'The use of knowledge in society', *American Economic Review*, **35**(4): 519–30.

Hayuth, Y. (1987), *Intermodality: Concept and Practice*, Colchester: Lloyds of London Press.

Hedlund, G. (1994), 'A model of knowledge management and the *N*-form corporation', *Strategic Management Journal*, **15**: 73–90.

Hedlund, G. and I. Nonaka (1993), 'Models of knowledge management in the West and Japan', in P. Lorange, B. Chakravarthy, J. Roos and A. Van de Ven (eds), *Implementing Strategic Processes: Change, Learning and Cooperation*, Oxford: Blackwell, pp. 117–44.

Heidegger, M. (1962), *Being and Time*, New York: Harper & Row.

Held, D., A. McGrew, D. Goldblatt and J. Perraton (1999), *Global Transformations: Politics, Economics, and Culture*, Cambridge: Polity.

Henderson, J. (1989), *The Globalisation of High Technology Production: Society, Space and Semiconductors in the Restructuring of the Modern World*, London: Routledge.

Henderson, J., P. Dicken, M. Hess, N. Coe and H. Yeung (2002), 'Global production networks and the analysis of economic development', *Review of International Political Economy*, **9**(3): 436–64.

Henderson, R.M. and K.B. Clark (1990), 'Architectural innovation', *Administrative Science Quarterly*, **35**: 9–30.

Hepworth, M.E., A.E. Green and A.E. Gillespie (1987), 'The spatial division of information labour in Great Britain', *Environment and Planning A*, **19**: 793–806.

Herod, A. (2000), 'Implications of just-in-time production for union strategy: lessons from the 1998 General Motors–United Auto Workers strike', *Annals of the Association of American Geographers*, **90**(3): 521–47.

Heshmati, A. (2003), 'Productivity growth, efficiency and outsourcing in manufacturing and service industries', *Journal of Economic Surveys*, **17**: 79–112.

Hicks, C.R. (1998), 'Places in the "Net": experiencing cyberspace', *Cultural Dynamics*, **10**(1): 49–70.

Hiebert, D. (2004), 'The political economy of immigration', paper presented to the Peter Wall Institute for Advanced Studies, University of British Columbia, Vancouver, 10 November.

Hill, P. (1977), 'On goods and services', *Review of Income and Wealth*, December, **23**(4): 315–38.

Hill, P. (1999), 'Tangibles, intangibles and services: a new taxonomy for the classification of output', *Canadian Journal of Economics*, **32**(2): 426–46.

Hill, C.W.L. and R.E. Hoskisson (1987), 'Strategy and structure in the multiproduct firm', *Academy of Management Review*, **12**: 331–41.

Hines, P., D. Jones and N. Rich (2001), 'Lean logistics', in Brewer et al., pp. 171–94.

Hipp, C. (1999), 'Information flows and knowledge creation in knowledge-intensive business services: scheme for a conceptualization', in J.S. Metcalfe and I. Miles (eds), *Innovation Systems in the Services Economy: Measurement and Case Study Analysis*, Norwell, MA: Kluwer, pp. 149–67.

Hipp, C., B. Tether and I. Miles (2000), 'The incidence and effects of innovation in services: evidence from Germany', *International Journal of Innovation Management*, **4**: 417–54.
Hislop, D. (2002), 'The client role in consultancy relations during the appropriation of technological innovations', *Research Policy*, **31**: 657–71.
Hitchens, D.M.W.N. (1997), 'The adequacy of the supply of professional advisory services to manufacturing firms in rural mid-Wales', *The Service Industries Journal*, **17**(4): 669–90.
Hitchens, D.M.W.N., P.N. O'Farrell and C. Conway (1994), 'Business service use by manufacturing firms in mid Wales', *Environment and Planning A*, **26**: 95–106.
Ho, K.C. (1991), 'Studying the city in the new international division of labor', Department of Sociology Working Paper 117, National University of Singapore.
Ho, K.C. (1998), 'Corporate regional functions in the Asia-Pacific', *Asia Pacific Viewpoint*, **39**: 179–92.
Ho, K.C. (2005), 'Service industries and occupational change: implications for identity, citizenship and politics', in Daniels et al. (eds), pp. 93–109.
Hochschild, A.R. (1983), *The Managed Heart: Commercialization of Human Feeling*, Berkeley, CA: University of California Press.
Hoekman, Bernard (1995), 'Assessing the General Agreement on Trade in Services', in Will Martin and L. Alan Winters (eds), *The Uruguay Round and the Developing Countries*, World Bank Discussion Paper No. 307, Washington, DC: World Bank. Revised version published in Will Martin and L. Alan Winters (eds), Cambridge: Cambridge University Press, 1996.
Hoekman, B. (2000), 'The next round of services negotiations: identifying priorities and options', *Federal Reserve Bank of St. Louis Review*, **82**: 31–47.
Hoekman, B. and C.A. Primo Braga (1997), 'Protection and trade in services: a survey', *Open Economies Review*, **8**: 285–308.
Holland, P. (1985), 'Banking in the eighties: adaptation or innovation?', *The Service Industries Journal*, **5**: 215–25.
Holmes, L. and A. Hardin (2000), 'Assessing barriers to services sector investment', in Findlay and Warren (eds), pp. 52–70.
Holzner, B., W.N. Dunn and M. Shahidullah (1987), 'An accounting scheme for designing science impact indicators', *Knowledge*, **9**: 173–204.
Howells, J. (1990), 'The internalisation of R&D and the development of global research networks', *Regional Studies*, **24**: 495–512.
Howells, J. (1999), 'Research and technology outsourcing and innovation systems: an exploratory analysis', *Industry and Innovation*, **6**(1): 111–27.
Howells, J. (2000a), 'Services and systems of innovation', in Andersen et al. (eds), pp. 215–28.
Howells, J. (2000b), 'Knowledge, innovation and location', in J.R. Bryson, P.W. Daniels, N. Henry and J. Pollard (eds), *Knowledge, Space, Economy*, London: Routledge, pp. 50–62.
Howells, J. (2001), 'The nature of innovation in services', in OECD, *Innovation and Productivity in Services*, Paris: OECD, pp. 55–79.
Howells, J. (2004), 'Innovation, consumption and services: encapsulation and the combinatorial role of services', *The Service Industries Journal*, **24**: 19–36.
Howells, J. and A. Green (1986), 'Location, technology and industrial organisation in UK services', *Progress in Planning*, **26**: 83–184.

Howells, J. and A. Green (1988), *Technological Innovation, Structural Change and Location in UK Services*, Aldershot: Avebury.

Howells, J. and J. Roberts (2000), 'From innovation systems to knowledge systems', *Prometheus*, **18**: 17–28.

Howells, J.R.L. and M. Wood (1993), *The globalisation of production and technology*, London: Belhaven Press.

Hoy, F. and J. Stanworth (eds) (2002), *Franchising: An International Perspective*, London: Routledge.

Hsu, J.-Y. and P.-H. Chen (2004), 'Financial service industry and the community of practice: a case study of Taipei financial center', paper presented to the IGU Commission Residential Conference, Birmingham, UK, 9–13 August.

Hu, J. (2001), 'Stubborn AOL may have last laugh', CNET News.com, June 6.

Hubbard, P., R. Kitchin, B. Bartley and D. Fuller (2002), *Thinking Geographically: Space, Theory, and Contemporary Human Geography*, London: Continuum.

Hudson, A. (2000), 'Offshoreness, globalization and sovereignty: a postmodern geopolitical economy?', *Transactions of the Institute of British Geographers*, **25**: 269–83.

Hugill, Peter J. (1993), *World Trade since 1451*, Baltimore, MD: Johns Hopkins University Press.

Huntington, S.P. (1973), 'Postindustrial politics: how benign will it be?', *Comparative Politics*, **6**: 163–91.

Husserl, E. (1931), '*Ideas: General Introduction to Pure Phenomenology*', W.R.B. (trans.), New York: Macmillan.

Hutton, T. (2000), 'Reconstructed production landscapes in the postmodern city: applied design and creative services in the metropolitan core', *Urban Geography*, **21**: 285–317.

Hutton, T. (2001), *Service Industries and the Transformation of Asia-Pacific City Regions*, Singapore: Centre for Advanced Studies, National University of Singapore.

Hutton, T. (2004a), 'Service industries, globalization, and urban restructuring within the Asia-Pacific: new development trajectories and planning responses', *Progress in Planning*, **61**(1): 1–74.

Hutton, T. (2004b), 'The new economy of the inner city', *Cities*, **21**(2): 89–108.

Hutton, T.A. (2005), 'Services and urban development in the Asia Pacific: institutional responses and policy innovation', in P.W. Daniels, K.C. Ho and T.A. Hutton (eds), *Service Industries and Asia Pacific Cities: New Development Trajectories*, London: Routledge, pp. 52–76.

Hyde, F.E. (1973), *Far Eastern Trade: 1860–1914*, London: Adam & Charles Black.

Ietto-Gillies, G. (1998), 'Location of affiliates and degree of internationalisation: an analysis of the world's largest 664 TNCs', CIBS Research Papers in International Business No. 14-98, South Bank University, London.

Illeris, S. (1985), 'How to analyse the role of services in regional development', in M.J. Bannon and S. Ward (eds), *Services and the New Economy: Implications for National and Regional Development*, Dublin: Regional Studies Association, pp. 1–22.

Illeris, S. (1989), *Services and Regions in Europe*, Aldershot: Avebury.

Illeris, S. (1994), 'Proximity between service producers and service users', *Tijdschrift voor Economische en Sociale Geografie*, **85**: 294–302.

Illeris, Sven (1996), *The Service Economy: A Geographical Approach*, Chichester: Wiley.

Illeris, S. (2002), 'Are service jobs as bad as theory says? Some empirical findings from Denmark', *The Service Industries Journal*, **22**(4): 1–18.

Illeris, S. and J. Phillipe (1993), 'Introduction: the role of services in regional economic growth', in P. Daniels (ed.), *The Geography of Services*, London: Frank Cass, pp. 3–11.

Indergaard, M. (2003), *Silicon Alley: The Rise and Fall of a New Media District*, London and New York: Routledge.

Inglehart, R. (1995), 'Changing values, economic development and political change', *International Social Science Journal*, **145**: 379–403.

Institute for Management Development (IMD) (2002), *IMD Competitiveness Yearbook*, Lausanne: IMD.

Institute of Innovation Research (IOIR) (2003), 'Knowing how, knowing whom: a study of the links between the knowledge intensive services sector and the science base', Report to the Council for Science and Technology, Manchester: Institute of Innovation Research.

International Accounting Bulletin (1983), 'The world's top 20 accounting groups', December, p. 13.

International Accounting Bulletin (1988), *World Survey*, December, p. 17.

International Accounting Bulletin (1993), *World Survey*, December, pp. 7–11.

International Financial Services London (2003), *International Financial Markets in the UK*, London: IFSL.

International Labour Organization (ILO) (1999), 'Statistiques de l'emploi dans le secteur public', Working paper SAP 2.84/WP.143, Geneva.

International Labour Organization (ILO) (2003), *ILO Migration Survey 2003: Country Summaries*, Geneva: ILO.

International Monetary Fund IMF (2002a), *Manual on Statistics of International Trade in Services*, New York: United Nations Publications.

International Telecommunication Union (ITU) (2004), *World Telecommunication Indicators*, Geneva: ITU.

Irwin, S. and W. Bottero (2000), 'Market returns? Gender and theories of change in employment relations', *British Journal of Sociology*, **51**: 261–80.

James, J. (1999), *Globalization, Information Technology and Development*, London: Macmillan.

James, J. (2003), *Bridging the Global Digital Divide*, Cheltenham, UK and Northampton, MA, USA: Edward Elgar.

Janelle, D. and M. Beuthe (2002), 'Globalization and transportation: contradictions and challenges', in W. Black and P. Nijkamp (eds), *Social Change and Sustainable Transport*, Bloomington, IN: Indiana University Press, pp. 49–54.

Jensen, M. (2000), *A Theory of the Firm: Governance, Residual Claims and Organisational Forms*, Boston, MA: Harvard Business School Press.

Johnson, G. (1993), 'Tsuen Wan: from Hakka enclave to post-industrial city', Department of Anthropology and Sociology, University of British Columbia, Vancouver (mimeo).

Johnson, G. (1996), 'From collective economy to collective economy? Spatial transformation in the Pearl River Delta in the post-reform period', paper presented to the International Conference on the Rural–Urban Transition and Development in China, Zhongshan University, Guangzhou, 11–15 December.

Johnson, G. (2002), 'Deconstructing construction: some social implications of economic transformation in Guangdong, South China', paper presented to an Exploratory Workshop on Service Industries and New Models of Urban Change within the Asia-Pacific, Peter Wall Institute for Advanced Studies, University of British Columbia, Vancouver.

Johnson, K.P. (1995), 'Redefining of the BEA economic areas', *Survey of Current Business*, **75**, February: 75–81.

Johnson, M., T. Gregan, G. Gentle and P. Belin (2000), 'Modeling the benefits of increasing competition in international air services', in Christopher Findlay and Tony Warren (eds), *Impediments to Trade in Services: Measurement and Policy Implications*, London and New York: Routledge.

Jones, A. (2002), 'The "global city" misconceived: the myth of "global management" in transnational service firms', *Geoforum*, **33**: 335–50.

Jones, A. (2003), *Management Consultancy and Banking in an Era of Globalization*, Basingstoke: Palgrave.

Jones, C., W.S. Hesterley, K. Fladmoe-Lindquist and S.P. Borgatti (1998), 'Professional service constellations: how strategies and capabilities influence collaborative stability and change', *Organization Science*, **9**(3): 396–410.

Kalirajan, K. (2000), 'Restrictions on trade in distribution services', Productivity Commission Staff Research Paper, AusInfo, Canberra, August.

Kalirajan, K., G. McGuire, D. Nguyen-Hong and M. Schuele (2000), 'The price impact of restrictions on banking services', in Findlay and Warren (eds), pp. 215–30.

Kang, Jong-Soon (2000), 'Price impact of restrictions on maritime transport services', in Findlay and Warren (eds), pp. 189–200.

Kang, N.-H. and K. Sakai (2001), *New Patterns of Industrial Globalisation: Cross-border Mergers and Acquisitions and Strategic Alliances*, Paris: OECD.

Karsenty, G. (2000a), 'Just how big are the stakes? An assessment of trade in services by mode of supply', in Pierre Sauvé and Robert M. Stern (eds), *Services 2000: New Directions in Services Trade Liberalization*, Washington, DC: Brookings Institution.

Karsenty, G. (2000b), 'Assessing trade in services by mode of supply', in *GATS 2000: New Directions in Service Trade Liberalization*, Washington, DC: Brookings Institution, pp. 33–56.

Kasarda, John, D. (2000), 'New logistics technologies and infrastructure for the digitized economy', 4th International Conference on Technology Policy and Innovation, Curitiba, Brazil, August 28–31 August, in3.dem.ist.utl.pt/downloads/cur 2000/papers/.

Kasarda, J.D. and D. Rondinelli (1998), 'Innovative infrastructure for agile manufacturers', *Sloan Management Review*, **39**: 78–92.

Katz, M.L. and C. Shapiro (1994), 'Systems competition and networks effects', *Journal of Economic Perspectives*, **8:** 93–115.

Kaufman, L. (1999), 'A behind-the-screens glimpse of an internet retailer', *New York Times*, May 24, www.nytimes.com/library/tech/99/05/biztech/articles/24web.html.

Keeble, D. (2000), 'Collective learning processes in European high-technology milieu', in D. Keeble and F. Wilkinson (eds), *Collective Learning, Networking and High-Technology Regions in Europe*, Aldershot: Ashgate, pp. 199–229.

Keeble, D., J.R. Bryson and P.A. Wood (1991), 'Small firms, business service growth and regional development in the UK: some empirical findings', *Regional Studies*, **25**: 439–57.

Keeble, D. and L. Nachum (2002), 'Why do business service firms cluster? Small consultancies, clustering and decentralisation in London and southern England', *Transactions Institute of British Geographers*, **27**: 67–90.

Kemp, S. (2000), 'Trade in education services and the impacts of barriers on trade', in Findlay and Warren (eds), pp. 231–44.

Keren, M. and G. Ofer (2002), 'The role of FDI in trade and financial services in transition: what distinguishes transition economies from developing economies?', *Comparative Economic Studies*, **44**(1): 15–45.

Keynes, John M. (1936), *The General Theory of Employment, Interest and Money*, London: Macmillan.

Kim, W.-B., M. Douglass, S.-C. Choel and K.C. Ho (eds) (1997a) *Culture and the City in East Asia*, Oxford: Oxford University Press.

Kim, W.-B., M. Douglass, S.-C. Choel and K.C. Ho (1997b), 'Introduction' to Kim et al. (eds).

King, A. (ed.) (1997), *Culture, Globalization and the World-System*, Minneapolis, MN: University of Minnesota Press.

Kirby, D.A. (1997), 'Small technology-based professional consultancy services in the United Kingdom', *The Service Industries Journal*, **17**(1): 155–72.

Kirby, K. (1996), *Indifferent Boundaries: Spatial Concepts of Human Subjectivity*, New York: Guilford.

Kirkegaard, J.F. (2004), 'Outsourcing: stains on the white collar?', *IEE Papers*, Washington, DC: Institute for International Economics.

Kitchin, R. (1998), *Cyberspace: The World in the Wires*, New York: John Wiley.

Klak, T. (ed.) (1998), *Globalization and Neoliberalism: The Caribbean Context*, Boulder, CO: Rowman & Littlefield.

Kleinknecht, A. and J.O.N. Reijnen (1992), 'Why do firms cooperate on R&D? An empirical study', *Research Policy*, **21**: 347–60.

Knight, G. and S.T. Cavusgil (1996), 'The born global firm: a challenge to traditional internationalization theory', *Advances in International Marketing*, Greenwich, CT: JAI Press, pp. 11–26.

Knox, P. (1995), 'World cities and the organization of global space', in R. Johnston, P. Taylor and M. Watts (eds), *Geographies of Global Change*, Oxford: Blackwell, pp. 232–47.

Knox, P., J. Agnew and L. McCarthy (2003), *The Geography of the World Economy*, 4th edn, London: Arnold.

Kobrin, S. (1997), 'Electronic cash and the end of national markets', *Foreign Policy*, summer: 65–77.

Kogut, B. (2002), 'International management and strategy', in A. Pettigrew, H. Thomas and R. Whittington (eds), *Handbook of Strategy and Management*, London: Sage, pp. 261–78.

Kogut, B. and U. Zander (1993), 'Knowledge of the firm and the evolutionary theory of the multinational enterprise', *Journal of International Business Studies*, **24**: 625–45.

Konopielko, L. (1999), 'Foreign banks' entry into Central and East European markets: motives and activities', *Post Communist Economies*, **11**(4): 463–85.

Koon, H. (1997), 'Robert Kuok and the Chinese business network in Eastern Asia: a study in Sino-capitalism', in Brook and Luong (eds), pp. 155–81.

Korpi, W. (2001), 'Class, gender and inequality: the role of welfare states', in M. Kohli and M. Novak (eds), *Will Europe Work?*, London: Routledge, pp. 52–72.

Kostecki, M. (2000), 'DHL Worldwide Express: providing just-in-time delivery services across customs borders in Central and Eastern Europe', in Aharoni and Nachum (eds), pp. 284–95.
Kostecki, M. and A. Fehervary (eds) (1996), *Services in the Transition Economies*, London: Elsevier Science.
Kostecki, M. and J. Pietras (1996), 'Foreign direct investment and the service economies of East–Central Europe', in Kostecki and Fehervary (eds), pp. 53–64.
Kovacs, Ilona (2002), 'Business services in the transitional economy of Hungary', in E. Kigossy-Schmidt (ed.), *Business Related Services in Central and Eastern Europe*, Wiesbaden: Deutscher Universitats-Verlag, pp. 67–94.
Kraft, K. (1990), 'Are product- and process-innovations independent of each other?', *Applied Economics*, **22**: 1029–38.
Kravis, I.B. and R.E. Lipsey (1988), 'Production and trade in services by U.S. multinational firms', NBER Working Paper w2615, June.
Kreibich, R. (1986), *Die Wissenschaftsgesellschaft. Von Galilei zur High-Tech Revolution*, Frankfurt am Main: Suhrkamp.
Kuhn, T.S. (1962), *The Structure of Scientific Revolutions*, Chicago: Chicago University Press.
Kurtzman, J. (1993), *The Death of Money*, Boston, MA: Little, Brown & Co.
Kutay, A. (1986), 'Effects of telecommunications technology on office locations', *Urban Geography*, **7**: 243–57.
Kwok, R. (1999), 'Last colonial spatial plans for Hong Kong: global economy and domestic politics', *European Planning Studies*, **7**(2): 207–29.
Kwok, R. (2002), 'Neo-liberalism, identity politics, and spatial development in the South China triangle: the case of Hong Kong and Taipei', paper presented to an Exploratory Workshop on Service Industries and New Models of Urban Change within the Asia-Pacific, Peter Wall Institute for Advanced Studies, University of British Columbia, Vancouver.
Lackoff, G. and M. Johnson (1999), *Philosophy in the Flesh: The Embodied Mind and Its Challenge to Western Thought*, New York: Basic Books.
Landefeld, J.S. and R. Mataloni (2004), 'Offshore outsourcing and multinational companies', Working Paper 2004-06, Bureau of Economic Analysis, Washington, DC.
Landes, D. (1998), *The Wealth and Poverty of Nations*, London: Little Brown.
Lane, R.E. (1966), 'The decline of politics and ideology in a knowledgeable society', *American Sociological Review*, **31**: 649–62.
Langdale, J. (1985), 'Electronic funds transfer and the internationalisation of the banking and finance industry', *Geoforum*, **16**: 393–409.
Langewiesche, William (2003), 'Anarchy at sea', *Atlantic Monthly*, **202**(2): 50–80.
Lash, S and J. Urry (1994), *Economies of Signs and Spaces*, London: Sage.
Latham, A. (2002), 'Retheorizing the scale of globalization: topologies, actor-networks, and cosmopolitanism', in A. Herod and M. Wright (eds), *Geographies of Power: Placing Scale*, Oxford: Blackwell, pp. 115–44.
Latour, B. (1993), *We Have Never Been Modern*, London: Harvester Wheatsheaf.
Law, J. (1994), *Organising Modernity*, Oxford: Blackwell.
Law, J. and J. Hassard (eds) (1999), *Actor Network Theory and After*, Oxford: Blackwell.
Lawson, T. (1997), *Economics and Reality*, New York: Routledge.

Leaf, M. (1996), 'Building the road for the BMW: culture, vision and the extended metropolitan region of Jakarta', *Environment and Planning A*, **28**: 1617–35.
Leaf, M. (1999), 'Vietnam's urban edge: the administration of urban development in Hanoi', *Third World Planning Review*, **21**(3): 297–315.
Leaf, M. (2004) 'New aspirations and old dilemmas: the new economy and development in Southeast Asia', paper prepared for ESRC Seminar on Geographies of the New Economy, University of Birmingham, 29 May 2002.
Leaf, M. (2005), 'The bazaar and the normal: informalization and tertiarization in urban Asia', in Daniels et al. (eds), pp. 110–28.
Leamer, E.E., M. Storper and N. Hsieh (2001), 'The economic geography of the internet age', *Journal of International Business Studies*, **32**(4): 641–5.
Lefebvre, H. (1991), *The Production of Space*, Oxford: Blackwell.
Leidner, R. (1993), *Fast Food, Fast Talk: Interactive Service Work and the Routinization of Everyday Life*, Berkeley, CA: University of California Press.
Leinbach, Thomas R. (1989), 'Transport policies in conflict: deregulation, subsidies and regional development in Indonesia', *Transportation Research*, **23A**(6): 467–75.
Leinbach, Thomas R. and John T. Bowen (2004), 'Air cargo services and the electronics industry in Southeast Asia', *Journal of Economic Geography*, **4**(3): 1–24.
Leontief, W. (1953), *Studies in the Structure of the American Economy*, Oxford and New York: Oxford University Press.
Letablier, M.T. and M. Lurol (2000), 'Les femmes entre travail et famille dans les pays de l'Union européenne', *La lettre du Centre d'Études de l'emploi*, La Lettre 63, Paris, July.
Levine, R. (2001), 'International financial liberation and economic growth', *Review of International Economics*, **9**: 688–702.
Levy, D. and S. Rosenbush (1999), 'Net's builders rake in biggest bucks', *USA Today*, June 10.
Lewis, M. (1989), *Liar's Poker*, London: Corgi.
Ley, D. (1996), *The New Middle Class and the Reshaping of the Central City*, Oxford: Oxford University Press.
Ley, D. and T. Hutton (1987), 'Vancouver's corporate complex and producer services sector: linkages and divergence within a provincial staple economy', *Regional Studies*, **21**: 413–24.
Leyshon, A. (2001), 'Time–space (and digital) compression: software formats, musical networks, and the reorganisation of the music industry', *Environment and Planning A*, **33**(1): 49–77.
Leyshon, A. (2003), 'Scary monsters? Free software, peer-to-peer connections and the spectre of the gift', *Environment and Planning D: Society and Space*, **22**(5): 533–58.
Leyshon, A., P. Webb, S. French, N. Thrift and L. Crewe (2005), 'On the reproduction of the musical economy after the internet', *Media, Culture and Society*, **27**(2): 177–209.
Li, J. and S. Guisinger (1992), 'The globalisation of service multinationals in the "Triad" regions', *Journal of International Business Studies*, **23**(4): 675–96.
Li, W., G. Dymski, Y. Zhou, M. Chee and C. Aldana (2002), 'Chinese-American banking and community development in Los Angeles County', *Annals of the Association of American Geographers*, **92**: 777–96.

Liebowitz, S. (2002), *Re-thinking the Network Economy: The True Forces that Drive the Digital Marketplace*, New York: AMACom.
Lin, G. (2002), 'The growth and structural change of Chinese cities: a contextual and geographic analysis', *Cities*, **19**(5): 299–316.
Lin, G. (2005), 'Service industries and transformation of city-regions in globalizing China: new testing ground for theoretical reconstruction', in Daniels et al. (eds), pp. 283–300.
Lin, G. and D. Wei (2002), 'China's restless urban landscape 1: new challenges for theoretical reconstruction', *Environment and Planning A*, **34**(9): 1535–44.
Lindblom, T. and C. von Koch (2002), 'Cross-border bank mergers and acquisitions in the EU', *The Service Industries Journal*, **22**(4): 41–72.
Lindsay, V., D. Chadee, J. Mattsson, R. Johnston and B. Millett (2003), 'Relationships, the role of individuals and knowledge flows in the internationalisation of service firms', *International Journal of Service Industry Management*, **14**(1): 7–35.
Longcore, T. and P. Rees (1996), 'Information technology and downtown restructuring: the case of New York City's financial district', *Urban Geography*, **17**: 354–72.
Lorenz, E. and A. Valeyre (2004), 'Organisational change in Europe: national models or the diffusion of a new "one best way"?', Danish Research Unit on Industrial Dynamics (DRUID) Working Paper N°04-04, www.druid.dk/wp/wp.html.
Lovelock, C.H. (1999), 'Developing marketing strategies for transnational service operations', *Journal of Services Marketing*, **13**(4/5): 278–97.
Lovelock, C.H. and G.S. Yip (1996), 'Developing global strategies for service businesses', *California Business Review*, **38**(2), Winter: 64–87.
Lowendahl, B. (1997), *Strategic Management of Professional Service Firms*, Copenhagen: Copenhagen Business School Press.
Lowendahl, B.R. (2000), 'The globalisation of professional business service firms: fad or genuine source of competitive advantage', in Aharoni and Nachum (eds), pp. 142–62.
Lowendahl, B., O. Revang and S.N. Fosstenlokken (2001), 'Knowledge and value creation in professional service firms', *Human Relations*, **54**: 911–31.
Luke, T. (1997), 'At the end of nature: cyborgs, "humachines" and environments in postmodernity', *Environment and Planning A*, **29**: 1367–80.
MacEwan, A. (1999), *Neo-Liberalism or Democracy? Economic Strategy, Markets, and Alternatives for the 21st Century*, London: Zed Books.
Machimura, T. (1992), 'The urban restructuring process in Tokyo in the 1980s: transforming Tokyo into a world city', *International Journal of Urban and Regional Research*, **16**: 114–28.
MacPherson, A. (1997), 'The role of producer service outsourcing in the innovation performance of New York State manufacturing firms', *Annals of the Association of American Geographers*, **87**: 52–71.
Madsem, T., E. Mosakowski and S. Zaheer (2002), 'The dynamics of knowledge flows: human capital mobility, knowledge retention and change', *Journal of Knowledge Management*, **6**: 164–76.
Mahajan, S. (ed.) (2005), *Input–Output Analysis: 2005*, London: Office for National Statistics.
Maister, D.H. (1986), 'The three E's of professional life', *Journal of Management Consulting*, **3**(2): 39–44.

Maister, D. (2003), *Managing the Professional Service Firm*, New York: Free Press.

Mallampally, P. and Z. Zimny (2000), 'Foreign direct investment in services', in Aharoni and Nachum (eds), pp. 25–51.

Mann, C.A. (2003), 'Globalization of IT services and white collar jobs: the next wave of productivity growth', International Economics Policy Briefs, No. PB03-11, Institute for International Economics, Washington, DC.

Mannheim, K. (1929 [1936]), *Ideology and Utopia: An Introduction to the Sociology of Knowledge*, London: Routledge & Kegan Paul.

Mao, Q. and Y. Jin (1996), 'Urban development and planning in Beijing metropolitan region', Paper presented to the Conference on Towards a Sustainable Urban Future: Mega-Cities, Regional Development and Planning, Tsinghua University, Beijing, 23–26 April.

Marcuse, H. (1964) *One-Dimensional Man: Studies in the Ideology of Advanced Industrial Society*, Boston, MA: Beacon Press.

Markides, C. and P.J. Williamson (1996), 'Corporate diversification and organisational structure', *Academy of Management Journal*, **39**: 340–67.

Marko, M. (1998), 'An evaluation of the basic telecommunications services agreement', CIES Policy Discussion Paper 98/09, Centre for International Economic Studies, University of Adelaide.

Markusen, A. and V. Gwiasda (1994), 'Multipolarity and the layering of functions in world cities: New York City's struggle to stay on top', *International Journal of Urban and Regional Research*, **18**: 167–93.

Markusen, A.R., Y.-S. Lee and S. Digiovanna (eds) (1999), *Second Tier Cities: Rapid Growth beyond the Metropolis*, Minneapolis, MN: University of Minnesota Press.

Marsh, D.C. (1977), *The Changing Structure of England and Wales: 1871–1961*, London: Routledge & Kegan Paul.

Marshall, A. (1892 [1899]), *Elements of Economics of Industry*, 3rd edn, London: Macmillan.

Marshall, A. (1909), *Elements of Economics of Industry: Being the First Volume of Elements of Economics*, London: Macmillan.

Marshall, Alfred (1920), *Principles of Economics*, London: Macmillan www.econlib.org/library/Marshall/marP7.html, 27 January 2005.

Marshall, A. (1932), *Elements of Economics of Industry*, London: Macmillan.

Marshall, J. and R. Richardson (1996), 'The impact of "telemediated" services on corporate structures: the example of "branchless" retail banking in Britain', *Environment and Planning A*, **28**: 1845–56.

Martin, L. and H. Matlay (2001), '"Blanket" approaches to promoting ICT in small firms: some lessons from the DTI ladder adoption model in the UK', *Internet Research: Electronic Networking Applications and Policy*, **11**(5): 399–410.

Martin, R. (1999), 'Stateless monies, global financial integration and national economic autonomy: the end of geography?', in S. Corbridge, R. Martin and N. Thrift (eds), *Money, Power and Space*, Oxford: Blackwell, pp. 253–78.

Martin, S. (2001), 'Heavy traffic: international migration in an age of globalization', *Brookings Review*, **19**(4): 41–4.

Marton, A. (1998), *Urbanization in China's Lower Yangzi Delta: Transactional Relations and the Repositioning of Locality*, Singapore: World Scientific and Singapore University Press.

Marton, A. (2000), *China's Spatial Economic Development: Regional Transformation in the Lower Yangzi Delta*, London and New York: Routledge.
Marx, K. (1939–41 [1973]), *Grundrisse: Introduction to the Critique of Political Economy*, New York: Vintage Books.
Maskell, P. (1999), 'Globalisation and industrial competitiveness: the process and consequences of ubiquitification', in Edward J. Malecki and Paivi Oinas (eds), *Making Connections: Technological Learning and Regional Economic Change*, Aldershot: Ashgate, pp. 35–59.
Maskell, P. and A. Malmberg (1999), 'The competitiveness of firms and regions: ubiquitification and the importance of localized learning', *European Urban and Regional Studies*, **6**(1): 9–25.
Mason, G. and K. Wagner (1999), 'Knowledge transfer and innovation in Germany and Britain: "intermediate institution" models of knowledge transfer under strain?', *Industry and Innovation*, **6**(1): 85–110.
Massey, D. (1999), 'Imagining globalization: power-geometries of time-space', in A. Brah, M. Hickman and M. Mac an Ghail (eds), *Global Futures: Migration, Environment and Globalization*, Basingstoke: Macmillan, pp. 27–44.
Mattoo, A. (1998), 'Financial services and the WTO: liberalization in the developing and transition economies', presentation at the Workshop, 'Measuring Impediments to Trade in Services', Productivity Commission, Canberra, April 30–May 1.
Mattoo, A. and A. Cazaniga (eds) (2003), *Moving People to Deliver Services*, Washington, DC: World Bank.
McDowell, L. (1991), 'Life without father and Ford: the new gender order of post-Fordism', *Transactions of the Institute of British Geographers*, **16**: 400–419.
McDowell, L. (1997), *Capital Culture: Gender at Work in the City*, Oxford: Blackwell.
McDowell, L. (2001), 'Father and Ford revisited: gender, class and employment change in the new millennium', *Transactions, Institute of British Geographers*, **24**: 448–64.
McDowell, L. (2002), 'Masculine discourses and dissonances: strutting "lads", protest masculinity and domestic respectability', *Environment and Planning D: Society and Space*, **20**: 97–119.
McDowell, L. (2003), *Redundant Masculinities? Employment Change and White Working Class Youth*, Oxford: Blackwell.
McDowell, L. (2004a), 'Masculinity, identity and labour market change: some reflections on the implications of thinking relationally about difference and the politics of inclusion', *Geografiska Annaler: Series B, Human Geography*, **86**(1): 45–56.
McDowell, L. (2004b), 'Work, workfare, work/life balance and an ethic of care', *Progress in Human Geography*, **28**: 1–19.
McDowell, L. and G. Court (1994a), 'Performing work: bodily representations in merchant banks', *Environment and Planning D*, **12**: 747–50.
McDowell, L. and G. Court (1994b), 'Missing subjects: gender, sexuality and power in merchant banks', *Economic Geography*, **70**: 229–51.
McGahey, R., M. Malloy, K. Kazanas and M. Jacobs (1990), *Financial Services, Financial Centers: Public Policy and the Competition for Markets, Firms and Jobs*, Boulder, CO: Westview Press.
McGee, T. (1991) 'The emergence of desakota regions in Asia: expanding a hypothesis',

in B. Koppel and T.G. McGee (eds), *The Extended Metropolis: Settlement Transition in Asia*, Honolulu, HI: University of Hawaii Press, pp. 3–25.
McGee, T. and G. Lin (1993), 'Footprints in space: spatial restructuring in the East Asian NICs 1950–1990', in C. Dixon and D. Drakakis-Smith (eds), *Economic and Social Development of Pacific Asia*, London: Routledge, pp. 128–51.
McGuire, G. (1998) 'Australia's restrictions on trade in financial services', Staff Research Paper, Productivity Commission, Canberra.
McGuire, G. and M. Schuele (2000), 'Restrictiveness of international trade in banking services', in Findlay and Warren (eds), pp. 201–14.
McGuire, G., M. Schuele and T. Smith (2000), 'Restrictiveness of international trade in maritime services', in Findlay and Warren (eds), pp. 172–88.
McKinnon, Alan (2001), 'Integrated logistics strategies', in Brewer et al. (eds), pp. 157–70.
McLaughan, G. and J. Salt (2002), 'Migration policies towards highly skilled foreign workers', Migration Research Unit, University College London.
McNair, M. (1958), 'Significant trends and developments in the postwar period', in A.B. Smith (ed.), *Competitive Distribution in Free High-Level Economy and its Implications for the University*, Pittsburg, PA: University of Pittsburg Press, pp. 1–25.
Meersman, Hilde and Eddy Van de Voorde (2001), 'International logistics: a continuous search for competitiveness', in Brewer et al. (eds), pp. 61–78.
Mellinger, Andrew D., Jeffrey D. Sachs and John L. Gallup (2000), 'Climate, coastal proximity, and development', in Gordon L. Clark, Maryann P. Feldman and Meric S. Gertler (eds), *The Oxford Handbook of Economic Geography*, Oxford and New York: Oxford University Press, pp. 169–94.
Methlie, L.B. and P.E. Pedersen (1999), 'Multimedia banking – bankenes strategiske situasjon, Ny teknologi. Ny konkuranseareana – ny struktur', Working Paper 41, Bergen: Institute for Economic and Business Administration.
Meyer, D. (2000), *Hong Kong as a Global Metropolis*, Cambridge: Cambridge University Press.
Michalova, V. (2001), 'Services in the era of globalization', *Ekonomicky-Casopis*, **49**(6): 1042–62.
Midoro, R. and A. Pitto (2000), 'A critical evaluation of strategic alliances in liner shipping', *Maritime Policy and Management*, **27**: 31–40.
Miles, I. (1993), 'Services in the new industrial economy', *Futures*, **25**: 653–72.
Miles, I. (1994), 'Innovation in services', in M. Dodgson and R. Rothwell (eds), *Handbook of Industrial Innovations*, Aldershot, UK and Brookfield, USA: Edward Elgar, pp. 243–56.
Miles, I. (2000a), 'Environmental services: sustaining knowledge', in Andersen et al. (eds), pp. 103–20.
Miles, I. (2000b), 'Services innovation: coming of age in the knowledge-based economy', *International Journal of Innovation Management*, **4**(4): 371–89.
Miles, I. (2001), 'Services innovation: a reconfiguration of innovation studies', Discussion Paper Series, PREST, University of Manchester.
Miles, I., B. Andersen, M. Boden and J. Howells (2000), 'Service production and intellectual property', *International Journal of Technology Management*, **20**: 95–115.
Miles, I. and K. Green (1996), 'A clean break? From corporate R&D to sustainable tech-

nological regimes', in R. Welford and R. Starkey (eds), *The Earthscan Reader in Business and the Environment*, London: Earthscan, pp. 120–44.

Miles, I., N. Kastrinos (with K. Flanagan), R. Bilderbeek and P. den Hertog (with W. Huitink and M. Bouman) (1995), *Knowledge-Intensive Business Services: Users, Carriers and Sources of Innovation*, Luxembourg; European Innovation Monitoring Service, Publication no. 15.

Miles, I., H. Rush, H. Turner and J. Bessant (1988), *Information Horizons: The Long-Term Social Implications of New Information Technology*: Aldershot, UK and Brookfield, US: Edward Elgar.

Miles, I. and S. Wyatt (1991), *Technological Change in Services and International Trade Competitiveness*, Geneva: UNCTAD.

Mill, John Stuart (1831 [1997]), *The Spirit of the Age: On Liberty, The Subjection of Women*, Selected and edited by Alan Ryan, New York: W.W. Norton.

Mill, John Stuart (1848 [1965]), *Principles of Political Economy*, W. Ashley (ed.), Reprinted, New York: Kelley.

Minkler, A.P. (1992), 'Why firms franchise: a search cost theory', *Journal of Institutional and Theoretical Economics*, **148**: 240–59.

Miozzo, M. and M. Ramirez (2003), 'Services innovation and the transformation of work', *New Technology, Work and Employment*, **18**: 63–80.

Miozzo, M. and L. Soete (2001), 'Internationalisation of services: a technological perspective', *Technological Forecasting and Social Change*, **67**: 159–85.

Mitchell, K. (1995), 'Flexible circulation in the Pacific Rim: capitalisms in cultural context', *Economic Geography*, **71**: 364–82.

Mitchell, K. and K. Olds (2000), 'Chinese business networks and the globalisation of property markets in the Pacific Rim', in H. Yeung and K. Olds (eds), *Globalization of Chinese Business Firms*, London: Macmillan, pp. 195–219.

Mollenkopf, J. and M. Castells (1991), *Dual City: Restructuring New York*, New York: Russell Sage Foundation.

Momigliano, F. and D. Siniscalco (1982), 'The growth of service employment: a reappraisal', *Banca Nazionale del Lavoro Quarterly Review*, **142**: 269–306.

Money, J. (1992), 'White collar jobs flow from Britain as data processors are lured by cheap labour', *The Guardian*, August 25, p. 1.

Moore, H. (1988), *Feminism and Anthropology*, Cambridge: Polity.

Moore, K. and J. Birkinshaw (1998), 'Managing knowledge in global service firms: centers of excellence', *The Academy of Management Executive*, **12**(4): 81–93.

Morgan, G. (2001), 'Transnational communities and business systems', *Global Networks*, **1**: 113–30.

Morgan, G., P.H. Kristensen and R. Whitely (eds) (2001), *The Multinational Firm: Organizing across Institutional and National Divides*, Oxford: Oxford University Press.

Morris, T. and L. Empson (1998), 'Organization and expertise: an exploration of knowledge bases and the management of accounting and consulting firms', *Accounting, Organizations and Society*, **23**: 609–24.

Morshidi, S. (1996), 'Producer services and growth management of metropolitan regions: the case of Kuala Lumpur, Malaysia', mimeo, Geography Section, School of Humanities, Universiti Sains Malaysia, Penang.

Morshidi, S. (2000), 'Globalising Kuala Lumpur and the strategic role of the producer services sector', *Urban Studies*, **37**: 2217–40.
Moss, M. (1987), 'Telecommunications, world cities, and urban policy', *Urban Studies*, **24**: 534–46.
Moss, M. and A. Dunau (1986), 'Offices, information technology, and locational trends', in J. Black, K. Roark and L. Schwartz (eds), *The Changing Office Workplace*, Washington, DC: Urban Land Institute, pp. 171–82.
Mowery, D. (1997), 'U.S. post-war technologies and the creation of new industries', in OECD Proceedings, *Creativity, Innovation and Job Creation*, Paris: OECD, pp. 199–218.
Mulgan, G. (1991), *Communications and Control: Networks and the New Economics of Communication*, Cambridge: Polity.
Muller, E. (2001), *Innovation Interactions between KIBS and SMEs*, Heidelberg: Physica-Verlag.
Muller, E. and A. Zenker (2001), 'Business services as actors of knowledge transformation: the role of KIBS in regional and national innovation systems', *Research Policy*, **30**: 1501–16.
Muller, L. (2002), 'Advanced business services in Southeast Asia: an opportunity for localizing international investment', School of Geography, Earth and Environmental Sciences working paper, WPSSS9, University of Birmingham.
Mullings, B. (1999), 'Sides of the same coin? Coping and resistance among Jamaican data-entry operators', *Annals of the Association of American Geographers*, **89**: 290–311.
Murakami, Y. (1992), *Han-koten no seijikeizaigaku* (The anti-classic political economy), Tokyo: Chuokoronsha.
Murdoch, J. (1995), 'Actor-networks and the evolution of economic forms: combining description and explanation in theories of regulation, flexible specialization and networks', *Environment and Planning A*, **25**: 731–57.
Murdoch, J. (1997), 'Towards a geography of heterogeneous associations', *Progress in Human Geography*, **21**:321–37.
Murdoch, J. (1998), 'The spaces of actor-network theory', *Geoforum*, **29**:357–74.
Murphy, A. (2002), 'The emergence of online food retailing: a stakeholder perspective', *Tijdschrift voor Economische en Sociale Geografie*, **93**(1): 47–61.
Murphy, A. (2003), '(Re)solving space and time: fulfilment issues in online grocery retailing', *Environment and Planning A*, **35**(7): 1173–200.
Murphy, M. and G. Vickery (1999), *Strategic Business Services*, Paris: OECD.
Murray, S. (2004), 'Importers pay the price of heavy security', *The Financial Times*, January 13, p. 12.
Nachum, L. (1999), *The Origins of the International Competitiveness of Firms: The Impact of Location and Ownership in the Professional Service Industries*, UK and Northampton, MA, USA: Edward Elgar.
Nachum, L. (2000), 'FDI, the location advantages of countries and the competitiveness of TNCs: US FDI in professional service industries', in Aharoni and Nachum (eds), pp. 75–92.
Nachum, L. and D. Keeble (1999), 'Neo-Marshallian nodes, global networks and firm competitivenss: the media cluster of Central London', ESRC Centre for Business Research Working Paper 138, University of Cambridge.

Naughton, J. (1999), *A Brief History of the Future: The Origins of the Internet*, London: Weidenfeld & Nicolson.

Nelson, K. (1986), 'Labor demand, labor supply, and the suburbanization of low-wage office work', in A. Scott and M. Storper (eds), *Production, Work, Territory*, Boston, MA: Allen & Unwin, pp. 149–71.

Nelson, R. and S. Winter (1982), *An Evolutionary Theory of Economic Change*, Cambridge, MA: Harvard University Press.

Newman, K. (1999), *No Shame in My Games: The Working Poor in the Inner City*, New York: Vintage Books and Russell Sage Foundation.

Nguyen-Hong, D. (2000), 'Restrictions on trade in professional services', Productivity Commission, Staff Research Paper, Ausinfo, Canberra, August.

Nicoletti, G. (2003), 'The economy-wide effects of product market policies', in OECD, *Quantifying the Benefits of Liberalizing Trade in Services*, Paris: OECD, pp. 14–31.

Nicoletti, G., S. Scarpetta and O. Boylaud (2000), 'Summary indicators of product market regulation with an extension to employment protection legislation', Working Paper No. 226, Economics Department, ECO/WKP(99)18, OECD, Paris, 13 April (revised).

Nishida, K. (1970), *Fundamental Problems of Philosophy: The World of Action and the Dialectical World*, Tokyo: Sophia University.

Nohria, N. and R. Eccles (1992), 'Face-to face: making network organizations work', in Nohria and Eccles (eds), *Networks and Organization: Structure, Form and Action*, Boston, MA: Harvard Business School Press, pp. 288–308.

Nohria, N. and S. Ghoshal (1997), *The Differentiated Network: Organizing Multinational Corporations for Value Creation*, San Francisco: Jossey-Bass.

Nonaka, I. (1991), 'The knowledge-creating company', *Harvard Business Review*, November–December, 96–104.

Nonaka, I. (1994), 'A dynamic theory of organizational knowledge creation', *Organization Sciences*, **5**(1): 14–37.

Nonaka, I. and N. Konno (1998), 'The concept of "*ba*": building a foundation for knowledge creation', *Californian Management Review*, **40**: 40–54.

Nonaka, I., V. Peltokorpi and H. Tomae (2005), 'Strategic knowledge creation: the case of hamamatsu photonics', *International Journal of Technology Management*, **30(**3/4): 248–64.

Nonaka, I. and H. Takeuchi (1995), *The Knowledge-Creating Company: How Japanese Companies Create the Dynamics of Innovation*, Oxford and New York: Oxford University Press.

Nonaka, I. and R. Toyama (2002), 'A firm as a dialectical being: towards a dynamic theory of a firm', *Industrial and Corporate Change*, **11**(5): 995–1009.

Nonaka, I. and R. Toyama (2003), 'The knowledge-creating theory revisited: knowledge creation as a synthesizing process', *Knowledge Management Research and Practice*, **1**(1): 2–10.

Nora, S. and A. Minc (1980), *The Computerisation of Society*, Cambridge, MA: MIT Press.

Normann, R. (1984), *Service Management*, Chichester: John Wiley.

Noyelle, T.J. and A.B. Dutka (1988), *International Trade in Business Services: Accounting, Advertising, Law, and Management Consulting*, Cambridge, MA: Ballinger.

Noyelle, T. and T. Stanback (1983), *The Economic Transformation of American Cities*, Totowa, NJ: Rowman & Allanheld.

NTIA (1995), 'Falling through the net: a survey of the "have nots" in rural and urban America', US Department of Commerce National Telecommunications and Information Administration, July.
NTIA (1999), 'Falling through the net III: defining the digital divide', US Department of Commerce National Telecommunications and Information Administration, July.
NTIA (2000), 'Falling through the net IV: towards digital inclusion', US Department of Commerce National Telecommunications and Information Administration, October.
Nusbaumer, Jacques (ed.) (1987), *Services in the Global Market*, Boston, MA: Kluwer.
O'Brien, R. (1992), *Global Financial Integration: The End of Geography*, London: Royal Institute of International Affairs.
O'Connor, K. and T. Hutton (1998), 'Producer services in the Asia-Pacific Region: an overview of research issues', *Asia Pacific Viewpoint*, **39:** 139–43.
O'Connor, K., R. Stimson and M. Daly (2001), *Australia's Changing Economic Geography: A Society Dividing*, Oxford and Melbourne: Oxford University Press.
O'Donnell, S.W. (2000), 'Managing foreign subsidiaries: agents of headquarters or an independent network', *Strategic Management Journal*, **21:** 525–48.
O'Driscoll, G. and M. Rizzo (1985), *The Economics of Time and Ignorance*, Oxford: Blackwell.
O'Farrell, P. and L. Moffat (1991), 'An interaction model of business service production and consumption', *British Journal of Management*, **2**: 205–21.
O'Farrell, P.N. and P.A. Wood (1994), 'International market selection by business service firms: key conceptual and methodological issues', *International Business Review*, **3**(3): 243–61.
O'Farrell, P.N. and P.A. Wood (1999), 'Formation of strategic alliances in business services: towards a new client-oriented conceptual framework', *The Service Industries Journal*, **19:** 133–51.
O'Farrell, P.N., P.A. Wood and J. Zheng (1998), 'Regional influences on foreign market development by business service companies: elements of a strategic context explanation', *Regional Studies*, **32(**1): 31–48.
Ochel, W. (2002), 'The international competitiveness of business service firms: the case of Germany', *The Service Industries Journal*, **22**(2): 1–16.
OECD (1996), *International Trade in Professional Services: Assessing Barriers and Encouraging Reform*, Paris: OECD.
OECD (1997), *Proposed Guidelines for Collecting and Interpreting Technological Innovation Data: Oslo Manual*, 2nd edn, Paris: OECD.
OECD (1999a), *Measuring Globalisation: The Role of Multinationals in OECD Economies*, Paris: OECD.
OECD (1999b), *The Economic and Social Impact of Electronic Commerce: Preliminary Findings and Research Agenda*, Geneva: OECD.
OECD (2000), *The Service Economy*, Paris: OECD.
OECD (2001a), *Communications Outlook 2001*, Paris: OECD.
OECD (2001b), *OECD Statistics on International Trade in Services 1990–1999*, Paris: OECD and Development and Statistical Office of the European Communities.
OECD (2002), *OECD Statistics on International Trade in Services: Partner Country Data and Summary Analysis, 1999–2000*, Paris: OECD.
OECD (2002a), *Statistiques des recettes publiques 1965–2001*, Paris: OECD.

OECD (2003b), *Structural Statistics for Industry and Services: Production Data*, Paris: OECD.

OECD (2003c), *ICT and Economic Growth: Evidence from OECD Countries, Industries and Enterprises*, Paris: OECD.

OECD (2003d), 'Service providers on the move. Labour mobility and the WTO General Agreement on Trade in Services', Policy Brief Paper, August, www.arm-wto.am/eng/analytics/Services ProvidersMove_August2003.pdf (accessed 30 October 2006).

OECD (2005), 'Potential offsharing of ICT-Intensive Using Occupations', Working Party on the Information Economy, DSTA/ICC/IE (2004) 19, OECD: Paris.

OECD (ICCP) (1993), *Usage Indicators: A New Foundation for Information Technology Policies*, Paris: OECD, Information Computer Communications Policy ICCP 31.

Ohmae, K. (1990), *The Borderless World*, London: Harper Collins.

Olds, Kris (1995), 'Globalization and the production of new urban spaces: Pacific Rim megaprojects in the late 20th century', *Environment and Planning A*, **27**: 1713–43.

Olds, K. (2001), *Globalization and Urban Change: Capital, Culture and Pacific Rim Mega-Projects*, Oxford: Oxford Geographical and Environmental Studies, Oxford University Press.

Olds, K. and N. Thrift (2005), 'Assembling the "global schoolhouse" in Pacific Asia: the case of Singapore', in Daniels et al. (eds), pp. 199–215.

Oliver, C. (1997), 'The influence of institutional and task environment relationships on organizational performance: the Canadian construction industry', *Journal of Management Studies*, **34**(1): 99–124.

Oulton,N. (1999), 'Must the growth rate decline? Baumol's unbalanced growth revisited', *Working Paper, Bank of England*, London.

Pacific Economic Cooperation Council (PECC) (1995), *Survey of Impediments to Trade and Investment in the APEC Region*, Singapore: PECC.

Palan, R. (1988a), 'The emergence of an offshare economy', *Futures*, **30**: 63–77.

Palan, R. (1988b), 'Trying to have your cake and eat it: how and why the state system has created offshore', *International Studies Quarterly*, **42**: 625–44.

Park, S. (1993), 'Industrial restructuring and the spatial division of labor: the case of the Seoul metropolitan region, the Republic of Korea', *Environment and Planning A*, **25**: 81–93.

Park, S. and J. Choi (2005), 'IT service industries and the transformation of Seoul', in Daniels et al. (eds), pp. 301–320.

Patterson, P.G. and M. Cicic (1995), 'A typology of service firms in international markets: an empirical investigation', *Journal of International Marketing*, **3**(4): 57–84.

Pavitt, K. (1984), 'Sectoral patterns of technical charge: towards a taxonomy and a theory', *Research Policy*, **13**: 343–3.

Pearson, G. (1983), *Hooligan: A History of Respectable Fears*, Basingstoke: Macmillan.

Pearson, Richard (2001), 'Malcolm McLean dies; revolutionized shipping', *The Washington Post*, May 27: C6.

Peck, J. and A. Tickell (1994), 'Searching for a new institutional fix: the after-Fordist crisis and the global–local disorder', in A. Amin (ed.), *Post-Fordism: A Reader*, Oxford: Blackwell, pp. 280–315.

Peneder, M., S. Kaniovski and B. Dachs (2001), 'External services, structural change and industrial performance', Enterprise Papers, No. 3, European Communities.

Perez, C. (1985), 'Microelectronics, long waves and world development', *World Development*, **13**: 441–463.
Perraton, J. (1997), 'The globalisation of economic activity', *New Political Economy*, **2**(2): 257–77.
Perroux, F. (1950), 'Economic space: theory and applications', *Quarterly Journal of Economics*, **64**(1): 89–104.
Perry, M. (1990), 'Business service specialisation and regional economic change', *Regional Studies*, **24**: 1331–47.
Peters, T.J. and R.H. Waterman (1982), *In Search of Excellence: Lessons from America's Best-run Companies*, London: Harper & Row.
Petit, P. (1986), *Slow Growth and the Service Economy*, London: Frances Pinter.
Philips, Don (2002), 'A rail model for urban congestion: LA project aids shippers, motorists', *The Washington Post*, May 21: A3.
Phillips, M. (1996), *Retail Franchising : A Strategy for International Expansion*, London: FT Retail & Consumer Publishing.
Pietras, J. (2002), 'Business services in the transitional economy of Poland', in E. Kigossy-Schmidt (ed.), *Business Related Services in Central and Eastern Europe*, Wiesbaden: Deutscher Universitats-Verlag, pp. 131–67.
Pilat, D. (2001), 'Innovation and productivity in services; state of the art', in OECD, *Innovation and Productivity in Services*, Paris: OECD, pp. 17–54.
Pile, S. and N. Thrift (eds) (1995), *Mapping the Subject*, London: Routledge.
Pilskog, G.M., L. Solheim and K. Ødegård (2002), *Bruk av informasjons- og kommunikasjonsteknologi i næringslivet 2001*, Konsvinger: Statistisk sentralbyrå.
Plantenga, J. and J. Hansen (1999), 'Analyse comparative de l'égalité des chances dans l'Union européenne', *Revue internationale du travail*, **138**(4): 387–419.
Polanyi, M. (1952), *Personal Knowledge*, Chicago: University of Chicago Press.
Polanyi, M. (1967), *The Tacit Dimension*, London: Routledge & Kegan Paul.
Poon, J.P.H. (1997), 'Inter-country trade patterns in Europe and the Asia-Pacific: regional structure and extra-regional trends', *Geografiska Annaler*, **79**: 41–55.
Poon, J.P.H., E.R. Thompson and P.F. Kelly (2000), 'Myth of the triad? The geography of trade and investment "blocs" ', *Transactions, Institute of British Geographers*, **25**: 427–44.
Popper, K. (1959), *The Logic of Scientific Discovery*, London: Hutchinson.
Porat, M.U. (1977), *The Information Economy: Definition and Measurement*, Washington, DC: US Department of Commerce.
Porter, M.E. (1980), *Competitive Strategy*, New York: Free Press.
Porter, M.E. (1985), *Competitive Advantage: Creating and Sustaining Superior Performance*, New York: Free Press.
Porter, M.E. (1990), *The Competitive Advantage of Nations*, Basingstoke: Macmillan.
Porter, M.E. (2000), 'Locations, clusters and company strategy', in G.L. Clark, M.P. Feldman and M.S. Gerler (eds), *The Oxford Handbook of Economic Geography*, Oxford: Oxford University Press, pp. 253–74.
Porter, M.E. (2001), 'Strategy and the internet', *Harvard Business Review*, **79**(3): 63–78.
Porterfield, S.L. and G.C. Pulver (1991), 'Exports, impacts, and locations of producer services', *International Regional Science Review*, **14**(1): 41–60.
Prahalad, C.K. and R.A. Bettis (1986), 'The dominant logic: a new linkage between diversity and performance', *Strategic Management Journal*, **7**: 485–511.

Pratiwo (2000), 'The future of traditional street markets in the urban of Java', paper presented to the Workshop on Southeast Asian Futures, Centre for Advanced Studies, National University of Singapore, 21–22 July.

Price, L. (ed.) (1954), *Dialogues of Alfred North Whitehead*, Boston, MA: Little, Brown & Co.

PricewaterhouseCoopers (PwC) (2003), *Global Annual Review*, www. pwcglobal.com, accessed 30 October 2006.

Pringle, R. (1988), *Secretaries Talk: Sexuality, Power and Work*, London: Verso.

Pringle, R. (1998), *Sex and Medicine: Gender, Power and Authority in the Medical Profession*, Cambridge: Cambridge University Press.

Pringle, R. (1999), 'Sex/sexuality', in L. McDowell and J. Sharp (eds), *A Feminist Glossary of Human Geography*, London: Arnold, pp. 248–51.

Pritchard, C., R. Hull, M. Chumer and H. Willmott (eds) (2000), *Managing Knowledge*, Basingstoke: Macmillan.

Quinn, J.B. (1988), 'Technology in services: past myths and future challenges', in Guile and Quinn (1988b) (eds), pp. 16–46.

Quinn, J.B. and K. Dickson (1995), 'The co-location of production and distribution: emergent trends in consumer services', *Technology Analysis and Strategic Management*, **7**: 343–54.

Quinn, J.B. and P.C. Paquette (1990), 'Technology in services: creating organisational revolutions', *Sloan Management Review*, **11**(2): 67–78.

Radebaugh, L.H. and S.L. Gray (1993), *International Accounting and Multinational Enterprise*, London: John Wiley & Son.

Raiser, M., M. Schaffer and J. Schuchhard (2003), 'Benchmarking structural change in transition', Discussion Paper No. 727, Institute for the Study of Labor, Bonn.

Rajan, A. and J. Fryatt (1988), *Create or Abdicate?*, London: Witherby & Company Ltd.

Ram, M. (1994), *Managing to Survive: Working Lives in Small Firms*, Oxford: Blackwell.

Ramirez, M. (2004), 'Innovation, network services and the restructuring of work organisation in customer services', *The Service Industries Journal*, **24**: 99–115.

Redding, S. (1990), *The Spirit of Chinese Capitalism*, Berlin: Walter de Gruyter.

Redfield, R. and M. Singer (1954), 'The cultural role of cities', *Economic Development and Cultural Change*, **3**: 53–73.

Reimus, B. (1997), *Knowledge Sharing Within Management Consulting Firms: Reports on How U.S.-Based Management Consultancies Deploy Technology, Use Groupware and Facilitate Collaboration*, Fitzwilliam, NH: Kennedy Information.

Rescher, N. (2003), *Epistemology: On the Scope and Limits of Knowledge*, Albany, NY: SUNY Press.

Reve, T. and E.W. Jakobsen (2001), *Et Verdiskapende Norge*, Oslo: Universitetsforlaget.

Richardson, R. (1994), 'Back officing front office functions – organisational and locational implications of new telemediated services', in R. Mansell (ed.), *Management of Information and Communication Technologies*, London: Aslib, pp. 309–55.

Richardson, R. (2002), *Information and Communications Technologies and Rural Inclusion*, Newcastle: Centre for Urban and Regional Development Studies, University of Newcastle.

Richardson, R., V. Belt and N. Marshall (2000), 'Taking calls to Newcastle: the regional implications of the growth in call centres', *Regional Studies*, **34**: 357–69.

Richardson, R. and J.N. Marshall (1999), 'Teleservices, call centres and urban and regional development', *The Service Industries Journal*, **19:** 96–116.
Richta, R. (1969), *Civilization at the Crossroads: Social and Human Implications of the Scientific and Technological Revolution*, White Plains, NY: International Arts and Sciences Press.
Riddle, D.I. (1986), *Service-led Growth: The Role of the Service Sector in World Development*, New York: Praeger.
Rimmer, P. (1996), 'International transport and communications interactions between Pacific Asia's emerging world cities', in F.-C. Lo and Y.-M. Yeung (eds), *Emerging World Cities in Pacific Asia*, Tokyo: United Nations University, pp. 48–97.
Rimmer, P.J. (1997), 'Trans-Pacific oceanic economy revisited', *Tijdschrift voor Economische en Sociale Geographie*, **88**(5): 439–56.
Roberts, J. (1998), *Multinational Business Service Firms: The Development of Multinational Organisational Structures in the UK Business Services Sector*, Aldershot: Ashgate.
Roberts, J. (1999), 'The internationalisation of business service firms: a stages approach', *The Service Industries Journal*, **19(**4): 68–89.
Roberts, S. (1994), 'Fictitious capital, fictitious spaces: the geography of offshore financial flows', in S. Corbridge, R. Martin and N. Thrift (eds), *Money, Power and Space*, Oxford: Blackwell, pp. 91–115.
Roberts, S. (1995), 'Small place, big money: the Cayman Islands and the international financial system', *Economic Geography*, **71**: 237–56.
Robertson, P.L. and T.F. Yu (2001), 'Firm strategy, innovation and consumer demand', *Managerial and Decision Economics*, **22:** 183–99.
Robinson, Ross (1998), 'Asian hub/feeder nets: the dynamics of restructuring', *Maritime Policy and Management*, **25**: 21–40.
Römisch, R. (2001), 'Trade in services in the Central and East European countries', Vienna Institute for International Economic Studies, No. 274.
Rostow, W.W. (1953), *The Process of Economic Growth*, Oxford: Oxford University Press.
Roth, V.J. and S. Klein (1993), 'A theory of retail change', *International Review of Retail, Distribution, and Consumer Research*, **3**(2): 167–83.
Rowthorn, R. and J. Wells (1987), *De-industrialisation and Foreign Trade*, Cambridge: Cambridge University Press.
Rubalcaba-Bermejo, L. (1999), 'Business services in the European industry: growth, employment and competitiveness', European Commission, Brussels.
Rubalcaba-Bermejo, L. and J.R. Cuadrado-Roura (2002), 'Services in the age of globalisation: explanatory interrelations and dimensions', in Cuadrado-Roura et al. (eds), pp. 27–57.
Rubalcaba-Bermejo, L. and D. Gago (2003), 'Regional concentrations of innovative business services: testing some explanatory factors at European regional level', *The Service Industries Journal*, **23**: 77–94.
Rubery, J., M. Smith, D. Anxo and L. Flood (2001), 'The future European labor supply: the critical role of the family', *Feminist Economics*, **7**(3): 33–69.
Rubin, P.H. (1978), 'The theory of the firm and the structure of the franchise contract', *Journal of Law and Economics*, **21**: 223–33.
Russell, Dawn. M and John P. Saldanha (2003), 'Five tenets of security-aware logistics and supply chain operation', *Transportation Journal*, **42**(4): 44–54.

Rusten, G. (1997), 'The role of geographic concentration in promoting competitive advantage: the Norwegian furniture industry', *Norsk geografisk. Tidsskrift*, **51**: 173–85.
Rusten, G., J.R. Bryson and H. Gammelsæter (2005), 'Dislocated versus local business service expertise and knowledge and the acquisition of external management consultancy expertise by small and medium-sized enterprises in Norway', *Geoforum*, **36**(4): 525–39.
Rusten, G. and J. Cornford (2003), 'Web-site strategies and performance in SMEs: performance indicators and regional challenges', Samfunns- og næringslivsforskning, Arbeidsnotat 15/03, Bergen.
Rusten, G., T.M. Ektvedt and O. Osland (2004a), 'Sjøforsvarets betydning for den regionale maritime klyngen i Hordaland', Institute for Research in Economics and Business Administration, report, 13/04, Bergen.
Rusten, G., H. Gammelsæter and J.R. Bryson (2004b), 'Combinatorial and dislocated knowledge and the Norwegian client–consultant relationship', *The Service Industries Journal*, **24**: 155–70.
Rusten, G., T. Kvinge and S.E. Jakobsen (1999), 'Internasionalt eierskap i norsk naeringsliv – omfang og effekter nasionalt og regional', SNF-report 24/99, Bergen.
Saccomano, A. (2003), 'Nowhere to hide: companies can no longer rely on inflation to mask logistics inefficiency', *Journal of Commerce*, **9**, June: 31.
Salt, J. (1988), 'Highly-skilled international migrants, careers and internal labour markets', *Geoforum*, **19**: 387–99.
Samers, M. (2002), 'Immigration and the global city hypothesis: towards an alternative research agenda', *International Journal of Urban and Regional Research*, **26**(2): 389–402.
Samiee, S. (1999), 'The internationalization of services: trends, obstacles and issues', *Journal of Services Marketing*, **13**(4/5): 319–28.
Sampson, G.P. and R.H. Snape (1985), 'Identifying the issues in trade in services', *The World Economy*, **8**: 171–81.
Sandoval, G. (2002), 'Airlines bristle at sale of vouchers', CNET News.com, March 21.
Sandvoss, C. (2003), *A Game of Two Halves: Football, Television, and Globalisation*, London: Routledge.
Sanghavi, N. (1990), *Retail Franchising in the 1990s*, Harlow: Longman.
Sassen, S. (1991 [2001]), *The Global City: New York, London, Tokyo*, Princeton, NJ: Princeton University Press.
Sassen, S. (1994), *Cities in a World Economy*, London: Pine Forge Press.
Sassen, S. (1996), *Losing Control: Sovereignty in an Age of Globalization*, New York: Columbia University Press.
Sassen, S. (1999), 'Whose city is it? Globalisation and the formation of new claims', in J. Holston (ed.), *Cities and Citizenship*, Durham, NC: Duke University Press, pp. 177–94.
Sassen, S. (2001), 'Cracked castings. Notes towards an analytics for studying transnational processes', in L. Pries (ed.), *New Transnational Social Spaces*, London: Routledge: pp. 187–207.
Sassen, Saskia (ed.) (2002), *Global Networks, Linked Cities*, London: Routledge.
Sassen, S. (2004), 'Local actors in global politics', *Current Sociology*, **52**(4): 649–70.
Sassen, S. (2005), 'When national territory is home to the global: old borders to novel borderings', *New Political Economy*, **10**(4): 523–41.

Saviotti, P.P. and J.S. Metcalfe (1984), 'A theoretical approach to the construction of technological output indicators', *Research Policy*, **13**: 141–51.
Saxenian, A. (1996), *Regional Advantage: Culture and Competition in Silicon Valley 128*, Cambridge, MA: Harvard University Press.
Saxonhouse, G.R. (2006), 'The integration of giants into the global economy', *Asian Outlook*, **1**: 1–11 (American Enterprise Institute for Public Policy Research).
Sayer, A. and R. Walker (1992), *The New Social Economy: Reworking the Division of Labour*, Blackwell: Oxford.
Schatzki, T. and W. Natter (eds) (1997), *The Social and Political Body*, New York: Guilford.
Scheler, M. (1924 [1990]), 'The sociology of knowledge: formal and material problems', in Volker Meja and Nico Stehr (eds), *Knowledge and Politics: The Sociology of Knowledge Dispute*, London: Routledge, pp. 17–36.
Schell, M.S. and C.M. Solomon (1997), *Capitalizing on the Global Workforce: A Strategic Guide to Expatriate Management*, London: Irwin.
Schelsky, H. (1961), *Der Mensch in der wissenschaftlichen Zivilisation*, Köln/Opladen: Westdeutscher Verlag.
Schement, J.R. and T. Curtis (1995), *Tendencies and Tensions of the Information Age: The Production and Distribution of Information in the United States*, New Brunswick, NJ: Transaction Books.
Schiller, D. (1999), *Digital Capitalism: Networking the Global Market System*, Cambridge, MA: MIT Press.
Schiller, H.I. (1981), *Who Knows: Information in the Age of the Fortune 500*, Norwood, NJ: Ablex.
Schoenberger, Erica (1994), 'Competition, time and space in industrial change', in Gereffi and Kornzeniewicz (eds), pp. 51–66.
Schoenberger, E. (1997), *The Cultural Crisis of the Firm*, Oxford: Blackwell.
Schonfeld, E. (2001), 'What ever happened to broadband?', *Business2.0*, October 16.
Schumpeter, J.A. (1942), *Capitalism, Socialism and Democracy*, Harper: New York.
Schumpeter, J. (1979), *Capitalism, Socialism and Democracy*, London: Allen & Unwin.
Scott, A.J. (1988a), *Metropolis: From the Division of Labor to Urban Form*, Berkeley, CA: University of California Press.
Scott, A.J. (1988b), *New Industrial Spaces*, London: Pion.
Scott, A.J. (1997), 'The cultural economy of cities', *International Journal of Urban and Regional Research*, **21**: 323–39.
Scott, A.J. (2000a), *The Cultural Economy of Cities*, London: Sage.
Scott, A.J. (2000b), 'French cinema: economy, policy and place in the making of a cultural-products industry', *Theory, Culture and Society*, **17**(1): 1–37.
Scott, A.J. (2002), *Global City Regions: Trends, Theory, Policy*, Oxford: Oxford University Press.
Segal-Horn, S. and D. Faulkner (1999), *The Dynamics of International Strategy*, London: International Thomson Business Press.
Selmer, J. (ed.) (1995), *Expatriate Management: New Ideas for International Business*, Westport CT: Quorum Press.
Seng, T.K. and P. Enderwick (2000), 'Global competition in industrial services: an analysis of aircraft maintenance, repair and overhaul services', in Aharoni and Nachum (eds), pp. 235–57.

Seristo, H. (2000), 'International alliances in service business: the case of the airline industry', in Aharoni and Nachum (eds), pp. 258–83.
Serres, M. (1997), *The Troubador of Knowledge*, Ann Arbor, MI: University of Michigan Press.
Serres, M. and B. Latour (1995), *Conversations on Science, Culture and Time*, Ann Arbor, MI: University of Michigan Press.
Servan-Schreiber, J.J. (1969), *The American Challenge*, Harmondsworth: Penguin.
Shah, Jennifer Balijko (2000), 'National hands off logistics task', *Electronic Buyers' News*, August 28: 10.
Shannon, T. (1996), *An Introduction to the World-System Perspective*, 2nd edn, Boulder, CO: Westview Press.
Shapiro, A. and H. Varian (1999), *Information Rules*, Boston, MA: Harvard Business School Press.
Shen, Y. (2004), 'Development of the third form of the car-making producer service industry in Shanghai, China', paper presented to the IGU Commission Residential Conference, Birmingham UK, 9–13 August.
Shields, R. (ed.) (1996), *Cultures of the Internet: Virtual Spaces, Real Histories, Living Bodies*, London: Sage.
Shiller, R.J. (2001), *Irrational Exuberance*, New York: Broadway Books.
Shön, D.A. (1983), *The Reflective Practitioner*, New York: Basic Books.
Sidaway, J.D. and J.R. Bryson (2002), 'Constructing knowledges of "emerging markets": UK-based fund managers and their overseas connections', *Environment and Planning A*, **34**: 401–16.
Sidorenko, A. (2001), 'The digital divide in East Asia', *Asia Pacific Economic Literature*, **15**(2): 18–30.
Silvestro, R., L. Fitzgerald, R. Johnston and C. Voss (1992), 'Towards a classification of service processes', *International Journal of Service Industry Management*, **3**(3): 62–75.
Simmie, J. (2002), 'Knowledge spillovers and reasons for the concentration of innovative SMEs', *Urban Studies*, **39**(5–6): 885–902.
Singelmann, J. (1977), *The Transformation of Industry: From Agriculture to Service Employment*, Beverly Hills, CA: Sage.
Singelmann, J. (1978), *From Agriculture to Services: The Transformation of Industrial Employment*, Beverly Hills, CA: Sage.
Sirilli, G. and R. Evangelista (1998), 'Technological innovation in services and manufacturing: results from Italian surveys', *Research Policy*, **27**: 881–9.
Sit, V. (1996), 'Mega-city, extended metropolitan region, desakota, and exo-urbanization: an introduction', *Asian Geographer*, **15**(1–2): 1–14.
SITPRO (Simpler Trade Procedures Board) (2004), *Letters of Credit: An Introduction*, www.sitpro.org.uk/trade/lettcred.html, 5 May 2005.
Sjøholt, P. (2001), 'Transfer of managerial knowledge by business related services', Department of Geography, University of Bergen, Norway, Working Paper No. 247 – 2001, presented at RESER (European Research Network on Services and Space) Conference on New Information Technology and Service Activities, Grenoble, October 2001.
Skyrme, D.J. (1999), *Knowledge Networking: Creating the Collaborative Enterprise*, Oxford: Butterworth-Heinemann.

Slack, Brian (2001), 'Intermodal transportation', in Brewer et al. (eds), pp. 141–54.
Slack, Brian, C. Comtois and R.J. McCalla (2002), 'Strategic alliances in the container shipping industry: a global perspective', *Maritime Policy and Management*, **29**: 65–76.
Slater, D. (2001), 'Markets, materiality, and the "new economy" ', paper presented to the Geographies of the New Economy seminar, University of Birmingham, 17 October.
Slater, R. (1999), *The GE Way Fieldbook*, New York: McGraw-Hill.
Slaughter, M.J. (2004), *Insourcing Jobs: Making the Global Economy Work for America*, Washington, DC: Organization for International Investment.
Small Business Research Centre (1992), 'The state of British enterprise: growth, innovation and competitive advantage in small and medium-sized firms', University of Cambridge.
Smith, A. (1776 [1977]), *The Wealth of Nations*, Harmondsworth: Penguin Books.
Smith, M. (1998), 'The global city – whose social construct is it anyway? A comment on White', *Urban Affairs Review*, **33**: 482–8.
Smith, N. (1993), 'Homeless/global: scaling places', in J. Bird, B. Curtis, T. Putnam, G. Robertson and L. Tickner (eds), *Mapping the Futures: Local Cultures, Global Change*, London: Routledge, pp. 87–119.
Soja, E. (2000), *Postmetropolis: Critical Studies of Cities and Regions*, Oxford: Blackwell.
Sorenson, O. and J.B. Sorensen (2001), 'Finding the right mix: franchising, organizational learning, and chain performance', *Strategic Entrepreneurship: Entrepreneurship Strategies for Wealth Creation*, **22**(6–7): 713–24.
SORS (2003), 'Rapid Reports: National Accounts', No. 114, Statistical Office of the Republic of Slovenia.
Spender, J.-C. (1996), 'Making knowledge the basis of a dynamic theory of the firm', *Strategic Management Journal*, **17**(2): 45–62.
Stanback, T.M. and G. Grove (2002), *The Transforming Metropolitan Economy*, New Brunswick, NJ: Center for Urban Policy Research.
Stare, M. (2001), 'Advancing the development of producer services in Slovenia with foreign direct investment', *The Service Industries Journal*, **21**(1): 19–34.
Stare, M. (2003), 'The scope for e-commerce in Central and Eastern European countries' services trade', *The Service Industries Journal*, **23**(1): 27–42.
Stare, M. and M. Bučar (2002), 'Innovation in services in accession countries: double trouble', 12th International Conference of RESER, Services and Innovation, Manchester, 26–27 September.
Stare, M. and J. Vanyai (1995), 'The increasing importance of the service industry in countries in transition', *Development and International Cooperation*, (**20–21**): 335–62.
Statistics in Focus (2001), 'Value added, employment, remuneration and labour productivity in the candidate countries: Theme 2', No. 13, Eurostat.
Statistics in Focus (2002), 'Information society statistics: Theme 4', No. 17, Eurostat.
Statistics in Focus (2003a), 'GDP of the candidate countries 2002, first results: Theme 2', No. 47, Eurostat.
Statistics in Focus (2003b), 'Acceding countries: still attractive to foreign direct investors: Theme 2', No. 51, Eurostat.
Statistics in Focus (2003c), 'High-tech and knowledge-intensive sectors creating employment in Europe: Theme 9', No. 10, Eurostat.
Statistics in Focus (2004), 'European employment increasing in services and especially in knowledge-intensive services, science and technology', No. 10, Eurostat.

Stehr, N. (1994), *Knowledge Societies*, London: Sage.
Stehr, N. (2001), *The Fragility of Modern Societies: Knowledge and Risk in the Information Age*, London: Sage.
Stehr, N. (2002), *Knowledge and Economic Conduct: The Social Foundations of the Modern Economy*, Toronto: University of Toronto Press.
Stehr, N. (2004), *Knowledge Politics: Governing the Consequences of Science and Technology*, Boulder, CO: Paradigm.
Stern, Robert, M. (2002), 'Quantifying barriers to trade in services', in Bernard Hoekman, Aaditya Mattoo and Philip English (eds), *Development, Trade, and the WTO: A Handbook*, Washington, DC: World Bank, pp. 45–62.
Stevens, B. and C. Moore (1980), 'A critical review of shift-share analysis', *Journal of Regional Science*, **30**: 420–50.
Stopford, Martin (2000), 'Defining the future of shipping markets', *ITIC Forum* 2000, 2 October, www.clarksons.net.
Stopford, Martin (2002), 'Is the drive for ever bigger containerships irreversible?', Containerisation International Shipping Forecasting Conference, 28 April, www.ci-online.co.uk.
Storper, M. (1995), 'The resurgence of regional economies, ten years later: the region as a nexus of untraded interdependencies', *European Urban and Regional Studies*, **2**(3): 191–221.
Storper, M. (1997), *The Regional World: Territorial Development in a Global Economy*, New York: Guilford.
Storper, Michael (2000), 'Globalization, localization, and trade', in Gordon L. Clark, Maryann P. Feldman and Meric S. Gertler (eds), *The Oxford Handbook of Economic Geography*, Oxford and New York: Oxford University Press, pp. 146–65.
Strambach, S. (2001), 'Innovation processes and the role of knowledge-intensive business services (KIBS)', in K. Koschatzky, M. Kulicke and A. Zenker (eds), *Innovation Networks: Concepts and Challenges in the European Perspective (Technology, Innovation and Policy)*, Heidelberg: Physica.
Ström, P. (2004), 'Internationalization of Japanese professional business services firms: dynamics of competitiveness in Southeast Asia', paper presented to IGU Commission Residential Conference, Birmingham, 9–13 August.
Sundbo, J. (1998), *The Organization of Innovation in Services*, Roskilde: Roskilde University Press.
Sundbo, J. and F. Gallouj (2000), 'Innovation as a loosely coupled system in services', in J.S. Metcalfe and I. Miles (eds), *Innovation Systems in the Service Economy*, Dordrecht: Kluwer, pp. 43–69.
Svetličič, M. (2003), 'Theoretical context of outward FDI from transition economies', in M. Svetličič and M. Rojec (eds), *Facilitating Transition by Internationalisation: Outward FDI from Central European Economies in Transition*, Aldershot: Ashgate, pp. 3–16.
Swyngedouw, E. (1989), 'The heart of the place: the resurrection of locality in an age of hyperspace', *Geografiska Annaler*, **71**: 31–42.
Swyngedouw, E. (1997), 'Neither global nor local: "glocalization" and the politics of scale', in Cox (ed.), pp. 137–66.
Tannock, S. (2001), *Youth at work*, Philadelphia, PA: Temple University Press.

Tapscott, D. (1996), *The Digital Economy: Promise and Peril in the Age of Networked Intelligence*, New York: McGraw-Hill.

Taylor, B. and R. Kwok (1989), 'From export center to world city: planning for the transformation of Hong Kong', *Journal of the American Planning Association*, **55**(3): 309–22.

Taylor, M. and A. Murphy (2004), 'SMEs and e-business', *Journal of Small Business and Enterprise Development*, **11**(3): 280–89.

Taylor, P. (2004), 'Leading world cities: empirical evaluations of urban nodes in multiple networks', *GaWC Bulletin 146*, Loughborough University.

Taylor, Peter J. (2000), 'World cities and territorial states under conditions of contemporary globalization', *Political Geography*, **19**(1): 5–32.

te Velde, D.W. (2004), 'Offshoring: opportunities and threats as services go global', *ODI Opinions 23*, Overseas Development Institute, London.

Teece, D. (1986), 'Transaction cost economics and the multinational enterprise: an assessment', *Journal of Economic Behavior and Organization*, **7**: 21–45.

TeleGeography (2004), *International Bandwidth Report*, San Diego, CA: Telegeography Research.

Tether, B.S. (2000), 'Analysis of CIS Data on Innovation in the Service Sector: Final Report', Report to European Commission DG12, CRIC, University of Manchester, November.

Tether, B.S. (2003), 'The sources and aims of innovation in services: variety between and within sectors', *Economics of Innovation and New Technology*, **16**: 481–506.

Tether, B.S., L. Green and G. Tampubolon (2000), 'What would constitute "success" for the UK in information communication technologies (ICTs) by 2005: a background report', report for the Director General of Research Councils' Study on the Future of Information Communication Technologies in the UK.

Tether, B.S. and C. Hipp (2002), 'Knowledge intensive, technical and other services: patterns of competitiveness and innovation', *Technology Analysis and Strategic Management*, **14**: 163–82.

Tether, B.S., C. Hipp and I. Miles (2001a), 'Standardisation and particularisation in services: evidence from Germany', *Research Policy*, **30**: 115–38.

Tether, B.S. and J.S. Metcalfe (2003), 'Services and systems', CRIC Discussion Paper No. 58, University of Manchester.

Tether, B.S., I. Miles, K. Blind, C. Hipp, N. de Liso and G. Cainelli (2001b), 'Innovation in the Service Sector: Analysis of Data Collected under the Community Innovation Survey (CIS-2)', Report for the Commission of the European Communities, Innovation Programme, CRIC, University of Manchester.

Tether, B.S. and G.M.P. Swann (2003), 'Services, innovation and the science base: an investigation into the UK's "system of innovation" using evidence from the UK's Third Community Innovation Survey', presented at the International Workshop on Innovation in Europe: Empirical Studies on Innovation Surveys and Economic Performance, Rome, 28 January (Institute of Socio-Economic Studies on Innovation and Research Policy; National Research Council, ISPRI-CNR and University of Urbino, Faculty of Economics).

Tharakan, P.K.M. and I. Van Beveren (2003), 'Exports and distance in a digitized world', Leverhulme Centre for Research on Globalisation and Economic Policy, Nottingham.

Therborn, G. (1995), *European Modernity and Beyond: The Trajectory of European Societies 1945–2000*, London: Sage.

Thiel, J. (2002), 'Reading the territorial restructuring of business services as an innovation process – the case of German advertising', Paper presented at the CURDS Anniversary Conference 'Cities and Regions in the 21st Century', Newcastle-upon-Tyne, 16–18 September.

THOCP (2002), 'The history of computing project', www.thocp.net, accessed 28 November 2005.

Thompson, J. (1967), *Organizations in Action*, New York: McGraw-Hill.

Thrift, N. (1994), 'On the social and cultural determinants of international financial centres', in S. Corbridge, R. Martin and N. Thrift (eds), *Money, Power and Space*, Oxford: Blackwell, pp. 327–55.

Thrift, N. (1995), 'A hyperactive world', in R. Johnston, P. Taylor and M. Watts (eds), *Geographies of Global Change*, Oxford: Blackwell, pp. 18–35.

Thrift, N. (1997), 'The rise of soft capitalism', *Cultural Values*, **1**: 29–57.

Thrift, N. (1999), 'The globalisation of the systems of business knowledge', in K. Olds, P. Dicken, P. Kelly, L. Kong and H. Yeung (eds), *Globalisation and the Asia Pacific*, London: Routledge, pp. 57–71.

Thrift, N. (2000), 'Performing cultures in the new economy', *Annals of the Association of American Geographers*, **90**: 674–92.

Thrift, N. (2001), '"It's the romance, not the finance, that makes the business worth pursuing": disclosing a new market culture', *Economy and Society*, **30**(4): 412–32.

Thrift, N. and A. Leyshon (1994), 'A phantom state? The de-traditionalisation of money, the international financial system and international financial centres', *Political Geography*, **13**: 299–327.

Thrift, N. and K. Olds (1996), 'Reconfiguring the economic in economic geography', *Progress in Human Geography*, **20**: 311–37.

Thurow, L. (1989), *Toward a High-Wage, High-Productivity Service Sector*, Washington, DC: Economic Policy Institute.

Tickell, A. and J. Peck (1995), 'Social regulation after Fordism: regulation theory, neoliberalism, and the global–local nexus', *Economy and Society*, **24**: 357–86.

Tiebout, C.M. (1962), *The Community Economic Base Study*, New York: Committee on Economic Development.

Toivonen, M. (2001), 'Megatrends and qualification requirements in the Finnish knowledge intensive business service sector', in Toivonen (ed.), *Growth and Significance of Knowledge-based Services*, Helsinki, Finland: Uusimaa TE Centre Publications.

Tomer, F. John, (2002), 'Intangible factors in the Eastern European transition: a socioeconomic analysis', *Post-Communist Economies*, **14**(4): 421–44.

Tomlinson, M. (2000), 'The contribution of knowledge-intensive services to the manufacturing industry', in B. Andersen, J. Howells, R. Hall, I. Miles and J. Edwards (eds), *Knowledge and Innovation in the New Service Economy*, Cheltenham, UK and Northampton, MA, USA: Edward Elgar.

Tomlinson, M. and I. Miles (1999), 'The career trajectories of knowledge workers', in Tomlinson, M. and I. Miles (eds), *Mobilising Human Resources for Innovation: Proceedings from the OECD Workshop on Science and Technology Labour Markets*, Paris: OECD.

Tordoir, P.P. (1994), 'Transactions of professional services and spatial systems', *Tijdschrift voor Economische en Sociale Geografie*, **85**: 322–32.

Tordoir, P.P. (1996), *The Professional Knowledge Economy: The Management and Integration of Professional Services in Business Organizations*, Dordrecht: Kluwer Academic.

Touraine, A. (1984 [1988]), *Return of the Actor: Social Theory in Postindustrial Society*, Minneapolis, MN: University of Minnesota Press.

Toynbee, P. (2003), *Hard Work: Life in Low Pay Britain*, London: Bloomsbury Press.

Treanor, J. (2003), 'Furse hits back at "frivolous" media', *The Guardian*, 27 February: 26.

Trefler, D. (1993), 'International factor price differences: Leontief was right!', *Journal of Political Economy*, **101**: 961–87.

Trewin, R. (2000), 'A price-impact measure of impediments to trade in telecommunications services', in Findlay and Warren (eds), pp. 101–18.

Triplett, J. and B.P. Bosworth (2004), *Productivity in the U.S. Services Sector: New Sources of Economic Growth*, Washington, DC: Brookings Institution Press.

Tübke, A. (2003), 'The patterns of industrial change in the post-communist EU candidate countries', *Post-Communist Economies*, **15**(2): 181–207.

Tucker, A.L. and A.C. Edmundson (2003), 'Why hospitals don't learn from failures: organizational and psychological dynamics that inhibit system change', *California Management Review*, **45**(2): 55–72.

Tung, R. (1988), *The New Expatriates: Managing Human Resources Abroad*, Cambridge, MA: Ballinger.

Uchitelle, L. (2002), 'Answering "800" calls offers extra income but no security', *New York Times*, March 27: 1.

Uchupalan, K. (2000), 'Competition and IT-based innovation in banking services, *International Journal of Innovation Management*, **4**: 455–89.

Ullman, E.L. and M.F. Dacey (1960), 'The minimum requirements approach to the urban economic base', *Papers and Proceedings of the Regional Science Association*, **6**: 175–94.

UNCTAD (United Nations Conference on Trade and Development) (1993), *World Investment Report 1993: Transnational Corporations and Integrated International Production*, Geneva and New York: UNCTAD.

UNCTAD (1994), *Liberalizing International Transactions in Services. A Handbook*, New York and Geneva: UNCTAD.

UNCTAD (1996), *World Investment Report 1996: Investment, Trade and International Policy Arrangements*, New York and Geneva: UNCTAD.

UNCTAD (1998), *World Investment Report 1998: Trends and Determinants*, Geneva: UNCTAD.

UNCTAD (2000), *World Investment Report 2000: Cross-border Mergers and Acquisitions and Development*, Geneva: UNCTAD.

UNCTAD (2003a), *World Investment Report 2003: FDI Policies for Development: National and International Perspectives*, New York and Geneva: UNCTAD.

UNCTAD (2003b), *Foreign Direct Investment and Performance Requirements: New Evidence from Selected Countries*, New York and Geneva: UNCTAD.

UNCTAD (2004a), *World Investment Report 2004: The Shift Towards Services*, New York and Geneva: UNCTAD.

UNCTAD (2004b), *Prospects for FDI flows, TNC Strategies and Promotion Policies: 2004–2007*, Geneva: UNCTAD.

UNECE (2000), *Economic Survey for Europe 2000*, No. 1, Geneva: United Nations Economic Commission for Europe.

United Nations (2004), *World Investment Report, 2004: The Shift Towards Services*, New York and Geneva: United Nations.

United Nations Center for Transnational Corporations (1988), *Transnational Corporations in World Development: Trends and Prospects*, New York: United Nations Center for Transnational Corporations.

United Nations Development Programme (UNDP) (2002), *Human Development Report*, New York: Oxford University Press.

United States Census Bureau (2003), 'E-commerce multi-sector report', www.census gov/estate.

Unni, J. (2000), 'Globalisation, information technology revolution and service sector in India', *Indian Journal of Labour Economics*, **43**: 803–28.

Urry, J. (1987), 'Some social and spatial aspects of services', *Environment and Planning D, Society and Space*, **5**: 5–26.

US Department of Commerce (2001), *E-commerce Multi-sector Report*, Washington, DC, www.census.gov/eos/www/ebusiness 614.htm, 19 March 2005.

US Department of Commerce, Bureau of Economic Analysis (2002), *Gross Domestic Product by Industry, 1987–93 and 1994–2001*, Washington, DC, www.bea.gov/bea/dn2/gpoc.htm#1994-2001, accessed 30 October 2006.

US Department of Transportation, Bureau of Transport Statistics (2003), *U.S. International Trade and Freight Transportation Trends*, BTS03–02, Washington, DC.

Van Ark, B. (2001), 'The renewal of the old economy: an international comparative perspective', STI Working Paper 2001/5, OECD, October.

Van Ark, B., L. Broersma and P. den Hertog (2003), *Services Innovation, Performance and Policy: A Review*, The Hague: Ministry of Economic Affairs.

Van Ark, B., R. Inklaar and R. McGuckin (2002), 'Changing gear: productivity, ICT and services: Europe and the United States', Research Memorandum GD60, Growth and Development Center, University of Groningen.

Van Krogh, G., K. Ichijo and I. Nonaka (2000), *Enabling Knowledge Creation*, Oxford: Oxford University Press.

van Zoest, A. (2004), *Offshoring Practices in the UK? Where are the Limits?*, London: Institute for Public Policy Research.

Venkatraman, N. and M. Subramaniam (2002), 'Theorizing the future of strategy: questions for shaping strategy research in the knowledge economy', in A. Pettigrew, H. Thomas and R. Whittington (eds), *Handbook of Strategy and Management*, London: Sage, pp. 461–74.

Vidovic, H. (2002), 'The services sectors in Central and Eastern Europe', Research Report No. 289, Vienna Institute for International Economic Studies (WIIW).

von Hippel, E. (1987), 'Cooperation between rivals: informal know-how trading', *Research Policy*, **16**(5): 291–302.

Waldman, A. (2003), 'More "may I help you?" jobs migrate from U.S. to India', *New York Times*, 26 May: A1.

Wallerstein, I. (1979), *The Capitalist World-Economy*, Cambridge: Cambridge University Press.

Wallis, R. (2003), *How Safe Are Our Skies? Assessing the Airlines' Response to Terrorism*, Westport, CI: Praeger.
Wang, Q. (1996), 'The pattern and structure of commercial areas in Beijing', paper presented to the Conference 'Towards a Sustainable Urban Future: Mega-Cities, Regional Development and Planning', Tsinghua University, 23–26 April.
Warf, B. (1993), 'Back office dispersal: implications for urban development', *Economic Development Commentary*, **16**: 11–16.
Warf, B. (1995a), 'Information services in the Dominican Republic', *Yearbook, Conference of Latin American Geographers*, **21**: 13–23.
Warf, B. (1995b), 'Telecommunications and the changing geographies of knowledge transmission in the late 20th century', *Urban Studies*, **32**: 361–78.
Warf, B. (2000), 'Compromising positions: the body in cyberspace', in Wheeler et al. (eds), pp. 54–68.
Warf, B. (2001), 'Global dimensions of U.S. legal services', *Professional Geographer*, **53**: 398–406.
Warf, B. (2002), 'Tailored for Panama: offshore banking at the crossroads of the Americas', *Geografiska Annaler*, **84**: 47–61.
Warf, B. (2004), 'Troubled Leviathan: the contemporary U.S. versus Brian Berry's U.S.', *The Professional Geographer*, **56**(1): 85–90.
Warren, T. (2000a), 'The identification of impediments to trade and investment in telecommunications services', in Findlay and Warren (eds), pp. 71–84.
Warren, Tony (2000b), 'The impact on output of impediments to trade and investment in telecommunications services', in Findlay and Warren (eds), pp. 85–100.
Waters, M. (2001), *Globalisation*, London: Routledge.
Webber, M.J. (1984), *Explanation, Prediction and Planning: The Lowry Model*, London: Pion.
Webster, D. (2002), 'On the edge: shaping the future of peri-urban East Asia', *Discussion Paper series*, Institute for International Studies, *Stanford University*.
Wechsler, W. (2001), 'Follow the money', *Foreign Affairs*, **80**: 40–57.
Wernerheim, C.M. (2004), 'Understanding regional high-order service growth in Canada: a cointegration approach', *The Service Industries Journal*, **24**: 131–54.
Westwood, S. (1984), *All Day, Every Day*, London: Pluto Press.
Wharton, A. (1993), 'The affective consequences of service work: managing emotions on the job', *Work and Occupations*, **20**(2): 205–32.
Wheeler, J., Y. Aoyama, and B. Warf (eds) (2000), *Cities in the Telecommunications Age: The Fracturing of Geographies*, London: Routledge.
Wheelock, J. (1992), 'The flexibility of small business family work strategies', in K. Caley, E. Chall, F. Chittenden and C. Mason (eds), *Small Enterprise Development: Policy and Practice in Action*, London: Paul Chapman, pp. 151–65.
Wickham, J. and G. Collins (2004), 'The call centre: a nursery for new forms of work organisation?' *Service Industries Journal*, **24**(1): 1–18.
Wighton, D. (2006), 'Movement of tasks overseas jumps up skills chain relentlessly', *Financial Times*, 25 January: 4.
Wiio, Osmo A. (1985), 'The information society: is it really like this? *Intermedia*, **13**: 12–14.
WIIW (2003), *WIIW Handbook of Statistics: Countries in Transition*, Vienna: WIIW (Vienna Institute for International Economic Studies).

Wilensky, Harold L. (1971), *Organizational Intelligence. Knowledge and Policy in Government and Industry*, New York: Basic Books.
Williams, C.L. (1989), *Gender Differences at Work: Men and Women in Non-traditional Occupations*, Berkeley, CA: University of California Press.
Williams, C.L. (1992), 'The glass escalator: hidden advantages for men in "female" professions', *Social Problems*, **39**, 253–67.
Williams, C.L. (1995), *Still a Man's World: Men Who Do Women's Work*, Berkeley, CA: University of California Press.
Williamson, O.E. (1975), *Markets and Hierarchies: Analysis and Antitrust Implications*, New York: Free Press.
Willis, P. (1997), *Learning to Labour: How Working Class Kids Get Working Class Jobs*, London: Hutchinson.
Willoughby, Christopher (2000), 'Transport services in the 21st century: seamless market or choiceless churning?', World Bank Discussion Paper, TWU-33, January.
Wilson, A.G. (1974), *Urban and Regional Models in Geography and Planning*, Chichester: John Wiley.
Windrum, P. and M. Tomlinson (1999), 'Knowledge-intensive services and international competitiveness: a four-country comparison', *Technology Analysis and Strategic Management*, **11**(3): 391–408.
Wolff, E.N. (2002), 'How stagnant are services?', in Gadrey and Gallouj (eds), pp. 3–25.
Wölfl, A. (2003), 'Productivity growth in service industries: an assessment of recent patterns and the role of measurement', OECD STI Working Paper, 2003/7.
Wood, P. (1991), 'Flexible accumulation and the rise of business services', *Transactions of the Institute of British Geographers*, **16**: 160–72.
Wood, P.A., (2002a), *Consultancy and Innovation: The Business Service Revolution in Europe*, London: Routledge.
Wood, P.A. (2002b), 'Services and the "new economy": an elaboration', *Journal of Economic Geography*, **2**: 109–14.
Wood, P.A. (2002c), 'Knowledge-intensive services and urban innovativeness', *Urban Studies*, **39**: 993–1002.
World Bank (2003a), *Transport Sector Overview*, Washington, DC, www.worldbank.org/transport/whytsimp.htm, accessed 30 October 2006.
World Bank (2003b), *World Development Indicators 2003*, Washington, DC: World Bank.
World Bank and International Finance Corporation (2004), *Doing Business in 2005: Removing Obstacles to Growth*, Washington, DC: World Bank Group.
World Trade Organisation (WTO) (2001), *Annual Report 2001*, Geneva: WTO.
World Trade Organisation (WTO) (2004), *World Trade Report: Exploring the Linkages between the Domestic Policy Environment and International Trade*, Geneva: WTO.
World Trade Organisation (WTO) (2005), *World Trade 2004, Prospects 2005*, Geneva: WTO.
Worthen, Ben (2001), '(Not sitting on a) dock of the bay', *CIO Magazine*, **14**(18), July 1: 108.
Wright Mills, C. (1953), *White Collar Work: The American Middle Classes*, Oxford and New York: Oxford University Press.
Wu, F. and A. Yeh (1999), 'Urban spatial structure in a transitional economy: the case of Guangzhou, China', *Journal of the American Planning Association*, **65**(4): 377–94.

Wymbs, C. (2000), 'How e-commerce is transforming and internationalizing service industries', *Journal of Services Marketing*, **14**(6): 463–78.

Yan, X., X. Xu and Y. Yang (1996), 'Study on CBD land use of Guangzhou, China: characteristics, causes, and prospects', *Working Paper no. 6, Centre for Urban and Regional Studies*, Zhongshan University, Guangzhou.

Yang, F. and G. Lin (2004), 'State strategy and the growth of services in China', paper presented to the IGU Commission Residential Conference, Birmingham, UK, 9–13 August.

Yeung, H. (2002), *Entrepreneurship and the Internationalisation of Asian Firms*, Cheltenham, UK and Northampton, MA, USA: Edward Elgar.

Yeung, H. and G. Lin (2003), 'Theorizing economic geographies of Asia', *Economic Geography*, **79**: 107–28.

Yeung, Y.-M. and X. Li (2000), 'Transnational corporations and local embeddedness: company case studies from Shanghai, China', *The Professional Geographer*, **52**: 624–35.

Young, I.M. (1990), *Justice and the Politics of Difference*, Princeton, NJ: Princeton University Press.

Zaloom, C. (2005), 'The discipline of the spectator', in A. Ong and S. Collier (eds), *Global Assemblages: Technology, Politics and Ethics as Anthropological Problems*, New York: Blackwell.

Zhou, Y. (1996), 'Inter-firm linkages, ethnic networks and territorial agglomeration: Chinese computer firms in Los Angeles', *Papers in Regional Science*, **75**: 265–91.

Zhou, Y. (1998), 'Beyond ethnic enclaves: location strategies of Chinese producer service firms in Los Angeles', *Economic Geography*, **74**(3): 228–51.

Zhou, Y. (2000), 'Bridging the continents: the roles of Los Angeles Chinese producer services', in H. Yeung and K. Olds (eds), *Globalization of Chinese Business in Globalization of Chinese Business Firms*, Basingstoke: Macmillan, pp. 167–94.

Zhu, Jieming, Han Swee Lean and Swee Kiat Ying (2002), 'The third-party logistics services and globalization of manufacturing', *International Planning Studies*, **7**(11): 89–104.

Zukin, S. (1994), *The Culture of Cities*, Oxford: Blackwell.

Index